READER'S DIGEST

BIRDS

THEIR LIFE · THEIR WAYS
THEIR WORLD

ILLUSTRATIONS BY
AD CAMERON

READER'S DIGEST EDITION

BIRDS

THEIR LIFE · THEIR WAYS
THEIR WORLD

The Reader's Digest Association, Inc.
Pleasantville, New York / Montreal

The birds shown on the preceding two pages are, from left to right,
Laughing kookaburra *(Dacelo gigas)*
Raquet-tailed kingfisher *(Tanysiptera galatea)*
Amazon kingfisher *(Chloroceryle amazona)*
Dwarf kingfisher *(Ceyx lepidus)*
Banded kingfisher *(Lacedo pulchella)*
Black-backed kingfisher *(Ceyx erithacus)*
Java kingfisher *(Halcyon cyanoventris)*
Shoe-billed kingfisher *(Clytoceyx rex)*
Mangrove kingfisher *(Halcyon chloris)*
Chestnut-collared kingfisher *(Halcyon concreta)*
Giant African kingfisher *(Megaceryle maxima)*

Text Author, pages 8–157:   Dr. Christopher Perrins
Consultant Editor, pages 158–412:   Dr. C.J.O. Harrison

Library of Congress Catalog Card Number 79-83553
ISBN 0-89577-065-2

Printed in the United States of America

Seventh Printing, May 1987

CONTENTS

(continued)

CONTENTS (continued)

INTRODUCTION

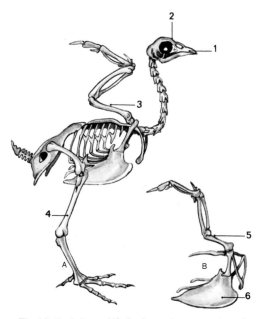

The bird's skeleton (A) displays a large number of modifications that make flight possible. Heavy teeth have been replaced by a light bill (1), the bones of the skull are thin (2) and those of the wings (3) and legs (4) composed of thin-walled tubes. The wing and shoulder girdle (B) are modified to accommodate large flight muscles which run between the forearm or humerus (5) and the keel (6).

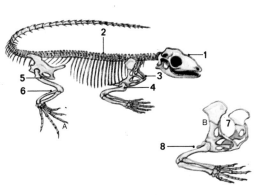

Birds evolved from a group of reptiles closely related to the dinosaurs about 150 million years ago. The skeleton of a reptile such as a lizard (A) is still similar in many respects to that of a bird. The skull (1) articulates with a backbone composed of elements called vertebrae (2). The pectoral or shoulder girdle (3) supports the forelimbs (4), and the pelvic or hip girdle (5) the hindlimbs (6). The pectoral girdle and forelimb are shown in more detail in (B). The girdle is heavily built (7) and articulates with the forelimb (8) which functions to support the front part of the body. This skeleton represents the basic plan seen also in birds, but in the latter, many modifications have taken place.

Man may be rightly accused of having a self centred view of the world. He is preoccupied both with himself and with the effects he has on this planet. Such preoccupations are understandable and certainly have profound significance, but there is a danger that lessons to be learnt from the study of other animals will be forgotten. This book is designed to stimulate an already considerable interest in birds and to illustrate some of the general principles that are demonstrated by the study of the life of birds.

Birds have always held a fascination for man. They have figured prominently in art and mythology since the Stone Age. More recently, the collecting of birds and their eggs and bird watching became popular especially in Europe and the United States. From these interests grew an enormous popular literature on birds, but most of it suffered from two major limitations. Firstly, books already published on birds concentrated on their external appearance and enabled their readers to do little more than identify bird species and tag on to them their scientific and common names. Secondly, these books were devoted to a description of birds which lived in particular regions such as Britain or the United States. As a result, the fabulous birds that lived in regions such as Antarctica and the Amazon basin remained relatively unknown. Furthermore, the life of birds, as opposed to their appearance, was not appreciated; witness for example the nineteenth century preoccupation with the collecting of birds' eggs which, once identified, simply became specimens for the museum cabinet.

There are about 8,600 different species of birds that are alive today. This diversity is reflected most obviously in the varied and often brilliant plumage patterns seen in birds, not only in temperate parts, but in a most spectacular way in tropical regions of the world. But this variation goes deeper, and one finds considerable diversity of anatomical structure and habit among birds. Many species are unable to fly, yet others are adapted to life on water. Again, birds feed on an incredible diversity of foods such as seeds, fruit, insects, fish and other animals. Certain birds are specialized to feed on certain food items, even limiting themselves, for example, to the fruit or seeds of a particular tree. All these aspects of bird life are described in the first pages of this volume. The author follows with a discussion of the habitats of the world that have been colonized by birds.

Birds: Their Life, Their Ways, Their World deals with two subjects that have stimulated much academic research and an enormous popular interest: social behaviour and breeding, and migration. Birds have evolved, to an extent rarely seen in other animals, intricate behaviour patterns particularly associated with the establishment of territories and breeding groups – sometimes small family units, sometimes enormous colonies. Much has been discovered of the complex ways in which birds relate to one another. Less is known about migration, which remains something of a mystery. Some facts are now well established, but others are the subject of ingenious experiments, the results of which are evaluated by Dr. Christopher Perrins.

Almost half the available space in this book is taken up by illustrations of every major type of bird. Special attention has been given to ensure that the birds are depicted in characteristic postures, just as they appear in life. In addition, a large number of smaller drawings illustrate specific points mentioned in the text.

EVOLUTION
AND CLASSIFICATION

The Black-headed gull is classified in the class Aves (1) because it has feathers, in the order Charadriiformes (2) because of features of its skeleton, and in the family Laridae (3) because it has long wings and webbed feet. It is included with other unspecialized members of the family Laridae in the genus *Larus* (4), and in the species *L. ridibundus* (5) because of its size and colouration. The classification of an animal enables its close relatives to be identified because these are included in the same groups, and provides an animal with two names, the generic and specific names, which are internationally recognized.

Evolution

150 million years ago the air was populated by flying reptiles called pterodactyls, but there were no birds. Birds are relative newcomers and most of their evolution has taken place since then, during a period following the so-called age of reptiles.

Our knowledge of the history of the evolution of birds begins in Germany, where an animal the size of a crow called *Archaeopteryx* lived in a fauna dominated by reptiles. Its fossilized remains have been found preserved in 150 million year old Jurassic limestone rocks quarried at Solnhofen, and they show that *Archaeopteryx* resembled a reptile in having a long, bony tail. But in one respect *Archaeopteryx* was unique, for it possessed feathers. Although this early bird may have been only able to glide, not fly, the development of feathers was one of the crucial steps in the evolution of birds, and it is from *Archaeopteryx* or a very similar creature that all the birds we know today have evolved.

The task of the paleontologist has been to fill in the details of avian evolution during the period between Jurassic times and today. Unfortunately his task has been a difficult one. The fossil record of birds is incomplete because birds rarely die under conditions favourable for preservation. Only when their carcasses fall into still or slowly moving water is there a chance of them becoming covered with sediment and their delicate bones saved from destruction. As a result, fossil birds have been limited to a few localities and the evolutionary story of birds is one composed of a few pieces in a jig-saw separated by gaps about which only guesses can be made. Even so, new discoveries are being made that help to provide a more complete picture.

The first well-preserved fossils to occur after *Archaeopteryx* are called *Ichthyornis* and *Hesperornis* from the 100 million year old Upper Cretaceous rocks of Niobrara in Kansas. These birds are preserved in chalk deposits, and they lived close to or over the sea, presumably taking a diet of fish. *Ichthyornis* was probably a good flier, but *Hesperornis* had already lost the power of flight and must have used its legs for swimming. Since the Cretaceous, the fossil record is vastly improved. The 60 million year old Eocene beds of the London Clay contain fossils of birds related to herons, vultures and kingfishers, while the somewhat younger beds of the Paris Basin and parts of America contain vultures, flamingoes, geese, rails, partridges and pheasants. By the end of the Miocene, some 11 million years ago, the majority of bird families in existence today and many of the genera are recorded as fossils.

This seemingly rapid increase in the number of different birds preserved in progressively younger sediments is due to two causes. Firstly, it is due to the fact that fossil remains are more readily found in recent rocks than in ancient ones but, more importantly, it reflects a real multiplication in the numbers of different birds during the past 50 million years. By flying, birds have been able to reach habitats everywhere in the world, and they readily colonized islands which could not be reached by amphibians, reptiles or mammals. This great mobility enabled birds to discover new sources of food, and much recent evolutionary change has produced groups with specialized feeding habits, as can be seen, for example, in the variety of bill shapes in birds described in the pages that follow.

Classification

Birds vary in size from the Ostrich which may stand 8 ft (2.4 m) high to the smallest hummingbirds which may measure no more than $2\frac{1}{2}$ in (6.3 cm) in length including a relatively long bill. Between these two extremes, there are over 8,600 different living species which occupy an amazing number of habitats and which display a variety of characteristics that enable them to pursue their different ways of life successfully.

This diversity is the result of rapid evolutionary change during the past 50 million years. For example, when a flock of birds were accidentally swept, perhaps by a freak storm, to the isolated Hawaiian Islands, they found an environment rich in new food sources which they had not before encountered. After many generations, different members of the original immigrant population became modified to take advantage of the variety of available foods. Some evolved short heavy bills with which to feed on nuts and seeds, while others developed long, curved, slender bills that enabled them to feed on nectar. Today there are 22 different species of honeycreeper on the Hawaiian Islands, and all have evolved from a single immigrant species.

The function of a classification is to make sense of the diversity of species by grouping together related forms. The Hawaiian honeycreepers are grouped together in a single family called the Drepanididae, not only because they have features in common, but because there is good evidence that they have all evolved from a common ancestor.

The family is not the only group to be used in bird classifications. In fact, there are five main groupings: classes, orders, families, genera and species. Species are defined as populations, the members of which are able to interbreed and produce fertile offspring. Closely related species are contained in a single genus, members of closely related genera are contained in the same family, and so on.

Representatives of each of the 34 orders of bird.
(1) Dinornithiformes, (2) Struthioniformes,
(3) Aepyornithiformes, (4) Rheiformes,
(5) Diatrymiformes, (6) Casuariiformes,
(7) Archaeopterygiformes, (8) Ciconiiformes,
(9) Sphenisciformes, (10) Apterygiformes,
(11) Ichthyornithiformes, (12) Pelecaniformes,
(13) Anseriformes, (14) Tinamiformes,
(15) Procellariiformes, (16) Gaviiformes,
(17) Podicipitiformes, (18) Hesperornithiformes,
(19) Odontopterygiformes, (20) Psittaciformes,
(21) Gruiformes, (22) Falconiformes,
(23) Strigiformes, (24) Trogoniformes,
(25) Coliiformes, (26) Galliformes,
(27) Charadriiformes, (28) Passeriformes,
(29) Apodiformes, (30) Piciformes,
(31) Coraciiformes, (32) Cuculiformes,
(33) Columbiformes and (34) Caprimulgiformes.

The principles of classification outlined above can best be illustrated by a particular example such as the Blackheaded gull. The Blackheaded gull is classified in the class Aves because, like other birds, it has feathers. This character alone distinguishes birds from all other animals, both living and extinct, and is evidence that they have all evolved from a 'feathered reptile' such as *Archaeopteryx*. The class Aves is subdivided into 34 orders, the Blackheaded gull being included in the order Charandriiformes along with the terns, skimmers and skuas as well as with other gulls. All members of the Charadriiformes are thought to have evolved from a common wader-like ancestor; evidence for this opinion is based on the fact that they all have similar characteristics of the skull and limb bones. The family Laridae is one of 16 in the order and can be defined as that containing gregarious sea birds with long legs, webbed feet and a relatively heavy bill. All members of the Laridae are efficient fliers. Passing down the hierarchy of groups we reach the genus *Larus*. Most gulls are in fact included in this genus, the only exceptions being rather more specialized forms such as the Kittiwake which, unlike most gulls, spends most of its time over the open sea rather than near the coasts, and which is classified in its own genus called *Rissa*. Finally, the species *L. ridibundus* is distinguished from other members of the genus because it is small, about 15 in (38 cm) long, it has a rather slender bill and is decorated with a brown hood during the breeding season and with a black spot behind each eye at other times of the year. The Blackheaded gull is thus classified as follows:

CLASS	Aves	GENUS	*Larus*
ORDER	Charadriiformes	SPECIES	*L. ridibundus*
FAMILY	Laridae		

In practice not all these names are used, and the Blackheaded gull is usually referred to by its generic and specific names, the generic name often being abbreviated to an initial letter.

ANATOMY, LOCOMOTION AND BEHAVIOUR

Anatomy

Almost every noteworthy feature of the anatomy of birds has evolved in order to make flight possible. The birds are one of the few groups of animals that have developed true flight, that is, powered flight not simple gliding. Insects, the flying reptiles called pterosaurs and bats share this ability and all these groups are, or have been, tremendously successful. Being warm-blooded has enabled birds to survive and even flourish in a wide range of areas of the world, including mountains and polar regions where some of these other groups have found it difficult to live.

The avian skeleton is based on the same general pattern as is found in the other vertebrate groups. The skull is joined to a backbone composed of bony elements called vertebrae, while the organs of the body are protected by a rib cage. At either end of the body the girdles support the limbs, the pectoral girdle articulating with the forelimbs which are modified as wings, and the pelvic girdle articulating with the legs. The special modifications of this basic plan are designed to reduce weight and to enable the legs to support the body when the bird is on the ground.

Lightness is achieved in several ways. The teeth have been lost and are replaced by a horny bill; many bones are extremely thin, for example those of the skull; and where strength is required, solid bone is replaced by structures that confer lightness with rigidity. Limb bones and the thicker parts of the bony structure are hollow, with thin internal struts for extra strength where necessary.

The bones of the backbone in the region of the pelvis are fused together. To compensate for this rigidity, the neck is flexible and sometimes extremely long. The wings are composed of the humerus or upper arm, the radius and ulna which comprise the forearm, and the wrist and finger bones. The secondary feathers of the wing are supported by the forearm while the wrist and hand bones are fused together to provide firm support for the primary feathers. The first and fifth fingers are absent and the second is modified to support the alula or bastard wing whose function is so important in flight and which will be discussed later. Still greater strength is achieved by the structure of the joints which do not allow movement except in the plane in which the wing is folded.

The wings articulate with the pectoral girdle. The wing sockets are braced apart by the clavicles, or collar bones, which are fused together to form the furcula or wishbone. As a whole, the pectoral girdle is designed to withstand the stresses which are imposed on the front part of the body when the powerful flight muscles contract. These muscles run from the head of the humerus to the keel of the sternum, a flat plate which projects downwards along the midline of the body.

Because the wings cannot support the bird on the ground, there are many profound modifications in the skeleton that enable the bird to walk on its hind legs—a method of locomotion called bipedalism. Firstly, the backbone between the pectoral and pelvic girdles is considerably shortened. This shortening has the effect of bringing the bird's centre of gravity far back enabling it to balance on its hind legs. The hind legs are modified so that their movement is restricted to a forward and backward swing below the body. It is interesting to note that some similar modifications took place in the evolution of bipedal man from his four-footed ancestors.

The bird's skeleton (1) may appear ungainly, but it is made streamlined by the body's covering of feathers. The all important forelimb supports the wing feathers which provide a large flight surface. To achieve strength and lightness (2), solid bone is replaced by structures composed of struts similar to those employed by engineers.

Bats are among the few animals that are able to fly as efficiently as birds. Their wings (1) are composed of a sheet of skin called a patagium which is stretched between four elongated fingers of the hand, and which extends backwards as far as the feet. The bird's wing (2) is almost entirely supported by the forearm, the fingers being reduced and playing a far less important role.

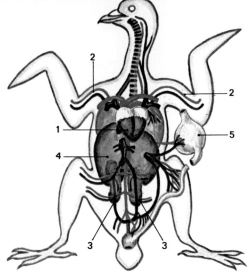

The blood vascular system. Blood functions to carry oxygen and food to the various organs of the body and carbon dioxide from the body to the lungs. Because birds are such active animals, their blood system needs to be extremely efficient. The arteries, depicted in red, are large and carry blood from the heart (1) to the body. Especially prominent are the innominate arteries (2) which supply the wings. Blood is returned to the heart via the veins, blue, from body organs such as the kidneys (3), liver (4) and stomach (5).

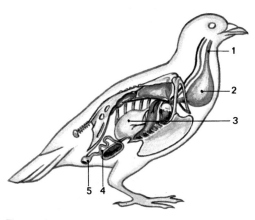

The bird's internal organs viewed from the side. The digestive system is composed of an oesophagus (1) which leads to the crop (2) and a stomach (3) which is divided into two chambers, the proventriculus and gizzard. The intestine (4) runs to the cloaca (5) which serves as the point of exit for the waste products. An important function of the cloaca is to extract water from the waste products.

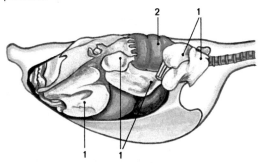

Much of the space inside a bird's body is taken up by air-sacs (1) which form extensions to the lungs (2). They assist the bird to get the large quantities of oxygen needed for flight.

Just as the skeleton is modified for flight, so too is the musculature. The most important muscles are the flight muscles which run between the upper arm and the keel—the 'breast' of poultry and game birds. There are two pairs of flight muscles. The larger pair is called the pectoralis major and provides the powerful downstroke of the wing when it contracts. The upstroke requires far less energy and is achieved by contraction of the second pair of flight muscles, the smaller pectoralis minor. These muscles also run between the humerus and keel, and lie between the pectoralis major and the sternum. They are not attached directly to the humerus. Instead, they terminate in a tendon which runs through a hole between the bones of the pectoral girdle to the upper side of the humerus. Thus the upstroke of the wing results from the pectoralis minor operating a simple mechanical pulley.

Another adaptation for flight is seen in the shape of birds. Their bodies may be elongated or compact but, whatever their shape, they are always streamlined. Streamlining is necessary to reduce friction to a minimum when the bird flies and is achieved, not only because the body itself is streamlined, but because the feathers provide a smooth outer surface. The tail, consisting entirely of feathers, may contribute a great deal to the bird's appearance and there is a great variety in tails, both in shape and length. Similarly with the length of leg: the long legs of, for example, storks are associated with the habit of wading in shallow water or marshy ground, but however long they are, the legs do not affect the bird's streamlining as they are usually tucked in under the body during flight.

When a bird flies, it is able to move in three dimensional space and thus has far more freedom than does an animal which is forced to crawl, walk or run on the earth's surface. However, birds are required to make extremely complex co-ordinated movements. Moreover, a bird such as a swift is capable of flying at 62 mph (100 kph), so these movements must be made extremely quickly. The part of the brain responsible for co-ordination of movement is called the cerebellum and, not surprisingly, this is large and elaborate in birds. Even larger, however, are the cerebral hemispheres, the lobes of the brain that are so well developed in man, which enable birds to perform complex behaviour patterns.

The digestive system is very efficient in birds. This is because, being such active animals, they are forced to assimilate food at an extremely rapid rate. A small bird such as the Goldcrest may eat food weighing one third of its body weight in a single day. Amongst birds there are herbivores, carnivores and omnivores. Herbivores, birds feeding on seeds, fruit and other vegetable matter, have rather more complex digestive systems than do carnivores. From the mouth the oesophagus runs to a storage sac, called the crop, which is particularly well developed in birds that feed on grain, such as the pigeon. Food stored in the crop is macerated before it passes to the two-chambered stomach where it is mixed with digestive juices in the first part, the proventriculus, and ground into a pulp in the second part, the thick-walled muscular gizzard. Herbivorous birds swallow small stones which assist the grinding of food in the gizzard. Carnivores do not usually have a crop or, if they do, it is small. The gizzard is also less muscular and functions as a normal stomach. Some carnivores, notably the owls, do not attempt to digest the bones and fur or skin of their prey. Instead, this material is regurgitated in the form of a hard pellet.

As has been noted above, birds are extremely active animals and, as well as having to assimilate large quantities of food, they must obtain the equally large amounts of oxygen required to transform this food into energy. Oxygen passes from the air into the blood through the thin walls of the lungs. In other vertebrates the lungs consist of blind sacs, but birds have extensions to the lungs called air-sacs. Inhaled air passes through the lungs into these air-sacs and then out again through the lungs. In birds that dive underwater, air may be passed through the lungs several times before it is exhaled, enabling them to stay submerged for long periods.

Oxygen is carried from the lungs to the tissues of the body in a blood vascular system which is basically similar to that of reptiles but which displays one or two

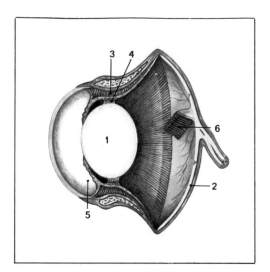

Many birds have more acute eyesight than any other animal. The eye of a hawk is relatively larger than that of man. The lens (1) focusses light onto the light-sensitive cells of the retina (2) and is held in position by a ring of bony plates called the sclerotic plates (3). Focussing is achieved by adjustment of the shape of the lens by the ciliary muscles (4), and the amount of light entering the eye controlled by the iris (5). The function of a group of cells called the pecten (6) is enigmatic. It may be responsible for increasing sensitivity to movement as it is especially well developed in birds of prey.

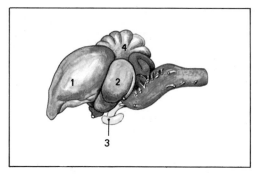

The main parts of the brain seen in side view: (1) cerebral hemisphere, (2) optic lobe, (3) hypophysis, and (4) cerebellum. The cerebral hemisphere and cerebellum are particularly large in birds.

notable modifications. In particular, there is complete separation between oxygenated and deoxygenated blood, that is, oxygenated blood from the lungs is not mixed in the heart with deoxygenated blood returning from the body tissues. The type of blood vascular system that makes this separation possible is found elsewhere only in the mammals, and enables the bird to maintain a high and constant body temperature. This is important, because it means that birds are to a large extent independent of the temperature of their surroundings. Reptiles, which cannot maintain a high body temperature, become torpid when the temperature of their environment drops. For this reason their distribution is limited to the warmer parts of the world and in temperate regions they are forced to hibernate during the winter. Birds do not suffer from these disadvantages, and they are found even in Arctic and Antarctic regions.

The bird's heart retains some reptilian features, but is powerfully built and beats rapidly. In large birds such as the turkey rates of 100 beats a minute have been recorded, but in smaller, more active birds, rates of 500 beats a minute are common.

As well as transporting oxygen, the blood functions to regulate the bird's temperature which is maintained at between 41° and 45°C (106° and 114°F). Heat loss from the body is reduced by the feathers which, as well as being essential aids to flight, provide an insulating layer. In addition, some aquatic birds such as penguins and petrels have a layer of fat which performs the same function. The only parts of the body which are not insulated are the feet and these are used as radiators. When the bird becomes too hot, the blood circulation to the feet and legs is increased with the result that heat is rapidly lost from the feet to the surrounding air or water. Additional heat may be lost through the lungs and air-sacs.

The reproductive organs of birds are not very different from those of mammals. Fertilization occurs inside the female's body and the male has an evertible cloaca to enable introduction of the sperm into the female. Some birds such as the ratite birds, swans, ducks and geese, have a penis. Patterns of behaviour involving courtship and breeding are well developed and will be discussed at length later in this book.

The bird's egg, like those of all other animals, is composed of a single cell. Only after it has been fertilized does this cell begin to divide to produce the chick, a process called embryonic development. Embryonic development is complex and in fact involves two processes, firstly, cell division and, secondly, cell differentiation. To begin with, the cells produced by division of the egg cell are similar to one another, but later they develop different characteristics so that it is possible to identify which parts of the chick's anatomy they are destined to become.

There are three essential components of the egg: the yolk, the egg white or albumen and the shell. The yolk contains fat and protein which nourishes the embryo during its later stages of development, while the albumen serves to protect the yolk by acting as a cushion which absorbs jolts and jars when the egg is moved. The shell also has a protective function and is often coloured so that it blends with its natural background —this is especially true of the eggs of birds which nest on the ground.

The yolk is suspended in the albumen on two strands called the chalazae which enable the yolk to rotate and remain in one position when the egg is turned. This is important because the cells that are destined to produce the chick are formed as a small disc on the upper surface of the yolk. By allowing the yolk to rotate, the chalazae enable this disc to remain always in the same position. The disc, or blastodisc as it is properly called, is at first composed of a single layer of cells but, within the first few days of incubation or even before incubation, these cells divide to produce a double layer called a gastrula. Later, a third layer is produced by which time not only cell division, but cell differentiation is taking place. If an egg which has just begun to develop is examined, a dark line is visible running across the blastodisc at right angles to the long axis of the egg. This line is called the primitive streak and represents the first obvious stage in the life of the embryo. At one end of the primitive streak, cells destined to become the head are visible, while along the streak there are blocks of cells which later grow into the bird's muscles.

The musculature of the wing is dominated by the pectoralis major (1), seen in side view in (A) and from below in (B). The triceps (2) and biceps (3) serve to extend and fold the wing, while a series of tendons (4) hold the feathers in their correct position.

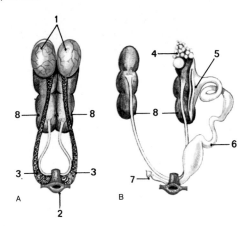

The male (A) and female (B) reproductive organs. Sperm are produced in the testis (1) which is joined to the cloaca (2) by a tube called the vas deferens (3). Eggs are produced in the ovary (4) and collected by a funnel (5) which leads to the oviduct (6) where the shell is formed. Normally, only the left ovary develops, the right one being present only in a rudimentary state (7). In both sexes, the reproductive organs are positioned close to the kidneys (8).

A hen's egg after 3½ days (A) showing the embryo (1) and its network of blood vessels (2), after 10 days (B), 15 days (C) and 20 days (D). ▶

One of the first organs to develop is the heart which pumps blood from the embryo through a network of blood vessels that run into the yolk. Food stored in the yolk is carried along the network to the embryo. Growth is rapid and, after a week of development in the case of the chicken *Gallus*, rudiments of the adult bill, eye, limbs and even feathers are clearly seen. The bill is formed at an early stage and in almost all birds bears on its upper part a structure called an egg tooth. It is with this horny 'tooth' that the chick breaks its shell immediately prior to hatching.

An important organ that grows with the developing chick is a sac of extremely thin tissue called the allantois. This sac begins as an outgrowth of the chick's gut and eventually completely surrounds the embryo and presses against the inner walls of the shell. Without the allantois the chick would never survive because, as the chick grows, it produces waste products in the form of uric acid and carbon dioxide. These products would poison the chick if they were not removed, so the allantois functions as the chick's waste disposal unit and stores uric acid safely away and allows carbon dioxide to pass through its walls and through the egg shell to the outside.

After a month, again in the case of the chicken, the chick is ready to break out of its confining egg shell. Before hatching takes place, however, a number of important events occur. These are necessary because the environment into which the chick emerges on hatching is completely different from that inside the egg. Firstly, the chick swallows the liquid in which it has been 'swimming' and stores the water thus acquired in its body tissues. Secondly, the yolk sac with the unused remains of yolk are pulled into the chick's body. Thus the chick is provided with a food store on which it can depend during its first few days of life outside the egg. Lastly, changes occur that enable the chick to breathe air. During most of its development, the chick obtains oxygen from the gases which diffuse into its blood via the thin membrane of the allantois. But when it hatches, the chick, cut off from this supply, must use its lungs. To make the transition easier, the chick begins to breathe while it is still enclosed in its shell. As a result of evaporation, an air space forms at the blunt end of the egg and, just before hatching, the chick pierces the membranes that enclose it, and breathes in the air from this space. For a while the chick derives oxygen from both the air inside the egg, and from the blood which is pumped from the allantois, but by the time the chick hatches, its lungs are fully operational. To make it easier for the chick to hatch, the shell enclosing it is weakened by the removal of minerals. This is a neat arrangement because these very same minerals are required to make the chick's skeleton hard and able to function when the bird finally emerges.

The time taken for a chick to grow from a single cell to an individual which is able, in almost all species, to break out of its shell is called the incubation period, and it is during this period that one or both of the parent birds is obliged to sit on the nest and prevent the eggs from cooling below the so-called incubation temperature, below which development ceases allowing the chick to die. Incubation periods vary considerably from bird to bird, and depend on the rate at which the chick embryo grows. In general, large birds have long incubation periods and small birds short periods. The Royal albatross, for example, has an incubation period of about 80 days, while many small passerine birds have a period of about 12–13 days.

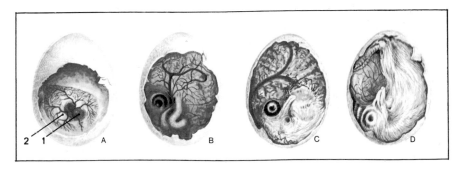

Beaks

The beaks of birds are extremely varied in shape, the individual design being related to the diet of the species concerned. Although some birds have large, well-built beaks designed for undertaking strong tasks, in general they are light compared with the toothed mouthparts of mammals, a factor necessitated by the need to reduce weight wherever possible so as to be able to fly. As a result, birds do not normally grind their food up in their mouths; this function is performed in the gizzard which is nearer to the centre of gravity of the bird. The two mandibles are basically bony structures covered with a layer of keratin—chemically very similar to feathers and to human finger nails. As with the feathers, these horny sheaths wear out and have to be replaced. Often worn sections peel away, but in some species whole sections may be shed at one time. The cutting-edge wears most and is replaced almost all the time.

The mouth is opened by the lower mandible being moved away from the upper mandible—in a way similar to that in humans. The upper mandible is not always rigidly fixed to the skull; usually there is a certain amount of movement, there being a hinged articulation between the skull and the mandible. At times the movement may be very considerable. The bill is not always a rigid bony structure; in some birds there is a considerable amount of movement in the bill. The long bill of the Snipe, for example, is very flexible. On the other hand, the bills of woodpeckers are extremely rigid and powerful in order to chip away at wood.

In many of the wading birds and some other species there are touch receptors in the tips of the mandibles. These organs, called Herbst's corpuscles, enable the birds to feel prey which they cannot see. They are particularly useful in species such as the godwits and curlews where the birds probe deep into soft ground in search of worms. Herbst's corpuscles are also present in the tips of the tongue of woodpeckers for the same reason. Other touch-sensitive cells, Grandry's corpuscles, occur in the palate and also in the tongue enabling a bird to feel the food that it has in the mouth. The tongue is often used, in association with the bill, to help a bird to hold and manipulate its food.

The upper mandible is pierced by the nostrils. Usually the nostrils are near the base of the bill. In some birds such as the Gannet, which dives into the sea from a considerable height, horny coverings lie over the nasal openings preventing water from being forced into them as it dives. Relatively few birds are known to use the sense of smell in their search for food; indeed in most species the sense of smell seems to be poorly developed. However, in the Kiwi it seems to be well developed and is presumably useful in the birds search for food. The nostrils are placed near to the bill tip and probably enable the bird to smell food underground when it is probing for food.

The bill is much used in the displays of birds. Often it is brightly coloured or ornamented. The horny sheath is shed from time to time and some species have different patterns on the sheath at different times of year. Many of the auks, especially the Puffin, have large sheaths over the bill during the breeding season. These brightly-coloured shields are shed after the breeding season and replaced with much smaller, duller sheaths for the winter. These in their turn are replaced prior to the next breeding season. Some pelicans also develop horny protuberances on the bill for the breeding season and shed them afterwards.

The tongue is frequently used in association with the mandibles in feeding. In the finches the tongue is used to position the seeds between the mandibles for cracking. In the Puffin the tongue holds small fish against the upper mandible, enabling the bird to open its beak and catch another fish. Each new fish caught is stacked between the tongue and the upper mandible and in this way the bird can gather a large number of prey before returning to its nest. The back of the tongue and the throat also house taste buds. Although less numerous than those in mammals, birds can distinguish the same tastes as mammals and the use of these is important in feeding.

The (Caribbean) Greater flamingo *Phoenicopterus ruber* (1) feeds with its head upside down. In this manner it is able to draw in large quantities of water from which it sieves out small organisms by means of the hair-like processes on the sides of its bill. The diving Goosander (or Common merganser) *Mergus merganser* (2) holds fish that it catches firmly with the tooth-like projections along its mandibles. The Fulmar *Fulmarus glacialis* (3) catches fish with its sharp beak-tip. It also feeds on offal, especially fish-waste dumped from fishing boats. The Brown kiwi *Apteryx australis* (4) probes in soft soil for worms and other small animals. Its nostril is close to the tip of the bill and the bird is apparently able to find its food by scent.

Variety of shape in beaks. (1) Scarlet ibis *Eudocimus ruber*, (2) Red crossbill *Loxia curvirostra*, (3) Anhinga *Anhinga anhinga*, (4) Toco toucan *Ramphastos toco*, (5) Laughing kookaburra *Dacelo gigas*, (6) Formosan kinglet *Regulus goodfellowi*, (7) Avocet *Recurvirostra avosetta*, (8) White-tipped sicklebill *Eutoxeres aquila*, (9) Swordbilled hummingbird *Ensifera ensifera*, (10) Crimson-backed woodpecker *Chrysocolaptes lucidus*, (11) Giant hornbill *Buceros bicornis*, (12) Hawfinch *Coccothraustes coccothraustes*, (13) Sparrowhawk *Accipiter nisus*, (14) Pennant-winged nightjar *Semeiophorus vexillarius*, (15) Great crested grebe *Podiceps cristatus*, (16) Shoebill stork *Balaeniceps rex*, (17) Mute swan *Cygnus olor*, (18) (Eurasian) Spoonbill *Platalea leucorodia*, (19) Great white pelican *Pelecanus onocrotalus*, (20) Indian skimmer *Rynchops albicollis* and (21) Masked lovebird *Agapornis personata*.

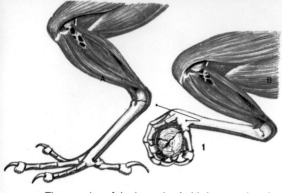

The muscles of the lower leg in birds are reduced for greater flying efficiency (A). In order to perch securely on a small branch or thin wire a bird must be able to grip hard with its toes. This grip is applied when the leg is bent and the flexor tendons (1) tightened (B).

The hind claw is an extremely variable feature in different groups of birds. In the stilts (1) it is absent, while in the herons (2) it is present but at a higher level than the other claws. In the terns the hind claw is much reduced, and does not appear in the footprint (3).

Legs

For reasons connected with flying, birds have evolved legs which have few large muscles except those at the top of the leg near to the centre of gravity. Unlike our legs, those of birds have three main sections. The femur is relatively short and buried in muscle. Forming a joint with the femur is the section equivalent to our tarsus, but this section, strictly called the tibio-tarsus, is not wholly comparable with our lower leg. The third and lowest section, usually called the tarsus, is basically a bone formed out of the upper bones of the foot. Since this bone is the one most easily seen in birds it is often the one called the leg, but really it is equivalent to parts of the ankle in man. The visible, backward-bending joint is not, anatomically speaking, the knee; which is higher up the leg and hidden by the feathers.

The femur tends to be shorter than the other two bones. The tibio-tarsus and the tarsus vary markedly in length, being very short in some birds such as swifts and penguins and very long in running and wading birds. In any species the two bones are closely similar in length. If they were not, the bird would have great difficulty getting up and sitting down since the centre of gravity would shift in relation to the foot.

Because lower parts of the legs have little musculature, they have to be controlled by a pulley system from the muscles at the top of the leg. A series of tendons run from the muscles at the top of the leg, operating the leg with a series of ropes and pulleys. One of the most important of these tendons runs round the back of the 'ankle' joint and into the toes. When the bird sits down onto its foot the tendon is tightened over the end of the joint so pulling in the toes. This action is particularly important in perching birds where the action of sitting down over the foot causes the toes to curl around the perch and lock the bird into position. By doing this, the bird can hold onto a branch tightly even when it is asleep. Indeed it cannot easily let go of the branch in a sitting position, but must raise itself up off its feet in order to release the toes.

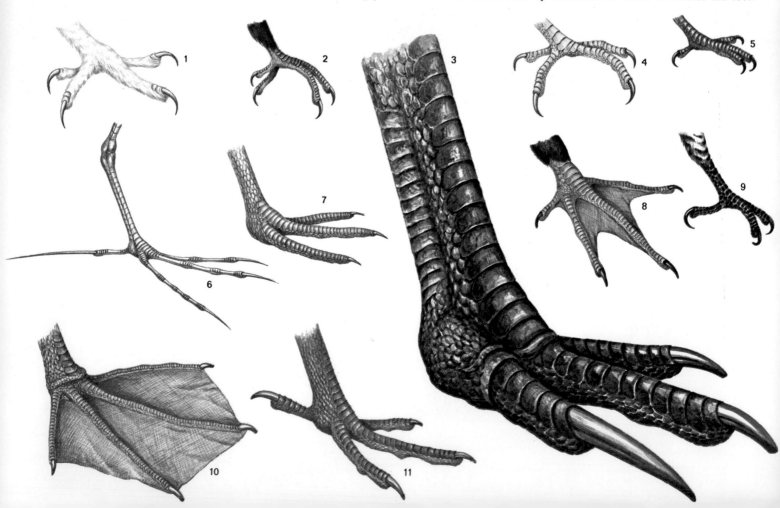

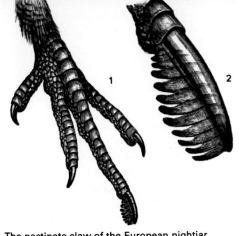

The pectinate claw of the European nightjar *Caprimulgus europaeus* (1), shown in detail in (2). Similar claws are found in some herons and in most pratincoles. Their function is not fully understood but they may be used in preening.

Variety in shape of feet. (1) Screech owl *Otus asio*, (2) Cuban trogon *Priotelus temnurus*, (3) Double-wattled cassowary *Casuarius casuarius*, (4) Oriental cuckoo *Cuculus saturatus*, (5) Common kingfisher *Alcedo atthis*, (6) Northern jacana *Jacana spinosa*, (7) Common oystercatcher *Haematopus ostralegus*, (8) Great frigatebird *Fregata minor*, (9) (Northern) Three-toed woodpecker *Picoides tridactylus*, (10) Blue-footed booby *Sula nebouxii*, (11) Turkey vulture *Cathartes aura*, (12) Ruffed grouse *Bonasa umbellus*, (13) (Black-crowned) Night heron *Nycticorax nycticorax*, (14) Slavonian (or Horned) grebe *Podiceps auritus*, (15) Ostrich *Struthio camelus*, (16) Meadow pipit *Anthus pratensis*, (17) Osprey *Pandion haliaetus*, (18) Mallard *Anas platyrhynchos*, (19) Pileated woodpecker *Dryocopus pileatus*, (20) Common swift *Apus apus*, (21) Red-necked (or Northern) phalarope *Phalaropus lobatus*, (22) Double-banded courser *Rhinoptilus africanus*, (23) Common (or Great) cormorant *Phalacrocorax carbo*.

This movement, together with ones made by the femur can, when done swiftly, cause the bird to be raised up very sharply and be almost thrown into the air. Advantage is taken of this action to launch the bird at the moment that it decides to take off.

Birds may either hop or run along the ground. In order to run really swiftly birds have had to develop very long and powerful legs. To be very fast, the bird has to be fairly large. Hence the development of high running speed has been one of the factors in the development of flightlessness. In some of these species, fast running has been made possible by a reduction of the size of the foot and by a reduction in the number of toes. This has been taken to the extreme in the Ostrich which has only two toes, one much smaller than the other.

Although bird legs have relatively little tissue in them and do not need much energy to keep them warm, birds that live in very cold climates have developed a further way of preventing heat loss through the legs. The arteries carrying blood to the legs divide into small vessels which intertwine with the returning veins, which are also greatly sub-divided. As a result, on leaving the body, the arterial blood passes much of its warmth to the returning, cooled venous blood. In this way the minimum of heat is wasted and the birds do not get chilled blood entering the body. The legs 'live' at a perpetually low temperature.

The foot has only four toes, the fifth having been lost early in the course of evolution —*Archaeopteryx*, which is known to have existed 150 million years ago, had only four toes. The toes show many adaptations to the birds way of life, often being modified for swimming. Perching birds may have two toes pointing forwards and two backwards, or three pointing forwards and only one backwards. The horny scutes of the legs and feet are, like those of the beak, formed of keratinous material. They are moulted regularly. In the Ptarmigan in winter the scutes of the toes have hair-like processes projecting from the sides enabling the bird to walk in the soft snow as if on snow-shoes. These scutes are moulted in the spring and replaced by normal ones.

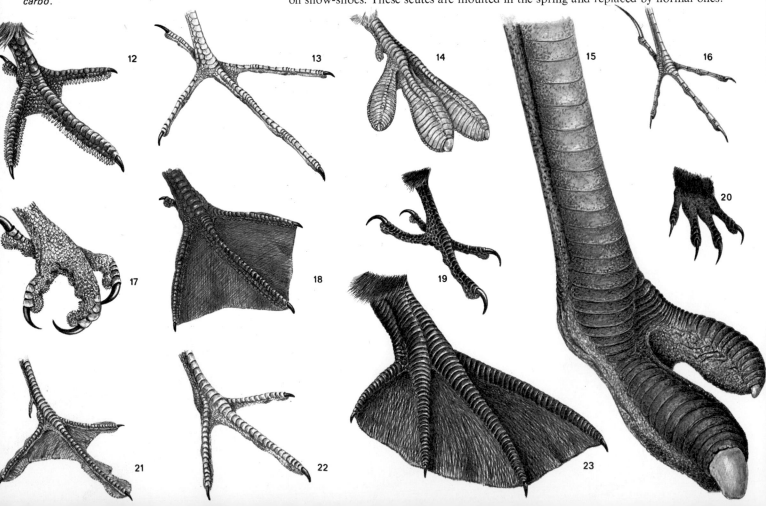

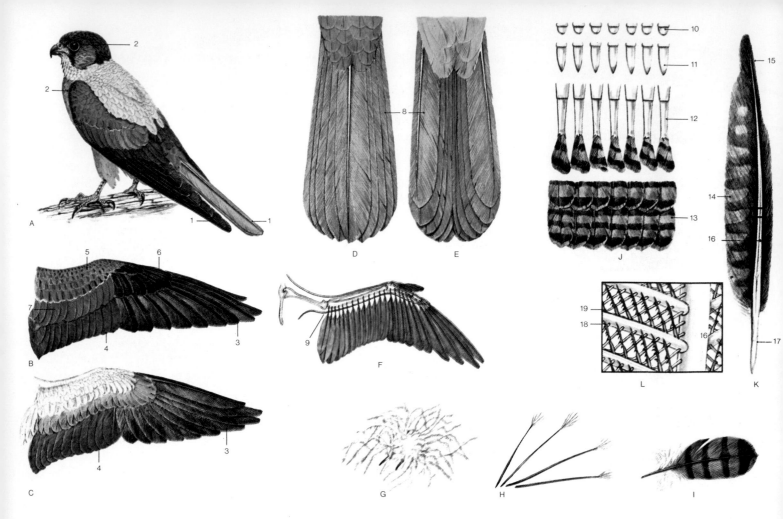

(A) Outer feathers or pennae are of two kinds,
flight feathers (1) and contour feathers (2). The
flight feathers of the upper (B) and lower (C) wing
surfaces are called primaries (3) and secondaries
(4). Smaller contour feathers, lesser coverts (5),
greater coverts (6) and secondary coverts (7), give
the wing its aerodynamic shape. The tail, seen
from above (D) and below (E), is composed of
flight feathers called rectrices (8). The primaries
and secondaries are held in position on the wing
(F) by an elastic tendon (9). Other feathers are
permanent down feathers (G), filoplumes (H) and
contour feathers (I). Growth of a feather (J) begins
with the development of a group of cells (10) into
a feather germ (11) which breaks through the skin
(12) before the vanes develop (13). Flight feathers
(K) are composed of inner (14) and outer (15)
vanes inserted on a rachis (16) which extends
from the basal calamus (17). The vanes are
composed (L) of barbs (18) and interlocking
barbules (19).

Some feathers have aftershafts which branch from
the underside of the base of the rachis. In this
example a contour feather (1) has a downy
aftershaft (2).

Feathers

The feathers of birds perform four important functions: they form an insulating
layer around the body; they create wing and tail surfaces that are essential for flight;
they keep the body waterproofed; and finally, their colouration can provide a bird
with camouflage by enabling it to blend with its surroundings or make it conspicuous
by providing colours and patterns that are used in displays particularly associated
with breeding behaviour and courtship ceremonies.

There are two principal types of feather: the pennae, which are the outer feathers,
divided into contour feathers and flight feathers; and the plumulae, or down feathers.
Other types of feather are either intermediate between pennae and plumulae, or are
derived from them. The pennae are shaped like the traditional quill pen, having a
flattened vane composed of many interlocking units growing out in one plane from a
supporting central mid-rib or rachis. The latter is a continuation of the basal calamus
which is hollow allowing passage of nutrient materials from the skin during the growth
of the feather. The structure of the feather vane is complex. Along each side of the
rachis project several hundred parallel filaments, or barbs, each of which has along its
length several hundred pairs of barbules which interlock, zipping the barbs together.
In most birds the feathers grow in special tracts with featherless areas in between, an
arrangement which is clearly seen in a plucked chicken. The feathers grow from
special papillae, 'goose pimples', which produce one, two, or even three sets of
feathers each year.

The down feathers are simpler and less varied than the pennae. The rachis is very
short and there are no barbules so that the barbs are not attached to each other. This
results in the fluffiness of down feathers.

A very important function of feathers is to help control the temperature of the bird's
body. Heat is retained by an insulating layer of air which is trapped close to the skin
by the feathers. When the bird becomes too cold, the outer feathers are fluffed up to
increase this insulating layer. The second function is to give the body a streamlined

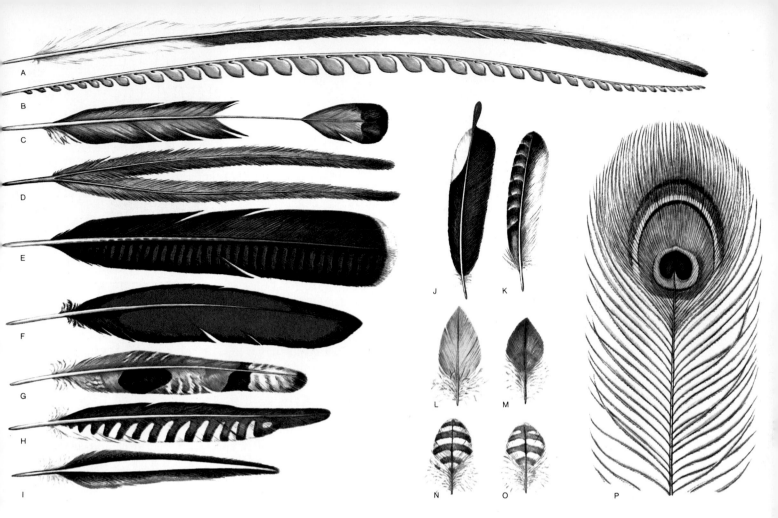

A variety of feather types. Trailing wing plume, Pennant-winged nightjar *Semeiophorus vexillarius* (A); head plume, King of Saxony bird of paradise *Pteridophora alberti* (B); racket tail feather, Turquoise-browed motmot *Eumomota superciliosa* (C); a feather with aftershaft, Emu *Dromaius novaehollandiae* (D); flight feathers, Anhinga *Anhinga anhinga* (E), Blue-crested plantain-eater *Tauraco hartlaubi* (F), Sunbittern *Eurypyga helias* (G), and the Hobby *Falco subbuteo* (H); neck hackle, Vulturine guinea fowl *Acryllium vulturinum* (I); secondary flight feather, Bohemian waxwing *Bombycilla garrulus* (J); wing covert, Jay *Garrulus glandarius* (K); contour feathers, Green woodpecker *Picus viridis* (L), Common kingfisher *Alcedo atthis* (M), the female (N) and male (O) Sparrowhawk *Accipiter nisus*; and the brilliant upper tail coverts of the male Peacock, *Pavo cristatus* (P).

The edge of an owl's wing feather has unconnected barbs which form a soft fringe. It is believed that this enables the owl to fly more silently.

shape and to provide flight surfaces, and is no less important. The streamlining of the bird is effected by the contour feathers, the main covering of the body. Measurements of flying efficiency suggest that the bird may be able to alter the shape of its body surface under different conditions, by altering the position of its contour feathers, in order to maximize the streamlining. The flight feathers of the wing, the remiges, and of the tail, the rectrices, can be spread to provide large, strong, light surfaces which can be varied to give the bird an efficiency of flight second to none in the animal kingdom. There are three groups of feathers on the wing: the primary feathers which are attached to the hand, the secondaries attached to the forearm, and the tertiaries attached to the humerus. The small group of feathers on the alula or bastard wing is also important during flight.

Another function of the feather covering is camouflage. Most birds are counter-shaded, being lighter beneath in order to counteract the effect of their shadow. The plumage of many species also blends well with the background of their normal environment, particularly in the case of hen birds which are therefore rendered inconspicuous when sitting on the nest. Plumage patterns also play important roles in keeping together members of a flock. The flashing of special wing or tail patches act as signals allowing birds to follow one another in flight.

Finally, feather patterns are important in species recognition. A major function of plumes, crests and feather patches on male birds which are shown during courtship displays is to enable the female to recognize the 'right' potential mate.

The number of feathers on a bird varies according to the species and the time of year. The larger the bird the greater the number of feathers in the plumage. For example, a Ruby-throated hummingbird has been recorded with a total of 940 feathers, while a Whistling swan had 25,216. The colder the climate the more feathers a bird has in the winter. It is a surprising fact that the total weight of a bird's plumage may be more than twice that of its skeleton. A Bald eagle weighing 144 oz (4,080 gm) with a skeleton of $9\frac{1}{2}$ oz (272 gm) carried 7,182 pennae weighing $20\frac{1}{2}$ oz (586 gm) and $3\frac{1}{4}$ oz (91 gm) of down.

Colour

Birds are amongst the most brilliantly coloured members of the animal kingdom, and to this they owe, to a large extent, their undoubted popularity. As far as the bird is concerned, colour has evolved, not to satisfy the aesthetic needs of man but to perform several important biological functions. These are discussed below, but it is first necessary to examine how colour is produced by birds.

There are two reasons why feathers appear coloured: they can have built into them structural elements that reflect light in different ways, as does a film of oil on the surface of water—these are called structural colours; or they can contain pigment or dyes—pigmentary colours. Structural colours are of two kinds, iridescent and non-iridescent. Iridescent colours change according to the angle at which light hits the feather's surface, and have a metallic appearance. They are produced either by the presence of a thin layer of a substance called keratin which occurs on the surface of the barbules, or by minute granules of a material called melanin which occur in a thin layer just below the surface of the barbules. In both cases, light hitting the feather is split into its component colours before being reflected back to the observer. Iridescent colours are most vivid in such birds as the hummingbirds.

Non-iridescent colours are produced by the scattering of light when it passes through minute air-filled cavities in the keratin of the barbs, and do not change according to the angle at which the light hits the feather's surface.

Pigmentary colours are less metallic in appearance than structural colours, and are not limited to the plumage of the bird. The bill, legs, feet and sometimes head and neck of birds are often pigmented. The most common pigment is a chemical called melanin which, when concentrated, shows black as in crows and the Blackbird. Other chemicals are the carotenoids, responsible for the red in the wattles of the pheasant and possibly also for the pink plumage of the flamingo. It is of interest to note that the flamingo is unable to manufacture its own pigment and must obtain it from its food. Red is also produced by the chemical turacin which is found in the turacos of Africa.

Some birds combine the effects of structural and pigmentary colours. For example the Blossom-headed parakeet has brilliantly purple plumage which is the result of the combination of blue produced by the physical scattering of light, and red pigment.

Colour functions in almost every aspect of life of birds and can be considered under two categories: colours that render a bird inconspicuous—cryptic colours; and colours that make a bird extremely conspicuous. Cryptic colours provide camouflage by enabling birds to merge with their backgrounds. A good example is seen in different species of larks which inhabit desert regions. Each species lives over ground which has a characteristic colour determined by the nature of the local rocks and soils, and each is appropriately coloured. Ptarmigan which live in northern climates are commonly white during the winter and assume a darker plumage in summer. Chicks of ground-nesting birds almost always have cryptic colouration, even though they may assume different colouration when adult. Cryptic colouration is often made more effective by the adoption of certain postures when predators threaten. For example, when a bittern is alarmed, it stretches its head to the sky revealing dark markings on its neck which merge with the pattern of the reeds in which it lives.

Colours that make birds conspicuous serve a number of different functions. Brilliant colours aid the recognition of species and sex by particular birds. Such colours are often used in conjunction with certain displays and with varying degrees of feather erection, and have enabled birds to evolve codes of signals indicating the mood and intentions of an individual. Examples of such signals are seen in threat and courtship.

Finally, some colours are used by colonial birds to keep together the flock. Sea birds are commonly white since white objects are able to approach fish more closely than black ones before they are seen.

Change of plumage colour in the Black-headed gull *Larus ridibundus*. (1) Juvenile plumage, (2) plumage of juvenile bird during its first winter, (3) immature bird during its first full summer, (4) adult plumage during winter and (5) adult plumage during summer.

Structural and pigmentary colours. (1) Quetzal *Pharomachrus mocinno*, (2) Cuban tody *Todus multicolor*, (3) Iiwi *Vestiaria coccinea*, (4) Keel-billed toucan *Ramphastos sulfuratus*, (5) Guianan cock-of-the-rock *Rupicola rupicola*, (6) Impeyan pheasant *Lophophorus impeyanus* and (7) African pitta *Pitta angolensis*.

23

The African scops owl *Otus leucotis* can conceal itself well beside a tree trunk. But if danger threatens it will open its eyes wide and simultaneously switch from a sleek camouflaged posture to one in which the feathers are all fluffed up, thus making itself look threatening.

Camouflage

Any animal that is in danger from attack by predators will be at an advantage if the predator cannot find it easily. Many birds resort to camouflage in order to increase their chances of survival; not only the birds themselves but their nests and eggs may be exceedingly well camouflaged.

Some examples of camouflage are obvious: the white of the winter plumage of the Ptarmigan, for example, obviously matches the background of snow very closely. However, the situation is not as simple as that since, in the summer, the snows melt and a white bird would be very striking at this time. Hence as spring arrives the birds moult progressively into a browner and greyer plumage which matches at first the broken patches of snow and open ground and later still the open ground. In autumn the bird moults slowly back into the white plumage.

Some of the most strikingly camouflaged birds are those that nest or live on the ground such as the Woodcock and the nightjars. These birds are so difficult to see that they are usually only found by the observer when he nearly treads on them and so causes them to fly away. Such patterns are called disruptive colouration, since they break up the outline of the bird. In some species such as the pheasants where the female alone incubates, the sexes may be of quite different colour. The female pheasants are almost as well camouflaged as the nightjars, though the males are very brightly coloured. Even in species with nests which are hidden in bushes the males tend to be less gaudily coloured if they help to incubate the eggs than if they do not. Not all birds that incubate eggs on the ground are well camouflaged. Many of the waders that nest in open country are quite brightly coloured. In these places, where it is relatively difficult for the birds to hide, the bird has a wide view and as soon as danger threatens, the bird leaves the nest and flies away, usually quite conspicuously. The predator has little chance of locating the nest of well-camouflaged eggs from this distance. In contrast, some of the well-camouflaged birds that nest in cover, such as the pheasants and the ducks, lay eggs that are quite conspicuous, often white or nearly so. The bird sits tight on the eggs and only leaves when almost trodden on; at that distance even cryptic eggs would be discovered.

An important aspect of animal camouflage involves the elimination of shadows. The undersides of animals are often more palely marked than the upperside. This is known as countershading since it serves to remove, or at least reduce, the darker colour that would result from the bird's own shadow on its underside. In the guinea-fowls, the pale spots are much smaller on the back than on the underside and this serves to reduce the amount of shadow showing on the underside. However, birds

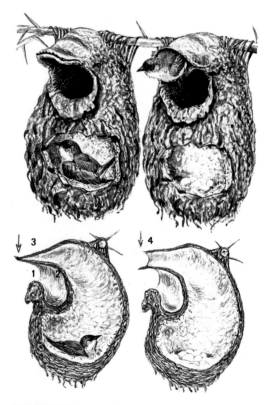

The Cape penduline tit *Anthoscopus minutus* builds a strong pliable nest of felt-like texture. It has a false entrance (1) to mislead predators which is seen to be a blind sac when viewed in section (2). The true entrance is narrower and lies above the false entrance (red arrow). It closes after the bird has forced its way in or out of the nest (3) and (4).

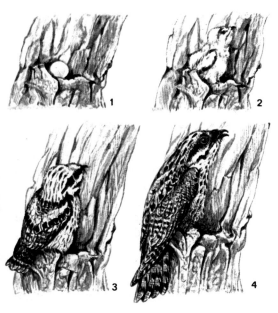

Like many ground-dwelling species, the Little bustard *Otis tetrax* will crouch low when a predator passes overhead. The bird is not only well-camouflaged, but by stretching out in this manner it eliminates all tell-tale shadows.

The Potoo *Nyctibius griseus* is related to the nightjars. Instead of laying its eggs on the ground as nightjars normally do, it lays a single egg on a tree notch (1). When incubating, the Potoo sits upright against the tree and in this position so resembles a dead branch that it is extremely difficult to see (4). The developing chick (2–3) also adopts this upright well-camouflaged posture.

stand above the ground on thin legs and if the light is bright, they tend to cast a conspicuous shadow on the ground which may give away their position. For this reason many birds crouch down on the ground when danger threatens so as to eliminate this tell-tale shadow. The head is drawn in or stretched out along the ground in front of the crouching bird.

In all aspects of camouflage the behaviour of the animal is crucial if the effects of the camouflage are not to be ruined. For example many young waders are beautifully camouflaged, but only if they crouch. If they stand up then their shadow gives them away at once. Hence they must immediately obey their parents' warning calls by crouching if they are to avoid the predator. Similarly, the bittern only achieves its best camouflage by drawing itself upright until it matches the vertical lines of the reed-bed in which it lives. Even the most beautifully camouflaged birds still have large eyes which might give their position away; they solve this problem by almost completely closing their eyes and watching the approach of the predator through very narrow slits. In a few species the nest site must be chosen with great care; the eggs of some sand-grouse match the colour of fallen leaves and the near-black eggs of Temminck's courser are said to match the droppings of antelopes. In both these cases the eggs would be conspicuous if laid in the wrong places.

A number of species of larks in Africa and Asia have local races whose colour matches the predominant soil colour of the area in which they live; some of these birds have been reported to be unwilling to leave the correct background when people have pursued them. Camouflage can only be considered in the correct ecological context. Even some birds that look conspicuous in a museum drawer are probably well-camouflaged in nature. The bright green parrots disappear when the birds enter a large tree; one can watch large numbers enter a tree and wonder wherever they have gone. Similarly birds such as the trogons with their bright red or yellow underparts can be exceedingly difficult to see in the tops of the trees in rain forest. Their colours blend with the patterns in the tree tops, where there are almost always dead and young leaves providing a wealth of different shades of colour.

A few species of predatory birds make use of camouflage in order to get close to their prey. The Snowy owl is cryptic against the background when perched; even sometimes when flying it can be extremely difficult to see. The white underparts of many seabirds are almost certainly camouflage in that a fish looking upwards can see a dark object approaching it from a greater distance than a white one and so have a greater opportunity to escape.

Young Siberian jays *Perisoreus infaustus*, birds of the cold taiga forests, huddling together to keep warm.

The Snowy owl *Nyctea scandiaca* lives on the open tundra where, since there is usually snow on the ground, it is capable of perfect concealment. The female Snowy owl is larger than the male and has light brown barring in her plumage.

Pigeons have been observed to hold one or both wings in a vertical position to expose their feathers to the rain, presumably to wash them.

A White-billed diver (or Yellow-billed loon) *Gavia adamsii* (1) and Tufted duck *Aythya fuligula* (2) rolling onto their backs in order to preen their undersides.

Care of the feathers in the Frilled coquette *Lophornis magnifica*. Hummingbirds practise head and neck scratching with the feet. Sometimes this is even attempted while the bird is airborne.

A Jay *Garrulus glandarius* engaged in anting. Having found a suitable ant-nest, the Jay fluffs out to allow the ants easy access to its feathers. It is believed that formic acid from the ants serves to kill parasites in the plumage.

Preening and Hygiene

All animals need to keep themselves clean and this is particularly true of birds which rely on the delicate and intricate structure of the feathers for so many of their activities. Dirty feathers stick together and reduce insulation and also would make good hiding places for a wide variety of parasites. The large flight feathers are in many ways a great improvement on the wings of bats, pterodactyls and insects; if pierced or hit while in flight the barbs separate, but sustain relatively little lasting damage; the bird just has to repair the feathers at a later stage by preening.

By far the greatest part of a bird's 'cleaning-up' time is spent on feather maintenance. The bird may bathe in water or, as is the case with the domestic hen, in dry dusty earth. This vigorous action helps to shake out foreign objects from the feathers. In preening the bird rubs its bill in the preen gland and distributes the preen oil over the surface of the feathers; particular attention is paid to the flight feathers. The action is very rapid and the preen oil dries extremely quickly. The full purpose of the spreading of this oil is not clear. One presumes that it must help to improve the condition of the feathers in some way, but it is not clear that, as was once supposed, it serves to water-proof the feathers; indeed many birds seem to wet the feathers before they spread the oil. The oil also has another function: on exposure to ultra-violet light it forms vitamin D; it is thought that this might be ingested by the bird in a later bout of preening or possibly absorbed through the skin. Whatever the real function of the oil, it is important to remember that a few birds, such as the frogmouths and some of the pigeons, parrots and woodpeckers, do not possess a preen gland and yet they too keep their feathers in perfect condition.

The bird uses its feet as well as its beak to preen the feathers. Some species of birds comb their feathers with their feet; in some, such as certain of the herons and night-jars, there is a serrated edge to the third claw; it is thought that this might help in preening. The claws are used most on the feathers, such as those of the head, which the bird cannot reach with its bill. In some species pairs of birds may preen one another, again concentrating on the head where the bird cannot easily preen itself. The bill, however, remains the most important structure for preening. There are two main actions. Either the feathers are drawn swiftly through the beak or the bird runs it more slowly along the barbs with a nibbling action. The latter action seems to function to repair small separations of the barbs and in addition the bird will stop and concentrate on a particular spot if it finds a break or a foreign body.

Anting is another aspect of feather maintenance which is imperfectly understood. A bird may settle among a group of ants and let them run around in its feathers or it may even pick up individual ants and pass them quickly across its plumage. Birds seem to prefer to use the acid-ejecting ants and the most obvious substance produced by these ants is formic acid. Assuming that it is this substance which the birds are trying to obtain, the most reasonable supposition is that the bird is spreading it over its feathers in order to kill parasites. Fleas and feather lice may live in numbers in the feathers and would almost certainly be killed by the formic acid. Although anting has been widely recorded in birds, all detailed records seem to relate to passerine birds.

Little is known about the maintenance of other structures. The beak receives frequent doses of preen oil during the action of preening the feathers and some birds also apply the oil to the horny scutes of the legs. The bill is kept clean by the feet or by being rubbed vigorously along a branch or other hard object.

Birds undertake a number of other hygenic activities; those that live in holes must be careful not to foul the site with their droppings, especially in the nesting season. This hygiene is carried to extremes in nestling birds which produce their droppings in small gelatinous bags—faecal sacs—which can be disposed of easily by the parents. When the young are very small the parents eat the sacs, but as the young and the sacs get larger the parents carry them away and drop them some distance from the nest in order not to reveal its site to predators.

Care of the feathers. (1) Anting by the American Blue jay *Cyanocitta cristata*, (2) preening in the Curlew sandpiper *Calidris ferruginea*, (3) scratching in the Ruby-crowned kinglet *Regulus calendula*, (4) care of the tail in the (European) Blackbird *Turdus merula* and of the wing (5) in the Southern carmine bee-eater *Merops nubicoides*, (6) scratching in the Ruby-crowned kinglet, (7) bathing in the House sparrow *Passer domesticus*, (8) bathing in dust by the House sparrow, (9) preening in the Tufted duck *Aythya fuligula* and (10) oiling the feathers by the Great crested grebe *Podiceps cristatus*.

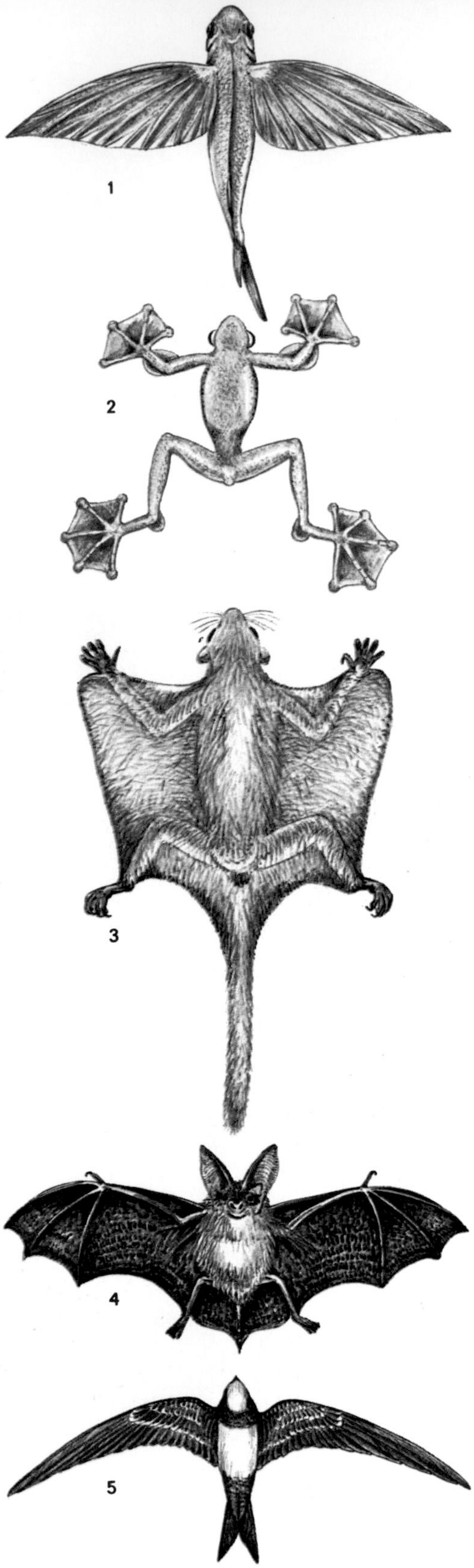

Flight and Flying

Although not all birds fly, flight is one of the most striking features of birds. In order to fly a bird must obtain an upward force; we call this force lift. A bird's wing is shaped to enable the birds to obtain this lift; we call a wing of such a shape an aerofoil. The leading edge of an aerofoil is thicker than the trailing edge and the upper surface is more convex than the lower surface. It is easiest to understand the forces on the wing by imagining a stationary wing with the air passing over it—this is the way that aeronautical engineers study the characteristics of a wing in a wind tunnel. The air strikes the leading edge of the wing and divides, some passing under the wing and some across the upper surface. It is here that the shape of the wing becomes important; the upper surface of the wing, because of its greater curvature, has a longer surface than the underside of the wing. In order to travel to the rear of the wing at more or less the same time as the air on the underside, the air on the upper surface must travel faster than the air underneath the wing. The faster air travels across a surface the lower the pressure it exerts on that surface; as a result, the wing's upper surface experiences a lower pressure than the under surface and so lift is produced. In practice, some 80 % or more of the lift results from this, and much less from the increased pressure on the underside.

Lift is only obtained by the wing when the flow of air is smooth over its surface. If the flow of air is turbulent, then lift is lost; we say that the wing is stalled. Stalling occurs when the wing is held at too high an angle to the flow of air so that the air cannot easily flow round the upper surface. Lift is also lost if the flow of air is too slow. Some of the lift is inevitably lost by air spilling round the wing tip; this is known as induced drag and is a more important factor in the flight of short-winged birds than in those with long wings.

Lift is not the only force which the passage of air exerts on the wing. As it passes over the wing the air tends to blow the wing backwards. This force is called drag and is roughly equivalent to the amount of wing exposed to the wind; the flatter the wing the less drag there is, the steeper the angle at which the wing is held—we say the higher the angle of attack—the greater the drag. Three factors affect the amount of lift: the surface area of the wing, the wind-speed and the angle of attack at which the wing is held. The same factors affect the amount of drag, so that the position of a bird in the air is determined by a large number of forces.

It is easiest to consider next a gliding bird in still air. Basically there are two ways in which a bird can glide in still air. Firstly, it can launch itself from a perch and open its wings. If it were to do this its path would be downward and, eventually, it would come to land. Such a glider is acting, effectively, like a toboggan on a hill. It is using the energy provided by gravity so that by losing height it can travel forwards. We have been looking so far at a stationary wing in moving air, though it is clear that the same forces apply if the air is still and the wing is moving.

The second method of gliding involves not the loss of height, but the loss of speed. A bird moving forward in flight may stop beating its wings and glide. As soon as it does this it starts to slow down because of the backwards force of drag. As it slows down it loses lift (because lift is related to the speed of air over the wings). The only way that it can increase lift without losing height or beating its wings is to raise the angle of attack (since lift increases with increased angle of attack). Hence our glider can remain in level flight only by steadily increasing the angle of attack, slowing down all the while. This method of gliding may seem short-sighted since in a relatively short period the bird will be flying so slowly that the wing will stall. Nevertheless the birds use this method of gliding frequently—it is the way they land. In order to land as softly as possible the bird needs to be at the point of stalling when it is just above the landing place. To do this it must judge the landing position from afar and glide into it in this manner, using up all its forward motion and so greatly reducing the shock to the body that a harder landing would entail.

Flying and gliding animals. The pectoral fins and lower lobe of the tail are greatly enlarged in the flying fish, seen here from above (1) which, after leaping from the sea, can glide considerable distances. The flying frog (2) and squirrel (3) glide, usually from tree to tree, supported by 'wings'. In the bats (4), which are capable of true flight, the wing membrane is stretched between the body and several of the fingers. Birds' wings (5) are more resistant to damage than are wings of the membranous type.

Early flying animals. A small pterodactyl, *Rhamphorhynchus* (1), and the earliest known bird, *Archaeopteryx* (2). In *Rhamphorhynchus* flight was by means of large wings of membrane attached along the body to the top of the hind legs and out along a greatly enlarged little finger. Unlike modern birds, the pterodactyls had relatively heavy heads and also teeth. *Archaeopteryx* had many features of modern birds while retaining a number of reptilian characteristics. It bore teeth and had an elongated tail which, however, was feathered throughout its length. Although the wing and feather attachments were similar to those in modern birds, the sternum (to which flight muscles are attached) was poorly developed. Hence it is almost certain that *Archaeopteryx* did not have muscles large enough for powered flight.

The shape of the wing in birds is determined by the contrasting needs of speed and manoeuverability. Wings built for speed tend to be long and pointed, while short broad wings make sudden changes of direction possible. (1) Wandering albatross *Diomedea exulans*, (2) White-tailed buzzard (or hawk) *Buteo albicaudatus*, (3) Willow grouse (or ptarmigan) *Lagopus lagopus*, (4) Sooty falcon *Falco concolor*, (5) Common swift *Apus apus*, (6) Rufous hummingbird *Selasphorus rufus*, (7) Wallcreeper *Tichodroma muraria*.

In itself, the first method of gliding will not enable the bird to travel very far, but in our example the bird was gliding in still air; in nature the air is often moving. In an efficient glider, such as a vulture, the speed at which height is lost—we say the rate of sink—is low. If the air were rising upwards at the same speed as the vulture loses height in still air, then the bird would stay at the same altitude; it is as if the toboggan in our example were racing down a hillside which was steadily rising into the sky—the toboggan would never reach the bottom of the hill. Rising air is found in a number of situations where birds can make use of it for hours, often hardly moving their wings at all. The vulture normally uses upcurrents or thermals that arise when the surface of the land is heated by the sun. Other species such as the gulls make use of the upcurrents caused when a wind strikes a cliff or hillside. The air is deflected upwards enabling the birds to ride in the updraught.

One group of birds glide in a different way. The albatrosses and related birds make use of the wind across the surface of the open sea. In many areas such as the Roaring Forties a strong wind blows more or less all the time. The albatrosses use this wind and, in particular, they make use of the fact that friction with the sea slows the wind down so that just above the surface of the sea the wind moves relatively slowly, blowing progressively faster as one climbs above the sea until at about 50 ft (15 m) above the surface it is more or less at full speed. The albatross glides very swiftly downwind, starting at about 50 feet above the surface and losing its height as it moves rapidly down-wind. When it has descended nearly to sea-level, it swings sharply into the wind and moves upwards until it is about 50 feet above the sea and once again in the fastest winds; it then turns downwind and the cycle is repeated. This type of flight can only be done at high speed; the albatross must have sufficient 'penetration' when it turns to enable it to move against the wind. The surprising aspect of this flight is that, without having to beat its wings, the albatross can progress against the wind. Where the winds are strong and steady the albatross can make a steady 5 mph (8 kph) upwind gliding downwind about 128 yd (118 m) and upwind about 180 yd (166 m) in each cycle, a net upwind movement of some 52 yd (48 m) on each gliding cycle.

1

3

4

Details of flight revealed by high-speed cine photography. Take off (1) is usually achieved by first jumping into the air. During landing (2) the wings tilt the body into an almost vertical position and act as brakes. A few birds such as the hummingbird (3) can hover. This is achieved by extremely rapid wing beats which may be as fast as 80 per second. In more normal flight (4) power for forward movement is derived from the downbeat of the wing.

Powered flight requires much more energy than gliding. When using their wings for powered flight many birds use the inner parts of the wings as gliding wings (they are held roughly steady) while the end of the wing acts as the oar. Forward propulsion is obtained when the great pectoral muscles drive the wing downwards. In order to fly forwards the downbeat must provide both upward and forward movement of the bird, so that it both stays airborne and moves forwards against the resistance provided by drag. The forwards propulsion comes about in two ways, the proportions contributing to the forwards movement from the two ways differing in different species. The wing bones are in the leading edge of the wing, the trailing edge being feathers. As the wing is flapped the feathers tend to bend so that the backward edge of the wing is above the bones. As a result, although the wing beats downwards, because of its shape it pushes the air not only downwards but also backwards and, of course, pushes itself in the opposite direction. The wing tips push the air in the same direction, but in a slightly different manner. Looked at from the side of the bird, the wing tip is composed solely of feathers pointing end on at the observer. These large flight feathers have their quills near to the leading edge. As the wing moves on the downstroke, the feathers meet considerable resistance from the air. Because the rear vane of the feather is far larger than the leading one, the feather twists along the quill, with the trailing edge above the leading edge. The result of this is that the feather, like the wing, imparts a backwards and downwards pressure. The swivelling of the feathers is particularly important in short, rounded-winged birds where the feathers separate for much of the length when the wing is opened; the Common partridge is a good example. The bending and twisting forces on the wing feathers are considerable and it is not surprising that they have to be replaced by moulting at regular intervals.

Once in flight, birds need to be able to steer themselves. They do this by a variety

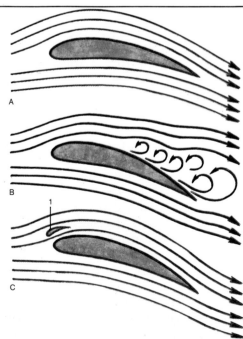

Air-flow across the wing must be smooth (A). When it breaks up and becomes turbulent (B), lift is lost; we say that the wing has stalled. This is likely to happen as the angle of the wing to the horizontal increases. Birds prevent stalling by raising the bastard wing (1) at the front of the wing proper and so smoothing the air flow (C).

of methods. They can turn solely by the use of the wings, as one can occasionally observe by watching a tail-less swallow or martin; their flight seems to be remarkably unimpaired. The bird has only to alter the angle or shape of one wing to throw itself off-balance. By slightly folding one wing, the bird can reduce the drag on that side and start to bank, or by turning any part of itself against the direction of motion the bird will be moved to one side and so turning will have been effected.

Taking off requires more energy than level flight since the bird must accelerate and climb. A small bird takes off in much the same way that it normally flies; merely by tilting the angle of the body at 45° to the ground, the backward and downward forces from the wings then become more nearly upward. In practice, the bird has to beat its wings more vigorously to obtain the extra lift needed. The larger the bird the greater this problem and large birds may have considerable trouble taking off; they have difficulty doing so because they cannot attain the air speed needed to prevent stalling. Most very large birds use additional aids to enable them to take off, they may run into the wind for example; by so doing they get an extra boost in that the air is already passing swiftly over their wings even before they start to fly. Another much favoured way of obtaining sufficient air speed is for the bird to launch itself from a cliff or tree and gain speed quickly by flying 'downhill'. Such a method is used not only by very large birds but also by those which have high stalling speeds such as auks and swifts. These species not only have difficulty gaining sufficient speed to fly, but they also have trouble losing this speed when they come in to land. Commonly they overcome this by aiming at a spot below their nesting site and at the last moment rising sharply, almost vertically upwards and using the force of gravity to slow them down. Such a technique requires considerable practice but may still be difficult, even for experienced birds, if the wind is unfavourable.

The smallest living bird, the Cuban Bee hummingbird *Mellisuga helenae* is here compared in size with the eye of the largest living bird, the Ostrich *Struthio camelus*. The hummingbird is only 2in (5cm) long and weighs less than 1/10oz (2.5g).

Wingspans compared. (1) The extinct pterodactyl *Pteranodon ingens* (not a bird) 26ft (8m); (2) the extinct albatross-like *Gigantornis eaglesomei* 20ft (6m); (3) *Teratornis incredibilis*, an extinct bird resembling the condors, estimated at about 16ft (5m); (4) the extinct relative of the storks and pelicans, *Osteodontornis orri* 16ft (5m); (5) Wandering albatross *Diomedea exulans* 11½ ft (3.5m); (6) Great white pelican *Pelecanus onocrotalus* 9½ ft (2.9m); (7) Andean condor *Vultur gryphus* 9½ ft (2.9m); (8) Lammergeier *Gypaetus barbatus* 9 ft (2.7m); (9) Rough-legged buzzard (or hawk) *Buteo lagopus* 5 ft (1.5m). All are compared with the artist (10) who has an arm-span of 5½ ft (1.7m).

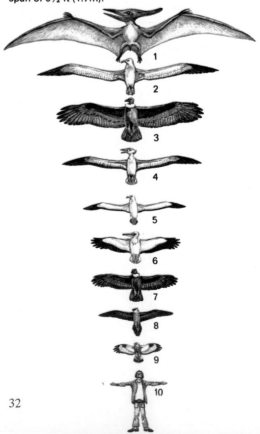

Size

Birds vary in size from the Bee hummingbird from Cuba which weighs around 1/10 oz (2.5 gm) or less, to the Ostrich. A large male Ostrich may weigh about 300 lb (135 kg). However, the extinct Elephant-bird *Aepyornis* of Malagasy was larger; this huge flightless bird stood over 10 ft (3 m) tall and is estimated to have weighed 1,000 lb (450 kg); its eggs contained around 2 gallons (9 litres) of liquid.

Two main factors impose limitations on the size of flying birds. Birds are very active and need to be warm-blooded. However, small bodies have relatively larger surface areas for their size than is the case with larger ones. Hence in small birds the heat of the body is lost more rapidly from the core through the exterior than occurs with large birds. As a result a very small bird such as a hummingbird uses up a great deal of energy merely trying to stay warm. Hummingbirds survive because for the most part they live in the warmer parts of the world (or in the USA only in the summer months) and in addition because they tend to go torpid at night. By reducing their high diurnal body temperature overnight they can economise on the amount of energy required to stay warm.

The limits imposed on the size of the largest flying birds are very different and are concerned with the energy required for flight. If one doubles the linear dimensions of a body the volume (or weight) increases by the cube, but the surface area increases only by the square. Hence if we compare two birds of the same relative proportions, but one twice as long as the other, the latter will have a wing area four times as large as the smaller bird but a weight eight times as great. Thus the wing loading (weight divided by wing area) of the larger bird will be twice that of the smaller. Flying for the larger bird is thus more difficult. In order to provide the same power, the larger bird must beat its wings more powerfully. Hence in practice our hypothetical pair of birds are not possible; the larger bird must have more powerful and therefore larger wing muscles than the smaller one. This in turn causes problems since the larger muscles weigh more.

The largest flying birds are likely to be as large as is practicable. It is probably no coincidence that birds of several different orders reach similar weights, in the region of 30–35 lb (13.6–15.8 kg). It is also no coincidence that we find that the large majority of such birds 'cheat' in that they find ways of getting extra help when taking off and often do not use powered flight to any great extent. Vultures, eagles, cranes, storks and albatrosses all fly under conditions when upcurrents help them to spend a great part of their time aloft soaring rather than flying, and all migrate by routes which minimise the distances over water where flapping flight would be necessary. Pelicans also use thermals to some extent and frequently flap for a few seconds and then glide for some distance.

In order to be able to fly, large birds have evolved more severe modifications to the skeleton than have smaller birds. Birds have hollow bones in order to reduce their weight, but larger birds have taken this to greater lengths than smaller ones. The larger eagles and albatrosses have more hollow bones than are found in smaller species; and in the larger storks, such as, for example, in the Marabou, even the toe bones are hollow.

Pelicans, swans and geese economise on the effort required for flight by flying in formation. When a bird flaps its wings it produces a slightly increased pressure on the underside in addition to the slightly reduced pressure that occurs on the upperside. As a result air spills round the tip of the wing in an upward direction in order to reduce this difference; this phenomenon is known as induced drag. The resultant air flow produces a little upward eddy of air at the tip of the bird's wing. By flying just above and behind another bird an individual can make use of the lift provided by this upward air current and so save itself effort. This is just what birds flying in V-formation are doing; by changing the leader from time to time, each bird saves itself a considerable amount of energy.

The world's largest birds, past and present, are found among the flightless species. Some of these fairly dwarf the human form. The man in the picture – the artist himself – stands at about 6ft (1.8m). The birds measure as follows: (1) The extinct penguin *Anthropornis* 5ft (1.5m); (2) Emperor penguin *Aptenodytes forsteri* 4ft (1.2m); (3) Double-wattled cassowary *Casuarius casuarius* 5ft (1.5m); (4) the extinct *Diatryma* 7ft (2.1m); (5) Emu *Dromaius novaehollandiae* 6ft (1.8m); (6) the largest member of the extinct family of moas, *Dinornis maximus* 10ft (3.1m); (7) Ostrich *Struthio camelus* 8ft (2.4m); and (8) *Aepyornis maximus*, largest member of the extinct family of elephant-birds 10ft (3.1m).

Flightless Birds

While flight may be the most striking form of locomotion used by birds, all birds also use other methods of progression, using the legs either for running or for swimming. A number of species of birds have become flightless during the course of evolution and so rely solely on one of these other means of locomotion. The penguins are one well-known group and the ratites, which include the moas, Elephant-bird, Emu, Ostrich, rhea, cassowary and Kiwi, are another. The rails have produced a number of flightless species usually on islands, the New Zealand Takahe being an example; other relatives of the rails, the Madagascan mesites and the Kagu from New Caledonia are also apparently flightless.

Other flightless species include the Dodo and the Solitaire of the Mascarene islands (probably related to the pigeons), the Kakapo (a New Zealand parrot), some steamer ducks, the Galapagos cormorant, a grebe from the lakes in the High Andes and. of course, the Great auk. Only one species of passerine is known—or believed—to have been flightless. This is the Stephen Island wren of New Zealand which is now extinct. Some other island passerines fly only very rarely.

We can say that these species have become flightless during the course of their evolution with some certainty, for it is most unlikely that any of these birds developed from lines of birds that never flew. Although all species have reduced wings and flight muscles that cannot support flight, all show many characteristics of flying birds. They have the hollow bones and the air sac-systems of flying birds together with the reduction in weight of the extremities, the shortening of the tail and so forth which are believed to be adaptations for flight. Almost all the species have wings and even when these are rudimentary they still show the same basic plan as the wings of flying birds; one can barely escape the conclusion that the wings of flightless birds were, in their ancestors, larger and more effective. Secondary flightlessness must have been developed at a relatively early stage in the history of birds. *Hesperornis*, a relatively early fossil bird, had a body rather like a diver, but very tiny wings; thus, already in the cretaceous, some 70 million years ago, there was a bird whose ancestors had clearly flown.

Why should birds become flightless? There are probably several reasons. Flying is an immensely expensive activity in terms of energy. In order to fly the bird must obtain much greater amounts of food than if it remains on the ground. This alone is an inadequate explanation; why should a bird not merely retain the wings but fly only when the need arises? The answer is that the maintenance of the flying apparatus, especially of the huge flight muscles, is expensive. These muscles may weigh up to about one sixth of the total weight of the bird and must be supplied with oxygen and food. It is an oversimplification to say that one sixth of a bird's food requirements go towards maintaining the flight muscles, but a bird with smaller muscles would need less food than the one with larger flight muscles. Hence at times of food shortage the former would have a greater chance of survival than the latter and so, under conditions where flying was not essential, evolution would favour reduction of the wings and their muscles. There could be other reasons for their reduction; birds the size of Ostriches could not fly anyway, they are too large, and so, in the course of evolution they have evolved large legs for running but have lost the power of flight. Birds such as auks which use their wings for 'flying' under water need small wings for this purpose and they do not fly well; the logical extension of such an adaptation is to become still more aquatic and lose the power of flight, as the Great auk and the penguins have done. There are grave dangers in this course since if a new enemy arrives and flight becomes necessary, these birds are relatively defenceless; even marine birds must come ashore to breed. Such dangers are all too obvious where man has arrived on the scene, and island forms such as Moas, Elephant-birds, the Great auk, the Dodo, the Solitaire, some of the rails and the Stephen Island wren have all been exterminated by man or by animals that he has introduced.

Some birds are efficient runners even though they retain the ability to fly. (1) Cream-coloured courser *Cursorius cursor,* (2) Greater roadrunner *Geococcyx californianus,* (3) Gallito *Rhinocrypta lanceolata* and (4) Steere's pitta *Pitta steerii.*

Running birds. (1) Emu *Dromaius novaehollandiae*, (2) Brown kiwi *Apteryx australis*, (3) Ostrich *Struthio camelus*, (4) Common rhea *Rhea americana* and (5) Crested tinamou *Eudromia elegans*.

Some ducks such as the (Green-winged) Teal *Anas crecca* (1) can take off from the water almost vertically. Other water birds such as the Moorhen (or Common gallinule) *Gallinula chloropus* (2) must run on the surface before take-off.

Common (or Great) cormorants *Phalacrocorax carbo* swim low in the water and can gently submerge by pressing their feathers to their bodies, thus decreasing their buoyancy.

The (Greater) Scaup *Aythya marila* (1) is able to dive for food, while the Whooper swan *Cygnus cygnus* (2) is able to tilt its body in the water to forage.

Most swimming birds have webbed feet, but the (African) Black rail *Limnocorax flavirostra* has long toes for walking on floating vegetation.

Swimming birds. (1) The Shoveler *Anas clypeata*, a dabbling duck found throughout most north temperate areas, (2) African finfoot *Podica senegalensis* from central and south Africa, (3) the Grey phalarope *Phalaropus fulicarius* which nests in the high Arctic in this red plumage and is hence sometimes called the Red phalarope. It spends the winter, in grey plumage, at sea. (4) The Pochard *Aythya ferina*, a diving duck from the Old World, (5) the Black-necked (or Eared) grebe *Podiceps nigricollis* which occurs in many north temperate areas and also in Africa and (6) the Smew *Mergus albellus*, a small saw-billed duck from temperate areas of the Old World. ▶

Swimming

Fresh and salt water cover great areas of the globe and birds would miss great opportunities if they were unable to make use of these habitats and their rich food supplies. Many species use them widely, their main limitation being that no bird nests on water, all must come ashore to breed. Birds from no fewer than 21 different families in nine orders swim often and well—penguins, divers, grebes, petrels, pelicans and their relatives, ducks, rails including finfeet, and waders (jacanas, phalaropes, gulls, terns and auks). All of these are groups that taxonomists consider to be ancient; none of the supposedly more modern groups have swimming representatives. No passerines swim with the exception of the Dipper and although this species both walks and 'flies' under water and obtains most of its food there, it can hardly be said to be well adapted to aquatic life in comparison with members of the other groups.

Many of these groups swim in very different ways from one another, some using their wings and others primarily their legs. The feet are adapted for swimming and here again this has been achieved in many different ways; the obvious way is development of webbed feet, but even here there are differences in that different groups have different amounts of webbing. By no means all swimming birds have webs; some groups have modified the feet in other ways. The grebes, coots, finfeet and phalaropes have lobed edges to the toes and these provide the birds' swimming power. The rails and jacanas have long toes with broadened and flattened undersides which provide their propulsion. Many of the most specialized swimming birds have extremely flattened legs which offer a minimum of resistance to the water. This adaptation reaches its height in the grebes and divers where, in cross-section, the leg is three to four times as long as it is wide.

Birds belonging to three orders swim mainly with their wings. These are the penguins, auks, some of the diving ducks and some of the petrels, especially the diving petrels. Water is a much more resistant medium than air and a bird could not 'fly' through water with a large wing as easily as it could do through air. Accordingly, both the auks and penguins have very small wings and while these act as good oars in the water, the auks find flying relatively difficult. Some of the diving ducks have solved the problem in a slightly different way in that they 'fly' under water with the wing folded, effectively using only the folded wing, and this perhaps only to a slight extent; the main propulsion coming from the feet. However, the wing may perform another function in these species in that the wing, or just the bastard wing, may be slightly spread so as to form a stabilizer in the same way that the forearms of dolphins act to stabilize during swimming. The wings of penguins are highly adapted for use in swimming. Although the bones are of the pattern and number found in flying birds, they are very flattened and expanded and take up most of the area within the wing; in addition, unlike other birds, the elbow and wrist joints are fused to give greater strength. The wing is covered with small, almost scale-like, feathers which provide a smooth surface to the oar. During the course of evolution birds have faced several problems which they have had to overcome in order to be able to swim efficiently, since the demands for swimming conflict with those for flying and walking. If a swimming bird is too buoyant it will never be able to submerge. Hence diving birds need to be heavier than they should be for flight alone; size for size, diving species have fewer hollow bones than have other birds and relatively smaller air-sacs. Most swimming birds have particularly dense layers of body feathers in order to insulate them from the cold water. The feathers of some aquatic species are specially adapted with very long barbules, many rather erratically arranged so as to form a dense matt. By trapping large quantities of air, these feathers aid the birds' buoyancy. Swimming birds spend a considerable amount of time preening their feathers with waxy substances from their preen gland. If these are removed by washing the bird in detergent, the bird cannot float. This is one of the problems associated with cleaning oiled seabirds; unless the detergents are extremely carefully removed afterwards, the bird cannot be

1

2

3

4

5

6

released to sea with safety. However, in order to dive, the birds must reduce their buoyancy and this they do by sleeking their feathers and squeezing out some of the air. Cormorants reduce their buoyancy by having less waterproof feathers than many other species; hence the reason why they are to be seen standing on rocks with their wings held out to dry. Other species such as grebes may carry stones in their stomachs; it has been said that these not only aid digestion by acting as grit, but also serve to help the bird submerge.

A diving bird such as a Gannet, which may drop into water from a height of 30 ft (9 m) or so, suffers a considerable impact on entering the water. Such diving species have fewer hollows in the bones of the skull, presumably in order not to damage themselves on impact with the water. Gannets have a dense mass of subcutaneous air-sacs over the front of the skull and these may help reduce damage from impact when diving.

Most diving birds do not descend to great depths nor do they stay underwater for long periods, two or three minutes being the normal maximum. However, some divers and the Long-tailed duck have been recorded as descending to about 200 ft (60 m) and certain birds, when forced to do so, can remain submerged for 15 minutes without breathing. In order to be able to do this, they possess certain adaptations such as being able to draw oxygen from the oxyhaemoglobin which is stored in the muscles. In addition, they have a high tolerance to carbon dioxide so that they are not forced to breathe until it reaches much higher concentrations in the lungs than would be the case in humans.

The feet of swimming birds are positioned towards the back of the body; as with the propellers of a ship, the most efficient propulsion comes from this position. However, such a position creates some difficulty for the bird when it comes ashore. It is not easy to walk with the legs placed so far back since the centre of gravity is far forward of the hips. Many of the shearwaters, the divers, the grebes and some of the diving ducks are extremely poor at walking. The penguins, and to a lesser extent the auks, have solved the problem in the same way that man has; they stand upright. However, they cannot move with any speed in this position and for their safety the auks are dependent on living near a cliff off which they can easily launch themselves if danger threatens. The penguins may lie down and 'toboggan' if they are in a hurry when on land.

The body of swimming birds is shaped more like a bullet than the more spherical body of most other birds; such a shape allows faster progress through the water. When diving to any depth the body is subject to great pressure from the surrounding water. Here again the more solid skeleton helps to withstand the pressures. To further aid the strengthening, the ribs are stronger than those of other birds and the uncinate processes, which in most birds occur on each rib and overlap the rib behind, in some seabirds overlap two other ribs and give much greater strength to the skeleton.

All birds have to cope with the problems of staying waterproof and keeping warm, but because of the contact with water these problems are more serious for swimming birds. If water penetrates the feathers the amount of heat lost by the body increases greatly; even if this does not happen, the cooling effect of water in close proximity to the bird is sufficient to cause the bird to use up a considerable amount of heat. Water birds have particularly densely packed plumage, often with an unusually thick layer of under-feathers. As already mentioned, water birds spend a considerable amount of time preening their feathers with waxy substances from their preen glands. During the moult, when the birds' feathering is temporarily reduced, they may have to stay out of the water for longer periods; some of the ducks and, in particular, the penguins spend almost the whole period of the moult on land; the penguins build up thick layers of fat on which they can draw during the fast that accompanies the moult. In spite of the good insulation, water birds still lose heat through the extremities, especially the beak and the legs which are not feathered. The legs of many swimming birds are adapted to save as much heat as possible.

Phalaropes such as this Grey (or Red) phalarope *Phalaropus fulicarius* disturb small organisms in the water on which they feed, by swimming in small circles, usually spinning on their own axes. This illustration shows a bird in several positions.

When danger threatens, the Moorhen (or Common gallinule) *Gallinula chloropus* submerges and retains its position in the water by holding onto underwater vegetation.

Instinct and Intelligence

Birds show a remarkable range of behaviour. Many of their habits are exceedingly intricate; for example nest-building in some species involves a wide range of activities including the choice of a good site, selection of the right materials—often different at different stages in the building operations—and a number of weaving and turning movements. Nevertheless, a pair of young birds breeding for the first time may successfully undertake these activities and go on to raise a family. Earlier observers tended to put all these activities down to 'instinct' and leave it at that.

Though much still remains a mystery, we now know a great deal more about the behaviour of birds. Careful study has shown that many of a bird's activities are learned and perfected during its life. However, a number of behaviour patterns are still innate in that the bird is born with the ability to do them. This can be tested by raising a young bird in isolation from all others and observing that it behaves in a way characteristic of its species even though there has never been the slightest possibility of learning the behaviour from others. Certain aspects of the songs of many birds are inherited. However, like so many inherited abilities, these are not perfect and the bird has to use them time and again in order to master them. Contact with others of its own species will certainly help the bird to perfect them, especially in the case of song. Again, a species may have a 'sensitive period' in which a certain ability is most likely to become fixed. For example young geese become 'imprinted', in that they learn to follow moving objects soon after hatching. In nature this is, of course, normally their parents, though in captivity it may well be a

Intelligent behaviour in (A) the Cedar waxwing *Bombycilla cedrorum* in which a bird close to a food source will pass fruit to a less well placed individual; (B) the European Goldfinch *Carduelis carduelis* which can lift food using its feet.

A

B

Intelligent behaviour in the Hooded crow *Corvus cornix* which behaves in a similar way as the Goldfinch to lift fish caught on lines set by Eskimos.

The Black-throated honeyguide *Indicator indicator*, renowned for its ability to guide other animals, especially ratels and more recently man, to the nests of honey bees.

The habit of storing food is well developed in some members of the Corvidae, particularly the (Eurasian) Nutcracker *Nucifraga caryocatactes* which is seen here recovering nuts in winter.

One of the best-known examples of learning in birds is the speed with which the Blue tit's habit of opening milk bottles spread once the birds had learnt that they contained an easily exploited food source.

man. In some species this tendency is very marked within the first 24 hours and then much less so; it is also difficult to reverse. In the case of song, the bird is most likely to modify its song in relation to its neighbours during the period prior to its first breeding season, many months after it was hatched. Hence many activities may include innate aspects as well as those perfected by practice and copied from other individuals.

Watching others of its own species and copying their behaviour is an obvious way in which young birds can learn to cope with their environment. In particular it is very important that young birds learn as quickly as possible which objects are dangerous and which impose no threat. For many species the early days after leaving the nest must be very important and the parents' guidance extremely valuable. Nevertheless, it must be stressed that in other species such as some of the megapodes, shearwaters, swifts and cuckoos, the young birds get no help at all from their parents after leaving the nest. Indeed in the case of the megapodes and cuckoos they may well never see their parents. Nonetheless the young birds survive sufficiently well for the species to prosper.

Learning by trial and error and continued practice may also be very important. New objects must be examined and efforts made to see if they will yield food. Several species can learn to pull up long pieces of thread so as to reach food attached to the end; a combination of feet and bill may be used to do this. Once a bird finds a new source of food, others may swiftly copy it and the new habit will spread rapidly through the population. The habit of opening milk bottles is a good example. In Britain it seems that this habit originated in Southampton in about 1929 and then spread rapidly outwards to different areas.

One must be very wary of discussing how intelligent birds may or may not be. For example parrots and members of the crow family are often thought of as being particularly intelligent. However, the criteria on which such an assumption is based are that the birds can learn to do things that man wants them to do. Birds have evolved their complex range of habits in relation to what has proved best for them in their natural surroundings. Under these circumstances they probably never need to be able to count (though in tests, crows show a simple 'numbers sense') or to do the tricks that man requires of them.

Similarly, actions that seem stupid to us are probably merely those that birds have not needed to adapt to in the wild. For example many species react to certain stimuli with a fairly stereotyped response. The red breast of a European robin acts as such a 'releaser' for other robins, the reaction depending on whether the other bird is a male or a female. However, a robin will show an almost identical response to a bunch of red breast feathers as it will to a live bird. Other species such as some of the waders prefer to incubate eggs larger than their own; these create a 'super-normal stimulus' and the bird may ignore its own eggs in its efforts to incubate giant dummy eggs. Both these activities seem stupid to us, but would never occur in the wild.

Similarly because different species may differ widely in their behaviour it does not follow that one is more less intelligent than another. For example, guillemots and penguins can learn to recognise their own young from a very early stage; in the former species at least, this happens before the young bird hatches since it calls from the pipping egg and the parent learns to recognise these calls. By way of contrast, parent tits cannot recognise their own young nestlings at all. In the guillemots the young birds may get muddled up with one another and the parents need to know which are theirs if they are to feed them. In the tits which nest in holes in trees their young could virtually never get mixed up with those of another brood and so there has been no need to evolve this habit of learning to recognise their own young.

Song

Humans tend to notice birds because they use the same sense organs as we do. The most important one is perhaps colour vision, but hearing lies a close second. Birds tend to have ears that detect the same kinds of sounds as man. They hear, and of course communicate, over a similar range of wavelengths as man. Possibly they are less good at hearing at either end of their scale than a human with good hearing. At any rate the outcome is that they make their calls within the range that is perceptible to humans and we thus appreciate their songs.

The ear of birds is in many ways similar to that of man; in addition, the voice of birds, although produced from a slightly different structure to that of man, bears some resemblances. The ability of some species of birds, such as mynahs and parrots, to mimic man's voice shows that they can produce sounds closely similar to those that we make. One distinctive feature of the voice of birds is that some can produce as many as three or four complex sounds that overlap one another in time; in other words the voice-producing organ can produce different sounds that are not just harmonics of one another simultaneously.

The other important feature of the voice, and hearing, of birds is the speed with which a message can be transmitted and received. Some complex songs may include as many as 80 notes per second. Such sounds seem like a single continuous note to the human ear and can only be seen not to be so by examination of sound spectrograph recordings of the song. Not surprisingly, if the bird can give such calls it can also receive them. The speed of the auditory response of birds may be of the order of ten times as fast as that of man.

The animal kingdom has developed many ways of transmitting messages, but sound is a particularly useful form of communication. Sound travels well in most of the habitats in which birds live and is a much better method of communication in habitats such as woodland than any other type. Thus it is not surprising that birds use sound as one of their most important forms of language.

Bird songs are the most elaborate series of message in the language of birds. Song

A Winter wren *Troglodytes troglodytes* in song. Wrens have well-developed songs which are often relatively loud. Several species maintain their territories for most of the year, and may be heard regularly throughout this period. Song is not only used in territorial defence, but also in a wide variety of other circumstances connected with courtship and nest-building.

(European) Coots *Fulica atra* defending their nest against a marauding polecat. Birds have many methods for defending their nest against predators including the giving of alarm calls so that the other member of the pair, or sometimes other birds, may come to their assistance.

(European) Blackbird *Turdus merula* feeding young. Young birds stimulate their parents to feed them by giving begging calls; the more intensely they call the harder the parents work to feed them. Only when the young are fully satiated do they stop calling for food.

During the breeding season the Common snipe *Capella gallinago* has an aerial display which it accompanies with a drumming noise, produced by the passage of air over the outermost pair of tail feathers. The noise can be reproduced by fitting a snipe's tail to a weight and whirling it overhead on a string.

has tended to be connected with the 'song-birds' (Passeriformes), but this is a very misleading view for two reasons. Firstly some non-passerine birds have complex and beautiful calls—the trilling song of Redshank or Greenshank and the laugh of the Kookaburra to take but two examples. Secondly, other birds with, to us, simpler calls use them apparently in the same way as do the more complex singers and therefore, at least to the other members of the same species, these calls also qualify as song.

Song is not usually produced equally at all times of the year, but is mainly concentrated during periods prior to breeding when territories are being set up and courtship undertaken. The tendency to sing appears to be closely correlated with the presence of sex hormones in the blood and these, of course, reach a peak around the time of breeding. In many temperate species, there is a brief resurgence of territorial behaviour and also of singing in the autumn just after moult has been completed. Song also varies within the day in relation to the bird's other activities, being commonest in early morning or in fine weather and less frequent at other times.

As has been mentioned, songs may be relatively complex. They are, however, highly characteristic, each species usually having a very distinct song. A complex song usually includes a series of notes that are formed into a recognisable pattern; also, the song is often of a fairly characteristic length though it may be repeated again and again.

There are probably three main functions of the song and the importance of each may vary between different species. By recognising their own type of singing, birds achieve reproductive isolation from other species. By singing, a male bird announces his claim to a territory and also endeavours to attract a mate.

Although the song of each species is characteristic of that species, each individual male bird usually develops a song that is slightly different from that of his neighbours.

Song is an ideal means of communication between birds especially in such habitats as woodland, where it is difficult to maintain contact between individuals by any means other than sound. The Three-wattled bellbird *Procnias tricarunculata* (1) lives in thick forest but its calls can be heard at a considerable distance. The passerines generally have the most complex songs, a good example being the (European) Blackbird *Turdus merula* (2). However, such birds as the Oriental hawk owl *Ninox punctulata* (3) which have simpler calls do not necessarily have simpler vocal organs, and there are many passerines, for example, the Jackdaw *Corvus monedula* (4), that also have relatively simple calls. Most birds sing with the bill wide open, but the doves make their cooing notes in the throat, usually with the bill closed, as in the Collared dove *Streptopelia decaocto* (5). The parrots, such as the Eclectus parrot *Eclectus roratus* (6), are well known for their harsh screaming calls but many of them are good mimics and can be taught to talk.

Although they may sound similar to us, there are subtle small differences. By recording the songs of individuals and playing them back to the birds it has been established that the birds themselves can easily distinguish between the songs of their neighbours and those of strangers. A territory holder does not respond vigorously to the song of a well-known and established neighbour, but reacts sharply to the song of a stranger. The known neighbour with whom the territory owner has already established some form of 'working agreement' does not pose the same threat to a territory holder as does the sudden appearance of a strange bird that might be trying to usurp his place. Hence the difference in the response. Curiously perhaps, the bird does not seem to recognise his own song, as some species may react to this as they would to that of a stranger.

Other variations within a species have been established. In many species not only does the individual have a recognisable song, but the individuals may have a variety of different songs; repertoires of up to six or eight different song types have been described within individuals. It is not known whether each of these variants carries a different message to others of the species. Attempts to find correlations between the

1

2

3

4

5

6

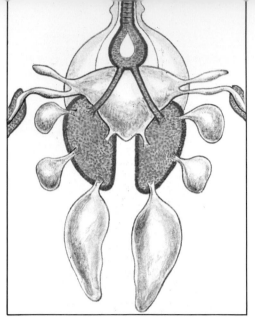

Birds are unusual in that they have air-sacs, thin bags through which air can flow after passing through the lungs. They are thought to aid respiration when the birds are in flight. The air sacs extend into the hollow bones.

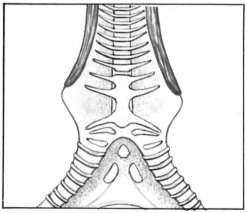

The syrinx is the bird's sound producing organ. The resonating chamber or tympanum is at the bifurcation of the windpipe and contains vibrating membranes formed from the connective tissue between the cartilages. Special muscles control the tensions and positions of the membranes, allowing different sounds to be made.

The trachea through which the air is passed from the nostrils to the lungs is a strong tube strengthened with cartilaginous rings which prevent it from collapsing.

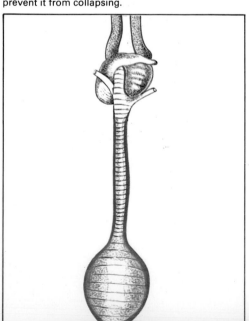

different songs in a repertoire and the circumstances under which they are given have so far proved unsuccessful. Birds appear to switch from one song to another after they have been singing one for a period of time; it is as if they get bored. However, when two birds are actively engaged in a border dispute, they may tend to use the same song type as each other. If one bird switches from one song type to another, the other bird will often follow suit.

One also commonly finds local variations in the songs of different species. These 'dialects' may occur over quite large areas or they may be local in extent. Simply by crossing over from one valley to the next one may find that the song of a given species has changed quite markedly. The European Chaffinch is a species with many different local dialects. Needless to say, on a wider geographical range the language of a species may differ much more than on the local scale.

In recent years some observations have helped to establish how some of these variations come about. Birds raised in captivity in sound-proof cages still develop a song which, although poor and rather muddled, is recognisably that of their own species. Such a song starts particularly poorly and slowly improves although it never reaches a very high standard of performance. It is clear therefore that such birds inherit some ability to produce a song of the basic pattern of their species. When these birds are allowed to hear the songs of others of their own species they rapidly incorporate details of the other songs into their own and so improve their song. Thus their songs could be said to comprise both inherited and learned components. If the birds that are raised in isolation are played songs of other species, even others with fairly similar songs, they do not copy these. Thus, to recognise the song of another species is an inherited ability.

There seems to be a period when the young bird is particularly sensitive to hearing the songs of others of its kind and is most likely to copy songs from other individuals. This sensitive period is often when the bird is approaching one year old—coming up to its first breeding season. Nevertheless, birds may go on adopting phrases from others and improving or modifying their own song throughout their life.

By and large, song is produced by the males and not by the females of a species. However, there are exceptions, some of which suggest that the females of many species may be capable of singing, but just do not do so very often. A female Great tit has been observed in full song defending the territory when her mate was sick for a few days. When he recovered she stopped singing. Female European robins sing regularly in autumn when they maintain their own independent territories. In the phalaropes (where the female takes the dominant role in courtship) the female sings and the male does not. Female Canaries, given doses of male hormones, have developed songs as good as those of males.

There are a number of species in which the female regularly sings. These include species where members of a pair sing to one another, a habit known as duetting. A particularly complex form of duetting is found in some of the African shrikes of the genus *Laniarius*. This type of singing is called antiphonal singing. One bird sings a short snatch of song and the other sings the next. Often the song may be composed of just the two parts, but in other species such as some of the Asian Laughing thrushes, the song may be much more complex with alternate snatches of the song given by each partner. Indeed the whole song is so well synchronized and given so rapidly that even a human observer watching closely cannot be certain which parts of the song are given by which bird. This can only be established by filming in conjunction with sophisticated tape-recording equipment. Such equipment can also produce sound spectrograms which can be analyzed in detail. Such analyses have shown that the speed of response of the second bird to the first bird is extremely fast, at least three times as fast as is possible for humans. This confirms a point made earlier, namely that although the auditory equipment of birds shows many similarities to that of humans, the ability to separate sounds that are close together in time is far superior in birds.

Hole nesting species such as the Great tit *Parus major* may defend themselves by making a loud hissing when a predator such as a squirrel tries to enter. This sound is said to resemble the hiss of a snake.

Displays and calls of Little ringed plover *Charadrius dubius.* When threatening another of its own species (1), the plover exposes the black facial breast bands fully to its opponent. When the parent bird warns the young of approaching danger (2), they scatter and crouch until the 'all-clear' is given. When a predator is close to the eggs or young (3), the parent may try to lure it away by dragging a wing and pretending to be unable to fly. Once the predator is a safe distance from the nest the bird flies off.

Warning and Fear

As with behaviour in general, one has to be extremely cautious in interpreting the behaviour of other animals in terms of love, hate and fear; it is all too easy to become uncritically anthropomorphic about such activities, to the extent that we think that we have explained them in terms of how we ourselves would feel, when in reality the reason for the animal's behaviour may be quite different. We can, however, see a number of circumstances where birds give calls that have the effect of drawing another bird's attention towards, say, an approaching predator and so enable it to take evasive action. Also birds plainly show avoidance of a number of objects that could be harmful to them; while the behaviour may not necessarily be fear in human terms, it is certainly adaptive for them to take such evasive action quickly.

For the vast majority of birds, there is almost always the threat of danger lurking somewhere and so caution pays off; discretion is the better part of valour. In practice birds soon learn to recognize the inoffensive from the enemy; in the first instance this is done by the young bird observing the reactions of its parents. Later, as knowledge accumulates, the bird only reacts to strange or unknown objects, being wary of these until it has had a chance to gauge the possible threat. Many birds can remember dangerous objects for long periods.

Once an enemy is identified, the bird can take appropriate action. If the marauder is a mammal, the bird can easily avoid it by staying clear of the ground. If, however, the threat comes from another bird then it must be avoided in another way. This might entail diving into thick bushes, onto or under water or trying to outpace it, depending on the species of bird threatened and the area in which it is. Often such flight is accompanied by alarm calls, warning the neighbouring birds of the threat. There have been a number of arguments about the dangers to the individual bird of giving an alarm call and so perhaps attracting the predator to itself. However, these

45

Woodpeckers may respond to seeing a predator or hearing an alarm call by hiding. Here a Great spotted woodpecker *Dendrocopos major* ducks as a Sparrowhawk *Accipiter nisus* passes over.

In some conflict situations, such as when a bird is uncertain whether to attack or flee from another, it may indulge in some quite different behaviour. Here (1) a Common oystercatcher *Haematopus ostralegus* hides its beak under its feathers in a sleeping posture. On other occasions, birds will mob a predator vigorously and often succeed in driving it away before it can find the eggs or young. In (2), Lapwings *Vanellus vanellus* mob a Carrion crow *Corvus corone*.

dangers may be outweighed by a number of other factors. Firstly parent birds have to give such calls in order to protect their offspring and secondly there are occasions when there is safety in numbers; by grouping tightly together the birds may be able to make it difficult for the attacking predator to single out and catch any one individual. Faced with a number of rapidly moving prey the predator becomes confused and is unable to make a decision. Thus European coots may pack in a tight group and splash up water when threatened by an attacking White-tailed eagle.

The alarm calls given under these conditions are very characteristic; they are thin, high notes which are particularly difficult to locate; hence they are unlikely to pose a great threat to the bird that gives them. Most species have a variety of warning calls that they give under different circumstances, enabling the other birds to gauge how frightened the calling bird is and of what it is frightened. Many species can 'understand' the notes of other species. For example the warning call described above is given by a number of small passerines, and the mobbing calls of Blackbirds when they have discovered a Tawny owl are also understood by many species. The mobbing probably helps each bird to learn where the potential danger lies and also, perhaps, to drive off the owl. The loud shrieking cries of captured birds may well be 'fear', but they also function to attract other birds to mob the predator and so, hopefully, distract his attention from the prey so that it may escape.

Young birds quickly learn to recognize many of their enemies from the reactions of their parents; they also learn to recognize and give the calls. Small birds, still in the nest, will crouch and remain silent when they hear their parents warn of an approaching predator; they learn to do this before they are a week old. Young nidifugous birds may learn to crouch when warning calls are given at still younger ages, sometimes when they are only a few hours old.

1

2

Bobwhites *Colinus virginianus* roosting in a circle. These birds haunt large open areas and by using this formation can guard against predators approaching from any point of the compass.

Masked wood-swallows *Artamus personatus* huddled together for roosting. By choosing a secluded site and keeping close together, they reduce the amount of energy needed for overnight survival.

Chimney swifts *Chaetura pelagica* roosting in a huddle. Several other species of aerial insectivore have been recorded clumping together in bad weather.

Sleep

Birds tend to sleep at those times of the day when they cannot feed. Thus not only do day-feeding birds sleep at night and nocturnal birds during the day, but birds such as waders and wildfowl sleep when the tide is high and they cannot feed. Typically, many sleeping birds insert their bill under their feathers and many of the smaller birds sit down on their legs, covering these with their fluffed-up feathers. By doing this, the birds cover the parts of the body from which heat can be most easily lost and so help to conserve energy. When perched in this way the birds are able to lock their feet to the branch securely. The tendon that curls the toes around the branch tightens as the joints bend and loosens as they straighten. Hence, as a bird sinks down onto its feet and relaxes its leg muscles, its feet become firmly locked around the branch.

Birds may roost singly or in huge numbers. Quelea roosts in Africa often contain many millions of birds and starlings may roost in small areas of woodland in numbers reaching into the millions; at times they may roost in such numbers that their droppings kill the trees. Some small birds, and some penguins, roost together in clusters in order to obtain warmth from one another. Long-tailed and bush-tits roost huddled together more closely in cold weather than in mild weather. Migrating swallows, confronted with cold weather, may occasionally clump together in large groups for the same reason. Some small birds that roost in holes or in their domed nests may also roost together. In Europe many Winter wrens are sometimes found roosting together in a single hole. Others, such as some of the sparrows, may build themselves a winter nest in which the pair shelters from the cold.

Some other birds conserve energy by becoming torpid at night. By doing this, the difference between the body temperature and that of the air is reduced and so the rate of heat loss is reduced. The best known example of this type of torpidity occurs in the hummingbirds. These very tiny birds would lose relatively large quantities of heat overnight unless they were able to go torpid. Some of the small birds such as the tits may lower their body temperature at night in very cold regions.

In order to minimize heat loss, roosting sites are normally chosen in sheltered positions where the wind and rain and most intense cold will not penetrate. A few Arctic species such as the Redpoll and some of the game birds roost in burrows in the snow. Such a position enables them to get some protection from the severest night temperature though presumably a few must perish by being buried in a very heavy snowfall and being unable to dig their way out in the morning.

Finding a position that is relatively sheltered from the weather is only one of the main prerequisites of birds. They must also find one where they are relatively safe from predators. This need undoubtedly dictates the use of a well-sheltered place in thick foliage where the bird will not be visible to owls. Some ground-dwelling birds, for example the Common pheasant, fly up into trees to roost where they are safe from predators such as foxes. Others may roost in the middle of open ground where they have ample warning of approaching enemies. Quail are reported to sleep in a small circle, facing outwards, so that they have a good opportunity to see any predator. Almost certainly one of the functions of the very large roosts is protection from predators. If one bird sees, or is attacked by, a predator it gives the alarm to all the others.

Many water birds roost either on islands where they are relatively safe from predators or in the middle of a large expanse of water. The flights of gulls towards reservoirs at dusk are now a familiar sight in many areas of the world. Under such conditions, deep sleep is impossible because the birds need to swim from time to time to avoid drifting to the bank.

A few species have odd roosting habits. Woodpeckers roost on the vertical trunks of trees in much the same position that they are seen to cling during the day. European treecreepers also roost in this position, but in crevices in the soft bark of trees. At

The Poorwill *Phalaenoptilus nuttallii,* a nightjar, is the only bird known to hibernate. Whether it spends the whole winter in a state of torpidity or merely a few days at a time is not, however, known. Several other groups of birds become torpid for short periods, often only overnight. These include the swifts, hummingbirds and colies, all species closely related to the nightjars. In the Colorado Desert in California, a Poorwill has been recorded hibernating in the same rock crevice during four successive winters.

Dunlin *Calidris alpina* roosting on tidal flats. Many waders have to feed at low tide and so sleep at high tide regardless of whether it is night or day. Much of their feeding is done by touch.

times they may hollow out the bark for this purpose and several birds may roost in adjacent hollows. The bat-parrots, *Loriculus,* hang by their feet, upside down, from the branches where they roost; hence their name.

Among the most extraordinary roosting habits known is that of the Common swift of Europe. Very many of these birds spend the whole of the night on the wing. These birds do not find it easy to land or take off from the ground and seem unwilling to touch down. The breeding birds, of course, have to have a nest site, but many of the non-breeding, younger birds do not appear to have a site where they can spend the night. These birds can be observed circling in the evening over reservoirs and then rising upwards at dusk. Radar observations show that they spend the whole night aloft. Since the same birds seem to be involved each night, it is possible that individuals may not land at all during the whole of the summer. Since roosts have not been noted in their winter quarters, it is just possible that Common swifts do not land at all except to breed and may spend their early non-breeding years totally aloft. It is not known how they are able to do this or to how many species of swift this may apply. Individuals of other species are known to roost in caves and rock crevices. The dusk ascent is thought to be associated with the need to be above the level where there is any danger of flying into obstacles.

Many birds cannot sleep deeply since they are quickly on the wing if disturbed. One suspects that it is necessary for many of them to sleep lightly for fear of predators. However, those birds such as the hummingbirds that go torpid become so deeply asleep that they may take several minutes to awaken since it is necessary for them to re-heat their bodies before they can become active again.

FEEDING

Eating and Drinking

Many birds need to drink frequently. The majority of species do this by dipping the beak into water, filling the mouth and then raising the head to let the water run down the throat, as shown in the Song thrush *Turdus philomelos* (1). The pigeons differ in being able to drink continuously, sucking the water up with a pumping action as in the Turtle dove *Streptopelia turtur* (2).

The Golden eagle *Aquila chrysaetos* drinking.

As a result of their lack of teeth, birds feed rather differently from mammals. The food is not chewed at all, but transferred to the gizzard where it is ground up. Many birds eat their prey whole. At times this may involve the swallowing of lizards, snakes, large insects or fish that are large in relation to the size of the bird. The majority of birds, however, take smaller prey than this; finches, warblers and thrushes for example take prey that are usually of sufficiently small size for them to be easily swallowed. Others such as the gulls and many birds of prey tear up larger prey with their beaks. Yet others such as the ducks and game birds may eat foliage.

Birds do not usually prepare their food, but there are exceptions. Many bee-eaters remove the stings from their prey before swallowing them. The bee is beaten against the perch and then vigorously wiped along the perch removing the sting. Birds that eat large insects, for example caterpillars which have powerful biting mouthparts, usually peck the head of their prey. This prevents the possibility of the insect biting the bird after it has been swallowed. In some cases the head capsule of the insect may be completely discarded. Occasionally birds remove the gut of caterpillars.

Feeding is a dangerous occupation since the bird must concentrate upon it and therefore run the risk of not noticing the approach of a predator until it is too late. In some cases the use of the crop may be advantageous since it enables the bird to feed in an exposed site for a very short period and then to retire to a safer place where it can digest the food that it has collected. Another situation when feeding may be dangerous is when sea birds come down to catch fish driven to the surface by larger fish. The birds risk becoming the prey themselves. Drinking is often dangerous too. Some birds obtain most of their water from their food, especially the insectivores and birds of prey which may never need to drink, but many other species must come down to water. In doing so the birds expose themselves to predators. This is especially true in the drier areas of the world where birds must congregate in large numbers at the few water holes available. The birds of prey know only too well where these are.

Many small birds may satisfy their needs from the dew or rain by merely sipping drops off the vegetation. Others such as the swallows and swifts collect water by accurate dives across the surface of lakes and rivers. Most birds use the same method as does the domestic hen; the beak is lowered into the water, the mouth filled and the head raised so that the water runs down the throat. The pigeons, sandgrouse and buttonquails are able to drink by dipping the beak into the water and sucking it up with a pumping action.

Sea birds face special problems since the available water is very salty. When they drink seawater, the majority of the salt is transported, through the blood supply, to the nose where it is transferred to large nasal glands which eliminate most of the salt from the body—their kidneys are relatively inefficient in this respect. When it has drunk a large quantity of salt water, a sea bird looks as if it has a cold. Droplets of highly concentrated salt run to the tip of the bill and are shaken off with a flick of the head.

The Two-barred (or White-winged) crossbill *Loxia leucoptera* feeds largely on pine seeds. The male is red and the female greenish-brown.

The bills in seed eating birds are modified to cope with a variety of size and hardness of seed coats. Short, stout bills are required to crack heavy seeds.

A male European Goldfinch *Carduelis carduelis* forages for thistle seeds.

Seed Eaters

Compared with mammals, birds do not always digest plant material efficiently; they do not have the ability to break down cellulose and digest leaves and grass in the same way that mammals do. Even those species that feed to a large extent on grass, such as the geese, do so by consuming great quantities of vegetation from which they extract relatively little of the available nutrients. The parts of plants which birds can and do eat in quantity are the seeds and fruits. A wide variety of birds consume one or other of these as a regular and major component of their diets. Amongst non-passerines one might list many of the ratites, the tinamous, a number of the ducks, the game birds, a number of gruiform birds, the sandgrouse, the pigeons, the parrots and the woodpeckers. Amongst the passerines, some tits, nuthatches and crows eat seeds for long periods of the year; however, the seed eaters *par excellence* are the finches of the four families Emberizidae, Fringillidae, Estrildidae and Ploceidae. Together there are some 600 species within these groups and the large majority are seed eaters for a major portion of the year. Not only are they very numerous, in terms of species, but also many of the species are exceedingly abundant; for example the pest of African grain crops, Quelea, may occur in colonies or roosts of many millions and devastate an area.

Seeds are hard structures and many are relatively difficult to break open and eat; often they are covered by a very thick outer shell or by a spiny case. A few species such as the Emu and the proverbial Ostrich seem able to swallow exceedingly spiky seeds and to digest them somehow or other. Most of the other birds that tackle the stronger seeds have ways of breaking into them: many such as the ducks and pigeons take only smaller seeds without strong coverings so that the problem does not arise to the same extent. Nobody who has seen one of the larger parrots opening seeds would readily put his finger near its beak! Indeed some of the finches can exert a considerable crushing force and, for its size, even the Blue tit has a powerful bite.

The larger parrots and macaws can crack open very large seeds with great ease; the bill of the Palm cockatoo is so deep and powerful that it can open the hard nuts of palms with relative ease. Some of the finches have equally remarkable strength. The Hawfinch opens cherry and olive stones to get at the seeds inside; it has been demonstrated that a cherry stone requires a crushing load of from 65–80 lb (30–36 kg) to break it open while the equivalent power required to open an olive stone is 106–159 lb (48–72 kg). Yet this two-ounce (56 gm) bird is able to achieve these strengths and split the stones. Hawfinches have immensely heavy, powerful skulls and beaks with extremely large muscles; the mandibles are protected from dislocation by a strong ligament that is partly ossified.

It is normally accepted that closely related species survive alongside one another by virtue of each species taking different foods; in this way they divide up the resources of the habitats. In the finches the different species tend to take seeds of different sizes, the larger species taking the larger seeds. The bills of the finches are specially adapted to deal with seeds and each size of bill is best suited for husking seeds of different sizes. The sharp edge of the lower mandible fits into a V-shaped cleft in the upper mandible. Using the tongue, the finch positions the seed in this cleft so that the joins in the husk or stone are in a position against the sharp edge of the lower mandible.

The shape of the bird bill has been modified to take advantage of a large variety of foods. (1) The Galapagos Woodpecker finch *Camarhynchus pallidus* uses a twig to probe for insects, (2) the European nightjar *Caprimulgus europaeus* has bristles round the mouth which help to trap insects, (3) the North Atlantic Gannet *Sula bassana* has a stout, pointed and conical bill and dives from a considerable height into the water, (4) the Anhinga *Anhinga anhinga* impales the fish with its sharp bill, (5) the (Caribbean) Greater flamingo *Phoenicopterus ruber* has marginal hooks for filter feeding, (6) the African spoonbill *Platalea alba* feeds while wading, sweeping the partly open bill from side to side.

The Palm (or Black) cockatoo *Probosciger aterrimus* uses its powerful beak to crack open hard palm nuts and extract the contents with the pointed tip of the bill.

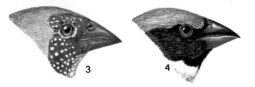

The Hawfinch *Coccothraustes coccothraustes* (1) has a very powerful beak capable of splitting cherry stones while the Redpoll *Carduelis flammea* (2) with its weaker bill eats small seeds such as those of birch. The Australian Star finch *Bathilda ruficauda* (3) and the South African waxbill *Estrilda melanotis* (4) are both members of the Estrildidae family of small finches that feed mainly on small grass seeds.

After part of the husk has been cut through by the mandibles, the seed is rotated and another crack made, until all the husk has been removed. The groove in which the seeds are held is wider at the back of the skull than at the front so that seeds of different sizes can be accommodated. If the seed is too large it shoots out of the cleft when pressure is applied. Hence there is an upper limit to the size of the seeds that each species can handle efficiently. Since large finches find it uneconomic to eat small seeds, each species tends to be restricted in its diet to a range of seed sizes related to the structure of its bill.

Seed eating birds face other problems in relation to their diet; they need powerful gizzards with a good supply of grit in order to break up the seed. Seed eaters usually possess a crop, a bag-like extension of the side of the lower throat in which food can be stored. Those birds that bring seeds back to their young carry them in the crop. Many of the birds, especially the smaller finches, go to roost in mid-winter with a crop full of seeds, enabling them to have a 'snack' in the middle of the night and so increase their chances of survival. Lastly, the possession of a crop enables the birds to feed rapidly in exposed places and digest the seeds later in safety.

Relatively few of the seed eating birds eat seeds the whole year round. For example the tits are largely insectivorous during the summer season and many of the finches raise their young on insects as well as seeds; there is a tendency for birds that have late broods to feed the young larger quantities of seeds than they brought to their earlier broods. This may reflect the increase in the number of available seeds, but caterpillars are becoming scarcer at this time as well and this may, in part, account for their diminuition in the diet. The full reasons for feeding insects to the young are not known, but insects are probably richer in certain proteins necessary for animal growth than are seeds. In addition, insects contain large quantities of water which are essential to a growing chick; seeds do not. The periods of the year when birds change over from a diet of seeds to one of insects and back again may be difficult ones for the birds. The digestive tract is more powerful and muscular when the bird is eating seeds than it is when the bird is eating insects; little is known of what happens during the period of changeover from one diet to the other.

Four different seed eaters. (1) Cardinal *Pyrrhuloxia cardinalis* of North America, (2) Greenfinch *Chloris chloris* of Europe, (3) Evening grosbeak *Hesperiphona vespertina* also of North America, and (4) Red-checked cordon bleu *Uraeginthus bengalus* which occurs on the southern side of the Sahara from Senegal to the Sudan.

Two of the most northerly seed eaters, the Snow bunting *Plectrophenax nivalis* and the Lapland bunting (or longspur) *Calcarius lapponicus*. Both these birds breed in the high Arctic though the Snow bunting also breeds in mountains further to the south. Both migrate southwards for the winter.

◀

Some finches remain on a diet of seeds the whole year round and feed their young on them. Their breeding seasons closely match the timing of their main food stocks of seeds. In many parts of Britain the Crossbill feeds its young on the seeds of pine cones, finding them most plentiful when the cones open in spring. In order to have its young in the nest in March and April when these seeds are available, the Crossbill lays its eggs before this date, often in February or early March; hence the females may be incubating during some of the coldest weather of the winter. In many parts of continental Europe, the Crossbills feed their young on the seeds from spruce cones which open even earlier; under these circumstances the birds may be found breeding at almost any time during the winter. As a result, the Crossbill has perhaps the most variable breeding season of any species of European bird. By way of contrast, the Goldfinch brings very small seeds of herbaceous plants to its young and often does not start breeding until May, having young in the nest from June onwards when the new crop of seeds is plentiful. If conditions are suitable the Goldfinch may go on nesting through until late summer; it is one of the latest European passerines to nest.

Seeds keep well and as a result, many seed eating birds store seeds so that they can find them during the winter when food is more difficult to come by. Jays and Old World nutcrackers store large seeds such as acorns and hazel nuts as do the Acorn woodpeckers. Smaller birds such as tits and nuthatches store small seeds in crevices in the bark from which they retrieve them later. During late summer and early autumn the birds may spend a high proportion of their time storing seeds.

The Toucan barbet *Semnornis ramphastinus* (1) lives in the mountains of northern South America. Like other members of the family it eats large quantities of seeds and fruits though, like many finches, it takes insects to its young. Head of Toucan barbet *Semnornis ramphastinus* (2). The powerful beak has serrations on the side which enable the bird to grip and cut into fruits easily. Barbets also use their bills for tearing wood when making nesting holes.

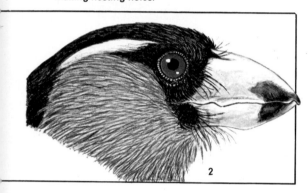

The Green imperial pigeon *Ducula aenea* of India and South East Asia takes very large fruits which it can swallow because it has a distensible gape. Such fruits often have large stones which the birds void undamaged.

Fruit eaters. (1) Knysna turaco *Tauraco corythaix* from Africa, (2) Bar-tailed trogon *Trogon collaris* from South and Central America — many trogons also eat insects which they catch on the wing, and they take fruits by hovering alongside branches, (3) Toco toucan *Ramphastos toco* from South America, (4) Yellow-bellied fruit pigeon *Leucotreron cincta* from the East Indies, (5) Double-toothed barbet *Lybius bidentatus* from central and east Africa and (6) Blue-crowned hanging parrot *Loriculus galgulus* from South East Asia. ▶

Fruit Eaters

Seed eating birds remove the offspring from a plant. Because of this, plants have evolved many mechanisms which make it more difficult for animals to remove seeds. For example, seeds may have hard shells or the trees may have short, well-synchronized seeding periods so that the animals have more food than they can possibly eat at one period and a dearth of food at another. From the evolutionary viewpoint, the strategy of a fruiting plant is quite different; we may say that it 'wants' the bird to eat the fruit in order that the seeds may be spread around. Although the fruits are highly digestible, the seeds are extremely resistant to the digestive juices of birds and usually pass through the gut undamaged.

In order to encourage the bird to eat and so distribute the seeds, the plant provides the fruit as a 'reward'. However, in order to have as many fruits as possible the plant grows fruits that are only just nutritious enough to attract birds; if they were less nutritious the birds could not survive on them and if they were more nutritious the plant would not be able to set so many seeds. Hence fruit eating birds eat a diet that is often poor in nutrients and they may have to spend long periods of the day feeding in order to get sufficient food. In further contrast to seed bearing plants, fruiting plants often bear fruits over long periods of the year in order that all their fruits may be taken by the birds. The relationships between fruit ripening and seed ripening have not been well worked out, but many fruits are bitter and distasteful as well as green in colour until the seeds are ripe; at this point the sugars are put into the fruit and it becomes highly coloured as a 'signal' to the birds that the fruit is ready to be eaten.

Fruits are often relatively large in size and, as a result, many of the fruit eating species have wide bills and gapes, enabling them to swallow the fruits whole; the toucans not only have a large bill, but a long one which enables them to reach small fruits from a strong perch. Once swallowed, the soft fruit is relatively rapidly broken down and digested. Although small seeds are passed through the digestive system, the large seeds of some of the tropical fruits are regurgitated.

In temperate areas fruits are not available all the year round so that many species that eat fruit at one time of the year may have to have other diets at other times of year. Many of the insectivorous migrants hunt for fruit in late summer and may concentrate upon the rich supplies of blackberries during the period when they are laying down the fat for their migration.

In Europe many fruits ripen at the time that small migrants are most abundant in the area. For example, plants may flower first in southern areas of Europe such as the Mediterranean and flowering occurs progressively later the further north one goes; however, the same does not hold for the fruiting seasons of many plants. The fruits ripen first in the northern areas, fruits in the southern areas maturing so slowly that they ripen after those in the north, but at the same time as the migrant warblers are passing through. It is difficult to escape the conclusion that the plants are timing their fruiting so as to coincide with the presence of the largest number of fruit eating birds.

In the tropics fruit may be available all the year round and several groups of birds feed largely on such a diet. The manakins and cotingids of South America and the fruit pigeons of Africa and southern Asia are good examples of such species, but many other less specialized species will take fruits when they are in abundance.

One tropical fruit eating species which deserves special mention is the Oilbird of northern South America. Although probably related to the insectivorous nightjars, it has taken to a diet of fruit. Like its relatives it is nocturnal, spending the day in dark caves where it finds its way about by echo-location. The Oilbirds leave their caves at night and set out in search of fruits. They feed mainly on the fruits of palms and of species of the family Lauracae, all highly aromatic fruits. Since the Oilbird has particularly well-developed olfactory lobes to the brain, it seems virtually certain that they possess a good sense of smell and track down these fruiting trees by scent.

Insect Eaters

Insect eaters. (1) Scarlet minivet *Pericrocotus flammeus* from India to South East Asia, (2) Firecrest *Regulus ignicapillus* from western Europe, (3) Bearded tit (or Reedling) *Panurus biarmicus* from Europe to central Asia, (4) Black-billed scythebill *Campylorhamphus falcularius* from South America, (5) Paradise flycatcher *Tersiphone paradisi* from India to South East Asia, and (6) Greater raquet-tailed drongo *Dicrurus paradiseus* from India and Malaya.

Although typically one tends to think of the small passerine insectivores, a wide variety of birds eat insects. Many of these are, at first sight, relatively unspecialized for this purpose—those such as the warblers having small all-purpose bills. One reason for this is that many insectivorous species turn to other diets at other times of year. It has already been mentioned that tits and other temperate birds such as the warblers eat fruit extensively prior to migration. For all-too-obvious reasons it is not possible to be a full-time insectivore in temperate areas.

The truly specialized insectivores that take insects the whole year round may, broadly, be divided into two types—those with stubby bills and huge gapes and those with long pointed bills. The latter group, which includes birds such as the bee-eaters, catch large flying insects and then return with them to a perch where they prepare them for eating, if necessary beating out the sting of the bees. Bee-eaters occur throughout much of the warmer areas of the Old World, with one species migrating for some distance up into the temperate areas. In South and Central America there is a remarkably similar group of birds, the jacamars, which feed in the same way.

The birds with stubby bills and broad gapes include a few that take large insects, such as the nightjars and the puffbirds, but many others take much smaller prey. These include the swifts and swallows. Some of these species take very tiny prey such as aphids and young spiders that are being blown along on their gossamer threads. When raising young, swifts take back large bolusses of insects to their brood. It may take some hours to collect such a large ball of small insects and some young swifts may only get fed four or five times a day or even less frequently if the weather is cold and insects are not plentiful. All these birds that feed on aerial insects are dependent on good supplies the year round; they do not change their diet. Almost all those that hunt prey in the temperate areas depart to spend the winter in more tropical climates.

Nightjars (Caprimulgidae) (1), swallows (Hirundinidae) (2) and swifts (Apodidae) (3) have extremely broad gapes which enable them to scoop insects out of the air.

Birds that catch insects on the wing. (1) European bee-eater *Merops apiaster* from southern Europe and west Asia, (2) Rufous-tailed jacamar *Galbula ruficauda* from Central and South America, (3) Vermilion flycatcher *Pyrocephalus rubinus* from Central and South America and (4) Puerto Rican tody *Todus mexicanus*.

The Great reed warbler *Acrocephalus arundinaceus* breeds in Europe and southwest Asia. Like almost all insectivores it migrates south outside the breeding season, spending the winter in tropical Africa. Here, a parent bird shades its young from the sun.

In North America a nightjar, Nuttall's poorwill, hibernates to overcome this difficulty though even this species may not hibernate for the whole winter; it may come out to feed on occasions when the weather is favourable.

A wide variety of other species of birds take insects, though not quite as dramatically as the swallows, bee-eaters and flycatchers which hawk them on the wing. The warblers feed primarily on insects which they glean from the foliage. Treecreepers and nuthatches climb up and down the trunks of trees searching for insects hidden behind the bark; the nuthatches may probe deep into the bark in their searches. In South America the woodhewers have evolved a wide range of birds that, like treecreepers, probe amongst the bark of trees. Perhaps the most specialized of insectivores that hunt for their food in the trunks of trees are the woodpeckers which drill holes into the burrows of beetle larvae and withdraw the grubs with their long tongues; the tip may be barbed or sticky to help them grip their prey. In the Galapagos Islands the Warbler-finch uses a sharp thorn to probe in holes for grubs, spearing them and pulling them out; it is one of the few animals known to use a tool regularly.

Many large birds also feed on insects. Birds such as rollers, hoopoes and hornbills take many large insects in their diet. Storks and herons may feed on large grasshoppers; the Cattle egret has acquired its name from its habit of closely following the cattle so that it can pick up the insects disturbed by them as they walk through the grass. Many of the marsh-dwelling terns eat insects. Birds of prey too may feed on insects: some of the smaller falcons include a high proportion of insects in their diet and even larger birds such as kites may descend on swarms of locusts and devour them. At times of great abundance such as these, many birds that do not regularly make use of insect food will join the hunt; for example, large numbers of species may be seen feeding on termites when these hatch.

The Red-throated diver (or loon) *Gavia stellata* nests on islets or beside freshwater lochs and feeds on the sea; it is often seen flying between the two places, bringing food to the young.

The (Common) Puffin *Fratercula arctica* is a highly colonial fish eating bird. It digs its burrows in soft soil, often preferring burrows already made by rabbits or other birds. The parents bring as many as 20 or 30 small fish to the young at a single feed.

Common eider *Somateria mollissima* is a seaduck that is widespread along north temperate coasts. It feeds in shallow water on a wide range of shellfish, crabs and mussels.

Fish and marine invertebrate feeders. (1) Common oystercatcher *Haematopus ostralegus* eats shellfish and crabs and also takes worms and insects inland, (2) Ruddy Turnstone *Arenaria interpres* turns over small stones and seaweed in its search for invertebrate food, (3) Arctic tern *Sterna paradisaea* takes a wide variety of small fish, (4) Black-throated diver (or Arctic loon) *Gavia arctica* takes larger fish, in the breeding season these may be freshwater species from near the nest, (5) Razorbill *Alca torda* feeds its young mainly on small sand eels and (6) Rockhopper penguin *Eudyptes crestatus* is widespread in the Antarctic. ▶

Fish Eaters

Species of six orders of birds (penguins, divers, grebes, petrels, pelicans and herons) feed predominantly on fish, though not all the individual species do so. In addition to these a number of ducks, a few birds of prey, most gulls and terns, skimmers, auks and kingfishers feed largely on fish, as also do a few species of owls. Curiously no passerines do this, though the Dipper may eat eggs of various fish.

The different species hunt their prey in a wide variety of ways. Some dive and swim after them catching them from behind; these include the cormorants, mergansers, auks, penguins, divers, grebes and petrels. Others, including pelicans, Gannets, terns and kingfishers, dive upon them from above; all these must chase their prey briefly except for a few of the terns that pluck their prey from the surface. The fish eating birds of prey and owls plunge down on the prey and catch them in their talons. Herons stalk them along the bank or in the water and then pounce on them.

Fish are extremely slippery prey and birds have evolved several adaptations which reduce the chances of their escaping. Some, such as the petrels and cormorants, have a sharp hook on the end of the upper mandible with which they grab their prey. Others, such as the herons, darters, kingfishers and penguins, use the open mandible to 'spear' the prey, giving them two chances of striking home, though more often they catch the fish accurately between the mandibles. The darters have two specially adapted neck vertebrae which enable them to catch their prey more easily; the birds swim with their necks folded back, but when they reach forward to try and catch a fish, the configuration of these vertebrae enables them to 'snap' the neck over at great speed. Similarly the long necks of the herons enable them to reach forward a great distance when they stretch out to strike at prey.

Once captured, the prey must be held firm so that it cannot escape. Again, a wide variety of methods are used. Many herons have backward facing serrations along the sides of the bill, penguins have them mainly on the tongue. Mergansers have toothlike extensions to the sides of the bill which they clamp into their prey. Some such as the auks and cormorants may bite the prey hard on its initial capture in the hope that it will not be able to struggle any further. The owls, Ospreys and sea eagles have particularly long talons which sink into their prey and greatly roughened pads on their toes which enable them to prevent their prey from slipping. Most of these fish eating birds, including the owls, have unusually long legs which are bare of feathers; presumably this reduces the amount of water-logging when the bird strikes the water.

Some of the terns take their prey without ever settling on the water; they just snatch them off the surface. Indeed a number of sea birds are only poorly water-proofed and do not normally settle on the water. Such species include not only some of the terns, but also the frigate birds and some of the storm petrels. Whether they rest or how they do so is not known; certainly since they only make landfall in the breeding season the storm petrels do not come to land to rest.

Another group of species which do not usually catch their prey by settling on the water is the skimmers; these species have a remarkable way of catching fish. They feed on tiny fish and prawns that lie just below the surface of the water. A skimmer's beak is unusual in that the lower mandible is half an inch or so longer than the upper one and also in that it can raise its upper mandible well out of the way of the lower mandible. The bird flies along maintaining a very precise level just above the surface of the water with the tip of the lower mandible cutting through the water. As it makes contact with a small fish beneath the surface the bill snaps shut as a result of a reflex action and the fish is caught. It does not seem that sight is involved in the capture though it must be in the maintenance of the bird's position above the water. Skimmers will even fish in drying pools only an inch deep, so accurate is their flight.

Sight is important for predatory birds, but fish eaters have two problems to contend with that other species do not encounter. A heron aiming at a fish underwater has to be able to allow for the refraction of the water, since the fish is not exactly

The American Anhinga (or Darter) *Anhinga anhinga* catches fish by stabbing with its beak open, thus doubling the chance of successfully spearing its prey. It then surfaces and turns the fish round so that it can swallow it head-first.

The Shelduck *Tadorna tadorna* searches through fine estuary mud for small snails. It uses a scything action while hunting and may leave tracks in the mud.

The King penguin *Aptenodytes patagonica* is one of the largest living penguins. Penguins eat crustaceans and squid as well as fish and may dive to considerable depths while hunting.

where it appears to be. No one is sure exactly how they do this: it may be that the young have to learn how much to allow for when they are fishing with their parents; in some species even birds of one year old are not as successful at fishing as are the older individuals so that the learning process may be long. Birds swimming after fish underneath the water have a different problem. The optical characteristics of water are different from those of air—as anyone who has opened his eyes underwater in a swimming pool will testify. Mammals such as seals have evolved eyes that suit the underwater conditions better than those in air, hence their, at times, apparent blindness when one approaches them. Some diving birds have come up with a better solution. Birds have a second, inner eyelid—the nictitating membrane. In diving species the central area of the membrane is clear but thickened; the membrane is kept across the eye while the bird is underwater and acts as a supplementary lens which makes the eye suitable for seeing underwater without the loss of good vision when the bird is in the air.

Fish eating birds have a wide variety of ways of bringing the fish back to their young. Some such as the skimmers bring back a morsel of prey each time that one is caught; this is a time-consuming operation and severely restricts the distance from the colony at which they can profitably feed. Other birds such as some of the terns bring back a small number of prey in the bill. Many of the auks do this also, though they may return with still larger numbers of prey. The Puffin is noted for its beakful of food; as many as 30 or more small sand eels may be brought in on a single visit. The Puffin catches the prey underwater, nipping it between the two mandibles and then transferring it so that it is held between the tongue and the upper mandible, thus allowing the bird to open its beak and catch further prey. Others such as the Gannet may bring the food back in their crop and the pelicans use their pouch. These birds usually travel further in search of food and so would waste too much time travelling if they did not bring back large quantities at irregular intervals. The extreme example of this habit is reached in certain oceanic sea birds such as some petrels and shearwaters where the birds may not return to the nest more frequently than every four or five days. In order to bring back the maximum amount of food they partially digest the fish they catch. Since fish are about 70% water, by doing this the birds can get rid of the water in the prey and bring back a full load of food which, weight for weight, is much more nutritious than if they brought it back undigested.

Although one tends to think of all sea birds as fish eaters, a number of species may specialize in other prey. Many of the smaller storm petrels patter along the surface of the water taking small crustaceans or other plankton. Some of the larger shearwaters and petrels specialize in feeding on krill, the widespread shrimp-like animals. Some albatrosses take jellyfish, including some of the venomous ones, having apparently developed some form of immunity to their stings. Albatrosses and penguins also take a large number of squid in their diet as do some of the terns and smaller shearwaters.

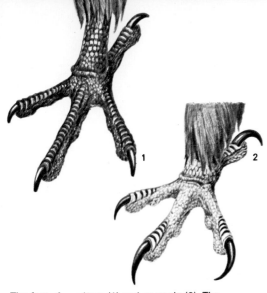

The feet of a vulture (1) and an eagle (2). The vulture can walk and run well on the ground but does not have the powerful gripping talons of the eagle. The eagle, however, cannot walk on land as well as the vulture.

The Palmnut vulture *Gypohierax angolensis* is an unusual bird of prey in that it has adapted to feeding on the fleshy parts of the fruits of the Oil palm.

The Everglade kite *Rostrhamus sociabilis* feeding exclusively on large aquatic snails. Its specific name *sociabilis* was given to it because of its colonial nesting habits.

The Secretary bird *Sagittarius serpentarius* is an aberrant bird of prey which feeds largely on snakes. It strides around on its long legs and kills the snakes with powerful blows from its feet. When attacking a snake it holds its drooped wings in front of itself, apparently to avoid being struck in the body by its poisonous adversary.

Birds of Prey

Two orders of birds, the Falconiformes and the Strigiformes, are usually classified as the 'birds of prey', often being referred to as the diurnal and the nocturnal birds of prey respectively even though a few of the owls are also diurnal. Although not closely related, the two groups have evolved a number of remarkable similarities that enable them to take their prey. There are similarities in the shapes of their bills and talons, both of which perform the same functions in the two groups, namely those of grasping their prey and of tearing it up to eat it. The positioning of the eyes in both groups is also similar, facing well forwards; possibly this increases the stereoscopic vision so essential to a bird that hunts moving prey.

The size of the prey taken—and the savageness of the larger birds—has usually been grossly exaggerated. Eagles may occasionally attack sheep, but almost always the sheep is seriously ill or dying before the eagle will risk doing so. Carrying off lambs or even small children are way beyond their capabilities; they could not hope to fly with such a load. As a result of this reputation however, the birds have been greatly and almost always unnecessarily molested and even exterminated. Sadly this habit still goes on, not only in the uneducated parts of the world but also in Europe and North America.

The largest birds of prey are the eagles, condors and vultures. The largest species may have wingspans of as much as eight or nine feet (about 2.5 m); a few much larger records are almost certainly exaggerations. Not all these birds kill their prey and most are not above scavenging from carcasses if they get the opportunity. Indeed these are the staple diet of the African vultures which usually, contrary to legend, feed only on freshly dead prey, if only because it is so swiftly consumed that they would get no other chance. The vultures do not carry food in their feet, but may so gorge themselves that they have difficulty taking off. The South American vultures, but not apparently the Old World species, have strong powers of scent and can locate decomposing bodies by this means; since some of these birds hunt over dense forest presumably they would have no chance of finding carrion there by any other means. One of the largest vultures, the Lammergeier, has learned to drop bones from a height onto rocks so that they break open and the bird can extract the marrow.

The larger eagles take a wide variety of prey, though on average much of this is smaller than believed; large objects tend to take longer to consume and so are noticed more frequently. Hares and rabbits are common prey for many species. The Wedge-tailed eagle of Australia takes some small wallabies, but now in many areas feeds largely on introduced rabbits. The Golden eagle takes many birds such as grouse and Ptarmigan. The White-tailed eagle takes many sea birds, and some tropical eagles specialize in taking monkeys from the tree-tops. The long-legged Secretary bird (usually put by itself in a separate suborder of the Falconiformes) is well known for its habit of taking snakes. A few other eagles also specialize in taking snakes as for example the Short-toed eagle—often called the Serpent eagle—which occurs through much of southern and western Europe and western Asia. Hence the prey taken is quite different for different species, but few prey are excessively large.

The Osprey *Pandion haliaetus* is a widespread, fish eating bird of prey. It has long, unfeathered legs and roughened pads on the toes which help it to grip its slippery prey.

Many predatory birds move their heads from side to side before attacking their prey; apparently this enables them to judge the distance more accurately. The bird shown here is a Black-and-white hawk-eagle *Spizastur melanoleucus* from Central and South America.

The Peregrine falcon *Falco peregrinus* attacks an American bittern *Botaurus lentiginosus*. Although the Peregrine does not often take prey as large as that figured here, from time to time it takes very large prey, such as geese.

Many of the smaller eagles have similar diets to the larger eagles though they take still smaller prey. The falcons are noted for fast flying and many of them swoop onto their prey at speeds which they could not reach in level flight. Many of the faster falcons take other birds as food, though a few of the smaller ones take insects. In contrast the goshawks, also bird eaters, have broad wings and fly much more slowly; they have much greater powers of quick manoeuvre and can chase small birds through the thick branches of a forest, something a falcon could not do. The kestrels are relatively slow-flying falcons with the ability to hover in light winds over grassy meadows where they hunt for small mammals on which they drop from a considerable height.

A number of birds of prey are specialized for odd careers. The African Bat-hawk hunts bats in the twilight, and hawks of the genus *Daptrius* have become vegetarian. However, taken as a group, it is the predatory habits and their speed that has attracted man and certain species have been tamed and used for falconry for many centuries. Falconry dates from over 1,000 years BC and at times was the prerogative of royalty.

The method used by birds of prey in hunting require considerable skill and, like most such, the hunters can meet with bad luck or scarcity of prey. Success at hunting affects the breeding of the birds of prey. They usually have only a small number of young, say one, two or three, though a few of the smaller species may lay more eggs. The young hatch one after the other rather than all together; hence during growth there is considerable disparity in size between nestlings in the same brood. If food is scarce the largest easily gets sufficient and the smallest quickly perishes having taken little food that might otherwise have been given to the larger. If the birds were all of equal size, then all might have been weakened. Hence this habit of hatching asynchronously increases the chance that some young may be raised successfully even when food is scarce. Once the young have left the nest they are cared for by their parents for some time while they develop the necessary hunting skills. Some of the largest eagles and condors look after their young for more than a year and so only breed every second year. The young birds may not breed for many years until they have perfected their skills to the extent where they can get sufficient food not only for themselves but also for their brood.

In many species the two sexes differ markedly in size. Apparently such differences have been evolved since they enable the two birds of a pair to hunt for a different range of sizes of prey and so increase the potential food available to the pair.

The owls are in many ways similar to the diurnal birds of prey, except that most of them hunt at night. They have exceptionally good night vision, they have high numbers of rods—the light sensitive cells of the eye—and few cones—the cells associated with colour vision; hence they see well in poor light but probably can only see in black and white. The ears of owls are positioned asymetrically on the head; apparently this helps them to locate a sound with great accuracy since something heard most clearly with one ear at one position of the head will be heard more clearly by the other ear when the head is in a different position. Using hearing, some owls can locate the position of a prey with an accuracy of at least one degree in both the horizontal and vertical planes and probably a good deal more accurately than that. To increase its chances of striking its prey, the owl spreads its talons as widely as possible along the direction that the animal is moving.

Many owls specialize in catching small mammals while others take birds. The European Tawny owl eats many earthworms. On damp nights these come to the surface in the dark and rustle on the leaves in the same way that a mouse would do, and under such conditions the owls take them in large numbers. Like the diurnal birds of prey, owls tend to have relatively small clutches and the young hatch asynchronously. When food is scarce, clutches may be small or the birds may not breed at all. However, in a few cases such as the Short-eared owl and the Snowy owl which feed on voles and lemmings, the birds may have large clutches in years when their prey are very numerous; as many as six or eight eggs may be laid and raised.

Birds of prey. (1) Steller's sea eagle *Haliaeetus pelagicus*, an inhabitant of the Pacific coast of Asia, eating a Steller's eider *Polysticta stelleri*, (2) Swallow-tailed kite *Elanoides forficatus* which is found from southern USA to South America, (3) Bateleur eagle *Terathopius ecaudatus* from Africa eats a wide variety of small animals and also carrion, (4) (European) Scops owl *Otus scops* and (5) Collared red-thighed falconet *Microhierax caerulescens* from Eurasia and Africa and from India and South East Asia respectively are very small birds of prey that feed mainly on insects, though the owl may also take very small mammals and reptiles.

The (European) Nuthatch *Sitta europaea* takes a wide variety of insects in summer but feeds mainly on seeds and nuts in winter. It wedges nuts into a crack and hammers them open with its powerful bill.

Many species store seeds in autumn in order to increase their winter food supply. The species shown here are (1) Acorn woodpecker *Melanerpes formicivorus* from western USA and (2) Grey jay *Perisoreus canadensis* from north Canadian forests. The woodpecker wedges nuts into holes it has made in the trunk of an oak tree, the jay sticks insects and seeds into crannies with the help of its own saliva.

The finfeet are represented by three species in different parts of the tropics. They take a wide variety of molluscs and crustacea and occasionally flying insects. This species is *Heliopais personata* from Asia.

Omnivores

As will have been apparent from the previous sections a great many birds take more than one type of food. Many show seasonal variation while others will not ignore a temporary abundance of any food that they can eat. Nevertheless there are birds that take a wide variety of foods at all times of the year, the jacks-of-all-trades. The Common starling is perhaps a good example of such a species; it may live in rural or urban areas, dig for small animals such as worms and wireworms in the meadow or plunder bird tables for food put out for other birds. In many areas they retire to the woods at the end of their nesting season, taking their fledged young with them to reap the caterpillars that have not yet completed their development. Soon after that they may return to gardens for the early soft fruits that are ripening; in places they may be a very serious threat to fruit growing.

The Common starling owes its great success in spreading over the wide areas of the world where it has been introduced to its ability to tackle such a wide variety of foods; in large measure it owes this ability to its 'all-purpose' beak. The medium length, straight beak enables it to probe the soil, pick caterpillars from leaves and reach and pull down fruits. In addition its strong feet enable it to perch easily in many places and on many types of twig. The Blackbird too is almost as successful at eating a wide variety of foods and has a similarly shaped beak.

Some of the gulls have also shown themselves able to cope with a wide variety of foods. The Herring gull has a longish bill with a slightly hooked tip. With this it is adept at catching fish; it probably did this most of the time before urban man appeared on the scene. The young gulls, in their brown plumage, stay on the shore much more than the older birds who are out at sea. Apparently the young gulls, being inexpert at fishing, augment their diet with quantities of odds and ends scavenged off the beach. A boat trip across the North Sea will be sufficient to show that the young gulls, although often prominent followers of ships close inshore, mostly drop out when the open sea is reached and only white birds follow the boat the whole way across. The hooked tip of the gull's beak serves not only to enable the adult birds to catch their prey, but also to help the young ones tear up dead fish and other offal on the beach. With this background of scavenging at least for part of the time, Herring gulls were well placed to make use of sources of food made available by man. Firstly they took the offal from fishdocks where the fish were cleaned, then they moved in and scavenged on the rubbish dumps that were placed on the outskirts of towns to deal with man's ever-growing piles of rubbish. In addition they discovered that the plough turned up huge quantities of earthworms and so they started to follow tractors across the fields. In recent years many gulls have spent more and more time in and around the coastal cities and are now spreading inland further and further and are also tending to remain there for longer periods each year. As a result of their ability to use these varied sources of food, the gulls have increased greatly in numbers until they have become quite a serious problem in some areas. They are therefore a good example of a species that has gained from the presence of man, unlike many others that have suffered from his influence.

Other scavengers are also good at eating a wide variety of foods. The Black kites normally scavenge dead animals or fish, but they too have learned the values of rubbish dumps; at other times they will turn to eating anything available and may descend on swarms of locusts in large numbers. As with gulls and the Common starlings, Black kites may be numerous in areas occupied by man.

All these birds could be called omnivores. There are, however, few birds that are truly omnivorous: seed eaters tend to remain seed eaters (though as we have seen, they may take insects in the breeding season) and relatively few other birds eat seeds in addition to their normal diet. It appears that either the bills, the digestive systems or the digestive enzymes of birds limit them to taking only a section of the full range of foods taken by all birds.

Omnivores. (1) Carrion crow *Corvus corone* from Eurasia, (2) (Black-billed) Magpie *Pica pica* from much of the north temperate areas of the world, (3) House sparrow *Passer domesticus*, (4) Starling *Sturnus vulgaris*, (5) Spotted bowerbird *Chlamydera maculata* from Australia and (6) King bird of paradise *Cicinnurus regius* from New Guinea ; bowerbirds and birds of paradise are closely related and take a wide range of fruits and insects. As a result of their omnivorous habits the House sparrow and Starling have successfully followed man's civilization.

The Hoatzin *Opisthocomus hoazin* is an unusual bird in that it feeds mainly on the leaves of certain riverine bushes. Here one of its young is seen reaching for food that the adult is about to regurgitate from the crop.

Specialized feeders. (1) Cattle egret *Bubulcus ibis* catches many large insects disturbed by big-game, it has spread through many parts of the world making use of man's cattle for the same purpose. (2) The Everglade kite *Rostrhamus sociabilis* and (3) Limpkin *Aramus guarauna* both live in American swamps feeding on large snails.

Specialized Feeders

As we have seen, most birds are specialized to some degree in the types of food they take or in the way that they take it. However, there are species that have particularly specialized ways of feeding; such methods often involve a highly specialized beak and this usually prevents them from being able to take a wide range of other types of food. Some birds, for example, are wholly dependent on a single species or group of species. The Limpkin, an American bird related to the rails but looking rather like a cross between a rail and a heron, feeds on large snails which it takes from shallow marshy ground. It apparently feeds on almost nothing else and even brings snails to the young which, at least at times, swallow them whole and later regurgitate the shell. Curiously, another species of bird is also dependent on these large snails. The Everglade kite, a rare bird in the USA but more numerous in tropical America, takes these large snails when they are near the surface; it picks them up in its feet and flies with them to a perch where it hooks the snail out of its shell with the long, curved tip of its upper mandible.

The African oxpeckers specialize in taking the ticks and mites off big game animals and, since the advent of man, have extended this habit to 'looking after' domestic cattle also. Not everyone believes that they are wholly beneficial since although they remove the parasites from open wounds in cattle they also sometimes eat the flesh and fat around the wound and so, it is believed, may extend the period for which the wound is open or even considerably enlarge it. Oxpeckers hang on the sides of large animals in the same way that woodpeckers hang on trees, and their feet are so adapted to perching in this position that they are not normally seen elsewhere.

It may not always be the bill that is specialized for taking an unusual diet. The

The hummingbirds of the New World and the sunbirds of the Old World, here depicted by (1) Purple-crowned fairy *Heliothryx barroti* and (2) Regal sunbird *Cinnyris regius* are highly specialized for the feeding on nectar. (3) The (European) Dipper *Cinclus cinclus* feeds on insects which it catches in fast-flowing streams.

The (European) Dipper *Cinclus cinclus* is adapted to take insects from the bottom of fast-flowing streams. It runs along the stones, at times flapping its wings to aid its progress. It is the only passerine bird that could be said to be a 'waterbird'.

honeyguides of Africa have a relationship with the Honey badger whereby they lure the animal to a bees' nest that they have found and once the badger has opened the nest they share the contents with him; they may also lure hunters to the nest. The unusual factor in the diet of these birds is that they eat not only some of the insects but also the bees' wax; this is not normally digestible by birds, but the honeyguides must have some special means of breaking it down. One species has even been recorded eating candles from a church altar!

In the warmer parts of the world there are a number of groups that specialize on feeding on nectar. In the New World the most striking group is the hummingbirds, over 300 species of tiny, brilliantly coloured birds. Their powers of hovering at flowers to obtain the nectar are well known: the smaller species may beat their wings as fast as 80 times per second. In Africa and much of the Oriental region we find the sunbirds which have a total of a little over 100 species. Again these birds are often brilliantly coloured and very small. They too may hover at flowers to obtain nectar, but they are not so proficient at doing so as are the hummingbirds. In the Far East, especially in New Guinea and Australia, another group of birds take nectar. They are the honey-eaters; about 170 species in all, these again include a number of small species, but lack the brilliant metallic hues possessed by many of the sunbirds and hummingbirds. In order to eat nectar many of these birds have the tip of the tongue divided into many hair-like processes. The white-eyes can roll the tongue into a tube. With this they 'brush' up the nectar and then suck it into their mouths. Even some of the lories and lorikeets of the Far East, have brush-tips to their tongues.

Specialization carries with it inherent dangers. Such birds are dependent wholly on a very special diet and if this becomes scarce or disappears then they face extinction. The very nature of their specializations does not enable them to switch easily to another type of food. Highly specialized birds have rarely been able to take advantage of man in this changing world; more often they find any change is for the worse. It is the omnivores such as the Common starling or the grain eaters such as the House sparrow that have benefited from the presence of man and have increased and spread widely.

67

HABITATS

Polar Regions

The polar areas of the world may be roughly defined as those where the mean temperature does not rise above 50°F (10°C) in the warmest month, and in which snow and ice cover the ground for long periods of the year. The polar regions of the south and north—the Antarctic and Arctic—differ in that the former area is frozen land surrounded by sea, whereas the latter is an area of frozen sea surrounded—in several places—by extensive land masses. These land masses support a variety of plant life during the short northern summer, but the Antarctic does not have a flora of equivalent richness.

Plant life forms the basis of all food chains. In order to grow, plants need sufficient light, warmth and nutrients; the first two of these are scarce in polar regions. Throughout the winter months there is little or no sunlight and thick layers of snow may cover the plants, cutting out what little light there is. As a result, plants in polar regions can grow only for short periods of the year. The animals which feed on these plants can likewise flourish only during these short periods.

In such inhospitable lands most birds cannot find food outside the summer period. In winter either there is no food at all or what there is lies covered with snow and ice and is totally inaccessible. An additional problem for the birds at such low temperatures is that they need very large amounts of food in order to provide the fuel to maintain their body temperature. It is not surprising therefore that most birds living in polar regions do so for only the short period of the summer months. Even so, their visit may be fraught with difficulty. The timing of both the spring thaw and the autumn freeze is very variable and so the breeding season tends to be a race against time in order that the birds may be able to raise their young and get away before winter returns. Many geese arrive in the Arctic with sufficient reserves to lay their eggs almost immediately and even to incubate them before food becomes available in the area. Hence they are able to start breeding well before they could if they were dependent on finding the necessary food on the breeding grounds. Many waders do not have time to moult after breeding and pause to do so on their southward migration. In some years a thaw may not come at all or comes so late that the birds fail to breed.

The presence of extensive land masses close to the pole in the Arctic, but not in the Antarctic, probably explains some of the differences between the birds found in these two areas. The Arctic tundra is covered with open valleys, streams and lakes in which plant life abounds. These areas are visited in summer by large numbers of birds which could not find a place for themselves in the Antarctic. Hence in the north there are many waders and wildfowl together with a few passerines, while few such birds visit the Antarctic.

The other habitat much favoured by birds of these regions is the sea, which is rich in nutrients and supports diatoms (microscopic plants), crustaceans and small fish. As a result we find an abundance of sea birds rarely matched in any other area of the world. The Antarctic is particularly rich in species, including large numbers of procellariform birds and, of course, the penguins.

The Adélie penguin *Pygoscelis adeliae* builds a nest of pebbles, probably in order to keep its two eggs above the ground so that they are not swamped by melting snow and ice.

The Sheathbill *Chionis alba* is a common scavenger in penguin colonies, taking eggs and unguarded small young and any food spilled during regurgitation, as is seen here.

Many polar species are white in colour, presumably as camouflage against enemies. Two high Arctic gulls, (1) The Ivory gull *Pagophila eburnea* and (2) Ross' gull *Rhodostethia rosea*. (3) The Snowy sheathbill *Chionis alba*, (4) McKay's bunting *Plectrophenax hyperboreus* from the Bering Straits, (5) Snow petrel *Pagodroma nivea* from the Antarctic, (6) Snow goose *Chen hyperborea* which breeds in Arctic Canada and (7) an adult Emperor penguin *Aptenodytes forsteri* standing by a creche of young. ▶

The Eagle owl *Bubo bubo* is found over a large area of the Old World and north Africa. It eats a wide variety of prey, some quite large. Here it is seen swallowing a hedgehog. It will later regurgitate the spines.

Nutcrackers occur in the temperate forests of both the New World and the Old World. (1) Clark's nutcracker *Nucifraga columbiana* from western USA and (2) the (Eurasian) Nutcracker *Nucifraga caryocatactes*. Both store seeds for winter use.

Temperate Forests

Temperate forests once covered huge expanses of the northern hemisphere but being on soil that made good farming land they have been progressively reduced. These forests are very different in type and may be divided into coniferous and broad-leaved woodlands. The most northerly forests are coniferous, and conifers are also to be found in the higher, cooler zones on mountains where lower temperatures again prevail. To the south of the conifers lie the broad-leaved woods and these may again be subdivided into two: the northern broad-leaved trees such as the oaks, beeches and maples are deciduous, while the more southerly ones, occupying such areas as the Mediterranean and southern USA, are evergreen. As their name suggests, these forests occur in places where the climate varies greatly around the year.

Although the temperate forests of the northern hemisphere are much more extensive than those of the southern, the latter are very important habitats for a wide variety of animals. There are four main areas of broad-leaved temperate forest in the southern hemisphere: there is a restricted area of Mediterranean-like forest on the southern tip of Africa; secondly, Australia, with its rich and unique fauna, has a variety of sclerophyll forests—the trees are primarily eucalypts, some growing as high as 300 ft (90 m); and lastly, both South America and New Zealand have extensive areas of Southern beech *Nothofagus* forests which contain a large number of animals and birds that occur nowhere else. The inroads presently being made into these latter forests are of considerable concern to conservationists.

In forests the large trees are constantly striving to get as much light as they can in order to grow well or to set seeds and fruit; they grow upwards and outwards, reaching for the sky and forming a closed canopy. As a result, in a mature woodland little light may reach the forest floor and plant growth there is poor. Most of the bird life follows this trend with many more species living in the trees than on the ground.

The temperate forests of the Old and the New Worlds have many similar species of birds.
(1) Sparrowhawk *Accipiter nisus* from the Old World, (2) Sharp-shinned hawk *Accipiter striatus* from the New World; both hunt small birds amongst the forest trees.

Woodpeckers are common in temperate forests. Here a pair of Great spotted woodpeckers *Dendrocopos major* tap to one another at a potential nest chamber they have made. The male has the red on the back of the head.

(1) Lesser spotted woodpecker *Dendrocopos minor* and (2) Red-headed woodpecker *Melanerpes erythrocephalus*; both these are birds primarily of deciduous woodland, though the latter is larger than the sparrow-sized former species.

Two features of temperate forests have overwhelming effects on the bird life in them. Firstly, the food supply varies markedly with the seasons; even the evergreen trees put on their new growths in the spring and usually produce their fruits in the autumn. The insect larvae grow best on the young tender leaves and so appear soon after bud-break. In European broad-leaved woods these caterpillars grow up very rapidly and soon disappear to pupate—often in the ground out of the reach of birds; those present in conifers grow a little more slowly and so are available to the birds for a longer period. Later in the summer, flying insects are more abundant, but both these and most other small animals become scarce as soon as the first autumn frosts occur. The insect eating birds then face a dilemma. Either they must go away or they must change their diet. Many, such as the warblers, leave the northern woods at this time and migrate southwards to spend the winter in much milder areas in or near the tropics. Others such as the finches and tits may stay, living largely on seeds. The thrushes also switch from worms and other small animals to fruits, at least when the ground is too hard to permit them to forage for the former. Hawthorn berries are a well-known winter diet for these birds.

Very few birds are resident in the northernmost forests; these are too cold and too thickly covered with snow for most birds to be able to survive and so they must move further south, though not as far as their insectivorous cousins. Another factor also governs whether or not these birds will migrate. The trees in temperate forests produce huge crops of seeds, but only in some years; in others there may be a great scarcity of seed and the birds may be forced to leave. Such sporadic fruiting occurs in many tree species, both conifer and broad-leaved. Years of great plenty are almost always followed by a year of crop 'failure', when no seeds are produced. It is not unlikely that such periodic fruiting has evolved as an adaptation against the seed eating birds and mammals; in one year there is no seed and the animals die in large

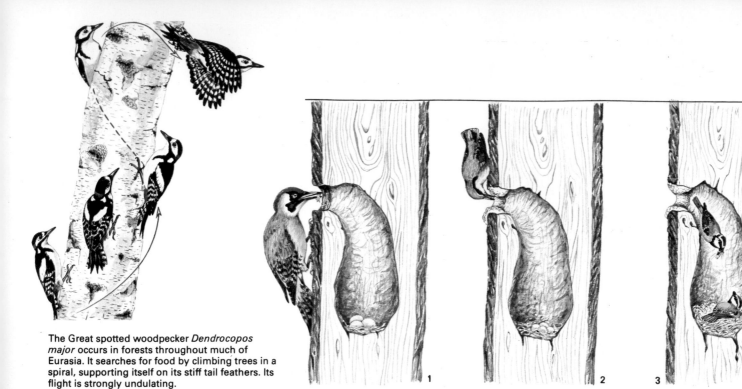

The Great spotted woodpecker *Dendrocopos major* occurs in forests throughout much of Eurasia. It searches for food by climbing trees in a spiral, supporting itself on its stiff tail feathers. Its flight is strongly undulating.

The Tawny owl *Strix aluco* may defend itself and its nest by fluffing its feathers up so as to make itself look as threatening as possible while hissing at the same time.

The Wryneck *Jynx torquilla* is an aberrant woodpecker which is found in Europe and Asia; it occurs primarily in broad-leaved deciduous forests. Most of the birds that breed in the north of its range migrate south for the winter.

numbers, in the next there is so rich a supply of seeds that the birds and mammals cannot eat it all and some of the seeds are certain to survive to germinate; by use of such a strategy the trees have a good chance of leaving offspring to fill the future woodlands. Whether such an idea is true or not, the numbers and movements of many birds of north temperate forests are markedly affected by the seed supply; waxwings, nutcrackers, crossbills and many other finches, nuthatches and tits move south in great numbers when seed crops fail.

Another bird was once dependent on seed crops—the Passenger pigeon which is now extinct. This bird once roamed the North American continent in huge flocks in search of the seeds of beech and oak. Some estimates suggest that there were as many as 1,000 million Passenger pigeons in a single flock. This gives some indication of how abundant seeds must have been. The pigeons nested colonially in great numbers and were easy game for hunters. However, the removal of the forests in order to create farmland must have greatly reduced their populations long before man, as a hunter, made serious inroads into their numbers.

When seeds are readily available, many birds may store them in large quantities so that they can find them more easily during midwinter when days are short and searching times reduced. Tits, jays, nutcrackers and nuthatches are among those that store food in this way. Many, such as the European jay, store large quantities of acorns in the ground, where some remain unfound and germinate in spring. Jays are important in the dispersal of these heavy seeds and may be the main agent in the uphill dispersal of the heavy acorns. The tits in Scandinavia tend to store their seeds in the bark of trees and crevices in branches since the ground is covered by deep snow in winter. Among the food-storers pride of place must go to the Acorn woodpecker of the western USA. This bird lives in small parties in open oakwoods. The party selects a tree or trees and drills large numbers of holes in the trunk; an acorn is placed in each hole and these storage trees are jealously guarded throughout the winter; indeed if a party loses its 'larder' it may well starve. The same trees are used as stores for many years.

Woodpeckers are an important part of the avifauna in temperate woodlands. Mostly they drill for, and extract beetle larvae from dead or damaged timber with their long tongues which have barbed or sticky tips. Many of them also eat seeds such as hazel nuts and acorns. In summer some species may not distinguish between insects and small birds. Broods of tits in holes in trees may be dug out and fed to the young woodpeckers. Another American species of woodpecker, the Sapsucker,

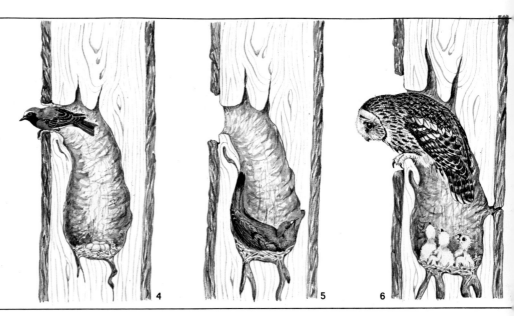

Many birds nest in holes in trees and at times these may be in short supply. Some birds, such as the Green woodpecker *Picus viridis* usually excavate a new hole for themselves each year (1). These may be used by (European) Nuthatches *Sitta europaea* which partly fill the entrance with mud to prevent other larger birds entering and evicting them (2). Tits, such as the Blue tit *Parus caeruleus* may use the hole also (3). When the entrance becomes slightly larger again (4), the (European) Redstart *Phoenicurus phoenicurus* may nest. As the hole starts to decay and the entrance becomes still larger, birds such as the Stock dove *Columba oenas* (5) or the Tawny owl *Strix aluco* (6) may use the site.

Jays are important members of the avifauna of many temperate forests where they store tree seeds for food in winter; since they fail to find many of them, they help to sow future trees. This species is *Garrulus glandarius*, found over much of Eurasia.

The Honey buzzard *Pernis apivorus* occurs in woodland throughout much of Eurasia. It is unusual for a bird of prey of its size in that it takes a large number of insects, including larvae from wild bees nests.

drills a series of holes in live wood and, as its name suggests, feeds on the sap that runs from these; it may also take the insects that gather on the sap. Woodpeckers nest in holes in trees, normally ones that they have excavated for themselves, often in sound timber.

Holes in trees provide nesting sites for a very wide variety of birds and are particularly valuable since they are relatively safe from predators such as large birds and most ground mammals. In addition to the woodpeckers, owls, tits, Jackdaw, Redstart, nuthatches, some flycatchers, doves and some American warblers all nest in holes in trees. In the relative safety of such sites they tend to have larger broods than do their relatives nesting in more exposed sites; although the large broods need more food, this can be brought to them over a longer period and hence the young birds raised in holes tend to stay there a little longer than birds reared in open, cup-shaped nests. Although many other birds build their nests in trees, a number perhaps surprisingly descend to the forest floor for nesting, especially if this has thick vegetation of brambles, ferns or mosses.

Although towards the poles the temperate forests are extremely cold in winter, the same is not true of forests nearer to the tropics where the winters may be relatively mild and many birds are resident the whole year round. For example, many honey-eaters and parrots are resident throughout the year in the forests of southern Australia. Some even breed in winter. Not all these birds are nectar feeders; many of the parrots eat seeds and many of the honey-eaters eat insects. However, some flowers and insects are available throughout the winter and these are plentiful enough to allow these birds to breed.

In the forests of the Mediterranean and of the southern USA the weather is much less harsh in winter than is the case further north and insects can still be found in these evergreen woodlands in winter. Some of both the European and the American warblers spend the winter in these habitats; others go much further afield—into Africa and Central America respectively.

The wide range of animal life in temperate forests has resulted in a number of predatory birds. The sparrowhawks *Accipiter* are specialists at catching birds by chasing them among the branches. Though relatively slow compared with the falcons, their great manoeuvrability makes them experts in this habitat. Many owls live in woodland, and kill both small birds and mammals by hunting them in the dark. They live in relatively restricted territories which they come to know so well that they can fly around even on a very dark night; they locate their prey by sound.

Tropical Forests

Tropical forests are one of the most exciting and richest habitats in the world. The huge, towering trees and the stillness inside the forest have a quality all of their own. True tropical forests are found only in the equatorial regions of the earth in areas of high rainfall—central America, Malaysia and the Far East, small areas of north-eastern Australia and the huge forests of Central and South America, in particular the vast Amazon basin. A common factor in these areas is the high year-round temperature and the heavy rainfall; the latter is also usually spread right round the year. Although there may be wetter and drier periods of the year, there are not pro-longed dry seasons; these would result in different, more seasonal woodlands. The warmth, with few extremes of temperature, makes relatively small demands on warm-blooded creatures and the high humidity results in a perpetually damp climate with little chance of fire spreading any distance. Tropical rain forests probably owe their continued presence today to their resistance to fire, for elsewhere man has used fire widely as a way of clearing forests.

The majority of the trees in tropical forests are evergreen; though some species shed all their leaves together they are usually leafless for a very brief period. The trees are often very large, the closed canopy being some 100 or even 120 ft (30–36 m) above one's head with even larger emergent trees towering over this. As a result, little light reaches the forest floor and there may be relatively little plant life there, possibly only a few small shrubs and many small saplings of the large trees.

Many of the trees in tropical forests have much in common with each other. They are straight and tall, with few side branches until 60 or 70 ft (18 or 21 m) above the ground, a result of their rapid race against other small trees to fill the space left by a dying canopy tree. Many have large buttresses or stilt roots at their base—outward projections that enable the tree to be more firmly rooted in the soil. The

Tropical forest birds. Trogons are found in most tropical forest areas of the world; this species (1) the Coppery-tailed trogon *Trogon elegans* is from Central America. There are some 320 species of hummingbirds all of which come from the New World. The species shown here (2) are, from left to right, the Sappho comet *Sappho sparganura*, the Scale-throated hermit *Phaethornis eurynome* and the Ruby-topaz hummingbird *Chrysolampis mosquitus*. Most birds of paradise occur in New Guinea; the two shown here are the Superb bird of paradise *Lophorina superba* (3) and the King of Saxony bird of paradise *Pteridophora alberti* (4), so-called because of the enamel-like blue gloss on the elongated head feathers.

The Quetzal *Pharomachrus mocinno* is a trogon. The male is unusual in having very long tail feathers. The species is found in tropical forests of Central America where it nests in holes in trees.

Tropical forest birds. Woodcreepers are birds that are found mainly in the tropical forests of the Americas; they climb up tree trunks, foraging for insects in a manner similar to treecreepers. The Barred woodcreeper *Dendrocolaptes certhia* (1) is the size of a large thrush. The Long-tailed hawk *Urotriorchis macrourus* (2) occurs in the forests of western Africa. The two species of rockfowl are found in highland forests of west Africa where they build mud nests on cliff-faces, the Grey-necked rockfowl *Picathartes oreas* (3) and the Bare-headed rockfowl *Picathartes gymnocephalus* (4). Pittas, such as the Garnet pitta *Pitta granatina* from South East Asia (5), live on the forest floor.

Many New World orioles build hanging nests in groups around wasp nests from which they gain protection from predators such as monkeys. The nests may even resemble the structure of a wasp nest. This species is Wagler's oropendola *Zarhynchus wagleri*, a crow-sized bird.

mature leaves are dark green with 'drip tips', pointed ends which are said to enable the rain to be rapidly shed from the leaf. The young leaves are often pink or red and hang vertically to avoid the sun's rays until they are fully developed. With these and other characters the tropical forests of the different parts of the world have a great deal in common even though the actual tree species may belong to totally different families. Unless he is an experienced botanist, the observer could find himself in any tropical rain forest in the world and be hard put to know where he was.

Rain forests are noted for the rich variety of species of both animals and plants and the trees that form the forest are no exception to this. There may be as many as 600 different species of tree in a single square mile (2.5 sq km) of rich rain forest. Because of this great diversity there tend, of course, to be relatively few individuals of any given species. This is a considerable contrast to a temperate woodland where the majority of the tree species may belong to perhaps half a dozen different species. Some idea of this diversity can be obtained by looking out over the top of one of these forests; perhaps this week one may see that a tree with orange flowers is in bloom and that these orange-flowered trees are widely scattered over the forest, but very few in number; next week the same may be true for a purple-flowered tree and then a red one and so on, each tree being relatively uncommon but all the individuals of that species flowering together.

Such successional flowering has important effects on the avifauna. Although all the individuals of a given species of tree tend to flower within a fairly short period, there are usually some species in flower or fruit at all times of the year. As a result, birds specialized to feed on nectar can exist. Even if there were no flowers or fruits for only one month of a year many of these birds could not survive. Among the most specialized are the hummingbirds of South America, the sunbirds of Africa and Asia, and the honey-eaters of Australasia. Many of these take insects in addition to a nectar diet, but nevertheless they need a reliable source of food that can only be

The White-faced antcatcher *Pithys albifrons* belongs to a large family of antbirds which occur in Central and South America. Most species live low down in the forest or even on the ground.

The Magnificent bird of paradise *Diphyllodes magnificus* is another inhabitant of New Guinea. The male bird clears a display ground some 20 ft (6 m) across, removing also the leaves of the saplings above so that more light filters through.

Like many other hornbills, the Giant hornbill *Buceros bicornis* from India and South East Asia walls the female into a nest cavity. The male feeds her through the small crack during the laying and incubation periods and through the early part of the nestling stages.

Silvery-cheeked hornbills *Bycanistes brevis* may travel long distances for food. Here a pair attacks a snake, a habit that does not, however, occur very often. ▶

found in such relatively stable areas as the tropics. The same applies to fruit eaters such as the fruit pigeons and the cotingids; they could not exist in areas without a plentiful supply of fruit in every month of the year.

The birds show some of the features described for the trees. Within the rain forest there are large numbers of different bird species, but by and large each species tends to be rather rare. Further, their breeding seasons show similarities to those of the trees in that although each individual species tends to breed only at certain times of the year some are breeding in every month. The length of each species' breeding season may be long compared with the breeding season of most birds in temperate areas, but nevertheless each species has a well-marked period when breeding does not take place; at this time the adults may moult to replace their worn plumage and generally prepare for the next breeding season. Hence if one goes into the forest in each month of the year, one may be able to find some species breeding on each visit, but not the same species on every visit.

People who walk through tropical forest often think that the forest is rather empty of birds. This is to some extent true; birds are not very common compared with the high densities of birds that one may at times find in other habitats. It is also partly a false impression. Firstly, most of the life in such forests goes on above one's head—most birds are in the canopy where the leaves, flowers, fruits and insects are and only a few ground- or trunk-foraging birds are to be found by the pedestrian observer. Climb up and sit in the canopy—especially near a flowering or a fruiting tree—and the story will be quite different. Another feature of the forest birds may aid this impression of scarcity. Many of the smaller birds go about in foraging flocks of 20, 30 or sometimes many more birds, a variety of species all foraging in the same flock. These travel steadily through the forest in each other's company. Suddenly, the air is full of birds and, just as suddenly, before one has had an opportunity to look at or identify them all, they have disappeared. After that one may walk for an hour or two and hardly see a bird, and then, another flock. The reasons why birds live in these mixed parties are not fully known, but the birds may be of use to one another by being on the look-out for potential predators—more watchers are better than one. In addition, some birds catch insects disturbed by others and so may gain from being in a flock.

Nonetheless birds are not as abundant in these forests as they are in many temperate regions. One possible reason for this may be that there are other animals which though relatively rare in temperate regions are common in the tropics. For example

Keel-billed toucans *Ramphastos sulfuratus* mobbing an Ornate hawk-eagle *Spizaetus ornatus*. As with small birds of temperate woodland, toucans will join together to mob a predator or potential enemy.

The Bare-headed rockfowl *Picathartes gymnocephalus* from west Africa builds its nest of mud on a rock wall; it may nest in groups. The birds hop along the forest floor catching insects and other small animals.

The Sulphur-crested cockatoo *Cacatua galerita* occurs over extensive parts of the eastern half of Australia. It lives in rather open forest from the tropics to the temperate areas, and nests in holes in trees.

The Superb lyrebird *Menura novaehollandiae* lives in cool sclerophyll forests of the southeastern part of Australia. The males display from small mounds that they scratch up. They are remarkable mimics of the other birds. The female builds a large domed nest of twigs and lays a single egg.

frogs and lizards abound in rain forest, living in the tops of trees where they must take a heavy toll of insects. Possibly because of this competition for food there cannot be so many birds as where these competitors are absent. This is a guess, but the fact remains that these rich forests do not harbour the high number of birds that one might expect; the richness is in species rather than in numbers.

Birds in the tropics tend to lay rather fewer eggs than those in temperate areas and birds in the rain forests tend to have the smallest clutches of all. Many reasons have been suggested for this but conclusive proof is lacking. Firstly, the birds have a shorter day in which to feed in the tropics than is the case in the temperate areas in the breeding season and so could not collect so much food each day for their growing young. Secondly, food rarely becomes so plentiful in the rain forest as in the spring flush of insects in temperate regions so that the parent birds may have to search harder and for longer in the tropics than in the temperate areas in order to find food.

Birds nesting in tropical forests face enemies that are less common in the temperate regions; among the enemies of nests, snakes and monkeys rank high. Many of the smaller tropical birds hang their nests from slender tips of branches or from creepers to make them difficult to reach; also they build a domed nest so that the potential predator cannot see whether there are eggs or not. Some birds build their nest close to a colony of wasps so that prospective raiders will have to face a barrage of angry wasps to get their prey; somehow or other the birds themselves seem to safely avoid antagonizing the wasps.

Many groups of birds are specialized for living in tropical forests. The South American family of woodhewers Dendrocolaptidae has produced a wide range of treecreeper-like birds which forage on the enormous area of trunks in the forests. These birds range in size from about that of a sparrow to about the size of a crow and have a wide variety of beak shapes for probing and pecking into the bark of trees. The trogons, including the beautiful Quetzal of Central America have a wide distribution in the tropics; they sit just below the canopy and make quick flights out after passing insects. In several parts of the world birds follow the big movements of ants around the forests. Some of the ant thrushes Formicariidae of South America specialize in this; they do not often take the ants, but rather specialize in catching the other insects that dash for safety from the approaching columns of ants.

Sadly, huge areas of tropical forests are currently being cleared by man; often they are not in fact good areas for cultivation. Once cleared of the big trees the heavy rain usually washes the nutrients out of the soil and within a year or two the land is no longer fit for cultivation; the farmer must move on and clear another area.

Two unrelated grassland species have remarkably similar plumage. The Eastern meadowlark *Sturnella magna* (1) of the USA and the Yellow-throated longclaw *Macronyx croceus* (2) of Africa look remarkably alike although the meadowlark is much larger than the longclaw.

Grasslands provide living places for several species of large cursorial birds. The Old World has some 22 species of bustard including (1) the large Kori bustard *Ardeotis kori* from east and southern Africa. These birds are omnivorous. The Carmine bee-eater *Merops nubicus* often rides on bustards, catching insects flushed by them as they walk through the grass. (2) The Secretary bird *Sagittarius serpentarius*, also of Africa, runs on the open grassland and catches reptiles. (3) The Crested seriema *Cariama cristata* lives on the pampas of South America; it is an aberrant gruiform bird. Like the bustards, seriemas are omnivorous.

Grasslands

Grasslands occur mainly in areas of relatively low rainfall; they lie between the deserts and the forests and grade into both. The temperate grasslands are mostly in the centres of large continents, away from the rain-bearing sea-winds. The great prairies of North America, the pampas of South America and the steppes of central Asia are of this type. Since they are distant from the warming influence of the oceans some of these places are very cold in winter. The great savannahs of central Africa and the grasslands of Australia are different in that they are warm the whole year round. In Africa the high temperature induces high evaporation and this, coupled with long periods of little or no rain, produces the grasslands. Trees find such conditions difficult especially since extensive fires may burn the dead grass in the dry season and cause them severe damage. Such fires may be caused by lightning strikes, but the grasslands of India and perhaps much of the Australian eucalypt woodland are partly the result of man's burning activities.

In grasslands totally devoid of trees, the number of bird species is usually low; once there is a scattering of trees a much wider variety of bird life is found. Many more birds are found in areas which are within easy flying distance of water, for most birds seem to need this addition to their diet.

A striking group of birds occurs in grasslands—the Ostrich, rhea and Emu, in Africa, South America and Australia respectively (though fossils show that the Ostrich was once widespread in parts of the Palearctic). These huge flightless birds have many features in common, but there is some dispute as to whether or not they

Birds of grassland. (1) Black-tailed godwit *Limosa limosa* nests in damp grasslands and spends the winter in estuaries, (2) Meadow pipit *Anthus pratensis* nests in open rough grassland and on moorland, (3) Lapwing *Vanellus vanellus* nests on rather drier grasslands; many of the birds from central Europe move westwards to damper areas for the hottest part of the summer, they may also leave for milder areas if the grasslands freeze in midwinter. Kestrels also live in grasslands, hunting small mammals. Shown here are the American kestrel (often called a 'Sparrow hawk') *Falco sparverius* (4) and the Kestrel *Falco tinnunculus* (5) from Eurasia and Africa.

Although living in grassland, the Kestrel *Falco tinnunculus* needs trees for nesting in. If cornered in its nest it may lie on its back and defend itself with its powerful talons.

are closely related. They live in grasslands or open forest where their large size combined with long legs and necks gives them the opportunity to spot danger from afar and to make a rapid getaway, at speeds of up to 40 mph (64 kph). They all feed primarily on vegetable diets and although they drink when water is available, they are able to extract some of the water they need from seeds and berries. Other powerful runners occupy the grasslands, though these can also fly if they have to. They include the bustards and the guineafowl.

A number of smaller birds also occupy the grasslands, among them the partridges and quail, the sandgrouse and some waders—in particular the stone curlews, dotterels and coursers—and some American orioles and Old World pipits and larks.

Another group that is particularly abundant in grassland deserves special mention —the finches. These birds live primarily on a diet of seeds though some of them feed on insects and many bring insects to their young. From the time that the seeds start to ripen (when many of the birds begin to nest) until the start of the next rainy season, there are large quantities of seeds. Only when rain has fallen and the seeds have started to germinate is food in short supply, and this apparent time of 'spring' is when some finches suffer the greatest hardships. To avoid this difficulty, many may wander from area to area avoiding the periods of dearth or switch from the seeds of one plant to those of another. In the grasslands of central Africa some species may follow the passage of the rain northwards and southwards, arriving in each area when the grass seeds have begun to ripen.

By their very nature the finches have sometimes come into severe conflict with man. Our cereal crops are grown in the grassland areas of the world, or in extensions of them where we have removed the forests. To these birds, man's extensive crops are just another seed to eat and they descend on them in thousands or in millions. In no area is this problem so acute as in Africa where colonies of many millions of a small finch, the Quelea, do untold damage. They take many crops but are especially partial to millet, possibly because in some areas this ripens at a time when there are few natural grass seeds available.

Waders that live in deserts. (1) Cream-coloured courser *Cursorius cursor* lives in very dry areas of north Africa and the Middle East and western Asia and (2) Collared pratincole *Glareola pratincola* is widespread through the drier parts of the Old World. It is often found near dried up areas near water.

The Hoopoe lark *Alaemon alaudipes* lives in the deserts of north Africa and the Middle East. It has striking display flights during which the male spirals upwards and then glides down again.

Desert birds. (1) Pallas' sandgrouse *Syrrhaptes paradoxus* breeds in the steppe country to the east of the Caspian Sea, but has occasionally visited Europe in large numbers, (2) Pygmy seedsnipe *Thinocorus rumicivorus* is one of the four species of seedsnipe and is an aberrant wader. They live in the very dry grasslands of South America. (3) The Bar-tailed desert lark *Ammomanes cincturus* from the Sahara and the deserts of the Middle East, (4) Greater roadrunner *Geococcyx californianus* a ground-dwelling, aberrant cuckoo from southern USA and Central America and (5) Black vulture *Coragyps atratus* which occurs in deserts and a wide variety of other habitats in southern USA, Central and South America. ▶

Deserts

We tend to think of deserts as areas of great heat and they may be, but they may also be extremely cold at night or in the winter. This is because they tend to occur far from rain-bearing winds which modify the climate on land near the sea by bringing warming winds in winter and cooling winds in summer. Since such winds have spent their warmth or moisture before they reach the desert areas, the extremes of temperature are not moderated in this way. Rainfall is not only slight but its timing is often unpredictable, hence animals must survive as best they can from one period of rainfall to the next. Because of water shortage the growth of plants is slow and if damaged by over-grazing they may take many years to recover. The sandy areas such as the great Sahara Desert of North Africa are, in many places, man-made. As a result of over-population and over-grazing by man's herds, especially by the all-destructive goat, the slow growing plants are being progressively eliminated and their slender hold on the poor soil removed so that the desert is allowed to spread.

Few natural deserts are sand blown wastes devoid of life. Most have grasses and small plants and many are even rich in plants and trees. Such places often house a wide variety of animals though these may not be conspicuous. For both the animals and plants, water conservation is of overriding importance. The desert adaptations of the plants are well known; in those such as the cacti, limited leaf surfaces reduce evaporation and the large stems have the ability to store water. Other plants are ephemeral, they grow rapidly from seeds once rain has fallen, set seed and die leaving the next generation of seeds to survive the dry period until the advent of more rain.

The rate of water loss by animals is related to their exposure to the sun and so animals take what steps they can to avoid unnecessary activities in the heat of the day. They may lie inactive in the shade of a bush or a rock or even shelter down burrows where the changes in temperature are less marked. The closer one is to the sandy soil, the hotter it is; only a few inches above the surface the temperature is markedly lower. This may in part explain why desert animals, including birds, have relatively long legs, for it is clear that the higher they can stand or walk, the less water they will lose.

Compared with mammals, the birds of deserts are not especially well adapted to such areas. Mostly they do their best to avoid exposure to the sun in the full heat of the day; they take a siesta and are most active in the early and later parts of the day. A few are able to go without water for long periods; some small finches can obtain much of their water supplies from their vegetable diet. When food material is digested, water—so-called metabolic water—is formed and the birds may be able to exist on this. However, most desert birds need to get water and must therefore live within flying distance of a source; normally they come both night and morning to the water holes. Huge flights of sandgrouse may be seen coming in to water during the evening in some parts of Africa. If these areas of water dry up the birds must move away. As a result, the birds of desert areas may be nomadic, settling to breed after rain and remaining as long as the area is suitable then, when the land dries out, departing in search of better areas.

Desert birds also have a problem with their nests since the eggs and young must be shielded from the worst of the sun's heat. Some of the smaller birds such as wheatears seek shelter for their nests down burrows or in crevices in rocks. Others such as some of the waders may have to stand over their eggs or young during the heat of the day in order to shield them from the intense heat. Since the young birds cannot fly to water, the parents may bring the water to them; when drinking, sandgrouse soak their breast feathers in the water and bring this water to the young. The feathers are specially adapted to absorb and hold large quantities of water. Kittlitz' plover in South Africa has been recorded burying its eggs in the sand during the heat of the day, and the Indian Yellow-wattled plover brings back water on its belly feathers to dampen the eggs and so help to keep them cool.

Mountains

Great mountain ranges or immense isolated mountain peaks occur in most continents. The mountain tops present considerable challenges to the animals which try and live on them. Two vital needs, oxygen and warmth, become scarcer with increasing altitude. Above about 16,000 ft (4,875 m) the air is rarefied and oxygen notably scarcer than at lower altitudes; many animals living at such heights have a higher proportion of red cells in their blood than animals of lower areas—this helps them to supply the body with oxygen in these difficult conditions. Temperature drops by about 3°F for each rise of 1,000 ft (6°C per 1000 m). Even on equatorial Mount Kenya one may find snow all the year round.

The effects of variations in temperature dominate the vegetation. As one goes up the mountainside one may pass from rich lowland forest through coniferous forests to poor, stunted trees, then through the treeline to alpine meadows of increasing paucity of vegetation until one reaches permanent snow. The passage up such a mountainside is like a compressed journey from the temperate areas of the world to polar regions.

In temperate areas, the mountains are subject to the same seasonal fluctuations as the surrounding land itself; as winter comes the snowline marches downwards, as spring returns the snow recedes. Many animals also show corresponding seasonal movements, spending the winter at lower altitudes than those at which they spend the summer. Because of the colder climate, birds that live on mountains tend to find themselves with a shorter summer period than their relatives in the adjacent lowlands and often have shorter breeding seasons. On high mountains in the tropics there may be little annual change in climate, but even so the animals face very rigorous conditions. High up on such mountains there may be a frost every night of the year with a sharp rise in the temperature during the day. Thus high on Mount Kenya, the daily temperature can fluctuate from 45°F (8°C) at the warmest to 10°F, or 22°F of frost (−14°C) at night, so animals find life difficult and may have to take shelter. Under such conditions many small birds roost deep down in the vegetation or down burrows in the ground since the temperature does not fall so low in such places. Some small birds such as hummingbirds and sunbirds 'hibernate' each night, becoming torpid during the cold hours and regaining their high body temperatures in the early morning in order to be able to carry out their daytime activities.

Many species of birds are restricted to particular habitats on mountains. Where the mountains are isolated, as in the case of many of those in Africa, they act like islands in a sea of lowlands; the montane birds are restricted to small groups of mountains or even to individual mountains. This coupled with their habitat restrictions may result in one particular species existing in only very small numbers and being very sensitive to changes in these habitats. In one area two closely related species may exist in neighbouring altitudinal zones. However, in an area where one of the two species is absent, the other may occupy the combined range of both species. How such partitioning of the habitat occurs is not understood.

Mountain ranges affect the lives of birds in other ways; for example, they cause changes in climate. Rain carried by winds is precipitated as the winds climb up and over the windward face of mountains; as a result this face is wet and often covered with lush vegetation. By way of contrast, the leeward side gets little rain and may have much poorer plant life. Hence the presence of mountains may have an important effect on the lowland birds as well as on the montane species. Mountain ranges have a further important influence in that they act as barriers to the passage of lowland birds and, if birds manage to cross them, the high ranges serve to keep the two populations apart. Thus isolated, the two groups may evolve differently during the course of time and may eventually become distinct species. The rich avifaunas of related species in and around the Himalayas and the northern end of the Andes testify to the importance of such barriers in the evolution of species.

The Lammergeier *Gypaetus barbatus* lives in mountainous areas, where it scavenges like other vultures. It has learned to drop bones onto rocks so that they break enabling it to extract the marrow.

The Wallcreeper *Tichodroma muraria* inhabits high mountains of Europe, the Middle East and through to the Himalayas. It climbs up rock faces searching for its insect food.

Choughs *Pyrrhocorax pyrrhocorax* live in mountainous areas or on rocky cliffs. Outside the breeding season they commonly live in flocks, often of several hundred birds.

Birds of mountainous regions. (1) Isidor's eagle *Oroaetus isidori* from Central and South America, (2) Golden eagle *Aquila chrysaetos*, an inhabitant of the highland areas of much of the north temperate areas of both the Old and New Worlds, (3) Snow finch *Montifringilla nivalis*, a bird of the high mountains of Eurasia which lives well above the tree-line, (4) Malachite sunbird *Nectarinia famosa* lives on high mountains in Africa, (5) Chough *Pyrrhocorax pyrrhocorax* and (6) Alpine chough *P. graculus*. Both these last named species are primarily birds of mountains of Eurasia, the Alpine chough being generally found at higher altitudes than its relative. Both species may live at lower altitudes during the winter.

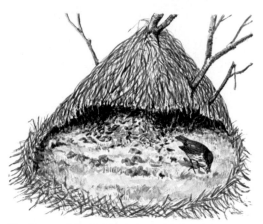

The bower of the Gardener bowerbird *Amblyornis inornatus*, a species that occurs in the mountains of western New Guinea. The bird brings new fruits and flowers to the moss-covered court almost daily.

Two Australian species of bowerbirds, both of which occur in the sclerophyll forests of eastern Australia, (1) The Regent bowerbird *Sericulus chrysocephalus* and (2) the Satin bowerbird *Ptilonorhynchus violaceus.* Both these species have avenues through which they pass while displaying.

Island birds. (1) The Wattled false sunbird *Neodrepanis coruscans* is a member of the family Philepittidae. Only four species are known and all are confined to Madagascar. The honey-eaters, family Meliphagidae, are an important part of the avifauna of Australia and the south parts of the Pacific; shown here are the Cardinal honey-eater *Myzomela cardinalis* from the New Hebrides (2) and the O-o *Moho nobilis* (3), an almost certainly extinct species from Hawaii. The Laysan teal *Anas laysanensis* (4), probably best regarded as a subspecies of the Mallard, displays the dull plumage characteristic of many island forms. The Weka *Gallirallus australis* (5) is a large flightless rail from New Zealand. ▶

Islands

Islands may be oceanic or close inshore, large or small, barren or thickly vegetated. Such characteristics have important effects on the birds. Even large land masses, the largest of which we call continents, can from the biological point of view be considered as islands. The main factor that influences the chances of a bird getting from one island to another is the width of the sea that it has to cross without a place to rest.

The relation of an island to the continents, and the history of the island's evolution, markedly affects its bird life. Basically islands may be inshore or oceanic. The former are usually on the continental shelf of a larger land mass and probably became islands when the action of the seas eroded their connection with the adjacent land. Hence they inherited the normal flora and fauna of the mainland and may retain a varying amount of it. Oceanic islands on the other hand have formed without former connections to the mainland. Some major movement of the land at the bottom of the oceans—often a volcanic eruption—has thrown up an area near to or above the surface of the sea. This may still remain, or it may have slowly sunk again until it is crowned by a coral atoll. Such islands are, at first, devoid of terrestrial plant and animal life and these must colonize them from afar. If the nearest land masses are far distant, obviously the build-up of flora and fauna will be exceedingly slow.

Most birds need other life on which to feed before they can successfully settle, but this is not so for the sea birds. These birds use the islands only for nesting and collect their food from the sea; the barrenness of the island is of no concern to them. Indeed the absence of potential predators is a positive advantage. Sea birds may even contribute to the paucity of life; if they nest in sufficiently large numbers their massive deposits of guano cover the surface and help to discourage the growth of plants.

Once an island has emerged from the sea and erosion of the surface of the new land has begun, there is the possibility that wind-blown and water-carried seeds may reach the land and slowly, over the course of time, the island will be colonized by plants, insects and then other animals. Apart from sea birds who use the islands purely as a nesting site, most other birds require a fairly well-developed community before they can settle easily.

The chance of settlement is closely related to the position of the island. The further the island from a source of possible colonists, the more difficult it will be to colonize and the more slowly this will occur. The chances of colonization are also markedly affected by the prevailing winds; if they are towards the island the colonists will be more likely to arrive than if they have to fly against head winds all the way. In addition, not only must the bird successfully make landfall and quickly find both food and water, but also it must find a mate. In order for a pair of birds to meet on such a place, either the sea crossing must be made fairly frequently or the birds must fly in flocks. As one might expect, the abilities of different species to make such crossings vary markedly. In many oceans a particular group of birds may be well represented on most islands while several other groups are missing. Among small birds, the white-eyes seem to have been successful colonists in many areas, while among the large birds, rails have also reached a great number of offshore islands.

Within any group of islands, the size of the island markedly affects the number of bird species that are present: the larger the island the more species there are. The full reasons for this are not understood, but it is likely that the number of species present on an island is related to the richness of the flora, since islands with a richer flora have more bird species.

Extinctions are a regular occurrence on islands. All bird populations fluctuate to some extent, but the smaller the population the more likely it is that the numbers will drop to nil. The total bird populations on islands, especially on small ones, are of course low compared with those on an adjacent mainland so that the chances of extinction on islands are much higher than on the mainland.

Extinctions do not in themselves explain the paucity of birds on islands, for if one

The Hawaiian goose (or Ne-ne) *Branta sandvicensis* (1) was almost extinct on Hawaii until many were bred in captivity. It lives on rough lava and has reduced webbing on the feet as can be seen here when compared with those of the Barnacle goose *Branta leucopsis* (2).

The Kakapo *Strigops habroptilus* is an almost flightless aberrant parrot from New Zealand. It feeds to a considerable extent on grass seeds, often leaving well-marked trails where it has been feeding. The species is extremely scarce.

The Kagu *Rhynochetos jubatus* is an almost flightless relative of the rails. It is confined to the montane forest of New Caledonia where its future is not secure. It is at least partly nocturnal, and its habits are not well known.

The Large cactus finch *Geospiza conirostris* is one ▶ of Darwin's finches and is confined to the Galapagos. This species has been seen to move small stones to get at seeds; it puts its head against a larger rock and thrusts the stones out behind it with its feet.

looks at the bird species that are there, one finds that they are not just a random selection of the birds present on the mainland, but rather, there are a few representatives of a wide range of families. For example, each of the islands in the Caribbean, including the large ones, has only one species of small hummingbird. Yet the Caribbean is surrounded by land where hummingbirds of many species abound. It is not even merely that only one or two of the species of hummingbird have been able to colonize the islands, for there are in all some 17 species on the islands. These and other examples make it difficult to escape the view that islands can only support a narrow variety of species, that there is only 'room' for one or two related species even if there are a number on the mainland, and that a new species can only establish itself after one of the residents has become extinct and so left a vacancy.

Island birds show some peculiarities: for example a number of them have become flightless—as have some island insects—and many others fly only very poorly. Others, related to brightly coloured stock, may have lost their bright plumage; some of the male ducks retain dull plumage like that of the female and never attain the bright colours of their mainland relatives. Both songs and plumage have probably evolved, at least in part, in order to enable each species to distinguish itself from those of other species. On a continent where there are many closely related species elaborate distinctions may be necessary, but these are not so necessary on islands where the problems of identification are much simpler.

Where, as is often the case, the colonists of islands receive few immigrants of their kind from the parental stock they will, as they evolve adaptations to their new environment, begin to differ from their relatives until, eventually, they may become a new species. This can happen even within archipelagos of islands. Here the birds on different islands may gradually evolve small differences, until eventually when they meet as a result of inter-island movements, they no longer interbreed, having become different species. Where this has happened on a number of occasions over a period of time one may find that a group of islands holds a considerable number of bird species—clearly all from the same ancestral stock. The honeycreepers of the Hawaiian islands are a good example of this; here there were once 22 species (some are now extinct) that had probably descended from a single invasion of a tanager from the New World. Perhaps less striking, though more important for another reason, are the Galapagos finches. These birds, some 14 species in all (13 in Galapagos,

The Yellow-tailed cockatoo *Calyptorhynchus funereus* lives in the forests of southeastern Australia. It may tear off the bark of trees and even rip into the wood with its powerful beak in its search for food.

The extinct Dodo *Raphus cucullatus* of Mauritius. This large, flightless bird may have been related to the pigeons. It was unable to survive in the face of man and his animals and became extinct around the end of the seventeeth century.

one on Cocos) were in part responsible for Charles Darwin's understanding of evolution. He wrote, 'Seeing this gradation and diversity of structure in one small, intimately related group of birds, one might really fancy that from an original paucity of birds in this archipelago, one species had been taken and modified for different ends.'

Speciation can occur not only in archipelagos, but on large islands; the prerequisite for speciation is that there should be two areas where a bird can live, separated by some form of physical barrier which cuts down movement between the two groups so that they can evolve sufficient differences to become separate species. This can, and has, happened within large islands such as Malagasy and New Guinea; once again the distinction between such islands and the continents is not a biological one.

A great many of the bird species on islands are represented on earth by very small populations and they are in many ways extremely vulnerable. In the natural course of events these species are relatively short-lived compared with many on the continents. They are often extremely vulnerable to small changes in their environment. Hence many are threatened today by man's activities. Of the birds that man has exterminated in the recent past, many were species restricted to small islands. Man has seldom exterminated these species intentionally, though he undoubtedly hunted the larger ones such as the Dodo of Mauritius and the Solitaire of Rodrigues. More often he has altered the natural balance on the islands, either by destroying the habitat or by introducing other animals. Introduced goats have eaten away the natural forests, and rats and cats have hunted and destroyed the birds, often ill-adapted to defend themselves against predators since many of them lived on islands virtually devoid of mammals apart from a few bats. The legendary tameness of island animals is a result of long periods of time during which they have had nothing to fear; with the advent of predatory animals this has proved their downfall. Introduced birds have also made their mark. Many, such as the starling and the mynah, have evolved successfully in areas where there were large numbers of competing species; they may be considered 'tough' birds, evolved in the rough and tumble of a continent. In contrast, island birds have had a sheltered life and are often ill-adapted to withstand such successful competitors whether in their search for food or for nesting sites. In some cases also it is possible that the introduced birds have brought with them diseases to which the native birds had no immunity.

The Palmchat *Dulus dominicus* is usually placed in a family of its own and is confined to the island of Hispaniola. The birds build a large, communal nest, often incorporating large twigs. As many as four pairs may occupy the same nest structure though each pair has a separate entrance.

Most kingfishers live along lake and river banks. Two Australian species are shown here: (1) the Azure kingfisher *Alcyone azurea* and (2) the very small Little kingfisher *Alcyone pusilla*. Both species fish from twigs along the sides of rivers and streams.

Birds of rivers and lakes. These are the main habitats for storks and herons, three of which are shown here: (1) the Jabiru stork *Jabiru mycteria* from Central and South America, (2) the massive-billed Shoebill stork *Balaeniceps rex* from central Africa, which catches lungfish, such as the *Protopterus* shown here, mainly in the dusk and at night and (3) the Little bittern *Ixobrychus minutus*, a small species only about 1 ft. (0.3 m) long which is widely distributed in Europe, eastern Asia and Africa. A number of species of terns live primarily on fresh water; this is the Black tern *Chlidonias niger* (4), a species which breeds in temperate areas of both the Old and New Worlds and spends the winter in warmer areas. In the marshes of most warmer parts of the world one may find stilts; this species, (5) the Black-necked stilt *Himantopus mexicanus*, comes from the New World.

Rivers and Lakes

Life depends on water; the sun's heat evaporates water, often from the sea, and it rises into the atmosphere, forms clouds and is subsequently precipitated once again as rain or snow. Eventually this finds its way back into the sea and so the cycle is repeated. Water that falls on land eventually flows into lakes and rivers and these provide rich habitats for birds.

Rivers start as small streams which join together to form larger and larger bodies of water, until they reach the sea. They may flow for 3,000 mi (4,800 km) as is the case with the Mississippi and the mighty Amazon. Not all rivers flow into the sea: they may flow into large inland lakes or even into areas of desert where they slowly weaken, eventually cease to flow and dry up altogether. The different stages of a river provide quite different habitats for birds. By and large the upper reaches are steep and fast-flowing; plants find these difficult to grow in and small animals are easily washed away. Hence food for birds is not always rich at these levels of the river and birds are scarce, both in species and in total numbers. Nevertheless, some species are specially adapted for living in such places. The torrent ducks of South America and the Blue duck of New Zealand inhabit fast-flowing streams where they are able to collect algae by gleaning them from the rocks. The Dipper is also a bird of fast-flowing reaches, foraging on the bottom of the streams for small insects. By walking upstream, holding on with its powerful claws and keeping its head down, it allows the pressure of the running water to keep it against the bottom of the stream; it may also beat its wings underwater, apparently to help keep itself submerged.

Further downstream the rivers run across less mountainous land and tend to flow more slowly. Plant life, and hence animal life, is richer and so the birds have more food available to them. Fish eating birds such as herons, kingfishers and mergansers become more common here. Towards the seaward end of their length,

Bitterns are relatives of the herons; usually they are well camouflaged and live secretively in reed beds. This species, the European bittern *Botaurus stellaris*, occurs through much of Eurasia. It is shown here preening after fishing.

Rails are most commonly found in marshes: (1) the (European) Purple gallinule *Porphyrio porphyrio* is a large species found in a number of areas of the Old World and Australia, (2) the Moorhen (or Common gallinule) *Gallinula chloropus* is even more widely distributed in the Old World, though unlike the Purple gallinule it does not reach Australia, and is also widely distributed in the New World and (3) the elusive Water rail *Rallus aquaticus* from Europe and Asia.

rivers may be very large; often they flow slowly and meander gently. They are also tidal; large mud-banks show at low tide. Here one may find an even wider variety of bird life, including cormorants, gulls and terns, and many wildfowl. Where the rivers are particularly large, they may impose a barrier to the landbirds on either side; the dangers of crossing such large bodies of water with no cover from marauding predators are so great that many small birds rarely take the risk. In extreme cases, such as the lower reaches of the Amazon, the other bank may not even be in sight! As a result, one may find that different subspecies or even species of bird inhabit the opposing banks.

In temperate areas of the world one tends to think of rivers as flowing, more or less steadily, throughout the year, but in many places this is far from the case. In some, marked seasonal fluctuations in rainfall result in widely varying levels in the river; in others, spring brings thawed snow from mountain areas with large rises in level. During the wet season or the thaw the rivers may overflow their banks and inundate wide areas of the surrounding country. The marshlands burst into growth and huge areas of reed beds and seasonal grasslands flourish. Later, during the dry part of the year, the waters fall back within their banks, shrink and even disappear completely. The birds respond to such changes according to their way of life. Birds that feed in marshes breed when the areas are most extensively flooded and the growth of vegetation is most marked. Those that feed in the river may take almost the opposite approach; for example, kingfishers and some herons need to be able to see their prey and this is not easy in turbulent, discoloured floodwaters. However, when the fish are confined within small areas of clearer, slower-flowing water, fishing is much easier; then is the time to breed. The kingfishers are also able to use their favoured nesting holes in the banks of rivers only when they are not flooded. Not only the flow of water but the vegetation tends to obscure the fish. Hence even in temperate areas one tends to find some herons breeding early in the year, before the waters warm up and become covered with a profuse growth of plant life.

The Black heron *Melanophoyx ardesiaca* of Africa raises its wings over its head while hunting. Apparently this helps the bird to catch fish either because they flee into the shade, or because the heron can see better with the glare of the bright sun removed.

The Reddish egret *Dichromanassa rufescens* of Central America and southern USA is a medium-sized heron. It is found chiefly in brackish lakes and saltmarshes. There is also a white form.

When danger threatens, bitterns stretch themselves upright and stand very still hoping that they will blend with the surrounding reeds. If discovered they may flap their wings and make themselves appear as large as possible in the hope of frightening the enemy away. This species is the European bittern *Botaurus stellaris.*

Other seasonal variations pose problems for the water bird. Although in most parts of the temperate zone the rivers do not dry up in summer, they may freeze over in winter. Fresh water freezes at a higher temperature than does salt water, so the birds of salt water areas do not suffer from this problem so acutely. In the polar areas the waters freeze every year and the birds have no option but to migrate to milder areas, and this they do. However, in areas that are further from the poles many birds try to remain for the winter. Their success is dependent upon the harshness of the winter. If the winter is unusually cold, then most inland waters freeze and the birds are in trouble; they must try to reach areas of open water either on or by the sea or to get to milder areas where the water has not frozen. Severe winter weather in Europe causes many of the wildfowl to move further west into Britain in an attempt to find areas where they can survive. However, these areas tend to become over-crowded so that it is still a struggle to get sufficient food. Birds that are dependent on getting their food from the water may starve at such times; herons and coots die in large numbers once the water freezes over and their food supply disappears beneath the ice; kingfishers are equally susceptible.

Some rivers never reach the sea but pour into lakes. These may vary in size from quite small to the size of Lake Superior, at some 31,000 sq mi (80,000 sq km) the largest body of fresh water in the world, or to as deep as Lake Baikal, almost a mile (1.6 km) from the surface to the bottom. The richness of the fauna of lakes varies in relation to their depth. The deep montane lakes—oligotrophic lakes—are too deep for light to reach the bottom and so plant life cannot flourish there and the whole fauna is poor as a result. Lakes of less than 20 ft (6 m) or so in depth—the eutrophic lakes—are much richer. Here plants can obtain sufficient light to grow freely on the bottom and a rich animal life is to be found. Such shallow waters have the highest productivity of almost any habitat. As a result they tend to fill with dead and dying vegetation and to become marshland and it is difficult to distinguish between where lakes end and swamps begin.

Such rich lake and swamp-lands abound in birds. Herons and cormorants, ducks, grebes, gulls, terns, kingfishers, rails and waders are among the groups that flourish there. Some ducks and rails may feed on the vegetation of the lake, but large numbers of the birds feed on the fish; grebes, cormorants and ducks dive for them and hunt

Kingfishers commonly breed in dry sandbanks along rivers. They usually breed in the summer or dry season when the banks are not liable to flooding; at the time when the rivers are low the small fish can be more easily seen and caught. This species is the Common kingfisher *Alcedo atthis* from Eurasia and Africa.

The Boat-billed heron *Cochlearius cochlearius* (1) is an inhabitant of mangroves and other dense vegetation in Central and South America. The (Black-crowned) Night heron *Nycticorax nycticorax* (2) is a secretive, largely nocturnal species which has a very wide distribution in the warmer areas of the world.

Many of the rails have slender bodies so that they can slip quickly and quietly through the reeds or other waterside vegetation. This species is the Water rail *Rallus aquaticus*.

them underwater, terns and kingfishers dive on them from the air as do the Ospreys and fish eagles, though the latter catch them in their feet not in their beaks. Herons stalk from the bank; one species, the Shoebill, hunts for eels and lungfish in swampy ground and grabs them with its immense beak.

Not all lakes are fresh, many are either brackish or salt; some are even highly saline as are the soda lakes of East Africa. The Caspian and the Black Sea are the two largest salt lakes in the world. Again the bird faunas are rich on all but the saltiest of lakes. The species concerned are often similar to those of fresh water, except that the species that seek shelter in or feed on the vegetation may be scarcer since this thrives less well in salt conditions. Pelicans may be common on salt lakes where they breed and feed in groups, taking large quantities of fish. Sometimes they dive from a height into a shoal of fish and catch them during the ensuing confusion, but they have also learnt how to hunt in groups and may encircle shoals of fish and come in on them from every side.

The most saline lakes of all harbour another group of birds, the flamingoes. These nest on small mounds that they construct for themselves in shallow water offshore or on low islands. They live in great aggregations and nest in very dense colonies. They feed on small shrimps or tiny algae which they collect by sweeping the water through their bills; having got a mouthful of the water, they close the beak and pump the water out leaving the food collected on fine hair-like strainers along the sides of the bill, from where it is removed and eaten. Flamingoes are widely spread around the warmer areas of the world and used, in addition, to inhabit Australia during wetter times when the central lakes of the continent were full.

Many fish eating birds are white, at least on their undersides. The fish cannot see the white against the sky as easily as darker colours and hence the birds stand a better chance of getting close before they are spotted by their prey. This is particularly true of many of the diving birds, less so of those that, like the cormorant, swim after the fish on the bottom of the lake. Herons catch their fish by moving very little and very stealthily; they hope to catch them without being seen at all. At least one species, the Black heron, puts its wings up as a shade and catches the fish beneath; whether they swim into the apparent cover or whether the raised wings help the bird to see better by eliminating the glare is not clear.

The Herring gull *Larus argentatus* has a wide range of feeding habits, including making use of man's rubbish. Here a bird is seen dropping cockles to break them on the rocks.

The Common oystercatcher *Haematopus ostralegus* has a powerful beak which it uses to hammer open shells and crabs and then chisel out the contents.

The Herring gull *Larus argentatus* may dive into the water for fish; like most gulls it does not usually dive very deep, seldom disappearing from sight.

Coastal species. (1) The Mangrove kingfisher *Halcyon chloris* is a largish kingfisher with a wide distribution in South East Asia and Australia. (2) The Sanderling *Calidris alba* and (3) Kentish (or Snowy) plover, *Charadrius alexandrinus*, both common on sandy shores. The former breeds in the Arctic but winters further south; the latter is widespread through much of the world. (4) The Great black-backed gull *Larus marinus*, a large predatory gull of the North Atlantic. (5) The Crab plover *Dromas ardeola*, an extraordinary wader that lives on the coast of East Africa and southwestern Asia. It nests colonially, breeding in burrows. Finally (6) the Black guillemot *Cepphus grylle* of north temperate seas. It is largely resident, nesting in loose colonies in small holes in the rocks. ▶

Coasts

Where the land ends and the sea begins one can find a wide variety of different habitats. In some areas wind may blow sand behind the beach, build up impressive dunes and so impede the flow of rivers, forcing them to flow parallel to the sea and form extensive salt marshes. Larger rivers flow out into the sea carrying with them great quantities of silt brought down from further inland. The extensive mud-banks so formed in the mouths of estuaries are very popular feeding grounds for many species of birds, especially waders. In the warmer parts of the world the muddy edges to the rivers and the coast may carry a thick covering of mangroves. In places where the land is higher the sea eats into its edge and cliffs, rocky shores and small islets are formed. Many of the birds that inhabit these areas are specially adapted to one of these habitats.

On first inspection sandy beaches and estuarine mud flats may seem barren land for birds, but a second glance shows the holes and worm casts of the small animals that live beneath the surface; when the tide starts to wash over the flats they come to life. A myriad of small shrimps, worms and shellfish live in the waters between tide marks. Although each of the waders does not always stick to just one method of feeding but will alter it to match the conditions prevailing, each species does have a feeding habit which differs from those that the other species use.

Of the many species of waders that occupy these habitats, only a few appear to prefer sand to the mud-flats. The Sanderling is one of these; it runs at top speed along the edge of the waves using its short bill to pick food off the surface of the beach in the narrow belt where the sand is wettest. The Ringed plover also has a short beak and takes small worms from the surface of the shore while the Dunlin, with its slightly longer beak, probes a little further into the sand for its food. Many rather larger waders have much longer beaks and probe more deeply into the mud in search of larger animals, especially worms, that are lying in their burrows well below the surface. The godwits and curlews are amongst those with the longest beaks. The Bar-tailed godwit is of special interest in that the female is much larger than the male and her bill is almost twice as long; it is one of the few species of wader that one can easily sex in the field. The godwits search for food in the edge of the sea, the females slightly further out to sea, in deeper water than their smaller mates. Other waders are specialized for different diets. The Oystercatcher probes in the sand for cockles or mussels, hammers them open with its powerful bill using the sharp tip to chisel the flesh from the shell. The Avocet 'scythes' through very soft, almost liquid, mud with a sideways motion, extracting small worms that come into contact with its beak.

All these waders feed on the sandy shores or the mud of estuaries. Many need a low tide to feed so that their lives are governed by the tides rather than by whether it is night or day. Many feed by touch so that visibility, except at relatively low intensity for flying, does not matter too much. When the tide is high the birds must roost on the beach above the tide line, in meadows or fields inland or on small islands waiting for the sea to ebb so that they can start to feed again.

Not many waders feed on the shingle beaches; there are few prospects for obtaining food there unless the sea has brought up large quantities of sea-weed; there one may find the Turnstones busily turning the debris in their search for small animals that live among it. True to their name, Turnstones will also turn over stones on rocky beaches in their search for animals sheltering underneath. Shingle beaches are, however, used for nesting by some waders such as Ringed plovers, Oystercatchers and some terns. Their eggs are beautifully camouflaged on stony beaches. Nesting on beaches is not a common habit among birds and may become less common; most of the birds that do so in heavily populated areas of the world are under threat from the continued human pressures on the beach throughout the summer period; in some areas such disturbance has considerably reduced the nesting success of the birds.

Cormorant feathers can become more water-
logged than those of many other diving birds.
By compressing the air from the feather, buoyancy
is lost and so diving is easier. However, the birds
then have more trouble drying out when they
leave the water and so have to sit with
outstretched wings for some time. This species is
the widespread Common (or Great) cormorant
Phalacrocorax carbo.

The Black skimmer *Rynchops nigra* from the New
World. This bird has the lower mandible much longer
than the upper one. It skims along just above
the surface of the water with just the tip of the lower
mandible in the water, snapping up shrimps
and small fish. It is a relative of the terns and gulls.

The dunes behind the beaches are not rich in bird life. The shifting sands and monotonous vegetation of marram grass do not provide rich feeding areas and only a few birds such as the Skylark live there. However, in isolated areas large colonies of gulls and terns may nest among the dunes. When the young are ready to fly they may gather on the beach in large parties waiting for their parents to come in to feed them.

Where the large dune systems divert the course of rivers large areas of saltmarsh may be found. Saltmarsh may also occur where low areas of land are found around the mouths of estuaries. These may be richer in plants than are the dunes and in consequence we find more birds there; again it is a good breeding ground for gulls, terns and waders, but here also we may find more small birds, larks, pipits and some of the New World sparrows.

A few birds that use the beaches also use the rocky shores, especially waders such as the Oystercatcher and the Turnstone. Some Oystercatchers specialise in eating limpets. Undisturbed, limpets are relaxed and not gripping tightly to the rock; the Oystercatcher catches its prey by stalking up to them quietly, smartly inserting its beak underneath them and knocking them from the rock before they can grip tightly. This can be dangerous since there are the odd records of Oystercatchers drowning when the limpet has tightened to the rock with the Oystercatcher's bill still caught beneath. The Rock pipit lives exclusively on rocky shores and eats large numbers of small winkles—almost its sole diet during the winter; each bird may eat as many as 14,000 per day.

Many birds use the cliffs above the shore though some of these are not in any way dependent on the sea. Peregrines and other birds of prey, the Black redstart, and the wren may spend their lives in these places oblivious of the sea beneath; they would live in just the same way on inland cliffs. Some cliff-nesting birds, however, are more intimately connected with the sea; once there, they are much safer from mammalian predators, including man, than are their cousins on the dunes. The Gannet, the fulmar, gulls, Kittiwakes and some of the tropical terns nest on cliffs, often in huge numbers. In the north Atlantic and the north Pacific many auks nest, often in countless thousands, on the cliffs. They use their wings for 'flying' underwater and as a consequence have small and stubby wings which need to be beaten fast for take-off before flight is possible. By launching themselves from cliffs and gaining speed by use of gravity, they are much less vulnerable to predators than they would be if taking off from flat ground. Some auks, among them the Puffins, live above the cliffs but they too need to get up speed before they can fly properly. They nest close to the cliff

Guillemots (or Common murres) *Uria aalge* nest on small ledges on sheer cliffs where they are relatively safe from predation. Nevertheless, marauding gulls such as the Herring gull *Larus argentatus* still manage to snatch eggs and chicks if the parents are not on their guard.

Many terns nest on sand dunes where they make only small scrapes for their nests. These are dug out by the bird lying on its belly and kicking out the sand with its feet. This is the Common tern *Sterna hirundo*.

(Black-legged) Kittiwakes *Rissa tridactyla* nest on very narrow ledges, the nest often overlapping the edge. The birds have a number of displays which prevent undue fighting on such limited areas.

The young of many water birds are able to swim freely soon after hatching, which enables them to move long distances; exceptionally, as here with the Goosander (or Common merganser) *Mergus merganser* the young may be carried by the female.

edge and run down the grassy slope before launching themselves into the air. They are poor at taking off from flat land and so easily chased by gulls and robbed of the fish that they are bringing to their young. Those that nest on the very edge of the cliff are more successful in raising their young than those that nest a little inland. Just these few yards may be enough to cause the difference between successful and unsuccessful breeding. In North America the increase in numbers of gulls has been held to be one of the main reasons for the decline of Puffins.

In warmer parts of the world coasts may be thickly fringed with mangroves. These plants, which live part in the sea, part on the land, may stretch for hundreds of miles in a thin belt along the shores. Being tidal, the floor of the mangroves is not a suitable area for birds to live but there are a wide variety of species which spend their whole lives in the mangroves and, in addition, many sea birds build their nests in them. A wide variety of warblers, flycatchers and other small birds live in them and, as anyone who has walked amongst the mangroves knows to his cost, there is a large stock of small insects present for their food, especially mosquitoes. Large birds also inhabit mangroves such as cuckoos, butcherbirds, bitterns and other small herons; there is often a kingfisher or two. Many of the species that live in mangroves are specific to that habitat occurring almost nowhere else.

Other birds also occupy the coastal habitats; some ducks such as eiders, scoters and the Common shelduck live on the shore. When winter comes in the northern hemisphere many birds that have spent the summer in inland Arctic areas migrate southwards to milder climates for the winter, some even reaching the southern hemisphere. Amongst these migrants are many ducks, geese, terns and waders, and many of them spend the winter in coastal areas. Indeed in many coastal areas of Europe and North America the avifauna in winter is much richer than in summer. In areas of mud-flats, especially where the eel-grass *Zostera* grows, ducks and some of the geese, especially Brent, may gather in large numbers. However, it is the waders that in many places are most impressive. Leaving their breeding grounds all over the Arctic they concentrate on the coast in winter. Some species, such as the Dunlin and the Knot may gather in flocks of thousands, or even tens of thousands. They fly in close formation, performing wonderfully co-ordinated movements, almost acting like a single bird.

Sadly many of the coastal habitats are severely threatened by man's activities. Pollution, reclamation, barrages to hold fresh water, all threaten the coast, especially the estuaries on which the waders rely so heavily.

Terns, such as the Arctic tern *Sterna paradisaea* bring fish to their chicks in their beaks. The young spend much of their time hiding in cover, but rush out to beg for food as soon as the parents appear. Occasionally the parents may feed the chicks while still in flight.

The male Magnificent frigatebird *Fregata magnificens* has an inflatable red pouch which he uses during his displays. The birds breed, often in large numbers, on small tropical islands.

The Gannet *Sula bassana* nests in large colonies, each nest being placed just out of pecking range of the next pair. The single egg is incubated under the webs of the feet.

The Inca tern *Larosterna inca* is found on the west coast of South America. It is the only species of tern known to nest in holes in rocks; most other species nest on the open ground.

Sea birds. Albatrosses live predominantly in the windy areas of the southern seas. This species (1) is the Wandering albatross *Diomedea exulans*; its wing span of nearly 12 ft. (3.5 m) exceeds that of any other bird. Tropicbirds are confined to the warm seas; the Red-tailed tropicbird *Phaethon rubricauda* (2) inhabits the Indian and Pacific Oceans. Storm petrels are the smallest sea birds; this species (3) is Leach's storm petrel *Oceanodroma leucorhoa*. Phalaropes are waders which spend the winter out at sea picking up small animals from the water's surface; this example (4) is the Red-necked (or Northern) phalarope *Phalaropus lobatus* in winter plumage. Frigatebirds live by chasing other sea birds and forcing them to regurgitate their last catch of fish. This species (5) is the Ascension Island frigatebird *Fregata aquila*. ▶

Oceans

Oceans cover over three fifths of the surface of the world and stretch from the frozen waters of one pole to the ice packs of the other; only at one point, where the Americas stretch across the globe, are they almost completely divided. As on the land, the animal life of the seas depends on the plant life that grows there. This in turn is dependent on the light, temperatures and minerals in the water. Apart from exceptional circumstances, light does not penetrate more than the top 200–300 ft (60–90 m) of sea in sufficient strength for plants to photosynthesise at all, and in most seas the water is not clear enough for light to penetrate this far. The greatest plant growth occurs within close reach of the surface. Yet many of the minerals in the water tend to fall to the bottom of the ocean where they cannot be utilised by plants unless they are in some way brought to the surface of the sea. Hence the areas of greatest plant— and therefore animal—life tend to be where upwellings occur within the sea. Two factors produce such upwardly-directed currents. Where an onshore current meets a continental shelf the water is thrust upwards to the surface in turbulent masses. The Humboldt current off Peru brings rich waters to the surface and is famous for its anchovies and for its great sea bird colonies. Wherever such upwellings occur there are rich supplies of fish for the birds; the Benguela current off southwest Africa produces another rich area for sea birds.

Upwellings also occur where cold and warm waters meet. In the Antarctic a warm current flows southwards below the northward-flooding surface current. Because of differences in density of the water, caused by the different temperatures, the warm water rises to the surface bringing with it rich supplies of nutrients. During the summer season at the poles, the long periods of light enable the phytoplankton to grow richly and form the base for the food chain through fishes to birds. Because of these upwellings, the polar regions of the oceans tend to be much richer in animals than are the tropical waters. Large numbers of auks, gulls, penguins and shearwaters breed in and around the polar areas of the oceans; they stay only for the brief summer season, leaving as soon as they have bred and before the winter closes in. One bird, the Arctic tern, makes use of both rich seas. It breeds in the north temperate areas in the northern summer and migrates southwards to spend the northern winter in the rich seas of south temperate and Antarctic waters.

Many of the birds in the tropical seas breed in huge colonies around areas of upwelling, but others breed in places where the food supply is not so richly concentrated; they must spread out to forage for their prey, often ranging over large areas of ocean. Some species appear to be dependent on large fish such as tuna chasing their smaller prey to the surface. As soon as a shoal of tuna attacks a shoal of smaller fish, some of the latter come to the surface in an attempt to escape. Birds congregate seemingly from nowhere and grab the food while it is near the surface. These birds may search for prey for longish periods without success and then have a brief period of very successful fishing. For at least some of the species this means of fishing, although highly rewarding, may be dangerous; by landing on the surface in the vicinity of very large fish the birds themselves are in danger of becoming prey. Not infrequently sea birds can be seen to be missing pieces of foot or leg, apparently nipped off by a fish; presumably some of their number suffer more serious injuries from which they die and still others are eaten—indeed rings from sea birds have been found in the stomachs of large fish. Many of the birds that roam the open waters of tropical seas in search of food have small numbers of young, often only one, and these must wait long intervals between the times that they are fed and so grow slowly. Presumably these habits are related to the difficulties of raising young in these conditions and to the large distances that must be covered in search of food.

The staple diet of most oceanic birds is, of course, fish but others take a large number of small squid; these do not seem to be easily caught in nets of the fishery research vessels so that their movements and behaviour are not well-known.

SOCIAL BEHAVIOUR

The nest of the Sociable weaver *Philetarius socius*. This species is one of the few birds where a communal nest structure is built. A large dome is made of strong twigs and the individual nests are underneath.

Colonial species. (1) The Antarctic Emperor penguin *Aptenodytes forsteri*, (2) Magnificent frigatebird *Fregata magnificens* from warm seas of the Atlantic and eastern Pacific, (3) Grey (or Common) heron *Ardea cinerea*, (4) Black-headed weaver *Ploceus cucullatus* from Africa, (5) Arctic tern *Sterna paradisaea* and (6) the Southern carmine bee-eater *Merops nubicoides* from South Africa.

Colonial Behaviour

Although a number of bird species nest in huge and sometimes spectacular colonies, these represent only a small proportion of the total numbers of birds. Only some 13% of birds nest in colonies; the remainder are solitary nesters. Many birds both nest and roost in colonies; such colonies may be small or very large—some of the larger colonies of the African finch, Quelea, which is a pest of seed-crops, may number many millions. A number of explanations for large gatherings have been suggested though probably none explain them all. Colonial nesting is common amongst sea birds; penguins, shearwaters, Gannets, cormorants and terns may nest together in great numbers. Their colonies are usually on small offshore islands where the birds gather near rich feeding grounds. Such feeding grounds need to be rich since a large colony of sea birds requires many tons of fish per day. However, the main reason that the birds nest on these islands is probably that they are relatively safe in such places as they are out of easy reach of mammalian predators—including man.

Another group of fish eating birds commonly found nesting in colonies are the herons. Heronries may often contain a number of different species of birds: herons, egrets, darters, spoonbills and fresh water cormorants. Other birds that nest in

The extinct Passenger pigeon *Ectopistes migratorius* used to nest in some of the largest colonies ever recorded among birds. An average colony might have covered an area of 30 sq mi (77 sq km).

Colonial nesting birds. (1) The (Common) Puffin *Fratercula arctica* nests in burows, usually on rat-free islands, (2) Cliff swallow *Petrochelidon pyrrhonota* from the New World builds its bottle-shaped nests on cliff faces or buildings, (3) Eleonora's falcon *Falco eleonorae* breeds in the Mediterranean region and raises its young in the autumn when it can feed them on the small migrants heading south to spend the winter in Africa and (4) the Monk parakeet *Myopsitta monachus* builds large communal nests in trees.

colonies on fresh water include the pelicans and the flamingoes, and the inland gulls and terns.

Amongst the smaller birds, a number of seed eaters nest in colonies, though during the period when they are in the colony, the birds may be primarily insectivorous. The same is true of some of the American orioles; the Yellowheaded and Tri-coloured blackbirds eat insects during the nesting season, but much seed at other times of the year. Most colonial land birds are probably insectivores. The groups that nest in colonies most frequently are those that take flying insects such as swallows, swifts, bee-eaters and some of the smaller falcons. By way of contrast, almost all those birds that feed on insects such as caterpillars collected from the trees nest solitarily; such birds include the warblers and the tits.

Some of the sea birds that nest in huge colonies probably do so because the small area of land available necessitates that they crowd into it; there is no other land nearby. Others may get more positive advantage from nesting in large colonies. The Wide-awake or Sooty terns nest in such large concentrations that any individual's chance of being taken by a predator is small. This too is one of the likely explanations for the huge colonies of nesting Quelea; they arrive in an area in great numbers, breed quickly and have raised their young before any significant build up in numbers of their predators can occur.

The nesting terns—and many other species—get additional advantages from being in a colony as they can 'gang-up' to attack a predator. When danger threatens, the numbers of birds attacking a potential predator are often sufficient to drive the animal away, although the attacks of a single pair might be of no avail. In an experiment, hen's eggs scattered in a colony of Black-headed gulls were taken by Carrion crows less frequently than those scattered just outside the colony. As soon as the crows penetrated the colony, the gulls rose and attacked in force, thus keeping them off the hen's scattered eggs as effectively as they kept them off their own. A few other species of birds are reported to nest within the colonies of aggressive gulls and terns in order to use these birds' ability of combined attack to protect their own nests.

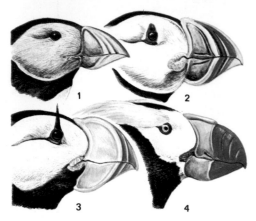

Many species grow breeding plumage for the period of courtship and nesting. In some this may involve the production of new scutes on the bill. Here three species of puffins in breeding dress are compared with a winter specimen of the (Common) Puffin *Fratercula arctica* (1); (2) (Common) Puffin, (3) Horned puffin *Fratercula corniculata*, (4) Tufted puffin *Lunda cirrhata*.

Cranes are noted for their wild courtship dances, often associated with powerful bugling calls. This species is the African Crowned crane *Balearica pavonina*.

In many species pairs may feed each other during courtship. Here a pair of Hawfinches *Coccothraustes coccothraustes* are indulging in social feeding.

Pair Bonds

Some birds are noted for their unusual mating systems, such as the lek displays of the Black grouse or some of the birds of paradise. Nevertheless, we should not lose sight of the fact that the large majority of birds, well over 90% of them, have normal monogamous breeding partnerships; in spite of the interesting adaptations of the few, simple pair bonds are the norm.

Complicated mating systems are more common in vegetarian birds than in those that eat animal food; large groups of birds such as sea birds, birds of prey and aerial insectivores (swifts and swallows) are all monogamous. Most of the other birds that raise their young in the nest are also monogamous; the unusual mating systems tend to be in nidifugous species where the precocious young leave the nest soon after hatching. However, such broad generalizations are not without exceptions.

Although most birds are monogamous, it is an old wives' tale that many, such as the swans, mate for life or will not remate if they lose their partner. Birds are by no means always so faithful. Partners may change between one year and the next, even between the beginning and the end of a season. With some of the longer-lived birds such as the shearwaters, a new pair may not settle down with one another very quickly; even if the pair is formed well before the start of the new season they may not breed in their first year together. In these longer-lived species, pairs are more likely to separate if they lose their eggs or young than if they nest successfully. Clearly there are advantages in staying with a partner with whom one has bred successfully. Further, well-established pairs breed earlier and more successfully than those breeding together for the first time.

Some species are polygamous, the males taking several mates: the weaver finches and some of the New World orioles are amongst these. Often the males will court a single female, mate with her and accompany her while she builds and lays, only to desert her as she starts to incubate the eggs and then go through the same procedure with the next female. In other species the males may take no interest whatever in the nesting, but merely congregate, often in the company of other males, at a display site where the females come for mating. The females then leave, build the nest, incubate and rear the young entirely on their own. Many American game birds, cotingids, manakins, birds of paradise and a few waders have these communal leks; so do some hummingbirds though the mating systems of relatively few birds from this large group are known.

A few other unusual mating systems may be mentioned. In the phalaropes and a few other waders the female lays the eggs and leaves the male to incubate and raise the young; in the phalarope the female also has the brighter plumage in the breeding season. In a few cases the female may lay two clutches, leaving the male to raise the first while she goes on to lay and raise a second; this may happen in a few waders and also has been suggested for the Red-legged partridge. In the Ostrich and the Emu the male mates with several females who all lay eggs in a single nest; the male incubates and looks after the young. In some tinamous several females lay together in a single nest and then go on to lay 'clutches' for other males to care for.

In many bird groups, especially passerines in warmer parts of the world, there are species where groups of birds, often as many as ten or more, care for the young in a single nest; these are the so-called co-operative breeders. The full details of many of these groupings are not yet fully understood, but many of the non-breeding birds are young that were raised in the territory in previous years and are not yet old enough to breed. As far as the pair bond is concerned, however, most of these groups do not appear as complicated as they were first thought to be. It seems that there is usually an older, dominant pair which mate and lay eggs and that the pair bond is therefore a simple monogamous one, except that the pair are accompanied by large numbers of additional birds which, though they may help raise the young, are not involved in the production of the clutch.

Courtship and nesting. (1) The male Winter wren *Troglodytes troglodytes* builds the nest by himself and then displays to attract a female to it. Once the female is incubating he may go on to build another nest and find another mate. (2) Common kingfishers *Alcedo atthis*, the male offering the female food. During the time that the female is forming eggs she needs considerably more food than usual and the male may help her. (3) Courtship flight of the Black-and-white warbler *Mniotilta varia*. Many small birds, especially those that nest in grassland or shrubby areas, have striking aerial displays. (4) The male (European) Redstart *Phoenicurus phoenicurus* leads his mate to a nest site by displaying his red tail; he may then enter the hole and display to her by moving his white forehead back and forth across the entrance. (5) In some species, such as the Roseate spoonbill *Ajaia ajaja*, nesting material is offered during courtship.

A pair of Black woodpeckers *Dryocopus martius*.
The male attempts to assess whether the bird on
its left is a female or a male intruder in its territory.
The female has a smaller red cap than the male
and, by turning away, a bird discloses its sex.

Territorial disputes occur in most species. In the
Gannet *Sula bassana* (1) disputes are confined to
keeping rivals out of beak range enabling the birds
to nest very close together. (2) In the Winter wren
Troglodytes troglodytes disputes take place on the
edge of the territory. In many species actual
fighting is rare and the disputes are confined to
threat. (3) In the European robin *Erithacus
rubecula* the male bird displays his red breast as
fully as possible to his opponent while (4), in the
Golden eagle *Aquila chrysaetos*, a bird may make
close passes at his opponent as if about to attack. ▶

Territorial Behaviour

A territory is an area which a bird defends against other birds. Many definitions of
territory have been proposed, but there are so many types of territory that none of the
definitions fit them all; the simplest and safest definition is probably 'a defended area'.
Birds vary markedly in the type of territory they defend. One tends to think of birds,
such as the Blackbird, which may defend an area in a garden and live and nest in
that area most of their lives. However, in other birds such as some hole-nesting
species, each male may defend only the area around the nest-site, leaving the woodland area between it and the next male undefended. Cliff-nesting species such as the
guillemot may merely defend a tiny piece of ledge where they lay their egg and raise
their youngster; all the feeding is done in the sea away from the territory. By way of
contrast, the shelduck defends a feeding territory on the estuary and nests in an
undefended area in the dunes away from the river. The drake stays on guard in the
territory while the duck goes to the nest. Some species such as the Woodchat shrike,
may hold territories while on migration; at each place they stop, they will vigorously
defend an area for the few days that they are there. Other species may defend
territories in winter quarters. In the European robin both sexes hold separate
territories in winter, defending them equally against intruding males or females. Only
as spring approaches does the female relinquish her territory and join the male in his;
often, where the two territories are adjacent, they may be amalgamated into a single
larger territory.

Once a bird becomes established in a territory—either as a result of driving the
previous owner out or, more frequently, by taking over one vacated as a result of
the death of the previous owner—it tends to retain this territory for the rest of its
life. Even if the bird is a migrant, it usually returns to the same patch of country each
year to breed. Once established, the right of 'ownership' seems to give the bird ascend-
ancy over most challengers. When two neighbours quarrel on their common boundary
they may be equally matched; however, if one enters the territory of the other it is
likely to back down in the ensuing dispute. If chased back into its own territory by
the owner of the land, the tables become turned and the fleeing bird becomes the
pursuer. Hence ownership gives some sort of strength to the competitor; it is not
only in humans that possession is nine tenths of the law! Once they get to know their
neighbours, birds tend to abide by the agreed boundaries and so avoid energy-con-
suming and potentially dangerous battles. Even with the species which live in one area
the whole year round, the vigor with which they defend their territories varies with the
stage of the year. During moult they tend to be quiet, but when feeding young and in
mid-winter, they may be much too busy searching for food to spend time defending
their territories.

One of the major functions proposed for territories is that of population regulation.
By spacing the birds out over the available habitat the territory holders may
prevent some of their kind from obtaining territories. When all areas are 'full' the
remainder have no place to go and either perish or, wandering as outcasts, do not
breed. The higher the population the greater the number of outcasts there might be.
There is strong evidence that some birds are forced, as a result of territorial disputes,
into poorer and more marginal territories, though less evidence that there is any
appreciable number of birds that fail to become established in a territory at all and
so perish. Experiments have been undertaken to see whether there is a surplus of
birds; these have involved the removal of established territory holders in spring in
order to see whether other birds filled the vacancies made. The results have often
been rather inconclusive at this time. However, earlier in the year, especially during
the brief period of autumn territorial behaviour, there is some evidence that a number
of birds may be excluded from holding territories. Further understanding of the
functions of territory is badly needed; once again it may be wrong to expect that the
same explanation will hold for all species.

Courtship display of the Magellanic penguin *Spheniscus magellanicus*. When displaying, many species of penguin draw themselves up to their full height, spead their flippers and give a trumpeting call.

Many birds of prey, such as the Goshawk *Accipiter gentilis*, have remarkable aerial displays, the members of the pair stooping at one another high in the air.

Courtship activities of (1) Buzzard *Buteo buteo*, (2) Great bustard *Otis tarda*, (3) Grey (or Common) heron *Ardea cinerea*, (4) Red-breasted merganser *Mergus serrator*, (5) Superb lyrebird *Menura novaehollandiae*, (6) Standardwing (or Wallace's) bird of paradise *Semioptera wallacei*, (7) Greater prairie chicken *Tympanuchus cupido*, (8) Wandering albatross *Diomedea exulans* and (9) Yellow wagtail *Motacilla flava*.

Courtship

Courtship covers the behaviour by which birds recognize others of the same species, find a member of the opposite sex and become established members of the breeding population. Much of the behaviour depends to some extent on the type of pair bond which is formed; for example, in species where groups of males hold communal display grounds or leks, the females go to these for mating and no lasting pair bond is formed. However, in most normal, monogamous birds a lasting bond is established.

Courtship serves to ensure that each individual bird successfully pairs with a mate from the correct species. Elaborate displays or songs are characteristic of each species enabling the females to select a correct partner more easily; the more prolonged the courtship the more likely that one or other bird will recognize its mistake if it is courting with a member of another species. It is said that hybrids are more common in species where the female only briefly visits the male at a display ground for mating, such as with some of the birds of paradise. Since mistakes might be more likely where there are a greater number of closely related species it is not surprising that one finds bright, distinctive plumages or songs in males where several species are gathered together and less distinctive ones where species are not so intermixed. The ducks provide a good example of this. In several areas of the northern hemisphere many species of ducks gather in the same areas and the plumages of the drakes are very distinct. In contrast, the drakes of isolated oceanic islands, where there is only one species in each area, have plumages which tend to be dull and female-like; problems of correct identification do not exist. As one would expect, birds tend to emphasize those patterns which distinguish them from other species by using them as central parts of their displays. The mechanism may be visual or auditory. Commonly where one finds closely related birds in very similar plumage, one finds that their songs are very different. A good example is the Willow warbler, Wood warbler and Chiffchaff where the songs are easily distinguished though the birds themselves are not.

Courtship performs a second important function. Apart from the cases where the species are promiscuous and only come together for mating, the continual presence and display of one bird to the other enables them to increase their confidence in one another so as to behave as a pair and, eventually, to breed. Close 'understanding' of one another is sometimes important, since in some species the female helps her mate in territorial conflicts with rival pairs. Further, the male's presence and display may induce the female to start nest-building and, in some species, also to start ovulation.

Normally a pair come together gradually through courtship. This may be so where new pairs are formed and also in others such as the European robin where the pairs split up between seasons; indeed in this species individuals of both sexes maintain an exclusive territory against all others of their species. However, as spring approaches, the two sexes must reduce their aggression towards one another if they are to pair successfully. In the case of the European robin, the female is attracted by the male's song and leaves her own territory to approach him. He, seeing an intruder in his territory, attacks. If the intruder were a rival male he would either contest this challenge or flee. The approaching female however, does neither; although she will flee if persistently attacked, initially she stands her ground and crouches—in a submissive as opposed to a threatening posture. This has the effect of inhibiting the male's aggressiveness and although he may still threaten he does not usually push home his attack. By persisting in approaching in a submissive manner the female becomes gradually accepted by the male, his aggression wanes and he turns to courtship; slowly the pair is formed. Full acceptance of each bird by the other may take days or even weeks. Under these conditions the female is normally submissive to the male for most of the period that she shares the territory formerly occupied by him alone. However in some species she may come to be the dominant member of the pair during the height of the nesting period, particularly near the nest.

The Great skua *Stercorarius skua* is a relative of the gulls. Both members of the pair take an active part in the courtship displays. Here they are bowing to each other.

Courtship pairs of grebes have a 'dance' in which both members of the pair rise up on the water and swim very rapidly along side-by-side. These are Red-necked grebes *Podiceps grisegena*.

The Common tern *Sterna hirundo* in one of its display postures. Note the raised head and tail and the drooped wings.

The plumage and displays of the birds of paradise have long been known as being some of the most dramatic among birds. The display involves the erection of bizarre plumages and is often accompanied by loud whip-like or cracking calls; frequently the bird's posture is upside down on a branch. The species shown here are (1) Magnficent riflebird *Ptiloris magnificus*, (2) Magnificent bird of paradise *Diphyllodes magnificus*, (3) White-plumed bird of paradise *Paradisaea guilielmi*, (4) Blue bird of paradise *Paradisaea rudolphi*, (5) Count Raggi's bird of paradise *Paradisaea raggiana* and (6) Twelve-wired bird of paradise *Seleucides ignotus*.

The first stages in the prelude to courtship involve the recognition of the sex of the other bird; in many cases this is by no means easy from the appearance of the plumage. In birds such as the European robin it is done initially through the female's recognition of the the male as a singing bird; thereafter behavioural differences separate the sexes. However, in many species the plumages of the two birds are clearly distinct. The ducks are a good example; in many of these the drakes are clearly different from the duller females and separation is easy. In many other species the individuals need to get close to one another to identify the sex; even then behavioural clues may be essential.

There is an almost infinite variety of ways in which courtship leads to pair formation, but the above description for the European robin probably covers the most common way in which it comes about. The male occupies a territory, advertizes his presence and the fact that he is without a mate; the female approaches and there follows a prolonged period during which the female's appeasement gradually reduces the male's aggression until the pair can co-exist. This happens in many species whether the territory be a large area of woodland or a small part of a colony as in the case of a gull.

Many birds appear at their breeding site already paired and, in cases where they are known not to have been paired the year before, they must have paired either in winter quarters or in their winter flocks; ducks and tits are examples of these two. The males are not isolated as in the case of the European robin, but are often in flocks so that the details of courtship must be slightly different. Most birds in flocks maintain small individual distances from one another; again this must be broken down for pair formation. In some such cases the courting male may accompany the female closely and defend a small area around her.

In most of the species covered by the description given above, the male displays and the female comes to him, but takes a small or negligible part in the displays. In many species however, both members of the pair undertake equal shares of often very elaborate displays; Gannets, swans and some herons may be cited as examples, while the elaborate bill-scissoring displays of some of the albatrosses show them to be on even terms. In the grebes, the courtship is also mutual and may occur at any time of the day or night. Courtship displays often involve highly vocal aspects as well as the upright 'penguin' dances, often accompanied by the birds rushing side-by-side across the surface of the water in an almost vertical position.

In many of those species where the female takes little part in the courtship display, the males are much more strikingly coloured than their mates. The species where the male holds a lek are good examples; the highly coloured or ornamented males (some of the American game birds, the Ruff, cotingids, manakins and birds of paradise) use striking displays to court the females who stay only briefly at the leks for mating and do not take part in the display. In a very few species, such as the phalaropes, the female is the larger and more brightly coloured; she arrives first at the breeding ground, takes and defends a territory against the other females and displays to attract the attentions of the male. Having paired and mated, she lays the eggs and leaves the male to incubate them and to care for the young. Apart from the laying of the eggs, the female takes over almost every aspect of breeding which, in most species, would be the responsibility of the male.

The female lays eggs and in many species she does all the incubation. Both these activities place a strain upon her; she requires more food than usual in order to form the eggs and in addition, when she is incubating, she has little time to collect food since she must spend much of the day keeping the eggs warm. At this time in many species the male provides what is known as 'courtship-feeding'. The female starts to behave like a small fledgling, gaping and quivering her wings and the male begins to bring her food. This behaviour often commences around the same time as copulation occurs. The male's contributions to the female's diet may be considerable—in some species up to 40% of her daily requirements are supplied by the male at this

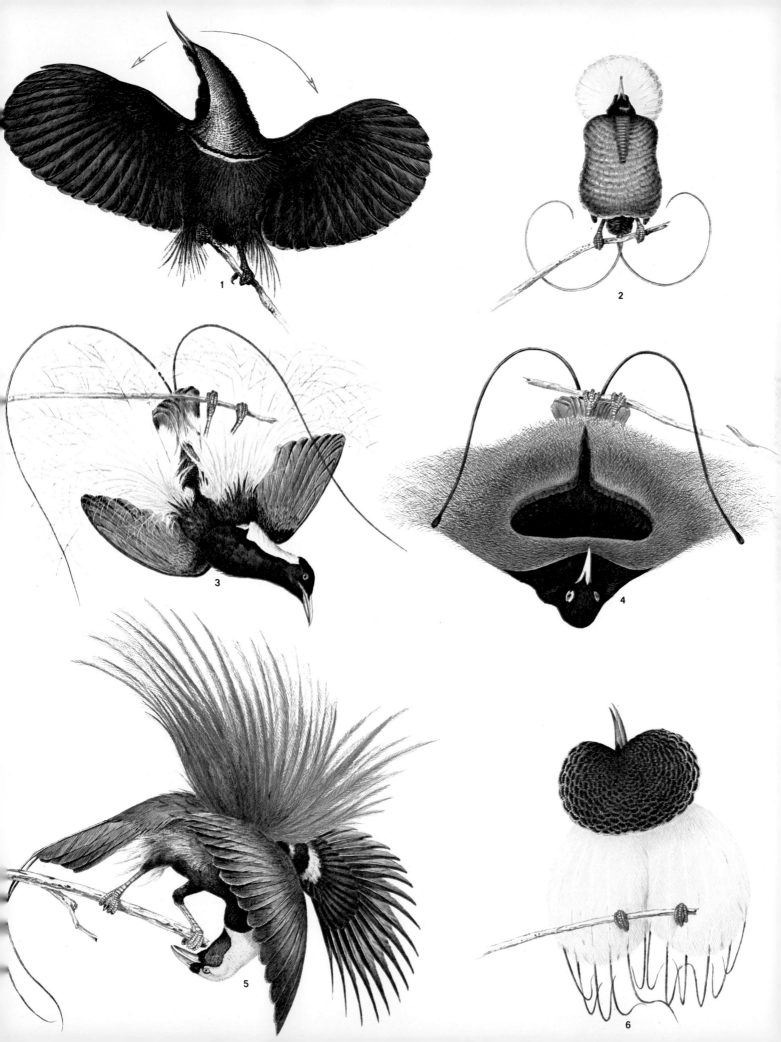

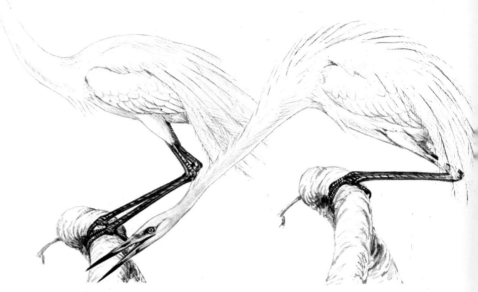

The Blue-footed booby *Sula nebouxii* is a relative of the gannets. Although they have dull brown plumage, they have very bright blue feet which they display to full effect during courtship, walking with a high-stepping action to draw attention to them.

Sarus crane *Grus antigone* displaying. The bird stands erect with wings drooped and uttering a loud call. In many species of crane, at the peak of their display, the pair indulge in a wild dance.

time. The male continues so-called courtship feeding during the incubation period, either calling the hen off the nest when he has brought her food or, while she is off, by foraging with her and so enabling her to get twice as much food in the time. In some game birds where the male does not feed the female he may scratch up the ground in order to make it easier for the hen to search for food.

In certain species courtship feeding is a prelude to copulation, the male bringing his mate an item of food and, in some passerines, accompanying the feeding with a special pre-copulation song. In other species the feeding has become ritualized in that the actual food is replaced in the courtship ceremony by other items such as nesting material.

Courtship feeding may have another function besides helping the female with her material needs at this time; it may help her to gauge how good a parent the male will be and thus how much help she will get from him when the young are in the nest. It has been shown in the USA that female Common terns lay more eggs if the male brings the female more food during the laying period; if he is of very little assistance she may leave him and look for another mate. It is unlikely that the number of eggs laid is solely dependent on the amount of food that the male brings, but more likely that the female can estimate the assistance that she will receive with the hungry broods and modify her clutch accordingly.

In those species where a proper pair bond is formed, the pair may remain together all the year or they may re-pair each spring. Geese and swans tend to remain paired the whole time even on migration. Other species such as some of the tits and many of the small tropical birds tend to remain within their territories all their lives and hence stay paired. Others re-pair each spring. In order to find each other again, they must come back to the same place. It seems likely that the birds that do re-mate remember one another. Courtship and acceptance seem to be faster amongst previously mated pairs than among those that are pairing for the first time. Indeed in the Kittiwake, pairs which have bred together in a previous year not only lay earlier than pairs breeding together for the first time, but also raise more young.

Since part of the function of courtship is to ensure that birds obtain a mate of the correct species, even the patterns of display between closely related species may be quite different. In many species the initial contact between a pair is made through

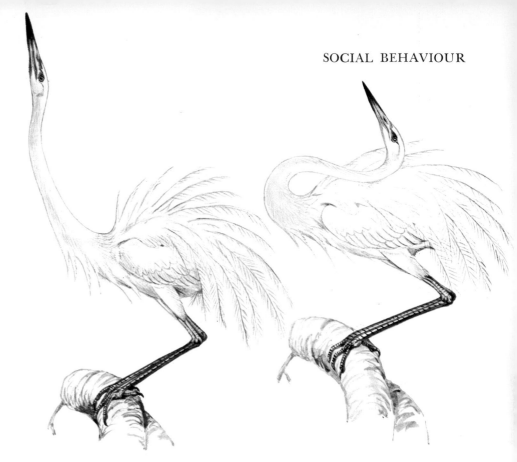

The American Common egret *Casmerodius albus* in a variety of the display postures it uses during courtship. In some species of herons, the beak colour can change at the peak of excitement during courtship, apparently as a result of a flush of blood. Note also how the plumes on the back are raised. It was these feathers that caused the rush of collectors to kill so many herons for the plume trade earlier during this century.

Bustards display on the ground. They enlarge their necks and frequently move their tails forward and puff up the back feathers. The species shown here is the Kori bustard *Ardeotis kori*.

Many herons grow plumes with which they display in the nesting season. During courtship they may also expand the neck by raising the neck feathers. This species is the (Black-crowned) Night heron *Nycticorax nycticorax*.

the female being attracted to the male's song. These are usually very distinct between related species, especially in cases where the plumage is only slightly different. Under circumstances such as these the female's initial discrimination for a mate of the correct species may be made from afar. Once close, the male is able to make use of visual displays. The male may undertake a wide variety of displays, including aerial acrobatics and song flights in order to further attract his mate. During these displays the male shows off the most striking parts of his plumage. One can think of an almost endless variety of such adornments all of which are usually spread, fanned or enlarged in order to make them more striking. An obvious example is the peacock's train, which is erected into a fan and rustled vigorously in front of his prospective mate. The birds of paradise are also brilliantly coloured and display—often in groups at communal display grounds—in most eye-catching ways; some even hang upside down and fluff out their feathers at the height of their displays. A closely related group of birds, the bowerbirds, are much less strikingly coloured and build bowers or arenas where they display to the visiting females. The bower of each species is of different design or decorated with stones and fruits of different colours. Although basically not brightly coloured, the males of some species possess bright crests of coloured feathers which are normally concealed beneath the other plumage. A wide variety of birds keep their brightest colours concealed beneath their normal plumage, presumably for reasons of camouflage and safety; only at the peak of their displays are these flags of bright colours unfurled. It is not only the plumage that may be brightly coloured. The male frigatebird has an inflatable throat pouch of bright red. He sits on his nest and throws his head back so as to display the bright red balloon to females passing overhead; he utters a loud call while doing this display. The male Blue-footed booby is a dull brown bird except for his brightly coloured feet. These he displays to his mate by continually 'goose-stepping' before her or by taking off, and circling around; on coming into land he throws his blue feet up and waves them prominently before touching down.

Although pair formation is not always smooth at first, gradually through courtship the two birds get to know one another better and settle down to a more regular routine. The territory is often chosen by the male, but the pair spend more and more time in each others company and begin to prospect for a suitable nest site.

During copulation, the female usually closes her tail and moves it to one side allowing the mounting male to bend his body over to bring the two cloacae into contact. These are Common terns *Sterna hirundo*.

Perhaps surprisingly, most water birds normally copulate on land. The ducks, however, are an exception; the male mounts the female on the water, often almost submerging her. Ducks have a penis-like structure, possibly to aid the transfer of sperm when copulation occurs in water. These are Shovelers *Anas clypeata*.

Black redstarts *Phoenicurus ochruros* copulating. The male positions himself on the back of the female and is very dependent on her remaining still if mating is to be successful.

Copulation. (1) Common swift *Apus apus*, who sometimes copulates on the wing, (2) Common kingfisher *Alcedo atthis*, (3) Black-winged stilt *Himantopus himantopus*, (4) Little ringed plover *Charadrius dubius* and (5) Bewick's swan *Cygnus bewickii*. ▶

Copulation

Normally even birds who are not strikingly territorial maintain some form of 'individual distance'; they keep at least a little way away from one another. Even within flocks, an individual distance is kept and birds do not normally come close together. Courtship functions not only in order to get a pair of birds used to one another so that their behaviour may be synchronized for breeding, but also to break down the maintenance of these individual distances. Until birds are sufficiently well acquainted with one another for individual distances to be dispensed with, the close approach necessary for copulation cannot be achieved. In certain birds, such as those where the males maintain leks, the prelude to copulation is very short; the females only come to the lek for brief visits when they are ready to be fertilized. Nonetheless, even in such cases, the pair may be more familiar with each other than one might think from such brief encounters; it is quite possible that each female visits the same male for the successive matings required for her clutch.

Unlike mammals, most birds do not possess a penis; sperm must be transferred by contact of the cloaca of the male with that of the female. In order for this to be achieved the male must mount the female and she must move her tail to one side so that he can bend the back of his body over so that the two cloacae can meet. The positioning of the two birds is such that the male is rather finely balanced and in order to complete copulation he requires the full co-operation of the female; she must remain still. Hence by his previous displays the male must have fully prepared his mate. When the two birds have their cloacae in contact, that of the female is usually somewhat everted so that the male can more easily reach over and make contact with it. When she withdraws the cloaca to the normal position, she draws the sperm into her and hence aids them in their journey up the oviduct towards the unfertilized egg.

Because of the close co-operation required by the two birds, many attempts at copulation appear to be unsuccessful, the male failing to get into the right position. Because there are no external differences in the sex organs of the two sexes 'reverse mountings'—where the female tries to copulate with the male—are frequently recorded in birds. These are said to be particularly frequent in species where there is little difference in the appearance of the plumage of the two sexes. Also homosexual pairings are relatively frequent; 'matings' within such 'pairs' of birds are commonly observed.

In the prelude to copulation, the male bird displays and sings to the female and, in some species, brings her presents of food; this is the basis for the phrase 'courtship-feeding', though the act is also important to the female in that it helps her to get sufficient food to form the eggs. In certain species, a particular song has been associated with the final prelude to copulation. Sexual chases are frequent in some species prior to the final display which leads to copulation.

Matings take place primarily during the period in which unfertilized eggs are present in the female; at this time she is most responsive to the male. The period is normally about two days before the egg is laid, but its length will depend greatly on how many eggs are to be laid in the clutch; the ten eggs of a tit or game bird may require several fertilizations over a period as opposed to one mating needed to fertilize the single egg of other species. As far as is known the females of most species do not store sperm for long periods of time so that a series of successful copulations may result in better fertilization of large clutches. However, there are exceptions, for in some of the ducks one successful copulation may be all that is necessary for the fertilization of the whole clutch. In addition, hornbills must be able to store sperm. The females are walled into the nesting chamber by the male some time before the first egg is laid. Thereafter, although copulation is impossible, the female lays five or more eggs; it seems that sperm from earlier copulations must remain viable for two or even three weeks in order for such eggs to be successfully fertilized.

BREEDING

The nest of the Lesser noddy *Anous tenuirostris*, a tern from the Indian Ocean. The nest is of seaweed, cemented together and to a branch by the birds' excreta. Only one egg is laid.

The Lesser treeswift *Hemiprocne comata* at its nest. In this species the nest is tiny, a very small patch of material being cemented to the side of the branch with the bird's saliva. The nest barely holds the single egg; the incubating adult, and later the growing young, have to support themselves on the branch.

Nests in a variety of species. (1) Long-tailed tit *Aegithalos caudatus*, (2) Goldcrest *Regulus regulus*, (3) Ruby-throated hummingbird *Archilochus colubris*, (4) Common (or Barn) swallow *Hirundo rustica*, (5) Wagler's oropendola *Zarhynchus wagleri*, (6) Osprey *Pandion haliaetus*, (7) Baya weaver *Ploceus philippinus*, (8) African palm swift *Cypsiurus parvus*, (9) Kentish (or Snowy) plover *Charadrius alexandrinus* and (10) Fairy tern *Gygis alba*. ▶

Nests and Nest Building

Birds build nests in order to raise young and hence it is most important that the nest should be safe from disturbance. However, as man well knows, both eggs and young birds are highly edible; in nature a wide variety of predators share this view and search diligently for the nests of birds; often the predators themselves are breeding at the same time as the birds and so they have a greater need of food than at any other time of year. Many mammals such as squirrels, raccoons, stoats, weasels, monkeys, pigs, foxes and many members of the cat family make short work of any nests and adults which they can find. While some of these predators are confined to the ground, others are good climbers and many can reach nests in trees. Birds also are serious raiders of the nests of other species; gulls, birds of prey and many members of the crow family are among the worst offenders, but herons, toucans, woodpeckers and other birds may also take their toll. In the tropics snakes are responsible for the loss of many a nest; there are even egg-eating snakes, especially adapted with 'teeth' far back in the throat so that they can puncture the eggs and eat the contents only when the egg has been completely swallowed; the snake can then close its mouth so as not to risk spilling and losing any of the contents. Ants may often take a nest and kill the occupants. Sometimes one wonders how, in the face of so many enemies, birds manage to raise their young at all!

There are, perhaps, two main ways in which birds seek to protect their nests. The most widely used one of these—especially amongst small birds—is concealment. By hiding the nest in an out-of-the-way place, covering it with camouflaging materials and taking great care to visit it cautiously so as not to draw attention to it, the birds hope to protect their young. A second method of protection is to put the nests in inaccessible places; here the value of secrecy is less since the birds rely on their enemies being unable to reach the site at all. Rooks and herons in tall trees, swallows in sand cliffs or building mud-nests on a wall and sea birds on islands are all examples; often many members of the family may group together, possibly because safe sites are hard to find. This method is also used by large birds which are relatively well able to defend themselves. These, such as some eagles and the swans, build large and sometimes more easily accessible nests. Here, too the nests are reasonably well protected from mammals, but are readily found by birds though they easily can be defended by the large owners. Concealment is by far the widest method practised: it is better to avoid conflict with a potential predator than to look for trouble. Small predators pose a threat even to large birds since they may sneak up to the nest in unguarded moments and take the eggs or small chicks.

Small birds have almost no chance of defence once they have been found, though many may use both concealment and inaccessibility to try and prevent this. In the tropics in particular many small birds suspend their nests from thin vines or the tips of twiggy branches; these nests may be roofed, making it particularly hard for potential predators to establish whether or not there is anything worthwhile there anyway and, by using stealthy approaches, the birds may get through the nesting stage untouched. Nevertheless, the life of small birds in the breeding season is diffi-

The Rufous ovenbird *Furnarius rufus* from South America builds a strong mud nest with two chambers. The nests are often built on fence posts or in close proximity to man.

Owls use a wide range of nest-sites, often taken over from other birds that have finished with them. (1) The New World Elf owl *Micrathene whitneyi* often nests in a saguaro cactus using old woodpecker holes, (2) another New World species, the Burrowing owl *Speotyto cunicularia* uses abandoned lairs of the prairie dog, (3) the Short-eared owl *Asio flammeus* nests on the ground, sometimes under the edge of a bush, (4) the Great grey owl *Strix nebulosa* of the northern forests uses old nests of birds of prey, (5) the Snowy owl *Nyctea scandiaca* nests on hummocks in the arctic and (6) the Eagle owl *Bubo bubo* nests in crevices and small caves, hollow trees and old nests of other birds.

cult. In a study of Blackbirds in English woodland only some 14% of the nests produced fledged young, while in Trinidad Black-and-white manakins raised young from only 19% of their nests. Such low figures do not mean that the birds are quite as unsuccessful as they might at first appear. Persistence is the other quality necessary for such birds; each time they lose their nest they start again and perhaps eventually each female may lay three, four or even five clutches. Hence she may have about a 50:50 chance of raising a brood within the season. The nesting success of larger birds is usually higher than this and one group of small birds, the hole-nesters, also have a high success. Small birds which nest in holes in trees cannot be reached by the large ground-dwelling predators and most bird predators also cannot reach them. Not surprisingly therefore, their nesting success is much higher, only some 15–30% of the nests being lost to predators. One wonders why more species do not nest in this way. Two factors probably contribute to this. Firstly, such sites may be in great demand, so great in fact that some birds may be unable to find a suitable nesting site, a situation that almost never occurs in birds that choose a bush to nest in. Some birds of course, such as the woodpeckers, make their own holes, but these are hard work to construct and may take several weeks; even then another bird may come along and evict the rightful owner. Secondly, there are dangers associated with nesting in holes. If a predator finds the nest while the female is incubating, she cannot easily escape. In a study of tits in England some 20% of the females were taken when the predators took the eggs; in a more conventional open nest, the female must have a much higher chance of escape. Hence the advantages of holes as nesting sites may be in part offset by the difficulties of finding one and by the dangers to the female of being caught in it.

A few species make large holes smaller so as to reduce the chances of larger stronger

The Penduline tit *Remiz pendulinus* builds a finely woven nest of a felt-like material. This is usually suspended from a thin twig at the tip of a branch, often over water.

Unusual nests. (1) The Sunbittern *Eurypyga helias* builds a precarious nest of vegetation and mud on a thin horizontal branch. (2) The Shelduck *Tadorna tadorna* is unusual for a duck in that it nests in sand-dunes. (3) The Long-tailed tailorbird *Orthotomus sutorius* stitches two sides of a leaf together as a support for its nest. The edges are held together by knotted fibres passed through holes made in the leaf edge. (4) The Horned coot *Fulica cornuta* builds a foundation for its nest by dropping stones into shallow water offshore. The platforms may grow to a considerable size over a period of years.

birds trying to take them over. The nuthatches plaster the entrance of a hole with mud until they themselves can only just squeeze through. In most hornbills, the female enters the nest chamber and then the male walls her in with mud until only a tiny opening is left. He feeds the female through this hole and she is wholly dependent on him throughout egg-laying, incubation and the earlier part of the nesting stage. After this she breaks out, and the young then help wall themselves in again until they are full-grown, but get fed by both parents.

Many species nest in even more inaccessible sites and suffer much less predation as a result. Sea birds are the most obvious examples of this. Their nests are often on cliffs or on small offshore islands. Mammalian predators cannot easily reach the nests on cliffs and even if they could reach the offshore islands they could not survive there at times when the sea birds were not breeding. There would be no food during the 'off-season'. Moreover these islands are often without fresh water, so that drinking would also pose a problem. Certain other species such as divers nest on small islands in lakes in temperate areas; again mammalian predators cannot easily reach them. Some Arctic species such as eider ducks, gulls and terns that nest on small islands just offshore are said to delay their nesting until after the ice has thawed and the Arctic fox can no longer reach the islands; the birds are then safe from their main predator.

Nesting on islands does not confer total protection; some birds are serious enemies of other nesting species. The larger gulls, for example, are predators of auks, shearwaters and storm petrels. Most of the latter species protect themselves by either nesting on tiny cliff ledges where the gulls cannot easily land, or by nesting underground—in burrows or under fallen rocks. Even then the marauding gulls may attack the parents, either to eat the birds themselves or to get the food that was being

brought to their chicks. To reduce this danger the Puffin nests close to the edge of the island in places where it can quickly land and get down its burrow and equally quickly take off again. The shearwaters and the storm petrels are even more defenceless than the Puffin and the only way that they can safely come to their nests is to do so in the dead of night when the gulls are asleep; one small auk, the Cassin's auklet, has also become completely nocturnal. In tropical seas frigate birds are a constant threat to nesting terns on many islands.

A small number of species build their own 'islands' and some of the marsh-dwelling terns build floating nests of vegetation, anchored to sticks or reeds protruding from the water. These too deter many of the mammalian predators which would have to swim to reach them. In South America the Horned coot builds its nest by dropping stones in shallow water until the tip of the small island emerges above the level of the lake; there, safe from mammalian predators, it builds its nest.

The nest itself varies markedly in complexity in different groups of birds. Some birds such as the waders or shore birds do little in the way of building a nest: their eggs are laid in mere scrapes on the ground. The same is true of some of the penguins, though the Adélie penguin builds a small mound of stones on which it lays its eggs; by raising them just this much above the ground it keeps them out of the melting ice on their nesting grounds. The Emperor penguin, which lays its egg and incubates it through the long winter nights period (so that it hatches early in the Antarctic spring) has no nest at all. The single egg is kept on top of the feet and warmed by a flap of skin that hangs over it. During its vigil, the incubating bird is free to shuffle around and huddle against other birds in periods of blizzard.

Many other birds, such as auks, build little or no nest though sometimes they may put small amounts of material around the egg. Others, such as the shearwaters and petrels, do not produce much in the way of a nest lining though they may have to dig a burrow in which to nest. Many gulls and terns put only little or no material into the nest though others may build more elaborate structures, especially those mentioned above which make floating nests. Some birds that nest in holes in trees, such as some owls and parrots, also put little material into the nest. Yet others 'steal' nests that were constructed by other birds; some owls may take old nests of other species in which to place their own young and one of the cowbirds of North America is said to specialize in nesting in old nests of other species.

The simplest type of nest is probably that of a pile of sticks in a tree where a flimsy platform is formed on which to put the eggs; pigeons, birds of prey, herons and cormorants for example build nests of this type, those of cormorants often being built on ledges on cliffs. The nests of some members of the crow family are similar though better constructed and often lined with small rootlets well woven into the structure. A wide range of other species build nests of increasing complexity, though nearly all the most elaborate forms of nests are built by passerines. Only a few non-passerines go beyond the level of nesting on the ground, in holes in trees or in a nest of twigs in the branches of a tree. The latter type of nest may be large, in some of the eagles it is immense, but the structure remains simple. The Hammerkop, an aberrant stork, is an exception, building a completely domed nest of sticks with one, or sometimes two, entrances to the nest chamber. Amongst other non-passerines, the hummingbirds build neatly woven nests held together with spiders web and some of the

Weavers of the family Ploceidae build some of the most intricately woven nests found among birds, some having long funnel-like entrances. They are built of grass strands or strips of palm leaf. Usually the male alone builds the nest; being polygamous, he may build a succession of nests for different females.

The male Mallee-fowl *Leipoa ocellata* builds a large mound in which the female lays her eggs. The male opens the nest daily to check the temperature. Initially the mound is kept warm by heat generated from decomposing vegetation placed inside the mound (1), but as this begins to lose effect later in the season the bird may spread the sand from the top of the mound over a large area so that it is heated by the sun and then pile the warm sand back into the mound (2).

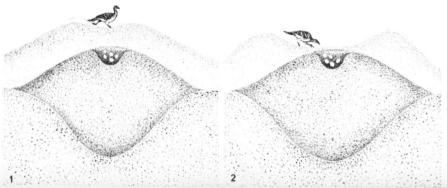

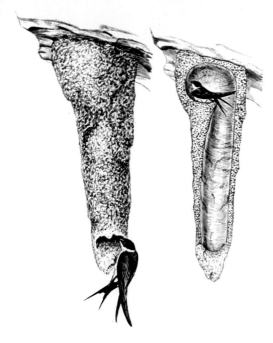

The Great swallow-tailed swift *Panyptila sancti-hieronymi* builds a long tubelike nest, using its saliva to hold the structure together. The nest chamber is at the top of the tube. In nature, the nests are usually built on rock faces, but they are sometimes placed on buildings.

The Golden oriole *Oriolus oriolus* builds a flimsy nest towards the end of the branch. Usually the nest material is composed of thin strips of grass or bark.

Stages in the building of the nest of the Edible-nest swiftlet *Collocalia fuciphaga*. The nest, built virtually entirely from the bird's saliva, is cemented to a rocky surface, usually in a cave. These are the nests which form the basis of birds' nest soup.

swifts, whose edible nests we use for soup, build nests projecting from a cliff face.

The basic passerine nest is also built of twigs on a branch of a tree, or in the undergrowth in birds such as the Blackbird or American robin. The nests tend to be better constructed than is the case with the non-passerines and most of them are lined with grass or rootlets; some birds, such as the Song thrush, neatly surface the interior of the nest with mud, making a smooth lining. The methods of construction used in nest building are about as varied as the sites chosen. A great many nests are domed: all the birds in the wren family for example build domed nests and, as mentioned previously, a great many of the nests built by tropical species are also domed.

Some of the smaller species using lichens, mosses and similar materials build nests held together with cobwebs. These nests are extremely warm and well-insulated enabling the incubating birds to snuggle down inside with a minimum of heat loss. The extremes of design of this type of nest are reached in the long-tailed tits of the Palearctic, the penduline tits of Africa and the bush-tits of America. The nests are purse-like structures of great intricacy, made of moss and lichens bound together with spiders web and often richly lined with feathers; in the case of the European Long-tailed tit more than 2,000 feathers may be used to line the nest and a considerable variety of complex building behaviours are needed during the course of construction. So pliable are these nests that they seem to expand to hold the growing brood; in Africa the nests of penduline tits are used by natives as purses. The European Long-tailed tits start to roost in the nest as soon as it is roofed and weather-proofed even though the birds may not lay eggs for some weeks.

The sunbirds also often build intricate domed nests, though these are not usually as neatly built as those of the tits; they may be suspended from the very tip of a branch so as to be very difficult to reach. A small group of warblers, the tailorbirds, from southeast Asia build their nests between two large leaves which they have sewn together—hence their name. These birds take a pair of more or less opposing leaves and make small holes in their borders through which they pass their 'thread'—either plant material or spiders web. Each stitch is made separately and the ends of the threads are bent over or knotted to prevent them slipping through. Not only is the nest difficult to reach, it is also very difficult to see.

Pride of place among the avian architects is usually given either to the Old World weavers or to the New World orioles. Some of both groups make magnificently woven nests of grass or other strips of vegetation. These are hung from trees, often in small colonies. Many are long pendulous structures. Apart from size—the orioles are larger than the weavers and their nests may be as much as 6 ft (1.8 m) long—the main difference is that the entrance and nest chambers are in different places in the two groups. In the weavers, the bird enters the nest at the bottom and climbs up through a long tube to the nest chamber at the top; in the orioles the entrance is at the top and the nest chamber at the bottom. The passage down the long tube presumably deters any predators that may reach the nest, though some of the orioles are heavily parasitized by other orioles—the cowbirds. The Social weaver of southwest Africa builds a nest of an entirely different kind; the woven nest is similar to that of other weavers though simpler in design, its main difference being that it is interwoven with many nests of adjacent pairs, forming a single gigantic mass, one of the very few truly communal structures built by birds.

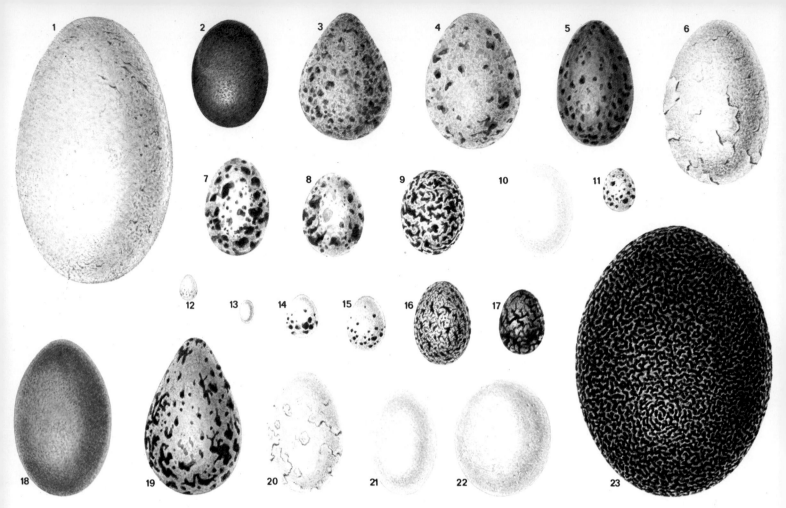

Eggs

Eggs of (1) Brown kiwi *Apteryx australis*, (2) Crested tinamou *Eudromia elegans*, (3) Eurasian curlew *Numenius arquata*, (4) Herring gull *Larus argentatus*, (5) Black-throated diver (or Arctic loon) *Gavia arctica*, (6) American White pelican *Pelecanus erythrorhynchos*, (7) Black skimmer *Rynchops nigra*, (8) Common tern *Sterna hirundo*, (9) Guira cuckoo *Guira guira*, (10) Snowy egret *Egretta thula*, (11) Hawfinch *Coccothraustes coccothraustes*, (12) Goldcrest *Regulus regulus*, (13) Broad-billed hummingbird *Cynanthus latirostris*, (14) Scissor-tailed flycatcher *Muscivora forficata*, (15) Song thrush *Turdus philomelos*, (16) Common crow *Corvus brachyrhynchos*, (17) Northern jacana *Jacana spinosa*, (18) Scrub fowl *Megapodius freycinet*, (19) Guillemot (or Common murre) *Uria aalge*, (20) Common (or Great) cormorant *Phalacrocorax carbo*, (21) Great crested grebe *Podiceps cristatus*, (22) Eagle owl *Bubo bubo* and (23) Emu *Dromaius novaehollandiae*.

The egg of the Guillemot (or Common murre) *Uria aalge* is very pointed. When pushed, it rolls around in a small circle and it is thought that this shape may reduce the chance of the egg being knocked off cliff ledges.

The hard shelled, often distinctively shaped, eggs of birds are well known. They are composed of three main parts—yolk, albumen and shell. The yolk is the most nutritive part, being relatively rich in fats and proteins. On the surface of the yolk there is a small patch, the germinal spot or blastodisc, which houses the tiny unfertilized ovum. After fertilization this develops into the embryo and, eventually, into the young bird. The growing embryo 'floats' on the surface of the yolk throughout its development. The egg white or albumen surrounds the embryo and, although relatively low in nutrients compared with the yolk, holds much of the water essential to the growing chick's survival. Two cords, the chalazae, attach the yolk to the shell keeping it central to the albumen and enabling it to turn as the incubating bird turns the egg; when small, the embryo stays uppermost on the yolk all the time. The albumen is surrounded by two layers of shell membranes just internal to the shell itself. The egg shell is a porous structure composed mainly of calcium carbonate; an average-sized hen's egg weighs about 2 oz (60 gm) and of the 0.2 oz (6 gm) of shell some 0.08 oz (2.25 gm) are calcium.

The developing chick must obtain all its nutrients from within the egg shell. The chick draws on these as it develops and also obtains the calcium it needs for its bones by withdrawing calcium from the shell. In most small birds the yolk is almost completely used up at hatching, but what remains is drawn into the body as a yolk sac just prior to hatching; this store helps the baby bird to survive if, for example, it hatches in the night when the parents cannot feed it. In a few species a considerable amount of the yolk remains at hatching. Young swans may hatch with 25% of the yolk still unused in the yolk sac; they are able to survive for a week or more on this food store. The largest yolk stores at hatching are found in penguins where some species hatch with as much as 50% of the yolk unused.

In order to metabolize its food the developing chick must be able to breathe and for this oxygen must be absorbed into the egg and carbon dioxide expired; a series

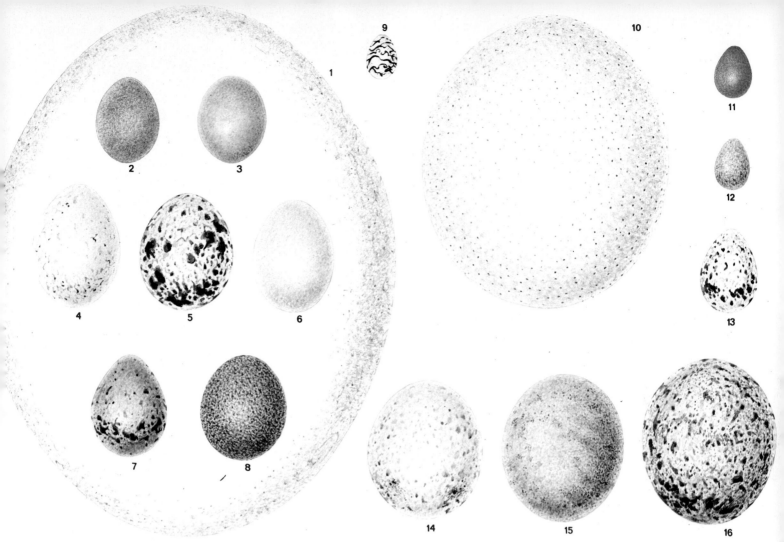

Eggs. (1) Extinct Elephant-bird *Aepyornis maximus*, (2) Glossy ibis *Plegadis falcinellus*, (3) European bittern *Botaurus stellaris*, (4) (Eurasian) Spoonbill *Platalea leucorodia*, (5) Osprey *Pandion haliaetus*, (6) Steller's eider *Polysticta stelleri*, (7) Long-tailed skua (or jaeger) *Stercorarius longicaudus*, (8) Gyrfalcon *Falco rusticolus*, (9) Northern oriole *Icterus galbula*, (10) Ostrich *Struthio camelus*, the largest egg laid by any living bird, (11) American robin *Turdus migratorius*, (12) Redwing *Turdus iliacus*, (13) Roseate tern *Sterna dougallii*, (14) Golden eagle *Aquila chrysaetos*, (15) Lammergeier *Gypaetus barbatus* and (16) Black vulture *Aegypius monachus*.

Some birds have a single large incubation or brood patch that covers all the eggs; others, such as the Black-headed gull *Larus ridibundus*, may have discrete patches for each egg, three in this species. The Emperor penguin *Aptenodytes forsteri* keeps its single egg on the top of its feet and incubates it with a fold of skin which hangs down and covers the egg.

of blood vessels throughout the egg, outside the chick, enable such respiration to occur. The egg shell is surprisingly porous to these gases and, during the latter stages of incubation as much as 30 ml of oxygen and a similar amount of carbon dioxide may pass through the shell of a gull's egg each hour, a considerable amount for a seemingly solid object. The difficulty for the embryo is that the egg also loses water through the shell during incubation; this is why a fresh egg sinks if placed in water whereas a well-incubated one floats: the loss of water has reduced its density. If too much water is lost the embryo may dry out and die. In many species, the loss of water produces an air space within the egg; this space forms between the two shell membranes and is called the air sac. Just before hatching the young bird forces its beak into this space and starts to breathe air through its nostrils in addition to that still being 'breathed in' through the embryonic blood system still visible in the egg. In this way the change-over to air breathing on hatching is facilitated. The growing embryo also produces waste products which are excreted into a bag within the egg— the allantois—where they are kept separate from still unused food resources. The small packet of waste materials is left in the egg on hatching.

The laying bird must find extra amounts of food in order to form eggs. It is estimated that this may increase her food demands by as much as 40 % during the laying period; in addition she may have to search for particular foods at this time. For example the female Quelea finch takes more insects than her mate just prior to laying, apparently needing the high protein content of the insects. Other birds have to collect the calcium required for the egg shell: they may take calcareous grit, snail shell, egg shell or other materials at this time. Laying Dunlin in the Arctic eat the bones of dead lemmings in order to get calcium. Fish eating birds probably get sufficient calcium from the bones or their prey; one insect eating marsh tern is known to switch to a diet of fish during the laying period.

The size of eggs varies markedly. The smallest eggs are laid by the smallest hum-

BREEDING

Variation in egg colour in the Guillemot (or Common murre) *Uria aalge* (1) and the Kestrel *Falco tinnunculus* (2). In certain species the variation in the egg colour may be considerable. In the case of the Guillemot, which nests very densely on cliff ledges, the variation may help a bird to recognize its own egg. Individual birds tend to lay eggs similar in colour throughout their life-times.

Depicted here are a range of egg shapes that are found in different species, varying from elliptical to conical in shape. (1) Steppe buzzard *Buteo vulpinus*, (2) Red-necked grebe *Podiceps grisegena*, (3) Crowned sandgrouse *Pterocles coronatus*, (4) Barbary falcon *Falco pelegrinoides*, (5) Moorhen (or Common gallinule) *Gallinula chloropus*, (6) Pygmy cormorant *Phalacrocorax pygmaeus*, (7) Tufted guineafowl *Numida meleagris*, (8) Sabine's gull *Xema sabini*, (9) Golden plover *Pluvialis apricaria*, (10) Lapwing *Vanellus vanellus*, (11) Spotted redshank *Tringa erythropus* and (12) Greenshank *Tringa nebularia*. Owls and kingfishers lay some of the most spherical eggs while swifts and woodpeckers lay some of the most slender elliptical ones. The most conical eggs (such as 8-12) are often laid by waders and gulls; in the waders these are commonly kept in a tight cluster, pointed ends inwards to minimize the surface area occupied.

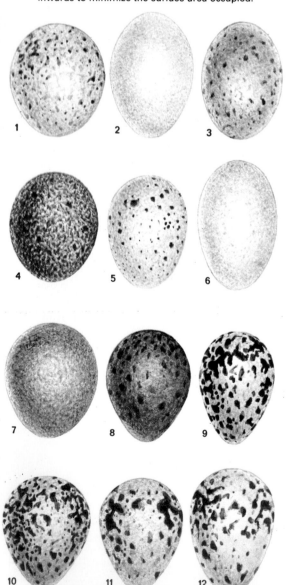

mingbirds and weigh about 0.02 oz (0.5 gm), while the largest, those of the Ostrich, weigh about 3.3 lb (1.5 kg); the eggs of the extinct Elephant-bird were much larger and, it is estimated, would have weighed about 20 lb (9 kg). Larger birds tend to have larger eggs, but there is considerable variation for other reasons as well; for example the Razorbill and the Carrion crow weigh about 2.8 lb (800 gm) and 1.8 lb (500 gm) respectively, but the former species lays an egg weighing about 3 oz (90 gm), the latter one of about 0.6 oz (18 gm), one fifth the size. If the clutch is large, eggs tend to be small, but perhaps the greatest factor is whether or not the young are precocial or altricial, the former hatching relatively larger than the latter.

The shape of the eggs also varies greatly, being almost spherical in some birds such as kingfishers and owls and long and pointed in some such as the woodpeckers, swifts and the guillemots; in the last species the egg, when knocked, spins round in a small circle; it is said that the egg is this shape to reduce the chance of its being knocked off a narrow ledge into the sea. The quality of the egg surface may be very chalky as in some of the cormorants, or smooth or even highly polished as in the tinamous and some babblers. Eggs of some babblers are so glossy that one can see reflections in them.

The most striking aspect of the appearance of eggs is their colour; this to some extent has been their downfall since their attractive colours and patterns have encouraged egg collectors. The reasons why there is a wide variety of egg colours have not been well explained except that in the waders and certain other ground nesting species such as some terns and the nightjars, they are beautifully camouflaged against their background. In the Indian Yellow-wattled plover, the ground colour of the eggs differs in different areas, but matches the general colour of the soil within that area. Eggs in dark sites such as nests in burrows tend to be either white, white with faint reddish spots or light blue. While eggs of these colours can be found in nests in other situations, the predominance of these colours in such sites—laid by birds from many different and often only distantly related groups—strongly suggests that there must be some good reason for having such colours. In more open places many eggs are beautifully marked with spots, blotches and streaks. The highly patterned eggs of the Common guillemot are said to enable the birds to recognize their own eggs from those of others—certainly the individuals tend to lay eggs of similar patterns in successive years.

There is some evidence that the eggs of a few species may not be highly palatable; in these cases they are often quite conspicuous; possibly since the risk of predation is lower, the predators may learn that the eggs are unpalatable and leave them alone.

Young and their Care

Young birds hatch from the eggs at the end of the incubation period; this may be as short as 11 or 12 days in some small birds or as long as 11 to 12 weeks in some of the larger albatrosses. The young weigh around 70 % of the weight of the freshly laid egg and this amount is relatively constant in different species. Hence the size of the hatching chick is closely related to the size of the egg. On average, smaller birds produce relatively larger eggs and therefore relatively larger chicks than larger birds.

Young birds are normally divided into two sorts, precocial and altricial. Precocial young, such as those of the domestic hen, can run around within a few hours of hatching whereas altricial young such as those of the Blackbird or American robin are relatively smaller and incapable of looking after themselves. Not only is there a difference in relative size between the two groups, but also different parts of the body have developed to a different level at the time of hatching. Comparing a wader with a crow the former has a brain 6 % of its total weight, compared with the latter's 3 % and the wader's eyes are 10 % of its total weight compared with 5 % in the crow. By way of contrast, the digestive tract of the crow is some 13 % of the total compared with the wader's 6 %. Those parts of the body needed for activity—sight and brain— are well developed in young precocial birds while the young altricial birds are little more than a food processing machine. These differences are lost by the time the young birds are fully grown as a result of differential growth rates in different parts of the body. In the altricial young the legs grow relatively earlier than the wings; legs are needed to help the young birds reach up above its brothers in order to gain the food brought in by the parents while wings are not needed until the young birds fly at the end of the nestling period.

Altricial young hatch from the egg with little or no down and are usually blind. They are entirely dependent on their parents, not only to bring them all their food, but also to brood them and to keep them warm. In most cases if they did not get this warmth from the parents at least intermittently throughout the day and especially overnight, they would die of cold. Such young are also usually nidicolous—nest-dwelling—and remain in the nest for more or less the whole of the nestling period. Almost all the passerines are altricial.

Precocial birds hatch from the egg as well-developed chicks, covered with down and with open eyes; they are nidifugous—nest-fleeing—leaving the nest within a few hours of hatching. Almost all precocial young are still dependent on their parents for care, though the megapodes are not. Megapode eggs are laid in areas where the sand or rotting vegetation is warm enough to provide the heat for incubation and the young may not even see a parent bird when they hatch and emerge from the sand; even if they do, they do not recognize them and run away into the bush. They are well-

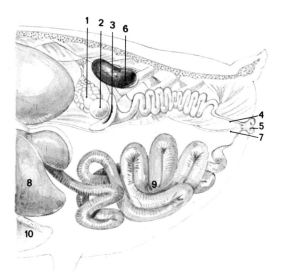

Section of an egg showing (1) shell, (2) shell membranes, (3) albumen, (4) air space, (5) chalaza, (6) and (7) vitelline membranes, (8) white layers of yolk, (9) yellow layers of yolk and (10) germinal disc.

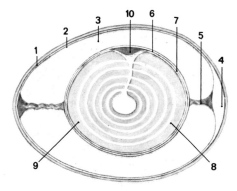

The reproductive system of a female bird, showing (1) ovary, (2) ovum (egg) passing into the top of the oviduct (3), (4) vagina and (5) cloaca. The reproductive system lies close to the kidney (6) and the ureter (7) which runs from the kidney into the cloaca. Also shown in the lower part of the diagram are the stomach (8) and intestines (9); the lower tip of the breast bone (10) is also just visible.

The shape of eggs may be related to the shape of ▶ the pelvic girdle. Birds with a deep pelvis lay rounder eggs than those with narrower, more flattened ones. Shown here are the eggs and pelvic girdles of (1) Buzzard *Buteo buteo*, (2) Barnacle goose *Branta leucopsis*, (3) Great crested grebe *Podiceps cristatus* and (4) Eagle owl *Bubo bubo*.

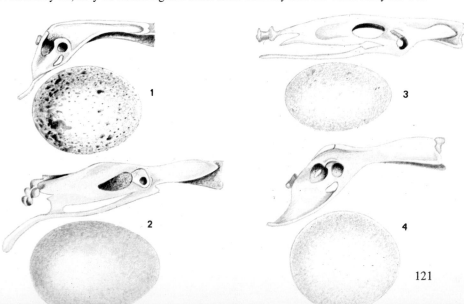

Most small birds keep their nests very clean. During the nestling period this usually involves the removal of faeces, wrapped in gelatinous faecal sacs. These sacs may be eaten or carried from the nest and dropped some distance away. This bird is a Sedge warbler *Acrocephalus schoenobaenus*.

Parent birds search the nest lining for foreign material, perhaps looking for parasites. They may also shake the lining vigorously; possibly they are then 'making the bed' by fluffing up the lining and improving the insulation.

Care of the young. (1) a Black vulture *Aegypius monachus* carries water in its bill to its young, (2) an adult Common (or Barn) swallow *Hirundo rustica* (left) feeds its newly fledged young, (3) a young Herring gull *Larus argentatus* pecks at the red spot on its parent's beak, so stimulating the adult bird to regurgitate food, (4) a Water rail *Rallus aquaticus* removes egg-shell from hatching young and (5) young Hoatzins *Opisthocomus hoazin* which apparently may be cared for by a number of older birds. ▶

feathered and look after themselves entirely from the moment of hatching. Uniquely among birds they are able to fly within a very few hours of hatching. The amount of care and attention given to other young precocial birds varies markedly though most will remain in contact with their mother during the day and will run to her for warmth and shelter during rainstorms and at night. Some, such as many of the ducks and shore birds, gain little more than this since they search for food for themselves and are self-sufficient in this sense. However, they still gain great advantage by remaining in the presence of their mother so as to benefit from her warning cries and general watchfulness. Others such as some of the game birds are shown where to feed by their mother, indeed as in the domestic hen the mother may scratch up food for them. Yet others may actually be fed by the parents bringing them food: some rails, the Oystercatcher and the Magpie goose do this; gradually the young birds take over feeding for themselves. Parent grebes also bring food to their young in the early nestling period though they may well carry the young on their back to good feeding areas.

So many groups contain exceptions to the above rules that generalizations are unwise. The auks provide a good example of variation in the nestlings though all would be classified as precocial; they hatch well-feathered and with open eyes. Some such as those in the genus *Synthliborhamphus* leave the nesting ledge within a day or two and swim out to sea in the company of their parents, completing their development at sea. The Common guillemot and Razorbill fall into the next category, the young departing from the nesting ledges when they are about one third grown. They leave in the fading light of the evening, bouncing or tumbling down into the sea in ways that one would think were almost certain to injure them and yet they arrive safely. Although the main flight feathers have not grown at this stage, some covert feathers provide them with little wings that help them to break their fall. The apparent purpose of departure at this time is that it is then too dark for marauding gulls to see them and so they can be safely away to sea before dawn. At the other extreme from those that leave soon after hatching, birds such as the Atlantic Puffin and the Black and Pigeon guillemots stay in the nest until they are fully grown, about six weeks in the case of the Puffin. Well able to fly, it sets off to fend for itself without the help of its parents; the Puffin leaves its burrow nest in the dark, again presumably since it is safer from predators at this time.

Like some of the auks, other birds fall between the definitions of altricial and precocial. Herons and birds of prey usually hatch with their eyes open and with a good covering of down, but they nevertheless remain in their nests for the whole of the nestling period. Owls are similar except that in their case they are born blind. Gulls and terns hatch with their eyes open and with a good covering of down, usually well camouflaged in this case. These birds stay near the nest though often they move a little distance away to hide under cover of grass or bracken; when necessary they can run well. Young nightjars are beautifully camouflaged against their backgrounds and though able to move away from the nest (the barest scrape on the ground) they do so only to a very slight extent.

Parental duties are many; if the young are vulnerable to predation the parents must take great care to conceal their nest from predators and make sure that they do not give the location away by careless visits. They must also ensure that the nest area is kept clean of tell-tale marks or droppings. Most small birds produce their droppings neatly packaged in small gelatinous bags—faecal sacs. The parents eat these when they are small but as the young grow and the sacs get comparatively larger, they carry them away to drop them at some distance from the nest. In birds such as the waders where the nest is in an exposed site, the parents also remove the egg-shells to some distance; their white inside is conspicuous to crows or other marauders passing overhead and could endanger the brood.

Many parent birds try to deter a predator that approaches the nest by 'dive-bombing' it and mobbing it in order to distract its attention. Others may press home

A few waders that live in very hot areas bring back water to dampen and cool both eggs and young. This bird is the Egyptian plover *Pluvianus aegyptius*.

Most species of birds will vigorously defend their young against any predator which they can physically hope to defeat. Here an Adélie penguin *Pygoscelis adeliae* attacks an Antarctic skua *Stercorarius skua* which is trying to take its chick. Penguin chicks which wander any distance from the parent are at risk since the skua moves so much faster than the penguin.

their attack; even a Blackbird can deal quite a hard blow with its feet or beak as it passes overhead. Others—especially ground nesting species—may feign injury, dropping to the ground and pretending that they are unable to fly; the predator, thinking that it has found an easy meal, runs after it only to find that the bird is always just out of reach; only once it has lured the predator to what it believes to be a safe distance from the nest does the bird fly off again.

The parents must also keep the young warm and, particularly with small and naked young, the female must brood them in order that they get sufficient warmth. As soon as the young are sufficiently warm she will go in search of food for them, intermittently staying to brood them on her return if they are getting chilled. The amount of brooding that she has to do will therefore depend upon the weather: the colder it is the more that she will have to brood the young and the less time she will have to collect food for them. In really bad weather the female may have to spend almost all her time brooding the young and leave the feeding solely to the male. Hence the young only get about half as much food as they would otherwise have done and many perish.

The food and the rate at which it is brought into the brood varies markedly in different species. Some, such as the small woodland insectivores, may bring in caterpillars almost every minute of the day; their trips to collect food may be very short and if food is relatively easily found there will be few delays. Most of the small insectivores bring food back to the nest at frequent intervals; in the Blue tit the pair may make as much as 1,000 visits to the nest each day in order to feed the rapidly growing young. No other bird is known to make so many visits, but many birds may return every three or four minutes during a sixteen or eighteen hour day, a rate of over 200 visits per day. Birds such as swifts tend to feed their young on great bolusses of food that they bring back from their long aerial foraging flights; they carry these masses of small insects in their throats and many visit their young only a few times during the day with these large meals. Similarly finches which bring seeds back to their young may bring cropfuls of seeds at infrequent intervals. Many of the larger birds such as gulls, herons and storks make irregular visits with large quantities of fish

Care of the young by carrying. The European nightjar *Caprimulgus europaeus* was first observed to carry its eggs (1) and young (2) from danger by Audubon, a habit questioned ever since by naturalists. However, there are better authenticated sightings of the European Woodcock *Scolopax rusticola* (3) carrying its young in flight.

Although thrushes *Turdus* use stones as anvils on which to break the shells of snails when feeding themselves, the habit almost certainly ensures that their young receive food that is easy to digest.

or other food which they regurgitate to their young from their crops. Owls and other birds of prey also visit their young relatively infrequently but with large amounts of food. In these cases the prey may have to be broken up for the young before they can swallow it. At one extreme some of the most oceanic sea birds search for food over wide areas of sea; these birds may come to feed their young only every four or five days, sometimes at even longer intervals. Even with both parents feeding, the young may not get more than two or three meals per week. The birds such as the shearwaters and petrels which fly great distances to collect food for their young must expend great amounts of energy flying back to their nest with food; in order to economize in energy consumption and to fly back to the nest with as much food as possible, they have gone one stage further than other species of birds, they predigest the food to some extent so as to reduce the water content. Fish, like most animal matter contains a very high proportion of water—up to 70%. The thick soup that the birds feed to their young is therefore much richer than plain, raw fish.

The pigeons have an unusual method of feeding their young. During the nestling period the inner crop lining swells and the cells in this tissue break off forming a whitish liquid, the so-called crop milk. The young birds are fed on this; they obtain it by putting their heads into the parents' mouths and drinking it from the crop. This habit is unique among birds. Most species feed their young on food similar to that which they normally take for themselves, though it may vary slightly in size. Some of the finches are an exception to this rule since they may feed their young on an insect, instead of a seed, diet. Probably the need for a rich supply of protein for the rapidly growing young dictates this move though it is also possible that the water content of seeds is too low to enable the young birds to grow since they would not get enough water to drink. A few birds such as the American Wood-ibis bring their young water in their beaks. Sandgrouse have special absorptive feathers on the breasts. They soak these in water and carry this back to their young who then sip it from the tips of the feathers.

Large prey may have to be broken up for the young, as in the case of that brought back by birds of prey. The parents may have to take steps to ensure that the young are not injured by the prey. Bee-eaters remove the stings of wasps and the Secretary bird

The Royal albatross *Diomedea epomophora* feeding its chick. Albatrosses raise a single chick; some of the largest species take over a year to care for the one young and so only breed every alternate year. They bring their young a regurgitated mush of fish and squid.

When disturbed, young terns and gulls may swim out to sea in order to try to escape from their enemies. This is a dangerous habit since they might easily get lost, but the risk may be worth it if the danger of remaining behind is great. At times some adults may accompany them. These are Lesser crested terns *Sterna bengalensis*.

Fledgelings. (1) Song thrush *Turdus philomelos*, (2) Lapwing *Vanellus vanellus*, (3) Dotterel *Eudromias morinellus*, (4) Crab plover *Dromas ardeola*, (5) Red-breasted merganser *Mergus serrator*, (6) Great black-backed gull *Larus marinus*, (7) Gannet *Sula bassana*, (8) Golden eagle *Aquila chrysaetos* and (9) Greater flamingo *Phoenicopterus ruber*. Numbers (1), (7) and (8) are nidicolous and remain in the nest until they can fly. The gull (6) only wanders a short way to find cover. Numbers (2), (3), (4), (5) and (9) are nidifugous and are able to follow the parents from the nest within a few days of hatching. However, the Crab plover (4) does not usually do so until it is older; unique among waders, its parents bring food to the young bird. ▶

pulls off the heads of snakes before feeding them to its young. Even birds bringing in large caterpillars to their young beat in the head or remove it so that the strong jaws cannot injure the young bird while it is being swallowed.

There may be subtle changes in the diet during the course of the nestling period. In the tits small young are fed only small caterpillars, possibly because these are the only ones that can easily be swallowed then. When the young get larger, they are fed larger prey. As yet unexplained is the increase in the proportion of spiders brought in around the middle part of the nestling period, just before the young birds start to get their feathers. It is not known why this happens, but it has been recorded in several different habitats in different countries and at different times of the season. Presumably spiders provide some essential substances that are not found in sufficient quantity in caterpillars.

The young bird communicates its needs for food to the parent birds by begging: the hungrier it is the more incessantly it begs. Begging has the effect on the parents of making them go out to search for more food. When the young beg incessantly the parents, wherever possible, step up their feeding rates. A noisy brood is in danger of attracting predators; more large than small broods of tits are taken by predators because they are hungrier and noisier. Hence the parents endeavour to keep their young satisfied. If a predator is in the vicinity the parents' warning cries will immediately silence the calling young, but by then it may already be too late.

The number of young in a brood varies widely from species to species. In the case of many species the number of young can be related to the maximum that the pair can successfully raise. The larger the brood the more mouths there are to feed and so the parents have to speed up their efforts. However, the possible increase in feeding frequency is not proportional to the increase in the number of young so that in larger broods the individual young get less food than those in smaller broods. As a result of this lack of nourishment, the young in larger broods leave the nest at a lower weight than those in smaller broods and they stand less chance of surviving.

Apart from the availability of food, other factors affect whether the young birds will get sufficient for their needs. As mentioned, the temperature while they are in the nest will affect how much food they need. As with man, young birds need more food in cold than in warm weather in order to maintain their body temperature since the colder it is the greater the heat loss from their body. Although in terms of feeding young birds suffer if too many brothers and sisters are present, in one way they gain from their presence also. The larger the number of young the more easily they can huddle together and keep each other warm. At times in cold weather this is a considerable advantage since the young can keep each other warm for longer periods in the larger broods, so freeing the hen bird from the need to brood and allowing her to go and get more food.

Each species of bird has a fairly characteristic number of young in its brood. Many nidifugous species such as rails, ducks and game birds have large numbers of young in a brood—say 6 to 15, though waders have a smaller number—2 to 4. Small birds tend to have larger broods than large ones (though hummingbirds have only 1 or 2) and many of the very large birds of prey, albatrosses and penguins have only one young at a time. Once again there are many exceptions to these rules, but some other general trends are also apparent. Species breeding in the tropics tend to have smaller clutches than those breeding in temperate areas; this has been explained in terms of a greater upsurge in spring food supplies in temperate areas making the feeding of a larger brood more practicable there than in the tropics. Sea birds that feed far out in the ocean and visit their young infrequently tend to have smaller clutches than those that feed inshore. Hole-nesting species tend to have larger broods than birds in more exposed sites; in this case the birds are in relatively safe nest sites and spend longer in the nest, growing more slowly than is the case with young in open nests.

Where the food supply is very sparse the brood size may be adjusted during the

Woodpeckers nest in holes in trees, usually ones that they have excavated for themselves. Large young may race to the entrance when they hear the parents arriving with food and so the parent does not have to enter to feed them. These are Green woodpeckers *Picus viridis.*

nestling period through starvation. In many species the bird does not start incubating until all the eggs have been laid, with the result that the young all hatch at more or less the same time. However, if the bird starts to incubate before all the eggs are laid then a number of the young will hatch after the others. Where such asynchronous hatching occurs the young are staggered in size and, if food is scarce, the larger young can easily get what food is necessary; the smaller young cannot compete and so may die. Only when the larger young have been satisfied will the smaller receive food. Hence in times of food shortage the smallest quickly starve without taking much of the food that could have been fed to the larger young. If the young did not hatch asynchronously all would compete on equal terms and, even if any survived, all would be weakened and light in weight. Nature's way is to give some the maximum chance of surviving even if others quickly starve. Asynchronous hatching is found in many groups of birds that hunt live prey such as herons, birds of prey, owls and swifts. In other groups it is not uncommon for the last one or two young to hatch a little behind the others and so stand slightly less chance of surviving.

If well-fed, the young may reach almost adult weight before they leave the nest. In a few cases they may greatly exceed it. Some shearwaters leave the nest weighing about $1\frac{1}{2}$ times the weight of their parents. They apparently use this surplus fat for their first migration, before they seriously start to feed for themselves. In these and a few other species the young are not cared for after they have left the nest; as soon as they have fledged they are on their own. A young Common swift left its nest in Oxford, England and was killed in Madrid, Spain, four days later when its parents were still roosting in the nest. Relatively few birds are like this, most need intensive parental care in the dangerous period when they enter the wide world and start to learn to fend for themselves.

The parents of most species look after their young during this period. In some small passerines, this may be only for a week or so and even then the care may be somewhat desultory on the part of the female if she is preparing to start another brood. Others may remain with their parents for many months or even years getting some limited care from them; many of the birds that hold group territories fall into this category. Others such as some of the northern geese may remain as family parties throughout the southward migration and the ensuing winter; during this time the young birds can learn the traditional routes and feeding areas of their parents. Others such as frigatebirds, other large sea birds and the large birds of prey may look after their fledged young for many months after they have left the nest, so long in some species that the adults do not breed the following year, continuing to care for the young of the previous season. Even the European Tawny owl which leaves the nest in May or early June may be cared for by its parents until at least September.

After this the young birds are on their own. Learning to fend for themselves, finding a territory and breeding are hazardous occupations for young birds and many perish before they themselves can attempt to raise their own young.

Many ground-nesting species can recover eggs that are accidentally knocked out of the nest. Here a Grey-lag goose *Anser anser* retrieves an egg by rolling it with the underside of the bill.

A young Black-throated honeyguide *Indicator indicator*, a species which parasitizes other birds such as barbets and woodpeckers. The newly-hatched honeyguide kills the young of the host species with sharp hooks on its bill tip; hooks that later fall off. Note the large protective pads on the ankles; the bird spends much of its nestling period sitting on these.

A newly hatched European cuckoo *Cuculus canorus* can evict eggs or young of the host species; here a Hedge sparrow *Prunella modularis*. The young cuckoo has a dip in its back into which it can manoeuvre the eggs. After leaving the nest, the young cuckoo continues to be fed by its foster parents, even though it may be many times larger than they are. Here a Winter wren *Troglodytes troglodytes*, a rather unusual host, feeds the young cuckoo.

Brood Parasites

A small number of birds have specialized in laying their eggs in the nests of other species so that the young are raised by foster parents; in this way the birds themselves may go on to lay more eggs in other nests. Although rather few species have developed this method of breeding, this habit has been evolved at least five and probably six times in birds. To a varying extent it is found in ducks, honeyguides, cuckoos, New World orioles and amongst the weavers where it has probably evolved independently on two occasions, in the Parasitic weaver and in the Viduinae, a group of estrildine finches.

Although some of the parasitic birds are extremely specialized, one can see a possible way in which the habit may have evolved by looking at the different species, since they show a whole range of different degrees of specialization. An American cowbird looks after its own young in the normal way, except that it lays its eggs in old nests of other species. The Black-headed duck lays its eggs in a wide variety of nests of other species and leaves the owners of those nests to incubate and hatch its eggs. Since this species is nidifugous and most ducks can feed themselves after hatching, possibly the young Black-headed ducks need little after-care from the foster parent. In the Common cowbird of North America the female lays eggs fairly indiscriminately in a wide variety of species nests of small birds; the eggs are not at all well-camouflaged and may be rejected by the host species. At the other extreme, some cuckoos lay eggs which often closely match the colour of the eggs of the host and in some cases the plumage of the young is also a close match with that of the foster parent. In the viduine finches the patterns of the mouthparts of the young parasite, together with its calls, are remarkably similar to those of the host.

The degree of perfection of these adaptations is, of course, the result of the behaviour of the hosts. It is a major disadvantage for the host to raise the young parasite; by so doing it decreases the number of its own offspring which it raises. In species such as those parasitized by the European cuckoo, which ejects the eggs or young of the host, the host raises no young of its own. Even where the young parasite is raised alongside the young of the host, there is often some mortality and so the host would raise more of its own young if it avoided being parasitized. The host can do this in a variety of ways; it may chase the female cuckoo away before she can parasitize the nest or if it finds a strange egg in its nest it can desert and nest again, thus being more certain of only raising its own young. Possibly also it could learn to recognize its own young and not feed young that differ from these. As a result of any of these actions on the part of the host, the parasite would die. Hence there has been strong selection for the parasite to evolve better and better camouflage in order that its young may be successfully raised and also strong selection for the host to learn to discriminate between its own young and those of the parasite. Such evolution of two species that are closely associated with one another frequently produces quite remarkable specializations, and it is not surprising to find many among parasitic birds.

The cuckoos, Cuculiformes, are probably the most highly adapted brood parasites; although by no means all the species of cuckoos are parasitic, many raise their own young. The European cuckoo has been the most studied; it lays its eggs in the nests of small passerines such as the European robin, Meadow pipit or Reed warbler. Each young cuckoo weighs about as much as the whole brood of the host. Presumably this is one of the reasons why only a single egg is laid in each nest: the host birds could not raise more than one cuckoo. In addition to being a close match in pattern, the egg is unusually small for a bird the size of a cuckoo, being only some 2.5% of the weight of the female. In contrast, the related Great spotted cuckoo lays its eggs in the nests of birds such as the Magpie which are about the same size as itself. In this case the cuckoo's egg is about 7% of the female's weight, a much more usual size. The young cuckoos are raised alongside the young Magpies and more than one cuckoo egg may be laid in a single nest. Not only can the female European cuckoo lay her egg

The European cuckoo *Cuculus canorus* (1) is one of the most highly specialized brood parasites. Here it is seen removing an egg of the Meadow pipit *Anthus pratensis* prior to laying one of its own. The Giant cowbird *Scaphidura oryzivora* (2) is a New World oriole which specializes in parasitizing nests of other members of its own family, here a Montezuma oropendola *Gymnostinops montezuma*. The Black-headed duck *Heteronetta atricapilla* (3) lays its eggs in the nests of a variety of other species of waterfowl and leaves the other birds to incubate the eggs.

remarkably quickly, but she has a protrusible cloaca enabling her to place the egg more nearly into the nest than she would otherwise be able to do. Nevertheless, the egg often has to be dropped into some nests. Not surprisingly the egg has an unusually thick shell in order to reduce the chance of its being broken by the fall.

Parasites have evolved a wide range of adaptations to enable them to carry out their strategies successfully. In honeyguides, the male attacks the barbet hosts and draws them away from their nest while the female slips in to lay the egg. In some other species the female may lay the egg elsewhere and fly to the nest carrying it in her beak. In a few species such as the European cuckoo the eggs may bear a remarkable resemblance to those of their host; each female lays only one pattern of egg and specializes on a particular host species. The close match is believed to have been brought about as follows: young hatch only if their eggs are not recognized by the host; the females that are successfully raised carry with them an image of the nest site or of the parent which raised them so that when they return as adults they specialize in parasitizing that particular type of nest.

The eggs of many parasites hatch very quickly, before those of the host. Hence the young can grow faster than the host young and, being larger, can dominate them in their demands for food. In the European cuckoo, which lays eggs only every other day, it is possible that 'incubation' starts while the egg is in the female's oviduct, so giving it the ability to hatch a day or two before the normally incubated eggs of the host. The European cuckoo is raised alone in the nest, being roughly equivalent in weight and food demands to the whole of a brood of the host. This cuckoo evicts the eggs or small young of the host by manoeuvring them into the small of its back and then standing up, so tipping them out of the nest. Young honeyguides kill the host young with a specially adapted egg-tooth which enables them to stab the young to death. This sharp point drops off after a week or so.

Young of some parasites show a remarkable series of adaptations that enable them to pass for young of the host. The Indian Koel (a cuckoo) parasitizes crows. The young of both sexes are black like the crows, but when the young have fledged the females moult into a brown plumage which they wear for the rest of their lives, though the males remain black. The young parasitic weaver and the young of the host warblers are identical in appearance—on the back; if one turns them upside down the belly feather colour is quite different—the host parents cannot see this in the nest so the parasite has not needed to evolve matching plumage here. The young of the whydah finches are raised by the parents of closely related estrildine finches. The latter have a remarkable series of protuberances and coloured marks around the gape which are different in each species; apparently these have been evolved to enable the parents to distinguish between their own young and the young whydahs. However, the latter have evolved identical marks to combat this. They have even evolved almost identical calls and so are exceedingly difficult to distinguish from the young of the host while they are in the nest.

Parasitic birds. (1) The viduine finches parasitize the nests of other small finches. The males of the Paradise whydah *Steganura paradisaea* hold leks to which the females come for mating; the females then go and lay their eggs in the nests of the host species, here a Green-winged pytilia *Pytilia melba*. (2) Each female European cuckoo lays eggs of a characteristic pattern which resembles that of one of the host species. Here cuckoo eggs (the left of each pair) are compared with eggs of the following host species: (3) Reed warbler *Acrocephalus scirpaceus*, (4) Great reed warbler *Acrocephalus arundinaceus* (5) Dunnock (or Hedge sparrow) *Prunella modularis* and (6) Meadow bunting *Emberiza cioides*. (7) A pair of Black-collared barbets *Lybius torquatus* chase away a parasitic Lesser honeyguide *Indicator minor* from their nest.

MIGRATION

Wintering

When autumn comes, birds that spend the summer in temperate areas must make a 'decision' as to whether or not they should remain. Migration involves long flights over often inhospitable or dangerous areas where there is little on which to feed, into areas which the young birds have never experienced before. On the other hand, to remain means that the birds must face the rigours of the winter in the hope that it will not be too severe. This 'choice' is not, of course, made every year but, as a result of natural selection, each species has evolved the habit which has proved to be safest. For some the 'choice' has been clear; birds that breed in the high Arctic or are wholly dependent on insects for their diet must leave. Others may go southwards only if their food supply fails. We call such birds irruptive species; many of the seed eaters such as the tits and finches are included in this category as are some predatory birds such as the Snowy owl and the Rough-legged buzzard.

Another group of birds, known as partial migrants, face a slightly different dilemma. In species such as the Chaffinch, Blackbird and European robin, some individuals migrate and others winter near to their birthplace or their breeding place. It has been said of the Chaffinch that one can see the even balance of the two alternatives; over the course of a series of mild winters more and more birds spend the winter in the breeding area while after a severe one almost all the birds are migrants. If the weather is mild in winter those that remain survive better than those that risk the dangers of migration, but if a hard winter prevails then migration proves less dangerous than wintering. Presumably the offspring of each type of bird inherit the same tendency as their parents and the relative number of each type depends on the hardness of recent winters. Over a period of time the advantages of each habit are fairly evenly balanced and so both habits persist.

In species where partial migration is observed more young birds than old ones migrate and more females migrate than males. Both young birds and females are less successful than old birds and males in competition for food; if fighting occurs for food, the latter groups tend to be the ones that are successful. Hence the young birds and the females are the groups which are less likely to be able to survive the winter on the breeding ground and so it is not, perhaps, surprising that larger proportions of these birds migrate.

Most birds that winter in temperate areas must search hard for sufficient food; the insects and fruit are gone so that the birds that eat these in the summer must change their diet. Many of the birds that remain are waterfowl and waders. In fact the large majority of these spend the summer in the higher latitudes and migrate some way southwards, but still spend their winter in temperate regions; marshlands and shore may be occupied by more birds in the winter than in the summer. Since these birds need water that does not freeze and make their food disappear, many of them move not north and south but from the centres of land masses to the edges where, with the warming influences of the oceans, the weather tends to be milder. In Western Europe many of the waterfowl, lapwings, starlings and blackbirds have come from as far east as Poland and Russia.

Winter wrens *Troglodytes troglodytes* may conserve energy in cold weather by huddling together in a communal roost. As many as 30 to 40 birds have been found together in a single hole. Here they are seen (viewed from behind) in the nest of a House martin *Delichon urbica*.

(Rock) Ptarmigan *Lagopus mutus* live in very cold areas. They conserve energy overnight by making tunnels into the snow and roosting in these. The temperatures down such holes is higher than on the surface and the birds are also sheltered from bitter winds. They may have to dig their way in and out of their burrows in snowy weather. Here a Ptarmigan is seen leaving its burrow.

Species that spend the winter in cold climates. At least some populations of all these species spend the winter in areas where there is thick snow on the ground. (1) Pine grosbeak *Pinicola enucleator*, (2) Steller's jay *Cyanocitta stelleri,* (3) Crested tit *Parus cristatus* and (4) Snowy owl *Nyctea scandiaca.* Jays and tits store food in the autumn which they use to help them survive the cold, short winter days. Some, such as the Snowy owl and some of the crossbills, may move south in winter when their food supplies fail in the north.

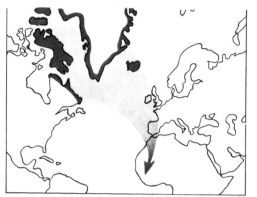

Wheatears *Oenanthe oenanthe* breed over much of the north temperate area of the world. Those that breed around the Atlantic may have to make long sea crossings to their wintering grounds in Africa. Birds leaving the southern tip of Greenland may not make landfall until they reach northern Spain, a flight of 1,850mi (3,000km) over sea, taking perhaps three days.

A range of migrants. (1) European cuckoo *Cuculus canorus*, (2) Lazuli bunting *Passerina amoena*, (3) Long-tailed skua (or jaeger) *Stercorarius longicaudus*, (4) Yellow-throated vireo *Vireo flavifrons*, (5) Red-headed woodpecker *Melanerpes erythrocephalus*, (6) Common crane *Grus grus*, (7) (Eurasian) Nutcracker *Nucifraga caryocatactes*, (8) Sooty shearwater *Puffinus griseus*, (9) Grey-headed albatross *Diomedea chrysostoma*, (10) Common (or Barn) swallow *Hirundo rustica* (American race), (11) Storm-petrel *Hydrobates pelagicus*, (12) American avocet *Recurvirostra americana*, (13) Common swift *Apus apus*, (14) Rufous hummingbird *Selasphorus rufus*, (15) Blue-winged teal *Anas discors*, (16) Sandwich tern *Sterna sandvicensis*, (17) Pomarine skua (or jaeger) *Stercorarius pomarinus* and (18) Short-eared owl *Asio flammeus*. ▶

Eleonora's falcon *Falco eleonorae* breeds in the winter in the Mediterranean region. Its own range is not well known, but some of the birds from the eastern Mediterranean spend the northern winter in Malagasy, some 3,700mi (6,000km) away.

Migration

At the end of each Ice Age, as the sheet of ice covering the land retreated, progressively more birdless land appeared. In the height of summer these areas provided rich breeding grounds and any bird living further to the south that moved up into the empty areas would have found food in plenty, though they would have had to move back south again for the winter. Gradually, as the ice receded further, the birds that could make use of the empty lands in the north found that they had to fly progressively further and further to reach them. This, we believe, is how the migration routes of birds evolved. At the present time we see the outcome of migratory routes that have evolved gradually over many thousands of years of changing climate.

One may consider true migration to involve a major shift of the majority of a population from a reasonably well-defined breeding area to a reasonably well-defined non-breeding area and back again, each movement taking place once a year. Under such a definition, cold weather movements and the altitudinal movements of birds on mountains are excluded. Practically no species is known which breeds in both the areas where it spends part of the year.

Birds usually migrate because the area in which they spend the non-breeding season is not as good an area to breed on as their summer grounds and because they cannot survive on their breeding grounds during winter. In the latter case they must feed up and get ready to migrate before the bad weather comes; it is no good waiting until conditions are already poor before leaving since by that time it will be difficult to lay down the fat needed for migration and the whole journey may be put in jeopardy. Normally, long-distance migrants lay down considerable stores of fat to provide the fuel for the long journey. Small warblers such as the Blackpoll or Sedge warbler, which normally weigh about 0.4 oz (12 gm) at most times of year, may set off on migration weighing twice as much as this. The Sanderling, a wader, may double its weight from 2 oz (60 gm) to 4 oz (120 gm) just prior to departure. Larger birds such as geese put on rather less fat, but even they may weigh as much as 50% more than normal just before they set off on their long flights to the north. These fat stores are laid down shortly before departure and plainly highly rich supplies of food must be available if the birds are to be able to fatten up to this extent.

Some migration routes cover considerable distances. Even birds as small as a Willow warbler, weighing about 0.3 oz (8 gm) may undertake very lengthy migrations. A small population of this species breeds as far east as Alaska and, like their more easterly colleagues, they apparently fly to Africa for the winter—a flight of some 8,000 mi (13,000 km) or more. The Arctic tern which spends the northern winter in the Antarctic waters and so gets two summers in each year, flies about 9,000 mi (14,500 km) each way. Some journeys involve a long non-stop flight. When small land birds make long sea-crossings one can be certain that they have found no place to rest en route. Wheatears from Greenland make land-fall on the north coast of Spain, a distance of 2,000 mi (3,200 km), and Golden plovers from Alaska reach the Hawaiian islands some 2,500 mi (4,000 km) away.

A few small birds get lost on the eastern seaboard of North America each autumn and arrive in Europe; such flights are even further than the figures quoted. However, many of those that successfully make the journey undoubtedly owe their survival to having been able to rest on a ship. Others probably only arrive if they have had strong tail-winds that decrease the amount of flying time involved.

Sea-crossings are not the only ones where the birds find landing unrewarding. In the autumn, many of the small birds leaving Europe may have to cross as much as 600 mi (960 km) of the Mediterranean, yet cannot expect to find anything worth stopping for in North Africa. At its driest in the autumn, the Sahara is almost as daunting as the sea. For small birds the total distance of inhospitable surface may be at least 1,500 mi (2,400 km) and possibly more. The recent droughts on the south side of the Sahara coupled with man's clearance of the vegetation to feed goats and cattle

Although birds making long journeys may have to fly both during the day and night, most can be classified as primarily day or night migrants. Day migrants: (1) Brambling *Fringilla montifringilla*, (2) Redwing *Turdus iliacus*, (3) Common (or Barn) swallow *Hirundo rustica*, (4) Red-winged blackbird *Agelaius phoeniceus* and (5) Chimney swift *Chaetura pelagica*. Night migrants: (6) Blue grosbeak *Guiraca caerulea*, (7) Rose-breasted grosbeak *Pheucticus ludovicianus*, (8) Black-and-white warbler *Mniotilta varia*, (9) Bluethroat *Cyanosylvia svecica* and (10) female Blackcap *Sylvia atricapilla*.

The Bristle-thighed curlew *Numenius tahitiensis* breeds around the Bering Strait and winters in remote Pacific Islands. Its nearest landfall is the Hawaiian islands, a non-stop flight of some 2,500mi (4,000km).

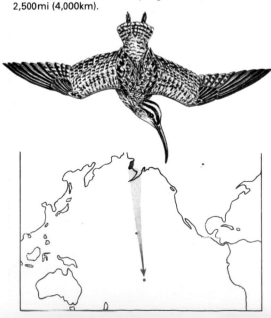

may well be making life much more difficult for some species by increasing the distance that they have to cover in order to reach good feeding areas. Some species which migrate to this general area, such as the Whitethroat, seem to have become scarcer.

Small wonder then that the migrants put on so much fat as fuel for the journey. Warblers fly at barely 30 mph (48 kph) though the larger waders fly a little faster. In order to cover 1,500 mi (2,400 km) some of these small birds must face non-stop flights of at least 48 hours; flying time will be longer for more extensive journeys or when they are slowed down by unfavourable head-winds. Normally they set out with enough fat to have some reserves in case this happens.

Warblers are night migrants at least in the sense that they take off at dusk. However, on these long journeys they must fly both day and night. Other species, in particular the finches, usually fly by day but these birds make, on average, much shorter journeys. In the Caribbean, the warblers tend to fly across the sea from the USA whereas the finches and buntings fly around the edge; they do not go so far south in any case.

Birds of prey, storks and cranes also usually fly by day, but they do so for a different reason. These large, relatively heavy birds try to save energy by soaring rather than using flapping flight. In order to do this they have to make use of thermals—which occur only in the day—and the upcurrents off mountainsides. Both these manoeuvres require careful positioning and accurate vision. Soaring species not only migrate by day, but they also stick to relatively narrow routes—along mountainsides for example; their course is largely plotted for them by the geography. In Europe, where many soaring birds leave to spend the northern winter in Africa, the birds avoid possible long sea-crossings by crossing the Mediterranean either at the Straits of Gibraltar or from Greece to Turkey over the Bosphorus. Other diurnal migrants fly on relatively narrow routes. In North America the waterfowl use 'flyways' that

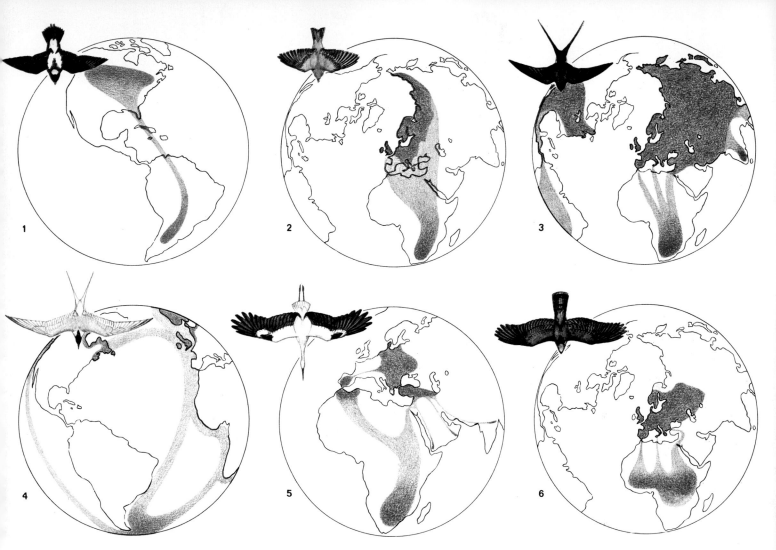

Long-distance migrations of (1) Bobolink *Dolichonyx oryzivorus*, one of the longest migrations of a New World passerine; (2) Willow warbler *Phylloscopus trochilus*; (3) Common (or Barn) swallow *Hirundo rustica*; (4) Arctic tern *Sterna paradisaea* has the longest journey of any species; and (5) White stork *Ciconia ciconia* and (6) Honey buzzard *Pernis apivorus*, which both cross the Mediterranean by the shortest routes so as to avoid long sea crossings.

The Short-tailed shearwater (or Mutton-bird) *Puffinus tenuirostris* breeds in southeastern Australia; during the non-breeding season at least some of the birds make a long journey in a figure-of-eight around the Pacific.

largely follow the course of some of the major rivers; in this way they can stop wherever they want to and are never out of sight of their favourite habitat. Many diurnal land birds such as the finches and the crows follow the coast, not straying out to sea if they can avoid it. The Chaffinches that visit Britain for the winter from northern Europe do not make the crossing of the North Sea direct, but fly down the coasts of Holland and Belgium and cross into Britain from Cap Gris Nez, the shortest route.

Nocturnal migrants again contrast with diurnal ones in that they usually fly on a broad front; also they tend to fly singly, perhaps in order to avoid collisions. Vast numbers of these small birds cross the coast of North Africa on their southwards migration in the autumn. Over 200 species of birds leave Europe for the winter and there must be at least 1,000 million individuals involved, possibly as many as 3,000 millions. Since the north coast of North Africa is about 2,500 miles (4,000 km) long, this is equivalent to something of the order of 0.5 million birds (possibly 1.5 million) crossing each mile of coast or some 4,000–12,000 birds per day for each day of a two month migration period.

The figures given here are obviously only crude estimates based on calculations of the numbers of breeding birds in Europe and the numbers of young they raise. Yet they must be roughly correct and similar huge numbers of birds must move southwards from USA and Asia seeking warmer climates for the winter. There is no equivalent migration on this scale for land birds from south temperate regions, there being insufficient land masses at that latitude. Nevertheless a few birds migrate to warmer climates for the winter; the Swift parrot leaves Tasmania and flies northwards into other parts of Australia for the southern winter. Within the tropics also, many birds migrate, avoiding areas when these are dry. In Africa a number of species cross back and forth across the equator to take advantage of two rainy seasons.

Navigation and Orientation

From early times it has been known that birds could find their way rapidly over long distances, hence the use of pigeons, and occasionally other species, for carrying messages. The Egyptians certainly used pigeons for carrying messages and the Romans are reputed to have tied coloured cottons to the legs of swallows so as to give early information to those at home about the results of chariot races. In more recent times the technique of ringing birds has demonstrated that individuals can find their way accurately over very long distances. The European swallow nesting in a barn in the northern hemisphere migrates to South Africa for the northern winter and returns, each summer of its life, to nest in the same place. In recent years it has also become apparent that most migrant birds also spend the winter within a relatively confined space, rather than wandering at large over wide areas. In addition there are now a few records of small migrants which, on their way between Europe and North Africa, stop in the same place each year. Hence an individual may acquire not only two 'homes' but also known 'ports of call'. Obviously if this is possible, it confers upon the bird the benefits of stopping at places that were safe the year before and where the bird can gain advantage of previous knowledge. Nevertheless in order to do this the birds must be able to navigate accurately and each individual bird must have a relatively restricted flight path.

A number of experiments have been performed with birds taken from their breeding grounds and released some distance away. Often these birds have returned to their nest in a remarkably short time. A Manx shearwater from Skokholm Island, Wales was released in Boston U.S.A. and returned to its nest within $12\frac{1}{2}$ days, and a Laysan albatross made a journey of a similar length back to Laysan in 10 days. These times imply that the birds must have headed more or less directly back to home from their release point; they had no time for wandering around while searching.

In order to find one's way from one place to another, one requires two sets of information, a map and a compass. A map is useless unless one knows how to find the direction between one place and another. Similarly a compass is no use if one does not know in which direction one wants to go. Migrating birds plainly possess both a map and a compass inasmuch as they know where they are going and, in addition, can take up a compass bearing. However, although the bird may be born with certain parts of this information, other parts may have to be learned. For example, Common starlings migrating southwestwards through Holland spend the winter in northwestern France. Some were caught and moved to Switzerland. When released the young and old birds behaved differently. The old birds adjusted to being moved off course and, flying northwestwards, returned to northern France (where they had been before). The young birds, on the other hand, flew in a southwestward direction from Switzerland, along a route parallel to their original course, and spent the winter in the vicinity of the Pyrenees. Hence the old birds had a map-sense in that they could somehow appreciate that they had been displaced and could rectify the situation. The young birds did not possess this map knowledge; they had no experience of the place where they were going to spend the winter. They could however fly in what was the correct direction, and perhaps also had some means of gauging the correct distance they had to fly to reach their winter quarters, since the area where they stopped in southern France was about the same distance from the place of release in Switzerland as was their normal wintering place from their place of capture in Holland. These young birds later returned successfully to the area in which they had been raised and after that some continued to migrate to the area in which they had, 'wrongly', spent the winter. Hence although they had a 'compass sense' they were not able to fly to an area unless they had previously visited it.

Many birds obtain their direction by use of the sun. Common starlings, kept in chambers from which they can see no land-marks but from which they can see the sun, will take up a direction relative to the sun. By altering the direction from which the sun

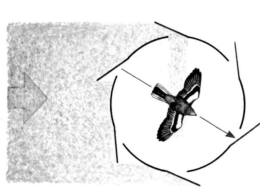

Orientation. Birds primarily establish their direction by use of the sun or stars. In order to be able to do this, they must know the time of day; it has been shown that they have an accurate internal clock. Here a Chaffinch *Fringilla coelebs* is in an orientation cage; it can see the sun through a series of windows (upper picture). If the windows are covered by mirrors (lower picture), the sun's rays cannot be seen directly, but only indirectly where they are reflected in off the mirrors. Under such experimental conditions the Chaffinch changes its orientation so as to maintain the same position relative to where it believes the sun to be.

Almost unique amongst birds, oilbirds of the genus *Steatornis* are able to navigate within dark caves by means of echo-location: They emit a series of clicks and use their echoes to determine whether there are rock sufaces nearby.

appears to come, the experimenter can cause a bird to alter its orientation thus showing that the bird is really using the sun and not some other celestial clue. If the weather is cloudy, the bird does not take up a fixed direction in the cage. The sun's position changes during the day, so that in order to maintain a constant compass direction, the bird must adjust its bearing to the sun in relation to the time of day. In other words, it must know the time; in addition to its map and compass senses it must also have a clock. Curiously, it is more difficult to train a Common starling to maintain a constant bearing to the sun throughout the day, than it is to train it to keep a fixed compass direction. In many ways the former is, at first sight, easier since it does not require information about the time.

Man can pin-point his position accurately with a good clock and sextant. These tell him the height of the sun at midday, and the time at which it reaches that highest point, and are sufficient to enable him to calculate both the latitude and longitude of his position. It seems clear that a bird can do something of this kind and, in addition, do it at times other than midday. It has been suggested that in order to do this the bird needs to be able to observe the movement of the sun along a tiny section of its arc and extrapolate the rest of the arc. There has been much controversy as to whether or not a bird is capable of taking such measurements. However, there is growing evidence that the discriminatory powers of many animals are far sharper·than those of man and that therefore birds may be able to do such things. Further, it is a weak argument to say that such-and-such a measurement could not be taken accurately enough. Birds make many very striking journeys and arrive safely. Whatever means they use seem to be beyond our abilities; small wonder then that we find the explanations that have been proposed hard to believe.

In addition to being able to use the sun, birds can navigate by the stars. A great many migrant birds normally fly at night and experiments similar to the ones testing birds' abilities to use the sun have been made by putting birds in orientation cages at night under starry skies. Hand-raised warblers that have never seen the sky can take up an orientation under the star patterns in a planetarium, hence at least certain aspects of the direction-finding techniques of birds are inherited from their parents. It appears that the birds use only certain portions of the star patterns in order to enable them to find their way. Indeed one of the greatest dangers to a migrating bird, especially a nocturnal migrant, is that it will fly into a change of weather. Not only may this obscure the stars but it may also bring a change of wind direction. The birds, bereft of navigational clues, cannot then maintain their direction and are in danger of getting swept off course into inhospitable areas, perhaps blown out over the sea. It is under such conditions that bird-watchers have a 'good' day at a bird observatory, many rare birds having arrived in the area. However, such a day is a bad one for the birds, many of which have become lost, may never find their way back on course, and so will perish. However, at least some of the older, more experienced birds may be able to re-orientate themselves and get back on course if only they can find sufficient food to survive until the weather improves. As with birds migrating during the day, thick cloud reduces the ability of night migrants to maintain a fixed flight path.

Under normal circumstances it seems likely that birds usually find their way either by use of the sun or the stars. However, recent research suggests that there may be occasions when birds can use some form of magnetic clue to find their way. How they do this is not known, but it may be only a subsidiary method to the normal use of sun and stars. Nevertheless, although at times discredited, it seems that magnetic, and possibly other clues, may be used by birds in addition to the more usually accepted methods. We still do not know how birds get home so quickly. However, in many of the release experiments (often made with homing pigeons) the birds determine which is the home direction within a few moments of being released from their light-proof carrying cases. Long before the birds have flown out of sight of the release point, most of them have turned in the direction of home. Indeed, a great many of them are flying in roughly the right direction within 30 seconds of release.

BIRD POPULATIONS

The Royal albatross *Diomedea epomophora* is an example of a very long-lived seabird. A study of this species showed that only some 3% of the breeding adults died each year. This means that the average age of the breeding adults is about 38 years.

Longevity

Many studies, usually involving ringed birds, have been made of the age to which birds live and of the numbers that die each year. Small birds of the temperate regions are among the best studied, and it is known that many have short life-spans. In birds such as tits and the European robin, only about 50% of the individuals that breed in one year survive to breed again in the following year. In a few other, larger, species such as the Common starling or Blackbird, the adult survival rate may be as much as 66%. Although there are some exceptions, large birds tend to live longer than small ones, and the greatest ages known are found amongst sea birds and large birds of prey which may reach an age of 30 years. Some bird species are known to have adult survival rates of 95% which means that the average age of individuals is 20 years. It is thus likely that some members of the population live to an age considerably older than 30 years.

The generalizations above appear to hold true for many birds in temperate regions but few intensive studies have been made elsewhere. In particular, survival rates in the tropics appear to be quite different from those quoted above. There are now several studies of small forest species suggesting that the birds may live much longer there than do those in temperate areas. The Black-and-White manakin, a tit-sized bird of Trinidad, has an annual survival rate of about 90%.

The death-rates of birds follow a rather different pattern from those in mammals (including man). In mammals after initial, often high, juvenile mortality there follows a period of 'middle-age' when relatively few animals die. After that the death rate increases again; we say the animals have reached old age. In birds, once the initial period of high mortality has been passed, the death rate remains fairly steady throughout the rest of the bird's life-span; there is no plateau in middle-age followed by an increasing death rate in old age. Hence, for birds it is more meaningful in most cases to say that the annual mortality is, say, 10% than to give an age to which birds of that species usually survive. It does not follow from this that birds never die of old age, but only that most studies have been unable to show that they do. One can say, however, that very few birds normally die of old age and that ages, such as those recorded occasionally in captivity, are very rare indeed. Hence the information on longevity of individual birds in zoos has little, if any, relevance to what happens in natural populations in the wild.

Bird-ringing has produced a number of records where wild birds have attained quite high ages. It must be emphasized however, that only a tiny proportion of wild birds live for very long periods. For example, if 50% of Robins die each year (the average figure) then only 1 out of every 1,000 Robins will survive 10 years. Ringing records show that a few gulls, Manx shearwaters and a Curlew have reached ages of 30 years or more, while a number of other gulls, terns, and birds of prey have survived between 20 and 30 years. For the smaller passerines in temperate areas, 10 years is a very good age, though there is a record of a 15-year-old swallow.

The European robin *Erithacus rubecula* is fairly typical of a small temperate passerine in that around 50–60% of the adults die between one year and the next. Hence only a tiny fraction of the birds will survive to reach 10 years of age.

The Black-headed gull *Larus ridibundus* has an adult mortality of around 25% per year, meaning that once they reach breeding age these birds may expect to live about 3½ more years on average. As with other species, the survival rate of the young birds is lower than that of the adults.

In many species of small birds living in temperate areas mortality during the summer is surprisingly high, almost equalling that in a normal winter. The effort required for breeding, together with the dangers of being caught by predators, either at the nest or while searching for food for the young, offset the milder weather and the longer hours for feeding. Often females live slightly less long than their mates since they are more closely associated with the nest and so more likely to be taken by predators.

The survival and mortality rates discussed above are for adult birds. Juvenile birds suffer much heavier mortality than their parents. Since numbers of birds remain stable in the long-term, it follows that the numbers of young birds reaching breeding age must balance the numbers of adults dying. For example if, as is roughly the case, 50% of adult Blue tits die between one year and the next, one adult per pair dies and so one young bird per pair is needed to replace it. Hence, on average, one chick must be produced by each pair and survive in order to maintain the numbers. Since Blue tits lay, and often raise, ten or more eggs, it follows that only one of these eggs can produce a young bird which survives long enough to become a breeding adult. Ringing studies support such theoretical calculations. In the Great tit where about 50% of the adults die each year, the birds fledge about 5 or 6 young per pair, on average, and about 17% of the resulting population survive to breed.

In larger birds, losses may be slightly lower, but there is still a very high loss of young before they reach breeding age. Many of the larger species have an immature age of several years during which they do not breed. Most of the mortality usually occurs in the first year of life, but throughout the immature stage the young birds have a higher mortality than do the adults.

Deaths of young birds are high throughout the nestling stage, but in many species it is thought that there is a very high loss during the period just after the young have left their parents and when they are learning to fend for themselves. This high loss of young birds has important implications in population studies.

The Mute swan *Cygnus olor* (1) lays a clutch of about six eggs. Some 40% of these hatch, but only about half reach the flying stage. Less than a quarter of the young that fly survive to breed at four years of age. Once adult, the birds may expect to live about five years; about 18% die each year. The equivalent figures have not all been worked out for the Trumpeter swan *Cygnus buccinator* (2), but are likely to be similar.

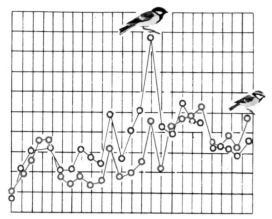

The number of pairs of Great tits *Parus major* (red graph) and Blue tits *Parus caeruleus* (green graph) breeding in a small wood in central England. In spite of their large broods, the numbers remain remarkably stable. Large increases in numbers usually follow a winter in which beech seed was in plentiful supply.

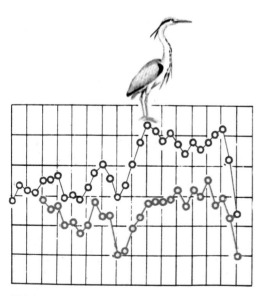

The numbers of Grey herons *Ardea cinerea* in two regions of Britain. The synchronous declines result from high mortality of herons in severe winters when their fishing grounds freeze over. If the succeeding winters are mild, the populations quickly recover to their previous levels.

Population Changes

Perhaps one of the most surprising features of bird populations is how little their numbers vary from year to year. We say that they are stable. Each spring a householder will notice that his garden contains perhaps a pair or two of Blackbirds, a pair of European robins and one or two pairs of tits. Numbers remain similar each summer; there are never five or six pairs of Blackbirds or none at all. When one considers the hazards that birds face and the numbers of young that they can sometimes raise this stability is rather surprising.

Such casual observations are borne out by accurate counts of the numbers of breeding birds in different areas. Although, of course, the numbers vary from time to time, the size of the fluctuations is surprisingly small in relation to the amount that they could theoretically change. Consider, for example, a pair of small passerines such as the Blackbird or the American robin; they may have two or three broods each year and may raise eight young in the season. If all these birds survived, then there would be ten birds (or five pairs) the following season. If all the parents and young lived, this single pair would increase to 25, 125 and 625 pairs in the third, fourth and fifth years.

One does not need accurate counts to know that this does not happen, but what prevents it? The numbers of birds in an area are dependent on the numbers of births and the numbers of deaths. If there are more births than deaths then the numbers will increase, if there are more deaths than births the numbers will decrease. When the population is stable, the numbers of births will equal the numbers of deaths. Hence in our example of the garden birds, the number of birds that die each year must be the same as the number of eggs laid. This may not happen in each garden but on average this must be the case.

One factor which could affect such calculations is the movement of individuals into and out of the area of study. This undoubtedly happens, with the populations in some areas over-producing and birds subsequently moving into other poorer areas where the population has been unable to maintain itself.

Ornithologists tend to conduct surveys of breeding birds during the summer. At this stage the birds are resident and, often, more easily counted than at any other time of year. However, one should always remember that all these counts of numbers hide one important facet of bird populations, namely that there are large changes in numbers within a year. At the start of the breeding season the number of birds is at its lowest. Once the young birds have hatched, a mere two to three weeks later with small birds, the numbers rise rapidly reaching a peak at the end of the nestling period. Thereafter when the young birds leave the nest there is a sharp decline in numbers since many of them perish. The large majority of the young birds have probably perished by the autumn and thereafter there is a slower decline in numbers until, once again, low numbers are reached just prior to the following breeding season.

Although taken as a whole populations are relatively stable, there are of course changes. Most populations show changes in numbers from year to year and at times these may be quite large. However, in most cases such fluctuations are of a temporary nature and the population soon reverts to its previous level. The reasons for these year to year changes are many and varied. Often, as in the case of the Grey heron, Common kingfisher and other birds dependent on open water for their livelihood, severe winter weather may bring about large numbers of deaths. Once the water has frozen over, these birds can no longer reach their food and so perish in large numbers. Similarly, severe cold affects many of the birds that feed on the ground, such as the thrushes and waders. Unless they can move elsewhere, they suffer the same fate as the water birds. It is not the cold weather in itself that brings about the birds' deaths. Even small birds are remarkably resistant to severe cold, provided that they can get their food. In the early part of 1963, southern England suffered its coldest winter for about 200 years and there was thick snow on the ground for 2–3 months. Nevertheless some species survived well because their food supply was plentiful. Bullfinches were

The (Common) Puffin *Fratercula arctica* is a relatively long-lived species; about 6% of the adults die each year, and the average age of the breeding population is about 20 years. However, each pair only produces a single chick each year, many of which do not survive. Hence if there are heavy losses for some reason, the numbers of breeding pairs will not recover nearly so quickly as is the case with the heron which may raise three young each year.

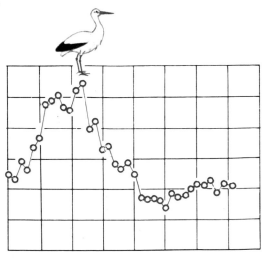

The numbers of White storks *Ciconia ciconia* in part of Germany. Here a long-term decline seems to have been taking place, possibly as a result of drainage of the wet meadows where the storks like to feed. The birds spend the winter in Africa and may also be suffering increased mortality there.

able to take seeds from the ash trees and this seed was unusually plentiful that winter. As a result, in spite of the weather, many Bullfinches survived the winter. In contrast Chaffinches, which feed largely on the ground, perished in considerable numbers.

Unfavourable weather in winter may not be the only cause of reduction in numbers. Heavy rain during the chick stage can cause large numbers of deaths amongst young gulls and terns. Even prolonged dry and sunny weather may not be good for certain birds. Blackbirds are dependent on soft, wet soil if they are to collect worms for their young. When the ground dries out and hardens, they may not be able to feed their brood properly and they may starve. During unusually dry summers they may have fewer nesting attempts than in wet moist summers.

Sharp increases in numbers of birds can often be related to unusually favourable conditions, especially to occasions when the food supply is unusually abundant. Many birds depend on seed crops during the winter and when these are plentiful, the birds will feed on them in large numbers. In Europe, seeds are an important source of

Sharp increases in numbers of birds can often be related to particularly favourable food for Common pheasants, Wood pigeons, Chaffinches, Bramblings and several of the tits. When the beech mast is plentiful, the tits tend to feed on it throughout the winter and large numbers survive to breed the following summer.

As has been mentioned already, most populations show year to year changes, but these are still relatively small compared with the changes that are theoretically possible. The potential power of increase described earlier for a pair of Blackbirds practically never occurs. Normally the doubling or halving of the breeding numbers of small birds between one year and the next is rather exceptional, though drastic reductions in numbers of some small birds were noted after the very severe winter of 1963 referred to above. In Europe, the Long-tailed tits, the Winter wren, the Green woodpecker, the Barn owl and several water birds suffered marked reductions in their numbers. However, these species recovered their numbers during the years following the hard winter.

Figures approaching those theoretically possible have, however, occurred under certain conditions, especially when a bird has been introduced to an area of the world where it had not previously lived. Often such changes have been brought about by man's introductions. A classic example is that of the introduction of the Common pheasant to Protection Island in the state of Washington, USA. Two cocks and six hens were released early in 1937. The area was obviously highly favourable for this species since within only six years there were almost 2,000 birds. Even this rapid increase was not so fast as is theoretically possible since there was always a lower number in spring than in the previous autumn; in other words, considerable numbers of birds must have died each winter.

Increases such as this do not occur within a small area, but only when a bird arrives in a new area which it can successfully exploit. The introductions of both the Common starling and the House sparrow to the USA have been well documented. About 150 Common starlings were introduced into New York State in 1890. Within a mere 60 years the birds were estimated to have increased by at least a millionfold and had spread throughout most of the country. Some of the birds reached Ontario in 1919 and within 15 years Common starlings were estimated to be the commonest bird in southern areas of Ontario. Similarly, the House sparrow, introduced in 1850, has reached all the states within about 50 years and must have increased by about the same amount. Elsewhere in the world these two birds and other species have shown dramatic increases in numbers after arrival in a new area. For example the Indian mynah is now widespread in many of the warmer areas of the world. In all these cases birds showed some of their potential for rapid increase in numbers.

We have seen that birds, introduced into a new area, can increase rapidly—at least for a number of years. However, most bird populations do not achieve these vast increases in numbers although, theoretically, we know that they could. What prevents them doing so? We get some insight into the problem by looking at the numbers

The Fulmar *Fulmarus glacialis* used to nest in Britain only on St Kilda. In 1878 the first nests were found elsewhere. Since that time the species has steadily expanded until it now breeds throughout the coasts of the British Isles. In 1970 it was estimated that there were more than 300,000 nests. This expansion has been achieved even though the Fulmar only lays one egg each year and does not normally breed until it is seven or eight years old.

of Grey herons, which have been recorded in Britain for many years. The numbers remain relatively stable for many years then, when a severe winter occurs, the numbers drop as birds starve to death. Breeding numbers are low the following year, but rapidly build up to around their previous numbers when they then level off once more. There seems to be a ceiling to their numbers which the birds cannot easily exceed.

We see this phenomenon in many species; birds are reduced in numbers after some natural disaster, but rapidly recover until they are around the previous level. Only during the few years after a marked reduction in numbers do the birds increase in numbers rapidly. Nature puts a ceiling to the numbers because there is a limit to the resources available. As a result of competition between individuals for these resources an upper limit is set. When a resource is scarce fewer birds (in relation to the number of birds present) can obtain sufficient to survive and breed. When the resource is plentiful in relation to the numbers of birds, more birds find sufficient and so a higher proportion survive and the population increases. We call such a response 'density dependent' since the survival of the birds is dependent on their own density. Many different resources have been held to limit the numbers of different species. Food is an obvious example. Nest sites may be in short supply, especially where a special type of site is needed such as a hole in a tree or a cliff site on a safe island. In some cases there may not be enough for all the birds to obtain a territory suitable for breeding.

We can now see what happens in the case of the Grey heron and a hard winter. After the winter, numbers are reduced and so each bird finds it easier to obtain food. However, as numbers increase again it becomes more difficult for each individual to find sufficient food and so the mortality increases until there is no more room for additional herons and the numbers level off once more.

This interaction between the individuals in a population has another important facet. It is that since there is an upper limit to the numbers which can survive, the death of one bird may mean that another—which would have otherwise perished—may be able to survive in its place. The relatively high reproductive rate of birds ensures that the population will be high at the end of the breeding season. Density dependent mortality reduces the numbers to a point where the resources can support the numbers remaining.

The interplay of these two factors—high production followed by high numbers of deaths—has important consequences for those concerned with the conservation of rare birds, the wildfowler and those concerned with the control of pest species. In a natural state, birds will produce far more young than will survive to breed. Hence, after a natural disaster, when numbers are low and survival rates high, the birds will rapidly recover to a higher population level. The protectionist, therefore, need have no fear for birds following such a disaster. After the very cold weather of the 1963 winter, Long-tailed tits disappeared from many areas and were rare for a year or two. However, their natural productivity enabled them to spread back into almost all their normal habitats within a few years.

The wildfowler shoots some of the doomed surplus. Provided he does not kill more than would have died anyway he can crop the population without danger. Properly controlled, such 'cropping' can provide not only food, but sport for man without in any way endangering the species concerned. Indeed, in a way, it may be beneficial since in many parts of the world, political pressure from huntsmen is an important factor persuading governments to preserve marshlands and forests. The farmer wishing to control a pest such as a pigeon faces a harder task. To reduce numbers he must kill more than the doomed surplus or the breeding level will remain the same. Further, even if he does reduce the number, keeping it at a lower level is extremely difficult. Again the high reproductive rates coupled with the high survival rates of the birds when living at low density enable the pest species to quickly recover its numbers. Temporary reduction in numbers is of little use and permanent reduction very difficult.

Long-term Changes

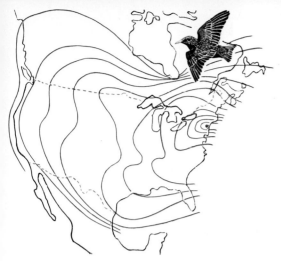

Rapid colonization. The Starling *Sturnus vulgaris* was introduced to New York in 1890. It spread extremely rapidly and within a little over 50 years was widespread throughout the whole of the United States. This probably reflects an increase of about a millionfold.

Although most species of birds were found and named many years ago, there is still a steady trickle of new discoveries. (1) *Conioptilon mcilhennyi*, a cotingid from Peru (1965); (2) *Amytornis barbatus*, a grass-wren from Australia (1968); (3) *Pseudochelidon sirintarae*, an aberrant swallow from Thailand (1968); (4) *Grallaria eludens*, an antpitta from Peru (1967); (5) *Monarcha sacerdotum*, a flycatcher from Flores (Indonesia) (1973); and (6) *Hemispingus parodii*, a tanager from Peru (1968).

While populations tend to be stable from year to year, changes take place over long periods. The history of the evolution of the avifauna has been one of change, with one species taking over from another. Such changes happened very slowly, often over millions of years. As one habitat declined, so another increased and the species adapted to those earlier habitats either had to adapt to the changes or suffer the same fate.

Not all such changes happened over millions of years. The habitats in most areas of the world have changed considerably even in the last 10,000–20,000 years. Some 12,000 years ago the temperate regions, in the grips of the last Ice Age, were dominated by ice and snow. Gradually as the ice receded new areas became more habitable to birds, but areas of central Europe did not become richly forested with deciduous woodland for several thousand years after the ice started to recede. It should be stressed that the woodlands which we know today still existed, probably in very similar form, during the Ice Age, but much farther to the south. As the successive Ice Ages have come and gone so the habitats have ebbed and flowed across the world. Thus the birds that have evolved to live in particular habitats have usually been able to find that type of habitat somewhere else; the habitats did not disappear, but merely shifted.

Still more recently many other changes have been brought about by man. These are usually different from those described above. Often they have involved the reduction of habitats without equivalent replacements elsewhere. Only those species which have been able to adapt to the new artificial man-made habitats have benefitted. The long-term changes brought about by man differ from the natural ones in that they have occurred more rapidly and hence the birds have had less chance of adapting to them. It is perhaps worth pointing out that man-made changes are occurring ever more swiftly as man becomes progressively more mechanised. In Mediterranean regions man has been changing the habitats for more than 5,000 years. In many other areas the small numbers of natives clearing tiny patches of trees caused

Rapid natural increases. (1) The Collared dove *Streptopelia decaocto* has spread rapidly across Europe during the last 50 years. It first bred in Britain in 1955 and within 10 years it was thought that there were probably at least 20,000 birds in the country. It is likely that the original colonists were further augmented by other birds. (2) The Cattle egret *Bubulcus ibis* is an Old World species that was found breeding in Guyana, South America, in 1930. Since then it has spread round the Caribbean into the United States where the increase continues. During the last 15 years there has been about a 20-fold increase. Unlike the Collared dove in Britain, further waves of colonists from Europe are likely to have been negligible, so that all the increase must have sprung from the original colonists.

Extinct birds. For birds which have become extinct in recent times, dates are given. For those known only or virtually only from fossils (1–5, 10 and 11) the colours are hypothetical. (1) *Ichthyornis*, (2) *Hesperornis*, (3) *Archaeopteryx*, (4) *Diatryma*, (5) *Teratornis*, (6) Great auk *Alca impennis* (extinct by 1844), (7) Reunion starling *Fregilupus varius* (1832), (8) Passenger pigeon *Ectopistes migratorius* (1914), (9) Huia *Heterolocha acutirostris* (1907), (10) Moa *Dinornis maximus* (the last species of moa to become extinct, perhaps as late as the eighteenth century), (11) Elephant-bird *Aepyornis titan* or *A. maximus* (possibly one species survived until the seventeenth century), (12) Dodo *Raphus cucullatus* (1681) and (13) Madagascar coua *Coua delalandei* (1930).

▶

almost no effect on the habitats which remained unchanged until the last 50 years or so when western man arrived with powerful tools. Hence the chances of birds being able to adapt to the changes brought about by man may have been different in different parts of the world.

We have, of course, very little quantitative data on the effect such changes have had on birds. We can usually only guess which species would have been in a certain area by working out what the habitats were. However, within the last 100 and more especially the last 50 years, there are better data and we know what has happened to some species. Many of these changes, such as the introduction of the Common starling and the House sparrow to the USA have been brought about by man. Changes in other species also may be a result of man's alteration of the habitats in ways which we have not recognized. The Cattle egret, however, certainly reached South America by its own efforts. It was first recorded breeding in Guyana about 1930 and then spread rapidly up the coast, reaching Florida within eleven years. In 1956, fifteen years later, there were estimated to be 1,100 nests in Florida and the bird is still spreading north today.

In Europe there have also been some large expansions in numbers of certain species during recent years. In Britain the Fulmar formerly only bred on the islands of St. Kilda. In 1878 this species was recorded breeding in the Shetlands and since then has spread throughout large areas of Britain, breeding in all the coastal counties. In 1959 there were estimated to be some 100,000 nests in the country. Even this figure is thought to be an underestimate and 305,000 sites were located in Britain and Ireland in 1969. This species has achieved its remarkable spread although each pair lays only one egg each year and the young birds do not normally start breeding until they are about 7 or 8 years old.

The Collared dove spread rapidly across Europe from the Middle East, first breeding in England in 1955. By 1964 there were estimated to be 20,000 birds in Britain. In this case, and perhaps in the case of the Fulmar, the increase may have been speeded up through further immigration after the first arrivals started to breed.

147

The Indian myna *Acridotheres tristis* is a relative of starlings and has been successful at colonizing many areas where it has been introduced. It is now widespread in parts of southern Africa, Australia and many oceanic islands.

Endangered species. (1) The Everglade kite *Rostrhamus sociabilis* is primarily a South American species which occurs in very small numbers in Florida. It is highly specialized for feeding on snails in marshes. Drainage of this habitat throughout its range represents a great hazard. (2) The American Bald eagle *Haliaeetus leucocephalus* has been greatly reduced in numbers in recent years, primarily as a result of toxic chemicals polluting the rivers and the fish on which it feeds.

Effects of Man

Man has had a profound effect on the landscape and has often markedly affected the habitats which birds use. Basically man has altered the natural habitats in two ways, either by changing the landscape physically or by poisoning it with toxic substances.

In many areas of the world man has made a few simple, but often drastic, changes. He has drained the marshlands and cut down the forests replacing them by farmland and later, often, by cities. In the early days man was a wandering hunter who made no more impact on his surroundings than any other animal, perhaps less than some. As he began to settle down, especially when he started to use fire and tools and to grow crops, he altered the landscape in more significant ways. First he cleared the light hill woodland for farmland, then, as his tools improved, he started to clear the larger trees from the fertile lowlands. Forest clearance has often been on an enormous scale. In Britain and other parts of Europe and in Australia the clearance was often done for sheep-farming. It is difficult nowadays to realize the scale on which this was done since so much has re-grown or been re-planted. In the United States almost all the lowland hardwoods of the eastern states were cleared for farming; again the forests we see now are those that have re-generated. In the wetter areas of the tropics clearance is often short-sighted; crops can be grown on such ground for only a few years before the heavy rainfall washes away the nutrients and the area must be abandoned. Even where forests have not been cleared, the selective use of certain trees (such as oaks for building ships) resulted in a change of the composition of the forests,

The Starling *Sturnus vulgaris* has been one of the most successful birds in coming to terms with the changes brought about by man. It likes open country and has made good use of farmland and cities. As a result it must now be more numerous than it was before man altered the landscape.

The House sparrow *Passer domesticus* has probably been even more successful than the Starling in adapting to the changes brought about by man. Both species have successfully used man's transport to colonize new areas and both have used his buildings for nesting and obtained their food from gardens and farms. The House sparrow was probably even more numerous in the centres of cities at the beginning of the century. At this time, the sparrows obtained much of their food from the grain supplied for horses. The advent of the car has probably led to a decrease in their numbers.

at times to the detriment of birds which depended on particular tree species for their livelihood.

As man's abilities increased he dug ditches to improve the drainage and straightened and widened rivers to increase the flow and to provide reliable transport routes. These changes had, and still have, profound effects on the birds. Marshland birds seem to have suffered more than woodland ones. Many of the latter seem to have been able to exist in small areas of woodland whereas the marshland species could no longer find suitable habitats.

By no means all birds have found man's changes deleterious, the species which live in open land have benefitted considerably. In some temperate areas it is not clear how, or where, these species existed when the land was completely covered with woodland. Birds such as the Common starling and the House sparrow have found the arable lands greatly to their liking. Other species such as some of the swallows and swifts nest nowadays almost exclusively on man's buildings, so much so that it is difficult to imagine where they nested previously, at least in such large numbers as they do now.

In recent times man has made yet other changes to the habitats, often including the planting of new forests. In many cases these are of different trees from the original ones such as, for example, the new coniferous plantations and eucalypt forests which have been extensively planted all over the world in suitable localities. Some of these are not easily colonized by local birds, perhaps because conifer and eucalypt forests have poor insect faunas for the birds to feed on. Other such forests may attract bird species that are different from those that occurred in the natural forests. In many parts of Europe, conifers are planted where broad-leaved deciduous woodlands would be the natural forests. However, there are coniferous woodlands in such areas, at higher altitudes or latitudes, and the birds that specialize in living in such places have spread into the extensions of their natural habitat. In particular, the Coal tit and the Crossbill have benefitted from these plantations in many parts of Europe. Modern forest management involves the removal of dead and dying wood, often to the disadvantage of birds, such as woodpeckers, that depend on such wood for their food.

Even the use of the term natural becomes difficult. For example the loss of the Great bustard from the downland areas of Britain occurred when the huge areas of sheep grazing lands were dissected by new plantations; doubtless more modern firearms were also a contributory factor. The loss of this species was regretted by many. However, this bird could only have become established in Britain after man had cleared the woodland, and so it was a temporary resident, staying for only a few centuries before disappearing.

Man has also built large reservoirs which have provided living quarters for many species of waterfowl. As with the new coniferous forests, the reservoirs provide a livelihood for many species of birds, but not the ones that lived in the habitat that was there previously. Marshland species are adapted to reed beds and shallow water, the birds on reservoirs are predominantly those that are adapted to diving in deep water for their food.

The changes brought about by man's pollution of the environment are a different matter altogether. These do not merely change the landscape so that different species can occupy a new area, their changes make it difficult for any species to survive there. Birds may not be able to raise enough young under these conditions to replace the adults that die, especially if the adult death rate also rises. Chemical poisoning of the land, and even more seriously, of the seas and rivers, is continuing at an alarming rate. Persistent poisons such as DDT have been implicated in the decline of the Peregrine and the American Bald eagle. These two species have declined because poisons have accumulated in these birds to levels which have affected their breeding success. Similarly, poisoning of the seas may be having a drastic effect on the life there. The birds die because the areas become either devoid of prey or because the prey are full of poisonous substances.

The Japanese ibis *Nipponia nippon* is probably now extinct in China and is very scarce in Japan where some 12 birds remain.

Although it has a very extensive range, the Peregrine falcon *Falco peregrinus* has become much reduced in numbers in the last 20 years.

Endangered species. (1) The Imperial eagle *Aquila heliaca adalberti*. This race, from Spain and North Africa, is probably reduced to fewer than 100 birds. They perhaps no longer breed in North Africa. This bird, like many eagles, has been much persecuted by man. (2) Mauritius kestrel *Falco punctatus*. Never a large population, this species has been frequently shot. There may only be one remaining pair living in the wild. (3) Seychelles owl *Otus insularis*. Very few individuals remain. Its habitat has been destroyed and it may have suffered in competition with the introduced Barn owl *Tyto alba*.

Endangered species. The numbers given relate to the most recent estimates made in the last 10–15 years and may well be now inaccurate. (1) Monkey-eating eagle *Pithecophaga jefferyi* from the Phillippines (less than 100 birds), (2) Californian condor *Gymnogyps californianus*, California (about 40 birds), (3) Takahe *Notornis mantelli*, New Zealand (perhaps 200 individuals), (4) Ivory-billed woodpecker *Campephilus principalis* (the races of this species that occur in Cuba and USA are reduced to very small numbers indeed), (5) Kakapo *Strigops habroptilus* (perhaps only about 20) and (6) Cahow *Pterodroma cahow*, Bermuda (some 30 pairs, possibly increasing slightly with protection). ▶

Endangered Species

In the last 200 years or so some 70 to 80 species of birds have become extinct. Many of these, perhaps almost all of them, have disappeared as a result of man's activities. In addition, a number of other species are known to have disappeared in the few centuries prior to recorded history; most of the moas of New Zealand and the Elephant-birds of Malagasy survived until their homelands were occupied by man. In all probability man was responsible for their demise.

One can make a few generalizations about the species which have become extinct and from these and other evidence deduce which living species are likely to be most endangered. A large proportion of the species which have become extinct lived on small islands; over two thirds of the extinct species lived on islands of less than 1,000 sq mi (2,600 sq km), only nine on large continents. A number of them were flightless (Elephant-birds, moas, Dodo, Great auk and several rails).

The reasons why each of these birds became extinct are not always known, but four, possibly five, causes probably explain most of them. Some (Great auk, Dodo) were hunted by man, others were exterminated by his introduced animals such as dogs, cats and rats, others could not survive in the face of the loss of their habitats; the Passenger pigeon may fall into this category. Yet others may well have been unable to survive in the face of competition with other, introduced, species of birds which competed with them for food or nesting sites; in general, species which have evolved on a large land mass appear to win in competition with species evolved in the more sheltered environment of small islands. For example, several of the Hawaiian honeycreepers disappeared shortly after introduced species spread throughout certain habitats. The fifth possible cause of extinction is that the introduced species did not compete directly with the resident species, but brought with them diseases to which they were reasonably resistant, but to which the native birds had no such immunity. Western man almost eliminated certain native populations on islands by carrying diseases such as measles to which he was largely immune (in the sense that

151

During the last century, perhaps a million Steller's (or Short-tailed) albatrosses *Diomedea albatrus* nested on several small islands south of Japan. It was heavily preyed upon by Japanese plume traders, and was later believed to be extinct. However, a small colony has formed on one island, Torishima and, with rigorous protection, the birds seem to be increasing in numbers.

Endangered species. (1) Audouin's gull *Larus audouinii*, a scarce species from the Mediterranean, breeding in a number of places, but in only small numbers. There may be some 1,000 pairs left. (2) Kagu *Rhynochetos jubatus* is an aberrant relative of the cranes. It is very rare, being found only on New Caledonia. It is virtually flightless and the forests in which it lives have been severely reduced and many injurious mammals such as pigs, cats, rats and dogs have been introduced. (3) The Night parrot *Geopsittacus occidentalis* is a ground-dwelling parrot of open country in Australia; it has only occasionally been reported during the present century and has at times been thought to be extinct.

The Whooping crane *Grus americana* breeds in freshwater bogs in northwestern Canada and spends the winter on the coastline of Texas. Only some 100 individuals remain.

he did not usually die) but to which the natives had no resistance. It could have been the same with birds. A number of New Zealand species disappeared very swiftly after western man colonized the islands, bringing with him many species of birds. These may well have carried diseases to which the native birds had no resistance.

The species which are most endangered at the present time are roughly in the same categories as those listed above. Many island species, never represented by large numbers of individuals, are threatened in part by habitat destruction and in part by man's introduced mammals. Rats, cats, mongeese, pigs, monkeys and other animals have all done damage. Several flightless species are extremely rare and threatened including the Kakapo and Takahe, both from New Zealand. At least 100 species of living birds are represented by fewer than 2,000 individuals. Although man is now aware of the threat he poses to such species and may be able to prevent hunting of these species (in contrast to the situation in the early part of this century when collectors were rushing to get the last few remaining specimens) the outlook for such species is not bright.

On mainland areas very large birds such as eagles, and birds that nest colonially such as herons and egrets, are at times severely threatened by man. The former group are not only large and therefore easy to shoot, but also they reproduce slowly, making it easier to reduce their numbers. Some egrets were brought to the verge of extinction by the plume trade earlier this century. They nested in a few large colonies and these continued to be worth a visit by the hunters even when the birds were becoming relatively scarce.

Hopefully, in many parts of the world such intentional slaughter is now being reduced, but this is not the case everywhere. Even if man can reduce his own direct threats to such species, further unintentional changes brought about by man's carelessness may always spoil the habitats in which they live. If the species concerned is rare and confined to a local area it may be exterminated. The greatest threat of this sort for the future lies in pollution which may result not only in the extermination of birds but of many men as well.

Domestic Birds

Only about a dozen birds can be thought of as successfully domesticated. However, four of these, the hen, duck, goose and turkey are important economic foods for man. All the species that are domesticated on any scale have two features in common; they eat grain and live, at least at times, in flocks. As a result, they are easily fed by man and will survive when kept in crowded conditions, a thing that many highly territorial species would not do.

The hen, a derivative of the Jungle fowl *Gallus gallus*, is by far the most important species of domestic bird, and is kept almost everywhere in the world. Presumably it was domesticated by primitive peoples who, when they could capture food animals alive, kept them until they were needed for a meal. The hen proved easy to keep alive in captivity and its additional advantage, that it laid edible eggs, led to its being kept for increasingly long periods. There is evidence that the species was domesticated in China about 1500 BC and may have been kept in India as much as 1,500 years before that. Early Neolithic men in Europe kept chickens so the habit obviously spread westwards at an early state. Most of the birds were kept for meat and eggs and little care was given to them. However, selective breeding (and therefore the necessary segregation of stocks) must have started relatively early since there were a number of distinct breeds by Roman times. Nowadays there are well over 200 breeds. Excluding the forms which could be said to be more ornamental, selective breeding has in recent years been along two main lines. First there has been selection for rapid growth rates since this produces more meat per kilogram of food than does a slow growth rate. Second there has been selection for high egg production; the natural clutch of about 6–8 eggs has given way to almost continual egg production. At their peak, birds of the best strains will lay at virtually the rate of an egg per day for the whole year.

The turkey is also a very important domestic bird. Although the history of its

All the birds on this plate have been commonly kept by man, sometimes as pets. Some, through selective breeding, have been modified by man. Others have escaped in new areas and may have become a nuisance. (1) Budgerigar *Melopsittacus undulatus* from Australia where the wild form is green, (2) Zebra finch *Taeniopygia guttata* from Australia, (3) Hill myna *Gracula reliogiosa* introduced into many of the warmer areas of the world, (4) domestic pigeon derived from the Rock dove *Columba livia* as is the racing pigeon; birds often show the white rump of the ancestral stock, (5) African Grey parrot *Psittacus erithacus* and (6) Java sparrow *Padda oryzivora,* both introduced to many new areas.

Birds that have been kept by man, mainly for food. (1) Domestic hen derived from the Jungle fowl *Gallus gallus,* (2) Turkey *Meleagris gallopavo* from the New World, not Turkey, and (3) Peacock *Pavo cristatus.*

domestication is less well known than is that of the hen, it may have been kept in Mexico for almost as long as the hen was kept in the East. In this species breeding has been for heavy birds with high growth rates more than for egg production. The largest marketable birds are currently running at about 30 lbs (13 kg). Although one bird brought to a National Turkey Federation convention weighed more than 70 lbs (31 kg), its weight was definitely the exception rather than the norm.

Ducks and geese are the other important food species. Most ducks, except the Muscovy which is derived from the wild Muscovy duck *Cairina moschata* from South America, are derived from the Mallard *Anas platyrhynchos.* Most geese are descended from the Greylag *Anser anser* though the Chinese goose is descended from the Swan goose *Anser cygnoides.* Other important commercial species include the Japanese Quail *Coturnix coturnix* and the Ostrich, though the latter species is kept for its plumes as much as for its food value.

A number of other birds are raised in large quantities. These are the game birds such as the Pheasant which are released, often in very large numbers, for shooting at a later date. Such species can barely be considered truly domesticated, but a number of the more ornamental pheasants are kept and bred under conditions of domestication. The Peafowl is a good example.

One species of pigeon, the Rock dove *Columba livia,* has been domesticated and a large number of fancy breeds are kept. However the most important form of this species is the homing pigeon which has been used for carrying messages since at least Roman times, has played a significant role in two World Wars and is now kept in huge numbers for racing as a hobby. It is also widely used in scientific research into the homing abilities of birds. Egyptian paintings suggest that this bird has been kept in captivity, if not used for homing, since about 2500 BC.

BIRD STUDY

Bird Observation

Man has probably always watched birds. Early observations were usually closely related to man's need for survival. Vultures gathering were an indication that an animal had recently died and that meat might be available. Many explorers have watched the flight lines of birds for signs of the nearest source of water. Mariners used the flights of sea birds to lead them to the nearest land. Even today many of the more primitive tribes know a considerable amount about their birds—often having names for each of the more common or conspicuous species. Knowledge of the habits of these birds may be useful in a variety of ways. The birds may be used as food, the feathers for decoration or their call for indicating the presence of other animals (or men) in the vicinity. Often, in the more civilized industrial societies, we have lost this knowledge; only the wildfowler or gamekeeper knows many of these things. He learns them from others and from his own observations.

Modern industrialized societies, with more time for leisure, have started to observe birds for different reasons, often for pleasure rather than survival. In such societies one may find many people making observations and these may range from the purely casual enjoyment of bird-watching to the detailed studies of the research scientist. The latter may be organized to discover information about any aspects of birds and their lives including how we can reduce the damage caused by certain species to our crops. Hence, though a far cry from the interest in birds as food shown by primitive societies, some of man's most sophsticated observations of birds may be related to the interests in our food and hence, ultimately to our survival.

Historically, observations on birds have followed a similar sequence in many areas of the world. Early explorers made casual observations and brought back a few specimens. They were followed by more experienced naturalists who made more detailed collections, bringing back large numbers of specimens for museums where they could be compared with other specimens, described and named. After reasonably complete collections and check-lists were made available, people started recording the abundance of these species, the habitats in which they lived and their ranges in greater detail. Only where there is detailed information of this sort, where one knows the bird that one is watching, can more detailed studies of individual species easily be made. It may be difficult for people living in Europe or North America, surrounded by a plethora of bird-books and an overwhelming selection of field guides, to appreciate that in many areas of the world this basic information is not available. Most species have been identified, but new ones are still being discovered at the rate of one or two a year and the ranges and movements of many of these species are very inadequately known. Yet more detailed knowledge, such as details of the eggs and nests, the breeding behaviour and survival rates are known for very few species. As might be expected, most detailed studies have been made of birds in North America and Europe. That these may not be typical of all birds is only now becoming clear. For example, we tend to think of birds as living in pairs and defending territories. However, many tropical species have community structures which are different from this. Many live in groups: often up to a dozen or so birds live together during the

Not only do the tits frequent houses and gardens during winter, but they will willingly accept nest-boxes that are provided for them. In the absence of these, the birds will use almost any kind of hole. Here (below) a Great tit *Parus major* leaves its nest in a hollow fence post.

Many people have first become interested in birds through keeping them in captivity. For many centuries birds have been kept for their singing abilities. Finches have proved particularly amenable to such treatment, being easy to feed and maintain in small cages and having pleasing songs. This species is the (European) Goldfinch *Carduelis carduelis*.

The Herring gull *Larus argentatus* has been one of the most studied species of birds. It is a common colonial species which has proved relatively easy to observe and was the basis of Professor Niko Tinbergen's *A Herring Gull's World*, one of the classic ornithological studies.

entire year, and help raise the young produced by a single pair. In some of these and other species territorial defence appears to be poorly developed. Hence, some of the aspects of the biology of temperate birds may well not be applicable to others.

As the background knowledge has increased, so more sophisticated and detailed studies have become possible. Although distributional studies established where birds were to be found at all times of the year, early observers were not able to discover where different populations of migrants went at the different times of year. Detailed studies of this sort have only been possible with the advent of ringing, the practice of putting small numbered rings on the legs of birds. Normally these rings have the address of the organization in the country where the ringing was undertaken and the hope is that the finder of a dead bird will return the ring. For most species, however, the chance of a small dead bird being found, especially in some of the larger forest areas of the tropics, is almost infinitesimally small. Nevertheless, by ringing very large numbers of the common species it is often possible to describe not only the breeding and wintering areas of migrants but also the routes by which they reach these places. Detailed information is, of course, only known for a relatively small number of the common species. Rarer species are still very poorly known.

It is a common misconception that ornithologists ring birds just to get information about their movements. One even meets people who think that so much is known that there can be no need for further ringing. Even if this were true, it would hold for only a tiny proportion of species. There are in fact many reasons for ringing birds and from almost no species have enough birds been ringed for us to be able to understand their movements completely. There is some evidence that movements of the Blackbird may have changed somewhat in the last 30 years. Hence, these studies may need continual reassessment. In some species there may be different movements in different winters. The Redwings from northern Europe migrate to different parts of southern Europe in different years. Another important reason for studying birds by use of ringing is that it enables one to measure the longevity and the mortality of birds at different stages in their lives. Here again we have too few data for almost every species. We need to have studies of population structure over long periods of time. In particular, where we have a landscape that is changing as rapidly as it is at present, we need to know whether the birds are continuing to face the challenge of man's changes, if only because changes in the numbers, or survival rates, of birds might stem from changes which may also affect man. Again, we need continuing measurements of these facets of the life of birds.

The studies mentioned above involve the use of small numbered rings with addresses. Many detailed studies of ecology, migration or behaviour require the research worker to be able to identify individual birds without having to catch them frequently and so disturb their everyday lives. For this reason many ornithologists use different types of marks, often coloured rings or sometimes wing-tags. These can be put on the birds in such a way, or in such a combination of colours, that each bird is individually recognizable by the research worker without its having to be caught.

Such detailed studies require a great amount of observation and therefore take time. Hence many, but by no means all, of the most detailed studies are undertaken by professionals working in universities or other large organizations. In the twenties and thirties, there were very few posts for professionals to undertake field studies of birds. The earlier pioneer studies such as Eliot Howard's *Territory in Bird Life*, David Lack's *Life of the Robin* and Mrs. Nice's *Studies in the Life History of the Song Sparrow* were all done by busy people in their spare time. However, as more became known, and as ornithological field work became possible for professional biologists, more and more of the very detailed studies, especially those requiring a number of people and the use of sophisticated equipment not available to amateurs, were undertaken by professionals. It should not be thought, however, that this means that the role of the amateur in bird observation is over. Only the professional can make

Common (or Barn) swallows *Hirundo rustica* are particularly well-known to man, in both the Old and the New World. They have nested on man's buildings for at least 2,000 years and are now rarely seen nesting elsewhere, Here birds are collecting mud to build their nests.

The Yellowhammer *Emberiza citrinella* and the Winter wren *Troglodytes troglodytes* are two other species well-known to Europeans. Both are widespread in Europe (the Winter wren is also found in North America) and both have distinctive and far-carrying songs. The Yellowhammer has been introduced to New Zealand and some of the nearby islands.

(1) The Common swift *Apus apus* is well-known to city dwellers. It nests under the eaves of houses and tall buildings. It forages, often some distance away, for aerial insects. (2) The (European) Blackbird *Turdus merula* is another well-known urban bird which has been much studied. It nests more densely in urban areas than in woodland. (3) The Reed bunting *Emberiza schoeniclus* is a bird of marshes. It was the subject of Eliot Howard's classic study, *Territory in Bird Life*.

very long-term, detailed or expensive studies necessary to learn more about certain aspects of the ways that birds live, but the amateur can make the wide-scale studies of distribution or surveys that need perhaps hundreds of people to count birds throughout a country simultaneously. For example, professionals could not undertake the detailed counts of waterfowl made in many parts of Europe once a month. Nor could they provide the stock of ringed birds all over the country for certain mortality studies. Only a small army of dedicated amateurs can do this. Many of the individuals concerned will never publish any of their material. Nevertheless, they spend their holidays making surveys in out-of-the-way parts of the world, contributing invaluable information and, at the same time, getting a great deal of enjoyment from their hobby.

As with ringing, the need for surveys does not end when they have been made. The changing face of the countryside requires that surveys of birds be made at relatively frequent intervals if we are to observe the changes that are doubtless taking place. Even in the most intensively-watched countries, such as Britain, with a small area and many watchers, there are areas that are not at all well-known, and the changing ranges of bird species go unrecorded. While some of these may well be due to changes brought about by man we are by no means certain that they all are, and further documentation is essential. In many parts of the world simple basic distributional data do not exist at all and are badly needed.

In all aspects of bird biology there is much to be learned as well as the continuous changes which need to be monitored. Not only the smaller detailed studies of individual species, but also the larger problems all need further study. To give but one example, we do not really understand the way that migrating birds find their way from one end of the world to the other. Migration may not be quite as much of a mystery as it was in Gilbert White's day 200 years ago, but much remains to be found out. The amateur who rings large numbers of birds and the professional who watches birds on migration with the help of radar and radio transmitters and investigates in detail the homing ability of pigeons, may well expect together to provide further insight into these subjects. The same is true of many aspects of the study of birds; often different approaches may combine to help provide us with a fuller picture. Bird observation remains as challenging, and enjoyable, as it has ever been.

BIRD FAMILIES OF THE WORLD

In the pages that follow we are offering an overall picture of the birds of the world. No one would really find a series of descriptions or an enumeration of the 8,600 or so known species to be a useful way of comprehending the whole, and in order to discuss them it is necessary to group them in some way. This is not easy. In spite of the apparent diversity of form and pattern, beneath all those feathers birds are rather uniform in structure.

The simplest ways of quickly subdividing birds are those sometimes used by authors of field guides. To aid identification in the wild, the obvious subdivisions are those of size, colour and pattern, and of the habitat in which the species occurs. Convenient as such divisions may be, obvious anomalies are immediately apparent, with very similar and apparently closely related species occurring in different categories. Differences in colour and pattern may even divide young and adults of the same species, or separate the two sexes; the size range may be considerable within an otherwise uniform group such as ducks, typical birds of prey, or gamebirds; and a group as uniformly recognizable as the typical waders, or shorebirds, can occur from sea coasts and mountain rivers to grassland, marsh, and the forest floor. ➡

Birds display an extraordinary range of size and shape. The largest species, the Ostrich *Struthio camelus* (1), towers over the man standing at its tail. Male ostriches grow to 8ft (2.4m) and weigh about 300lb (135kg). In descending order of size are (2) the Emperor penguin *Aptenodytes forsteri*, (3) the Wandering albatross *Diomedea exulans* which has the longest wingspan of any bird at 11½ft (3.5m), (4) the Grey heron *Ardea cinerea*, (5) the Peregrine falcon *Falco peregrinus*, (6) Pallas' sandgrouse *Syrrhaptes paradoxus*, (7) the Yellow wagtail *Motacilla flava* and (8) the Bee hummingbird *Calypte helenae*, the smallest species, at 2½in (6.5cm).

Anomalies such as these can be avoided by using evidence based on the structure of birds rather than their external features to establish relationships. Clues may be found in similarities of structure of many parts of the skeleton, especially the skull. Other internal parts such as muscles, tendons and even the loops of the gut may furnish supporting evidence; and external features such as the type, number and arrangement of feathers, scaly pattern of the legs and type of bill-shape and bill-sheath may also help. Our present systems of bird classification, based in the main on such structures, have evolved gradually over about a century, changing at times as new information emerges.

An early arrangement was a subdivision of birds into two groups: the carinate birds which have a keel on the breastbone and are able to fly; and the ratite birds which lack a keel and are flightless. Later studies of flightless birds occurring in families where most species can fly as, for example, in the island rails, showed that the keel could become greatly reduced fairly rapidly in bird evolution. This might have totally invalidated these earlier categories but for the fact that a study of bird skulls showed that it was possible to divide birds into four groups on the basis of the arrangement of their palate bones. The flightless ratites had a palate thought to be of a very early evolutionary type and continued to be a discrete unit but were now joined by an additional group of birds which possessed the power of flight, the tinamous.

The classification of birds has been closely bound up with ideas about evolution. However, because adaptiveness and general intelligence are regarded as special attributes most highly developed in man and justifying his self-appointed place at the head of the animal kingdom, these were regarded as equally relevant in birds, and the crow family was placed at the top of the scale as the group in which these characters were most apparent. This meant that the order of passerine birds as a whole came at the top of the list and below this the other bird groups were arranged in what was regarded as a descending order of increasing antiquity or 'primitiveness'. Later the whole list was usually reversed, with the crows coming last and the whole series of orders and families of birds arranged in this hypothetical sequence from the most 'primitive' to the most 'advanced'. The order was influenced to some extent by the knowledge of the existence of avian fossils attributed to existing bird families and occurring at different geological periods. In view of our incomplete knowledge of fossil birds, however, any inference about their evolution derived from this source must be treated with considerable caution, and more recent discoveries have modified some of the ideas that were used to produce the sequence of groups.

The concept of 'primitiveness' in birds, which was often used in earlier studies of evolution, is difficult to defend, but it persisted for a long time. Primitiveness should imply that the animal possessing this feature has retained the characters of the ancestral form. The evolutionary divergence within the early toothed birds was such that by the time we arrive at our present birds it is difficult to be certain what is primitive and what is not.

The groups of birds which are sometimes described as primitive are actually those which diverge most widely from the typical passerine pattern. The mainly flightless ratite birds appear the most divergent, while the penguins, with their loss of flight, lower legs modified into squat feet, and many elements flattened in the forelimbs to form the flippers, are a close second. Then come the divers (loons) with long bodies, legs set so far back on the body for propulsion in water that movement on land is difficult, and wings reduced to the necessary minimum; and the grebes, similarly modified but with structural differences indicating a separate origin. These all show a high degree of specialization.

The presence of some of the other orders and families early in the sequence may be due in part to a preponderance of larger birds and water birds in the fossil record, and probably merely reflects the accidental result of the way in which bones of such birds are preserved. It is also due to some groups being composed of highly diverse and numerically few species which appear to be the isolated relics of larger and more complex groups at earlier periods. Such groups may therefore be suspected of having an evolutionarily earlier origin. The order comprising albatrosses, shearwaters and petrels that follows the grebes is a fairly uniform group which is suspected of having early origins because of the early occurrence of fossil forms. Next come the pelican and stork orders, which fulfil the criteria of early groups in having small numbers of highly modified and diverse forms with fossil evidence of early origin. After these are a series of distinct and diverse orders—the waterfowl, diurnal birds of prey, and the game-birds. These well-defined entities are followed by two broad and varied groups, first the crane order comprising not only the big cranes, but also the rails and the tiny buttonquails; and then the wader order ranging from the typical shorebirds through gulls and terns to the highly modified auks.

This list has been generally accepted, but doubts arise since some recently-described early fossil birds show, not only a link between shearwaters and pelican-like birds, but also apparent triple links between the previous two and the waders; and between waders, ducks and flamingos. In attempting to reconcile possible modifications of this type with the old sequence one is faced, not only with relative changes in position of various orders, but also with the impossibility of representing in a single sequence of groups the situation in which there is an apparently equal relationship between three different groups. With problems such as these it becomes apparent that, however accurate the arrangements of orders and families was felt to be at the time when it was devised, such a sequence must now be regarded as an arbitrary but convenient arrangement which does not necessarily reflect the true relationships of the various groups.

Following the waders there is a series of small orders and families about which there has been little controversy although in terms of the fossil sequence the owls are now known to have had a very early separate origin, and it has been argued that the differences between the sandgrouse and pigeons are large enough to justify their separation into two orders. The main differences of opinion in the latter part of the sequence concern the passerines. As stated earlier, these had been arranged in a sequence of families finishing with the crows, because they were considered to be the most intelligent of birds. It had, however, been argued that the lack of anatomical specialization in the crows was not indicative of a high degree of evolution but represented a more generalized condition. The seed eating birds—weavers, finches and buntings, were proposed as the group that should occupy their position. Against both proposals it can be argued that the arrangement represents a departure from the criteria used at an earlier stage in the sequence, in that the most highly specialized and divergent groups were now being placed last instead of first.

From a purely practical point of view the main result of this controversy is that there are now two widely accepted sequences which may be used for the passerine families. The second sequence, finishing with the buntings, has been more widely accepted in North America but is sometimes used in European publications. However, the only complete sequence of birds, including genera and species as well as orders and families, is the fifteen volume work begun by J. L. Peters, and this uses the earlier sequence ending with the crow family. Since this is the work most frequently used by museums and scientific collections for arranging their material it occurs widely as a sequence in ornithological literature, and is the one chosen for the present work.

It has already been explained that the sequence of orders and families used here has a logical basis, albeit one that may have altered with time; but for practical reasons, it is an arbitrary arrangement and alternative sequences are recognized. It has the advantage that it is sufficiently well-known for the bird enthusiast to be able to find with little difficulty the group in which he is interested. Its disadvantage is that it does not necessarily reflect the latest views on the relationships of the various groups involved. For anyone who is working on the taxonomy of birds there is always a conflict of choice between a re-arrangement of groups that would reflect new ideas which are being put forward, and the retention of an earlier recognized, but possibly erroneous, sequence which will be familiar to the reader. This conflict is resolved in the pages that follow by the inclusion at the end of each entry of a section headed 'Composition'. In this section, the possible alternative positions of the family under discussion in the sequence are mentioned, as well as its composition.

ARCHAEOPTERYGIFORMES

The fossil link between reptiles and birds. Only five skeletons have been discovered

ARCHAEOPTERYX — *Archaeopterygidae*

ARCHAEOPTERYX

Archaeopteryx lithographica, the earliest recognized bird, is the only representative of its family and displays a mixture of features that are typical of both reptiles and birds.

Fossils of *Archaeopteryx* were first discovered over a century ago in the 150 million year old Jurassic lithographic limestone deposits of southern Germany. These specimens and subsequent finds have been examined in great detail by many scientists who have reached different conclusions as to the significance of *Archaeopteryx*. Two things are certain however; it is a bird, but it closely resembles extinct reptiles called coelurosaurs which were carnivorous, bipedal dinosaurs.

The information obtained from the five known skeletons makes it possible to say that *Archaeopteryx* was a land bird about the size of a large crow, possibly capable of perching, but with limited powers of flight, and that it probably lived in or about the trees surrounding the lagoons and shallow seas found in Germany during the Jurassic period. In life it must have superficially resembled a coucal which is a clumsy, partly ground-living member of the cuckoo family that has short rounded wings and a long ungainly tail. Here the similarity ends, because some of the features of the skeleton of *Archaeopteryx* are reptilian. In fact many of the scientists who have studied this bird agree that it is very fortunate that its feathers were preserved, for without them it would have been difficult to identify the remains as belonging to a bird at all.

The skull, for instance, has rows of sharp, pointed teeth in both the upper and lower jaws, which are situated in sockets and are not unlike those of certain lizards. It also possesses large narial, pre-orbital and temporal fossae and a post-temporal bar separating the orbit from the latter – all features expected in a reptile. In one specimen the cast of the brain can be seen which is reminiscent of reptiles in both shape and structure, and is very different from that found in all other known birds.

The rest of the skeleton is also atypical of those found in all other birds whether fossil or living. The elements of the backbone, the vertebrae, have biconcave articular ends and nowhere exhibit the saddle-shaped articulations characteristic of birds. Further, the tail vertebrae are not reduced to a pygostyle (parson's nose) but are arranged in a long chain numbering about 20.

The pectoral girdle is well preserved, and from it one can see that although the elements found in flying birds are represented they are not as well developed. For instance, the coracoid is only one third the length of the scapula, and the sternum, to which the flight muscles are attached in flying birds, is only a short, flattened plate, lacking a keel. The forelimb is unusual being as long as the hindlimb with the humerus being longer than the radius and ulna which are weakly developed. The bones of the wrist and hand are not fused as in living birds although the number of individual elements are reduced. There are three fingers which were apparently functional in life, each of which terminates in a claw. The feather impressions

The Berlin specimen of *Archaeopteryx lithographica* (1). A fairly complete restoration of its skeleton is possible (2), but its colours (3) must always remain a subject for speculation.

Restoration of *Archaeopteryx*. (1) Feeding on insects, which are known to have evolved 150 million years ago, and (2) in an aggressive posture. The posture is hypothetical; there is no fossil evidence for such displays.

which are well preserved on two specimens show that they were well formed, and consist of eight primaries and 10 secondaries.

The pelvic girdle is distinctly dinosaurian in appearance, however there is at present some controversy concerning the way in which two bones of the girdle, the pubis and ischium, are joined to one another. In all reconstructions these two paired bones are shown pointing backwards, as they do in all birds, but it has been suggested recently that the pubis could have taken up a more forward position in life. The characters of the hindlimb are well authenticated, and again display several reptilian features such as a long femur, separate tibia and fibula which are almost equal in length, and what appears to be four metatarsals. The most striking feature, however, is the first digit which is rotated backwards, and is consequently capable of being opposed to the others.

The Origin of Flight. Although powered flight is one of the most demanding means of locomotion it has been successfully evolved independently by three different vertebrate groups. The pterosaurs (flying reptiles) popularly known as pterodactyls were the first. Their remains are recorded from as early as the late Triassic (200 million years ago) but they became extinct towards the end of the Cretaceous some 70 million years ago. It was towards the end of their existence that they produced *Pteranodon*, the largest known flying animal, which had a wing-span of at least 27ft (8m). Birds were the next to take to the air during the Upper Jurassic about 150 million years ago, followed by the mammals in the form of bats some 100 million years later. Many other animals are said to fly, but they are really only passive gliders or parachutists – for example among living animals certain fish, frogs, snakes, lizards, opossums, squirrels and lemurs are all gliders of varying efficiency. It should be

pointed out that the pterosaurs did not evolve into birds nor did the birds give rise to the bats, but each group evolved flight independently.

Whether *Archaeopteryx* was capable of powered flight has long been the subject of much argument amongst scientists. Some have stated that, because of the structural limitations in the skeleton of the pectoral girdle (unkeeled sternum, short coracoids and poorly developed pectoral crest of the humerus – all concerned with the attachment of flight muscles), *Archaeopteryx* must have been a glider or at best a very poor flier. It has also been stated that the spread of the wing was less than that found in birds with weak flight, and that, as a result, the wing loading would have been too high. These observations are now known to be of doubtful significance: the spread of the wing was probably comparable with that of arboreal birds of similar proportions. Also, we know that bats possess no significant keel, nor was it well developed in the pterosaurs, yet bats at least are capable of powered flight. Finally, it has recently been pointed out that, although the shortness of the coracoids would limit the size of the flight muscles, this would only affect the speed of the wing beat and not its power.

More research needs to be undertaken before it is known for certain how flight originated and whether *Archaeopteryx* was an efficient flier. My personal view is that *Archaeopteryx* was capable of powered flight over short distances.

If one believes that *Archaeopteryx* was a mainly cursorial carnivore it would be reasonable to assume that it captured and fed upon small ground-living reptiles and insects. It probably achieved this by gliding down from an elevated position, making quick dashes, and seizing its prey in its toothed jaws.

Composition. The two original skeletons (housed in museums at London and Berlin) were thought by some workers to be distinct from one another and the name *Archaeornis siemensi* was erected for the Berlin specimen. A theory was also put forward stating that *Archaeopteryx* was the originator of the ratites and *Archaeornis* of the carinates. This idea has now been completely rejected, and all of the specimens are now placed within the same genus and species, that of *Archaeopteryx lithographica*.

HESPERORNITHIFORMES

Extinct marine birds. Fossils have been found in
Montana and Nebraska

HESPERORNIS — *Hesperornithidae*
ENALIORNIS — *Enaliornithidae*
BAPTORNIS — *Baptornithidae*

HESPERORNIS

The family Hesperornithidae is at present made up of two genera, *Hesperornis* (3 species) and the monotypic *Coniornis*. Like members of the contemporary order Ichthyornithiformes, these birds are distinct from birds of a modern type because of the possession of true teeth in their jaws. Until recently, however, there has been some doubt as to whether the jaws were in fact toothed, but further preparation of fossil remains, followed by a detailed re-examination of the material, proved that the original description published by Marsh over one hundred years ago was correct.

By the end of the Cretaceous period, about 70 million years after *Archaeopteryx* had evolved, the bird fauna apparently consisted of birds of modern aspect referable to Tertiary orders. The only well preserved specimens intermediate in age and structure between the dinosaurian-like *Archaeopteryx* and modern birds are two genera *Hesperornis* and *Ichthyornis* which were found in marine sediments deposited during the late Cretaceous.

The best example of the Hesperornithidae, by which we can obtain a good idea of the outward appearance of these birds, is *H. regalis*. This species is represented by one almost complete skeleton with a partial skull, and other less complete material, and next to

Archaeopteryx is without doubt one of the more famous fossil birds.

In life this bird probably resembled the present-day divers or loons in having become extremely well adapted to an aquatic mode of life. It was some 6ft (2m) long, long-bodied with relatively short, powerful legs placed far back on the body. The positioning of the legs makes it unlikely that the bird could have balanced on them and walked on land, but would have improved its swimming ability. It was unable to fly as the wings were reduced to mere vestiges and the keel of the breast-bone, to which the flight muscles are attached, was virtually absent.

The three species of *Hesperornis*, *H. regalis*, *H. crassipes* and *H. gracilis* are all separated on size with the former species being the largest. The second genus, *Coniornis*, is distinguished from *Hesperornis* by certain characters known from a single fragment of leg bone. The validity of this genus has been questioned in the past, and one author believed that it was in fact just a small species of the former genus. He regarded the osteological differences as representing merely individual variation or distortion caused by crushing during the process of fossilization.

Distribution. From the osteological and geological evidence it is possible to say that *Hesperornis* was a flightless swimming bird which lived in a warm marine environment, towards the end of the age of reptiles that included the great dinosaurs.

During an expedition in 1871 to the Niobrara Chalk, a marine sediment of western Kansas, Marsh collected the first example of this family. Shortly afterwards a more complete skeleton of *Hesperornis* was discovered and four years later Marsh described the two other species which came from the same horizon in Kansas. *Coniornis* was originally thought to have come from geologically younger rocks near the mouth of the Judith River in Montana. All

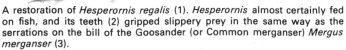

A restoration of *Hesperornis regalis* (1). *Hesperornis* almost certainly fed on fish, and its teeth (2) gripped slippery prey in the same way as the serrations on the bill of the Goosander (or Common merganser) *Mergus merganser* (3).

specimens are now regarded as being the same age and are about 80 million years old, coming from the Upper Cretaceous period.

Feeding. Being a flightless aquatic animal that possessed a body shape similar to the modern-day divers one can say without hesitation that *Hesperornis* obtained its food, which would almost certainly have consisted of fish, by diving. The toothed jaws would have helped in seizing and holding a struggling, slippery fish, but they could have been a hindrance when trying to swallow the prey. This bird appears to have overcome this problem by retaining the dinosaur-like joint between the lower jaw bones. It is thought that this articulation probably permitted rotation of the back part of the mandible independently of the front part, thus allowing a disengagement of the lower teeth from the prey as the mandible protruded.

Nesting. Although there is no evidence to show the type of nest this family would have built, it is reasonable to assume that because of its similarity to the modern divers, it would have had great difficulty in manoeuvering on land and would, therefore, have chosen a similar site: flat land that shelved gently to the water edge.

Composition. The Hesperornithidae are classified in two genera with four species and are: *Hesperornis regalis*, *H. crassipes*, *H. gracilis* and *Coniornis altus*.

As the fossil evidence of these early birds is so poor, one cannot say where this family should be placed on the evolutionary tree. The Lower Cretaceous family Enaliornithidae could have been an early forerunner of this family, but to what group of modern birds it is related is impossible to say.

ENALIORNIS

The Enaliornithidae consists of a single genus *Enaliornis* which has two species, *E. barretti* and *E. sedgwicki*. The remains of these two species were originally discovered over a hundred years ago in the Lower Cretaceous deposits in England, and are some of the earliest examples of birds known to man. The material, although fragmentary, includes many parts of the skeleton of at least two species,

distinguished from each other by their size and minor osteological characters. The larger of the two forms, *E. barretti*, includes a partial skull, vertebrae, pelvis and all the larger limb bones of the legs; the smaller species, *E. sedgwicki*, is more incomplete and only dorsal vertebrae and leg bones are known. The size of the larger species would have been considerably smaller than the smallest of our living divers. One author has likened its size to that of a large pigeon.

The characters of the hind portion of the skull appear to be diver-like, but it is impossible to say whether the jaws were toothed as in *Hesperornis*. No bones of the forelimb having been found, it seems reasonable to assume that *Enaliornis* was probably flightless.

Distribution. From the osteological evidence it is possible to say that *Enaliornis* was an aquatic bird that evolved early in the Cretaceous from an unknown ancestor. Its remains were discovered in 1858 in the Upper Greensand (Lower Cretaceous) deposits at Coldham Common between Grantchester and Cambridge in England, and are approximately 100 million years old.

Feeding. Taking all the evidence into account, it would seem reasonable to assume that this family consisted of flightless, diving species which lived upon marine animals, presumably fish.

Composition. The exact taxonomic position of the family Enaliornithidae is at present the centre of some controversy, for one author regards it as an early member of the order Gaviiformes which includes the divers or loons of our present-day avifauna, while another believes it to be an early example of the order Hesperornithiformes, an extinct group of diver-like birds which died out towards the end of the Cretaceous period about 80 million years ago, without leaving any obvious relatives. The latter view is reflected in the classification adopted for this volume.

BAPTORNIS

The Baptornithidae is composed of two genera, each with a single species; they are *Baptornis advenus* and *Neogaeornis wetzeli*. The fossil material from which *B. advenus* was described in 1877

Restoration of three members of the Hesperornithiformes: (1) *Enaliornis*, (2) *Hesperornis* and (3) *Baptornis*. Such restorations contain much guesswork: for years *Baptornis* was known from a single fossilized leg bone.

consisted only of a single leg bone; however, this material was enough to convince the author that he had a new extinct form. Although there is now some doubt as to whether the two halves of the bone belong to the same individual, one end appears to be from a young bird while the other is definitely adult in character, both undoubtedly belong to a diver-like bird somewhat larger than the present-day diver *Gavia immer*. Further bones have now been discovered, including a humerus and coracoid, which indicate that the forearm was small for a bird of its size, but perfectly formed and displaying the muscle impressions normally found on much larger wing bones. The impressions appear to imply the presence of quill feathers suggesting that the wings may have been functional and used in conjunction with the feet for locomotion under water. The genus *Neogaeornis* was founded upon a single leg bone in 1929.

Distribution. *Baptornis*, like its contemporaries *Hesperornis* and *Ichthyornis*, was found in the richly fossiliferous Niobrara Chalk of Kansas which is Upper Cretaceous in age and was deposited over 80 million years ago. *Neogaeornis* was collected from slightly younger rocks in Chile.

Feeding. As this family appears to have resembled the present-day divers or grebes, it is reasonable to assume that they dived for, and lived on marine organisms such as fish.

Composition. There has been much discussion during the past decade on the true affinities of this Upper Cretaceous family. Some authors would prefer to place it within the Hesperornithiformes, an extinct order of toothed, diver-like birds, while others have suggested that it should be included with the grebes in the order Podicipitriformes, and regarded as an early ancestor of the true grebes. The former view is adopted in this volume. The genus *Baptornis* is currently under review.

ICHTHYORNITHIFORMES

Unlike living birds these extinct species were equipped with teeth

ICHTHYORNIS — *Ichthyornithidae*
APATORNIS — *Apatornithidae*

ICHTHYORNIS

The family Ichthyornithidae is made up of a single genus *Ichthyornis*, which has seven species. These, and the species of the family Apatornithidae are at present the only known representatives of the extinct order Ichthyornithiformes. Like its contemporary *Hesperornis* (dawn-bird), *Ichthyornis* is commonly referred to as the 'fish bird', and is undoubtedly one of the more famous fossil birds. Since the first specimen was described by Marsh just over a hundred years ago, reconstructions of the skeleton can be found in many text-books as well as popular writings dealing with fossil birds.

The species often used for these reconstructions is *I. victor* and from its remains it is possible to obtain a good idea of what this family of birds looked like in life. *I. victor* was just over 8in (20cm) in height, had short legs, and is said to have resembled a tern. The characters of the skeleton, except for the rows of true teeth in the jaws, are similar to those found in modern flying birds, and include a well developed keel on the sternum (breast bone) which indicates good powers of flight.

Distribution. The remains of all the forms placed within the Ichthyornithidae have been found in North America. All but *I. lentus*, which was collected from the Austin Chalk of Texas, have been found in the Niobrara Chalk of Kansas. Both deposits are marine sediments, are Upper Cretaceous in age and are just over 80 million years old.

Feeding. Early work indicated that *Ichthyornis* was a toothed bird. Later, however, this conclusion was doubted because it was thought that the imperfect remains of one species, *I. dispar*, had been mixed with toothed jawbones from a young extinct marine reptile called a mosasaur. Subsequent discovery of new fossil material has shown that there is little doubt that *Ichthyornis* did, in fact, have teeth. It is reasonable to suppose that these teeth were used to hold slippery prey such as fish. What methods were used to catch these fish must remain purely speculative, but as the skeleton superficially resembles that of a modern tern, it is possible that *Ichthyornis* used the same methods found in that group.

Composition. The Ichthyornithidae and the closely related Apatornithidae can no longer be regarded as early ancestors of the Laridae (gulls and terns) as is shown in many family trees. It has been said that the skeleton of *Ichthyornis* is similar to that of a gull, but these similarities are only superficial, and it should be remembered that similarities do not necessarily indicate a direct relationship between animals. If a particular environment provides a niche for a certain mode of life, and demands a particular body type, then this structure is likely to evolve more than once in completely unrelated animals. This type of development is known as convergent evolution. A good example of such convergence is that between the Little auk *Plautus alle* of the Charadriiformes and the Diving petrel *Pelecanoides urinatrix* of the Procellariiformes. These birds are unrelated, but almost indistinguishable, and it would be difficult to tell them apart if they lived within the same region of the world.

APATORNIS

The Apatornithidae contains a single genus *Apatornis* which has two recognized species *A. celer* and *A. retusus*. The former species was originally thought to belong to the closely related genus of *Ichthyornis*, while the latter was until recently placed in the

Restoration of *Ichthyornis*. There is some doubt as to whether *Ichthyornis* had teeth, and its taxonomic position is therefore debatable.

Restorations of (1) *Ichthyornis* and (2) *Apatornis*. These birds may be closely related, but *Apatornis* is known only from fragmentary fossils.

Cimolopterygidae, an extinct family related to the gulls, terns, auks and waders of our modern bird fauna.

Unlike *Ichthyornis* the remains of this family are very fragmentary. The original material consisted of only a sacrum in the case of *A. celer*, although other material has now been found, while *A. retusus* is only known from the front portion of part of the shoulder girdle, the coracoid. From these bones, however, it is possible to say that the species of *Apatornis* fall within the same size range as those found in the family Ichthyornithidae, being approximately 7–8in (18–20cm) high. The wing elements appear to be not as well developed as those of its famous contemporary *Ichthyornis*, and it was probably a less capable flier. *A. retusus* appears to have been slightly larger than *A. celer*. In life this family, like the Ichthyornithidae, possibly resembled the modern terns.

Distribution. Like the closely related Ichthyornithidae the skeletal and geological evidence shows that this family lived close to water in a marine environment.

The fossil remains of this family are entirely restricted to the Upper Cretaceous deposits of North America and are approximately 80 million years old. *A. celer* was found in the Smoky Hill Chalk of Kansas, and *A. retusus* was collected from the Lance Formation of Wyoming.

Feeding. As the fossil evidence is so poor it is almost impossible to say how this family of birds obtained its food. If, however, one accepts that *Apatornis* is closely related to *Ichthyornis* it would be reasonable to assume that it possessed toothed jaws, and hunted for its food in the same way.

Composition. The two species placed within this family, *A. celer* and *A. retusus*, are founded upon very incomplete material and for this reason some doubt still remains as to the exact relationship between the Ichthyornithidae and Apatornithidae. *A. celer* was originally regarded as being a species of *Ichthyornis*, while *A. retusus* until 1963 was recognized as belonging to another order and was included in the Charadriiformes. This error was discovered when a close examination was made of the shoulder girdle of the two birds which showed that the two species were closely related. They were therefore included in the same genus. At the same time it was noted

that the coracoid of *A. retusus* bore some resemblance to those found in cormorants (Phalacrocoracidae). More complete material needs to be collected before it can be discovered if *Apatornis* is, in fact, related to cormorants, or if the current view, that the genus is related to *Ichthyornis*, is correct. If *Apatornis* is related to *Ichthyornis*, the similarities with cormorants must be regarded as the result of convergent evolution.

STRUTHIONIFORMES

The world's largest living bird lays eggs 6 inches long and 5 inches wide

OSTRICH — *Struthionidae*

OSTRICH

The Ostrich *Struthio camelus*, largest of living birds, is the only member of the family Struthionidae. Like most other flightless birds it is highly adapted for a terrestrial life, having very long and powerful legs, which, together with the elongated neck, make up a considerable part of the bird's height. A large male may stand at 8ft (2·5m) and weigh up to 300lb (135kg). The male body plumage is black while the more plumey wings and tail are white. The smaller females are duller, having a generally grey-brown plumage. In both sexes the head looks small in relation to the rest of the bird. Ostriches have unusually prominent black eyelashes, apart from which the head and most of the neck are almost bare, being sparsely covered with down and bristle-like feathers. The legs are also largely bare, the skin of the neck and legs being greyish or reddish.

The head of the Ostrich *Struthio camelus* showing the almost bare neck and long eyelashes.

In its bush environment the Ostrich is tolerated by herbivorous mammals and may even be of use to them, spotting danger from afar.

The Ostrich has only two toes on each foot, the original third and fourth digits – that corresponding to the third being much the larger. This is an adaptation to a predominantly running and walking mode of life, giving greater strength and thrust to the foot, as in the reduction of the horse's foot to one strong digit. Ostriches, with their long necks and keen eyes, are able to see considerable distances and their powerful legs make them capable of speeds up to 40mph (64kph), so that they can outpace most pursuers. They are commonly found, therefore, in open country where cover is slight, and are very difficult to approach, except in nature reserves where the birds have become accustomed to man.

Distribution. Up until about the first decade of the 20th century Ostriches were found in large numbers in many parts of Africa and southwest Asia, but they are now common in the wild only in parts of East Africa. There are also considerable numbers in Ostrich farms in South Africa and domesticated birds have become feral in South Australia.

There are six subspecies of *Struthio camelus*. The Arabian ostrich *S. c. syriacus*, now extinct, was fairly common in the deserts of Syria and Arabia until about 1914, but none has been recorded since 1941. It was ruthlessly hunted for its plumes and for sport. The southern form *S. c. australis* was once widely distributed through southern Africa but is now largely restricted to parts of Southwest Africa and Angola. This is the form which was first successfully domesticated for its plumes. The northern subspecies *S. c. camelus*, formerly much more widely distributed, is now found in steppe country south of the Sahara from the Niger in the west to Ethiopia in the east. Further to the west in Mauritania and Rio de Oro a fourth form *S. c. spatzi*, has been described. This is separated largely on the grounds of size, though the validity of the distinction has been disputed. The fifth and best known form is the Masai ostrich *S. c. massaicus* of southern Kenya and Tanzania. The Somali ostrich *S. c. molybdophanes*, a bird of the bush country, is found from northern Kenya to Ethiopia and Somalia.

Feeding. Ostriches are omnivorous, though the bulk of their food is usually of plant origin. They take a variety of fruits and seeds and also the leaves and shoots of shrubs, creepers and succulent plants. Some invertebrates and smaller vertebrates, such as lizards, are also eaten. Quantities of grit and stones are swallowed, aiding digestion by assisting in the grinding of resistant foods. Succulents provide a certain amount of moisture, while other elements in the diet, such as fruits and animals, also contribute. It is the acquisition of water in this way that has probably given rise to the supposition that ostriches can survive for long periods under desert conditions without water, which of course is not the case. They must either obtain water from their food or else have access to drinking water. They also bathe when they have the opportunity.

Nesting and the Young. Ostriches are polygamous. Varying numbers of females are recorded as forming the harem of a single male but this may be the result of differences in the availability of females rather than racial differences. The nest is a shallow pit dug in sandy soil and in this the eggs of all the females of a particular male are laid. Varying clutch sizes are recorded, from 15–60 eggs. It seems that each female lays from six to eight eggs, usually one every other day. The eggs vary in surface texture in the different subspecies, some smooth, some pitted, and there is also a certain amount of variation in size. The average egg is around 6in (15cm) long and 5in (13cm) wide, with a weight only 1·4% of that of the laying female. This is an unusually low figure for such a large bird.

The incubation period is around 40 days, rather short compared with other ratites, or flightless birds, possibly a development resulting from the considerable amount of predation to which the nests are subject. The male bird incubates at night but one or more of the females takes over for much of the day. A large proportion of eggs fails to hatch. An 'injury-feigning' distraction display may be performed by either or both of the sexes if danger threatens the eggs or young and, as in other birds, this is more frequent around the time of hatching. The young are precocial, following the parent as soon as they are dry, and being able to run as fast as the adult when only one month old.

Economic Importance. Ostriches have been farmed for their plumes in Cape Province in South Africa since the 1850s. In the early part of this century there were over 700,000 birds in captivity and Ostrich farming enterprises had also been started in North Africa, the USA and various European countries, as well as South Australia. But the First World War almost eliminated the industry and now there are

The courtship of a male Ostrich *Struthio camelus*.
Males are polygamous and
commonly have harems of ten females.

only about 25,000 birds in captivity in South Africa, principally for the production of high-quality leather.

Composition. The Struthionidae contains a single species which is divided into six subspecies, one of which, the Arabian ostrich *Struthio camelus syriacus*, is extinct.

RHEIFORMES

Large flightless birds from South America. A male may weigh more than 50 pounds

RHEAS – *Rheidae*

RHEAS

The rheas – South American equivalents of the Old World ostriches – are large, flightless birds capable of running long distances at high speed in the open country they generally inhabit. The larger of the two living species, the Common or Greater rhea *Rhea americana*, is the largest American bird – a male Common rhea might stand 5ft (1·6m) high and weigh 55lb (25kg). Like other flightless birds, rheas lack the keel on the breastbone which in flying birds supports the pectoral flight muscles. It is, however, quite certain that the ratites – flightless birds – are all descendants of flying forms that lost their powers of flight as they evolved into medium-sized grazing animals. Like the ostriches, rheas have characteristically long necks and legs. Similarly, they have no aftershaft to their loose, soft feathers, though this is a prominent feature of the Australasian emus and cassowaries. Rheas lack a hind toe (or hallux) and have only three toes, while ostriches have but two.

Distribution. Members of the Rheidae range from eastern Brazil, southern Bolivia and southeast Peru to Tierra del Fuego, where Darwin's rhea *Pterocnemia pennata* has been introduced. The

Common rhea is a bird of the pampas but Darwin's rhea has been found in the Andes at heights of up to 16,000ft (5,000m). Both species are gregarious and usually found in small parties of between 5 and 20 but flocks of up to 50 are sometimes encountered.

Behaviour. Although normally vegetarian, grazing, eating roots and seeds, rheas will readily eat insects, lizards and small mammals if the opportunity arises. Adult males, which are larger than the females, will fight for dominance at the beginning of the breeding season using their necks, beaks and powerful legs as weapons. Victorious males then choose territories encompassing some stretch of cover and set about courting the females. This entails wing-fluttering displays and an accompanying deep booming call by the male, who ultimately chooses the nest site and prepares it, by removing

The Common rhea *Rhea americana*, the largest American bird. A male is seen incubating on the nest which consists of a scrape on the ground.

vegetation from a natural hollow or making a scrape. He leads his harem of females to the nest and they often literally queue up to lay. Each female may lay up to as many as 18 eggs, though 15 is a more common figure, so that a male with a group of six or eight females might be responsible for around 100 eggs. Clutches of this enormity are, however, relatively rare.

The male, alone responsible for incubation, defends the nest, even against his own hens who may wish to lay further eggs. Often they will only manage to lay nearby and on such occasions the male will sometimes be prepared to roll the eggs into the nest. Incubation lasts about six weeks and the young then stay with their father who looks after them for a further four or five months, by which time they are almost fully grown. Parties of rheas will join other groups of grazing animals, like deer or even domestic cattle. If disturbed they will run far and fast with their wings raised above their backs to help them balance. Sometimes rather than flee from danger they will hide flat on the ground and, for birds of such considerable size, they are able to make themselves surprisingly inconspicuous.

Composition. The two living species differ in size; the Common rhea *Rhea americana* stands, on average, about 4·5ft (1·45m) and Darwin's rhea *Pterocnemia pennata*, just over 3ft (90cm); in colour of underparts, which are white in the Common rhea and brown with white spots in Darwin's rhea; and in the initial colour of the egg; that of the Common rhea starts golden, while that of Darwin's rhea starts green, though both fade. Four other species of rhea – all South American – have been described from fossils, the earliest being from an Eocene deposit about 50 million years old.

CASUARIIFORMES
Flightless birds with peculiar quills on their wings

CASSOWARIES – *Casuariidae*
EMU – *Dromaiidae*

CASSOWARIES

The cassowaries consist of three species of large flightless birds which are closely related to the emu. The Double-wattled cassowary is 6ft (1·8m) tall, the Single-wattled cassowary 5ft (1·6m) tall, and the Dwarf cassowary only 3½ft (1·1m) tall. Cassowaries live in the dense undergrowth of rain forests, and many of their most characteristic features are associated with life in these habitats.

They are flightless because they can find abundant supplies of food close to the ground and, because their habitat affords ample cover, the power of flight is not required to escape from enemies. The feathers on the wings are peculiar in that they consist only of quills which appear more like coarse hair than feathers, and which hang at the bird's side as it stands. The advantage of such feathers is that they are not easily damaged in dense, thorny vegetation. Another distinctive feature of the cassowary is the casque, a flattened horny crown which embellishes the head. In the Double-wattled cassowary the casque may be as high as 6in (15cm). The casque functions to protect the head from undergrowth by parting it as the cassowary thrusts forward in search of food.

Distribution. Cassowaries are found only in Australasia. The Double-wattled cassowary lives mainly in the rain forests of New

The three cassowary species. (1) Single-wattled cassowary *Casuarius un-appendiculatus*, (2) Papuan cassowary, once named *C. papuarius*, but now thought to be conspecific with the Single-wattled cassowary, (3) Double-wattled cassowary *C. casuarius* and (4) the Dwarf cassowary *C. bennetti*.

Guinea and the surrounding islands, as well as in northeastern Australia, while the Single-wattled cassowary is found in riverine and coastal swamp forests of New Guinea and adjacent islands. Finally, the Dwarf cassowary is also found in New Guinea and the surrounding islands, and inhabits montane forests, rarely below a height of 3,500ft (1,000m) and sometimes above a height of 10,000ft (3,000m).

Behaviour. Wild cassowaries have been recorded eating the fruit of various native and cultivated plants throughout the year, sometimes swallowing whole items as bulky as a large plum. Leaves have also been found in their gizzards, but it is also likely that other plant, and probably animal, food is taken at times when fruit is in short supply.

Cassowaries appear to have two distinct calls. The more usual call is a throbbing sound similar to that produced by the emu, while just before breeding, a grunting call is employed.

Very little has been recorded about the habits of any of the cassowaries. The birds appear to live in pairs and family parties, each pair defending a territory during the breeding season. Eggs are laid from May onwards, and have been found even in September in North Queensland. Incubation probably takes about seven weeks, and in captive birds the male undertakes the whole of the incubation, as does the emu. The clutches so far recorded range

Little is known of the habits of cassowaries, but they have been seen bathing, and appear to be good swimmers.

from three to eight eggs, and the nest is a scrape on the forest floor in the dense vegetation of the bird's normal habitat. The chicks are striped with a dark and light longitudinal pattern.

Composition. The three cassowary species are classified in a single genus *Casuarius* and are: *C. casuarius* the Double-wattled cassowary, *C. unappendiculatus* the Single-wattled cassowary, and *C. bennetti* the Dwarf cassowary. The first two species have, as their common names suggest, small wattles which hang from their throats. The bare head is brightly coloured in purple, red, orange or yellow, and is probably used in sexual display, the colour developing and changing as the young bird matures.

EMU

The only extant member of the Dromaiidae, the Emu *Dromaius novaehollandiae* is the most widespread of the Australian continent's flightless birds and, after the African ostrich *Struthio camelus*, the world's second largest living bird. Emus vary in height from 5–6ft (1·5–1·8m). Adult females weigh about 90lb (41kg) and

Cassowary feathers are unlike those of flying birds in that they lack barbules and are coarse and hair-like. Their structure prevents damage by the dense undergrowth in which cassowaries live.

males 80lb (36kg). The female of a pair is usually larger than the male, in other dimensions as well as body weight.

Emus are brown, although when the feathers are new after the moult, they look almost black, fading to pale brown with age. The bases of the feathers are white. Each feather has two identical shafts, with the barbs so widely spaced that they do not interlock to form the firm vane as do the feathers of most birds. Rather they form a loose, hair-like body covering. The feathers growing out from the back near the base of the spine differ from those covering the rest of the bird in having longer barbs and being set very far apart indeed, looking even looser than the body feathers and giving the appearance of a mop-like 'tail'. The skin on the neck and head is often free of feathers and has a more or less bluish tinge. The intensity of this colour varies according, apparently, to the season of the year and also in response to moment-to-moment changes in its surroundings and the behaviour of other nearby birds. The sexes are similar in plumage except in the period prior to egg laying, when the female's head and neck are densely covered with black feathers. In addition the dense white feather bases of the male's lower neck feathers are conspicuous at this time, giving his neck a striking, pale appearance, particularly from the front.

The legs are unfeathered and so long that a running bird can make a stride of 9ft (2·7m) with ease. Emus have three toes, compared with the two of the ostrich, and the underside of each toe is flattened with a broad pad. The bill is broad and soft, adapted for

Cassowaries have long claws and a dagger-like spike on each foot with which enemies are attacked. They are known to have killed humans in their native New Guinea.

browsing and grazing. The wings, though only one tenth of the body length, appear to assist the bird in cooling itself. In hot conditions they are held out from the side and the bare 'under arm,' with its plexus of superficial blood vessels, is exposed to facilitate cooling by evaporation.

Distribution. Nowadays only one species exists but at the time of the first European settlement three other island species occurred along Australia's southern coast: the Kangaroo Island emu, the King Island emu and the Tasmanian emu. All three species were exterminated soon after permanent settlements were established. Today Emus occur throughout the Australian mainland, from the highest mountains to the coast.

Feeding. Adult Emus feed mainly on fruits, flowers, insects, seeds and green vegetation. Caterpillars, beetles and grasshoppers are taken in large quantities when abundant. The seeds and pods of many pea-like shrubs and trees are a staple food source in summer. The large fruits of a wide variety of shrubs and trees of other species, differing from locality to locality, are commonly eaten in the spring. Grass and herbage form the bulk of the autumn and winter food and Emus will sometimes graze clover leys at this season. Quite large stones are ingested into the gizzard to aid the grinding process, single pebbles as large as 1in (2·5cm) in diameter being quite commonly taken.

Nesting and the Young. The birds usually breed in the winter months, May–August, throughout their range, but occasional out-of-season nests are found, particularly after rain in the interior. Most breeding units are of a single pair. The nest is a low platform of twigs or leaves, generally placed so that the sitting bird has a clear outlook, often downhill. The male does not begin sitting until five to nine eggs have been laid. In average seasons a hen will lay from 9–12 eggs, each weighing 1–1½lb (0·5–0·7kg). The male carries out the whole incubation process which takes about eight weeks and during this time he hardly eats and does not drink. Indeed he seldom leaves the nest, rising daily only to turn the eggs. The incubation temperature of 91°F (33°C) is low compared with that of most birds.

The tiny chicks leave the nest after two or three days and may often be seen leading their father rather than being led by him. They feed extensively on green vegetation and insects in their first weeks. At first their plumage is cream with brown longitudinal stripes, and dark dots on the head, but as they grow the stripes become less conspicuous and the chicks gradually acquire a dappled appearance, differing from their parents in the dense black feathering of the head.

Emus have two main calls, a guttural grunt and a throbbing drum. The grunts are most commonly given by the male in the two or three months prior to egg laying. The drumming call is also frequently given at this time, and again by the hen towards the end of incubation. Both sexes drum when alarmed.

Composition. The Emu *Dromaius novaehollandiae* is the sole surviving member of the Dromaiidae. Three island species, the Kangaroo Island emu, the King Island emu and the Tasmanian emu, became extinct soon after the colonization of Australia. All three were considerably smaller than the mainland species.

AEPYORNITHIFORMES
Extinct ostrich-like birds known only from Africa

ELEPHANT BIRDS — *Aepyornithidae*

ELEPHANT BIRDS

The family Aepyornithidae is at present made up of four extinct genera; *Eremopezus*, *Stromeria*, *Mullerornis* and *Aepyornis*, and is placed within its own order Aepyornithiformes. This group, commonly referred to as the 'Elephant birds', belongs to the rather loose assemblage of flightless running birds collectively called the ratites, which includes the Ostrich, rheas, cassowaries, Emu and kiwis amongst our living bird fauna.

Eremopezus and *Stromeria* are thought to be the earliest representatives of the family, their remains having been found in Tertiary rocks of North Africa that are up to 60 million years old. Both genera have been described from single leg bones although fragments of egg shell, sometimes referred to as *Psammornis*, have been attributed to *Eremopezus*.

The remains of *Aepyornis* and the smaller *Mullerornis* are 2 million years old or less, having been found in Pleistocene and Holocene deposits of Madagascar. Their skeletons are well-known, and must have resembled the Ostrich in life. The head was small. The wings were reduced to mere vestiges, but the legs were long and powerful and used for running. The foot, unlike that of the Ostrich, normally had four toes although the rear toe is sometimes absent. The largest species *A. maximus* (*A. titan*) attained a height of over 10ft (3m) and probably inspired some of the legends of the past such as that of the Rukh, or Roc of Sinbad the sailor and Marco Polo.

Distribution. The whole family, except for a single record of *Eremopezus* from Arabia, appears to have been restricted to North Africa and Madagascar. *Eremopezus* is recorded from Eocene deposits of Egypt, Libya and Algeria that are about 40 million years old. The genus *Stromeria* is found in Egypt in rocks that are thought to be from the slightly younger deposits of the Lower Oligocene.

Aepyornis and *Mullerornis* are only known from Pleistocene and Holocene rocks of the island of Madagascar. The exact date of their extinction is not known, but dates acquired from some egg shells show that at least some species were still alive less than one thousand years ago.

Eggs and Nests. The nests of the Madagascan aepyornithids probably resembled those of the present-day ratites. The eggs which are creamy-white, are still found buried in the sand on the shores where they were laid many thousands of years ago. The largest known specimen measures 3ft (1m) in its largest circumference and its liquid content would have been over 2gal (4·5l). It is possible that both *Aepyornis* and *Mullerornis* were used as a food source by man and eventually exterminated by him through over exploitation.

Composition. The exact relationship between *Eremopezus* and *Stromeria* of mainland Africa and *Aepyornis* and *Mullerornis* of Madagascar must remain in doubt until more complete material has been found. If the two Tertiary genera are indeed ancestral to the later forms then one can say that the concentration of species in

The Emu *Dromaius novaehollandiae*. The adult head (1) is bare, but covered with dark feathers in young birds (2). A male is seen in its typical sitting position (3) and protecting its chicks (4).

Madagascar represented the last stand of the order which once had a wider distribution.

The interrelationships between the ratites have long puzzled zoologists as it is uncertain whether they are a natural group or merely an assemblage of unrelated forms that have followed parallel lines of evolution. It has been stated recently, however, that the ratites are related through a common ancestor from South America which, by successive invasions via the Antarctic before the breakup and migration of the continents into their present global positions, reached their final destinations. The Madagascan birds probably reached that island before its separation from Africa.

DINORNITHIFORMES

Huge birds from New Zealand. One or more species survived until the last century

MOAS — *Dinornithidae*
ANOMALOPTERYX — *Anomalopterygidae*

MOAS

The Dinornithidae is one of two families of extinct, extremely large running birds of New Zealand. Sub-fossil and even unfossilized remains have been recovered and make it possible to attempt an accurate classification. The six species in the genus *Dinornis* include the largest and best-known of the moas, *D. maximus*, which stood some 10ft (3m) or more in height and was entirely wingless, with appropriately strong hindlimbs. Like other moas it had a relatively small head, but one equipped with a strong beak for the collection and manipulation of the plant materials on which it fed.

Distribution. The moas were at one time a highly successful group of flightless birds, related to the Ostrich *Struthio camelus*, and found in both islands of New Zealand. Like certain other flightless birds such as the Dodo and the Great auk, moas were able to develop so successfully because of their isolation from significant competitors or predators. It seems that they evolved rapidly in the favourable New Zealand environment, though the fossil record does not go back very far. But during the late Pleistocene and early recent times in New Zealand there was a great deal of geographical and ecological instability and the moas suffered accordingly. Man undoubtedly contributed to their extinction but not so significantly as in many other specialized faunas. One or more species apparently survived well into the 19th century, but the majority are thought to have become extinct by the end of the 17th century.

Behaviour. Moas were almost entirely herviborous, taking a wide variety of plant food. They had to eat a larger amount of food than a carnivore of corresponding bulk to obtain the same food value, and their adaptations are centred around this feeding requirement. Their carriage resembled that of the emus, the neck being looped forward rather than held upright as in the Ostrich. (This is shown by their skeletal structure though most illustrations fail to make the distinction.) And they had large muscular gizzards, some of which have been found complete with grinding stones.

Such large, and at one time plentiful, species were of course an important item of food for the local human population and the early Polynesians, who settled in New Zealand rather less than 1,000 years ago, developed a moa-hunting culture. Findings of the most recently-existing moa remains indicate a continuing importance to Maori hunters. Even the smallest moas – roughly turkey-sized – would have been useful food items. But the full story of the extinction of the moas is not known.

Composition. The Dinornithidae contains a single genus, *Dinornis*, which is composed of six species. New Zealand's North and South Islands each have three species which are distinguished according to height.

ANOMALOPTERYX

The Anomalopterygidae (Emeidae) is one of the two families which make up the extinct order that contains the Moas, the Dinornithiformes. The family is now divided into two subfamilies Anomalopteryginae and Emeinae, each of which has three genera. The fossil record shows that the whole order is restricted to the islands of New Zealand.

From the vast amount of material collected it is possible to obtain a good idea of the size and outward appearance of many members of the family. The larger forms, *Emeus* and *Pachyornis*, attained a height of 5ft (1·75m) while the smallest, *Anomalopteryx*, was no larger than a Turkey. Like the larger Dinornithidae they were powerful running birds which were completely flightless for they had no wings. Although the original remains were likened to the Ostrich it is now known that they must have had the looped neck stance of the Emu and cassowaries rather than the erect carriage seen in the Ostrich and rheas. A few feathers have been found with the remains of *Megalapteryx* and are said to be much less 'degenerate' than those of other struthios birds. There is enough vein structure preserved to show that at least some of the plumage was purplish-black with buff tips.

Distribution. The sites where the remains of Moas have been found show that they favoured the foothills adjacent to low country. The smaller and more agile, *Megalapteryx* and *Anomalopteryx*, however, appear to have been montane in habit.

Behaviour. Like the Dinornithidae members of this family were herbivorous, and the remains of their stomach contents show that they ate a wide variety of plant material.

The largest moa *Dinornis maximus* (1) and the largest Elephant bird *Aepyornis maximus* (2). Both birds lived until relatively recent times and may well have been seen by primitive man; their colours are hypothetical.

Two species of kiwi. (1) The Brown kiwi *Apteryx australis* and (2) the Little spotted kiwi *Apteryx owenii*.

Very little is known about the nest and nesting habits of this group, but discoveries of several nests of *Anomalopteryx* in two North Island districts by W. H. Hartree has provided some information. He found, without exception, that the nests contained the remains of only one egg or single chicks in scooped nests, situated in sheltered positions in forested areas. The eggs were not particularly large or their shells abnormally thick and they were either white or pale green in colour.

One cannot put an exact date on the extermination for each genus, but *Euryapteryx* was still plentiful on Stewart Island and the east coast of South Island 600–800 years ago, but had disappeared 300–400 years later. *Anomalopteryx* is thought to have been still part of the avifauna 200 years ago and, according to an eye-witness account, *Megalapteryx* was still in existence during the nineteenth century. There is no doubt that the moas were very important to Maoris as a source of food and for tools which they made out of their bones.

Composition. The family Anomalopterygidae has been divided into two subfamilies which have three genera allocated to each and are: *Anomalopteryx*, *Megalapteryx*, *Pachyornis* (Anomalopteryginae); and *Emeus*, *Euryapteryx*, *Zelornis* (Emeinae).

APTERYGIFORMES

These flightless nocturnal birds are the national emblem of New Zealand

KIWIS — *Apterygidae*

KIWIS

Kiwis are flightless birds from New Zealand. They rival penguins or dinosaurs for a place in popular illustration and, like them, still lack much fundamental scientific elucidation. The kiwi is the national emblem of New Zealand, but rather few New Zealanders (themselves commonly termed 'kiwis') have seen a live kiwi even in zoos where their nocturnal habits necessitate special conditions for viewing. In many parts of New Zealand, however, kiwis are abundant and the tramper in dense forests, modestly called bush, will almost certainly hear their characteristic calls even if he is ignorant of the identity of the animal making them.

With a rounded body, some 14 to 22in (35 to 55cm) in length, no tail and only a hint of wings, the kiwi is some 15in (38cm) high. Females are noticeably larger than males. A small, compressed head leads to a long, curved bill with nostrils at its tip, the upper mandible bent over the end of the lower. The whole body is covered with feathers resembling a shaggy coat of ruffled brown hair. The eyes are very small. At the base of the bill are long hair-like feathers, probably organs of touch, standing out like whiskers. Strong, short legs and claws, used for defence and feeding, are conspicuous.

Kiwis, the smallest and most anomalous of the ratites, that group of flightless birds with wings reduced, lacking barbules on the feathers, and with little or no keel on the breastbone for the attachment of flight muscles, may be polyphyletic, that is, derived from more than one evolutionary line. Their German name 'Schnepfenstrauss', or woodcock-ostrich, reminds us of their complex relationships, but there is little doubt that kiwis are descendants of early birds that were able to fly. The enormous egg is also a remarkable feature, one of considerable evolutionary and physiological significance.

Distribution. Kiwis are found only in New Zealand. Of the three forms of Brown kiwi, one is limited to the North Island in forest areas north of about latitude 40° S. The South Island form lives in high rainfall districts in the west and southwest. A third form lives only on Stewart Island, the most southerly of the main islands of New Zealand. Of the two kinds of Spotted kiwi, the smaller occurs in high rainfall districts of the South Island although mainly to the west of the dividing alps, and the larger is found in the South Island also west of the main divide but not so far to the south and northeast although its range crosses the mountain passes to the eastern foothills.

Feeding. Kiwi feeding grounds can be readily recognized by the series of deep, crater-like beak marks in the soil showing where the birds have been probing, using their long beaks to enlarge an initial opening from which their prey is gradually eased out. As many as 30 holes up to 5in (12·5cm) in diameter have been seen in one area of 25sq ft (2·3sq m).

According to popular belief, kiwis feed largely on worms. However, insects and their larvae, other arthropods, as well as berries and other plant material, are regularly taken. The North Island kiwi can be a significant predator of pasture pests, especially scarabaeid beetle larvae. Their diet may vary from time to time and from place to place. Cultivated vegetables, such as peas, marrows and cabbage, are also taken.

A Brown kiwi *Apteryx australis* at its nest (1). It rarely lays more than three eggs. A subspecies of the Brown kiwi, the North Island kiwi *Apteryx australis mantelli* (2) drinking.

Because of the problem of getting sufficient food for numbers of injured kiwis often held at its Mt Bruce Native Bird Reserve, the New Zealand Wildlife Service is experimenting with artificial diets including milk powder and vegetable oil mixes, though with dubious success.

Feeding range is limited by suitable habitats. Where extermination of browsing animals allows regrowth of forest floor plants, kiwis extend their feeding areas noticeably. Feeding on pastures shows that they take advantage of new sources of food. Although kiwis do not normally drink water, presence of fatty acids in the skin has suggested that they may feed on aquatic animals and that their distribution may be related to watersheds.

Nesting and the Young. Kiwis nest in holes beneath tree roots or in burrows, one of which with an entrance resembling a large rabbit hole was 12ft (3·6m) long, and set in an open area of bush near the top of a steep bank. Two tracks, kept free of debris, led away from it. Twigs, grass and feathers are sometimes used as a lining.

The eggs weigh about 1lb (450g) and measure 5 by $3\frac{1}{2}$in (13 by 9cm), and are laid between July and February. One or two eggs, very rarely three, form the clutch. Twin chicks have been reared in captivity. Only the male incubates although the female may help in building the burrow. Kiwis are the only birds in which both left and right ovaries consistently occur (in other birds only the left ovary is normally functional). The kiwi lays an egg which, relative to its body weight, is the largest known. The egg of the North Island kiwi is about 12·5% of the body weight.

Incubation lasts 75 to 78 days or longer, during which the male may stay with the egg for as long as a week at a time. Chicks are not fed for the first 6 to 12 days but are then able to pick up food helped by the male. The chick does not have a downy stage being feathered at birth. Growth is slow and breeding age may be reached in five or six years although the mating and egg-laying of a female North Island kiwi of estimated age of two years with a male of three years was reported at the Otorohanga Zoo in 1972.

Behaviour. The Maori people alluded to the kiwi as 'Te manu huna a Tane', the hidden bird of Tane, god of the forest, drawing attention to its nocturnal habits. Relatively little is known about the behaviour of the kiwi for this reason although a few daytime observations of feeding have been made. By day, kiwis hide in burrows or under logs. At night, they become active and, calling loudly and continuously snuffling dog-like, move through the forest scratching at the undergrowth with their strong feet and probing into soft soil for food. Mating behaviour has been observed at the Otorohanga Zoo. Pre-mating calling is done by the male but displays as such do not occur probably because of the poor vision of the birds and the lack of display apparatus such as coloured feathers.

The voice of the kiwi is a shrill, rather mournful, two-part whistle emitted by the male. The female, in contrast, has a lower, hoarser, deep-throated cry. Although the *ki-wi* call has given the bird its name, the Maoris also distinguished the male call as *koire!*, the female as *ho! ho! ho!* and the young birds as *pio* or *rire-rire*. Some differences in pitch and intervals are evident amongst the three forms of the Brown kiwi.

Economic Importance. In pre-European times the kiwi was widely used for food. Its feathers were greatly sought for ornamenting fine cloaks of woven flax, now among the more historic and prized of Maori heirlooms. European settlers also took the kiwi for food and there was a considerable export of skins and feathers for ladies' costumes. Even by 1877, kiwis were becoming rare, the famous Austrian collector Andreas Reischek paying £40 for four pairs of '*Apteryx australis*, the Alpine kiwi . . . regarded as extinct, no specimen having been found for the last five years.' Since 1908, kiwis have been totally protected by law. To-day there is great public appreciation and interest in their conservation. Kiwis often fall victim to traps or poison laid for such vermin as the introduced Australian Brush-tailed opossum. The New Zealand Wildlife Service has tried, with notable success, to educate hunters in methods of setting traps that do not harm kiwis as well as in breaking dogs from chasing them. Farmers and landowners are encouraged to save small areas of forest or scrub from clearing. Kiwis are now in a healthy state, having made a pleasing return from their former threatened position, but a continual regard is still held for their safety and welfare.

Composition. The family Apterygidae, comprising the entire order Apterygiformes, contains only the single genus *Apteryx* which is divided into two groups based largely on differences in external appearance. The striated kiwis consist of the Brown kiwis which are divided into three races: the North Island subspecies *Apteryx australis mantelli*, the smallest and darkest coloured with dark legs and stiffened tips to the feathers giving a harsh touch; the South Island kiwi *A. a. australis*, with duller, lighter and softer plumage and pale legs; and the Stewart Island race *A. a. lawryi*, rather browner but larger with dark legs. The Spotted kiwis differ considerably in size and colouring although often regarded as subspecies. The Little spotted kiwi *Apteryx owenii* is predominantly grey, but the Great spotted kiwi *A. haasti* has a more chestnut-brown colouring on the back apart from its much larger size. The phylogenetic relationships of the kiwis are by no means settled. As recently as 1960, Verheyen proposed a new genus for *Apteryx owenii*. Other forms, including a large variety of *A. owenii* described as *A. occidentalis*, have been recognized but all are now generally accepted within the three readily definable species despite their considerable geographic variation.

From studies of the tongue, McCann recently concluded that the spotted kiwis are distinct from the striated forms and suggested evolutionary divergence following early separation in type of habitat occupied. Feather lice of the genus *Rallicola* found on kiwis indicate the validity of the taxonomic divisions in that there is one species *R. gadowi* on each of the three subspecies of *Apteryx australis* with different species *R. gracilentus* and *R. pilgrimi* on *A. haasti* and *A. oweni* respectively. The two latter species of lice are more closely related to each other than to *R. gadowi*. Such ancillary studies, together with evidence from serology, egg white proteins and other biochemical techniques, may well assist the purely morphological analyses of interspecific relationships of the kiwis.

TINAMIFORMES
Partridge-like birds probably related to the rheas

TINAMOUS — *Tinamidae*

TINAMOUS

Tinamous are partridge-like birds with plump bodies and short, rounded wings. The 45–50 species of tinamous are all rather closely related to each other, but their distinctness from other groups of birds is emphasized by their being placed in their own order, the Tinamiformes. Various anatomical characters suggest they are more closely related to rheas (Rheidae) and other large ratite birds than to other groups, although they differ from the ratites in being

Two species of tinamou. (1) The Martineta (or Crested) tinamou *Eudromia elegans* and (2) the Chilean tinamou *Nothoprocta perdicaria*. A Variegated tinamou *Crypturellus variegatus* is shown hiding in grass. Tinamous are weak fliers and often escape from danger by hiding rather than flying.

able to fly and consequently in having a keel on the sternum for attachment of the flight muscles.

Tinamous range from 8–21in (20–53cm) in length and bear a superficial resemblance to short-tailed game-birds. Like many game-birds, they have a proportionately small head, a rather long and slender neck, a plump body, rather short and rounded wings and strong legs and feet with the hind toe either absent or inserted some way up on the back of the tarsus. The bill tends to be longer than in most game-birds, and rather slender with a decurved tip. The tail is very short and soft; commonly it is hidden beneath a thick pad of rump feathers which makes many tinamous seem to have the rear part of the body held high.

Distribution. The family Tinamidae is entirely confined to the Neotropical zoogeographical region, with the greatest diversity of species on the South American continent. Four species are found in southern Mexico, although one of them ranges south to Costa Rica (Slaty-breasted tinamou *Crypturellus boucardi*) and the other three range south to South America (Great tinamou *Tinamus major*, Little tinamou *Crypturellus soui* and Rufescent tinamou *Crypturellus cinnamomeus*). Besides these four, the only other tinamou occurring north of South America is the Highland tinamou *Nothoprocta bonapartei* which ranges from the highlands of Costa Rica and western Panama to northwest South America.

In South America tinamous range south to southern Argentina and Chile. They are absent from Tierra del Fuego, although Ingouf's tinamou *Tinamotis ingoufi* occurs south to Magallanes in Chile and several other species occur in the cold puna zone of the southern Andes. The Chilean tinamou *Nothoprocta perdicaria* was introduced to Easter Island in the 1890s and still survives there.

All five Central American tinamous and a majority of the South American species inhabit forests, woodland and scrub. Some species are confined to high elevations in montane forests, but the majority are found only in the lowlands or range up to middle elevations.

Some of the South American species inhabit open grasslands. For example, the Chilean tinamou inhabits wheat fields and semi-arid grasslands and Pentland's tinamou *Nothoprocta pentlandii* occurs in grasslands and terraced alfalfa fields at around 10,000ft (3,300m) elevation in the Chilean Andes.

Feeding. Very little detailed information is available on the food of tinamous. The contents of crops and stomachs of specimens suggest that seeds, fruit and other vegetable matter such as roots and buds make up the bulk of the diet. Insects and other small animals are also eaten, especially by species of the genus *Nothoprocta*, and the young of some species may subsist almost entirely on insects. Species of *Rhynchotus* have been recorded occasionally swallowing mice.

The presence of a large crop and caeca suggest that the diet consists mainly of vegetable matter, but more detailed investigation is needed as soft insects tend to pass unnoticed in investigations of bird stomach contents due to the rapidity with which they are digested.

Nesting and the Young. Tinamous are one of a few unrelated groups of birds in which the sexual roles are largely reversed in care of the eggs and young. Similar systems occur in button-quail, phalaropes and a few plovers. So far as is known, only male tinamous incubate and care for the young, and it is known that in *Nothoprocta* only the male acquires a bare incubation patch on the abdomen. The larger average size of female tinamous compared to males (as with phalaropes) is probably related to this reversal of the usual sexual roles.

The nest is built on the ground and varies from an unlined hollow to a substantial cup of grass or sticks. Clutches vary from 1–12 eggs, the larger clutches probably resulting from more than one female. The eggs are relatively large with a very glossy surface and are variously brown, purple, nearly black, grey, yellow-green or deep green. The incubation period is rather short, being 19–20 days in several species.

The chicks are active soon after hatching and can run well within a few days. They have thick down with concealing patterns of dark colours.

Behaviour. Most tinamous have mellow flute-like whistling calls. These are often loud and may be the only indication that the birds are present in the concealment of forest undergrowth. These whistling and trilling calls, given by both sexes in some species, may function in territory defence.

Many species occur solitarily or in small groups throughout the year, but some open-country species flock outside the breeding season. Up to 100 adult Martineta tinamous *Eudromia elegans* may occur in a single flock, although smaller groups are more usual.

Economic Importance. Tinamous are not of great economic importance, although a few species cause slight damage by eating grain and other seeds. In much of Central and South America they are prized as sporting birds or simply trapped for their meat, which is very tender with a strangely translucent appearance.

Composition. There are about 50 species classified into nine genera. Further study may extend or decrease the number of species recognized, as many forms are rather similar in appearance or replace each other geographically.

SPHENISCIFORMES

Seabirds almost entirely restricted to the southern hemisphere. The largest stands 3 feet tall

PENGUINS — *Spheniscidae*

PENGUINS

The penguins are a distinctive group of seabirds, restricted almost entirely to the southern hemisphere and commonest in the cooler waters of the southern ocean. The largest, the Emperor penguin *Aptenodytes forsteri* of the Antarctic, stands 3ft (1m) tall and weighs on average 65lb (30kg); the smallest is the Little blue penguin *Eudyptula minor* of Australia and New Zealand, standing 1ft (30cm) high and weighing 2–2½lb (1–1·2kg). Flightless, and highly adapted for swimming, penguins have a compact, stream-lined and powerful body with a large strongly-keeled breastbone and massive pectoral muscles. The wings lack flight feathers and cannot be folded; in use they form flat, scimitar-shaped paddles, which propel the birds rapidly through the water. The legs are set well back along the body, giving upright stance and rolling gait; penguins walk, run, hop and climb efficiently on rock and ice. The feet, with fleshy webs and strong nails, trail behind in the water and are used for braking and steering.

Short, curved feathers cover the body, each with an aftershaft of dense down. The tips of the feathers overlap, like tiles on a roof, forming an oily and watertight outer garment; the down forms a warm shirt beneath, keeping the skin dry. This double layer of plumage, often enhanced by a wadding of blubber beneath the skin, protects the birds against excessive heat losses both in the sea and on land.

Most penguins are white on chest and abdomen; Emperors alone are pale lemon yellow. Most are black dorsally, fading to brown when exposed to strong sunlight; dorsal feathers are usually blue-tipped and may be slate grey (King penguins *Aptenodytes patagonicus*), pale powder blue (White-flippered penguins *Eudyptula albasignata*) or darker blue turning green when wet (Little blue penguins). In some species of warm climates the throat and chest are banded or dappled with black, perhaps making the birds more difficult to see from below in sunlit surface waters. Nearly all the features distinguishing genera and species are borne on the head and neck, showing clearly when the birds are swimming on the surface with head erect. The feathered crest of penguins in the genus *Eudyptes*, the golden auricular patches in the genus *Aptenodytes*, and the cranial crest and white eye-ring of the Adélie penguin *Pygoscelis adeliae* are featured in courtship and aggressive displays.

Penguins are intensely social, and usually found in groups both at sea and on land; distinctive rallying calls help them to find each other. Most polar and sub-polar species breed communally in huge

colonies, some numbering several million pairs. Tropical and temperate species generally breed in smaller groups, usually in caves or burrows, among tall tussock grass, or in forests close to the water's edge, where they are safe from strong sun and aerial predators.

Resting or swimming slowly at sea they lie low in the water, like grebes or cormorants, paddling gently with the flippers. In more active swimming they submerge completely, 'porpoising' at intervals: this allows them to breathe without reducing swimming speed, which is normally 5–10mph (8–16kph) but might reach 15mph (24kph) in short bursts. Most of the small penguins live and feed close to the surface. Emperor and King penguins are believed to dive deeper for their food: one Emperor fitted with a depth recorder was found to dive to 880ft (268m). Small species seldom dive for longer than two minutes; Emperors often stay under for four to six minutes and have been known to dive for 18 minutes or more.

(1) An Emperor penguin with a chick protected from the cold by its parent's feet and (2) Adélie penguins *Pygoscelis adeliae* diving.

Distribution. Of the 18 living species three (the Emperor, the Adélie and the Chinstrap penguin *Pygoscelis antarctica*) live entirely in the Antarctic region, where the largest colonies and greatest densities of penguins are found. Three species (the Galapagos penguin *Spheniscus mendiculus*, the Peruvian penguin *S. humboldti*, and the Blackfoot penguin *S. demersus*) are entirely tropical. The remaining species are widely distributed in the southern oceans, with the greatest variety in cold temperate and sub-Antarctic waters. Six species breed on New Zealand and its offshore islands, five on the Falkland Islands, and four on South Georgia. Most of the small islands of the South Atlantic and Indian Oceans have two or more resident species. In South America the Magellanic penguin *Spheniscus magellanicus* breeds on the mainland coasts of Patagonia and Chile, the Peruvian or Humboldt penguin on guano islands off the Peruvian coast. Australia has resident Little blue penguins along its southern coasts, almost to Fremantle in the west and Sydney in the east. Offshore islands of southern Africa are the home of the Black-footed penguins. The most northerly species is the Galapagos penguin, which breeds in small numbers on the western islands of the group.

Feeding. Penguins feed exclusively at sea. In every species mouth

Penguin species drawn to scale to show size variation. (1) Emperor *Aptenodytes forsteri*, (2) Chinstrap *Pygoscelis antarctica*, (3) Schlegel's *Eudyptes schlegeli* and (4) the Little blue penguin *Eudyptula minor*.

and tongue are lined with fleshy, backward pointing spines, which help in holding slippery prey. All have powerful bills with sharp cutting edges, and the different shapes of bill may to some degree be related to food preferences. Emperors and Kings, the largest penguins, hunt in deep water for squid and fish; smaller species feed in surface waters, taking shoaling crustaceans, small squid and fish. Polar penguins take krill – red shrimp-like crustaceans of the genus *Euphausia* – and larval fish, both plentiful in the cold ocean throughout summer. Species of warmer waters take 'false krill' (larvae of bottom-living crabs) and fish, including the shoaling forms which abound in the rich, cool currents off South America, South Africa and Australia. The largest breeding colonies occur where the sea is richest and the food most plentiful.

Penguins usually have to swim several miles to offshore feeding grounds. Chicks are fed by regurgitation: the freshly caught food is held in the parent's capacious crop, preserved from digestion during the long journey home, and meted out to the chicks on demand. Penguins drink both fresh water and sea water; salt glands above the eyes help them to excrete surplus salts from their body when fresh water is not available. Polar species eat snow copiously, especially on warm summer days when they lose water by panting.
Behaviour. Most penguins breed once a year. Polar and temperate species generally breed in spring, so that the chicks reach independence while food is still plentiful; tropical penguins have a less restricted season. Adélie penguins cross the sea ice to their traditional Antarctic breeding grounds in mid October; individual partnerships often re-form on the site of the previous year. Pairs

build pebble nests and lay two eggs; courtship, which is often marked by boundary disputes and fighting, lasts two to three weeks, during which neither partner feeds. Males take the first spell of incubation (a further two weeks of fasting); the females return to sea, over ice which by this time is usually starting to disperse. Incubation lasts 42 days, with the partners taking turns at four to seven day intervals. By hatching time the ice has dispersed, allowing the birds to feed close at hand. The chicks, clothed in heavy down, are fed by both parents: they moult and leave for the sea in February and March. Adults moult in late summer, leaving the colony areas as the inshore ice begins to form. Both adults and young winter on the pack ice offshore.

Emperor penguins return to their Antarctic colonies in early winter, courting and laying a single egg on newly formed sea ice in May–June. Only the males incubate, holding the single egg on their feet for two months, huddling together for warmth in the coldest part of winter at temperatures of $-58°F$ ($-50°C$). Females return as the eggs hatch, and both parents feed the growing chicks through late winter and spring. This regime ensures that the chicks, which take longer to grow than Adélies, reach independence as the sea ice begins to disperse in summer. King penguins, breeding in the sub-Antarctic, lay a single egg in spring but keep the partly-grown chicks on the colonies through their first winter; the chicks complete their growth, fatten, moult and leave for the sea in the following spring. Most temperate and tropical species build nests of stones, sticks or moss, often in burrows, and lay two or three eggs.
Composition. There are six genera: *Aptenodytes* (Emperor, King, with golden auricular patches and mauve bill plates) and *Pygoscelis* (Adélie, Gentoo, Chinstrap) both genera of the Antarctic and sub-Antarctic; *Spheniscus* (Black-footed, Magellanic, Peruvian, Galapagos), burrowing or cavern-dwelling species of South America and South Africa; *Eudyptula* (Little blue or Fairy, White-flippered) living in caves and burrows in southern Australia and New Zealand; *Megadyptes* (Yellow-eyed) with yellow 'coronet', restricted to New Zealand, Campbell and Auckland islands; *Eudyptes* (Macaroni, Royal, Rockhopper, Erect-crested, Snares crested, Fiordland) with yellow or golden crests, distributed on sub-Antarctic and temperate islands in the southern ocean.

Three methods of locomotion seen in penguins. (1) Chinstrap penguins *Pygoscelis antarctica* 'porpoising', (2) Emperor penguins *Aptenodytes forsteri* sliding on ice and (3) Rockhopper penguins *Eudyptes crestatus* jumping.

1

2

3

GAVIIFORMES

Aquatic birds called divers, or loons, need a
lengthy runway for take-off

DIVERS (LOONS) – *Gaviidae*

DIVERS

The divers, or loons as they are known in the New World, bear superficial resemblance to the grebes; members of both families – respectively the Gaviidae and the Podicipitidae – are tailless, with moderately long necks and pointed beaks, their elongated bodies having the legs placed well to the rear (so that they walk on land with difficulty), and are specialized to an aquatic way of life. However, the similarities are probably the result of convergent evolution, with adaptations to the same aquatic environment; these two families are evidently unrelated (despite the fact that they are generally placed side by side at the primitive end of classifications), and one recent authority placed the divers close to the auks (Alcidae). Divers differ

Three divers in summer plumage. (1) Red-throated diver (or loon) *Gavia stellata*, (2) Black-throated diver (or Arctic loon) *Gavia arctica* and (3) Great northern diver (or Common loon) *Gavia immer*. Divers can swim with their bodies almost completely submerged (4).

externally from grebes in being larger and bulkier, with thicker necks, lacking paddle-like lobes on the toes, and in having plumage of a harsher texture. All divers have distinctive breeding and non-breeding plumages; in south Greenland the attractive skins of Great northern divers *Gavia immer* and Red-throated divers *G. stellata* are used to make ornamental blankets or wall-carpets. Divers are flightless during wing-moult but at other times they fly strongly, though to become airborne all but the smallest species need to 'patter' over the water in a lengthy take-off run.

Distribution. The divers are a Holarctic family, breeding in arctic and subarctic latitudes of North America and Eurasia, and on various islands in the Polar Basin. The Black-throated *Gavia arctica* and Red-throated divers *G. stellata* have a wide breeding distribution across both Old and New Worlds. However, the two larger species, the Great northern *G. immer* and White-billed divers *G. adamsii*, almost replace each other geographically, with the latter breeding in arctic Eurasia (mainly Siberia), and the former in North America with outposts in Greenland and Iceland; but there is limited overlap in Alaska and northwest Canada. The most northerly breeding divers are Red-throateds at 83° N in Greenland and Ellesmere Island, and the most southerly are Great northerns at about 41° N in North America (Great Lakes region). All are highly migratory, breeding on freshwater lakes of the tundra and boreal zones, and wintering in inshore tidal waters. Migrations consist of southward shifts to warmer, ice-free regions, mainly within the temperate zone. Such southward movements are less pronounced in the White-billed diver, which in North America winters mainly off British Columbia and in Europe mainly off Norway. Some divers are even trans-continental migrants; Red-throateds ringed as chicks in Greenland have been recovered in England and France, while Black-throateds ringed on passage in the Baltic have been recovered in summer across Russia and Siberia east to the Lena delta, movements of more than 3,500 mi (5,630km).

Feeding. All divers are principally fish-eaters, taking their prey by seizing (not spearing) in underwater pursuit; they are, therefore,

skilled at diving – hence the European group vernacular. They can dive to depths of 30ft (say 9m), and can remain submerged for up to two minutes. Other food items recorded at various times include crustaceans, molluscs, frogs, annelid worms and water insects. If a breeding lake contains inadequate quantities of fish, the birds will make regular feeding flights to the sea or to better fishing lakes.

Nesting and the Young. Divers nest on inland, freshwater lakes, generally choosing a deep one, with little or no cover around the margins; the nest-site, close to the water edge due to the bird's clumsiness on land, may be on the lake shore, but more often on a low-lying islet. These bare sites afford protection to the incubating birds, since mammalian predators have little chance of sneaking up unobserved. However, there is an exception in Canada, where Great northerns sometimes nest on the edge of a reed-bed; while Red-throated divers, which have less trouble getting airborne, are able to nest on smaller pools than the others. Divers are generally solitary nesters, though there may be two or three pairs on a really large lake; the Red-throated has been reported as breeding socially in Finland and Iceland, with nests sometimes only a few yards apart, but this would be exceptional elsewhere. The nest is no more than a flattened scrape on the ground, lined with grass or aquatic vegetation. All species are determinate layers, the clutch being two elliptical or ovate eggs, coloured olive-brown with black spots, blotches or streaks. Both adults share the incubation, which lasts 26–29 days and begins with the first egg. The chicks leave the nest after no more than 1–2 days, and they take to the water straightaway, swimming to meet their parents when food is brought. The pre-fledging period is a long one, for the young acquire the ability to fly after 55–60 days. This is followed by a long period of immaturity, and divers do not begin breeding until their third calendar year.

Behaviour. In territorial behaviour, divers fly over their domains uttering mournful, eerie, wailing cries, which have been likened to the screams of a child in pain, and this call is also used in response to similar calls from neighbouring pairs. On the water, intruders are warned off by a variety of displays, including a remarkable 'plesiosaur-race,' so called from the way the birds swim with the rear halves of their bodies submerged but with their necks extended stiffly and bills lifted.

A Red-throated diver *Gavia stellata* in 'plesiosaur display'(1) and a White-billed diver *Gavia adamsii* chasing an intruder (2). In North America divers are called loons, and the White-billed diver is known as the Yellow-billed loon.

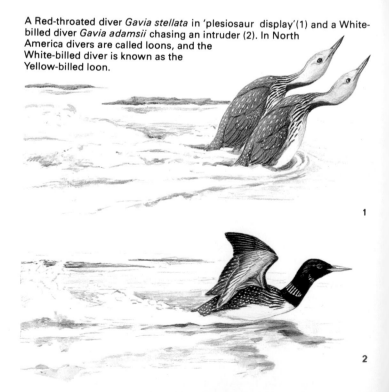

Composition. The family Gaviidae consists of a single genus *Gavia*, and four species are generally recognized: *Gavia immer*, *G. adamsii*, *G. arctica* and *G. stellata*. Black-throated divers breeding in North America and northeast Siberia are sometimes considered a separate species, *G. pacifica*; while it has been suggested that *G. immer* and *G. adamsii*, which have rather little geographical overlap, might be conspecific.

PODICIPITIFORMES

Aquatic birds with elaborate courtship rituals

GREBES — *Podicipedidae*

GREBES

The grebes are highly specialized aquatic birds closely related to one another but to no other known birds, living or fossil. For this reason, the family is included in its own order, the Podicipediformes.

Grebes are adapted for diving from the surface and for underwater swimming. Their strong legs are situated at the rear of a rotund or somewhat elongated, virtually tailless body. The large feet are partly webbed with well-developed, paddle-like lobes on each of the three main toes, and are used to propel the bird at speed under the water with a powerful, figure-of-eight movement. Most grebes can fly well, but do so rather infrequently once settled down on a particular water. Their wings are relatively small, necessitating a fast rate of flapping, and when not in use are usually folded right away under the body plumage. Three species – the Short-winged grebe *Rollandia micropterum*, Taczanowsky's grebe *Podiceps taczanowskii*, and the Giant pied-billed grebe *Podilymbus gigas* – are permanently flightless; each is confined to a single large lake, or lake system, in south or central America.

Grebes vary in size from 9–30in (23–76cm) in length. In nonbreeding plumage, they are typically countershaded, that is dark grey, blackish, or brown above (on the crown, hind neck, and upperparts), and paler, usually pure white, below (on the throat, foreneck, and underparts). The display and breeding plumage is quite different, both sexes developing special plumes, colours, or markings. These are most elaborate in the *Podiceps* grebes, often involving elongated crests, tippets, horns, fans, and filaments on the head, while the whole neck and breast may become red or black. In all plumages, the feathering is very dense and waterproof.

Distribution. Grebes have a world-wide distribution mainly in temperate and tropical areas, but are absent from the smaller, truly oceanic islands and from Antarctica. They extend into the sub-Arctic in Canada, Alaska, Iceland, and northern Eurasia. In the southern hemisphere, the most southerly point of their range is Tierra del Fuego. Most species are found in the New World, especially within the Neotropical Region.

In the breeding season, grebes typically inhabit both natural and artificial, standing fresh water such as lakes, reservoirs, gravel-pits, and marshes. Some species, for example the Little grebe *Tachybaptus ruficollis* and Lesser golden-grebe *R. chilensis*, also frequent slow-moving streams. When not breeding, many populations move away, especially from smaller ponds, to large lakes or coastal salt water to complete their wing moult in safety while flightless and to

avoid drought or ice. Those species that summer in high latitudes – such as the Western grebe *Aechmophorus occidentalis*, Slavonian (or Horned) grebe *Podiceps auritus*, and Pied-billed grebe *Podilymbus podiceps* – perform true, seasonal migrations. When travelling, grebes usually fly by night and move by foot, swimming and feeding, by day.

Feeding. Aquatic animals caught under water are the staple diet of grebes. Many species eat fishes, in particular the larger, streamlined grebes with their long bodies, necks, and bills; of these, the Western grebe is unique in its method of spearing fishes in the manner of the unrelated darters. Some of the smaller species eat invertebrates to the partial or total exclusion of fishes, at least while nesting. Of these, the Black-necked (or Eared) grebe *Podiceps nigricollis* has a specialized upturned bill for skimming insects off the surface. The two pied-billed grebes, with their powerful beaks, can deal with hard-bodied crustaceans such as crayfish.

Courtship. Grebes form monogamous pairs and both sexes take part in ritual courtship ceremonies, both during pairing and later before the eggs are laid. These are particularly well developed in the genus *Podiceps* and in the Western grebe, and are associated with vocal

Details of the heads of members of the grebe family. (1) Western grebe *Aechmophorus occidentalis*, (2) Black-necked (or Eared) grebe *Podiceps nigricollis*, (3) Pied-billed grebe *Podilymbus podiceps*, (4) Red-necked grebe *Podiceps grisegena*, (5) Slavonian (or Horned) grebe *P. auritus* and (6) the Little grebe *Tachybaptus ruficollis*.

'advertising' by lone birds seeking a partner or by paired birds wanting to re-establish contact with the mate. All species perform 'head-shaking' and 'habit-preening' in some form, as male and female face or swim side by side. The *Podiceps* grebes all have a complex 'discovery ceremony', especially likely to occur when birds meet after total separation, in which one swims towards the other under water, then surfaces close by in the 'ghostly-penguin' display, rising vertically out of the water, while the second bird assumes the 'cat-display'. In species such as the Great crested grebe, this display involves the sideways spreading of the partly inverted wings showing their white markings. At the climax of their discovery ceremony, the males and females of most species rise vertically in a mutual 'penguin-dance', but the Great crested grebe just head-shakes. The latter species, however, has an elaborate 'weed ceremony' at the climax of which the two birds meet and rise breast to breast in a spectacular 'weed-dance' carrying weed in their bills.

In all the grebes, courtship is quite distinct from the mating ceremonies leading to copulation which occur at specially built platforms. Reversed mounting has been recorded from a number of species.

Nesting and the Young. Male and female share more or less equally

The Western grebe *Aechmophorus occidentalis* is a large North American species with an extremely long bill.

America and the Great crested grebe in Europe) were formerly used for making women's capes, muffs and hats, while those of the Short-winged grebe of South America served as saddle blankets for the local Indians.

Composition. Depending on taxonomic judgement, there are at least 19 and perhaps up to 22 species of grebes; of these, 12 are found only in the New World, seven only in the Old World, while three are common to both. The family can conveniently be divided into two groups which differ from one another in the musculature of the leg and in certain aspects of behaviour: (1) the pied-billed grebes *Podilymbus*, the golden-grebes and the Short-winged grebe *Rollandia*, and the true dabchicks *Tachybaptus*; and (2) the ornamental grebes *Podiceps* and the Western grebe *Aechmophorus*. Of these, *Podilymbus*, *Rollandia*, and *Aechmophorus* are solely New World and *Tachybaptus* solely Old World, while *Podiceps* is cosmopolitan. Within the latter, as presently constituted, the generic affinities of the two hoary-headed grebes *P. poliocephalus* and *P. rufopectus* (of Australia and New Zealand respectively), the Least grebe (New World), and the Great grebe *P. major* (South America) require final assessment, as does that of the newly described Hooded grebe *P. gallardoi* of Patagonia.

in all reproductive activities. Grebes' nests are simple structures of piled-up weeds, reeds, and the like built in the water, either tethered to aquatic vegetation, sometimes floating, or anchored to the bottom. The eggs are pale and unmarked but become stained brownish during incubation which lasts from three to just over four weeks, according to species. Clutch-size usually ranges from two to six eggs but some of the smaller grebes lay up to eight. Incubation starts before the clutch is complete and the young hatch out at approximately two-day intervals, at least in the larger species. The eggs are covered by material when the sitting bird is disturbed from the nest, this habit serving both to conceal them and reduce chilling.

At hatching, grebe chicks are covered in down which in all species but the Western grebe is conspicuously striped, especially on the head and neck. Those of many species have bare patches of skin on the head which flush deep red if the bird is excited in any way. Though active, they are fed by the parents which carry them in turn on their backs in the nest and for a while after the family takes to the water. Later, the chicks are completely aquatic and follow the adults for food. Division of the brood between the parents and the favouring of certain young is well established in the Great crested grebe and probably widespread. In this species, the young are dependent on the parents for 10–11 weeks or longer. Chicks of the Black-necked grebe, however, are said to be fully independent in as little as three weeks. With its long cycle, the Great crested grebe is only occasionally double brooded but some of the smaller grebes will attempt two or more broods regularly in one season.

Economic Importance. The breast pelts – the so-called 'grebe fur', of some of the larger species (such as the Western grebe in North

PROCELLARIIFORMES

Large seabirds with a wingspan measuring up to 12 feet in the largest species

ALBATROSSES — *Diomedeidae*
SHEARWATERS — *Procellariidae*
STORM PETRELS — *Hydrobatidae*
DIVING PETRELS — *Pelecanoididae*

ALBATROSSES

Albatrosses are very large, long-winged seabirds with long hooked bills and separate raised tubular nostrils. The body is $2\frac{1}{2}$–4ft (76–122cm) long, while the wingspan has often been exaggerated but may range up to 12ft (3·6m) across in the largest species, which weigh 15–20lb (6·8–9kg). They are fairly closely related to petrels, but much larger than any of them except the Giant petrel *Macronectes giganteus*, which looks rather similar but has shorter wings and united nostrils. Like it they differ from the other petrels in having in most cases a distinct immature plumage and in nesting on the ground in the open.

In general, three types of plumage are found: an all-white adult

plumage with dark wingtips; a white body with a dark brow, back, upperwing and tail; or a more-or-less uniformly dark plumage, sometimes characteristic of immaturity in species which adopt the first plumage later. The bill of each species is constructed of distinctively shaped and coloured horny plates, while the legs are set in the middle of the body and are moderately long and sturdy so that, unlike most petrels, they can stand upright and walk fairly easily. The toes are webbed, and they also swim on the water surface easily, though apart from shallow plunges to seize food they cannot dive.

Distribution. Albatrosses are pelagic, and are widely distributed at sea but are never seen over land except at the breeding-places and exceptionally after storms. Nine species are found in the Southern Ocean and adjacent seas, most breeding on islands near the Antarctic and some off southern South America, southeast Australia and New Zealand. One species frequents the eastern tropical Pacific and breeds on the Galapagos, and three species occur in the North Pacific, breeding on the central archipelagoes. All species disperse very widely from the breeding-places, especially while they are young, but they only exceptionally cross the equator. Fossil remains indicate that they also occurred in the North Atlantic while it communicated with the Pacific through the Strait of Panama in the Tertiary period about 20 million years ago, but they are no longer found there now except as rare wanderers from the Antarctic. Black-browed Albatrosses *Diomedea melanophris* have twice started to visit Atlantic gannet *Sula bassana* colonies in the Faroes and Britain for periods of years during the last century, and if such birds could find mates they might well start to breed again.

Feeding. The main diet of most species appears to consist of large squid seized at the water surface, perhaps often at night, though several birds often gather to dismember sick individuals if they come to the surface by day. They also catch fish and various invertebrates, and in recent years have taken to scavenging freely after fishing-boats in some areas, notably off South Africa and New Zealand. Very large flocks may gather with other seabirds behind trawlers at times, and also in areas where there is an exceptional food supply as, for example, along the borders of the Falkland Current off southeastern South America. Elsewhere they scatter to feed alone at sea, often following passing ships.

Behaviour. The birds are silent and undemonstrative at sea, soaring endlessly back and forth or round and round a ship, and sometimes settling to rest on the water. Young birds do not appear to return to the breeding places until they are several years old, where they spend several more before starting to breed somewhere between five and ten years old. Where they are undisturbed, they form large scattered

Black-browed albatrosses *Diomedea melanophris* are able to soar long distances (1). They build high nests in large colonies (2).

breeding colonies, usually on the flatter, more open parts of oceanic islands, though some species nest on rock stacks or even cliffs. The southern species build a definite nest of compacted earth and vegetation up to 18in (45cm) high and 24in (61cm) across with a hollow cup on the top, whereas the northern ones lay on the bare earth. They defend its immediate vicinity but are not otherwise territorial. Courting birds spend much time soaring back and forth around the colony, and indulge in bowing, bill-clapping, fencing and dancing displays on or near the nest, in the course of which the distinctive head and bill markings of each species are exhibited.

A single large egg with a coarse white shell is laid, and the male then takes the first incubation shift, which normally lasts several days and may last weeks. Incubation lasts for over two months, and is carried out by the two sexes in turn. The chick is covered in long down, and is fed by regurgitation on a mass of half-digested food and oil secreted by the parent's stomach. It becomes very fat towards the end of the period of growth, but loses some weight again before fledging. It is guarded by one parent at first, but as it grows, it is left alone. It fledges at somewhere between four and nine months, depending on the size of the species. It follows that the largest species in the southern hemisphere, the two great albat-

Courtship behaviour in the Great crested grebe. (1) The discovery ceremony in which one bird approaches with the cat-display (left) while the other stands in the ghostly-penguin display. (2) Habit preening then takes place, each bird flicking up its own wing feathers. (3) The weed ceremony follows in which water weed is carried and presented by each bird. Finally, the birds patter-fly across the water in the retreat ceremony (4). After mating (5), there is evidence of considerable parental care, each bird taking turns to carry the young (6).

rosses, the Wandering albatross *Diomedea exulans* and the Royal albatross *Diomedea epomophora*, and also the Grey-headed albatross *Diomedea chrysostoma*, have such a long breeding cycle, approaching an entire year, that they cannot breed successfully every year, and if they succeed in rearing chicks only nest every other year. The smaller species nest annually, usually in the spring in the south, though the North Pacific species lay in the autumn in the southern part of their range and disperse north after breeding.

Economic Importance. In the past, albatrosses which had presumably been caught at sea formed an important article of diet for the inhabitants of islands around the North Pacific and at such sites as the Chatham Islands east of New Zealand, and they were also often eaten by whalers and sealers visiting the Antarctic islands in the past. In the last half of the nineteenth century the North Pacific species were also exploited on a very large scale by the Japanese for their feathers, millions of birds being killed over a few years so that most of the western colonies were exterminated and the eastern ones in the Hawaiian Leeward Islands were severely reduced. Following the creation of a reserve, these last colonies have increased again during this century to hold hundreds of thousands of birds of two species, the Laysan and Black-footed albatrosses *Diomedea immutabilis* and *D. nigripes*. The third north Pacific species, the Short-tailed albatross *Diomedea albatrus*, which had a more westerly breeding distribution, was nearly wiped out by first continued collecting and then a volcanic eruption at its breeding place, Torishima, between the wars, and was thought to be extinct at one time. Young birds which had been away at sea eventually reappeared, however, and there are now about 50 pairs again. The southern populations are now very healthy.

Composition. The southern species include the two great albatrosses already mentioned, which are very large and adopt a white adult plumage, five rather similar mollymawks showing the second type of plumage with a dark back and tail, and two sooty albatrosses of the genus *Phoebetria* with dark plumage and long, wedge-shaped tails. The north Pacific species show a similar variety of plumages, the Short-tailed albatross resembling the Wanderer with a dark immature and a white adult plumage, the Laysan resembling the mollymawks, and the Black-footed the Sooty albatrosses in colour, though it has a shorter tail and tends to scavenge offshore rather like a Giant petrel.

Three species of albatross. (1) The Wandering albatross *Diomedea exulans*, (2) Grey-headed albatross *Diomedea chrysostoma*, (3) Sooty albatross *Phoebetria palpebrata*. Courtship behaviour in the Galapagos (or Waved) albatross *Diomedea irrorata* (4). Wandering albatross feeding (5), mating (6).

SHEARWATERS

The shearwaters are a group of some 15 species of fairly large seabirds in the family Procellariidae which also includes the typical petrels. They are tubenosed birds, having nostrils opening through horny tubes lying on top of the upper mandible. Like other tubenosed birds, they produce large amounts of oil in the gut and discharge it through the mouth. The oil, rich in vitamin A, is secreted by special glands lining the part of the stomach preceding the gizzard. In some species it is used defensively, being vomited up and directed at an intruder. It is also used to feed the young and in courtship feeding.

Shearwaters' bills are generally rather long, deeply grooved – being covered with separate horny plates – and hooked for the retention of prey. The feet are webbed, all species swimming well and some capturing their food beneath the surface of the water. The plumage, dense and strongly waterproof, is usually black above and white beneath, or else uniformly dark.

As the general adaptations of shearwaters are connected with an oceanic existence, their legs are placed far back for efficient swimming while their wings are long and narrow for efficient high-speed gliding flight, which means that on land they have difficulty in taking flight in windless conditions. On the wing, shearwaters are commonly seen in small parties gliding over the waves with occasional wing beats, tipping from side to side as they follow up currents of air and appearing to shear the water.

Distribution. One of the best-known of all seabirds is the Manx shearwater *Puffinus puffinus*. Discontinuously cosmopolitan in distribution, being found, for example, in Britain, the Mediterranean, New Zealand and off the southwest coast of North America, it is a bird of shallow coastal waters rather than the open ocean.

The Manx shearwater is some 14in (36cm) long. The closely-related Little shearwater *Puffinus assimilis* is some 3in (7·5cm) shorter and has a more fluttering flight. The Sooty shearwater *P. griseus*, only a little larger than the Manx shearwater, has a wholly dark plumage. British colonies of the Manx shearwater fly considerable distances to feed, Welsh birds, for example, feeding in the Bay of Biscay on the abundant sardine crop. Some British birds winter as far afield as the east coast of South America. Even the birds of the year take part in this migration, recently-fledged young from Britain having been found on the coast of Brazil.

The Short-tailed shearwater *Puffinus tenuirostris* is another species with an impressive annual migration. From its breeding grounds in south Australia and Tasmania it circumnavigates the North Pacific; a journey of some 20,000mi (32,000km).

The Great shearwater *Puffinus gravis*, of the Tristan da Cunha group of islands in the South Atlantic, has a breeding poulation of some 4 million birds, which easily maintains itself although the islanders annually take 15–20,000 eggs and the same number of young birds. The post-breeding migration of this species takes it to the coast of western Europe.

Feeding. The prey – zooplankton, fish, cephalopods and offal – varies according to species and conditions. It is taken both on and below the water's surface.

Nesting and the Young. Shearwaters breed colonially in burrows on offshore islands which most species visit only at night. Some nest in hilly inland areas. The birds spend several days or even weeks prospecting for suitable nest sites and will often take over a burrow from some other owner. Normally only one large egg is laid. Both parents take part in incubation and care of the young, procedures taking several weeks. The young are fed by regurgitation of partially digested food, mixed with the stomach oil.

Shearwaters have a low mortality once they have successfully left the nest and are long-lived, reaching 15 years of age or more. There is a long period of immaturity in which the young birds spend almost all of their time at sea, coming to land progressively earlier and with increasing interest each breeding season but they do not show interest in a particular colony or a particular site and mate until they are five years old or more.

Colonial Behaviour. At the breeding grounds shearwaters perform complex displays involving flights over the breeding colony while producing their specific – and perhaps individual – calls. These vocalizations are somewhat unusual in that they involve harsh cackling, screaming, gurgling and wailing noises.

Economic Importance. Shearwaters, particularly when young, have for centuries been valued by man as a source of food. The greatest utilization of shearwaters has been in Australasia where the species known as 'mutton-birds' are taken as well-grown chicks for their valuable stomach oil and their down which is used to make bedding.

Composition. The shearwaters can be divided into two groups on the basis of two different kinds of adaptation to oceanic life. The genera *Procellaria*, *Thyellodroma* and *Calonectris* have longer wings and tails, being adapted for soaring over the open oceans. *Adamastor* and *Puffinus* are more aquatic, with shorter wings and tails.

The Manx shearwater *Puffinus puffinus*, one of the best-known seabirds (1), and the closely related Little shearwater *Puffinus assimilis* (2) in which the young are as large, or larger than, the adult bird just before feathering.

STORM PETRELS

The storm petrels are a group of small, web-footed seabirds about 6–10in (15–25cm) long which specialize in feeding on small marine animals caught from the air far out at sea. At times in the past they have been classified in the family Procellariidae with the larger fulmarine petrels and shearwaters, but they differ from them in

(1) The Fulmar *Fulmarus glacialis*, (2) Kermadec petrel *Pteroderma neglecta*, (3) Capped (or Black-capped) petrel *Pteroderma hasitata* and (4) Great (or Greater) shearwater *Puffinus gravis*.

having only a single, joint opening to their tubular nostrils, and in recent years they have normally been placed in a separate family. They are otherwise very similar to the large petrels in their habits and life-history. This distinction is possibly best expressed by calling them all 'storm petrels,' a name originally restricted to the main European species, though they are often also referred to simply as 'petrels.' They fall naturally into two groups. The northern species tend to be long-winged and often fork-tailed with a swooping flight rather like the terns, and a fairly uniform black to grey colouration. The southern species have short, round wings, square tails, and long legs with small feet; they are dark above but may be either dark or white below, polymorphism sometimes occurring within the same species. Many species have distinctive white rumps.

Distribution. Storm petrels are found throughout the larger oceans and in the Mediterranean but not normally in enclosed waters such as the Caspian Sea. The majority of species have a fairly local distribution in middle latitude areas of water-mixing, but a few species breeding in higher latitudes and migrating into lower ones are much more numerous and widespread. These include Leach's storm petrel *Oceanodroma leucorrhoa* in the north Atlantic and Pacific and especially Wilson's storm petrel *Oceanites oceanicus*, which breeds around the Antarctic and is one of the world's famous long-distance migrants, moving north in all oceans to reach a maximum of about 45°N in the North Atlantic.

Behaviour. At sea, storm petrels tend to feed alone or in small, loose groups, though congregations of hundreds or even thousands may gather to feed together in good areas, around a plankton-slick, for example, where from a distance they may look like a gathering of butterflies. Wilson's storm petrel commonly follows ships and others species may do so at times though some, such as Leach's storm petrel, normally avoid them entirely. The southern species show variations in the style of flight alleged to have given rise to the name 'petrel,' walking on the water with their wings spread like St Peter and stooping to pick small food-items from the surface, though the northern species swoop, skim, and soar more. They do not normally mix freely with other bird flocks feeding over fish-shoals or around fishing boats, but wait around the outer edge,

A petrel, the Prion *Pachyptila vittata* strains water through its bill, retaining minute organisms for food (1). Three species of storm petrel: (2) Leach's storm petrel *Oceanodroma leucorrhoa*, (3) Storm petrel *Hydrobates pelagicus* and (4) Bulwer's petrel *Bulweria bulwerii*.

possibly attracted by the smell of food, since they will assemble from long distances when hot fat is thrown overboard.

They normally stay out of sight of land by day, possibly to avoid birds of prey, which wreak havoc on storm petrels when they accompany ships in any number. They visit their breeding places on offshore rocks and islands and sometimes mainland cliffs or in inland deserts normally only on dark nights, though in a few remote areas some species also come in by day. Courting birds carry out complex aerial displays, weaving back and forth over the colony with crooning or whistling cries, which are continued as more subdued purring when they visit the nest-holes. These may be situated among boulders, in rock crevices or vegetation, or in burrows dug by the birds, according to the terrain. The nest-chamber may be barely shielded from daylight, or many feet down the hole, and may be bare or lined with miscellaneous debris probably dragged in by accident. The birds may prospect several colonies for two or three years before starting to breed, when they normally return to their natal colony. They lay one large white oval egg with a rough shell and sometimes small rusty spots, which is normally incubated by both parents in turn for spells of days at a stretch for about six weeks before hatching. The chick is at first small and helpless and is covered with long dark down; it is soon abandoned by day and fed by regurgitation at night, becoming very

Wilson's storm petrels *Oceanites oceanicus* foraging for food (1). The poisonous Tiger snake may occur with chicks of the Slender-billed shearwater *Puffinus tenuirostris*, but does not harm them.

fat before it fledges in 8 to 10 weeks, when it presumably has to fend for itself out at sea.

Economic Importance. The birds are often very fat, and wicks used to be passed through their bodies which could then be burnt like a candle. Their appearance may indicate the presence of fish or whales at sea.

Composition. The two main groups are perhaps best treated as subfamilies. There are seven species of Oceanitinae in the south, including in addition to Wilson's storm petrel the White-faced storm petrel, which is very numerous around Australasia with outlying colonies in the North Atlantic. There are 14 species of Hydrobatinae in the North Atlantic and Pacific, including in addition to Leach's storm petrel the British storm petrel, which breeds from islands off Norway and Iceland south down the west coast of Europe into the Mediterranean, and winters off South Africa.

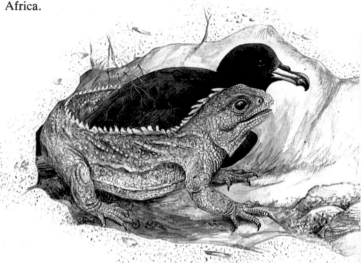

A famous example of co-habitation. The Tuatara, a reptile found only in New Zealand, shares a nesting burrow with a variety of petrels, here *Procellaria parkinsoni*.

DIVING PETRELS

Diving petrels are a numerous group of small aquatic petrels about 6–9in (15–23cm) long which replace the smaller northern auks in the southern hemisphere, and resemble them remarkably closely except for their retention of the raised tubular nostrils characteristic of the petrels, which in this case have separate openings facing upwards. Like such northern species as the Little auk or Dovekie they have black backs, white underparts, short stout bills, short pointed wings, very short tails, and short stout legs with webbed feet set far back, adapted for swimming and 'flying' underwater as easily as they fly in the air. They also show a variable amount of white flecking on the upper part of the body, or mantle, and dark streaking across the breast in some species, blue legs, and they lack the back toe.

Distribution. Diving petrels occur throughout the Southern Ocean, breeding on islands off the Antarctic, and where cool currents extend north off southeast Australia, New Zealand, and especially western South America.

Behaviour. The habits of diving petrels, like their appearance, resemble those of the smaller auks. They spend most of their time on the water, diving freely to feed on planktonic invertebrates, which they collect in a distensile pouch under the tongue to bring back to their young. They swim low, just showing the head, and have a rapid, whirring flight, often pitching soon, though they can at times

Three related species. (1) Wilson's storm petrel *Oceanites oceanicus*, (2) Great (or Greater) shearwater *Puffinus puffinus* and (3) Giant fulmar *Macronectes giganteus*. (4) A Fulmar *Fulmarus glacialis* deters a predator by projecting musky stomach oil.

fly long distances. They are most easily seen feeding off the coast in tide-rips in straits and around headlands, individuals feeding alone though many may congregate in a small area. It does not seem clear how far they disperse out to sea, where they may be hard to detect, though it seems unlikely, in view of their manner of flight, that they travel as far as the larger petrels. The fact that they visit their nest sites frequently also suggests they do not go far.

They normally come to land at night like other petrels, and also nest in holes, often in rocks, though they may be in vegetation or dense warrens of burrows shared with several other species of petrel on the subantarctic islands. In some areas at least they seem to visit the burrows for a good deal of the year to display and clean them out. A single, remarkably large, white egg with a coarse surface is laid at some time between July and December, with a good deal of local variation even within the same species, and incubated by the two sexes in turn for spells of a day for about eight weeks. The downy chick is incubated for a longer period than in most petrels, one to two weeks, and then fed by both parents nightly until it fledges and starts to care for itself at about eight weeks. The parents are then unusual among petrels in that they loose all their flight feathers, in a single moult in at least one species, and become flightless whilst regrowing them.

The White-faced storm petrel *Pelagodroma marina* uses the updraft from the edge of a wave to sustain it in flight. Cape pigeons *Daption capense* are shown taking advantage of the movement of water within the waves.

Economic Importance.

Economic Importance. Diving petrels were clearly once harvested in large numbers by primitive people for food. They are one of the commonest species in Morjori middens in the Chatham Islands, and were being taken by fishermen in Peru until quite recently. It is not known whether they are still hunted on a large scale in any part of the world.

Composition. The classification of the group has been difficult to determine because, not only do diving petrels resemble the auks, they also resemble each other. The latest view is that there are four species that are included in a single genus *Pelecanoides*: the Peruvian diving petrel *P. garnoti*, the Magellanic diving petrel *P. magellani*, the Georgian diving petrel *P. georgicus* and the Common diving petrel *P. urinatrix*.

The Common diving petrel *Pelecanoides urinatrix* (1) and diving petrels (2) shown feeding by diving through waves.

ODONTOPTERYGIFORMES

Extinct long-winged seabirds pose many unanswered questions

BONY-TOOTHS — *Odontopterygidae*
FALSE-TOOTHED BIRDS — *Pseudodontornithidae*

BONY-TOOTHS

The Odontopterygidae is a member of an extinct order of birds, the Odontopterygiformes, which evolved and died out during the Cenozoic Era between 70 and 3 million years ago.

In 1873 the paleontologist Owen described an incomplete skull

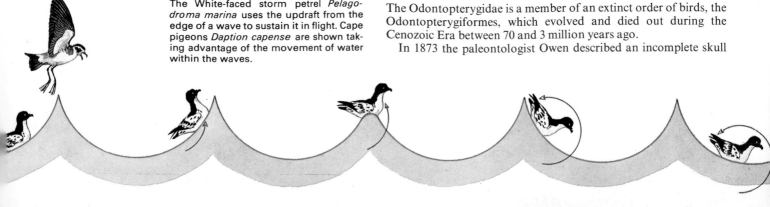

Restorations of the bony-toothed bird *Odontopteryx*. The known evidence suggests that *Odontopteryx* was possibly similar in feeding habits to such birds as albatrosses.

lacking the front part, which had been found in the 50 million years old Lower Eocene deposits of Britain, and named it *Odontopteryx toliapica*. It possessed a character which no other known fossil or living bird has, in that it had a series of bony, tooth-like projections on both the upper and lower jaws. For this reason a new family thought to be related to the pelicans, the Odontopterygidae, was later founded to include this form. It is impossible to say exactly what *Odontopteryx* would have looked like in life. It was certainly the smallest member of the group, and was probably a long-winged seabird, about the size of a large cormorant or gannet, with a gannet-like bill about 5in (12·5cm) long, and short stout legs. In its original condition, the skull resembled that of the gannet, except for the 'teeth', in having a small rounded cranium which lacked evidence of any salt glands above the orbits, powerful lower jaws, and a stout upper jaw with a well-marked hinge between the frontal and nasal bones.

Distribution. *Odontopteryx* is the only known representative of the Odontopterygidae. Its remains have been found in the London Clay deposits of the Isle of Sheppey, England. The fauna and flora found with *Odontopteryx* resemble those which are normally associated with a tropical environment similar to that of Malaysia today, and include numerous sharks, turtles, crocodiles and *Nipa* palms.

Feeding. It is not known how *Odontopteryx* and its relatives obtained their food, but the possession of the tooth-like projections on the jaws would certainly assist in catching fish and other aquatic creatures. How they performed this task is difficult to say, but if the body form was similar to that of the gannet, there is no reason why they should not have dived for their prey in the same way as does the modern bird.

Composition. Howard, in 1957, with the aid of material collected since the late nineteenth century noted that the bony-toothed birds possessed characters in common with two present-day orders, the Pelecaniformes, the pelicans and related birds, and the Procelariiformes, the albatrosses, shearwaters and petrels, as well as having their own distinct structures. She therefore placed them in a new order, the Odontopterygiformes, which contains two families, the Odontopterygidae and the Pseudodontornithidae. Nevertheless some palaeontologists do not agree with her conclusions, and still regard this group as a suborder within the Pelecaniformes.

FALSE-TOOTHED BIRDS

The family Pseudodontornithidae, comprising two genera *Osteodontornis* and *Pseudodontornis*, is the only family apart from the Odontopterygidae at present recognized as belonging to the extinct order Odontopterygiformes. The two families placed in this order are separated basically on the arrangement of the bony, tooth-like projections along the edges of both the upper and lower jaws, with the Odontopterygidae having rather small projections that resemble a saw. In the Pseudodontornithidae the teeth are more widely spaced, and are longer and narrower with smaller projections placed between them.

The best preserved pseudodontornithid specimen, from which we can obtain some idea of the basic appearance of the family, is *Osteodontornis orri* which was found in marine sediments deposited during the Miocene period. From the skeleton one can see that this species was a large-headed, long-winged, short-legged seabird. The skull, which was crushed during fossilization, measures over 16in (41cm) and the wing span has been estimated as being close to 16ft (5m). This animal therefore, may have possessed the largest wing span of any known flying bird, be it fossil or recent. As in the albatrosses the wings were probably relatively narrow thus allowing efficient gliding over the sea.

Distribution. Members of this family are known from the Lower Miocene, marine deposits of North America *O. orri* and New Zealand *P. stirtoni* and are approximately 20 million years old. The age of the latter species, however, is rather uncertain and it has been suggested that it may come from the lowermost part of the following

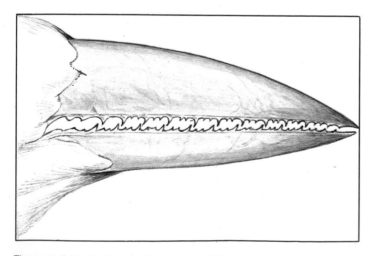

The most distinctive feature of bony-toothed birds, a series of bony tooth-like projections on the bill. The shape of the bill is unknown.

Pliocene period. One other species, *P. longirostris*, has been described, but was obtained from a seaman, and its age and origins are completely unknown.

Composition. The Odontopterygiformes is at present under review, and it is probable that several previously unrecognized forms will be added to this order. The relationship between the Pseudodontornithidae and Odontopterygidae is not yet fully understood, and it is possible that they may eventually be placed within a single family.

PELECANIFORMES
Large birds with webbed feet. Some fish for a living; others steal their food

TROPICBIRDS — *Phaethontidae*
PELICANS — *Pelecanidae*
BOOBIES AND GANNETS — *Sulidae*
CORMORANTS — *Phalacrocoracidae*
ANHINGAS — *Anhingidae*
FRIGATEBIRDS — *Fregatidae*

TROPICBIRDS

Tropicbirds are adapted for obtaining their prey by plunge-diving in tropical and sub-tropical seas and for nesting in cavities in cliffs, under bushes and in tall rain forest trees. Their wings are short and

Three species of tropicbird. (1) Red-billed *Phaethon aethereus*, (2) Yellow-billed *Phaethon lepturus*, (3) Red-tailed tropicbird *Phaethon rubricauda*. Tropicbirds feed by diving into the sea to catch fish and squid (4).

stout. In flight they resemble a heavy-bodied tern, their flapping and circling flight alternating with long straight glides. Their shrill calls also resemble those of terns and the similarity between these calls and the noise made by a bosun's whistle has led to their being called 'bosunbirds.' Tropicbirds are morphologically and behaviourally most closely related to gannets.

If we exclude the central tail streamers, the birds vary in length from 16–19in (41–48cm). The bill is stout, pointed and slightly decurved with serrated edges. Juveniles lack the serrations on the bill. The legs are very short and the birds are barely able to walk. The feet are totipalmate (all four toes webbed throughout their length). Adult tropicbirds have two elongated tail streamers which are much prized as ornaments by the Polynesians.

Distribution. The smallest species of tropicbird, the Yellow-billed or White-tailed tropicbird *Phaethon lepturus* is found throughout the world's tropical regions. Collectively the two larger species are also pantropical, but they have allopatric breeding distributions. The Red-billed tropicbird *P. aethereus* breeds in the eastern Pacific, Atlantic and northwest Indian Ocean; and the Red-tailed tropicbird *P. rubricauda* breeds in the central and eastern Indian Ocean and the western and central Pacific Ocean. Juveniles leave the vicinity of their natal island as soon as they can fly and do not return until they have attained adult plumage.

Feeding. Tropicbirds feed mainly on squid and fish, including flying fishes. Concentrations of fish are poor in tropical oceans and adult tropicbirds have been seen to forage hundreds of miles away from their nesting islands.

Nesting and the Young. Pair-formation in tropicbirds is achieved by courtship flights very similar to those of terns and gadfly petrels. In these flights the male advertises for a mate and prospective pairs circle, wheel and glide together calling loudly. Sometimes one of a pair hovers over the other, depresses its tail, and touches the lower bird with its streamers. Eventually the male leads the female to the nest cavity which is usually hidden from sight. The nest is normally a scrape with virtually no nest material in it. Members of a pair take turns guarding the nest until the chick is old enough to defend itself. Normally only one egg is laid. The chick is fed regurgitated squid and fish which is transferred from mouth to mouth without the chick putting its head down the throat of its parent as in other pelecaniform birds.

Composition. The three tropicbird species are very similar in plumage and behaviour and are all placed in a single genus, *Phaethon*. The flight of *P. lepturus* is more graceful and less ponderous than that of the other two larger species. The bill is red in *P. rubricauda* and yellow in *P. lepturus*. It is red in breeding and yellow in non-breeding *P. aethereus*. The tail streamers are yellow or white in *P. lepturus* and red or pink in the other two species. The plumage is white with fine black bars in immature birds.

PELICANS

Pelicans are large aquatic birds that are highly adapted for swimming and flying, but are ungainly on land. They belong to the diverse order Pelecaniformes which also includes the tropicbirds, gannets, cormorants, darters and frigatebirds. The order as a whole is very ancient and dates back to the Eocene period 60–40 million years ago, with the first identifiable pelican coming from the Lower Miocene rocks of France which are over 20 million years old. The geological species are so like the modern forms that they have been placed in the same genus, that of *Pelecanus*.

The genus can be conveniently divided into two, or perhaps three, groups. In the first are included the larger species, all of which breed in dense colonies on the ground and rarely perch on trees. The second consists of the remaining smaller forms which normally nest in trees in loosely packed colonies, and often perch and roost in trees. The Brown pelican *Pelecanus occidentalis* because of its more specialized method of fishing is sometimes placed in a group of its own.

Pelicans are amongst the largest of all flying birds, and have an overall length of between 50–72in (127–183cm); weigh 10–25lb (4·5–11kg), with the larger species having wingspans of up to 9ft (2·7m). The legs are short and stout with large feet which, like those of the majority of the families within the Pelecaniformes, are fully webbed. The most obvious character by which one can identify all pelicans is that of the bill. This is very long, straight, flattened, hooked at the tip, with a large elastic pouch suspended beneath the lower mandible. Their plumage, except for the Brown pelican, is white or mainly white with areas of grey, brown and black. The face, throat and area around the eyes have patches of bare skin, the colour of which becomes more intense during the breeding season. In the American white pelican *P. erythrorhynchus* a strange horn-like growth develops on the bill at this time, and in the Great white pelican *P. onocrotalus* the forehead becomes swollen, while other species grow crests. Males are considerably larger, and can be further separated from the smaller females by the colour of the bare skin, and the length of the crest if present. Despite their grotesque shape, pelicans in breeding dress are often beautifully coloured; in *P. onocrotalus*, for instance, a rosy flush derived from secretions of the preen gland tinges the silky white plumage. Brown and yellow tints found in other species are acquired from stains in the water upon which the pelicans swim.

Distribution. The entire family is restricted to the temperate and tropical regions of both the Old and New Worlds including Australia. All but the Brown pelican, which is almost completely maritime in its habits, are found on inland waters where there are large quantities of fish, although some species are sometimes encountered in estuaries and coastal lagoons.

The two species inhabiting the Americas range from the Great Slave Lake south through Central America to the Galapagos Islands, and part of the northeastern coast of South America. The Old World forms are found from Africa, except the northwest, southeastern Europe, southern Asia, the East Indies and Australia. They are basically sedentary in habit, but as they are not well insulated against cold weather, all the northern populations migrate

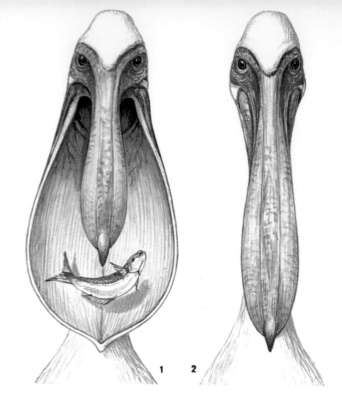

The pouch of the Great white pelican *Pelecanus onocrotalus* open (1) and closed (2). Contrary to popular belief, the pouch is used to catch fish and not to store food.

in winter, and even the tropical species undertake long local journeys in search of suitable feeding areas.

Pelicans are light, having numerous air spaces beneath the skin and in the bones, and are magnificent fliers capable of sustained soaring flight over great distances. When migrating or looking for good fishing areas they will take off in flocks, using thermal currents to give them height, and reach their destinations with the minimum of effort.

Feeding. The diet of the pelican is mainly fish, but crustaceans are sometimes eaten. The basic adaptation of the group for fishing is the bill, and contrary to general belief the pouch is not used for storage or holding fish, but simply a catching apparatus that acts as a scoop net. The pouch however, is not permeable like a net, but is highly expansible and elastic. When the bird plunges its bill into the water the flexible lower mandible expands automatically into a broad oval scoop. As the pelican raises its head from the water the fish are trapped in the pouch. The pouch then contracts to its original shape and the upper mandible closes like a lid over the lower jaw, thus preventing the fishes' escape. The prey is then swallowed whole, but can be transported long distances in the bird's gullet in a partially digested state.

This method of attaining food is elaborated in several ways. The Brown pelican, for instance, is unique amongst the family in that it often dives from the air for food. On sighting a fish it plunges

During the breeding season, a strange growth develops on the bill of the American white pelican *Pelecanus erythrorhynchus*. Its function is unknown.

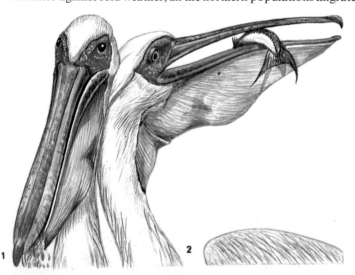

The pelican's pouch is used as a scoop net. When prey has been caught, the pouch contracts (1), squeezing out water. The prey is then turned round and swallowed whole (2).

vertically, and just before striking the water the neck, which is doubled up in flight, is shot straight out, thus the bird enters the water with its neck at full stretch. The fish are caught underwater and swallowed when the bird surfaces. Pink-backed *P. rufescens* and Spotted-billed pelicans *P. philippensis* use a different method. These species usually fish singly. They swim slowly along or remain stationary. On locating a suitable prey they dart out their head and neck to catch the fish. Occasionally they fish in groups using the 'scare-line' technique normally typical of the larger species. This is rare however, and is only used in deep water.

The 'scare-line' form of fishing is perfectly demonstrated by the Great white pelican. A group of 8–12 swim rapidly forward in a horseshoe formation with the open end of the horseshoe pointing forwards. At intervals, as if given a signal, all plunge their bills into the centre where the fish have presumably collected.

Nesting and the Young. Courtship is usually short and unspectacular. In some, pair formation probably immediately precedes egg-laying. The smaller species normally breed in trees, and make a platform nest of twigs. The larger forms lay their eggs in simple nests on the ground which can be made up of reeds or mud. The same nesting sites are used continuously, and in the tropics the breeding season may be protracted, sometimes continuing throughout the year. Two, three or occasionally more eggs are laid and are large, rather elongated and chalky white. Both sexes take turns in incubating which takes 35–37 days.

The newly hatched young are ugly, being pink and naked at first, turning black or grey, then growing a coat of grey or blackish down. After about three weeks the young are able to walk, and in the ground-nesting species collect in groups or 'pods'. The chicks are fed by both parents on small quantities of regurgitated liquid matter dribbled down the adults bill. Young pelicans take 60–70 days to reach the flying stage, but before doing so become much heavier than their parents. The adults usually stop feeding their young before the flying stage.

The Brown pelican *Pelecanus occidentalis* (1) is unique in that it dives for its food. Its entry into the water looks clumsy but is effective. The Great white pelican *Pelecanus onocrotalus* (2) does not dive but simply plunges its head under water.

Pelican chicks are fed by their parents on regurgitated food which is allowed to run down the bill.

Economic Importance. When found, pelicans are often seen in large numbers. In the breeding season they nest gregariously in large colonies. In the ground-nesting species it is dangerous to approach a nesting colony as they have a habit of deserting *en masse*. It is not unnatural that pelicans have been suspected of damaging fishing areas. They probably eat from 5–10% of their own body weight each day, that is between $\frac{1}{2}$–$2\frac{1}{2}$lb (0·2–1·2kg). While it cannot be denied that a large number of pelicans eat an enormous amount of fish each year, recent work in the Danube delta has shown that they take a higher proportion of diseased fish, therefore are beneficial to the fish population as a whole.

The Great white pelican *Pelecanus onocrotalus* has a wingspan of 9ft (2.7m) and, like other pelicans, has short stout legs and webbed feet.

Composition. The family Pelecanidae contains the single genus *Pelecanus*. The exact number of species varies from six to eight depending on the opinion of different ornithologists, and the relationships between them have not yet been ascertained.

BOOBIES AND GANNETS

The gannets and boobies, or sulids, form a closely knit family of marine plunge-divers placed, together with pelicans, cormorants, anhingas, frigatebirds and tropicbirds in the order Pelicaniformes. Fossil sulids probably date back at least 20 million years.

Sulids range in total length from about 2ft (60cm) (the male Red-footed booby, *Sula sula*) to $2\frac{3}{4}$ft (85cm) (the Atlantic gannet *S. bassana bassana*, the Masked or White booby *S. dactylatra* and Abbott's booby *S. abbotti*). They all have long, fairly narrow wings, cigar shaped bodies and longish tails. Within the family there is considerable variation in weight, from 2–8lb (0·9–3·6kg), and bill dimensions correlated with the nature of their prey. Bills are in all cases strong, with serrated cutting edges and sealed nostrils. The feet are webbed between all four toes. Unlike the cormorants, gannets and boobies possess waterproof plumage and some range hundreds of miles from land.

All sulids possess bare facial skin which in some species (gannets, Masked boobies, Abbott's booby) is blackish and in others, brightly coloured (yellow-green in the Brown booby *Sula leucogaster*, blue and red in the Red-footed, slatey in the Blue-footed *S. nebouxii* and Peruvian *S. variegata*). The bills are always colourful (blue in gannets, Red-footed and Blue-footed boobies; green in Brown boobies; grey or pink in Abbott's, male and female respectively; orange-pink in the White). These, and their 'stupidity' in allowing close approach by humans, may be responsible for the common name of the group, bobos or clowns.

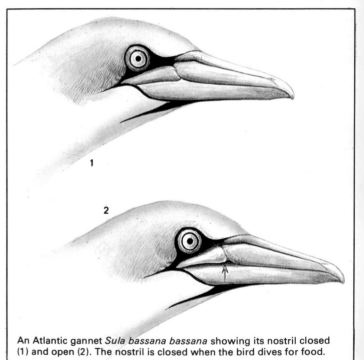

An Atlantic gannet *Sula bassana bassana* showing its nostril closed (1) and open (2). The nostril is closed when the bird dives for food.

Four species of gannet. (1) Atlantic gannet *Sula bassana bassana*, (2) Australasian gannet *Sula bassana serrator*, (3) Abbott's booby *Sula abbotti* and (4) Peruvian booby *Sula variegata*.

Distribution. The Red footed, Brown and White boobies are the most numerous and widely distributed sulids, breeding on thousands of islands in the pan-tropical 'blue-water' belt of the three major oceans. The Blue-footed booby is discontinuously distributed along the western seaboard of South America from northern Peru to the Gulf of Panama, on the Galapagos Islands and on islands in the Gulf of California; the Peruvian booby is restricted to offshore islands and headlands of Peru; Abbott's booby occurs only on the Indian Ocean Christmas Island; the Atlantic gannet has some 28 colonies in the eastern Atlantic and six in Canadian waters; the Cape gannet *Sula bassana capensis* has six colonies off southern Africa and the Australasian gannet *S. bassana serrator* some 25 colonies mainly in New Zealand. In many cases, distribution correlates closely with the presence of food fish.

Feeding. Sulids forage on the wing, scanning the sea with down pointed head from less than 10 to over 100ft (3–30m). On sighting fish they plunge into the water with angled wings. Occasionally they power dive. Gannets and Peruvian boobies often exploit shoaling fish, diving down from large gatherings with spectacular effect. Brown, White and particularly Red-footed boobies catch flying fish on the wing. Blue-footed and Brown boobies sometimes hunt in collaborative fashion (which differs from group diving in which each bird acts individually). In these species the difference in size between the sexes is particularly marked and the males, which are small, specialize in diving into shallow, inshore water. Gannets can swallow fish up to 14in (40cm) long and are capable of eating more than 2lb (1kg) in one short session. All sulids can survive for several days without food.

Nesting and the Young. White and particularly Blue-footed boobies nest on flat ground, though coping with a wide range of habitats; Brown boobies prefer slopes or cliff edges; Red-footed boobies nest in trees or bushes and Abbott's boobies high in forest trees. Atlantic gannets prefer cliff ledges but Australasian and particularly Cape gannets choose flat ground. With the exception of Abbott's booby, all are highly colonial, though colony size and density varies much between species. Peruvian boobies form the largest colonies (up to a million pairs on one island), followed by Cape gannets (over 100,000). The remainder are highly variable, ranging from scores of thousands to less than 10 pairs per colony. The densest nesters are Cape gannets (in some areas more than six pairs per square metre), followed by Peruvian boobies, Atlantic and Australasian gannets (all over two pairs per square metre). The other boobies nest at highly variable densities.

Important aspects of sulid ecology are the timing and frequency of breeding, the number of young reared and the nature of their growth and mortality, all of which are related to the nature of their food supply. Sulids are basically annual breeders but Abbott's booby lays only once every two years. Moreover, some Galapagos Red-footed boobies breed less often, and Ascension Brown boobies and Galapagos Blue-feet more often than once a year. The three pan-tropical boobies are, in many areas, non-seasonal breeders, that is, they lay throughout much of the year, whereas all the gannets are seasonal breeders. Where food and weather is non-seasonal, or unpredictable, breeding is often non-seasonal too, whereas where these factors are predictably seasonal, breeding is adjusted to produce young at the most favourable time. Single egg clutches are laid by most sulids, but the Blue-footed and Peruvian boobies commonly rear two or more young. In the White and Brown boobies, two eggs are laid, but the first chick to hatch always kills its

An Atlantic gannet *Sula bassana bassana* carries seaweed for its nest.

nest-mate. The eggs are relatively small (between 3·5 and 8% of the female's weight); four is the maximum ever laid by any species (the Peruvian booby) and eggs are incubated beneath the feet rather than against a brood spot. The chicks hatch almost naked, become fluffy white in two to three weeks, sprout feathers and become fully feathered and clear of down between 10 and 16 weeks depending on species and fledge between 12 and 20 weeks. Boobies guard their young for three–five weeks (until they can regulate their body temperature) but Atlantic gannets guard them unremittingly until they fledge. Gannets do not desert their young, nor do they stop feeding them before the young fledge. The young of the pan-tropical species, breeding in impoverished waters, typically grow slowly and often starve in the nest, whilst the gannets and Peruvian boobies, breeding in rich waters, rear their young quickly and have a high breeding success.

Gannets showing colour variation in the webbed feet. (1) Red-footed booby *Sula sula*, (2) Blue-footed booby *Sula nebouxii*, (3) Brown booby *Sula leucogaster* and (4) Masked (or Blue-faced) booby *Sula dactylatra*. Gannets incubate their eggs beneath their feet as is this Cape gannet *Sula bassana capensis* (5). A Blue-footed booby displays its feet in courtship (6).

The newly independent young of the Atlantic gannet migrate southwards to northwest African water, those of the Cape gannet northwards (the two overlap in the Gulf of Guinea) and Australasian gannets migrate to the south and east coastal waters of Australia. Young boobies disperse, those of the pan-tropical species sometimes moving several thousands of miles. Movements of adults of all species are usually restricted to within a few hundred miles of their breeding place.

All sulids are strongly territorial. Gannets and the Peruvian booby often fight ferociously during the process of establishing a site (usually when four or five years old); other boobies usually negotiate by display, which is highly developed in all species and basically consists of exaggerated and stereotyped head, and often wing, movements. Males establish the site and 'advertize' to females. Subsequently, the pair engage in elaborate mutual ceremonies prior to copulation and nest-building. All species build either a functional or a symbolic nest and the behaviour involved is an important pair-bonding activity. Only male gannets regularly attack their mates (nape-biting) and bite her during copulation. Incubation and care of young is fairly evenly shared by the two sexes. The tiny young are brooded on top of the webs of the feet and (in the tropical boobies) carefully shaded. They are fed straight from the parent's throat. When well feathered, young ground-nesting boobies wander and exercise and fledge gradually. Young Atlantic gannets fledge precipitously by leaping off cliffs, after which they swim away unaccompanied and do not return until, usually, in their third year. There is considerable fidelity to site and mate (partners can recognize each other by sight and voice) but also, divorce is common.

Variation of colour in cormorants. (1) Common (or Great) cormorant *Phalacrocorax carbo*, (2) Shag *Phalacrocorax aristotelis*, (3) the Galapagos Flightless cormorant *Nannopterum harrisi* and (4) Spotted shag *Phalacrocorax punctatus*. These are compared with a member of a related family, the Anhingidae, the Anhinga *Anhinga anhinga* (5).

Economic Importance. The only economically important sulids are the guano species (Peruvian booby and Cape gannet) but the eggs, young and adults of the Red-footed and Brown boobies in particular are widely taken by natives and the young (gugas) of the Atlantic gannet are still taken annually from Sula Sgeir, the Westmann Islands and Myggenaes (Faroes).

Composition. The three gannets, which are very similar, may belong to a single species *S. bassana* and are regarded here as subspecies. Some authorities separate gannets from other sulids and include them in their own genus *Morus*, others include them in the genus *Sula* that contains the other sulids, the boobies. The boobies are all closely related, but the Red-footed and Abbott's boobies probably separated from the ancestral sulid stock at an early date.

CORMORANTS

Cormorants are long-necked, long-billed diving birds, sometimes known as 'shags,' contained in the family Phalacrocoracidae. There are some 30 species, the exact status of some of them, particularly the Antarctic forms, being uncertain. They vary in length from 19–40in (48–101cm).

In most species the plumage is black, or black with a green or blue metallic sheen, hence the etymological development: corvus marinus ('sea crow'), cor marin (some French patois), cormorant. In the southern hemisphere a few species are grey and others white on the throat or underparts. The eyes, bill and facial skin are often brightly coloured. In the breeding season many species have crests, or patches of white on the head, neck or flanks. The bill is long, though strong, and is hooked. The feet are large and fully webbed, and the legs are short and strong – all contributing to the cormorants' abilities as swimmers.

Distribution. Cormorants are found in most parts of the world on sea coasts and large lakes and rivers, the major exceptions being parts of northern Canada, northern Asia and certain islands in the Pacific. Some species are strictly marine, some restricted to freshwater, while others habit both. The Common cormorant *Phalacrocorax carbo* (the Great cormorant of eastern North America, and the Black cormorant of Australasia) for example, is almost cosmopolitan in its distribution, ranging from Canada eastwards to Japan and Australasia. In many countries it is found on both fresh and salt water, and will nest in trees or on rocks. It takes a wide variety of animal food but feeds largely on fishes. Although in some years large numbers of Common cormorants die as a result of human activities, including pollution, their numbers remain, nevertheless, relatively stable.

Possibly the most extensive fluctuations in numbers to be seen in the bird world are those which occur in colonies of the Guanay or Peruvian cormorant *Phalacrocorax bougainville* which breeds in enormous numbers on islands off the coasts of Chile and Peru. From time to time, most markedly at intervals of about seven years when the warm current from the north overcomes the cold Humboldt current from the south and thus displaces the upwelling which is essential for proper plankton production, the food supply of the Guanay fails and the birds die in millions. As with any animal which breeds in large numbers with much contact between individuals, any significant disturbance in the food supply will have indirect as well as direct effects on the population.

One group, sometimes placed in a separate genus *Halietor*, consists of four species of small size found mainly in tropical and sub-tropical lakes and rivers. The most unusual species is certainly the Galapagos Flightless cormorant *Nannopterum harrisi*. It has been flightless for a very long time, as indicated by the lack of a keel on the sternum (used principally for flight-muscle attachment) and the density of the plumage. Its isolation on the Galapagos, some 600mi (960km) west of South America on the Equator, has made this possible and has also resulted in its lack of fear of man – a common consequence of long isolation. As there are only about 1,000 individuals of this species left the conservation measures which have been adopted for its protection are clearly of importance.

Feeding. Cormorants are primarily fish-eaters, with crustacea or amphibia forming part of their diet. They dive in pursuit of prey, using their wings to a certain extent, particularly for steering and braking. Fish are generally brought to the surface before they are swallowed. The Guanay and North America's Double-crested cormorant *Phalacrocorax auritus* employ a communal fishing system often involving thousands of birds at a time. Schools of surface-feeding fishes are herded by large fan-shaped formations of birds which feed as they move forward.

When flying, the Red-faced cormorant *Phalacrocorax urile* breathes through its bill, its nostrils being closed as an adaption to diving.

ANHINGAS

Anhingas, *Anhinga anhinga*, and Darters, *Anhinga melanogaster*, are strikingly adapted for stalking fish underwater and do so in a manner similar to the way herons and egrets stalk aquatic prey from above the water surface. When they swim with only the slender head and neck sticking out above the water they resemble a swimming snake, hence they are often referred to as "snakebirds." With their very long neck, wings and tail they look cross-shaped when in flight, as they soar in thermals. Anhingas perch near water, in trees and on the ground. They make shrill rattling and clicking calls. Morphologically and behaviourally they are related to gannets, pelicans, cormorants and herons.

The Anhingidae vary in size from 34–36in (86–91cm). The bill is dowel-shaped with serrated edges. The neck is long, slender and G-shaped. The joints between the neck vertebrae are visible in the angular contours of the neck. A special hinge mechanism at the eighth neck vertebra enables the neck muscles to dart the bill rapidly forward to puncture the flank of a passing fish. In adults the long broad wings have slender lanceolate coverts on the upper surface. The central feathers of the long tail have wavy transverse corrugations. The feet are totipalmate (all four toes being united by a web throughout their length).

Distribution. Anhingas and Darters require a smooth water surface when stalking their prey. Hence they occur in the relatively quiet backwaters of sluggish rivers, estuaries, swamps, marshes and lakes. The Anhinga occurs in tropical, sub-tropical and warm temperate areas of the New World and the Darter in similar areas of the Old World including Australia and New Guinea.

Behaviour. Nests are built in trees or on the ground over or near water either singly or in loose aggregations, usually in association with the nests of herons, cormorants and other tree-nesting waterbirds. The male claims the nest site. He advertises for a mate by wing-waving and snap-bowing. Wing-waving consists of alternately raising and lowering the folded left and right wings by humeral (shoulder) rotation. During wing-waving the tail is down and the head is up with the bill more or less horizontal. Snap-bowing consists of raising both folded wings together by humeral rotation. During snap-bowing the tail is raised, the neck is arched and the bird snaps with its bill at a nearby twig. The female selects a male and his nest site and if accepted she builds the nest with twigs and other plant matter brought to her by the male.

After pair-formation male and female take turns at defending the nest site until their chicks are strong enough to defend themselves. Copulation takes place on the nest. The feet are used for warming the eggs during incubation. Small chicks are fed a regurgitated fluid which is poured down the upper bill as in pelicans and not the lower bill as in cormorants. Older chicks take their food by inserting their heads into the throats of their parents. Chicks beg for food by

Nesting and the Young. The sexes of cormorants are externally very similar and there is a reduction in the dimorphism of their sexual display. There has also been some confusion on the part of observers as to the relative roles of the two sexes during display. In the family as a whole it would seem that breeding may be promiscuous, polygamous or polyandrous, with reversed copulation being quite common. The Flightless cormorant, however, is monogamous, and other species probably are as well. Copulation normally takes place on the nest, or nest site.

Most cormorants are gregarious and breed colonially on rocky shores or cliff ledges or in trees. Cormorants' nests are commonly quite bulky structures, built of sticks, seaweed or other vegetation, or simply of rubbish from the shore. In a few species, which nest together in very large numbers in rainless regions where the droppings, or guano, accumulate in thick layers, the nest is little more than a depression in this material. The eggs are basically a pale blue or green colour but typically are more or less covered with a chalky encrustation. They are rather elongated and vary in number from two to six, according to species. Both sexes normally incubate the eggs, which hatch in the order in which they are laid. Thus in times of food scarcity the strongest young survive at the expense of the weakest. In the Flightless cormorant, although three eggs are laid, only two of them hatch and only one chick survives to independence.

Economic Importance. In China and Japan the practice of using cormorants to catch fish is centuries old. The birds are fitted round the neck with a ring, which prevents them swallowing the fish they catch, and then secured by a cord to the fisherman's boat. On a much larger scale is the fertilizer industry of South America, based on the collection of guano, the droppings of the Guanay. Being fish eaters, cormorants also compete with man. Of the 2lb (1kg) of fish taken each day by the Common cormorant about 50% is of marketable size and nature. This has led to a considerable amount of persecution of the cormorant by man, yet numbers have remained surprisingly stable over the years.

Composition. The Phalacrocoracidae consists of some 30 species in the genus *Phalacrocorax*. One species, *P. perspicillatus*, found on Bering Island has been extinct for over a century. Four species distinguished by their small size and length of tail are sometimes placed in the separate genus *Halietor*. Mainly found on tropical or sub-tropical lakes and rivers they are the Pigmy cormorant *P. pygmaeus*; the Long-tailed shag *P. africanus*; the Little cormorant *P. niger*; and the Little pied cormorant *P. melanoleucos*. The Flightless cormorant *N. harrasi* is contained in a separate genus *Nannopterum*.

Cormorants stand for long periods drying their wings after fishing. This is the Common (or Great) cormorant *Phalacrocorax carbo*.

195

An anhinga, the African darter *Anhinga rufa* in its characteristic swimming position with body almost totally submerged.

waving their head with the bill closed and the hyoid bones (at the base of the tongue) forward, thus giving the throat an angular appearance.

Composition. As indicated above there are only two species in the Anhingidae. The male Anhinga is all black with a median ruff on the back of the upper neck. The male Darter does not have a ruff. The female Anhinga has a brown head and neck and a black body with a straight division between the brown and black across the breast. Male and female Darters are dark dorsally, with a white stripe down the side of the upper neck. In southern Asia the nominate race *A. melanogaster* has a black breast and abdomen in adult males and females. In Africa, the Middle East, New Guinea and Australia the females are white ventrally while the males are various combinations of black, dark brown and white.

FRIGATEBIRDS

Frigatebirds are adapted for drinking and feeding on the wing from water surfaces and for nesting and roosting on the branches of trees and bushes. They are notorious for their habit of pirating food and nest material from other seabirds. Frigatebirds normally soar in thermals and in up-drafts of air near cliffs. Over the open ocean they fly very high, descending rapidly when other species of seabirds have located a school of fish. The body is small and hangs low like a gondola below the main surface of the huge wings. They are able to do stall turns and many aerial acrobatics in play and in pursuit of other birds. At rest they sun their wings by extending them laterally and turning them upside down by forward rotation. Morphologically and behaviourally they are most closely related to gannets and cormorants.

Members of the Fregatidae vary in size from 31–41in (79–104cm). The bill, long and stout with a strong terminal hook, is longer in the female than in the male. The long bones are very light tubes with paper thin walls. The legs are tiny with totipalmate (toes webbed throughout their length) and semipalmate (toes partially webbed) feet. Frigatebirds are able to perch but cannot walk. They have a huge forked tail. The dorsal plumage is black with, in some species, light brown bars on the wings. The distribution of black and white in the ventral plumage varies according to species, sex and age. When courting, males inflate a red balloon-like throat pouch, which acts as a resonating chamber for a variety of rattling and yodelling calls.

Distribution. Frigatebirds breed on small tropical islands usually in association with other seabirds. Occasionally they occur as vagrants in temperate regions including inland lakes after cyclonic storms. The Magnificent frigatebird *Fregata magnificens* occurs on both sides of Middle America and frequently flies across the Isthmus of Panama. The Ascension Island frigatebird *F. aquila* breeds only on Ascension Island in the Atlantic Ocean and the Christmas Island

frigatebird *F. andrewsi* breeds only on Christmas Island in the Indian Ocean. The Greater frigatebird *F. minor* and the Lesser frigatebird *F. ariel* are pantropical in their distribution, but do not normally occur in the Caribbean area. Young frigatebirds are easily tamed and communities in the South Sea Islands have used them as message bearers.

Feeding. The Fregatidae feed on squid and fish, including flying fish. They range hundreds of miles out to sea to find food, but they also wait near seabird colonies to intercept boobies as they fly in with food for their chicks. The frigatebirds grab the boobies by the tail or wing to make them regurgitate the food. In exposed situations frigatebirds take small tern chicks and will occasionally take the young of other birds, including their own species. Frigatebirds are attracted to pools of fresh water which, though they do drink both, they prefer to seawater.

Nesting and the Young. Nests are built in the tops of trees and on bushes near the seashore either singly or in loose aggregations usually in association with the nests of Red-footed boobies *Sula sula*. The male selects the nest site and advertises for a mate by loud repetitive calls and bill-clappering with the wings and tail spread and the red throat pouch inflated. The female approaches a male and his nest site and if she is accepted she builds the nest with sticks and twigs brought to her by the male. The male obtains nest material while on the wing, breaking it off trees and bushes as he goes, and by stealing it from other birds. Copulation takes place on the nest. Members of a pair take turns in guarding the nest until the chick is large enough to defend itself. After the egg has been laid both sexes bring in nest material as part of the nest relief procedures. Chicks put their head into the throat of a parent to obtain regurgitated food. They remain on the nest until fully grown and adults continue to feed them well after they have fledged; immature birds of at least a year old have been observed begging and obtaining food from incubating adults, presumably their parents.

Frigatebirds. Magnificent frigatebirds *Fregata magnificens*, male (1), female (2) and young (3). The Ascension Island frigatebird *Fregata aquila* with its throat pouch inflated (4). Christmas Island frigatebird *Fregata andrewsi* (5).

A female Lesser frigatebird *Fregata ariel* pursues a gannet, forcing it to drop its catch which the frigatebird then retrieves.

A Lesser frigatebird *Fregata ariel* catches flying fish on the water's surface.

Composition. As indicated above there are only five species of frigatebirds in a single genus *Fregata*. Males are all black, except that *F. ariel* has white axillaries ('armpits') and flanks, and *F. andrewsi* and rarely *F. aquila* have a white abdomen. Males of *F. aquila* have a green, and of *F. magnificens* a violet gloss. Males of the other three species have a brown band on the upper wing. Females differ by having a white breast except for *F. aquila* which has a dark brown breast and nape. Additional white areas occur in females as follows: the axillaries and flanks in *F. ariel*; the axillaries and abdomen in *F. andrewsi*; and the abdomen rarely in *F. aquila*. The throat of females of *F. minor* is grey. Immatures are white ventrally with white, yellow or red-brown heads and some have red-brown breast bands. The plumage of immature birds is very variable so that different species are indistinguishable in the field.

CICONIIFORMES
Fish-eating birds with long bills and necks, and long legs for wading in shallow water

HERONS AND BITTERNS — *Ardeidae*
BOAT-BILLED HERON — *Cochleariidae*
WHALE-HEADED STORK — *Balaenicipitidae*
HAMMERHEAD — *Scopidae*
STORKS — *Ciconiidae*
IBISES AND SPOONBILLS — *Threskiornithidae*
FLAMINGOS — *Phoenicopteridae*

HERONS AND BITTERNS

The herons and bitterns are generally large, wading birds in the family Ardeidae. Herons are long-billed and long-legged, slenderly built birds with short tails and long, broad wings and form the subfamily Ardeinae. Bitterns, more squat than the herons and distinguished by their deep booming call, belong to the subfamily Botaurinae. This article deals separately with each subfamily.

Herons vary in height from 16in (40cm) in the Green heron *Butorides virescens* of North America up to 50in (127cm) in the largest members of the subfamily. The Grey heron *Ardea cinerea* reaches a height of 3ft (91cm), has a wing-span of over 5ft (152cm) and varies in weight from $3-4\frac{1}{2}$lb (1·3–2kg). In flight the feet extend beyond the tail and the neck is withdrawn. A kink in the neck is caused by the sixth vertebra articulating differently from the others, an adaptation which permits the gullet to slide before or behind the vertebrae to facilitate swallowing large prey. It also acts as a fulcrum in catching prey.

Although more slender than the Grey heron, the Purple heron *Ardea purpurea* has adaptations to aid its foraging in swamps. Its toes, much longer than those of its relatives, span the aquatic vegetation but are apparently less suitable for perching in trees. When flying, Purple herons are easily distinguished from Grey herons by their extremely slender necks, and even their longer toes can often be seen.

Herons' feathers grow in narrow tracts, those of the Grey heron being blue-grey, black and white. The adult has a white forehead while that of the juvenile is grey. The undersurface has a disruptive pattern of black and white. Both sexes have a black crest of lanceolate feathers. The mandibles are yellowish, varying from straw-colour to yellow-brown, but with the approach of breeding they may assume a deep pink hue. The eyes are yellow, legs and feet dull brown, darker on the frontal surfaces. Herons have three pairs of powder-down areas composed of fine filaments without lateral offshoots and so friable that, when rubbed with the bill, they crumble into an amorphous powder, the function of which is to cleanse the contour-feathers of eel-slime. This powder, applied in preening, is combed out with the third toe, the claw of which is flattened and serrated.

Distribution. Among Old World species the Purple heron *Ardea purpurea*, the Great white heron *Egretta alba*, the Little egret *Egretta garzetta*, the Cattle egret *Ardeola ibis* and the Squacco heron *Ardeola ralloides* breed in Europe and are rare, or very rare, vagrants to Britain. Of the European herons only the Grey heron

Ardea cinerea nests in Britain where its insular population disperses but does not migrate.

New World species include the American (Great) egret *Casmerodius albus egretta*, the Snowy egret *Leucophoyx thula*, the Louisiana heron *Hydranassa tricolor*, the Little blue heron *Florida caerulea* and the Green heron *Butorides virescens*.

The Atlantic is the western boundary of the Grey heron which is replaced in North America by the Great blue heron *Ardea herodias*, a species so similar that it is probably a subspecies which has acquired specific rank, the two together forming a superspecies. The Great white heron, which has enjoyed specific rank, may well be merely a dimorphic subspecies of the Great blue heron.

While all the species are known somewhat arbitrarily as 'herons' or 'egrets' both names may be used indiscriminately for the same bird.

Some species occur across a vast stretch of land, for example the Grey heron is found almost continuously across Europe, Asia and Africa, there being three recognizable geographical races which replace each other in various parts of the range. From 17° W to 150° E the birds become progressively paler in colour, the races *A. c. cinerea* and *A. c. jouyi* being found at the ends of the 'cline.' The third subspecies *A. c. firasa* is the result of island isolation, being confined to Madagascar, Aldabra and probably the Comoros.

The Grey heron's most northerly breeding place is 70° N in Norway and extends eastwards following an isotherm marking the mean annual temperature of 32° F (0° C). The southern limit is in the region of 34° S, the birds breeding commonly in South Africa.

Four herons showing size and colour variation. (1) Great white heron (or Great egret) *Egretta alba*, (2) Purple heron *Ardea purpurea*, (3) Tiger heron *Tigrisoma lineatum* and (4) Yellow-crowned night heron *Nyctanassa violacea*.

Feeding. Adapted for wading, herons feed mainly on fishes and other animal life caught near water, although they also catch a surprising number of moles. The disruptive pattern of the Grey heron is an ideal adaptation for a wait-and-watch method of hunting. The Green heron has no such adaptation and catches its prey by diving. The Grey heron normally stands motionless at the water's edge waiting for prey to swim within grasping distance. It then uses its bill as a vice, not a spear. Occasionally it varies its method of hunting, as in deeper water where it may swim or dive after fishes. Prey is killed before being swallowed by battering on any convenient anvil. Whatever their diet herons need to disgorge pellets and, if they have been living exclusively on fish, which is completely dissolved by their digestive juices, and therefore lacks pellet-forming material, they will swallow rootlets, grass, feathers or twigs to repair this deficiency. When they feed on small mammals the fur and bones are sufficient to provide pellets.

Nesting and the Young. About the end of February the adult birds gather in the vicinity of the nesting trees, but do not immediately take to the tree-tops. Adjacent to the heronry is an area which can be called the 'standing ground' and there synchronization of breeding condition is achieved. At first only a few birds arrive, the number growing until the full complement is present. They stand all facing one direction, just waiting. Gradually, they begin to occupy the tree-tops – the males, now in full sexual condition, going first and each taking possession of an existing nest or a stance where one will subsequently be built.

At the nest a male advertises for a mate by formalized displays, vocal and visual. However, it is at the standing ground that the best opportunity occurs for seeing herons in full display with red bills and feet. This suffusion of red is not peculiar to the Grey heron, having been noticed in birds of related genera, and resulting from a more active metabolism, consequent upon lengthening daylight and a more adequate food-supply, which not only brings about maturity of the sex-organs but produces a surplus of endocrine secretions which effect colour-changes in keratinized structures such as the bill and feet.

Gradually the female responds to the male's display and, after some rebuff, is accepted and the nest is prepared for the reception of the clutch which, in Europe, averages four eggs. Incubation is shared and extends to the 26th day. The Grey heron, which breeds for the first time in its second or third year, is single-brooded but may lay a replacement clutch. Nestling herons are fed by regurgitation.

The Bitterns form the subfamily Botaurinae which comprises two genera, *Botaurus* and *Ixobrychus*. The sexes of all the *Botaurus* species have similar plumage, that of the bittern *B. stellaris* being soft golden-brown and owl-like, heavily mottled with black above, longitudinally streaked below. A mane of long feathers on the neck and throat can be erected at will. Their necks and legs are shorter than those of herons. The 3in (7·5cm) bill is yellowish-green, the eyes yellow and the legs and feet pale green. They have powder-down patches on the breast and rump, one pair fewer than the herons, and the toothed middle claw is used to apply powder-down to the contour-feathers in preening. The finely divided particles of the disintegrating filaments of powder-down coagulate slime which coats the plumage when bitterns feed on eels. The bittern measures 30in (76cm) and weighs about 3lb (1·3kg). Most *Ixobrychus* species are considerably smaller weighing not more than 5–6oz (140–170g).

The bittern's protective colouration is much enhanced by the bird's habit, when disturbed, of standing rigid with bill pointed skywards, presenting to the intruder the striped under-surface which blends so well with the surrounding reeds as to render the bird virtually invisible.

Distribution. The genus *Botaurus* contains the Eurasian bittern *B.*

stellaris, the Australian *B. poiciloptilus*, the American *B. lentiginosus* and the South American *B. pinnatus* which replace each other and together form a superspecies. Of the genus *Ixobrychus*, the Least bittern *I. exilis* of North America, the Little bittern *I. minutus* of Europe, Asia, Africa, and Australia and the Chinese little bittern *I. sinensis* form another superspecies.

The bittern *B. stellaris* is resident in British and European marshes while the smaller American bittern is a rare vagrant to Europe.

Distribution is restricted by nesting requirements to reedbeds and rank vegetation around sluggish water. The extensive marshes of North Jutland, the 'plassen' of Zuid-Holland and Utrecht, Austria's Neusiedler See and the Danube marshes provide typically ideal haunts for many bitterns. In Europe bitterns breed from 60° N to the Mediterranean basin and very large numbers are present in the USSR. The number of pairs that a reedbed can accommodate is not known for certain for, while there is evidence that a female does not require an extensive area from which to collect enough food to rear her brood and that several pairs may breed fairly close together, fighting and injured birds have been observed, which suggests territorial battles may occur under conditions of overcrowding.

In Britain and the Netherlands severe winter weather takes a heavy toll of resident bitterns, suggesting that not many from these areas migrate. Birds from colder areas probably do migrate, however, as an increased population in countries bordering the Mediterranean is apparent during winter months.

The American bittern *B. lentiginosus* is not so restricted to reedbeds as is the Eurasian species and is often observed feeding in open wet meadows. Its plumage lacks the black on the upperparts which are finely vermiculated and the primaries are uniform grey-brown without barring. It is smaller, only 23in (58cm) long. The American bittern ranges over the northern half of the USA and southern Canada in summer and migrates south for the winter.

Feeding. Extremely furtive, indeed mainly crepuscular, bitterns hunt within the reedbeds, grasping the stems as they progress although, occasionally, one will venture out onto open water. When flying over the reedbeds they skirt the tops of the stems with a slow wingbeat, quickly dropping back into cover. The prey consists mainly of fish, eels and frogs with small mammals, worms, insects, crustaceans and the eggs and young of small birds also taken.

Nesting and the Young. The nest is built up above water level on matted roots in a reedbed and is constructed of reeds and sedge, lined with finer material. Three to six olive-brown eggs, without gloss, laid at intervals of two or three days, are incubated by the female alone. The young, too, are fed entirely by the female. The Little bittern *Ixobrychus minutus* is the only European member of its genus. Sluggish rivers, backwaters, even small ponds satisfy its nesting requirements and it nests practically throughout Europe, building sometimes just above water level and sometimes in willows up to 10ft (3m) above the water.

Composition. The Ardeidae can be conveniently divided into two subfamilies, though some authorities make no such distinction. The Ardeinae comprises 64 species of heron in 15 genera. In the Botaurinae 12 species of bittern are divided into two genera.

BOAT-BILLED HERON

Historically, the peculiar Boat-billed heron *Cochlearius cochlearius* has been assigned to its own family because of its extraordinarily wide bill. It also differs from other herons in the structure of its skull (modifications associated with bill-support), in having an extra pair of powder-down patches (four pairs instead of three), in egg colour (some eggs have tiny spots), and in its nestling down colour. However, its body below the skull is amazingly similar to that of the Black-crowned night heron in size, plumage, and skeletal details. The Boat-bill's general habits of preening, locomotion, and nocturnal hunting also strongly resemble those of the night herons. It uses powder-down in the same manner as do other herons to dress its plumage, combing it out with a serrated middle claw.

Distribution. Boat-billed herons inhabit both fresh and salt water areas throughout much of the New World tropics. They are found most often along thickly vegetated rivers and estuaries but are also known to hunt along beaches. The range of the species extends from both coasts of Mexico through Central America and into the northern half of South America (where details of its distribution are not known). Boat-bills are probably non-migratory.

Behaviour. Boat-billed herons seem to be strongly nocturnal in their hunting behaviour. By day they preen and roost quietly in dense mangrove thickets near feeding areas, venturing forth at dusk to forage. Although Boat-bills can hunt in the wade-and-stab manner of other herons, there is reason to believe that they switch to touch-

Feeding in the Grey heron *Ardea cinerea*. (1) The fish is caught in the bill and manipulated to the correct position (2). It is then washed (3) and swallowed head first (4).

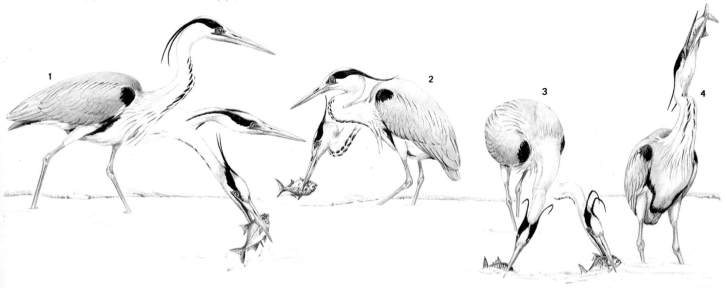

feeding during the breeding season when they consume shrimp and other mud-dwelling prey that cannot be located except by groping. Such blind captures are presumably facilitated by the extra-wide bill.

Boat-bills nest in colonies that may include other species of water birds. They choose nest sites low over water in the maze of branches and prop roots while the other species dwell above, in the canopy. Each pair defends a three-dimensional territory around the nest. Perhaps because of the unusual density of their nesting environment, the social signals of Boat-billed herons have evolved rather differently from those of herons living in more open sites. Indeed, only two of the 12 most common displays in the Boat-bill's

The Boat-billed heron *Cochlearius cochlearius*. It feeds on small turtles and other aquatic animals, spooning them up in its flattened bill.

repertoire are obviously the same displays as those used by other herons. Instead of the visual signals characteristic of most heron communication, the Boat-billed heron relies more on acoustic signals, both vocal and mechanical, that penetrate the mangrove tangle more efficiently. The large bill also serves as a resonator, producing single and multiple bill-pops that resemble loud human handclaps.

The postures and movements used in the displays are generally simple and slow. Many are enhanced by the erecting of broad crown plumes which produces a highly conspicuous black array above the white forehead. Between members of a mated pair there is a great deal of ritualized mutual preening behaviour (called bill-clappering) that probably serves to strengthen the pair bond.

It is not known whether Boat-billed herons form new pair bonds each year or retain the previous year's mate. Both sexes share in nest building, incubating, and feeding the chicks. Three or four pale greenish-blue eggs sometimes bearing small red flecks are laid at roughly two-day intervals. Incubation commences with the first egg, producing an asynchronous hatch. Later, if the chicks' total energy demands exceed the parents' ability to provide food, only the youngest chick starves. As in the other herons, chicks are fed by regurgitation by the parents.

Composition. The single species of Boat-billed heron is subdivided into three to five races. But the central question concerning the

Boat-bill is whether to include it in the family Ardeidae or to retain it in its own family. Most modern authors prefer to stress its similarities to the other herons by including it within the Ardeidae, arguing that it is no more aberrant than many other heron species. Indeed, most of the well-known differences between the Boat-bill and other herons can be explained by its specialized feeding niche and corresponding adaptations. Nevertheless it remains a poorly-known bird that deserves further research.

WHALE-HEADED STORK

The Whale-headed stork, Shoebill or Shoe-billed stork *Balaeniceps rex*, is a large bird that bears a superficial resemblance to a stork or heron. It stands about 3ft 5in (1.05m) high and is about 3ft 10in (1.17m) in length. Its most striking feature is the very large and long bill, which is broad and flattened with a massive hook at the tip of the upper mandible. The neck is rather long, and there is a short bushy crest on the upper nape. The wings are large and broad, the tail short and squared, and the legs and toes long with the tibiae partly bare of feathers.

The plumage is dark grey, with a slighty greenish gloss on the upperparts, and paler underparts. The large feathers of the wings and tail are blackish-grey, probably because a chemical called melanin, which imparts a dark colour, strengthens these vital feathers.

Distribution. *Balaeniceps* has a rather limited range in eastern tropical Africa, from the southern Sudan in the valley of the White Nile south to northern Uganda and the most easterly parts of Zaire. It inhabits swamps, marshes and the edges of lakes and slow-flowing rivers, often standing on 'islands' of floating vegetation. Typical habitats are the 'sudd' region of the White Nile and the vegetated swampy borders of lakes in northern Uganda. The species is non-migratory throughout its range.

Behaviour. The Whale-headed stork is usually seen singly or in pairs, rarely in groups. It is rather silent, calls being limited to a 'shrill kite-like' whistle and a laughing note. In display the huge bill is clattered, making a mechanical rattling sound like displaying Storks. This behaviour is probably evidence of its relationship to Storks.

The species is generally of a rather slow-moving disposition, characteristically standing motionless in a swamp or at the edge of water with its bill drawn back on the breast. Periodically a quick lunge is made to catch prey that has swum or walked within reach. The bill is also thought to be used for digging lungfish and other

The Shoebill (or Whale-headed stork) *Balaeniceps rex* (1) and Hammerhead *Scopus umbretta* (2) in flight. The Shoebill flies with its neck retracted, the Hammerhead with its neck stretched forwards.

The Shoebill *Balaeniceps rex* with its Lungfish prey (1). The Hammerhead *Scopus umbretta* (2) builds a large nest of branches plastered with mud, with an entrance situated at the side (3).

$19\frac{3}{4}$in (50cm) long, with a generally heron-like shape, but somewhat heavier build. The rather large and long bill is laterally compressed and has a small hook at the tip of the upper mandible. The neck is moderately long, the body plump and the wings rather long and rounded. The square-tipped tail is proportionately longer than in most herons and storks. The legs are fairly long, with the lower tibiae bare of feathers. There are four toes, the three forward-pointing toes being connected by a partial web, and the hind toe inserted at the same level. Like storks, but unlike herons, the Hammerhead lacks patches of specialized powder-down feathers on the sides of its breast, while having the pectinated edge to the middle toe, which presumably aids preening, in common with the herons.

The plumage is generally of rather drab appearance, being mainly dull brown, with a slight purplish gloss on the upperparts and flight feathers, faint grey streaking on the throat and faint dark brown barring on the tail. Both bill and legs are black. One of the bird's most striking features is its long crest of pointed, horizontally-carried feathers on the back of the head. This gives the impression of 'balancing the bill' and is presumably the reason for the common names of the species.

There are probably more African legends about the Hammerhead than about any other bird species. There is a general concensus of opinion that to molest Hammerheads brings bad luck, and some tribes regard them with awe.

Distribution. The Hammerhead has a wide range in the Ethiopian and Malagasy zoogeographical regions, extending from southwest

A peculiarity of Hammerheads *Scopus umbretta* is their habit of standing motionless for long periods of time.

prey from the bottom of shallow water while wading. The diet is varied, including a variety of fish, frogs and other amphibians, molluscs and snakes. Small dead animals of various kinds are also eaten, but probably all of the carrion taken is sufficiently small to be swallowed whole.

The flight is most often slow and direct with the legs extended behind, the head drawn into the breast, and slow flapping wing-beats. However, the broad wings are sometimes used for soaring on thermal upcurrents, when the bird may reach great heights and moves with the agility of soaring pelicans or vultures.

Nesting and the Young. The nest is a bulky platform of grass, rushes, leaves and other vegetable materials collected together among thick ground vegetation in a swamp or on an island in a lake or river. It is lined with finer dry grass or rushes. The clutch is of one or two large white eggs that have a chalky surface and a faint blue tinge showing from the deeper layers of shell. Incubation is carried out by each parent in turn, with regular changeovers occurring at the nest. When hatched the young are downy and helpless like young storks. Both parents feed them on food that is carried to the nest in the throat and regurgitated.

Many details of the Whale-headed stork's biology are still unknown. For example, detailed information on its displays and social behaviour might be of value in assessing its relationships to storks on the one hand and to herons on the other, as both of these groups have been studied in detail.

Composition. *Balaeniceps rex* is the only species of the family Balaenicipitidae. Its affinities to other families have been much disputed, so that different authors have included it in the stork family Ciconiidae, afforded it a separate family placed in the order Ciconiiformes, or even considered it a member of the Pelecaniformes.

HAMMERHEAD

The Hammerhead *Scopus umbretta* – also known as Hammerkop, Anvil-head or Hammer-headed stork – is the only member of the family Scopidae. It is an unusual-looking medium-sized bird about

Arabia through much of tropical Africa to Madagascar. The small subspecies *Scopus umbretta umbretta*, formerly known as the Lesser hammerkop, has a restricted range in coastal areas of West Africa, from Senegal to Nigeria. The more widespread subspecies *S. u. bannermanni* occupies the remainder of the range, from Arabia to the Cape and to Madagascar. The typical habitat consists of marshes, mangrove swamps and the edges of lakes and slow-flowing rivers, generally with trees nearby. The Hammerhead is non-migratory.

Behaviour. Hammerheads usually occur singly or in pairs, and are often seen wading in shallow water, where they can be observed to shuffle their feet, probably to disturb hidden prey. They will often stand on the backs of wallowing hippopotamus and sometimes use these animals as hunting platforms. The varied diet consists mainly of amphibians, fish, insects and crustaceans, most of which are obtained in shallow water. The young are fed mainly on tadpoles.

Hammerheads roost in trees, usually returning regularly to the same roosting place, but they are at least partly nocturnal and probably obtain much of their food at night. The flight is distinctive, with the neck partially drawn back (not drawn right back as in most herons), and a peculiar appearance given by the proportionately large wings and head and small body, the overall impression being rather owl-like. In display, elaborate dancing movements occur, accompanied by bowing and wing-flapping. A yapping, cackling call is also given. Other calls include a sharp shrill *taket taket* or *sikwee-sikwee-kwee-kwee* repeated in flight, and notes variously described as 'a harsh metallic croak,' 'an occasional metallic grunt' or a 'low *kar kar*.'

Nesting and the Young. The nest is an enormous structure, usually placed 15–40ft (5–13m) above the ground in the fork of a tree, or occasionally built in a fissure of the rocks of a cliff or inland crag. The nest is built mainly of sticks, lined, and partly held together by dried mud or dung, and measuring up to 3–4ft (1–1·3m) in diameter. It is a closed ball with a small round entrance hole and tunnel in the most inaccessible side. A common native legend has it that other birds help the Hammerheads by supplying them with nesting material, but in fact a pair may spend up to six months building its nest. Clutches are of three to seven white eggs with a slightly chalky surface. Incubation is shared and the newly-hatched downy and helpless young are tended by both parents. Breeding occurs in all months of the year.

Composition. The Hammerhead *Scopus umbretta* is the only member of the Scopidae. Its affinities are mainly with the storks Ciconiidae with which it is classified in the suborder Ciconiae, but it differs from all true storks in having the middle toe pectinated as in the herons Ardeidae. There are two subspecies *Scopus umbretta umbretta* and *S. u. bannermanni*.

STORKS

The Ciconiidae is a small family of long-legged birds that are most closely related to the ibises and spoonbills of the family Threskiornithidae and the Hammerhead (Scopidae). They are all large or very large birds, varying from 30–60in (76–152cm) long, with long necks, long and broad wings and a short tail. In some species the tail is hidden beneath elongated upper tail coverts. The bill is long and stout, without surface grooves. It is straight in most species, but downcurved in a few and upcurved in others. The openbills in the genus *Anastomus* have a downcurved upper mandible and upcurved lower mandible, leaving a conspicuous gap between. The legs are long, with the tibiae partly bare of feathers, and the toes moderately long with short webs connecting the front three toes.

A White stork *Ciconia ciconia* in its normal posture (1) and displaying (2) by rattling the bill.

Three species of stork. (1) Saddle-billed stork *Ephippiorhynchus senegalensis*, (2) Lesser (or Javan) adjutant *Leptoptilos javanicus* and (3) Black stork *Ciconia nigra*. Wagtails (4) often associate with storks because the latter disturb insects on which the wagtails feed.

Most species are boldly marked with black and white, mainly black with iridescent gloss, or mainly white. Several species have the face or the whole head and neck mainly bare of feathers, often with coloured skin. The genus *Leptoptilos* has a well developed throat pouch. The plumage of the sexes is alike in all species, but adults and young often differ in the colour of the legs, bill or facial skin.

Storks fly strongly, usually with the neck extended and legs trailing behind. Their broad wings enable them to soar like eagles on thermal upcurrents. Migrating European White storks *Ciconia ciconia* probably soar nearly all of the way from Europe to tropical Africa each year, concentrating at the Bosporus and Straits of Gibraltar to avoid crossing the open Mediterranean, where there are no thermals.

Distribution. The majority of species are found in the Old World tropics, but two species occur in Europe and northern Asia, and three in central and South America. Europe has the well-known White stork and the Black stork *Ciconia nigra*, both of which migrate to winter in tropical Africa. These two species also occur in northern Asia, although the White stork is replaced in the east by the closely related Asian White stork *C. boyciana*.

Besides the wintering Black and White storks, tropical Africa also has Abdim's stork *Sphenorhynchus abdimii*, the Saddle-billed stork *Ephipphiorhynchus senegalensis*, the Woolly-necked stork *Dissoura episcopus*, the Openbill *Anastomus lamelligerus*, the so-called Wood ibis *Ibis ibis* and the carrion-eating Marabou *Leptoptilos crumeniferus*. The range of the Woolly-necked stork extends to southern Asia, where the genus *Leptoptilos* is represented by the Adjutant *L. dubius* and Lesser adjutant *L. javanicus*, the genus *Ibis* by the Painted stork *I. leucocephalus* and Southern painted stork *I. cinereus*, and the Openbill by *A. oscitans*, which is known by the same English name. The Black-necked stork *Xenorhynchus asiaticus* has a wide range extending from India to Australia, being the only species found on the Australian continent.

Storks are absent from most of North America, although the

Jabiru *Jabiru mycteria* and Wood ibis *Mycteria americana* occur southwards through Central and South America from Mexico and South Carolina respectively. The third American stork, the Maguari stork *Euxenura galeata*, occurs from the Guianas south to Argentina.

The family occupies a wide range of habitats, varying from clearings in forests to dry open plains and agricultural land. The openbills and Saddlebill are usually associated with water or marshland, but the Marabou and adjutants commonly occur far from water in arid regions. The European and Asian White storks commonly nest on houses in towns and villages, but most species are shy of humans.

Feeding. The majority of species in the Ciconiidae feed on a variety of animals captured while walking in grassland, marsh vegetation or along the margins of lakes and rivers. Fish, frogs, large insects, snails, small mammals and small reptiles are the usual prey taken. Although, like waders, they have partly webbed toes, the majority of storks find their food in dry fields and open plains, and to a lesser extent in marshes and ditches. The Saddlebill is unusual in habitually wading in shallow water to catch fish and amphibians after the manner of a large heron. In Africa and the Near East several species will congregate to feed on swarms of locusts.

The Marabou, Adjutant and Lesser adjutant eat mainly carrion, often from the corpses of large game animals. These species circle high in the air like vultures, then congregate at food, often alongside vultures. Their bare heads and throats are probably an adaptation to reduce soiling while feeding on carrion. In some parts of Africa, Marabous cause considerable damage to breeding colonies of flamingos and pelicans by plundering eggs and nestlings.

The peculiar bill structure from which the openbills derive their name is a special adaptation to allow them to grasp and open the slippery shells of large water snails. Unlike other members of the family, these two species often feed at night.

Nesting and the Young. Storks of most species nest in trees, often high above the ground. A few species also use cliff ledges and the European White stork has come to prefer buildings or the special nesting platforms that are in some places erected for its benefit.

Storks fly with outstretched necks but herons with the neck retracted. (1) The Jabiru *Jabiru mycteria* with its crop filled with food and (2) the White stork *Ciconia ciconia* are contrasted with the Grey heron *Ardea cinerea* (3).

Nests are bulky structures of sticks and twigs, often with sods of turf and other vegetable materials. The clutches of 3–5, occasionally 6, unmarked white eggs are incubated by both male and female.

The nestlings are naked and helpless when first hatched, but later acquire a woolly down plumage before the feathers grow. Both parents take part in feeding, carrying food to the nest in the throat or crop, then regurgitating. Incubation starts as soon as the first egg is laid, the young hatching over a period of several days. As a result there is often a substantial size difference between the younger and older nestlings. When food is scarce the smaller, younger ones usually die, thus ensuring the survival of at least part of the brood.

Most if not all storks probably pair for life and do not breed until

The Black-faced spoonbill *Platalea minor* (1) and the American White ibis *Eudocimus albus* (2) in flight. (Eurasian) Spoonbills *Platalea leucorodia* (3) forage by swinging their bills from side to side to sieve food from the water.

several years old. Sexual displays include a variety of elaborate postures and a stylized dancing or walking on the spot during which the bill is often rattled or clattered.

Colonial Behaviour. Most storks are gregarious, at least at times, but some nest solitarily, others in loose colonies and a few species in dense colonies. In different regions the European White stork nests either as solitary, rather widely spaced pairs, in small colonies of a few pairs or in larger colonies where food and nest sites are both available in plenty. In contrast the Black stork normally nests solitarily in wooded regions.

Composition. The Ciconiidae is a natural group of about 17 species usually classified into 11 genera, although recent studies suggest fewer genera may suffice. The New World genus *Mycteria* and the Old World genus *Ibis* are usually placed in the subfamily Mycteriinae.

IBISES AND SPOONBILLS

Ibises are adapted for obtaining food by probing shallow water, mud and grass for small animals, whereas spoonbills are adapted for catching floating prey in shallow water. Both ibises and spoonbills find their food more by touch than by sight. They nest and roost in swamps and marshes, in trees and on the ground. Behaviourally and morphologically they are closely related to flamingoes and pelicans.

The Threskiornithidae vary in size from 19–42in (48–107cm). Ibises have long, slender, decurved, curlew-like bills and spoonbills have long straight spoon-shaped bills. Both have long necks and legs. The feet are semi-palmate (partly webbed). The wings are long and broad. In sustained flight, head and neck are stretched forward, and slow flapping wing beats alternate with short glides. The adults of some species have naked heads and upper necks. In other species the heads are feathered, and in some a large tuft projects back from the nape. A few species have a tuft of ornamental feathers on the breast.

Distribution. The distribution of ibises and spoonbills is worldwide in tropical and warm temperate regions. When the swamps and marshes in which they breed dry up, they may go thousands of miles in search of suitable habitat.

The Bald ibis *Geronticus eremita* at its nest situated on a cliff ledge.

Only one genus of ibis, *Plegadis*, has a worldwide distribution, from Central America to Australia. Sacred and related ibises *Threskiornis* occur in an arc around the Indian Ocean from South Africa to Australia. The genus *Geronticus* is now restricted to remnant populations in the mountains of Africa and the Middle East. Formerly it also occurred in the Alps of Europe. The remaining ibis genera are distributed as follows: *Eudocimus (Guara)*, *Thersiticus*, *Mesebrinibus*, *Harpiprion*, *Phimosus* and *Cercibis* in America; *Hagedashia*, *Lampribis* and *Bostrychia* in Africa, *Lophotibis* in Madagascar, and *Nipponia*, *Pseudibis* and *Thaumatibis* in Asia.

There are three genera of spoonbills, *Ajaia* in the New World, *Platibis* in Australia and *Platalea* in the Old World, including Australasia.

Feeding. Ibises feed on a wide variety of small animals, vertebrate and invertebrate. They are particularly noted for foraging in rice fields and in other irrigated crops. They will also feed on grasshoppers and mice in dry grasslands. The Australian White ibis *Threskiornis molucca* uses hard surfaces as anvils on which to break open fresh water mussels. It does this by holding the mussel under its foot and using its bill as a hammer.

Spoonbills feed by waving the open bill from side to side in shallow water. The bill snaps shut when a floating or swimming

The Painted stork *Ibis leucocephalus* (1) shakes its leg in shallow water to disturb fish and other aquatic prey. On other occasions, Painted storks may forage for food in groups (2).

object touches the inside of the bill tip. They feed both during the day and at night.

Nesting and the Young. Most species of ibises and spoonbills nest colonially in trees, on bushes, or among reeds near water. *Geronticus* nests in loose agregations on mountain cliff ledges, and *Nipponia* nests in isolated pairs in large trees on slopes of hills and mountains.

In colonies several pairs claim adjacent nest sites at the same time. Members of a pair take turns in guarding the nest site until the chicks are large enough to defend themselves. Nests are built of twigs, plants and debris. Up to five eggs are laid. Both parents feed the chicks which take regurgitated food from the parent's mouth and throat. The chicks are fed until they fledge and disperse from the colony.

Economic Importance. Ibises have been valued since prehistoric times for their rôle in controlling animal pests in irrigated crops but now many species are threatened with extinction because the crops are treated with biocides.

Composition. Despite the great difference in bill shape ibises and spoonbills are sufficiently closely related for hybrids between an ibis and a spoonbill to have been produced in captivity. The obvious difference between species groups is the extent in adult birds of naked areas on the head, upper neck and under the wings. There has been no satisfactory recent revision of the ibis genera.

The American ibises including the cosmopolitan species *Plegadis falcinellus* and the Australian Yellow-billed spoonbill *Platibis flavipes* have feathered heads without a large prominent crest on the nape in breeding birds. Feathered heads with a large prominent crest on the nape are a feature of breeding birds in the following Old World genera of ibises and spoonbills: *Hagedashia*, *Lampribis*, *Bostrychia*, *Lophotibis*, *Nipponia* and *Platalea*. Adults of *Geronticus* have a naked head with a prominent ruff of long plumes around the upper neck. The head and neck is naked in adults of *Threskiornis*, *Pseudibis* and *Ajaia*. *Threskiornis* has naked patches under the wings which are visible when the wings are raised or spread during courtship and in flight. The patches are scarlet in the Sacred ibis *T. aethiopicus* and the Australian White ibis *T. molucca* and orange in the Straw-necked ibis *T. spinicollis*. Adults of *Threskiornis*, *Ajaia* and *Platibis* have a tuft of long ornamental plumes on the breast.

Four species of ibis and a spoonbill. (1) Glossy ibis *Plegadis falcinellus*, (2) American White ibis *Eudocimus albus*, (3) Scarlet ibis *E. ruber*, (4) Japanese ibis *Nipponia nippon* and (5) the Roseate spoonbill *Ajaia ajaja*.

The trachea is straight in ibises of the genus *Platibis* and juveniles of the genera *Ajaia* and *Platalea*. It is bifurcated in adults of *Ajaia* and convoluted in adults of *Platalea*.

A pink feather pigment occurs in adults of the Scarlet ibis *Eudocimus ruber*, the Japanese ibis *Nipponia nippon*, the Roseate spoonbill *Ajaia ajaja* and the Yellow-billed spoonbill *Platibis flavipes*. Before nesting the Japanese ibis anoints itself with a dark pigment secretion to acquire a cryptic grey plumage.

FLAMINGOS

Flamingos are large, brilliantly colured, aquatic birds which inhabit alkaline and saline lakes and lagoons. They belong to the family Phoenicopteridae, one of the oldest birds groups still alive, with fossil evidence going back to the early Tertiary. The flamingos constitute an easily recognized group. All are large, 3–6ft (1–2m) in length, with long sinuous necks, long legs and webbed feet. The bill is highly specialized for filter-feeding, sharply bent in the middle, with the lower mandible large and trough-like and the upper one small and lid-like. The plumage is pink, red and black, often brilliant. No other large gregarious birds are quite so colourful.

Distribution. From fossils we know that flamingos were once widespread in Europe, North America and Australia as well as in the areas where they are found today. They are now a relict group occurring in isolated pockets mainly in the tropics. Being specialized ecologically, they are often superabundant in certain habitats and entirely absent in others. The Caribbean flamingo *Phoenicopterus ruber ruber* occurs in the West Indies with an outlying population in the Galapagos Islands. The Greater flamingo *Phoenicopterus ruber*, is the most widespread, ranging from West Africa to southeast India and Ceylon, and from Kazakhstan south to the Cape Province of South Africa. The Chilean flamingo *Phoenicopterus chilensis* occurs from central Peru southwards along the Andes to Tierra del Fuego. Major concentrations of the Lesser flamingo *Phoeniconaias minor* are found in soda lakes of the east African rift valley, and large populations also exist in southwest Africa, Botswana and northwest India. The Andean flamingo *Phoenicoparrus andinus* is found mainly above 8,000ft (say 2,500m) from southern Peru to central

Six kinds of flamingo to show size variation. (1) Greater flamingo *Phoenicopterus ruber roseus*, (2) Caribbean *P. r. ruber*, (3) Chilean *P. chilensis*, (4) Andean *Phoenicoparrus andinus*, (5) James's *P. jamesi* and (6) the Lesser flamingo *Phoeniconaias minor*.

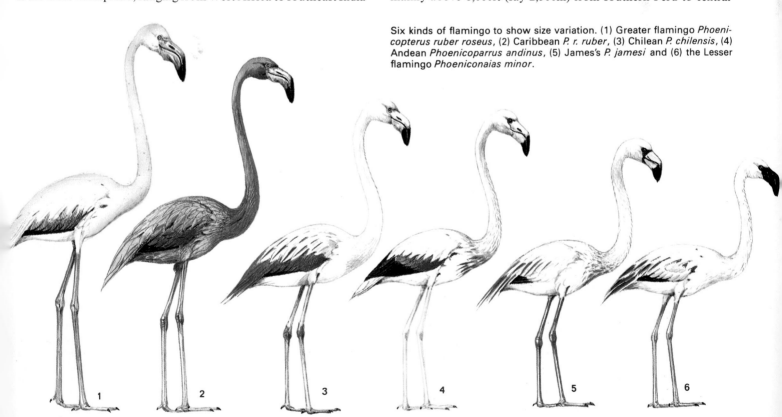

Chile and northwest Argentina. James's flamingo *P. jamesi* has the most restricted range of all, occurring mainly above 11,400ft (say 3,500m) with the Andean species.

Flamingos are confined to shallow soda lakes and salt lagoons, usually barren of vegetation and surrounded by almost desert-like wastes. Birds breeding at higher latitudes or altitudes move to warmer climates in the winter, the young travelling separately from their parents. Other, irregular, movements are suspected to be in relation to food supply.

Feeding. The feeding methods of flamingos are characteristic and peculiar. The bill is held upside-down in the water and minute organisms are filtered out by fine lamellae. The Caribbean and Greater flamingos feed mainly on invertebrates in the bottom mud, normally wading in shallow water, more rarely swimming, or upending like ducks. They are thus usually found feeding at a shoreline or on mud banks. The smaller Lesser flamingo feeds on blue-green algae and is a primary user of lake vegetation extracted from the top two or three inches or so, often while swimming. The feeding habits of the other species are less well-known.

Nesting and the Young. Males tend to be larger than females but the sexes are almost indistinguishable. Flamingos are among the most social of birds and display in large groups with sometimes hundreds of birds taking part. Both sexes participate, although displays are usually initiated by the males and their performances may be more intense and protracted. Displaying occurs months before, as well as after, actual nesting.

Many of the ritualized displays of flamingos are similar to the preening and stretching movements adopted in everyday activity, only they are more stiffly performed, more contagious among members of the group, and given in typical sequences. Head-flagging followed by wing-saluting is common: a bird in or near the displaying group suddenly stops head-flagging, spreads its wings to the sides and folds them again. The general effect is a flash of black in a pink field. A twist-preen may then follow: the bird twists its neck back, flashing a wing downward to expose the black primaries, and appears to preen behind the wing with its bill. In the inverted wing salute, the bird bends forwards and the wings are flashed partly open and held above the back. Marching is a display in which flamingos gather in a tight mass, standing erect, and march backwards and forwards in synchronized quickstep, sometimes making feeding movements with the bill in the water.

At a certain stage in displaying, pairs break away and start to build nests. They build with movements similar to those of waterfowl, picking up mud and stones within reach and placing them beneath their bodies to form a circular pile. Both sexes build and a single white egg is laid which both sexes incubate for 28–30 days. After hatching the chick is brooded and, unlike young waterfowl and screamers, it will not leave the nest until 5–8 days of age. While there, it is fed by its parents on a secretion formed by glands in the upper digestive tract. Initially the secretion is dark red in colour due to a high canthaxanthin content; after a while this fades and the secretion appears to be a pale straw colour. The length of time for which the chick is dependent for food varies: in the wild Caribbean flamingo it feeds itself from 4–6 weeks, but in captivity, parental feeding has been recorded at 12 months of age. In most

The Greater flamingo *Phoenicopterus ruber* at its nest (1). These are built of mud in large colonies. (2) Characteristic feeding displayed by James's flamingo *Phoenicoparrus jamesi* in which the bill is passed through shallow water and filters out minute organisms.

species the young are fully fledged in 3 months.

Territorial Behaviour. Flamingos nest in huge colonies; indeed, they seldom breed in flocks smaller than 20 birds. Nesting is synchronized, presumably in relation to food abundance for the laying females and the feeding chicks. Only the nest site is defended vigorously with various threat postures, and the nest mounds themselves are usually two neck-lengths apart. The flamingo's voice is loud and rather goose-like and appears important in keeping the flock together.

Composition. There are five species and three genera which differ mainly in bill and leg colour. The two largest are subspecies of *Phoenicopterus ruber*, the very bright pink Caribbean being *P.r. ruber*, and the paler Greater being *P.r. roseus*. On behavioural grounds, the Chilean flamingo *P. chilensis* is now considered to have specific status. *Phoenicoparrus andinus*, the Andean, and *P. jamesi*, the James's, differ from the others in lacking a hind toe. The smallest species is the Lesser flamingo *Phoeniconaias minor*.

ANSERIFORMES

Waterfowl are gregarious birds with webbed feet.
All lay plain, unspotted eggs

SCREAMERS — *Anhimidae*
SWANS, GEESE AND DUCKS — *Anatidae*

SCREAMERS

The screamers bear little resemblance to other anseriforms – swans, geese and ducks – although there are anatomical similarities which suggest that they form the link between the curassows (game birds) and the Magpie goose *Anseranas semipalmata*. Like the Magpie goose their legs are long and the feet large with a strong hind toe and little webbing. The bill, however, is game-bird like, with a pronounced downward hook and none of the filtering fringes (lamellae) so common in ducks. Flight feathers are moulted gradually so that, like the Magpie goose but unlike most waterfowl, they do not pass through an annual flightless stage. Practically all their bones are hollow and beneath the loose skin lies a network of small airsacs. The Horned screamer *Anhima cornuta* has a remarkable 6in (15cm) long caruncle or horn projecting from the forehead. The function of this is unknown but it is probably connected with display.

Distribution. Screamers are non-migratory and native to South America. The Black-necked, or Northern, screamer *Chauna chav-*

aria is restricted to Colombia and western Venezuela. The Horned screamer is also tropical and found from the Guianas, Venezuela and Colombia to eastern Bolivia and Argentina. The Crested, or Southern, screamer *Chauna torquata* occurs in Brazil, eastern Bolivia, Paraguay and Argentina.

They are mainly marshland birds, but found also in open savannas, and on the banks of ponds and slow-moving streams. Shallow water is used for roosting and they can swim, although, except for the young birds, they do so rather reluctantly. Once airborne, screamers fly strongly and can soar to considerable heights.

Behaviour. The Crested screamer in particular grazes in open grassland along with farm stock, but they and the other species typically feed on marsh plants while wading through, or walking on, floating vegetation. The Horned screamer, although primarily vegetarian, may take some insects.

Male and female look alike and seem to pair for life. Displays do not differ between the sexes and are inconspicuous, consisting mainly of antiphonal calling or duetting, rapid opening and closing of the bill, and mutual preening of the head feathers. A long breeding season is probably influenced by temperature and the rains. Copulation occurs on land and, as in all waterfowl, the male bird has a penis. Nests are placed in shallow water within 240ft (27m) of the shore and built of sticks and vegetation. Material is not carried but passed back to the nest in the bill so that it is constructed of items within easy reach. Both sexes build, and incubate the large white eggs which are laid at nearly two-day intervals. The Black-necked screamer produces four eggs, the Horned five and the Crested commonly five or six, although in all species the range may be from three to seven. Incubation generally lasts from between 40 and 44 days. On hatching, the chicks are covered in dense yellow down and follow their parents from the nest. Like Magpie geese, both parents may supplement feeding with items placed in the open gape of the chick, and they also pick up and drop food items,

The Black-necked screamer *Chauna chavaria* (1) uses its long toes to advantage when walking on floating vegetation. A Horned screamer *Anhima cornuta* adopts an aggressive posture to fend off an Ornate hawk-eagle that threatens its chicks (2). All screamers are native to South America.

(1) Horned screamer *Anhima cornuta*, (2) Black-necked screamer *Chauna chavaria* and (3) the Crested screamer *C. torquata*.

apparently to bring them to their chicks' attention. The juvenile Crested screamer is full grown in 3½ months.

Pairs establish territories before breeding and flock only in winter. Two sharp spurs measuring up to 2in (5cm) protrude from the wrist of each wing and are present as tiny thorns at hatching. These are used to attack intruders and broken off spurs have been found buried in screamer breast muscle. All species have loud, far-carrying voices with which they announce their possession of a territory and from which they derive their common name. The male's call is lower-pitched than the female's and is a double-noted 'cha-ha.' Both sexes also produce rumbling sounds by vibrating the airsacs, which seem to function as close-range threat.

Composition. Two genera and three species are recognized. The Crested screamer *Chauna torquata*, weighing 6–7½lb (2·7–3·4kg), is the best known. It is similar, and closely related, to the slightly smaller Black-necked screamer *C. chavaria* with which it has hybridized in captivity. Both species are grey, the Black-necked being darker with whiter cheeks and a longer crest. The Horned screamer *Anhima cornuta* weighs 8–10lb (3·6–4·5kg) and is almost black above with white underparts.

SWANS, GEESE AND DUCKS

The family Anatidae consists of swans, geese and ducks (known collectively as waterfowl) and is usually associated with aquatic or marine habitats. Members vary greatly in size, the largest, the Mute swan *Cygnus olor*, weighing some 33lb (15kg), and the smallest, the Ringed teal *Callonetta leucophrys*, about 10½oz (300gm). The bill also varies widely, as would be expected in species with diets as different as grass, fish and surface plankton, but is typically broad and somewhat flattened with a rounded tip, and with fine lamellae at the edges of the mandibles to aid in food handling and in straining

A Mute swan *Cygnus olor*
defending its young.

food organisms from water. The evolutionary trend within the group has been towards increasing adaptation to aquatic life. The more 'advanced' waterfowl have streamlined bodies, close and waterproof plumage and webbed feet.

Distribution. Waterfowl breed on every major continent and island, except Antarctica, and may undertake migrations over thousands of miles. Some species are extremely numerous and widespread; among these are the Pintail *Anas acuta* and Mallard *A. platyrhynchos*, both found throughout the northern hemisphere. Other species are represented by a few thousand, or even hundred, individuals confined to a single island; among these is the Hawaiian goose *Branta sandvicensis*.

Most waterfowl are associated with fresh water, at least during the breeding season. Preferred areas seem to be those which have been glaciated in the recent past and are rich in shallow lakes and marshes. An area with many small water surfaces supports more ducks than a single large lake, because an extended shoreline produces food, isolation for breeding pairs, cover from predators and shelter from winds. When small lakes dry out, their bottoms become colonized by plants; later re-flooding makes available a rich harvest of seeds and invertebrate animals.

The ability to migrate increases ecological flexibility. Waterfowl can exploit the resources of the northern tundras and then move great distances to a warmer climate in the winter. The longest duck migration is probably that of the Blue-winged teal *Anas discors* which nests up to 60° N in North America and winters to beyond 30° S – a distance of over 6,000mi (9,600km).

Feeding. Wildfowl have evolved along three main lines of feeding behaviour – diving, dabbling and grazing. Those that dive for food occur in two groups, first the inland species favouring shallow lakes and predominantly feeding on vegetation (leaves, roots and seeds), and secondly the sea ducks which use deeper marine waters and take largely invertebrates and fish. Dabbling ducks feed on the surface or just below, or up-end to reach food (largely plant material) on the bottom. Geese, swans and a few ducks take grasses and other pasture plants on dry land or in marshes, and may also take roots both on land and beneath the water surface. Many of these grazing birds have adapted to feeding on farm crops.

Nesting and the Young. Courtship produces social displays that are clearly derived in evolution from maintenance activities such as preening and body stretching. Pair formation displays are genetically 'fixed' and characteristic of a species, and this is necessary if mating between closely related species that winter in the same place is to be avoided. Displays that maintain the pair bond in the less advanced species, where the mates normally stay together for life, tend to be inconspicuous, such as mutual preening of the head and neck feathers. Swans and geese maintain their bonds with a 'triumph ceremony' which involves mutual head movements, wing lifting, and calling, typically after they have repulsed an intruder.

In sheldgeese, females incite their males to attack other birds by actually running between the two opponents, and female inciting is found throughout the rest of the family, although male behaviour is quite varied. Male dabbling ducks show a variety of movements to which ethologists have endeavoured to give objective names. Thus 'head-up tail-up' involves a simultaneous jerk of the head and tail upwards and a lifting of the folded wings to display the 'speculum' (a set of metallic-coloured secondary feathers on the upper surface of the wing). In the 'grunt-whistle' an arc of water is thrown at the female by a sideways flick of the male's bill, followed by rearing up the body and shaking the head and tail while giving two calls – a

grunt followed by a whistle. The sea ducks have particularly elaborate male displays, jerking the head back on the tail while kicking up a spurt of water, bowing while producing dove-like coos, or wagging the head from side to side. Some of the most bizarre displays are found among the stifftails such as the Ruddy duck *Oxyura jamaicensis* of North America; the males cock their tails over their backs, inflate their lower necks and beat on them with their bright blue bills, producing bubbles as they eject the air from their feathers, and then a burp from the open bill.

Copulation in all the advanced species occurs while the pair is swimming and as in all waterfowl, the male bird has a penis. Primitive species build their nests over water and among marsh vegetation. The protection thus afforded may have tipped evolution towards the progressively more aquatic existence of the rest of the group. Many nests, however, are found on dry land; some species

(shelducks) use burrows and others (the perching ducks and some small mergansers) cavities in trees. They do not construct these for themselves but take over whatever is available, such as rabbit warrens or woodpecker holes. Some successful species, like the Mallard, are adaptable and may nest in a variety of situations. In the more 'primitive' species, such as the Magpie goose *Anseranas semipalmata*, whistling ducks and swans, the building of the nest is done by both sexes; in the true geese and ducks, the task is undertaken by the female alone. Generally, waterfowl appear incapable of carrying items in the bill; therefore, the nest is constructed of materials within reach of the bill and present on the site. These materials are pulled in and dropped at the feet or passed sideways over the shoulder forming a pile as the bird rotates. With the exception of those species where incubation is shared and the eggs are never left uncovered, down feathers from the breast are used to line the nest. The down is normally pulled over the eggs when the female leaves to feed, thus keeping them warm, preventing loss of moisture and protecting them from the sight of predators.

Egg laying usually occurs early in the morning, and generally one egg is laid per day, although with the larger species an egg every two days is the rule. Clutch size is variable but the averages for all species range from 3–12 eggs, and there is a tendency for the larger clutches to be laid by species that devote little parental care to their offspring. Eggshells are uniformly white, green or brownish, and the texture is smooth.

A number of species lay their eggs casually in the nests of other birds; in the diving ducks and stifftails, this is sometimes common enough to influence the breeding biology of a population. The Black-headed duck *Heteronetta atricapilla* of South America is an obligate nest parasite, always laying in the nest of other birds, usually ibis or coot. Incubation periods, ranging from 22–39 days, are generally short in birds nesting at high latitudes and longer in those nesting in the tropics. Since incubation does not start until the clutch is complete, hatching is synchronous and the brood appears within six hours, remaining in the nest overnight and leaving the following morning behind the female. While they are in the nest, the chicks become imprinted with her appearance and her voice, and when they leave, she takes them to suitable feeding grounds. Apart from the Magpie goose and the Musk duck *Biziura lobata* of Australia, which are similar to the screamers in placing food items in the gape of begging chicks, none feed their offspring. The young are covered in thick down and swim from a day old. Some dive to obtain their food, but the majority peck at items on the surface, preferring green and yellow objects, and objects that move.

In the more primitive species, both parents stay with the brood. In all others, except the Black-headed duck, the mother remains to guard, guide and initially brood the ducklings at night and during inclement weather. The downy covering is retained for about two weeks in the small ducks, for up to six weeks in the large swans, and is then gradually replaced by the feathers of the juvenile plumage. After fledging, young ducks must make their own way, but in geese and swans, the parents remain throughout the first winter, migrating with their family to the wintering grounds.

Territorial Behaviour. Most waterfowl are gregarious, although few nest in true colonies. The eiders positively prefer to seek each other's company, and a number of other species, including the Gadwall *Anas strepera*, nest very closely, perhaps because of a shortage of protected situations in suitable habitats, rather than from a colonial preference on the part of the female choosing the site. One or two species with insectivorous young are territorial; for instance, the white swans maintain large territories, using their conspicuous pale plumage and visual displays and, in the far northern species, a loud call to advertise their presence. Others that maintain territories along river systems include the Torrent ducks *Merganetta armata*

Five species of swan. (1) Black-necked swan *Cygnus melanocoryphus*, (2) Whistling *C. columbianus*, (3) Trumpeter *C. buccinator*, (4) Coscoroba *Coscoroba coscoroba* and (5) the Whooper *Cygnus cygnus*.

and sub-species of South America, Salvadori's duck *Anas waiginensis* of New Guinea and the Blue duck *Hymenolaimus malacorhynchas* of New Zealand. The Kelp goose *Chloephaga hybrida* of South America also maintains a linear territory along a stretch of sea-shore and, like the swans, the male of this species is conspicuously white.

Vocalizations within the waterfowl are rather simple and not individually elaborate. A range of grunts, hoots, honks and coos is produced, mainly by males in social contact or courtship display, but the quack is almost always female. The voice of most territorial species is loud and used to announce the owner's presence. Some non-vocal sounds are produced by the wings or inflated airsacs.

Economic Importance. The large size of many waterfowl has long made them the quarry of man. The period of flightlessness, when all the wing feathers are moulted simultaneously, was early exploited, the birds being driven into netting or corrals and then slaughtered. Some populations are now threatened by the loss of wetland habitat, due to drainage for development and wildfowling has had such damaging effects that many countries have banned market shooting and made at least some attempts to impose bag limits on the individual hunter.

When diving, the Tufted duck *Aythya fuligula* (1) keeps its wings close to its body, while the Velvet (or White-winged) scoter *Melanitta fusca* (2) partly spreads its wings, the alula or bastard wing projecting.

Claims that waterfowl cause damage to farm crops are often exaggerated, for the majority of migratory waterfowl arrive after the harvest has been gathered and they then take only spilled grain or rejected tubers, performing a useful operation in cleaning the fields. Experiments have shown that geese grazing growing cereals in winter do not reduce subsequent grain yield. In certain cases, conflicts do arise, as when geese take carrots, turnips, or spring grass but these can often be resolved by changes in husbandry or by scaring.

Waterfowl are frequently kept in captivity and are popular zoo animals. In view of this ready adaptation, it is surprising that only four temperate zone species have been domesticated. The Mallard came into domestication 2,000 years ago in China and more than 10 varieties have been developed for meat or egg production. The Muscovy duck *Cairina moschata* was domesticated in South America before the arrival of the Spaniards. The eastern Greylag goose *Anser anser* has been domesticated for at least 4,000 years and eight varieties of farmyard goose are known. The Swan goose *A. cygnoides* of Asia has also been farmed. A remarkable form of exploitation has been that of the Eider *Somateria mallissima*; the down with which the female lines the nest is collected during and

Geese display a greater variety of plumage colours than do swans. (1) Red-breasted goose *Branta ruficollis*, (2) Brent goose (or Brant) *B. bernicla*, (3) Emperor goose *Anser canagicus*, (4) Cape Barren goose *Cereopsis novae-hollandiae* and (5) the Spur-winged goose *Plectropterus gambensis*.

after incubation for use in producing eiderdowns and padded clothing. Its insulating properties are unsurpassed by man-made fibres.

Composition. Within the family of ducks, geese and swans there are about 37 genera and 142 species. One subfamily, the Anseranatinae, contains only the Magpie goose *Anseranas semipalmata*, which is the least adapted to water and shares features with the screamers. A second subfamily, Anserinae, contains the large swans *Cygnus* and true geese, *Anser* and *Branta* plus the smaller whistling ducks *Dendrocygna* and the Australian Freckled duck *Stictonetta naevosa*. The subfamily Anatinae contains the burrow-nesting shelducks *Tadorna*, the grazing sheldgeese *Chloephaga* and all other ducks. These are further sub-divided into the perching

Six species of duck. (1) Garganey *Anas querquedula*, (2) Long-tailed duck (or Oldsquaw) *Clangula hyemalis*, (3) Torrent duck *Merganetta armata*, (4) Hooded merganser *Mergus cucullatus*, (5) White-faced tree duck *Dendrocygna viduata* and (6) the Steamer duck *Tachyeres brachypterus*.

ducks *Cairina*, dabbling ducks *Anas*, diving ducks *Aythya* and *Netta* (pochard and scaup), sea ducks (mergansers *Mergus* and eiders *Somateria*) and finally the highly aquatic stifftails *Oxyura*. There is general agreement on this taxonomic organization but controversy does exist about the correct positionings of certain species. These include the Whitebacked duck *Thalassornis leuconotus*, which seems curiously intermediate between the stifftails and whistling ducks; Cape Barren goose *Cereopsis novae-hollandiae*, which may be placed nearest to the sheldgeese, true geese or swans; and the Ringed teal *Callonetta leucophrys*, which is sometimes put within the genus *Anas*.

FALCONIFORMES

The birds of prey are a varied group. Some hunt rodents, others eat lizards and a few snatch insects from the air

NEW WORLD VULTURES — *Cathartidae*
SECRETARY BIRD — *Sagittariidae*
HAWKS AND EAGLES — *Accipitridae*
OSPREY — *Pandionidae*
FALCONS — *Falconidae*

NEW WORLD VULTURES

All of the living species of New World vultures, which include the condors, are placed in this family, and although they possess the same carrion feeding habits and adaptations as the Old World forms found in Africa, Asia and Europe, they are not thought to be closely related to them. They appear to be not far removed from the primitive types of wading and swimming birds, and like the marsh-dwelling cranes and rails have a completely perforate nasal septum. This obvious hole through the bill is one of the more conspicuous differences between the cathartids and the generally heavier-billed Old World vultures, which according to the geological evidence probably evolved some 30 million years later. The cathartid vultures once existed in both hemispheres with the earliest records coming from the Tertiary deposits of both Europe and America. The remains of the largest described form, fossil or Recent, have been found in the tar pits of Rancho La Brea in California and are Pleistocene in age. One species of condor-like bird collected from these pits is said to have had a wing span of at least 16ft (5m), and is called *Teratornis mirabilis*.

The archaeological record shows that certain species of this family were important to some ancient cults. The Mayan civilization of Central America for instance, was much concerned with animals, and used the King vulture *Sarcoramphus papa* as the hieroglyph for Cib, the thirteenth day of the month, often accompanied by a rain sign. It also appears in inscriptions relating to anthropomorphic gods. Carthartids vary in size from 24–44in (61–118cm) in length. Their plumage is typically brownish-black with a paler area on the

Details of the heads of Andean condor *Vultur gryphus* (left) and the California condor *Gymnogyps californianus*. The head of the male Andean condor is crowned with a fleshy caruncle.

under surface of the long, broad wings, the only exception being the King vulture which has a white and cream body. The larger species possess ruffs of lanceolate or downy feathers about the base of the neck. The head is warty, and like the upper portions of the neck is usually bare and can be either black, red or yellow in colour. In the King vulture, however, the head is elaborately patterned with black, hair-like feathers. The bills are always hooked and may be thick or slender. The legs are medium to short in length, with long toes and poorly hooked claws which are too weak for grasping.

Distribution. The New World vultures range from southern Canada to the tip of South America, including many of the Caribbean Islands. The more northerly breeding subspecies of the Turkey vulture *Cathartes aura* is migratory, and has been seen moving in large flocks of several hundreds. Other species, living in more tropical areas are sedentary, although the Black vulture *Coragyps atratus* can be a partial migrant, and the condor will descend to lower altitudes during the winter months.

Feeding. All species are basically carrion feeders, and all but the condors can be found eating casualties or picking over offal at abattoirs, refuse tips and even sewers around human habitation. They will, under certain conditions, attack and kill young animals including domesticated stock. Species living in densely wooded areas are known to eat fruit and other vegetable matter when meat is scarce.

The King vulture *Sarcoramphus papa*, which occurs from Mexico to Argentina, especially in the region of the Andes. The pouch hanging from the neck is a distended crop.

The bills and feet of the cathartids are relatively weak and are not strong enough to rip open a recently killed animal. They will, therefore, sit and wait for the skin to rot before attempting to eat. In the meantime, the eyes are usually plucked out, and appear to be one of the delicacies. When the corpse is 'ready' the stomach wall is punctured and the intestines are eaten immediately. After such a gruesome feast individuals can be so gorged with meat that, on being disturbed, they have to regurgitate their meal before they can take flight.

How these avian dustbins actually locate their food is still a matter of argument amongst ornithologists. Sight undoubtedly plays an important part, but is smell the first indicator in search for dead animals? Recent investigations have shown that the Turkey vulture has the largest olfactory system of all birds, and it is a known fact that no vulture will venture near a newly discovered carcass if a human is up-wind from it. Furthermore, they have been seen to ignore suitable carrion until they have picked up the scent.

Courtship. Much of the courtship display of this family takes the form of aerial displays, made up of much soaring and wheeling. This appears to be preceded by a courtship dance between a pair of birds, but in some species this display can be gregarious. The dance usually consists of hopping towards an intended mate with outstretched wings and lowered head. Much of this display is undertaken in silence, but normally ends with sighs, gutteral croaks or hissing.

Nesting and the Young. After pairing, a variety of nesting sites may be chosen. They may be in caves, hollow trees, deserted buildings, old nests of other birds or even on the ground. Little or no attempt is made to construct an actual nest, and the 1–3, white or pale grey-green, sometimes brown-blotched eggs are laid on the ground. They are incubated by both parents and take up to 58 days to hatch in the case of the Andean condor *Vultur gryphus*. On hatching the young are covered with down, completely helpless and are cared for by both parents. The young of the condors often remain up to six months in the nest.

Behaviour. The largest members of the family tend to be solitary, or occur in pairs or family groups. The smaller and much commoner forms are often encountered in large flocks around a suitable carcass, and out of the breeding season will often roost colonially.

Economic importance. In the primitive regions of South America the majority of the species were more than welcome around human settlements, as they cleared away all decaying animal matter, thus helping to prevent the spread of disease. Today, however, they are no longer welcome, as they are known to foul water supplies. At one time they were thought to be the carriers of hog cholera, anthrax and other contagious ailments because they fed on animals which died of these diseases, and before this was disproved many thousands were slaughtered by farmers. One such person boasted of shooting 3,500 Black vultures in one winter.

Composition. The family Cathartidae is made up of five genera: *Cathartes*, *Coragyps*, *Sarcoramphus*, *Gymnogyps* and *Vultur*, containing seven species. The Andean condor has the largest wing-span of all living birds, attaining a spread of something over 10ft (3m). The Andean and Californian condors, but more especially the latter, are in danger of becoming extinct, mainly because of the influence of man.

In some birds, arena behaviour occurs in which males parade in a circle in order to impress potential mates. Usually the females are promiscuous and choose their mate. In this example, a group of Turkey vultures *Cathartes aura* are shown performing.

Two of the largest birds of prey: (1) Andean condor *Vultur gryphus* and (2) Bearded vulture *Gypaëtus barbatus*.

SECRETARY BIRD

The Secretary bird *Sagittarius serpentarius*, a long-legged, diurnal, terrestrial bird of prey, confined to Africa south of the Sahara, is the sole living member of the family Sagittariidae. Although it is generally considered to belong to the order Falconiformes, some anatomical and other peculiarities suggest that it may be allied to the South American family of cariamas (Cariamidae).

Secretary birds stand almost 4ft (1·2m) high, and their wings span 6–7ft (1·8–2·1m). They are mainly grey, with black wing quills and thighs, and bare orange skin on the face. The head is adorned with a black-tipped crest, the central tail-feathers are very long and the grey legs are long with short stubby toes. The name comes from the

Secretary birds *Sagittarius serpentarius* can soar in air thermals like eagles (1). On the ground (2) they feed on snakes although such small prey items as rodents are more important sources of food.

A male Andean condor *Vultur gryphus* with the huge wingspan. Condors are the largest living flying birds, some weighing over 15lb (6½kg).

grey and black clerical livery and from a fancied resemblance of the crest to quill pens stuck behind the ear.

Behaviour. Secretary birds haunt open country, avoiding long grass and extreme desert, but sometimes adapting to cultivated areas. They roost on low thorny trees, usually in pairs, and early in the morning jump to the ground and begin hunting. They walk steadily through the grassland, nodding the head backwards and forwards as domestic fowl do. Now and again one makes a quick dart to catch an insect or mouse in the bill, or breaks its pace to stamp rapidly for half a minute or so, presumably to disturb prey. The food mainly consists of rodents, insects and snakes, in that order of preference. Secretary birds kill far fewer snakes than they are usually credited with.

Normally terrestrial, they can fly well and can soar like a vulture or an eagle. They soar mainly in nuptial display, but sometimes to move from place to place, and have been recorded at 12,000ft (3,650m) above the ground. They are probably nomadic, becoming more common in certain areas in response to rodent or insect plagues, but some pairs are permanently resident, occupying a territory of about 4,000 acres (1,600ha).

Secretary birds nest in low, very thorny trees, usually acacia or Desert date. They make a large, flat nest of sticks, lined with grass, and use it for several years. Two to three greenish white eggs are normally laid. Incubation, undertaken by both sexes, lasts for about 45 days.

When the chicks hatch their development resembles that of other

large falconiforms: helpless and downy at first, feathering by about 30 days and leaving the nest at 60–70 days. They do not fight with one another and two are often reared. They are at first fed by the parent with regurgitated liquid matter, probably pre-digested insects. Later the parent regurgitates a mass of grasshoppers, rats and snakes onto the nest and the young feed on it. Since the Secretary bird has short toes, it cannot carry prey in its feet, and so brings all food for the nestlings in the bill or the crop.

Secretary birds are wholly beneficial and should never be molested. They have disappeared gradually in many inhabited parts of Africa, probably because their nests are relatively easy to reach and rob.

Composition. The Secretary bird is the only extant member of the family Sagittaridae. It is generally thought to belong to the order Falconiformes, though it has been placed by different authorities either in the suborder Falcones or in the Sagittarii.

The Secretary bird *Sagittarius serpentarius* stands at 4ft (1.2m).

HAWKS AND EAGLES

With 217 species, the Accipitridae is the largest family of diurnal birds of prey, varying from tiny sparrowhawks of 4oz (100–120gm) to huge vultures and eagles weighing 13–17lb (6–8kg). With rare crepuscular exceptions, all feed by day, none by night. With one mainly vegetarian exception all feed on dead or live insects, molluscs, crabs, fish, reptiles, birds, or mammals. The predatory habit results in common characters of hooked beaks, very acute sight, and powerful feet with long curved claws, except among mainly non-predatory vultures, whose feet and claws are weak and blunt. Other common characters include eggs with inside shells that appear greenish against the light, and the habit of normally defaecating a white jet, expelled forcibly several feet. The family is so large and varied that it was formerly split into many subfamilies.

Distribution. Members of the Accipitridae occur on all continents except Antarctica, and many oceanic islands. They breed from the Arctic to the tropics, in every habitat from tundra and desert to tall forest. Some groups or genera have restricted distribution in certain areas; for example, Old World vultures and snake eagles are exclusively Old World, whereas the highly variable kites, specialized harriers, and goshawks and sparrowhawks (*Accipiter*) are cosmopolitan. Buzzards and their near allies (*Buteo* and related genera) are most abundant and varied in the Americas, while scavenging kites (*Milvus*) abound in the east. Australasia lacks both buzzards and vultures; but their function is partially performed by an aberrant kite *Hamirostra* and the Wedge-tailed eagle *Aquila audax* respectively.

The number of species and genera occurring anywhere depends primarily on ecological diversity. Thus, only one species, the Rough-legged buzzard *Buteo lagopus* breeds in tundra, and even this migrates in winter. In tropical forest savanna 20 or more species may occur, each occupying particular ecological niches and feeding on different prey. More species are found in South America than anywhere else; but these have been little studied so their relationships are obscure. Generally, species with similar functions are geographically separated; thus, at most, two of seven large Old World vultures (*Gyps*) occur together; and six African buzzards (*Buteo*) divide the continent between them. Where several species of a genus occur, they may be ecologically separate; thus in Europe three similar harriers, the Marsh, Montagu's and Hen harriers, prefer somewhat different country, but in North America the Hen harrier, and in Australia the Marsh harrier occupy all niches.

Many temperate zone species migrate; and a few migrate entirely within the tropics, for example, Wahlberg's Eagle *Aquila wahlbergi*. Others, such as many buzzards and some small kites (*Elanus*) are nomadic, moving irregularly perhaps in response to fluctuations in rodent populations. Movements of most tropical species are neither properly recorded nor understood; nor are tropical winter quarters of temperate species well-known. Thus, the Lesser and Greater spotted eagles and Honey buzzard enter Africa by well-known routes in numbers, but are thereafter little recorded. Some, for instance the European snake eagle *Circaetus g. gallicus* are completely migratory. Others, for example, the Common buzzard *Buteo buteo* have northern migratory populations, *B. b. vulpinus* and sedentary southern populations *B. b. buteo*. Populations subject to severe winters normally migrate; but migration of some subtropical species may be controlled by food supply, for instance in the Honey buzzard which feeds on wasp grubs and the European snake eagle which feeds on reptiles, neither of which are available during the winter; both these species have close tropical allies which are sedentary.

Feeding. Hawks and eagles eat anything from termites to dead whales or elephants. Most find or catch prey on the ground, a few of the swifter eagles sometimes in flight. Without exception prey is located by sight, aided sometimes by hearing (harriers) and, if necessary, killed with the powerful feet. Even vultures have no sense of smell. The most powerful eagles, *Aquila* and *Stephanoaetus*, occasionally kill prey up to five times their own weight; but most species habitually take prey half their own weight or less. Old World vultures seldom or never kill and subsist on carrion; but the Egyptian vulture *Neophron* is one of the few known tool-users and hurls stones at ostrich eggs, while the Lammergeier *Gypaetus* drops bones or rocks to split them.

Some species, for example, the scavenging kites *Milvus* or the Tawny eagle *Aquila rapax* are versatile, feeding on insects, small mammals and birds, as well as carrion. They also pirate prey from other species. Others are highly specialized, for example, the honey buzzards *Pernis* and *Henicopernis* which feed on wasp grubs; the

The Red kite *Milvus milvus* (1), Hen harrier (or Marsh hawk) *Circus cyaneus* (2) and Verreaux's eagle *Aquila verreauxi* (3).

crepuscular bat eating Bat hawk *Machaerhamphus*; or the snail eating kites *Rostrhamus* and *Chondrohierax*. The mainly vegetarian Vulturine fish eagle *Gypohierax angolensis* feeds on oil palm fruit, and its distribution coincides with that of the palm *Elaeis guineensis*. More adaptable species are more widespread, for example, the scavenging Black kite *Milvus migrans*, probably the world's most abundant raptor.

Appetite and food requirements are related to body weight, varying from about 25% of body weight daily in small active sparrowhawks to 5% or even less in large vultures and eagles. Small active species must feed daily or frequently, while large eagles and vultures can gorge and then starve for weeks.

Nesting and the Young. All Accipitridae build their own nests, of sticks or similar material, usually in trees, sometimes on cliffs (some eagles) rarely on the ground (harriers). Occasionally a nest is built on top of another raptor's nest. Nests may be used for one year

Ospreys *Pandion haliaetus* have roughened pads under their claws which enable them to hold such slippery prey as this small pike.

(small accipiters, snake eagles); or several or many years. Large species tend to have bigger nests occupied for many years; among the largest nests known are those of the genera *Haliaeetus* and *Aquila*. Even if a new nest is built annually, it is often near an old one. Normally both sexes build; the female doing most of the work. The way in which the sexes share their work has, however, been little studied.

One to ten eggs may be laid, but normal numbers are 2–4. They are usually rounded oval in shape, and white or greenish, sometimes spotted with brown and sometimes unmarked. Snake eagles and several booted eagles (*Polemaetus, Oroaetus, Spizaetus*) lay only a single egg. Large clutches of 5–10 are laid by ground-nesting harriers *Circus* and small accipiters. Since eggs are laid at 2–4 day intervals, and incubation normally starts at once, this leads to great variation in size of young. Incubation varies from 30–32 days in small accipiters to over 50 days in snake eagles and large vultures, even 60 days in the Philippine Monkey-eating eagle *Pithecophaga jefferyi*. In most species, females incubate all night and most of the day. They may be fed on the nest by males or may leave to catch prey; incubation by males is often associated with female feeding. Although there is no direct relationship between length of incubation and size, incubation periods are generally longer in large species.

The young hatch nearly helpless. They are clad in down, which is later replaced by a second, thicker down, and finally pushed out on the tips of the true feathers. Disparity in size leads in some species to inter-sibling aggression, the elder dominating and sometimes killing the younger. Sibling aggression is not connected with food supply, nor unusually aggressive adult behaviour and its evolutionary value is obscure.

Young leave the nest 25–120 days after hatching; large and

tropical species have longer fledging periods than small and temperate counterparts. The fledging period divides into three stages: downy, when the female remains on the nest brooding young and the male brings all the prey to the nest; feathering, when the body feathers cover the down, releasing the female from brooding duties, although she still stays near the nest and the male brings most prey; and feathered, when the young are left alone in the nest, and both adults share in bringing prey. Occasionally, the male continues to bring all prey throughout (*Accipiter*).

The young remain dependent on their parents for 1–11 months after their first flight. In most species this post-fledging period terminates with gradual independence of young, but sometimes they may be driven away. In the large forest Crowned and Harpy eagles the post-fledging period is so long that annual breeding is prevented.

Productivity varies from more than one young per adult per year in sparrowhawks and some harriers to one young per adult per 5 years in some tropical eagles. Some adults do not breed annually (up to 35% in tropical eagles). Failures in incubation due to inter-sibling strife, shortage of food, human interference, and rare predation by other carnivors reduce success when eggs are laid. In general, tropical species breed less often, lay smaller clutches, and rear smaller broods than their temperate counterparts.

Territorial Behaviour. This is either absent (colonial vultures) or strongly developed (fish eagles and buzzards). Colonial vultures (*Gyps*) defend only a few square yards or feet round the nest, and forage communally far from the breeding colony. Buzzards and fish eagles defend all or most of their total range from intruders. Most species maintain a home range without obvious territorial activity, with breeding pairs scattered evenly over available terrain. A territory may be like an inverted truncated cone of air, the airspace at the top overlapping with other pairs, but the ground space at the bottom discrete, separated by tracts of unused country. Territories are maintained by perching conspicuously in view of neighbours, by display flights near boundaries, and often by voice. Advertisement displays and voice are combined in many species to make the bird more conspicuous at long range; but in species living in open country the voice is used less. True song is unknown, but loud yelping, whistling, or barking calls, sometimes in duet, are common.

Economic Importance. Many species are accused of damaging human interests by eating lambs, game birds, or fish, while others are regarded as highly beneficial, eating rodents or carrion. Appetite

A pair of Lappet-faced vultures *Torgos tracheliotus* fighting.

An African fish eagle *Haliaeetus vocifer,* during its display call, throws its head backwards and forwards.

and territorial behaviour limits their effects either way. Those species claimed to be harmful never do much harm; equally those species thought beneficial in fact have little overall effect on their prey. The huge majority are either completely harmless or neutral; under 5% are potentially harmful, and when investigated carefully their harmful effect is always found to be negligible. There is no economic ground for the persecution of certain species such as large eagles or goshawks.

Composition. The 217 species are included in 64 genera, of which 38 contain one species (monotypic); ten have two species; and only four (*Circus* 10, *Spizaetus* 10, *Accipter* 47, *Buteo* 25) have ten or more. Although there is scope for generic amalgamation, this demonstrates a high degree of specialization.

The family splits conveniently into nine groups:

(i) Kites and honey buzzards; 31 species in 17 genera, many highly specialized and monotypic, varying in size from the tiny Pearl kite *Gampsonyx swainsoni* to the large, predatory Black-breasted buzzard-kite *Hamirostra melanosternon.* Extreme specialization occurs in honey buzzards (*Pernis, Henicopernis*) eating wasp grubs; the Bat hawk *Machaerhamphus* eating bats all caught in a short evening hunt; and snail kites (*Rostrhamus, Chondrohierax*) eating snails. Extreme adaptability is shown by the Black kite *Milvus migrans.* The kites are more varied and specialized than any other group.

(ii) Sea and fish eagles; 11 species in three genera, all large or very large, mainly aquatic, feeding on fish, water birds and carrion. The young are usually brown, and the adults have some white or grey plumage. All are found in the Old World, except the American bald eagle. The aberrant Vulturine fish eagle *Gypohierax* feeds on oil palm fruit, also some fish and crabs.

(iii) Old World vultures; 14 species in eight genera, of which griffons (*Gyps*) are colonial, the rest solitary. Most very large or huge, brown or dark brown, with bare heads and necks for carrion feeding. Males are larger than females, and their talons are reduced or blunt. Most lay one egg, sometimes two. The Egyptian vulture *Neophron,* largely commensal with man, is black and white when adult and breeds in caves; and the Lammergeier, dark grey above, rufous below, has a unique and unexplained 'beard' of stiff bristles, and colours its white breast with rufous iron oxide.

(iv) Snake eagles; 12 species in five genera, mainly African, one eastern, none New World. Large to very large, usually grey or brown, with large cowled heads and yellow eyes, short toes adapted to killing snakes. The aberrant Bateleur *Terathopius ecudatus* has very long wings and almost no tail, is black, chestnut and white in adult plumage, and glides swiftly over savanna and plains. All but the Bateleur hunt snakes, lizards and frogs mainly from perches; and can kill large venomous snakes.

(v) Harrier hawks and crane hawks; three species in two genera (*Polyboroides* and *Geranospiza*) medium-sized forest or woodland hawks, adults grey, young brown. Superficially resembling eastern snake eagles *Spilornis,* but uniquely adapted by 'double-jointed' legs which can bend either way at the tarsal joint. Hunt by slow, methodical searching for small animals.

(vi) Harriers; ten species in one genus (*Circus*), a uniform group of medium-sized, long-winged, long-tailed hawks that hunt by slow flapping flight over moors, grasslands and marshes. They feed mainly on small mammals and birds, and some reptiles and insects. Ears specialized to help locate prey in thick cover. Cosmopolitan, sexually dimorphic: the males are usually grey or black and white and the females and young are brown. Harriers are often polygamous, and their northern populations migratory. They breed on the ground except *Circus assimilis,* which breeds in bushes.

(vii) Chanting goshawks, goshawks, sparrowhawks; 53 species in five genera. *Accipiter* is the largest genus with 47 species. Medium-sized to small, generally grey or blackish above, white or rufous barred darker below; some are rufous. Goshawks and sparrowhawks are extremely varied and adaptable, but all have short rounded wings and long or very long tails, they live mainly in woodland or forest, feed entirely on birds and sometimes reptiles that they kill themselves, have yellow or red eyes when adult, are excitable and nervous, and, for their size, are powerful and swift predators.

(viii) Buzzards, buteonines, and harpies. A large, varied group of 53 species in 14 genera, many monotypic. They vary from small accipiter-like hawks (*Kaupifalco*) to huge Harpy eagles (*Harpia, Pithecophaga*). Mainly inhabiting woodlands and often deep forest, they prey mainly on mammals and some birds. Most abundant in South America, but one genus (*Buteo*) is widespread in any open

Cooper's hawk *Accipiter cooperii* (1), African fish eagle *Haliaeetus vocifer* (2) and the Harpy eagle *Harpia harpyja* (3).

country or woodland world wide except in Australasia. Buzzards are generally in combinations of brown, grey and white.

(ix) True or booted eagles; 30 species in nine genera. Differ from all other accipiters (except *Buteo lagopus*) in having feathered, not bare, legs. Medium-sized to very large or huge. Highly variable plumage, usually plain brown, more specialized forest species often strongly barred black and white. Immature plumage is often very different from adult. They feed mainly on live prey caught themselves, but *Aquila* takes some carrion and *Ictinaetus* (Indian black eagle) is specialized to feed on birds' nests and eggs. Some species (Tawny eagle) regularly piratical, partly commensal with man and highly adaptable, eating termites to dead elephants. They inhabit every type of country from tundra to tropics, desert to high forest. The northern species are mainly migratory.

OSPREY

The Osprey *Pandion haliaetus*, a large fish-eating bird of prey, known in North America as the Fish hawk, is the only member of the Pandionidae. Measuring up to 24in (61cm) long, the Osprey is unusual among birds of prey in being almost wholly dark above and white beneath. It has a white head with a dark streak through the eye, a barred tail, and angled wings with a dark patch beneath at the angle. The feet are very strong, the claws long and sharp and the toes bear spiny tubercles on their undersurfaces to give a good grip on a slippery fish. Furthermore, the outer toe is large and can be moved to face backwards as in the owls.

Distribution. Ospreys are found regularly throughout the world except for South America where they only occur on migration. They have, however, suffered considerably from shooting, reduction of their habitat and pesticides. The colony on Gardiner's Island off Long Island, New York, contained around 300 nests early in this century. Now there are only about 20 and the hatching success of these birds has dropped by a third. In Britain the Osprey ceased to breed in 1908 but in the 1950s it attempted to re-establish itself in Scotland. The first nest was found in 1955 and with increased protection the first young were reared in 1959. The efforts made by the Royal Society for the Protection of Birds to make it possible for this important species to re-establish itself have resulted in one of the success stories of conservation. Within 10 years the Scottish Ospreys had nested for 10 successive years; by 1969 there were four nests with eggs.

The future of the Osprey, however, remains in doubt. Like many other animals, particularly birds of prey, the Osprey suffers from a combination of misfortunes. The widespread use of chlorinated hydrocarbon pesticides such as DDT, which do not break down in the soil or in animals and accumulate as they progress up a food chain, are particularly dangerous to primary predators.

Behaviour. The Osprey feeds mainly on fish and occupies both freshwater and marine areas where there is sufficient food. It hunts by cruising above the water at heights up to 200ft (60m) and takes its prey by plunging in a shallow dive. The talons are brought forward to strike the prey just as the Osprey hits the water and it sometimes completely submerges. The grip following a good strike is so efficient that the bird may not be readily able to let go, and there is at least one record of an Osprey striking a very large fish and being dragged under the water. After a successful strike the Osprey rises from the surface, shakes the water from its plumage, arranges the fish head-forwards and carries it to its young or a suitable feeding place. In addition to fish, Ospreys take mammals, birds, Sea snakes and even large Sea snails. In some regions they are frequently robbed of their prey by eagles, such as the American bald eagle *Haliaetus leucocephalus*.

Ospreys usually nest in trees or on cliffs, though they also nest on the ground. In some regions, particularly eastern North America and northeast Africa, they nest in large colonies. The nests usually command a clear view of the fishing grounds, and are built of sticks, grasses or any other available material. They are often used year after year and may have material added to them annually. Ospreys usually mate for life, which may be 20 years or more. Two to four, usually three, eggs are laid and incubation, largely by the female, begins with the first egg. The eggs hatch after about 35 days. For five or six weeks the young are fed by the female with food brought by the male. Then, when the young can deal with the food themselves, it is dropped to them by both parents. The losses of eggs and young are high but successful young leave the nest after 8–10 weeks.

Composition. The Osprey *Pandion haliaetus* is the only member of the Pandionidae.

FALCONS

Falcons and their allies, the caracaras, forest falcons and falconets, constitute one of the two major groups of diurnal birds of prey. They resemble the hawks and eagles in having hooked beaks, taloned feet, and keen sight; but differ in laying eggs with inside shells that appear buff against the light, defaecating directly below the perch, and some habits such as head-bobbing and killing prey by breaking the neck with the beak. Some species have serrated upper mandibles believed to assist in killing. In some anatomical features they resemble owls.

All are mainly diurnal though some small falcons (hobbies) hunt much at dusk and the forest falcons *Micrastur* hunt in forest in almost complete darkness, their large eyes and specialized ears making this possible. All are predatory; but some caracaras also eat carrion and are piratical, robbing other birds of prey.

The Lesser kestrel *Falco naumanni* hunting insects. It consumes only the soft body of the prey.

Caracaras and milvagos are all rather large and broad-winged, and scarcely resemble the true falcons of the genus *Falco*, but they are related to the latter because they have features in common, such as the pattern of wing moult and egg shell colour. The forest falcons are short-winged, long tailed, with proportions resembling hawks and eagles rather than falcons. Colour in these aberrant falcons is extremely varied, often dark above, plain or barred below. Among true falcons, the kestrel group are mainly chestnut, barred and spotted black, Peregrines *Falco peregrinus* and Lanners *F. biarmicus* grey above, white or barred below, while others, for example,

Peregrine falcons *Falco peregrinus* are able to catch prey on the wing. In this example (1), a Great bustard is being attacked. Peregrines can also pass food to their mates in flight (2). The female flies under the male and turns upside-down to receive a Blackbird prey.

Eleanora's and the Sooty falcon *F. eleanorae* and *F. concolor* may be plain dark brown or grey. The largest falcons weigh 3–4½lb (1·3–2kg) and the smallest falconets *Microhierax* 1½oz (43gm).

Distribution. Falcons occur world wide, but only the genus *Falco* is cosmopolitan. Neotropical caracaras *Daptrius*, *Phalcoboenus*, *Polyborus* and *Milvago* are South and Central American, as are the Laughing falcon *herpetotheres*, forest falcons, and the Spot-winged falconet *Spiziapteryx*. Pygmy falcons *Poliohierax* occur in Africa and Asia while falconets *Microhierax* are exclusively oriental. The Peregrine falcon is cosmopolitan, with 16 races including many on oceanic islands; but some small kestrels occur only on one or a small group of islands, and include the world's most threatened raptor, the Mauritius kestrel *Falco punctatus* of which there were fewer than 10 individuals alive in 1975.

Falcons inhabit all types of terrain from Arctic to tropical and deserts to tall forest. The Gyrfalcon *F. rusticolus* is the only diurnal bird of prey resident during winter in the Arctic. Most species prefer open country, mountains, moorlands, or grasslands. Many *Falco* species migrate, including kestrels, Red-footed falcons *F. vesertinus*, and hobbies. The Eastern red-footed falcon *F. vespertinus amurensis* apparently crosses the Indian Ocean from India to southern Tanzania. Most tropical species, including all aberrant New World species, are resident or partly nomadic. Common kestrels *F. tinnunculus* include migrant northern races and resident tropical races. Adult gyrfalcons are resident, while young may migrate.

Feeding. Typical falcons all eat prey they themselves catch, often in flight (hobbies, Lanners, Peregrines) or on the ground after hovering (kestrels). Caracaras and milvagos also feed on carrion, and pirate prey from other raptors. One species of *Daptrius* feeds mainly on wasps, and the Laughing falcon *Herpetotheres cachinnans* eats snakes; these thus partially fill the roles of Old World honey buzzards and snake eagles. Apart from caracaras, most are rather specialized feeders, concentrating on birds taken in flight (Peregrine) small mammals taken on the ground (kestrels) or insects (hobbies). Forest falcons feed on both mammals and birds, locating prey partly by specialized ears. All others locate prey by sight, and kill with the feet, or carry prey to a perch and kill it with the bill.

Appetite, related to body-weight, varies from 2–25% of body-weight in small kestrels to 8–10% in Peregrines. The food

requirement of the larger caracaras is unknown; but probably like other carrion-eaters they can gorge and then survive for some time without feeding.

Nesting and the Young. Most species do not build their own nests, but caracaras and milvagos build small stick nests on trees or cliffs. The Laughing falcon breeds in cavities in trees; Pygmy falcons breed in other birds' nests, the African Pygmy falcon *P. semitorquatus* in those of Buffalo weavers or Social weavers. Falconets nest in old barbet or woodpecker holes; and members of the genus *Falco* in holes in trees, cliff ledges, on the ground, in other birds' nests, on buildings, even in nest boxes.

Courtship displays, where known, are largely swift and aerial and may be followed by courtship feeding, with special bowing displays. Male Peregrines fly from ledge to ledge, followed by females who eventually select and lay on one. Two to six eggs are laid by most *Falco* species and caracaras; the Laughing falcon lays only one. Eggs in *Falco* and caracaras are buff or whitish, and heavily or completely spotted dark red; those of Pygmy falcons and falconets are white or whitish.

Incubation does not normally begin till the second last egg is laid, and is normally by the female only, though males occasionally sit. Females are fed at or near the nests by males. Incubation lasts 28–30 days in all known species, including both the tiny Pygmy falcon which weighs 2oz (65gm) and Peregrine which weighs 2½lb (1,000gm).

Young hatch nearly simultaneously, helpless, clad in white or grey down, but a second voluminous coat of down supersedes the first after some days. Females may assist in bringing food to feathered young, but often the male supplies the entire family throughout the breeding season. The young later depend on the parents for 3–8 weeks after fledging, learning during this time to kill

Five species of falcon. (1) Gyrfalcon *Falco rusticolus*, (2) Red-footed falcon *F. vespertinus*, (3) Prairie falcon *F. mexicanus*, (4) Bat falcon *F. rufigularis* and (5) Black-legged falconet *Microhierax fringillarius*.

for themselves. Young Hobbies *F. subbuteo* learn to kill insects before they can catch birds.

Economic Importance. Several large bird-killing falcons are alleged to damage game-preserving or pigeon-keeping; but investigations prove that all such complaints are exaggerated. Carrion-eating caracaras are accused, without good evidence, of killing lambs; but probably cannot. Kestrels and many others are wholly beneficial or neutral, feeding on small rodents or insects. No species has any marked proven injurious effect.

Large powerful falcons are sought by falconers; the Peregrine is locally endangered as a result. Arabs especially value and pay large sums for good falcons. Most *Falco* species can be trained; but their usefulness to falconers depends on their wild habits. The insectivorous Hobby, though a marvellous flier, will not kill gamebirds.

Composition. The 61 species are contained in 10 genera which conveniently split into two groups: the aberrant New World caracaras, milvagos, forest falcons, and Laughing falcon (16 species in six genera); and the pygmy falcons, falconets, and true falcons (45 species in four genera). Pygmy falcons and falconets are regarded as being more primitive than members of the genus *Falco*.

GALLIFORMES

Game-birds are usually ground-dwellers. Many have elaborate courtship displays

MEGAPODES — *Megapodiidae*
GUANS — *Cracidae*
GROUSE — *Tetraonidae*
PHEASANTS AND QUAILS — *Phasianidae*
GUINEAFOWL — *Numididae*
TURKEYS — *Meleagrididae*

MEGAPODES

The megapodes are all robust, ground-dwelling birds that resemble hens or pheasants in many ways – for instance in their vaulted tails and manner of feeding by scratching around in leaf litter – and there is every reason to suppose that their closest relatives are the pheasants, hens and peacocks of the family Phasianidae. But in respect of breeding biology the resemblance ends, for the megapodes (or mound-builders or incubator-birds, as they are variously called) are uniquely distinguished by laying their eggs in a mound of earth or vegetation, in the warmth of which the eggs are incubated. Some of the megapodes attend the 'nest' until the last-laid eggs have hatched, and control the incubation temperature by varying the thickness of the mound, but beyond this there is no parental care. On hatching, the precocious chick struggles to the surface, can fly within hours, and leads an independent life. It may never see its parent; megapodes are thus the only birds in the world without parental bonds. Megapodes can be divided into three groups: the junglefowl, the brush-turkeys and the Mallee-fowl.

Distribution. The most widespread megapode is the Scrub-fowl *Megapodius freycinet*; it is found within about 50mi (80km) of the coast of northern Australia, from the Kimberley range in Western Australia to the Broadsound Range at the Tropic of Capricorn in

Two megapodes. (1) The Maleo *Macrocephalon maleo* and (2) the Scrub-fowl *Megapodius freycinet*. The Maleo (3) digs a simple nest in soil or, in this case, dark lava sand. The eggs are incubated by the sun's heat.

Queensland; it inhabits the New Hebrides, Solomons, Bismarck Archipelago and the whole of New Guinea, the Moluccas, Celebes and Philippines, Palawan, Sabah in Borneo and the Indian Ocean Nicobar Islands (in recent geological time it must also have inhabited the intervening areas). The closely related *M. laperouse* and *M. pritchardii* are endemic to the Mariana Islands and central Polynesia respectively; the Moluccan megapode *Eulipoa wallacei* is confined to those islands, and the junglefowl known as the Maleo *Macrocephalon maleo* is a native of the Celebes.

Of the brush-turkeys, the Australian bird, the Brush-turkey *Alectura lathami*, ranges east of the Great Dividing Range from the Manning River in New South Wales north to the tip of the York Peninsula, and the other five species included in the genera *Talegalla* and *Aepypodius* occur only in New Guinea and its outlying islands. Bruijn's brush-turkey *Aepypodius bruijnii* is an exceedingly rare bird

The Brush-turkey *Alectura lathami* builds a mound of vegetation inside which its eggs are laid. The heat generated by the decaying vegetation incubates the eggs.

of montane forests that has not been seen for 35 years. The Australian Brush-turkey occurs sparsely quite far from coastal forests and has even been found on the western slopes of the Great Dividing Range; it is said to have extended its range to the west with the spread of the prickly pear cactus, the fruits of which it eats.

The Mallee-fowl *Leipoa ocellata* is found from western New South Wales and northwestern Victoria, across southern Australia to the whole of Western Australia except the coastal forests, which it shuns.

Feeding. Megapodes feed in the manner of hens, by scratching industriously at the soil and pecking amongst the leaf litter for seeds, fruits and small arthropods. Mallee-fowl have been studied in much greater detail than any other megapode, and their diet consists mainly of fallen seeds of the shrubs Cassia, Acacia and Beyeria. Buds and flowers are also browsed, and during the transient rains, when insects become abundant, they become an important constituent in Mallee-fowls' diet. In agricultural areas they forage for spilt cereal grain. They are desert-adapted to the extent of being able to do without drinking.

Nesting and the Young. We can construct a series of increasing complexity of breeding behaviour among the megapodes. The Maleo and Moluccan megapode, and also occasional individual Scrub-fowl merely dig a hole in sand or loose unshaded soil for the reception of their eggs, fill the hole in and abandon the site. The only control that the birds can exert over the temperature of the 'nest' is in selecting the site in the first place; Dr H. J. Frith has reported that on some islands in the Solomons and New Britain the eggs are laid in soil warmed by volcanic steam, while on Dunk Island in the Great Barrier Reef Scrub-fowl manage to lay their eggs deep in rock fissures where they are shaded by day and the rock retains sufficient heat to keep them warm throughout the night.

In Queensland forests the same species builds huge mounds of earth or vegetation or a mixture of the two. Ancient mounds may be up to 36ft (12m) in diameter and 16ft (5m) high and at least some of them are constructed co-operatively by several adult birds. It appears that the relative admixture of soil and vegetable matter in the mounds varies according to the degree of insulation, humidity and other physical factors of the site affecting the mound's temperature; the more vegetable matter is used, the greater is the temperature of its fermentation. Heat generated during decomposition of a pure vegetable mound can exceed 90° F (32° C). Eggs are laid at daily intervals, the female excavating a hole in the conical mound for each one separately until a clutch of some 15 eggs is completed. Each egg begins to incubate as it is buried, and the adult birds remain in close attendance until hatching has finished, monitoring the incubation temperature by frequently digging into the mound and probing with the bill which evidently contains temperature sensors, probably in the tongue.

Brush-turkeys behave in much the same way, but the mound is made entirely of plant material and is only about 3ft (1m) high. Initially the heat of fermentation is too great and the male dissipates it by turning the rotting vegetation over from time to time; only then does he permit the female to start laying and digging-in her eggs.

Mallee-fowl show the greatest complexity of nest-care behaviour. Months before breeding commences, the male scrapes a hole $1\frac{1}{2}$ft (0·5m) deep in the soil and heaps leaves and rootlets into and over it until a conical mound 16ft (5m) in diameter and more than 3ft (1m) high is formed. In the arid interior of Australia the nights can be very cold while the days are very hot; yet by constantly attending the mound and scraping earth on or away from the central hotbed of fermenting vegetation, the pair of Mallee-fowl can keep the egg-pit, where up to 35 eggs are laid on top of the hot-bed, at about 92° F (33° C).

Two species of megapode, the Mallee-fowl *Leipoa ocellata* (1) and the Brush-turkey *Alectura lathami* (2), compared with two guans, the Great curassow *Crax rubra* (3) and the Piping guan *Pipile pipile* (4).

Hatching under the soil, the downy megapode chicks start life with an arduous and sometimes fatal struggle to the surface. Once there, they run strongly into the undergrowth and begin feeding. They can fly within hours of hatching.

Composition. Besides the Mallee-fowl there are five species of junglefowl (*Megapodius*, *Eulipoa* and *Macrocephalon*) and six of Brush-turkeys (*Alectura*, *Talegalla* and *Aepypodius*). The genera *Eulipoa*, *Leipoa*, *Alectura* and *Macrocephalon* have a single species each but despite this diversity, the megapodes constitute a natural family of galliform birds.

GUANS

The guans constitute a natural and well defined family of primitive gallinaceous birds, the Cracidae. Their geographical origin is uncertain, as fossils of the same age are known from France, northern and eastern United States, and southern Patagonia, but it is quite certain that they evolved most rapidly in South America which may have been the place of their origin.

An English name does not exist for the family as a whole and the birds are generally called, for the three groups into which the family is usually divided, the chachalacas, guans, and the curassows. 'Curassow' refers to the fact that the first live birds, or specimens, arrived in Europe from the island of Curacao in the Caribbean, to which they had been presumably introduced from Venezuela. The name 'chachalaca' is an imitation of the raucous song of the birds; but the etymology of 'guan' is unknown. Members of the family Cracidae are often compared to pheasants and turkeys which they resemble superficially in many respects; for instance, a chachalaca is easily compared to a rather scrawny hen and chachalacas are often seen at liberty in native villages and barnyards associating with hens; whereas a curassow is very similar to a turkey. The resemblance is increased by certain features of the Cracidae which undoubtedly play a part in the displays that help individuals recognize members of their own species, such as colourful wattles or fleshy knobs, areas of bare skin on the face or throat, 'horns' or 'helmets' at the base of the bill and forehead, or crests. In the curassows of the genus *Crax*, the colour of the wattles and knob varies from yellow and orange to bright blue and flaming red; the bare skin on the face and throat, and the 'horns' and 'helmets' can also be highly coloured, but the plumage of the Cracidae is never colourful as in the pheasants. It is chiefly brownish and plain in the chachalacas and guans, and black and white in the curassows, with the exception of the strange Nocturnal curassow *Nothocrax urumutum* in which it is chiefly chestnut, with very fine blackish vermiculations. The whole of the face of this bird is completely bare and its skin is very vividly coloured, bright yellow in front of, above, and behind the eye, and is blue below the eye, grading into purple. If we add to this the fact that the Nocturnal curassow has also a very long crest which projects well beyond the nape onto the neck, it is probably the most colourful of all Cracidae, although, paradoxically, it is almost completely nocturnal in its native habitat, though not in aviaries.

The Cracidae vary in size. The smallest are the chachalacas in which the mean wing length of adult males is about 7in (18cm) in the smallest species, and the largest are the curassows; the biggest is the Great curassow *Crax rubra* with a mean of 16in (40cm). But as all Cracidae have a very rounded and blunt wing, a better indication of relative size is perhaps given by weight. In representative species in which it has been recorded, the average weight of males is about $17\frac{1}{2}$oz (500gm) in the chachalacas; about 60oz (1,700gm) in large species of guans; and varies between 162 and 170oz (4,600–4,800gm) in the Great curassow mentioned above, that is, nearly ten times the weight of the chachalacas, a very large difference not made clear by the length of the wing. The tails of Cracidae are long, notably broad and 'heavy', and their legs are also long and strong, ending in very big feet with strong claws.

Distribution. Guans have penetrated into Central America and Mexico and, at present, the northern limits of their distribution are the lower Rio Grande Valley on the border of Texas and Mexico in the east, and southern Sonora in the west, while the southern limits are northern Argentina and Uruguay.

All the species are arboreal and their normal habitat is dense humid forest, with the exception of the 10 species of the genus *Ortalis* – the only genus of the chachalacas which frequent thickets, narrow gallery forest or brushy ravines, maquis, or other thin low forest, characteristic of the more arid parts of the range occupied by the family.

Behaviour. The food consists chiefly of fruits and seeds, or other vegetable matter such as leaves, flowers and buds, varied occasionally by small animals such as large insects, or small salamanders or frogs. Chachalacas and curassows spend a large amount of time on the ground scratching for food, but the guans come down to the ground seldom. All the members of the family are very agile in trees. The flight is poor and laboured and consists mainly of gliding or fluttering. The nest of all the species is not known, but when observed is said to be loosely constructed of twigs, generally in a tree not far above the ground, or, in some species, commonly directly on the ground.

Composition. The family can be divided in 11 genera and 44 species. The chachalacas form a single genus, *Ortalis*, with 10 species. The guans, with 20 species, are divided into five genera. In three of these, *Pipile*, *Aburria*, and *Chamaepetes*, the three or four outer wing feathers are modified by having their webs excised more or less

deeply for about one third or more of the length of the feather. These cut-out tips are also stiffened and produce a whirring sound when the wing is vibrated – a 'drumming' display common to most gallinaceous birds. The Horned guan *Oreophasis derbianus* is normally considered to form a group of its own. The curassows, with 13 species, have four genera, *Pauxi* and *Mitu*, which are related to *Crax*, and *Nothocrax* mentioned above.

GROUSE

The grouse are a well-defined family of birds, the Tetraonidae, which can be seen by even the casual observer to be members of a

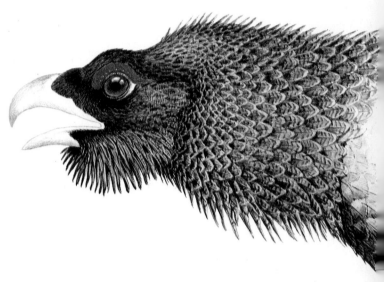

A Capercaillie *Tetrao urogallus* in a head-forward threat posture.

related group, with 'typical game-bird' shape and feathered legs. Within the group, they show diverse forms of adaptation and courtship behaviour.

Distribution. Grouse occupy many of the major natural habitats of the northern hemisphere and there are species adapted to the tundra, prairie, alpine meadows, coniferous forest, mixed forest, moorland, brushland and also to the successive regeneration stages of burned forest. Most are resident, although the Red or Willow grouse *Lagopus lagopus* moves southward from parts of its Arctic range in winter. Grouse of most open country species are powerful fliers, but they tend to use this power to range locally in winter in search of food plants blown clear of snow, rather than to migrate. Despite heavy hunting and their inability to adapt to man-made patterns of land use such as intensive agriculture and monoculture forestry, most species are still abundant. This is mainly due to close links between research and management which have resulted in limited shooting seasons, kill quotas and, especially in the case of the Red grouse, in direct manipulation of the habitat to benefit these highly valued game-birds. The main exception is the Prairie chicken *Tympanuchus cupido*, once found in very large numbers throughout the tall-grass prairies of Canada and the central United States. At first, this fine species benefitted from the introduction of grainfields into its habitat and thousands were shot for the markets of the East Coast cities. As the proportion of natural grassland steadily fell, however, the Prairie chicken went into decline and is now a protected bird in most of its former strongholds. Especially at risk is the subspecies, Attwater's prairie chicken, now restricted to a few sites on the Texas coastal prairies. The Heath hen, a subspecies once found on the coastal heaths of the East Coast, became extinct early in this century.

Feeding. Tetraonids are mainly vegetarians, eating buds and shoots, with additional animal food in summer. Some have highly adapted digestive systems for breaking down high-fibre diets (such as heather, pine shoots and sage tips). The relationship between grouse and their food sources is the subject of continuing research which gives some insight into the cycles of abundance of many birds. This has been studied especially in relation to the Red grouse in Scotland. The species is found on heather moorland, and it has been established that its entire life cycle and population numbers are dependent on the growth and nutritive condition of its foodplant *Calluna vulgaris*. Given good growth conditions, with base-rich rocks beneath the soil and an absence of spring frosts to check growth, the heather thrives, the grouse lay large clutches of eggs and their chicks survive well. This is especially noticeable where artificial patch-burning of the moor has given a varied pattern of ages and heights of heather. The males take smaller territories when growth conditions have been good and the population increases. But when the heather is poor, not only is breeding success lower, but the males become aggressive in their attempts to hold larger territories and a surplus population arises, formed of non-territorial birds. These homeless birds wander about, pursued by territorial cocks, and often form packs which leave the moor completely and turn up on neighbouring farm land or other unsuitable habitats. These surplus birds fall prey to disease, predators and accidents over the winter, although the territorial pairs have few losses. Shooting is not a major regulating factor on numbers.

Nesting and the Young. Most grouse are ground nesters and lay a clutch of 5–10 eggs, and the female alone incubates for 3–4 weeks. The eggs are cryptically coloured and the nest itself is no more than a scrape among ground cover. The downy chicks feed on insects as well as vegetable food and develop rapidly, especially where they

Various courtship displays by male grouse. (1) Greater prairie chicken *Tympanuchus cupido*, (2) Sage grouse *Centrocercus urophasianus*, (3) Ruffed grouse *Bonasa umbellus*, (4) Black grouse *Tetrao tetrix* and (5) Capercaillie *T. urogallus*.

benefit from the long daylight hours of the Arctic summer. Ptarmigan (a general name for many species of the genus *Lagopus*) and Red grouse are capable of fluttering flight 10 days after hatching. In some species the male links up again with the brood after hatching, but in the communal-display species the rearing is left entirely to the female, although cocks join winter flocks.

Behaviour. The display behaviour of male grouse ranges from simple 'song flights' on individual territories to communal frenzies of drumming, dancing and calling which are among the highlights of the northern spring. Ptarmigan, Red grouse and the Hazel hen *Bonasa bonasa* have the least complicated territorial displays, while the Ruffed grouse *B. umbellus* of North American woodlands is noted for his 'drumming', in which he thumps the air with vibrating wings. The Spruce and Blue grouse *Dendragapus canadensis* and *D. obscurus* and the Capercaillie *Tetrao urogallus* have special mating calls, display areas of coloured skin over air sacs or wattles and show off their tail plumage. They are often solitary. The heights of communal display are reached by the Prairie chicken, Black *Tetrao tetrix*, Sharp-tailed *Tympanuchus phasianellus* and Sage grouse *Centrocercus urophasianus*, in which the males gather at traditional sites (leks) to call, display their wattles, air sacs and plumage, and perform intricate, repetitive ritual dances. Females mate with males holding central, dominant position on the display ground.

As a unique adaptation to preserve their camouflage, Willow grouse and Ptarmigan moult three times during the year. The Ptarmigan is barred grey or brown in autumn, white in winter and has a yellower barred plumage in spring, with bolder patterning. The white primaries and belly remain unchanged throughout the year. The feathered 'snowshoes' on the feet become much larger and denser in winter. The Red grouse, now regarded as a subspecies of

Six species of grouse. (1) Spruce grouse *Dendragapus canadensis*, (2) Sage grouse *Centrocercus urophasianus*, (3) Greater prairie chicken *Tympanuchus cupido*, (4) (Rock) Ptarmigan *Lagopus mutus*, in winter plumage, (5) Black grouse *Tetrao tetrix*, (6) Capercaillie *Tetrao urogallus*.

A pair of male Black grouse *Tetrao tetrix* display at sites called leks. The female will mate with the male that becomes dominant in the lek.

the Willow grouse, does not turn white during the much less snowy winter of the British Isles.

Economic Importance. The grouse are important game-birds, both in terms of numbers and the value placed upon them by hunters. It has been estimated that 5–6 million Hazel hens were killed each year in the USSR alone earlier in this century. Sporting rents for Red grouse moors in the British Isles are reckoned in scores of pounds for every brace of birds killed annually. North American grouse provide the cream of upland hunting and the harvest is strictly controlled by bag limits and licensing systems. Many gamekeepers, wildlife managers and wardens are employed solely to preserve various species of grouse.

Composition. There are 11 main species of grouse, plus six others which may be considered as minor variations on these main themes, although usually given specific rank by taxonomists. The Family is divided into six genera: *Tetrao*, *Lagopus*, *Dendragapus*, *Bonasa*, *Tympanuchus* and *Centrocercus*.

Two species of pheasant showing how the male pulls its neck cape to one side of his head, revealing a large area of colour, during courtship display. (1) Golden pheasant *Chrysolophus pictus* and (2) the Lady Amherst pheasant *C. amherstiae*.

PHEASANTS AND QUAILS

The Phasianidae includes most of the so-called game-birds of temperate Europe, Asia and North America, and of tropical Asia and Africa, among them pheasants, quails, partridges, francolins, peafowl, snowcocks and domestic chickens. Although the family seems very diverse, with birds varying from quails only 5in (13cm) long and having short tails, to peafowl up to 78in (198cm) long with long tails, all of its members are closely related and share numerous structural and behavioural features. They are all rather heavily built

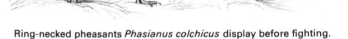

Ring-necked pheasants *Phasianus colchicus* display before fighting.

birds, with relatively short rounded wings and a short thick bill having the upper mandible overhanging the tip of the lower. The legs are stout and vary from short to rather long, with four toes, the hallux usually being shorter than the others and set somewhat higher. In many species there are from one to three pointed spurs on the back of the tarsus, but spurs are absent in the native American genera.

In most quail the tail is very short and weak, in partridges, francolins and others it is fairly short, but in the majority of pheasants it is long and ornate. Some pheasants also have elongated upper tail coverts. Development of the tail reaches an extreme in peafowl of the genus *Pavo* and in the Argus pheasant *Argusianus argus*, in which the broad and elaborately patterned tail is more than twice as long as the body. Most members of the Phasianidae have a rather long neck, while the head is always relatively small. Some pheasants and a variety of smaller species have coloured wattles or areas of bare skin on the head and throat, as in the familiar domestic cock.

The body plumage is generally soft and plentiful. In many species the male is brightly coloured with an elaborate pattern, whereas the female is cryptically marked in shades of buff and brown with darker streaking and barring. In some species the sexes are alike.

Distribution. The family as a whole has a wide distribution, being absent only from the Arctic, Antarctic, parts of South America, and most oceanic islands. However, except for introduced populations, the Americas have only the quails of the subfamily Odontophorinae, of which there are about 36 species. These range from southern Canada through the United States and Central America to Peru, Bolivia and Paraguay. Familiar American species are the Bobwhite *Colinus virginianus* and California quail *Lophortyx californica*.

The greatest diversity of Phasianidae is to be found in southern

Asia, where most of the pheasants, as well as a variety of francolins, quail and partridges occur. In the wild state the two species of peafowl, the Blue or Indian peacock *Pavo cristatus* and the Green peacock *P. muticus* are both confined to tropical Asia, as is the genus *Argus*. The Domestic fowl, which is now probably the most numerous bird in the world, is descended from the Red junglefowl *Gallus gallus* of southern Asia.

Europe has one species of quail, *Coturnix coturnix*, four species of partridge, and the Pheasant *Phasianus colchicus*, which is native only in southeast Europe, but has been widely introduced. Most quail breeding in Europe migrate to winter in tropical Africa, and Asian populations migrate to southern Asia. These are the only long distance migrants of the family. Africa has numerous species of francolins and other partridge-like Phasianidae. The only pheasant found in Africa, the Congo peacock *Afropavo congensis* is confined to the Congo. The discovery of this species in 1936 was a most sensational find, as the avifaunas of most of Africa were well known by then. The only members of the family native to Australia are quail, although various others have been introduced. New Zealand's only native member of the Phasianidae, the New Zealand quail *Coturnix novaezelandiae* is now extinct.

Nearly all Phasianidae are terrestrial birds, although many perch freely in trees. The range of habitats occupied by the family as a whole is vast, including dry desert, tropical rain forest, the bare slopes of high mountains and agricultural land. Most quails, partridges and francolins inhabit open grassland, brush or arid regions, but others are woodland or forest birds. The majority of pheasants inhabit woodland or forests, but some are found in open grassy areas around the tree-line in the Himalayas and others prefer cultivated areas or brushland.

Feeding. All Phasianidae feed mainly on the ground, although a few species will sometimes take food from bushes or the lower branches of trees. A variety of vegetable foods, including seeds, fruit, buds, roots and leaves, is supplemented by worms, snails, insects and other small animals. Many species scratch in the ground with their feet to expose food hidden among dead leaves or in the soil, and some will dig with the bill. Small chicks eat mainly insects, but the diets of adults depend partly on the seasonal availability of different foods and partly on the birds' preferences. Some species eat large quantities of fallen fruit from beneath trees and bushes, others feed freely from cultivated grain crops and other grass seeds.

Nesting and the Young. The nests of all Phasianidae are simple structures of dead leaves or twigs, usually placed in cover on the ground. The European pheasant sometimes nests in trees, on the old nests of other birds, and the Asian pheasants of the genus *Tragopan* habitually nest in trees. The nest is invariably built by the female bird alone. Eggs are white to buff or olive, speckled and blotched in some species, but unmarked in others. The clutch varies from two eggs in the Argus pheasant and other large pheasants to as many as 15 in partridges and quails. Incubation is by the female, lasting only about 17 days in small quails, but as long as 27–28 days in large pheasants. The young hatch within a few hours of each other; apparently, the peeping calls of the unhatched chicks allow them to communicate and synchronize the hatching process, an adaptation that probably reduces predation. The newly-hatched young are covered with thick down and soon leave the nest area in

Nine species of game-bird showing variation of size and plumage. (1) Black francolin *Francolinus francolinus*, (2) Chukar partridge *Alectoris chukar*, (3) Blood pheasant *Ithaginis cruentus*, (4) Mountain quail *Oreortyx pictus*, (5) Painted quail *Excalfactoria chinensis*, (6) the Silver pheasant *Lophura nycthemera*, (7) Elliot's pheasant *Syrmaticus ellioti*, (8) Mikado pheasant *Syrmaticus mikado* and (9) Swinhoe's pheasant *Lophura swinhoii*.

company with their mother. In monogamous species both parents tend the young to some extent; in polygamous pheasants this duty is performed solely by the female. Many species feed the small young on insects, but they rapidly learn to pick up food for themselves. The wing feathers grow quickly, allowing the young birds to fly long before they reach adult size. Juveniles become independent of their parents by the time they are fully grown, and are sexually mature in the next summer in all but the large pheasants.

Territorial Behaviour. Two distinct types of social organization occur in the Phasianidae. Most of the smaller species are monogamous and have little or no sexual dimorphism in colouration. In these species either both members of the pair or the male alone defend the breeding territory. During the non-breeding season family parties of some species remain together, sometimes amalgamating into larger flocks.

In contrast, most pheasants are polygamous and show striking sexual dimorphism in colouration. In the polygamous pheasants the males defend large territories in which there are several females. The male mates with each of the females in turn and takes no part in nesting or tending the young. The polygamous mating system probably enhances competition between males, leading to the evolution of such bizarre structures as the peacock's tail and the ornate wattles of domestic fowl cocks.

The monogamous species do not have the very elaborate sexual displays of polygamous pheasants. Each genus of the latter has a distinctive display, with the tail arched sideways and the male standing beside the female in *Polyplectron*, *Phasianus* and other genera, or the tail spread forwards and exposed in a frontal display in *Argusianus* and *Pavo*.

Most Pheasants have noisy wing-whirring territorial displays and give crowing, clucking and cackling calls. The calls of the smaller species are generally similar, with musical whistles in some, as in the characteristic 'bob-white' of Bob-white quail or 'wet-my-lips' of European quail. Chicks of all species have high peeping calls.

Economic Importance. Members of the Phasianidae are probably of greater economic interest than any other group of birds, primarily because of the domestic fowl, which is much the most important bird for production of both meat and eggs. This species has been kept in captivity for thousands of years and is now found almost throughout the world. Chickens are considerably more efficient in converting food to meat than domestic mammals, and can be kept at a much higher density.

Many members of the family are important game birds. In Europe and North America the shooting of quails, partridges and pheasants is often a highly organized concern, which provides employment for gamekeepers and others, although it is indulged in for sport rather than the meat that results. In Africa, francolins are widely hunted for food, and in Asia various partridges, quails and pheasants are also hunted. Because all pheasants are good to eat – most of them are large and conspicuous and many of them are brightly coloured – they have been constantly harassed by man. Many of the spectacular species with small ranges in Asia are now threatened with extinction. However, some of these are easily kept in captivity and it is to be hoped that the efforts being made to restock reserves with captive-bred birds will be successful.

Composition. The family includes about 166 species classified in two subfamilies, the Phasianinae which is native only in the Old World, and the Odontophorinae which is native only in the New World. Recent studies suggest that the Curassows (Cracidae), Turkeys (Meleagrididae), Grouse (Tetraonidae), Megapodes (Megapodidae) and Guineafowl (Numididae) are all very closely related and perhaps best included in a single family. If this were done, the Phasianidae of this account would become a subfamily Phasianinae, containing two tribes, the Odontophorini and Phasianini.

GUINEAFOWL

The guineafowl are medium-sized game-birds, included in the family Numididae, and varying from $17-29\frac{1}{2}$in (43–75cm) long. All guineafowl are rather plump and heavy bodied, with a moderately long neck and rather small head. The bill is short and stout, the wings short and very rounded, and the tail either of medium length or long. In accordance with their terrestrial habits, the feet are large and the legs strong. The two species of the genus *Agelastes* have spurs on the back of the legs.

Most species have predominantly dark grey or black body plumage that is uniformly spotted with white. The dark wing and

Helmeted guineafowl *Numida meleagris*. The adults are seen protecting their young from a snake.

tail feathers usually have white streaks. The Vulturine guineafowl *Acryllium vulturinum* has a bright blue neck and breast with long, pointed hackles, and the white-breasted guineafowl *Agelastes meleagrides* has the entire front of the body white. All species have the head and neck mainly bare of feathers, with the skin coloured yellow, red, blue or slate-grey. Some species are distinguished by having casques on the head, others by short vertical crests, short bristles about the face, or wattles or loose folds of coloured skin. The sexes are similarly coloured in all species.

Distribution. The family Numididae is probably restricted to the Ethiopian zoogeographical region, it being likely that the populations of Helmeted guineafowl *Numida meleagris* in Madagascar and the Comoro Islands are descended from introduced domestic birds. The Helmeted guineafowl has a wide range in Africa

Courtship display by a male Great argus pheasant *Argusianus argus*.

south of the Sahara and is also present in Morocco. Some of its varied subspecies were formerly regarded as distinct species. It inhabits dry bush covered country and savannas with scattered trees. The Crested guineafowl *Guttera edouardi* also has a wide range in tropical Africa, but inhabits dense bush or even forests. The two other members of the genus *Guttera* both have restricted ranges and also live in forests, the Kenya crested guineafowl *G. pucherani* in Kenya and the Plumed guineafowl *G. plumifera* in Gaboon.

The extremely rare White-breasted guineafowl is found in Ghana and Liberia. The Black guineafowl *Agelastes niger*, a forest bird of Lower Guinea, is also very rare. The Vulturine guineafowl has an extensive range in east and central Africa, where it inhabits the most arid bushy regions. All guineafowl are sedentary except for short local movements.

Behaviour. Guineafowl are mainly terrestrial, although several species habitually roost in trees. The diets of the well-known species include insects and vegetable matter of all kinds, especially seeds, leaves and roots. Molluscs and small frogs are also eaten at times. When feeding most species scratch in ground litter like chickens.

Several species are often seen in small groups that consist either of males with their harems or family parties. The species living in open country also form flocks during the non-breeding season. Most guineafowl calls are loud and repetitive, and often harsh, but softer clucking and squeaking notes are also given.

Nests are hollows in the ground with little or no lining, usually screened by ground vegetation. In the commoner species (the biology of the two rarest species is almost unknown) clutches are of 7–20 eggs which are white to very pale reddish-brown and either unmarked or finely speckled. Incubation is carried out by the female alone. The young hatch synchronously and leave the nest in the company of their parents soon afterwards. They are covered with thick down and are able to fly long before attaining full size. Fully-grown young flock together in some species.

Economic Importance. The Helmeted guineafowl *Numida meleagris* has been kept in captivity since at least the 4th century B.C. The Romans kept one of the east African subspecies which they called the 'Numidian fowl' and the Moroccan subspecies which they called 'Meleagris.' Both were kept mainly for their meat, and both were apparently lost to Europe after the fall of the Roman Empire, until the 15th and 16th centuries when Portuguese introduced *N. m. galeata* from West Africa. This subspecies has been kept in small numbers in Europe since then, latterly as much for ornament and as a pet as for its meat.

Composition. The seven species of Numididae are nowadays usually classified into four genera, *Acryllium, Agelastes, Guttera* and *Numida.* The Black guineafowl *Agelastes niger* was formerly separated in a genus *Phasidus.* The Numididae is a small natural group, but closely related to the family Phasianidae. Some taxonomists believe that the Numididae, Tetraonidae, Cracidae and other families of the Galliformes should be regarded as subfamilies of the Phasianidae.

TURKEYS

The two species of turkey, the Common turkey *Meleagris gallopavo* and the Ocellated turkey *Agriocharis ocellata*, are related to the pheasants but are sufficiently distinct to warrant inclusion in their own family, the Meleagridae. They are large, powerful birds, 36–48in (91–123cm) in overall length with strong legs, spurred in the male, but with rudimentary webs between the toes and with non-vaulted tails. The head and neck is naked, giving the birds a superficial resemblance to guineafowl. The male Common turkey has a curious growth on the breast during the breeding season. It is a thick mass of tissue which swells, serving as a reserve of oil and fat, on which the bird draws for sustinence to compensate for loss of energy during the breeding season. The plumage of turkeys is generally dark in colour with metallic reflections, most of the feathers margined with black. The naked head and neck are brightly coloured: red, white and blue in the Common turkey, blue and orange in the Ocellated turkey.

Distribution. Turkeys are exclusively New World in distribution and formerly extended from Maine to Guatemala, but their range is now reduced, particularly that of the Common turkey which began to retreat with colonization by white man. The spread of roads and railways too is believed to have helped cause a great reduction in range during the 19th century. The Common turkey occurs from eastern United States to Mexico and the Ocellated turkey from Yucatan to Guatemala. The family is known from the fossil record as far back as the Oligocene, and as a group doubtless evolved in North America. They are birds of woodland and mixed open forest, roaming in small flocks, feeding on the ground and roosting at night in trees. They are non-migratory but given to extensive wanderings in search of food.

Feeding. Turkeys are largely vegetarian, feeding on grain, seeds and berries, but about 15% of their food consists of insects and other small invertebrates. They are very fond of the oily peccan nuts and become very fat when these are in season. They are said to be able to survive for several days without food during periods of severe frost and snow.

Behaviour. Turkeys are polygamous, the male having a characteristic courtship display which consists of expanding the body plumage, spreading the fan-shaped tail, swelling the naked head ornaments, drooping and rattling the wing quills, all this being accompanied by gobbling and strutting. The males will fight to the death if they encounter each other, and by the end of the season are emaciated by their incessant displaying and copulating. The mating season begins in February and nesting commences in April. Nest building, incubation and care of the young is carried out entirely by the female. The nest is on the ground, usually in a well concealed position. Eight to fifteen eggs are laid, creamy in colour speckled with darker brown. The incubation period is 28 days; the female is a very close sitter and will seldom be persuaded to leave the nest. The young are precocious, and generally spend only the first night in the nest, thereafter leaving it and following their mother. At the age of about a fortnight they can fly to low branches to roost at night. They remain with the female till the following spring.

Turkeys are gregarious outside the breeding season, forming flocks which travel in search of food. They generally walk or run, the strong legs enabling them to travel long distances rapidly. They can also fly strongly when hard pressed or in order to cross wide rivers. They have a varied vocabulary of clucks, yelps, gobbling and gurgling sounds. They do not appear to show territorial behaviour.

A male Common turkey *Meleagris gallopavo* showing how the wattle is expanded during display.

Less appears to be known of the habits of the Ocellated turkey which inhabits thicker forest than its relative and is exceedingly shy.

Economic Importance. In the wild, turkeys are considered prime gamebirds and are extensively hunted. They were first brought to Europe by the Spanish, who found them already domesticated by the Mexican Indians in the 16th century. The domestic turkey is descended from the Mexican race of the Common turkey, and the name for the bird is said to derive from the fact that at the time of its introduction to England it was customary to refer to foreign traders as Turks – and Turkey meant, therefore, merely a foreign bird. Domestic birds, bred for their flesh exist in a number of breeds varying in colour from black to white.

Composition. The family consists of only two species, the Common turkey and the Ocellated turkey, usually placed in a separate genus though several authorities have expressed the opinion that the two species are so closely related as hardly to warrant generic separation. The Common turkey varies somewhat in colour, seven geographical races being recognized.

The two species of turkey. Male Ocellated turkey *Agriocharis ocellata* (1) and (2) Common turkey *Meleagris gallopavo*.

DIATRYMIFORMES

Large, extinct, flightless birds. Fossils have been discovered in Europe and North America

DIATRYMA – *Diatrymidae*

DIATRYMA

The diatrymas are extinct, giant birds of uncertain affinities. There are four species. The first example was described in 1876 from fragmentary fossil remains and it was not until 1916 that an almost complete skeleton was discovered in the Tertiary rocks of North America. This gave a good indication of what this extraordinary giant bird would have looked like in life. The skeleton was originally given a new specific name *Diatryma steini*, but was later recognized as being the same species as the original material, and is now referred to as *D. gigantea*.

The skeleton shows that the diatrymids were large, thick-set birds about 7ft (2m) tall, with long powerful legs and vestigal wings which rendered them flightless. The body probably resembled the modern cassowary's *Casuaria*, but had not undergone a reduction in the number of digits in the foot, as have the larger modern ratites. The most striking aspect is the size of the skull which for a bird is huge. It measures some 17in (48cm) in length, the greater part of which is made up of an enormous, laterally compressed beak $6\frac{1}{2}$in (16·5cm) high and 9in (22·5cm) long. It is very different from that of any modern bird although the parrots approach it to some degree. Superficially Diatryma resembles another giant ground living bird *Phororhacos*, known from younger Miocene rocks of South America, but the resemblance apparently does not involve a close relationship.

Distribution. With the extinction of the great land dwelling dinosaurs, and before the mammals had established themselves as the dominant terrestrial form, an ecological niche must have

A restoration of the Diatryma *Diatryma gigantea*, about 7ft (2m) tall.

become available for a large cursorial animal – Diatryma appears to have filled this gap.

The fossil remains of this family have been described from North America, France and Germany. They vary in age from Upper Palaeocene to Middle Eocene and are approximately 65–55 million years old. *D. ajax* was found in the Upper Palaeocene rocks of Wyoming, while *D. gigantea* is recorded from the Lower Eocene deposits of Wyoming, New Mexico and New Jersey, with the latter locality possibly being Middle Eocene in age. *D. sarasini* is restricted to the French Lower Eocene, while evidence of *D. cotei* has come from the Middle Eocene deposits of France and Germany.

Feeding. Being a large, flightless land bird, Diatryma obviously had to obtain its food either from the trees or the ground, but whether its diet was of a herbivorous or carnivorous type is open to speculation. It is generally thought that Diatryma was a flesh-eater, but a striking similarity can be seen between its beak and those of parrots which use their bills as crushing and cutting implements, and it can therefore be suggested that this bird used its beak for shearing vegetation rather than for tearing flesh.

Composition. The Diatrymidae contains a single genus, *Diatryma*, which has four species: *D. ajax, D. gigantea, D. sarasini* and *D. cotei*.

Some authorities believe that the Diatrymidae is related to members of the order Galliformes, but others prefer to include it in its own order, the Diatrymiformes, because its relationships with any living bird are so uncertain.

GRUIFORMES

Ground-feeding and ground-nesting birds. Most species rarely fly

ROATELOS – *Mesoenatidae*
BUTTONQUAILS – *Turnicidae*
PLAINS WANDERER – *Pedionomidae*
CRANES – *Gruidae*
LIMPKIN – *Aramidae*
TRUMPETERS – *Psophiidae*
RAILS – *Rallidae*
SUN GREBES – *Heliornithidae*
KAGU – *Rhynochetidae*
SUNBITTERN – *Eurypygidae*
SERIEMAS – *Cariamidae*
BUSTARDS – *Otidae*

ROATELOS

The roatelos or mesites consist of three species, the Mesite *Mesitornis unicolor*, the Varied mesite *M. variegata* and the Monias *Monias benschi*. All are included in the family Mesoenatidae (=Mesitornithidae), and all are confined to Madagascar. They are similar in size to large thrushes, being 10 12in (25–30cm) in length. All three have moderately long rounded tails, short rounded wings and moderately strong legs and feet with three toes pointing forwards and one backwards. In the two species of *Mesitornis* the bill is rather short and straight, recalling that of a thrush, in *Monias* it is as long as the head and downcurved. The nostrils are long and slit-shaped and partly covered by a horny operculum.

The plumage is brown, olive-brown or greyish on the upperparts and paler below. Two species have darker spots and bars on the pale throat and breast, but the Mesite has these parts unmarked. All three species have one or more white streaks on the side of the head or neck. There are five patches of powder down scattered among the body plumage. The short feathers of these patches abrade at their tips to produce a fine keratinous powder that functions in cleaning the plumage.

Distribution. The Mesite inhabits the lush rain forests of eastern Madagascar; the Varied mesite the dry forests of the northwest part of the island, and the Monias (or Bensch's rail) is restricted to arid brushlands of the semi-desert region of southwest Madagascar.

Behaviour. The mesites are entirely terrestrial, walking about on the ground with quick pigeon-like steps while bobbing the head and lowering the tail with each step. When alarmed all three species run rather than fly, although *Mesitornis* are evidently not entirely flightless as some writers have stated that they fly weakly or fly when forced to do so. However, *Monias* may be completely flightless.

Little is known of the diet, although stomach contents suggest that it consists mainly of insects and seeds picked from the ground. *Mesitornis* are usually found feeding in pairs, less often in small parties, but *Monias* has been seen in flocks of as many as 30 birds.

Nests are placed 2–6ft (0·6–2m) above the ground in bushes or saplings, in positions such that the birds can reach them without flying. The nest is a thin, flat platform of twigs with a scanty lining of leaves, grass stems and other soft materials. Clutches may usually be of a single egg, or of two or three eggs, but only scanty and to some extent contradictory information is available. The eggs are relatively large and nearly oval in shape, with slight gloss. Their background colour is nearly white and they are marked with small and medium-sized brown spots which often form a cap at one end.

The young hatch covered with down and soon leave the nest accompanied by a parent. In *Monias* the down of the chick is brown on the upperparts and white on the underparts, with a rufous tinge on the breast and throat. As the down is lost, immature birds acquire a juvenile plumage similar in colour to that of adults.

Little appears to have been recorded of the voice of the two species of *Mesitornis*. *Monias* gives short sharp *nak . . . nak . . .* calls when disturbed, and a low *creeu* note.

The Varied (or White-breasted) mesite *Mesitornis variegata*, a strange rail-like bird of Madagascar.

Mesites *Mesitornis unicolor* are poor fliers and climb to their nests which are built low down in trees and bushes.

Composition. There can be little doubt that the mesites are only distantly related to any other living family of birds. Most likely they are the remnant of some group that was formerly widespread, but which has survived in Madagascar because of the island's isolation from the competition of more recently evolved groups of birds.

Early naturalists had very varied opinions of their relationships to other groups of birds, but detailed study suggests that they should probably be regarded as relatives of the rails, although they are far too different from them to be included in the Rallidae. Thus, they are at present classified as a distinct family placed near the rails in the order Gruiformes.

BUTTONQUAILS

Buttonquails are diminutive ground birds that inhabit grassland and scrub country in warmer areas of the Old World, from the Mediterranean to Australia. The common alternative name bustard-quail may be preferable, as it draws attention to the family's likely affinity with the diverse assemblage of birds that comprise the order Gruiformes (cranes, rails, bustards and the like) as well as emphasizing the strong convergent resemblance with the true quails, unrelated but ecologically similar birds belonging to the pheasant family Phasianidae. Hemipode is another common name, meaning 'half-foot', in reference to the absence of a hind toe, which is the easiest way to distinguish buttonquails from quails.

They are plump, very secretive birds that mostly inhabit grass plains, crops, marsh flats and sandy wastes, feeding on insects and seeds and flying only with great reluctance. The plumage is buffy brown, richly patterned above with cinnamon, greys and creams which disrupt the bird's outline and effectively conceal it when it is still. In size the largest of the buttonquails is about the same as the smallest quails of America and Europe while the smallest species are the size of larks. In several species the female is appreciably larger than the male, in keeping with her dominant sexual role. They have rather a weak, whirring flight on short, rounded and arched wings, quickly dropping into cover.

In most buttonquails the bill is short, crake- or quail-like, but is arched and quite heavy in such species as the Australian Chestnut-backed buttonquail *Turnix castanota*. Their legs are strong, rather longer than quails'; the body is compact and the tail feathers soft and extremely short. All buttonquails belong to the single genus

Turnix except the African Larkquail, *Ortyxelos meiffrenii*. This is a creamy buff bird living in sandy sub-Saharan steppe; it flies rather more readily than other buttonquails, has boldly patterned black and white wings, a very thin beak and relatively long tail, features enhancing its lark-like qualities.

Distribution. The Larkquail inhabits the southern fringe of the Sahara and the thorn-bush zone from Senegal east to the Nile and northwest Kenya. Two species of *Turnix* range widely in sub-Saharan Africa, and one of them, the Andalusian hemipode *T. sylvatica*, has an enormous additional range from southern Spain and Morocco to India, Indo-China and the Philippines. Six *Turnix* species are Australian, but only the Little buttonquail *T. velox* is found over the entire continent. Red-chested buttonquails *T. pyrrhothorax* inhabit the eastern half of Australia but are very rare, and the other four species each have rather restricted ranges near the coast. The Black-breasted buttonquail *T. melanogaster* is a very rare bird found from north Queensland to northeast New South Wales. One *Turnix* species is endemic to Madagascar and two to the Philippines, including the largest buttonquail, the bright plumaged Ocellated *T. ocellata* of Luzon. Last, the Barred buttonquail *T. suscitator* and the Yellow-legged buttonquail *T. tanki* range from India to Manchuria, where the latter bird is migratory. Otherwise, buttonquails appear to be sedentary over most of their ranges, although some like the Australian Red-backed buttonquail *T. maculosa* are given to vagrancy.

Feeding. Grass seeds and small arthropods constitute the food, which is picked from the surface of the ground. Shoots are sometimes eaten, and the birds also scratch up seeds in the soil. Insects feature predominantly in the diets of some buttonquails. The birds have no crop in which temporarily to store food. They drink freely, without lifting the head.

Nesting and the Young. The breeding biology of button quails is of particular interest, because of the reversed roles of the sexes (buttonquails probably being among the very few birds which are polyandrous, one female serving several males) and because of the accelerated growth rates of the young. Knowledge of the breeding of these secretive, shy and often rare birds has been much improved by studies in the aviary, for buttonquails are as amenable in captivity as other game-birds, breeding readily.

The female, which is the larger and more brightly coloured sex, courts the male and proclaims her territory by repeatedly singing a resonant, low-pitched booming note that seems to vary little among the various species. Females, but not males, have an expanded trachea and adjacently a bulb in the oesophagus (throat), probably significant in relation to this song.

Both sexes build the nest, which varies from a pad or cup of dead leaves and bits of dry grass placed in a depression under a tussock, to a domed structure well concealed under long grass which sometimes makes a rodent-like covered runway to the entrance. The pale eggs are cryptically speckled and blotched, and the usual clutch is four. Throughout the breeding season the female vigorously defends her territory against other females, and is so pugnacious that in India females are captured and pitted against each other in 'cock fights'.

Incubation is left entirely to the male and there is strong evidence that his female then departs to court other males and lay other clutches sequentially. The incubation period is only 12 to 13 days, which is one of the shortest of any birds and certainly the shortest among species whose young are precocious. The chicks are covered in down, concealingly marked with black and rufous; they are active immediately after hatching and soon leave the the nest in the company of the male, who continues to brood and feed them, although they mainly feed themselves. By two weeks of age the chicks can fly and are virtually independent, and soon thereafter go their separate ways. Having replaced the down with feathers, there is a second complete moult which is accomplished by ten weeks of age, the new plumage in some cases being the nuptial one. Full adult size is attained at age six or seven weeks, but it is not known how soon they mature sexually.

Composition. The species fall into a natural genus *Turnix* to which the African Larkquail *Ortyxelos meiffrenii* is distantly related. The Plains wanderer *Pedionomus torquatus* of Australia, generally placed in its own family Pedionomidae, is probably related to the buttonquails.

PLAINS WANDERER

The Plains wanderer *Pedionomus torquatus* is the sole member of the Pedionomidae. It is often thought of as a buttonquail (Turnicidae) with a hind toe, but this is an oversimplification. It differs from the buttonquails also in many characters of the skeleton, in its paired carotid arteries instead of a single left, in its softer looser plumage and in its wader-like eggs.

The bill is of medium length and rather slender, the wings short and rounded, the tail very short, the legs quite long and unfeathered to well up the tibia, and the tarsus scutellate. The three front toes are fairly long, the hind toe short. The feathers of the upper surface present a pattern of fine crescentic barring of whitish, grey-brown and black; the under surface is pale buff with short dark brown bars on the upper belly and flanks. There is marked sexual dimorphism: the female has a wide complete collar of black and white spots and a light chestnut breastpatch and nape, whereas the male has the black of the collar replaced by buff and the chestnut areas much paler. As in the buttonquails, the female is larger than the male, $6\frac{1}{3}$–7in (15·8–17·5cm) in total length as against 4–$4\frac{1}{2}$in (10·2–11·4cm).

The bird rarely flies when disturbed, preferring to freeze or run. It

Two species of buttonquail (family Turnicidae). (1) the Andalusian hemipode *Turnix sylvatica* and (2) the Barred buttonquail *T. suscitator*, compared with a close relative, the Plains wanderer *Pedionomus torquatus* (3). The latter species differs from buttonquails in having a hind toe.

A female Plains wanderer *Pedionomus torquatus* showing the tiptoe posture with stretched neck adopted when nervous.

also has a characteristic upright posture for surveying its surroundings, standing almost on tiptoe with neck stretched upwards; in the open it also runs in this manner.

Distribution. The Plains wanderer is confined to the mainland of Australia, where it has been recorded from South Australia, Victoria, New South Wales and, very rarely, southeastern Queensland. It frequents mainly areas of low open herbage, including crops, and is usually found singly or in pairs rather than in the larger numbers in which buttonquail may occur.

It is believed that a great diminution of the population of this species has occurred in the last one hundred years or so. Several causes have been suggested, all connected directly or indirectly with European settlement. It should be pointed out, however, that fewer Plains wanderers have been brought to the attention of ornithologists during recent years because quail shooting has declined, and it was the quail hunters and their dogs that were once responsible for the collection of the majority of specimens of this species.

Behaviour. Little has been recorded of the diet of the Plains wanderer. Some early records of stomach contents mention bits of grass, small black granular seeds, minute fragments of insects, and grit.

Almost nothing has been published on its breeding biology. Nests have been described as grass-lined hollows in the ground, usually sheltered by a grass tussock or low shrub. One nest, found in a field

The Plains wanderer *Pedionomus torquatus* exhibits sexual dimorphism. The female (1) is larger and more colourful than the male (2).

of young oats, had horse dung as well as grass in the bowl. Eggs have been taken from June to early January. They differ markedly in shape and colouring from those of the button quails, recalling the eggs of some species of the wader genus *Calidris*. They are pear-shaped; the ground colour varies from yellowish stone to pale greenish cream and the patterning is of greenish brown and olive brown streaks and blotches with underlying blotches of light grey. The clutch is usually of four eggs, sometimes five. It is generally believed that, as in the buttonquails, the male incubates. There is a record, however, of a female having been collected from off a clutch of five eggs. The young are downy and presumably nidifugous.

The call has been described as a hollow sound like that produced by tapping on a cask, like one of the calls of the Emu but much fainter; and as a low-pitched resonant *oom*, delivered by day and by night.

Composition. The Plains wanderer is the only member of the Pedionomidae, a family that is probably related to the buttonquails.

CRANES

Cranes, members of the family Gruidae, are large, long-legged birds that are similar in some respects to the rails. Crane fossils have been found from the Eocene period, some 40 million years ago. Bones resembling those found in present day Sandhill cranes *Grus canadensis* have been found from the Pliocene period, four or more million years ago. Present-day cranes stand 2–5ft (0·6–1·5m) in height, have a wing-spread up to 7–8ft (2·1–2·4m). They have long straight bills, long legs and necks and an elevated hind toe. Most cranes have grey, white, brown or blue plumages with black primaries. They have long inner secondaries which hang over the tail. The two crowned cranes *Balearica* of Africa have a bare pink or red, and white cheek patch. They also have a beautiful 'crown' protruding from the hind portion of the head, 3–4in (7–10cm) in length. Demoiselle and Stanley cranes, *Anthropoides virgo* and *Tetrapteryx paradisea*, have ornamental feathers on their heads. All ten species of *Grus* and the Wattled crane *Bugeranus carunculatus* have a bare patch on the head, or the head and neck which is coloured red, orange, or black. A few hair-like feathers are scattered on this region. Cranes fly with their head and neck straight forward, their legs and feet straight out behind. Sometimes they circle on set wings at tremendous heights.

Distribution. Cranes are found in Asia, Europe, Africa, North America and Australia, and most species are migratory. Several species migrate from Asia to Japan. Common cranes *Grus grus* nest in northeastern Europe and winter in southern Spain and Portugal, northern Morocco, Sudan, Iran and Ethiopia. Siberian white cranes *G. leucogeranus* winter in India and Afghanistan; White-naped and Hooded cranes, *G. vipio* and *G. monacha*, in Korea, southern Japan and China. Manchurian cranes *G. japonensis* remain in Hokkaido through cold snowy winters. Black-necked cranes *G. nigricollis* in Tibet migrate to higher altitudes to nest. During drought Sarus cranes and Australian brolgas, *G. antigone* and *G. rubicunda*, migrate to wetter regions. Finally, Whooping cranes *G. americana* fly from Wood Buffalo National Park, Canada, to Aransas Refuge, Texas, where they spend the winter.

Six species and subspecies, Black-necked, Mississippi sandhill, Cuban sandhill, Whooping, Manchurian and Siberian white cranes are rare and in need of protection.

Feeding. Cranes eat a great variety of both animal and vegetable matter. During summer Sandhill cranes will consume daily four or five hundred grasshoppers, crickets and earthworms. One Whooping crane at Aransas Refuge is recorded to have eaten 800 grasshoppers in 75 minutes. Japanese cranes eat mud fishes. Most

Six species of crane to show variation of plumage and relative height. (1) Whooping crane *Grus americana*, (2) Manchurian *G. japonensis*, (3) Siberian white *G. leucogeranus*, (4) Crowned *Balearica pavonina*, (5) Stanley *Tetrapteryx paradisea* and (6) the Demoiselle crane *Anthropoides virgo*. An Australian brolga *Grus rubicunda* (7) is depicted to show how the neck and feet are extended in flight, and a pair of Common cranes *Grus grus* (8) are seen performing a courtship dance.

species eat crayfish and snakes, tubers and grain. Sandhill cranes have eaten mice, bird's eggs and young. Crowned and Stanley eat grass seeds. Australian brolgas dig with their bills for bulkuru sedge tubers, and for peanuts. At times, Sandhill and Common cranes damage wheat and other grain crops. In winter, some cranes fly 12mi (19km) daily from roost ponds to grain fields to feed.

Nesting and the Young. Most cranes build nests in shallow water, up to 24in (61cm) deep surrounded by protective plants up to 2–3ft (61–92cm) tall. Both birds assist in its construction, piling vegetation into a flat mass 2–8ft (61cm–2·4m) across. In the Arctic, Sandhill cranes nest on top of dry dunes or mounds, in Cuba on dry plains. In the sub-Arctic, Common and Sandhill cranes nest in slightly flooded bogs. In these last three situations, their meagre nests are regularly built near water. Crowned cranes lay 2, 3 or 4 eggs. Clutch sizes for other cranes are 2, rarely 1 or 3 eggs. Australian brolgas and Sarus cranes lay spotted white eggs; crowned cranes immaculate light blue eggs; other cranes lay heavily spotted, olive or drab-coloured eggs. Crane eggs measure 3 to 4in (8–11cm) in length and weigh 4 to 10oz (120–170gm). Both male and female incubate, changing roles 2 to 10 times each day.

Incubation requires 28 to 36 days and about 70% of eggs hatch successfully.

Chicks are covered with beautiful tawny, brown or grey down. They can swim and walk when a few hours old and are quite mature in one or two days. Although parents are very attentive, one chick occasionally pecks the other so severely that it runs away and is lost. Families remain intact for nine months or more. Just prior to the next breeding season, parents chase their full-grown young away. Joining with other members of their generation, these youngsters form flocks which remain together during the breeding season. Although some cranes breed when two years old, most wait until 3 to 5 years.

Behaviour. Both sexes of cranes have a spectacular dance, most often displayed prior to the breeding season. Sometimes lone cranes, pairs, or many birds in a large flock dance. They swing sideways, bow, bounce 6–8ft (1·8–2·5m) into the air, uttering simultaneously loud calls and bugles. With a nest or young nearby, a pair occasionally use the dance to distract would-be predators.

Most crane pairs give a 'unison call' during early morning, less often during mid-day and occasionally when they change incubation duties. Both birds extend their head and neck upwards. The female holds her wings tight against her side but the male holds his primaries stiffly below his sides, often extending them even to the ground. The male utters a series of bugles while the female gives a synchronized call so that it normally sounds like the call of but a single bird.

Composition. The family Gruidae is divided into two subfamilies. In the first, Gruinae, there are three genera: *Grus* which includes

A White-naped crane *Grus vipio* throws dry vegetation into the air, presumably the result of playful behaviour.

European, Black-necked, Hooded, Sandhill, Japanese, Whooping, White-naped, Sarus, Australian and Siberian white cranes; *Bugeranus*, the Wattled crane; and *Anthropoides*, Demoiselle and Stanley cranes. In the second Subfamily, Balearicinae, there is one genus, *Balearica*, which includes all the crowned cranes. Crowned cranes differ from other cranes in lacking tracheal convolutions (folds in the windpipe) and, as a result, having differently sounding voices. They also occasionally roost in trees, a habit not seen in other cranes.

LIMPKIN

The Limpkin *Aramus guarauna*, the only species of the Aramidae, is a slender wading bird about 23–28in (58–71cm) in length, with a long laterally-compressed bill that droops at the tip and is usually somewhat twisted along its length. The neck is long and slender, the wings broad and rounded, and the tail broad and of moderate length. The legs are notably long, with the tibiae partly bare of feathers and long slender toes having long, sharply-pointed claws. The plumage is a glossy brownish-olive, with greenish iridescence on the upperparts. The feathers of the head, neck and underparts are broadly streaked with white, these markings extending also to the back and wing coverts in some subspecies. Adults of each sex are very similar in both size and colouration. The fledged young resemble adults, but have less gloss on the feathers of the upperparts and shorter bills.

Distribution. The Limpkin is restricted to the Neotropical zoogeographical region, except for a few populations in the south of the Nearctic region. The subspecies *Aramus guarauna pictus* occurs

in the United States from southeastern Georgia through peninsular Florida, but is local everywhere. This form also inhabits Cuba, the Isle of Pines and Jamaica, and has occurred as a vagrant in South Carolina and the Bahama Islands. Three other subspecies together range widely from Caxaca, Veracruz, Tabasco, Campeche, Yucatán and Quintana Roo in Mexico southwards through Central America to South America east of the Andes. In South America Limpkins occur widely to as far south as the Province of Buenos Aires in central Argentina and to Uruguay.

All populations of the Limpkin are thought to be entirely sedentary, except perhaps for dispersal movements of young birds. In most parts of the range it inhabits wooded swamps or shaded places with abundant vegetation of herbs, bushes or trees, most of its food being obtained while wading in shallow water. On some islands of the West Indies it has been seen regularly in areas of arid brush, but there is no evidence of its breeding in such habitats.

Behaviour. In their usual swamp habitats Limpkins wade in shallow water, perch on the ground and on soft mud, and perch at varying heights in vegetation, sometimes in the tops of tall trees. They can swim well, despite having unwebbed feet, but they fly rather infrequently. In regions where they are unprotected Limpkins are shy and nocturnal or crepuscular, but on nature reserves in Florida where they are protected they have become both tame and diurnal, although continuing to feed also at night.

Although a few insects and seeds are eaten, the diet consists mainly of large water snails, mostly species of the genus *Pomacea* (formerly known as *Ampullaria*). These snails are obtained by wading in shallow water, being picked from the bottom or underwater vegetation. They are then carried ashore or into shallower water, where the snail is extracted and the undamaged shell dropped. Regular feeding places are generally littered with large numbers of such empty shells.

A shallow, rather flimsy nest of sticks and other dry vegetation is built either on the ground near water, or up to 17ft (5·2m) above the ground in a bush or tree. Clutches are of 4–8 buff eggs with blotches and speckles of light brown. Incubation, and care of the young are carried out by both parents. The newly-hatched young are covered with unmarked dark brown down, through which the feathers soon begin to grow. The young leave the nest within a few days of hatching and accompany their parents for at least a few weeks afterwards. Fledged young continue to obtain food from their parents for some time after they are able to fly, approaching the

The Limpkin *Aramus guarauna* is able to extract water snails from their shells by using both the bill and feet.

parent from behind while it is removing a snail from a shell, pulling the snail from the parent's bill, then swallowing it whole.

Calls of the Limpkin consists of loud screaming, wailing notes and clucking noises, all of which are made most frequently at night. These calls have given rise to vernacular names such as 'Wailing bird' and 'Crying bird' in some regions.

Composition. The Limpkin *Aramus guarauna* is the sole member of the Aramidae. Its general appearance is similar to that of a large, slender rail (Rallidae), a resemblance also found in some anatomical features, such as the way in which the intestine is looped. However, in several skeletal features and in the arrangement of the feather tracts it resembles a crane (Gruidae); other structural features are peculiar to the genus *Aramus*. For these reasons it is afforded a distinct family, Aramidae, which is placed in the order Gruiformes.

TRUMPETERS

The Psophiidae contains only three species of plump, chicken-like birds weighing around 2¼lb (just over 1kg) and measuring 17–21in (43–53cm) in length. They have rather long necks, a short, stout and slightly curved bill, moderately long legs, very rounded wings and a short tail which is usually hidden beneath the long, fluffy upper-tail coverts. The stance of trumpeters is characteristically hump-

The three species of trumpeter. (1) Pale-winged (or White-winged) trumpeter *Psophia leucoptera*, (2) Grey-winged (or Common) trumpeter *P. crepitans* and (3) the Dark-winged (or Green-winged) trumpeter *P. viridis*.

backed. Their plumage is very soft and long-webbed, being downy on the body and thick and superficially velvet-like on the head and neck. The outer webs of the secondary and tertial feathers are modified to long hairlike filaments that overhang the tail.

All three species are predominantly glossy black in colour. The Grey-winged or Common trumpeter *Psophia crepitans* has the tertials, scapulars and middle of the back grey; the Pale- or White-winged trumpeter *P. leucoptera* has white scapulars and tertials and a black back, and the Dark- or Green-winged trumpeter *P. viridis* has dark, glossy-green wing coverts, olive-green scapulars and tertials and a dark brown back. The sexes have similar colouration in all three species; young birds are less glossy than adults.

Distribution. Trumpeters are sedentary birds of the rain forests of South America. The Common trumpeter has the widest range, inhabiting the Guianas, Venezuela south of the Orinoco and locally further north, most of eastern Columbia, eastern Ecuador, northeastern Peru and various localities in Brazil, mostly in the

Amazon basin. The White-winged trumpeter occurs from Amazonian Brazil, mostly south of the Amazon, to eastern Peru and southwards to northern and eastern Bolivia. Some authorities have suggested that this bird may be a subspecies of the Common trumpeter, but this seems unlikely if the records of their occurrence in the same regions about the Negro and Solimões rivers are accurate. The Green-winged trumpeter has the most restricted range of the three species, occurring in Brazil south of the Amazon from the east bank of the Madeira river in Amazonas Province eastwards to the vicinity of Belém in the Pará Province.

All three species inhabit mature rain forests of the humid tropical zone, being absent from all but well-grown secondary forests and absent at high elevations. They are often intensively hunted by South American Indians, so are commonest away from habitations.

Behaviour. Trumpeters live on the ground, usually in groups which roam about the forest floor. They roost in trees, and fly only infrequently and with considerable effort. They run very fast when pursued, easily outstripping dogs and other potential predators. The diet includes fallen fruit, berries from low-growing plants and other vegetable matter, supplemented with insects. Stomach contents of the Common trumpeter have been found to include ants and flies of the family Tabanidae.

The name trumpeter describes the loud, deep-toned calls given by both sexes of all three species. The Common trumpeter typically gives several short *uh uh* notes in rapid succession, followed by two or three long *oooooo* booming notes. As this call is given the bill is opened and closed and the feathers of the back are slightly raised. An even louder trumpeting noise is made when members of a flock threaten each other. Native hunters imitate the booming calls in order to lure the birds within range. Soft *weet weet* calls and prolonged cackles have also been described.

In display the wings are spread widely as the birds strut about. Trumpeters often bathe in shallow pools of water, afterwards sunbathing to dry their plumage.

Surprisingly little is known about their breeding biology. Two nests of the Common trumpeter have been recorded in large holes in trees and a third in the crown of a palm. The eggs are dirty white and rounded, with a rough surface to the shell, and may be laid in clutches of as many as eight. The female bird incubates, apparently without assistance from the male, for an unknown period.

Old observations from British Guiana showed that the young

A pair of Pale-winged trumpeters jumping during courtship display.

leave the nest soon after hatching, and are then accompanied by one or perhaps both parents. Small young have elaborately patterned downy plumage, which is of blackish ground colour with elaborate streaks and bars of cinnamon and rufous.

Composition. There are three closely-related species in the family Psophiidae all placed in a single genus, *Psophia*. The family's closest affinities appear to be with the rails (Rallidae) and cranes (Gruidae), and related groups of the Gruiformes.

RAILS

The rails, including gallinules and coots, form a natural group of rather generalized birds, the Rallidae, somewhat fowl-like in appearance but actually most closely related to the finfoots Heliornithidae, and trumpeters Psophiidae, in the order Gruiformes.

Rails vary in size from species hardly bigger than a sparrow, to heavy flightless forms the size of a goose. They have short rounded wings, large legs and feet, and small, often degenerate tails. The bill shape is variable. Many forms have short chicken-like bills; the smaller of these species are frequently referred to as 'crakes.' Others, such as those in the genus *Rallus*, have long slender decurved bills for probing, while in some of the gallinules the bill is massive and conical. Coots and gallinules have a horny frontal shield extending back beyond the bill. The toes may be rather short and heavy, as in some of the flightless terrestrial species, or greatly elongated for walking on floating vegetation, as in the purple gallinules *Porphyrio*. Coots are notable for having the lateral fringes of the toes expanded into well-developed lobes as an adaptation for swimming and diving.

When the sexes differ in size, the male is usually the larger. In the more specialized marsh-dwelling species the body is markedly compressed from side to side, whence the expression 'skinny as a rail.' Marsh rails are often difficult to see, preferring to skulk and hide, or escape by running. When flushed they fly feebly for a short distance, with legs dangling, before dropping back into cover. Many of the forms occurring on islands have the wings and breast muscles greatly reduced and are flightless. This condition evolves rapidly (in some species there are both volant and flightless races) and is probably advantageous in conserving energy in predator-free environments. It has the effect, however, of rendering island rails extremely vulnerable to introduced predators, like rats and cats,

Water rails *Rallus aquaticus* seen in characteristic flight posture with legs hanging down, and washing its prey, in this case a young Reed warbler.

and the Rallidae has, therefore, a sad history of repeated extinctions.

The plumage of rails is lax and decomposed; in some flightless species it appears almost hairlike. The colouration usually consists of sombre hues of black, white, grey, brown, or chestnut. A number of species are nearly uniform in pattern, while many others are variously barred and streaked, sometimes ornately so. The undertail coverts are commonly white and used conspicuously in displays. The purple gallinules are gaudily attired in shades of green, turquoise, and purple. They share brightly coloured frontal shields with several other genera. The sexes are alike in plumage, with the exception of the genus *Rallicula* of New Guinea, the flufftails *Sarothrura*, the Watercock *Gallicrex*, and the Little crake *Porzana parva*. Only in *Himantornis* are the downy young cryptically coloured and countershaded. In other rails the chicks are covered with black down, mottled with brown in a few species, or frosted about the head in gallinules. The heads of downy coots bear peculiar orange or reddish filaments. Flight feathers are moulted one at a time in some species and simultaneously in others, causing them to undergo a period of flightlessness until the new feathers regenerate.

Distribution. Rails are perhaps the most widespread group of terrestrial birds. They occur on all continents, except Antarctica, and are most remarkable for their success at colonizing very remote oceanic islands. Living or sub-fossil rails are known from most of the world's temperate and tropical islands, regardless of their size or degree of isolation. Bones of recently exterminated species are being found with some regularity on islands where rails were previously unknown.

Rails are commonly thought of as being restricted to marshy areas, but in reality are extremely catholic in their choice of habitat, being excluded only from polar areas and the great deserts. Clapper rails *Rallus longirostris*, for instance, are found in salt marshes and mangrove swamps at sea level, while the Giant coot *Fulica gigantea* and the Horned coot *F. cornuta* are confined to small frigid lakes in the highest Andes. Many rails, particularly some of the more primitive ones, are found in forests; either lowland, as in the Congo and Amazon basins, or montane, as in New Guinea. Some, like the well-known Corncrake *Crex crex* of Eurasia, are found in grassy uplands. An endemic rail once occurred on Ascension Island, which is scarcely more than a barren heap of cinders in the middle of the South Atlantic. The Laysan rail *Porzana palmeri* lived out its foreshortened existence on a low sandy island only 1·4 square miles

Heads of rails to show variation of bill shape. (1) Luzon rail *Rallus mirificus*, (2) Takahe *Porphyrio mantelli*, (3) Spotted crake *Porzana porzana*, (4) Weka rail *Gallirallus australis* and (5) the Crested coot *Fulica cristata*.

in area. Rails, obviously, are extremely adaptable; still, it is true that the more familiar Holarctic members of the family are encountered in marshes, ponds and lakes.

Most of the Holarctic species, despite their seemingly feeble flight, perform considerable migrations, usually at night, retreating in winter to the southern portions of their range or to Africa and South America. Some, like the purple gallinules, are notorious oceanic wanderers and may turn up thousands of miles away from their normal ranges. Vertical movements in response to seasonal food supply are recorded for the flightless Takahe *Porphyrio mantelli* of New Zealand.

Feeding. In their food habits rails are for the most part unspecialized. Many species subsist on a wide variety of animal life such as insects, worms, snails, crustacea, fish and amphibians, with varying amounts of plant food also included. The gallinules tend to include more vegetable matter in their diet; some, such as the Takahe and the Tasmanian native-hen *Gallinula mortierii*, are almost entirely grazers of green herbage. Coots feed by diving for submerged vegetation. Some species are opportunistic and may feed upon the eggs and young of other birds or upon carrion. Purple gallinules are known to grasp and hold food in one foot while eating.

Nesting and the Young. Except for a few species that frequent open areas, most rails are secretive and difficult to observe; consequently our knowledge of their behaviour is limited and probably not representative of the family as a whole. Courtship behaviour appears to be simple, and may consist of duetting, displaying the undertail coverts, pursuits, and suggestive posturing. Either sex

Variety of shape and plumage in rails. (1) Inaccessible Island rail *Atlantisia rogersi*, (2) Madagascar rail *Rallus madagascariensis*, (3) Australian spotted crake *Porzana fluminea*, (4) Banded land rail *Gallirallus philippensis*, (5) White-spotted crake *Sarothrura elegans*, (6) Red-winged woodrail *Aramides calopterus*, (7) (European) Purple gallinule *Porphyrio porphyrio* and (8) the Nkulengu rail *Himantornis haematopus*.

may initiate courtship. Nests are built on the ground, in reeds, or on floating mats of vegetation. The aberrant *Himantornis* is reported to nest in trees. Clutch size varies from 2–16 but is usually fairly large. Eggs are white to dark tan in ground colour with darker brown splotches and speckles; in a few species they are immaculate. Both sexes incubate. The young are covered with down and are able to leave the nest with the parents within a few hours after hatching, although they may return to the nest at night. Several species build nursery nests in which the young are brooded for their first few weeks. Young are fed by the parents until proficient at capturing their own food.

Behaviour. At least some rails are highly territorial. Certain gallinules engage in spectacular fights, leaping up in the air and lashing out with the feet at invaders. Coots are particularly belligerent, even towards unrelated waterbirds. The nest may be defended pugnaciously and distraction displays are recorded for several species. The vocalizations of rails are not melodic, usually consisting of raucous cackles, whinnies, grunts and clucks.

Economic Importance. Rails are generally regarded as quite edible, although they seldom constitute a significant portion of human diet. An exception may have been the extinct flightless species *Nesotrochis debooyi* known only from bones found in Indian kitchen middens and caves in Puerto Rico and the Virgin Islands. Good sport is made of rail shooting in some places, especially on the east coast of the USA where, in the last century, the Sora *Porzana carolina* was taken in prodigious numbers and was highly esteemed as food. Its popularity has declined, however, and rail hunting is now practised by relatively few individuals. Purple gallinules are at times destructive to rice crops in the southern USA and in northern South America, control measures having been taken at least in Surinam. The larger species of Australia and New Zealand is likewise known for its occasional depredations on crops.

Composition. There are about 140 recent species of rails, at least 10 of which are extinct. In addition there are another 18 or so island species which probably became extinct in the period since the

beginning of European exploration and are known only from bones or travellers' accounts. For these 158 species, 40 genera are recognized, 5 of which are extinct. The family Rallidae is divided into two subfamilies. One, the Himantornithinae, contains only the primitive species *Himantornis haematopus* of west African forests, which differs markedly from other rails in details of its skeleton, natal down, appearance, and habits. The typical rails, Rallinae, are a rather homogeneous group and the more divergent forms are closely interconnected by intermediate forms so that further division into tribes is impractical. Two groups showing pronounced morphological adaptations are the purple gallinules *Porphyrio* in which the hindlimb is modified for walking on floating vegetation, and the coots *Fulica* in which the pelvis and hindlimb are modified for diving.

SUN GREBES

The family Heliornithidae includes three species: the Sun grebe *Heliornis fulica*, the Masked finfoot *Heliopais personata*, and the African or Peter's finfoot *Podica senegalensis*. The species vary from 12–24½in (31–62cm) in length. They have a long thin neck, small head and a strong bill that is rather long and tapers from base to tip. The wings are short and rounded, the tail moderately long and broad, the legs short, and the toes lobed as in coots (species of the genus *Fulica* Rallidae).

The plumage is brown or blackish-green on the upperparts, with white spots in the African finfoot, and light buff on the underparts. The neck and head are at least partly black, marked with white stripes that are conspicuous in two species, but faint in the African finfoot. The bill, legs and iris are brightly coloured in most forms. The feet of the Sun grebe being bright yellow with black stripes, those of the African finfoot bright red, and those of the Masked finfoot bright green. In the Masked finfoot the iris is bright yellow in the female and brown in the male, a tendency towards brighter colouration of females that also shows in the brighter plumage markings of females of all three species. However, females are slightly smaller than males and it seems likely that they fulfil the usual roles in nesting.

The African finfoot differs from the other two species in having a prominent 'spur' on the carpal joint of the wing and stiffer shafts to the tail feathers. The Masked finfoot is unique in having a prominent knife-like ridge on the base of the culmen (a ridge on the upper edge of the upper mandible) which appears to be developed only during the breeding season.

Distribution. The Heliornithidae has a wide range in the tropics, inhabiting the Neotropical, Ethiopian and Oriental zoogeographical regions.

The smallest species, the Sun grebe ranges from southern Mexico southwards through central America to Panama. It is widely distributed in tropical parts of South America, occurring south to northern Bolivia, Paraguay and the Misiones region of Argentina. Although absent from the West Indies, it has occurred as a straggler on Trinidad.

The larger Masked finfoot occurs only in southern Asia, from Bengal and Assam to the Malay peninsula and Sumatra. The African finfoot is the largest species and confined to Africa, excluding Madagascar and the offshore islands. Its four subspecies, which differ mainly in size, range from tropical West Africa to tropical parts of the eastern Cape Province of South Africa.

All three species are thought to be entirely sedentary, although young birds presumably make short dispersal movements. Their habitats are the vicinity of tropical lakes and rivers, waters surrounded by dense forest or scrub being preferred. The Masked finfoot sometimes occurs in swampy forests with very little open water. All three species are usually scarce, but tend to be commonest in wild and secluded regions. They adapt readily to life in river rapids and easily survive floods and spates of lowland rivers.

Behaviour. Sun grebes swim readily, although they usually remain close to the cover of marginal vegetation. They seem well adapted for diving, but infrequently do so, preferring to escape from predators by scuttering along the surface of the water. On land they clamber with agility among fallen trunks and branches and sometimes perch high up in trees near water.

Their food includes frogs, worms, crustaceans, molluscs and insects. It has been suggested that fish are also eaten, but there seems to be no reliable record of this. Most of the diet seems to be obtained on land or in shallow water, but their shyness and general scarcity makes observation difficult.

The voices and behaviour of all three species are poorly known. The Sun grebe has been recorded giving a double or triple barking call, the Masked finfoot has been thought to be the source of a strange bubbling note, and the African finfoot has been credited with such varied calls as hoarse croaks, a booming note, shrill screams and growling noises, some of which might well have been made by other birds.

Nests are built among vegetation, often on branches of dead trees or among flood debris. They are flat structures of sticks or reeds and contain clutches of two to five rounded eggs. The eggs have a cream ground colour and blotches of brown or purplish-brown. Incubation is carried out by both sexes and the newly hatched young are downy. It is not known when they leave the nest, nor which parent tends them.

Composition. The three species of sun grebes appear to be closely related to the rails (Rallidae), but their peculiar appearance combines resemblances to grebes (Podicipedidae), cormorants (Phalacrocoracidae), darters (Anhingidae) and ducks (Anatidae).

KAGU

The Kagu *Rhynochetos jubatus* was first discovered in the 1850s. It is 22in (56cm) long and the loose plumage is light ash-grey above, washed with brownish on the back and wings; and pale buffish-grey below. It has a large shaggy erectile crest of pale grey feathers.

The African finfoot *Podica senegalensis* showing the lobed feet (1). Finfoots are good swimmers and swim low in the water (2).

Powder downs are present, but as scattered feathers, and not grouped together as in the herons. The feathers of the broad, rounded wings are marked with broad bars of black, white and chestnut (resembling those of the Sunbittern), visible only when the wings are spread. The bill, legs and feet are orange and the nostrils are shielded by a membrane, presumably as a protection while digging for food. Opinion appears to be divided as to whether the Kagu is capable of flight. Most accounts say that it is able to fly but seldom, if ever, does so, and that the flight is very weak; others insist that it is flightless, the large wings used only in courtship.

Distribution. The Kagu is endemic to the island of New Caledonia, a rugged, ancient land over 250mi (400km) long, but comparatively narrow. It is believed by some to have formed part of a continent joining New Zealand and Australia; but even if this is not so it was certainly once a much larger island than it is now, and the Kagu is probably the last remaining member of a once larger bird fauna. It was formerly common and widespread in the island, but since the

The Kagu *Rhynochetos jubatus*, sole member of the Rhynochetidae (1). Its courtship dance (2) includes display of wing colouration and raising and lowering of its head crest.

arrival of man and domestic animals it has been declining rapidly and has been considered an endangered species since 1940. It is now restricted to the mountain forests in the southern third of the island, and it is considered that it is unlikely it will survive the 20th century as a wild bird. The bird's decline has been due to competition from alien predators such as dogs, rats and pigs, but also to the destruction of its native forests by cultivators and by prospectors after nickel, of which New Caledonia is a leading producer.

Behaviour. The food of the Kagu consists of worms, insects and other invertebrates, but the principal food item is the mollusc *Placostylus bavayi*, a type of snail which is extracted from the shell by a blow from the bird's bill and then shaken to remove fragments of shell.

The breeding season in the wild is said to be from August to January, but in captivity the bird usually lays between April and November. The pair have a courtship display in which they stand facing each other, standing very erect with the wings open revealing the spectacular barring. The nest has never been found in the wild, but in captivity birds build loose structures of sticks and leaves on the ground, both sexes sharing the tasks of building and incubation. The single egg is buffish with blotches of grey and brown and resembles a rail's egg. The incubation period is 36 days. The downy chick is dark brown, paler on the wings and with a very large head. It

leaves the nest after 3 days and can feed itself in a month. The total number of birds in captivity is not known but may be quite large: they live commonly for 20–30 years in warm climates, but the young are not easy to rear.

The Kagu has survived during recent years, probably because it is so shy and very difficult to locate. Consequently almost nothing is known of its habits in the wild; Orenstein recounts having met a New Caledonian who had heard Kagus on his estate almost every day for 15 years, but had only twice seen the birds. It has, however, been quite extensively kept in captivity, and much of what is known of it, is derived from observations of captive birds. It is said to inhabit the forest floor, though apparently birds have occasionally been seen in trees; and to escape from enemies by running rapidly for short distances and then standing still, turning, and flinging out its spectacularly patterned wings in front of its pursuer. The birds are very noisy at night, the call is a weird yelping, and it has been assumed to be nocturnal in the wild, though in captivity it is active during the day. Early accounts of captive birds indicate that they are extremely pugnacious and will tease and torment rails, waterfowl and other birds unmercifully, and that they are very quarrelsome among themselves. The Kagu sleeps with its head under its wing and also sometimes rests with the head sunk into the shoulders. It becomes very tame in captivity.

The Kagu is said to be excellent eating and in the nineteenth century many were snared for the table. A certain number have, of course, also been snared as captive birds for export to zoos, and some were formerly kept in barnyards in New Caledonia together with domestic fowls.

Composition. The Kagu consists of a single species *Rhynochetos jubatus*, though early accounts indicate that it was once believed that two species existed. Its systematic position puzzled zoologists for a long time. Originally it was thought to be a member of the Ardeidae, the family that contains herons and bitterns, but it is now believed to be more closely allied to the Sunbittern than to any other living bird, hence its inclusion in the order Gruiformes.

SUNBITTERN

The Sunbittern *Eurypyga helias*, a bird of quite unusual appearance, is the only species of the family Eurypygidae. It is about 18in (46cm) in length, with a long stout body, a long slender neck and a relatively small head. The bill is rather long and straight, the legs moderately long with the tibiae partly bare of feathers, and the toes rather long, excepting a half-sized hind toe that is set slightly higher than the other three. The wings are moderately long and notably broad and rounded, and the tail is rather long and graduated, consisting of 16 broad feathers. Body plumage is full and soft, although the feathers of the very slender neck are short. Almost the entire plumage is intricately barred with brown, grey, black and white. The head is almost black with white moustachial and superciliary stripes, the

Threat display in the Sunbittern *Eurypyga helias*.

neck, breast and shoulders brown, and the throat, belly and undertail coverts pale buff or white. The upperparts are marked with grey, brown and olive, with white spots and prominent black barring, and the tail has two broad black bands. The concealing nature of the brown plumage is broken by a rich orange-chestnut patch near the tip of each wing, an orange lower mandible, orange legs and deep ruby-red eyes. The sexes are similar in both size and colouration, but immature birds are slightly duller.

Distribution. The Sunbittern is confined to the Neotropical zoogeographical region. Three subspecies are currently recognized. The so-called 'Greater sunbittern' *Eurypyga helias major*, formerly regarded as a distinct species, ranges from Tabasco and Chiapas in southern Mexico southwards through Central America (excluding El Salvador) to western Colombia and western Ecuador. Two smaller subspecies of similar appearance inhabit tropical South America east of the Andes. They range from Venezuela and the Guianas south to southern Peru, southern Goiás, Mato Grosso and Amazonas in Brazil, and the La Paz, Beni and Santa Cruz departments of Bolivia.

All three subspecies are thought to be sedentary, although short dispersal movements may well occur. They inhabit the vicinity of watercourses in forests and woodland, and sometimes other swampy places in forests. In habitats of this kind they occur up to elevations of over 3,000ft (about 1,000m), following the clear streams of the hill forests, although elsewhere they frequent the fringes of muddy lowland rivers.

Behaviour. Sunbitterns usually occur singly or in pairs, walking with a deliberate gait along muddy stream or lake shores, among rocks by rushing water, or wading in shallow water. They walk for most of the time, periodically making short flapping flights to cross deep water. The flight is light and graceful with slow wing beats. When alarmed, sunbitterns will readily fly to perch high in trees, where they probably roost throughout the year.

The diet consists mainly of insects, small crustaceans and tiny fish, which are caught with pecking actions in shallow water or on the exposed rocky or muddy margins of water. Sunbitterns are rather quiet birds, seeming almost completely silent when observed from a distance in their normal forest habitats. However, when captive birds are studied at close range a variety of short piping notes and very long squeaky whistles is heard, most of them very high pitched. A mechanical rattling noise is also made, apparently by clattering the mandibles. In display the wings are held open and tilted forwards and the broad tail is fanned to fill the gap between the wing bases. In this posture the bird bows and makes strutting movements.

Nests on the ground have been reported, but it seems that they are usually placed in a tree or bush. They are rounded structures of decaying vegetable materials with a shallow cup containing the clutch of two or three eggs. The eggs are buff or light brown with dark spots and blotches. A pair that bred in captivity in the last century provided much of what is known of the breeding biology. With this pair both parents incubated for a period of 27 days. A nestling was hatched with thick down, but it remained in the nest where it was fed for 21 days, the parents carrying food in the bill. It is not known, however, whether the behaviour of this captive pair was typical.

Composition. The Sunbittern *Eurypyga helias* is placed in a family of its own, Eurypygidae. Its affinities are with the cranes, rails, seriemas and related groups in the order Gruiformes, but it has various anatomical pecularities that have led to its being classed in a monotypic suborder, Eurypygae.

SERIEMAS

The Cariamidae consists of only two species, the Crested or Red-legged seriema *Cariama cristata* and the Black-legged or Burmeister's seriema *Chunga burmeisteri*. The latter is about 36in (91cm) in length, whereas the smaller Crested seriema averages about 30in (76cm). Both have long muscular bodies, a long neck, long tail and rounded wings. The legs are long with the tibiae partly bare, coloured red in the Crested seriema, black in Burmeister's seriema. The toes are short and connected by a partial web at their bases and the bill is short, broad and downcurved. The forehead has a bushy crest of bristly feathers that extend forwards over the base of the bill. Both species have soft, loose-webbed plumage. That of the Crested seriema is light grey-brown with fine dark vermicu-

The Crested (or Red-legged) seriema *Cariama cristata* (1) and Black-legged (or Burmeister's) seriema *Chunga burmeisteri* (2).

lations throughout and broad black and pale bands on the wings and tail. Burmeister's seriema has a longer and heavier frontal crest and darker colouration, with heavy streaking on the throat, breast and belly.

In general appearance the seriemas resemble the African Secretary bird *Sagittarius serpentarius*, a peculiar hawk to which the seriemas bear no actual evolutionary relationship. All three are, however, large cursorial birds that include snakes in their diets and so it seems that their general similarity is a result of convergent evolution.

The common name 'seriema' derives from the Tupi word 'çariama', which was rendered in Latin as *Cariama* as early as 1648 and later became the accepted generic name. Nowadays seriema, which is used as a vernacular name in Brazil, has tended to replace the anglicized 'Cariama.'

The diet of seriemas includes insects, reptiles, small birds and mammals, fruit, seeds and leaves. Here a Crested (or Red-legged) seriema *Cariama cristata* is pursuing a small rodent.

Distribution. The Cariamidae is confined to the neotropical zoogeographical region, having a limited range in the subtemperate and temperate zones. A number of fossil species that seem to have been more closely related to the living Cariamidae than to any other birds have been discovered in geological deposits of mid-Tertiary age in Argentina, suggesting that the family was formerly richer in species. Another group of fossils, with four recognized species in a genus *Bathornis* (placed in an extinct family, the Bathornithidae), is known from the Great Plains region of North America. These fossils dating from the Oligocene seem to be closer to the seriemas than to any other living family of birds. Possibly the genus *Bathornis* represented an early type of seriema living in North America, or an offshoot of early seriema stock.

Both species of seriema have restricted ranges. The Crested seriema occurs in eastern and central Brazil from southern Piauí, Ceará, Paraíba, Pernambuco, Alagoas, Rio de Janeiro, Minas Gerais, Goiás and São Paulo to Rio Grande do Sul and west to Mato Grosso, throughout Uruguay and Paraguay, in northern Argentina south to San Luis and in eastern Bolivia in the department of Santa Cruz. Burmeister's seriema has a more southerly range, extending from Paraguay into northern Argentina, from Jujuy, Salta, western Chaco, western Formosa and Santiago del Estero to Córdoba, La Rioja and San Luis. This species inhabits open areas of thorny woodland and scrub, usually remaining in the concealment of thickets. The Crested seriema prefers more open areas, where patches of scrub, or occasionally light woodland, are interspersed with stretches of open grassland. Both species are entirely sedentary and almost entirely terrestrial, although they

roost and nest low in bushes or trees. They run rapidly to escape from enemies, flying only when hard pressed and then for no great distance. As both species are hunted they are shy of man and are normally seen only running away or at a considerable distance.

Feeding. Seriemas are omnivorous. They regularly eat small snakes, including venomous species, but an early belief that seriemas have immunity to the venom of snakes has been disproved.

Nesting and the Young. Crested seriemas build a substantial nest of sticks in a bush or low tree, at heights varying from about 1–10ft (0·3–3m). Clutches are of two, occasionally three, pale pink eggs which soon fade to white and are thinly spotted and lined with brown, grey and dull purple. The newly-hatched young are thickly covered with down and remain in the nest until they are nearly full grown. Both parents carry food to them in their bills. The nesting of Burmeister's seriema, which is not known in detail, seems to be similar to that of the Crested seriema, except that the eggs are more heavily spotted and the nest is infrequently placed more than a few feet above the ground.

Behaviour. The voice of both species consists of high-pitched yelping, screaming or barking calls. These loud notes are often given in chorus, especially at night, and may reveal the birds' presence when they would otherwise pass undetected. The calls of Burmeister's seriema appear to be higher-pitched than those of the Crested seriema, but both species have a varied vocabulary.

Economic Importance. Both species are regularly hunted as game, with guns or with dogs. Young Crested seriemas are often taken from the nest by country people and reared with domestic chickens. They readily become tame, and serve to warn the farmers of intruders by their noisy calls.

Composition. The Cariamidae contains two species of seriema in two genera, *Cariama* and *Chunga*, both until recently treated under the latter name.

The two species of seriemas share a number of anatomical features with the cranes (Gruidae) and rails (Rallidae), but also differ from these families in other characters. The Cariamidae is therefore classified with those families in the order Gruiformes, but in the separate suborder Cariami.

BUSTARDS

The bustards are a well-defined Old World family of birds, the Otidae, which may be medium to large in size 14½–52in (37–132cm)

Scarlet bee-eaters hunt insects disturbed by the Kori bustard *Ardeotis kori*.

in length. The upper plumage is cryptically patterned and is buff and grey, finely barred and vermiculated with black. The underparts may be pale buff, white or solid black with some species exhibiting bold black and white patterns on the head and neck. In flight some forms show large conspicuous white areas on the broad wings. The head, which is placed on a long neck that remains extended in flight, presents a characteristically low profile as does the bill which is also short and stout. Ornamental plumes are often present and occur as crests, and long bristly feathers on the sides of the head, nape, cheeks, throat or foreneck. The legs are fairly long and strong with the tibia almost devoid of feathering. They have only three front toes, the hallux is missing, which are short and broad and well adapted for running. Males are usually more brightly coloured than the smaller females.

Distribution. The bustards are normally birds of the wide open spaces, especially grasslands and the more arid regions of the Old World. The Australian bustard *Ardeotis australis* and certain other species, however, may be encountered in quite thick areas of scrub. They are difficult to approach on foot, but are less suspicious when approached in vehicles. Although they are capable fliers they are reluctant to take to the air and prefer to run or walk away from an intruder. On many occasions they may crouch in the grass and use their cryptic colouration to help escape detection.

The family is completely restricted to the Old World. Of the 22 species, a few are Eurasian, one is Australian, with the remainder being purely African in distribution. The Great bustard *Otis tarda*, which became extinct as a British breeding bird in around 1832, is a Palaearctic species with a broken distribution; its strongholds being in western and central Asia, although they still breed in isolated areas in Europe. The Little bustard *Otis tetrax* has a similar range to the Great bustard. The Houbara bustard *Chlamydotis undulata* occurs from the Canary Islands through northern Africa to southwestern Asia where it is known as the Macqueen's bustard. The largest examples of the family are placed in the genus *Ardeotis*

Great bustard *Otis tarda* in normal posture (1), during courtship (2).

which has representatives in Africa, southern Arabia, India and Australia. The smallest species is the Lesser florican *Sypheotides indica* and like the Bengal florican *Houbaropsis bengalensis* is restricted to India. The five remaining genera of the family (*Neotis, Laphotis, Afrotis, Eupodotis* and *Lissolis*) are all confined to various parts of Africa with the more southerly forms being commonly called korhaans.

Although basically sedentary some of the more northern species undertake migrations. The best examples being the Great and Little bustards.

Behaviour. All bustards are omnivorous. Large insects, especially grasshoppers and locusts are commonly taken, but lizards and young birds are also eaten. The courtship display of certain species is still not fully described, but those that are known consist of posturing and strutting. In the Great bustard the performance is well-known and is rather spectacular. In this species the male usually chooses a raised piece of ground upon which to perform his elaborate courtship to an audience of six or more females. He begins his display by extending his gular pouch, which is developed only in the breeding season, to expose a wide tract of bare skin. At the same time the underwing coverts are brought forward at the leading edge of the wing and scapulars are turned. The tail is then lifted and placed on the back to display a mass of white under-tail coverts. At this stage the male is unrecognizable as a bird. This pose may be held for only a few moments, but he may remain in this position for three or four minutes before reverting to his normal shape. The display normally takes place in the late afternoon, but the greatest activity occurs at dusk, and when there is a full moon it may continue through the night. Battles between courting males are rare. In some species an aerial display is known.

After mating, a depression in the ground is selected as the nest site which may be under a bush or in tall grass. One to five reddish brown to olive green, speckled and blotched brown eggs are layed in the hollow that may be partly lined. The incubation period is somewhat over three weeks. The downy young are sandy-coloured with dark spots and leave the nest shortly after hatching. The female undertakes all nesting duties. Males are sometimes polygamous.

Bustards can be extremely gregarious and up to 500 Great bustards have been counted in one party on their wintering grounds. Other species may be solitary. They are generally silent outside the

The Little bustard *Otis tetrax* showing differences between the heads of the female (1) and male (2), and between the wings of the female (3) and the male (4). Vibrations of the shortened fourth feather in the male (5) produce a singing note during flight.

breeding season except for barks and grunts. Both sexes hiss and whistle when alarmed.

Economic Importance. Being large and palatable the bustards are often hunted for food. Some species are in danger of becoming extinct while others have had their numbers greatly reduced through shooting and farming activities. Although they are protected in many countries their liking for the remoter areas makes it almost impossible to enforce the law. If they are disturbed, they do not always take flight, but just walk away from the intruder, or in many instances they will just crouch and for this reason they are easy prey for the would-be poacher.

Composition. The Otidae contains 10 genera (*Otis, Chlamydotis, Neotis, Ardeotis, Lophotis, Afrotis, Eupodotis, Lissotis, Houbaropsis* and *Sypheotides*), which have 22–23 species divided among them.

CHARADRIIFORMES

The waders and shorebirds often breed in large colonies and undergo long-distance migrations

JACANAS — *Jacanidae*
PAINTED SNIPE — *Rostratulidae*
OYSTERCATCHERS — *Haematopodidae*
PLOVERS — *Charadriidae*
SANDPIPERS — *Scolopacidae*
AVOCETS AND STILTS — *Recurvirostridae*
PHALAROPES — *Phalaropodidae*
CRAB PLOVER — *Dromadidae*
THICK-KNEES — *Burhinidae*
PRATINCOLES AND COURSERS — *Glareolidae*
SEED SNIPE — *Thinocoridae*
SHEATHBILLS — *Chionididae*
SKUAS AND JAEGERS — *Stercorariidae*
GULLS AND TERNS — *Laridae*
SKIMMERS — *Rynchopidae*
AUKS — *Alcidae*

Four species of jacana. (1) Pheasant-tailed jacana *Hydrophasianus chirurgus*, (2) Northern jacana *Jacana spinosa*, (3) African jacana *Actophilornis africanus* and (4) the Lotus bird or Comb-crested jacana *Irediparra gallinacea.*

Sexes are alike, but females are larger than males. The eggs are amongst the most striking of all birds' eggs, and in all jacana species the males takes the major role at the nest and in caring for the chicks. At least three species are polyandrous, a very rare condition in birds.

Distribution. One or two species (depending on taxonomy) occur in the tropical regions of the New World; two occur in Africa with a close relative in Madagascar; and three in India, the East Indies and part of Australia.

The Wattled jacana *Jacana jacana* is widespread throughout the tropical zone of South America from the northern provinces of Argentina, through Paraguay, Ecuador and Brazil to the Guianas, Venezuela and Colombia and northwestward through Panama to Veraguas. From here the closely allied population of Northern jacanas *J. spinosa*, regarded by some as conspecific with the tropical

The Northern jacana *Jacana spinosa* at its floating nest, usually built on a raft of vegetation.

JACANAS

Variously called jacanas (from an Amerindian name), lily-trotters or lotus-birds, the seven or eight members of the family Jacanidae are moorhen-like birds of tropical ponds, lakes and swamps. Here they live in pairs or small parties foraging along shore lines and beside sedge- and reed-beds, particularly where water-lilies (lotuses) grow. Jacanas have unwebbed feet but extremely long toes and toe-nails which enable them to walk over floating lily leaves without causing them to sink. They are often quite common and not being particularly shy are easy birds to observe. Most of the species have dark plumage – cinnamon is the basic colour – relieved by well-defined areas of white. Further, five species have yellow or straw-coloured plumage on the neck and three have bold white or lime-green marks visible in the outstretched wing. There is a bony knob or spur at the bend of the wing.

form, extends to Mexico from Tamaulipas to Yucatan and on the Pacific slope north to central Sinaloa. It is rare in southern Texas and widespread in the West Indies, on Cuba, the Isle of Pines, Jamaica and Hispaniola, where it passes under the delightful name of Banana coot. It is a 9in (23cm) long cinnamon bird with black head and neck, yellow frontal shield and bill, and lime-green wing feathers.

The African jacana *Actophilornis africana* is larger than the American birds, about 12in (30cm) from bill tip to the end of the short and weak tail, and it is found over the whole of sub-Saharan Africa except for the more arid regions. African jacanas are common inhabitants of almost every piece of permanent fresh water which has a fringe of green vegetation – roadside pools, marshes and lakes, vleis and the margins of rivers. It is rich dark brown in colour, with black crown and nape sharply defined from white face and throat merging into straw-coloured breast. The deep frontal shield and bill are sky blue and the legs grey blue.

A second species, the Lesser jacana *Microparra capensis*, is much less common and has a restricted African range. It lives on lily fields in larger lakes in otherwise drier country from the inland delta of the Niger river to Lake Chad and Uganda, the Rift Valley and the whole of east and southeast Africa to the Transkei. It is only 6in (15cm) in length, mainly golden above and white below, chestnut on flanks and tail. The crown is blackish and there is no frontal shield.

The Madagascar jacana *Actophilornis albinucha* is widespread on that island and clearly closely related to the African jacana, which it resembles, except that it has a white nape.

In the Orient from India to Indonesia is found the Bronze-winged jacana *Metopidius indicus*, which is the same size as the African jacana and alike in plumage except that the forepart of the body is all black (but for a white superciliary stripe) and that the frontal shield is red and the beak yellow. Another species with much the same range is the Pheasant-tailed jacana *Hydrophasianus chirurgus* – a large, striking, graceful and well-liked bird; and lastly, the Lotus bird *Irediparra gallinacea* is a 9in (23cm) long species ranging from Borneo and Mindanao to New Guinea and northern and eastern parts of Australia south on the Pacific coast to just south of Sydney. Its plumage is very like the African jacana's but the frontal shield is red and laterally compressed into a leaf-like comb.

Jacanas are sedentary birds, without any well-defined migrations; but like other birds dependant upon water they are obliged to wander if their pond or marsh dries out. For this reason they are sometimes recorded in foreign lands as rare vagrants. More localized conditions of flooding or drying sometimes cause jacanas to congregate into loose groups of scores or even hundreds of birds. **Feeding.** Jacanas feed by walking about on lily leaves and other floating vegetation, with high stepping gait and jerking tail; they sometimes pick their way through shallows. They make quick darts of the beak for insects, pick up seeds, poke under the water's surface for crustacea and small snails, and often turn over the edge of a large lily leaf with the bill, treading on the upturned edge before examining the glistening underside of the leaf for animal matter. Often they make a dash of a few quick steps after a passing insect, and flies and bees are caught as they visit lily flowers. Bees are always dipped into water before being swallowed. Small water snails are important in the diet, and gelatinous masses of snail eggs are also taken. In addition dragonfly larvae and small fish have been identified as jacanas' food.

Nesting and the Young. Polyandry is strongly developed among the jacanas, with a reversal of the role of the sexes. Males establish small territories which are defended from incursions by adjacent males by strident calls, chases with upraised wings and even aerial attack. Gallinules, rails, grebes and ducks are also repelled. Males of American, Pheasant-tailed and African jacanas (and probably

The Northern jacana *Jacana spinosa* during courtship display during which water plants are held in the bill by the male (1). A detail of the foot (2) shows the long unwebbed toes that enable the bird to walk on floating vegetation.

other species, though these have not been sufficiently studied), build the nest unaided by the female, but only begin to do so after repeated copulations have occurred within the male's territory. The nest is made of water weeds, a low raft usually on floating vegetation but sometimes a pad in a tussock at the edge of the water. The female visits the nest to lay a clutch of three to six eggs, usually four, and then departs to consort with a neighbouring male and lay a clutch for him. A female American jacana may have up to four males (although two is the commonest number) and a female Pheasant-tailed jacana will lay clutches for up to 10 males in the course of a season. When, as sometimes happens, a female has but a single mate, she may share incubation. Generally however, males incubate by themselves, for a period of 22 to 24 days. Eggs are strong-shelled, pear-shaped, and very highly polished owing to a water-proofing layer in the shell. They are olive brown, heavily scrolled with irregular twisting black lines. This makes them difficult to detect, and in addition, like grebe clutches, they are at times covered with scraps of vegetation when the parent is absent.

A parent will sometimes 'incubate' by standing knock-kneed over the eggs to shade them from a fierce sun. But usually the adults squats on the nest in a hunched position, with the legs and feet splayed out to each side, and observers watching closely from hides have claimed that the eggs are scooped up between wings and body and incubated without touching the nest. Certainly the newly-hatched young are similarly scooped up, and are sometimes carried a short distance by the adult like this, since their toes can easily be seen projecting from the folded wing. Nests and eggs in danger of flooding are sometimes moved, the eggs presumably being carried under the wings.

On hatching, the nestling African jacana is almost helpless, blueish-black with a sparse covering of thin down. The eyes remain closed for several hours and it seems very weak. The parent pushes the nestlings under its wings, where they dry out and can stand shakily on legs that are not particularly large after a few hours. By two days of age the chicks are fairly agile and can follow the parent; the legs are proportionally bigger and the down is denser, white below and chestnut brown above. There is a dark crown patch and pale lines down the sides of the neck, and black and white stripes over the shoulders. At three days the chicks can run swiftly over lily pads, and thereafter they forage with their parent further from the nest and are like typical precocious nidifugous chicks of many other birds.

Composition. The seven or eight species of lily-trotters have customarily been placed in six genera, and this classification has been adopted here. Most species, however, differ only in minor respects of size, pattern, and form and size of the frontal shield or comb, and it may be better to include these species in a single genus. Only the Pheasant-tailed jacana should remain generically discrete, differing from all the other species in its greater size, long tail, and peculiarly elongated and attenuated outer primary feathers. Furthermore this is the only species with a distinct breeding plumage, that differs markedly from the non-breeding dress.

Jacanas have no close relatives. The family is usually placed in the wader order Chardriiformes, but their freshwater habit, voice, plumage, gait, frontal shield, and young chicks are more reminiscent of rails, order Gruiformes.

The Old World Painted snipe *Rostratula benghalensis* (1) and the South American Painted snipe *Nycticryphes semicollaris* (2) to show variations in their size.

PAINTED SNIPE

The Rostratulidae is a family containing two species of marsh-frequenting snipe-like birds. The Old World Painted snipe *Rostratula benghalensis* varies in length from $8\frac{1}{2}$–10in (21·6–25cm) and the South American Painted snipe *Nycticryphes semicollaris* from $7\frac{1}{2}$–$8\frac{1}{3}$in (19·1–21·1cm). Resemblance to the true snipe is superficial, painted snipe being in fact closer to the jacanas (Jacanidae) in anatomy and behaviour. Painted snipe have a long bill which is decurved at the tip, a feature more pronounced in the South American species. The bill tip, flattened in the South American species, is semi-flexible and equipped with sensor cells. In colour the bill is pinkish-orange, shading darker towards the tip.

Painted snipe have a compact body, with broad wings that all but obscure the short tail, which is wedge-shaped in the South American species and rounded in the Old World species. Normal posture is almost horizontal, with the head frequently held lower than the tail. The greyish legs are relatively long, with partially bare tibia and long toes that are partially webbed in the South American species.

The head is compact, with a wide, high forehead. The dark brown eyes are set further forward than in the true snipe, allowing greater stereoscopic vision. In both species of painted snipe the female is larger and brighter than the male.

The female Old World Painted snipe has a deep chestnut-bronze head, neck, upper chest and back. There is a prominent buff 'V' in the middle of the back. The wings are metallic bronze-green, while the primaries and secondaries are strongly attenuated in bands, visible only when the wings are open, of black, buff and chestnut. A pronounced buff stripe bisects the head lengthwise. The eye is bisected by a broad white horizontal band, giving a spectacled appearance. The chestnut neck contrasts strongly with the white underparts and the broad white band between the neck and wings. From above, the bird looks dark and blends cryptically with its surroundings; from the side, the alternating dark and light patterns break up the body outline in a disruptive pattern. The male resembles the female, but is smaller and duller. The chestnut of the female is replaced by mottled greyish-brown, and the wings and back are widely barred in black, buff and white. The breast is transected by a broad black band. Juveniles resemble the male, but lack a continuous black band on the lower breast.

In the South American Painted snipe, plumage differences between the sexes are less marked, though the male's colouration is duller than the female's. The crown of the head is blackish with a pale buff median stripe. The back is very dark, mottled with chestnut and black. There is a striking rufous stripe, formed by the edges of the scapulars, on each side of the back. The wing coverts have conspicuous oval white spots. Throat and breast are brown and there are white crescent-shaped marks on the sides of the breast. The underparts are largely white.

Distribution. The Old World Painted snipe is found erratically in marshy lowland areas in southern Africa and in Madagascar, through southern Asia to southeastern China and Japan, with populations in the Philippines and Indonesia and in Australia. The South American species lives in similar habitats in Chile, Paraguay, Uruguay, Argentina and Brazil. The two species are therefore widely separated.

Behaviour. The Rostratulidae is poorly documented. Its members are difficult to observe, being generally unobtrusive, skulking birds,

The Old World Painted snipe *Rostratula benghalensis* adopts a position used in threat.

seldom common anywhere in their range and tending to move about nomadically according to the availability of rain. Painted snipe are active from dusk to dawn and invariably inhabit very muddy bogs and marshes, ricefields or sewer outlets – habitats that are difficult for man to enter undetected. They are also extremely alert and generally able to skulk away well before either predator or bird-watcher can come within view. If taken by surprise, however, painted snipe start suddenly up into the air in an erratic if somewhat feeble flight consisting of rapid wing beats alternated with gliding, the legs being left to dangle as they are in the rails. Painted snipe are nonetheless capable of strong flight over quite long distances, as when they wander in search of fresh wetland.

The diet consists mainly of insects and other invertebrates – particularly earthworms which are the family's most favoured food – and seeds are also taken.

When cornered, the Old World Painted snipe has a spectacular threat display in which both wings are fully spread out towards an intruder, forming two fan-shapes of bright butterfly patterning. At the same time the head is lowered and the tail raised and fanned. In such a position the bird presents a shape four times its normal size. The display is also used in courtship.

Breeding follows the rains, when food is readily available and the nest sites most unapproachable. The nest is a simple grass pad concealed under a tuft of grass or reeds and surrounded by mud. The Old World species is polyandrous, the females defending their breeding territories and mating with one or more males. Only the males incubate the eggs and rear the young. A normal clutch has 4 eggs, though clutches of 6 have been recorded. The ovate, semi-glossy eggs have a cream background with purple and black splotches. The precise duration of incubation is unknown but it probably lasts some four weeks. On hatching the young are covered with down and are straightaway able to feed and run about. They are dark brown in colour, streaked lengthwise with grey and black.

The South American species lays only 2 eggs per clutch, and only the female incubates. The eggs are white, heavily splotched with black. The young are probably cared for by both parents, but little is known of the behaviour of this species.

Vocalizations are not well documented. Whistles and soft croakings are made by the Old World species, with the females being able to hiss loudly or make a guttural growling noise when threatened. Only a plaintive whistle is recorded for the South American species.

Composition. The Rostratulidae consists of two monotypic genera, *Rostratula* found in the Old World and *Nycticryphes* of South America.

OYSTERCATCHERS

The oystercatchers, sometimes known as 'sea-pies,' are seashore wading birds of the family Haematopodidae. There are usually considered to be four species and 21 subspecies of which seven are completely black while the remainder have pied plumage. The pied forms are very distinctive, having a black head and upperparts, white belly and rump, white tips to the primary wing feathers and patches on the secondary wing feathers forming a broad wing bar. Oystercatchers vary in length between 16in (40cm) and 21in (53cm) which makes them comparatively large among marine waders. The feet and legs of all species are stout with three toes and the colour varies from bright orange-pink to a pale pink depending on age and subspecies. The bill is long, laterally compressed and about 3½in (9cm) long. It is bright orange in the breeding season, but becomes duller during the rest of the year. The iris is bright scarlet. The females are slightly larger than the males.

Immature oystercatchers have brownish tinges to the plumage and also differ from the adult in having darker legs, a black tip to the bill and a brown eye iris. They have a white half-collar on the front of the neck which is also common to the adult bird outside the breeding season.

Distribution. Oystercatchers are found on the shores of every continent except Antarctica. Most of them are separated geographically from their neighbours, but in certain areas two species exist together. In South America, the Falkland Islands, New Zealand and Australia, one of the pair of species is pied, the other black. The pairs also differ in their feeding and breeding habits which helps to maintain the species separation and permits peaceful coexistence.

The Haematopodidae are adapted to feeding on marine shellfish and worms and are hence restricted to coastal areas in winter. Most of them remain on coasts to breed on sand dunes, among rocks and shingle or on small islands. Inland breeding, though not at all common and nowhere extensive, does occur in northern Britain, the Netherlands (Friesland), New Zealand (South Island) and around the Aral Sea (USSR). In Britain the habit has increased very greatly in the past 35 years and continues to do so. Territories are taken in arable fields, although some birds will be found nesting at altitudes of up to 2,000ft (610m) in the Scottish Cairngorms. In low-lying parts of Scotland eggs are laid in mid-April, over 90% being placed in newly-sown fields. The food of the adults and young consists of earthworms and leatherjackets.

On average each pair in Britain manages to raise between 0·7 and 1·0 chick to the flying stage, but coastal breeders, studied in Scotland, appear to be less successful, perhaps due to a greater number of predators or to human disturbance in some districts.

Feeding. Many oystercatchers are specialist feeders on bivalve shellfish, a source of food tapped by very few other birds. They have evolved a complex pattern of behaviour to exploit this rich food supply. For example, when they are attacking mussels *Mytilus edulis* the oystercatchers pull the mussels off the bed, turn them over, hammer a hole in the flat surface and cut the strong adductor muscle

The Common oystercatcher *Haematopus ostralegus* (1) and its chick (2), and the Black oystercatcher *H. bachmani* (3) and its chick (4).

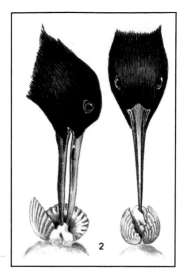

A Common oystercatcher *Haematopus ostralegus* in early winter plumage (1). It can use its bill to open bivalve shells before consuming the contents (2). Common oystercatchers *Haematopus ostralegus* 'piping' during protection of their breeding or feeding grounds (3).

which holds the two halves of the shell together. Once this muscle is severed the bird can use its bill as a lever prising the shells apart; the meat is then chiselled out with fine scissor-like movements of the bill. It has been shown experimentally that the ventral surface is the weakest area of the mussel shell and this fact ties in with the oystercatchers' behaviour which has become adapted to opening the mussel in the easiest possible manner. When the mussel is underwater the shell halves gape so that the bird can sever the adductor muscle with one quick stabbing action, without breaking the shell.

Nesting and the Young. In early spring the oystercatchers arrive on their breeding grounds where they set up territories. Each territory, comprising part of a mudflat, mussel-bed or sand beach, enables access to a good supply of food and also includes an area which will, subsequently, be used for nesting purposes. Nests are simply scrapes in the ground, crudely lined with small flat stones or pebbles, pieces of seaweed, fragments of shell – any suitable material near at hand. Scraping appears to be of great importance and a large number of scrapes may be prepared before the final choice is made. The first eggs are laid in May, about eight weeks after the birds arrive. A clutch of three is usual but two or four are not uncommon. The eggs are incubated by both parents for 25–28 days. When disturbed, nesting birds put on distraction displays, feigning injury and brooding at false nest sites occurs. The chicks are fed on shellfish and marine worms, again by both adults, until they fly at about five weeks of age.

Territorial Behaviour. Oystercatchers are noisy birds, particularly in the breeding season, and much of this noise results from their 'piping'. The birds strut around, shoulders hunched forward with their bills pointing almost vertically downwards and a continuous, loud, rapid trilling accompanies these movements. Previously thought to be solely part of sexual behaviour, it has recently been shown to involve aggressive tendencies associated with the driving away of intruders from a breeding territory or from the vicinity of a feeding ground.

Composition. The Haematopodidae consists of a single genus *Haematopus*, with four species and 21 subspecies. Melanistic populations are sometimes treated as races of *Haematopus ostralegus* and sometimes as distinct species, such as the Black

oystercatcher *H. bachmani* of North America. Other species are *H. ater*, a black form, and the pied *H. leucopodus*, found on South America's southern coasts and on the Falkland Islands; and the Sooty oystercatcher *H. fuliginosus* of Australia.

PLOVERS

The plovers constitute the second largest family, the Charadriidae, in the suborder Charadrii. They have straight bills, about equal in length to the head, with a characteristic hardened swelling at the tip and a narrow gape; only Mitchell's plover *Phegornis mitchellii* has a longish decurved bill. Plovers are moderately long-legged and long-winged, with wings pointed or rounded at the tip according to the species. Most have distinctive black and white wing markings or a white wing stripe visible in flight. Their tails are rather short, rounded and usually boldly marked with black, white or rufous. Most plovers have plain brown or grey colouration on their upper sides when markings have evolved in a few species adapted to tundra or arid habitats. The plumage on the lower part of the body in most plovers is white, often with one or two black, brown or rufous chest bands. Head patterns tend to consist of grey or brown on the crown, white on the forehead, and a black bar separating the two regions. The sexes are similar. Only a few species have a non-breeding eclipse plumage. The hind toe, if present, is rudimentary and raised above ground level. All plovers have the habit of scratching their heads with the foot over the wing.

Distribution. Plovers occur throughout the world, except in Antarctica. The smaller 'sandplovers' of the genus *Charadrius* are ubiquitous on marine or inland shores, but three Asian species and one in North America are adapted to deserts or open grasslands. The 'lapwings' in the genus *Vanellus* are largely tropical in distribution; most are African, but a few occur in South America, Europe, Asia and Australia. A number of lapwing species have forsaken the ancestral waterside habitat of the family for dry grasslands, savannas and semi-deserts.

Most northern hemisphere plovers migrate southward during the northern winter, some reaching as far south as Tierra del Fuego, South Africa and Australia. Tropical species are mostly sedentary. The few species of desert-dwelling plovers are either migratory (in the northern hemisphere) or nomadic (in the southern hemisphere). Regular seasonal movements occur in several species of African lapwings, but these have not been mapped.

Feeding. Nearly all the plovers feed entirely on animal food – insects, crustaceans, other arthropods, and a number of other invertebrates. The Australian dotterel *Peltohyas australis*, however, feeds chiefly on leaves, flowers and seeds of plants in its semi-desert habitat, although it includes some ants and grasshoppers in its diet. Most plovers pick up food at the waterside, either from the surface of the water or mud, or by probing in mud or sand. All species feed by running in short bursts and darting at the prey. The Australian dotterel pulls food off growing plants with vigorous head movements.

The Magellanic plover *Pluvianellus socialis* of Patagonia scratches on damp shorelines as it dances around in a circle, picking up small organisms as it uncovers them. This may be a modified form of 'paddling' or 'pattering' commonly used by members of the genus *Charadrius* on mud or sand; the bird stands on one leg while rapidly pattering the substrate with the other, possibly to bring small animals to the surface.

Nesting and the Young. Plovers of the northern hemisphere and South America breed during spring and early summer. Most species in Africa and Australia nest from July (midwinter) to October, but they may extend breeding activities if suitable conditions persist. Courtship involves mutual displays, many of them similar to threat displays. An essential part of pair-formation is the nest-scrape ceremony; both partners take turns in pivoting on the breast to form the scrape and tossing small objects sideways toward the scrape. The material thus collected eventually lines or encircles the scrape. Copulation occurs during courtship and even after the full clutch of eggs is laid.

Most plovers nest in the open on beaches, grasslands, tundra, gravelly shorelines or stony deserts. The clutch is four eggs in nearly all northern hemisphere species, in most lapwings and in the Slender-billed plover *Oreopholus ruficollis* of South America and the Red-kneed dotterel *Charadrius cinctus* of Australia. All other southern hemisphere plovers and a very few northern species lay

Plovers nest on open ground, and in spite of protective colouration the eggs are vulnerable to a wide variety of predators and intruders. Here a North American Killdeer *Charadrius vociferus* tries to drive cattle away from her nest with a display of aggression.

two or three eggs. The Red-kneed dotterel is also peculiar in nesting in concealed sites under plants on muddy islets of inland lakes.

The eggs of the small aquatic plovers are light yellowish or greenish grey, finely dotted or lined with black or grey. The eggs of lapwings and most non-aquatic plovers are richly coloured yellowish or olive, heavily marked with blotches of black and grey. Incubation periods vary from 14 to 30 days. Parental duties are shared equally by both sexes, except in the Mountain plover *C. montanus* in which each clutch is cared for solely by one or other parent. At least four of the smaller species of plover cover their eggs by kicking nest material over them with the feet when disturbed. Three of these are African representatives of the genus *Charadrius* and the fourth is the Australian dotterel. The habit seems to be mainly for concealment but it also protects the eggs from the sun when the parents are absent. Another protective device against overheating, so far recorded in about eight species, is that of wetting the eggs with water transported in the belly feathers.

Plover chicks characteristically have a white forehead and nape bordered by black bands; the back is mottled and usually marked with median and lateral patches of black. Plovers never feed their chicks, but parental care is otherwise well developed in both parents. Plovers with eggs or young often employ injury-feigning displays to distract intruders.

Territorial Behaviour. Most plovers are more or less gregarious when not breeding. Some flock to a certain extent even when breeding, but they tend to be monogamous, each pair maintaining a small territory, the size of which depends to some extent on the habitat. Thus the Three-banded plover *C. tricollaris* of Africa has small territories where food is abundant, so that it appears to be almost colonial, but pairs are more widely scattered on larger territories where food is scarce. Mitchell's plover of the Andes is well spaced along mountain streams, probably reflecting a relatively poor food supply.

An exception to the rule of monogamy among plovers is the Mountain plover of North America, in which the female mates with

The Double-banded plover *Charadrius bicinctus* (1), the Wrybill *Anarhynchus frontalis* (2) showing its asymmetrical bill, a chick of the Little ringed plover *Charadrius dubius* (3) and Mitchell's plover *Phegornis mitchelli* (4).

one or more successive males, leaving the first with a clutch of eggs, and then laying a clutch for herself. Plovers communicate by means of loud piping, clinking or screeching calls.

Composition. The family Charadriidae is divided into the subfamily Charadriinae with 39 species and the subfamily Vanellinae with 24 species. Included in the Charadriinae are 28 species of *Charadrius*, four of *Pluvialis*, and one each in the genera *Anarhynchus, Thinornis, Zonibyx, Pluvianellus, Oreopholus, Peltohyas* and *Eudromias*. The only charadriine genus not obviously related to *Charadrius* is *Oreopholus*. *Peltohyas* is peculiar in having vertical instead of horizontal eye and chest markings – an adaptation for camouflage among the upright stems of desert shrubs.

The Vanellinae all belong to the single genus *Vanellus*. Vanelline plovers weigh around 5½oz (160gm), being considerably larger than the charadriine species which usually weigh about 1oz (28gm) and seldom as much as 2½oz (70gm).

SANDPIPERS

The sandpipers are typically birds of the seashore, but the family Scolopacidae also includes forms of tundra, marsh and even woodland: the curlews and tringa sandpipers (or 'shanks'); the woodcock and snipe; the godwits, dowitchers, calidris sandpipers (also called 'peeps' in America and 'stints' in Europe); and the turnstones. Altogether there are about 82 species, distributed in some 22 genera, and they exhibit such diversity in form and size, 5–24in (13–60cm), much of which may be due to the often greatly elongated beaks, that it is difficult to define the family in a few words.

Two species of the plover genus *Vanellus* commonly called 'lapwings'. White-headed plover *V. albiceps* (1), Crowned plover *V. coronatus* (2).

Their principal characteristic is their high-latitude breeding range. Not many scolopacids breed south of 50° N and many of them range well into the Arctic Circle, birds like the Sanderling *Crocethia (Calidris) alba*, the Red knot *Calidris canutus* and the Ruddy turnstone *Arenaria interpres* nesting within 8° (550mi or 900km) of the North Pole. Since they feed by probing into mud, sand, silt or earth for insects, worms and crustacea, these northern

birds have to move when, at the end of the short Arctic summer, the substrate freezes over; and many species undertake spectacular migrations to the tropics.

Some species of the other large family of waders, the plovers (Charadriidae), also breed at high latitudes and have long migrations, but from them the scolopacids are readily distinguished by having a different beak shape dictated by their habit of probing rather than pecking at the surface for food. Curlews, godwits, snipe, woodcock and dowitchers have extremely long beaks, straight or decurved, but even in the quite short-beaked stints and Buff-breasted sandpiper *Tryngites subruficollis* feeding is mainly by probing.

The two species of turnstones are aberrant in respect of feeding and of plumage, which is boldly patterned russet, black and white. They may in fact more properly belong in the Charadriidae. The other scolopacids are mostly buffy brown above and white below. In winter plumage they are greyer, while in summer a warm buff or ruddy plumage is acquired, the feathers of the back usually having dark centres and pale margins; pictures may make this plumage look bold but in fact it serves to conceal the incubating bird on its ground nest. Many scolopacids have white wing or tail flashes that show in flight, or white rumps, helping to identify some birds which in winter plumage are otherwise notoriously difficult to tell apart in the field.

Distribution. The most northerly latitudes are occupied in summer by the stints *Calidris* and their allies the dowitchers and Surfbird *Aphriza virgata*, Buff-breasted sandpiper and Stilt sandpiper *Micropalama himantopus* in the New World and another dowitcher, the Ruff *Philomachus pugnax*, Spoon-billed sandpiper *Eurynorhynchus pygmeus* and Broad-billed sandpiper *Limicola falcinellus* in the Old. Some, like the Sanderling, have a circumpolar distribution, while several others evidently have a very circumscribed distribution; for instance, the strange Spoon-billed sandpiper is known to breed only on the Chukot Peninsula in northeast Siberia, close to the Bering Straits.

The sandpipers of the genus *Tringa* (including the familiar Greater yellowlegs *T. melanoleuca* and Solitary sandpiper *T. solitaria* in North America and Redshank *T. totanus* and Greenshank *T. nebularia* in Europe), as well as the godwits and curlews, are centred further south and breed mainly between 50° and 70° N in moorlands and tundra, in birch scrub and along streams.

Some snipe are species of the far north birds, but others, and the woodcock species, range well south into the temperate zone. Indeed this is the only group of scolopacids to have invaded the tropical regions. The Common snipe *Capella gallinago* has an almost unbroken breeding range between 45° and 70° N (south to 36° N in California); clearly derived from it – and by some authorities regarded as belonging to the same species – are the Ethiopian snipe *C. nigripennis* of east and south Africa and the Magellanic snipe *C. paragaiae* of South America. Five other Snipe are endemic to South America and one to Madagascar, while the Pintail snipe *C. stenura* (which has the remarkable number of 26 tail feathers) ranges from Siberia to southeast Asia, breeding as far east as Borneo. The East Indian woodcock *Scolopax saturata*, a close relative of the well-known Eurasian game bird, breeds from Sumatra to New Guinea. One species lives at high latitudes in the southern hemisphere; this is the New Zealand or sub-Antarctic snipe *Coenocorypha aucklandica* found on Ewing, Adams, Antipodes, Snares, South-East Islands and off Stewart Island, an extraordinary bird which, being more woodcock- than snipe-like, poses a major zoogeographical problem about the origin of these birds. It is not clear why the snipe and woodcock have been able to invade the tropics, but it may be related to the distribution of their preferred habitats, respectively

Four species of sandpiper to show variety of size and bill shape. (1) Black turnstone *Arenaria melanocephala*, (2) American woodcock *Philohela minor*, (3) Greater yellowlegs *Tringa melanoleuca* and (4) the Long-billed curlew *Numenius americanus*.

(1) The Willet *Catoptrophorus semipalmatus* in winter plumage. Only during flight are the striking markings of the underside of the wing visible. (2) The Sanderling *Calidris alba* probing sand for invertebrate prey.

marshes and – uniquely in the scolopacids – woodland and forest, where woodcock feed and breed among damp litter.

One last southern hemisphere bird is the Tuamotu sandpiper *Aechmorhynchus cancellatus*, found abundantly on fringing reefs of atolls of the Tuamotu Archipelago at 17° S, 144° W.

All of the northern hemisphere scolopacids are migratory, and those nesting at the highest latitudes perform journeys which put them among the world's greatest travellers. Surfbirds, to give an example, breed in mountains of the Alaska Range, above the timberline, and winter along the Pacific coast south to Tierra del Fuego, a journey for some individuals of over 10,000mi (16,000km) each way. The two yellowlegs, Red knots, Baird's sandpiper *Calidris bairdii* and other peeps, Upland plover *Bartramia longicauda* and Hudsonian godwit *Limosa haemastica* range to Argentina and Tierra del Fuego too. Africa is host to most of the Palaearctic-nesting sandpipers, and some frequently over-summer there instead of returning to the north. The Common sandpiper *Tringa (Actitis) hypoleuca* has two or three times remained to nest, authenticated instances being known from Uganda and Kenya. As vagrants, several North American sandpipers have turned up in Africa, like Baird's, and conversely Europeans have wandered to South America, like the Ruff.

Ruffs abound on their African wintering grounds; one million inhabit a small area at Lake Chad alone. Many have been banded, and recovered 6,000mi (9,650km) away on Siberian grounds east to the Lena River.

From Siberia and Alaska numerous waders make for wintering grounds in south Australia, where the commonest visitors are Bartailed godwits *Limosa lapponica*, Red knot and Ruddy turnstone. Others winter on Pacific islands, like the rare Bristlethighed curlew *Numenius tahitiensis* which breeds in western Alaska and winters up to 5,500mi (8,850km) due south on Central Pacific islands, an oceanic journey requiring prodigious feats of endurance and navigation.

Feeding. Scolopacids feed mainly by probing in soft earth or sand for a variety of invertebrates – earthworms, seaworms, molluscs, sandhoppers and many other small crustaceans, insect grubs and so on. Their beaks are short or very long, up to 8in (20cm), straight, decurved or perceptibly recurved as in the Terek sandpiper *Xenus (Tringa) cinereus*, godwits and large tringas. The beak tip is generally rather soft and pliable, and is heavily innervated and sensitive. Snipe thrust their long beaks deep into mud and can then part the mandibles at the tip to grasp whatever animal matter they sense. The expanded beak tip of Spoon-billed sandpipers, $\frac{1}{2}$in (12mm) wide, increases its tactile surface area and the bird is thought to hunt by touch. The shorter-billed sandpipers, like the Least sandpiper *Calidris minutilla* and other peeps, feed by pecking as well as by probing. Others feed substantially on sedge and grass seeds, and in Africa Ruffs are becoming an economic pest of wheat and rice fields. Ruffs will also run the beak along a grass blade coated with hundreds of midges, and some sandpipers occasionally snatch insects from the air. Curlews eat berries, and in the Pacific islands the Bristle-thighed curlew has a remarkable predilection for birds' eggs, spearing or breaking them by dropping. Turnstones feed on crustacea which they find by flicking over pebbles and seaweed.

Behaviour. While highly gregarious during the rest of the year, sandpipers breed as solitary pairs which are aggressively territorial. Many species have elaborate courtship flights and displays on the ground, accompanied by melodious calls. The 'rodent-run' of Purple sandpipers *Calidris maritima* serves to distract would-be predators. Mating systems are complex. Female Spotted sandpipers *Actitis macularis* nest with one male, or two or three in succession. Up to 30 pairs of Great snipe *Capella media* foregather at traditional spots in marshes and have an extraordinary collective courtship lasting through the twilit night, with choral singing, bill-sparing and formal battles between males. No less remarkable is the courtship of Ruffs. The elaborate 'ears' and collar for which males are named show great individual variability in colour – black collar and russet 'ears'; barred brown and black; white and white; and so on – and no two males are alike. Males gather on grassy hillocks, called leks, where each has a territory of about a square yard in size, hotly defended from other males and functioning as a private arena for frenzied courtship of visiting females (smaller, plain brown birds called Reeves); the species is promiscuous rather than polygamous.

Nesting and the Young. Sandpipers nest on the ground, a shallow scrape concealed in vegetation with a few grasses or rootlets for lining. Sub-antarctic snipe make a deep cup of fine grasses placed among tree roots or under logs, and tringa waders sometimes use abandoned tree nests. Two to four heavily mottled buffy eggs are laid, usually incubated by both sexes. Among Short-billed dowitchers *Limnodromus griseus* the female alone incubates and the male alone looks after the young. In all sandpipers the young are fluffy, cryptically marked, and leave the nest immediately to feed themselves in the company of attentive parents.

Composition. Of the 22 genera the largest are *Calidris* (18 species), *Gallinago* (16) and *Tringa* (10). The only genera not mentioned above are *Catoptrophorus* (the American willet, *C. semipalmatus*) and *Heteroscelus* (the two tattlers, from Alaska and Siberia). Fifteen genera contain only one or two species each.

AVOCETS AND STILTS

The four species of avocet and three species of stilt are proportionately the longest-legged waders. Their bills are also long, and curved upwards along the distal half in the avocets, but straight in the stilts. Avocets have partly webbed toes. The hind toe is absent in stilts, but rudimentary in the avocets. They have predominantly black wings and white bodies; the Red-necked avocet *Recurvirostra novaehollandiae* of Australia and the American avocet *R. americana* have chestnut heads, while the Banded stilt *Cladorhynchus leucocephala* of Australia has a chestnut chest band. Despite their long legs, avocets and stilts scratch their heads with the foot over the wing. Also placed in the Recurvirostridae is the curious Ibisbill *Ibidorhyncha struthersii*; as its name implies, its bill is long and downcurved. Its back is grey, its belly white, and it has a black breast band and facial mask.

Distribution. Recurvirostrids are all waterside birds, usually haunting the shores of shallow lakes, pans and lagoons, often where the water is brackish or salty. The Ibisbill inhabits glacial streams in the Sino-Himalayan region. The stilts and avocets have a worldwide distribution in the subtropical and temperate zones. The only species confined to cold climates are the Ibisbill and the Andean avocet *Recurvirostra andina*, both birds of high montane waters. Most members of the family are nomadic, moving about as conditions change; a few northern hemisphere populations are migratory over relatively short distances. The Ibisbill has altitudinal migrations, moving to lower elevations in winter, although some birds may be resident.

Feeding. Stilts and avocets take small aquatic animals from the surface of the water or from the surface of the submerged mud, at times immersing the entire head and neck. The Banded stilt feeds almost exclusively on minute crustaceans in saline waters. All species swim when necessary. The Ibisbill feeds either on the ground, making short darts at prey, or by probing with the long curved bill under pebbles and boulders in streams to find small invertebrates.

(1) Chick of the Black-winged stilt *Himantopus himantopus*, (2) South American form of the Black-winged stilt *H. melanurus*, (3) Banded stilt *Cladorhynchus leucocephala* and (4) the Ibisbill *Ibidorhyncha struthersii*.

The Black-winged stilt *Himantopus himantopus* in characteristic posture.

Nesting and the Young. Members of the Recurvirostridae always nest near water, usually on small islands or on boggy shorelines where access by predators is difficult. The nests of stilts and avocets are often substantial saucer-shaped platforms of plant stems; in very wet situations, stilts may build up a deep pile of vegetable matter with a depression at the top. The Ibisbill makes a more conventional wader nest-scrape among stones, lining it with tiny pebbles.

The clutch size in all members of this family is normally four eggs, although the Banded stilt often lays only three. The eggs of stilts and avocets are peg-top shaped, heavily blotched with black and grey on ground colours of dull yellow and olive. The Ibisbill lays a more rounded egg with greenish-grey ground colour and scattered small dark brown spots.

Incubation is by both sexes and takes between 22 and 26 days. The incubation period of the Ibisbill has not been recorded. The conspicuous pied plumage of stilts and avocets is correlated with

Avocet *Recurvirostra avosetta* protecting the nest. Avocets normally lay only one clutch of eggs, but if the eggs are lost another clutch will be laid.

colonial breeding and wary behaviour at the nest. The solitary nesting Ibisbill's grey, rounded back, on the other hand, camouflages it well among the water-worn boulders of its habitat, although it too tends to leave its nest early when disturbed. In all cases the eggs are protected by their cryptic coloration.

The chicks of avocets and stilts are grey on the back, and white below, with bold black mid-dorsal lines or patches. The Ibisbill chick is quite dissimilar; its back is plain brownish-grey and it has traces of darker coloration on the face and chest-band. The chicks of avocets and stilts feed by themselves and are never fed by their parents. The situation in the case of the Ibisbill is not known. Parents with young fly about calling loudly in alarm. Both stilts and avocets perform injury-feigning displays near eggs or young, sometimes on the shore and sometimes in the water. Where stilts and avocets are subjected to erratic rainfall, they are opportunistic in their nesting times, breeding whenever and wherever suitable sites occur. These consist usually of islets in shallow waters, either immediately after rain or as water levels are falling with the onset of drier conditions. The Ibisbill, however, because of its harsh and highly seasonal montane environment, breeds only in spring and early summer when the ground is free of snow.

Behaviour. Stilts and avocets are nearly always gregarious. They may form breeding colonies numbering scores of pairs. When breeding is over they gather in large flocks, sometimes of hundreds of birds. Even so, it is possible to find isolated nesting pairs. The birds are not especially vocal unless disturbed, when they have loud,

yelping cries. Like many waders, the Ibisbill is somewhat gregarious when it is not breeding, but flocks apparently seldom exceed 10 to 15 birds. At such times they are not very shy, allowing one to get within 150ft (45·7m) before they show fear. However, breeding pairs seem to be shy and solitary, each pair occupying a length of stream measuring about half a mile. Nesting Ibisbills are highly secretive.

Composition. The family Recurvirostridae as it stands probably does not constitute a natural grouping. The four avocets all belong to the genus *Recurvirostra* and are clearly closely related. The three stilts are also a natural group of one worldwide species and one New Zealand species in the genus *Himantopus*, and a third species confined to Australia in the genus *Cladorhynchus*; this generic separation of stilts is probably unwarranted. Stilts and avocets show clear relationships through skeletal structure, breeding biology, plumage patterns, behaviour and habitats. The Ibisbill, however, is very different from other recurvirostrids. It is unique among waders in its feeding habits, bill structure, plumage and other features that adapt it to Himalayan glacial streams. There is little doubt that it is not closely related to the stilts and avocets. Until its true relationships are known, some ornithologists believe that it would perhaps best be placed in its own monotypic family, the Ibidorhynchidae.

PHALAROPES

Phalaropes comprise three species of fairly small aquatic wading birds, included in the family Phalaropodidae. They are similar in build to the sandpipers and stints, having thinnish, though rather long, necks and small heads. All three species swim a great deal and have dense plumage on their breast, belly and underparts, to

The Grey (or Red) phalarope *Phalaropus fulicarius*. Its plumage is grey and white in the winter (1) and red in the summer (2).

Two phalaropes in summer plumage. (1) Wilson's phalarope *Steganopus tricolor* and (2) the Red-necked (or Northern) phalarope *Phalaropus lobatus*.

provide both water-proofing and buoyancy; legs with an oval cross-section so that the width of bone is much smaller in the direction of movement than at right angles to it, thereby cutting down resistance to the water flow without losing leg strength; and toes broadened or lobed and slightly webbed at the base. They have different plumages in summer and winter. In the breeding plumage females are more brightly coloured than males.

In their grey and white winter plumage the Grey phalarope *Phalaropus fulicarius* and the Red-necked phalarope *P. lobatus* are very similar, and both resemble the Sanderling in general colouration. The Grey phalarope is slightly larger than the Red-necked, but the main difference in winter is in bill proportions, that of the Red-necked being fine and delicate while that of the Grey is shorter and broader. In summer plumage the Grey phalarope is, confusingly, the more richly coloured of the two. This is reflected in its American common name, Red phalarope. The Red-necked phalarope is known as the Northern phalarope in North America, and this also is confusing, as the Red-necked has the more southerly distribution of the two. The third species in the family, Wilson's phalarope *Steganopus tricolor*, is placed in a different genus. It is slightly larger than the other two, with longer legs and a long needle-like bill (of the same shape but longer than the Red-necked's).

Distribution. Two of the species are of arctic origin. The Grey has a patchy circumpolar breeding distribution in the tundra zone, while the Red-necked is found usually to the south of the Grey, in both tundra and boreal climatic zones between about 60° and 70° N. However, in several parts of Canada the two species breed alongside each other. In Britain, the Red-necked phalarope breeds in small, but decreasing, numbers to the south of its normal range, while it is reported to be extending its breeding range northwards in other parts of the world. Both species reach their arctic breeding grounds in June, but stay there only a few months. After breeding they move first to coastal waters close to the breeding areas, where they gather in large concentrations on the sea to moult, in the same way as many ducks. Later, they migrate to tropical and sub-tropical oceanic regions where 'upwellings' occur, bringing cold water, laden with nutrients, to the sea surface. While both species are often found together outside the breeding season, the chief wintering areas of the Grey phalarope are believed to be off the coasts of northern Chile and West Africa, whereas concentrations of Red-necked phalaropes have been recorded chiefly in more tropical waters, off Peru, to the north of New Guinea and off the coasts of Arabia. Wilson's phalarope is restricted as a breeding bird to the North American

continent, where it is found between the latitudes of California (about 35° N) and northern Alberta (about 55° N). Both males in full reproductive condition and females, not yet ready to lay, reach the northern part of their breeding range in Canada in mid-May. Females leave the actual breeding grounds about a month later, and males and juveniles follow some two months after them. They move south to Central and South America, where they winter inland on and around freshwater.

Feeding. In freshwater habitats, phalaropes take aquatic insect larvae (chiefly mosquitoes) and small crustaceans from the surface layers of the water. They stir up these food items from lower levels, or at least cause them to move so that they become conspicuous, by rapid swimming movements with their feet. At the same time they spin their bodies round and round on the water, making many revolutions per minute. This behaviour marks off the phalaropes from other wading birds, as also does their occasional up-ending (like a Dabbling duck). Wilson's phalarope spins less than the other two species and often swims directly or wades. It also sometimes feeds on land. In addition, all three species pick flying insects from the surface of the water. At sea, phalaropes feed on zooplankton.

Nesting and the Young. Pair-formation takes place with the female selecting and chasing the male of her choice, and driving off other females. Phalaropes normally nest on the grassy margins of shallow freshwater pools. Wilson's may, however, nest in meadows up to 330ft (100m) from the water's edge. Usually several pairs nest around the same pool, and in some parts of the Canadian Arctic, Wilson's phalaropes may be described almost as colonial nesters, since they are so common. While it is possible that a small area around the nest may be defended against other phalaropes, breeding phalaropes do not have well-defined feeding territories, but rather feed communally. The nest consists of a scrape made by the female, to which some lining may be added later, either during the laying period, or during incubation, which is done entirely by the male. Often several scrapes are made before the female chooses one for laying the three, or more usually, four eggs. Incubation lasts about three weeks, and the chicks take to the water soon after hatching. Many females, particularly of Red-necked and Wilson's phalaropes, leave the breeding area before the young hatch, so that the male has sole responsibility for the chicks, and it is he who performs the distraction displays to lure away potential predators.

Composition. The Phalaropodidae is divided into two genera, *Phalaropus* consisting of two species, the Grey phalarope *P. fulicarius* and the Red-necked phalarope *P. lobatus*; and *Steganopus*, consisting of the single species, Wilson's phalarope *S. tricolor*.

The Grey (or Red) phalarope *Phalaropus fulicarius* winters at sea, often at considerable distances from the land, and may feed on parasites taken from the bodies of killer whales.

CRAB PLOVER

The family Dromadidae is represented by a single species – the Crab plover *Dromas ardeola*.

It is a unique and interesting bird. Though clearly a relative of the waders, it exhibits many unusual features of plumage, structure and behaviour. It is a white bird, with black back, mantle and flight feathers. A distinctive feature is the heavy, black dagger-like bill, rather resembling those of large terns or herons. The legs are long and grey, and in flight project beyond the short white tail, while the wings appear long and pointed.

The most strikingly unusual features of the Crab plover, however, concern its breeding biology. It nests in colonies, often of hundreds of pairs, situated on sandy plains near the sea. The nests are placed in tunnels, excavated by the birds themselves, a habit unparalleled among waders. The nesting tunnels are four or more feet long, and

The Crab plover *Dromas ardeola*, the only member of the Dromadidae, nests in tunnels constructed near the seashore.

shelving, ending in a chamber where the single egg is placed. The colonies are dense, and the ground is completely honeycombed with tunnels, making walking perilous for any human visitor. Compared to the size of the bird, the Crab plover's egg is one of the largest among birds; the bird itself is about as big as a Lapwing, but its egg is the size of a goose's. Both eggs and chicks are unmarked – the former plain chalky white, and the latter ash-grey, paler below. This lack of patterning is another departure from typical waders, and may be a consequence of the birds' subterranean nesting habits. These habits have probably evolved to give protection against the fierce heat of the sun, which is normal in their nesting areas, especially while the birds are away from the nest. In East Africa, burrowing is recorded as commencing in mid-May, and hatching takes place mainly in early July. Records for the Persian Gulf indicate a somewhat earlier breeding season.

Distribution. The Crab plover inhabits the northwestern shores of India, and includes the Red Sea and Persian Gulf, as well as Madagascar and smaller islands such as Aldabra and the Andaman, Laccadive and Comoro Islands.

Feeding. The Crab plover's name is well deserved, for crabs are indeed its main food, though worms and molluscs are also taken. The powerful bill enables the tough shells of its prey to be cracked

open with ease. The birds forage for them on mudflats and coral reefs in noisy flocks often of some hundreds. They are restless and active in their pursuit of prey, and frequently rise up and fly out over the sea briefly, before returning to resume feeding. The Crab plover's calls are raucous and insistent, and several collectors record how, when one bird had been shot, a flock gathered round calling loudly and following the gunner. At high tide, they gather on sand spits and reefs, travelling to them in long, low lines. They have been observed perching on the backs of basking hippopotamuses.

There is evidently a dispersal from the breeding areas when nesting is finished, and the available observations seem to indicate some migration between Arabian and African coasts. Detailed studies of this, and other features of the bird's life would be most desirable, as despite its unique features, there is a surprising lack of reliable and quantitative information about the Crab plover.

Composition. The relationships of the Crab plover are at present rather obscure, though it has been generally considered a distant relative of the coursers and pratincoles (Glareolidae).

THICK-KNEES

The nine species of thick-knees, also called stone-curlews, stone-plovers or dikkops, are fairly large long-legged waders with yellow eyes and mainly nocturnal habits. Their plumage is mostly brown and buff in colour, plain or patterned with spots or streaks on the back and chest, with a pattern of broad, dark and light stripes about the face. The long wings have striking white patches on the black flight feathers. The legs are greenish or yellow, the three front toes short and the hind toe absent. The bill is straight, relatively heavy (exceptionally so in the genus *Esacus*) and coloured yellow at the base and black at the tip. The ankle joint is characteristically enlarged, whence the name 'thick-knee.'

Distribution. Thick-knees are tropical to warm-temperate in

Two species of thick-knees. (1) The European stone-curlew *Burhinus oedicnemus* and its chick (2), and the Beach stone-curlew *Orthorhamphus magnirostris* (3).

distribution in both the Old and the New World. There are two species in Tropical America, three in Africa, two in Eurasia and two in Australasia. Apart from two exclusively beach-dwelling species and one restricted to African rivers and lakes, the thick-knees are mainly birds of open country, from savanna to semidesert. The two Central and South American species are almost entirely confined to arid country. Only some northerly populations of the European stone-curlew *Burhinus oedicnemus* are migratory; other burhinids are sedentary or locally nomadic.

Behaviour. Most thick-knees eat a surprising range of animal food, both vertebrate (lizards, small mammals) and invertebrate (arthropods, worms and molluscs). Coastal species feed on crabs and shellfish.

Courtship in thick-knees involves chasing, calling and displays which show off the flashing black-and-white patterns of wings and barred outer tail feathers. The nest is a shallow scrape in almost any

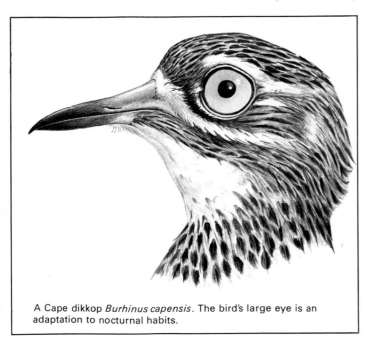

A Cape dikkop *Burhinus capensis*. The bird's large eye is an adaptation to nocturnal habits.

type of site, usually exposed, but sometimes under a bush or tree. The scrape is not lined, but may be ringed with a few small bits of earth or stones. Usual nest sites are open savanna or semidesert, stony hillsides, ploughed fields, urban parks or shingle beaches. The eggs of thick-knees are distinctive in being pale buff in ground colour with sharply etched, irregularly shaped markings of chocolate brown, sometimes in the form of longitudinal streaks. Most species lay two eggs per clutch, but the Beach stone-curlew *Orthorhamphus magnirostris* of Australia normally lays only one.

Both sexes incubate the eggs and care for the young. The off-duty parent usually stands nearby under a shady bush and may act as sentinel while its mate is on the nest. As a rule the sitting bird leaves the eggs long before an intruder is aware of its presence, but occasionally it will flatten itself on the nest and remain motionless until almost stepped on. Incubation lasts for between three and four weeks. The young hatch covered with down and with their eyes open, but they are fed to some extent by their parents for the first part of their dependent period. Burhinid chicks are characteristically grey above with a dark line or row of dark patches on either side of the midline; they are off-white below.

Nesting burhinids are not usually demonstrative towards man, but they will drive cattle from a nest by flashing out their wings.

Breeding thick-knees keep in isolated pairs and are probably territorial. Non-breeding birds, however, become gregarious, gathering in groups of up to about 30. They are generally highly vocal at night, giving loud, rich, piping calls which may drop in pitch and slowly die away. These calls are a particular feature of the African night, although the Water dikkop *Burhinus vermiculatus* of Africa commonly performs wild choruses in broad daylight, several birds participating at once.

Thick-knees are usually shy, spending the day under bushes, singly or in small groups. In some South African urban areas the Cape dikkop *B. capensis* has become almost as tame as the domestic fowl, and may be seen frequenting large lawns in city parks.

Composition. Seven of the nine burhinids occur in the genus *Burhinus*, characterized by patterned dorsal plumage and a relatively smaller bill than the two species of the genus *Esacus*, whose large bills equip them for feeding on the hard carapaces and shells of marine crabs and molluscs. The genus *Esacus* is further distinguished by its plain brown dorsal plumage, unmarked ventral plumage and overall greater size, It is confined to Asia and Australia. In Africa, at least two species of the genus *Burhinus* have tended to colonize marine shores, although species of *Burhinus* are usually birds of inland regions. The thick-knees' nearest relatives are probably the oystercatchers (Haematopodidae).

PRATINCOLES AND COURSERS

Members of the Glareolidae have strongly arched and pointed bills, wide gapes, long and pointed wings (especially in the pratincoles), large eyes (indicating crepuscular habits, mainly among coursers), and they scratch the head with the foot under the wing. Most pratincoles are short-legged, have retained the hind toe, and have forked tails. The Australian pratincole *Stiltia isabella* is exceptional in being long-legged and square-tailed. Coursers are long-legged and have no hind toe. They all have square tails. Most glareolids have collars or bands of black or brown across the throat, chest or belly. The Egyptian plover *Pluvianus aegyptius* has a unique plumage pattern, but is related to the pratincoles, sharing their short legs and riverine habitat. There is no sexual dichromatism in glareolids.

Distribution. Pratincoles occur from Africa and southern Europe across southern Asia to Australia. Coursers occur only in Africa, the Middle East and India. Pratincoles inhabit open grasslands when not breeding, but they nest near water; even the desert-dwelling Australian pratincole nests within 1·2mi (2km) of water. Coursers are never associated with water; most live in short grasslands, semi-deserts, or dry savanna woodland.

Most pratincoles are long-distance migrants. For example, the Black-winged pratincole *Glareola nordmanni* migrates from its breeding grounds in Central Asia to southern Africa and Australia. The Madagascar pratincole *G. ocularis* has a regular migration from Malagasy where it breeds, to the African mainland. The Red-winged pratincole *G. pratincola* is peculiar in having migratory breeding populations in both the northern and southern hemispheres. The Australian pratincole nests in the arid interior of Australia and migrates to northern Australia and the Indonesian Archipelago.

Coursers, like many desert birds, are nomadic. Species living in woodland tend to be sedentary. None has a regular migration.

Feeding. Glareolids are primarily insectivorous. Pratincoles catch much of their food in the air, but also feed on the ground, running in swift bursts to dart at prey. Some coursers augment their animal diet with seeds; all feed exclusively on the ground.

Nesting and the Young. Pair-formation in the glareolids is not well

(1) The Australian pratincole *Stiltia isabella*, (2) Double-banded courser *Rhinoptilus africanus*, (3) Cream-coloured courser *Cursorius cursor* and its chick and (4) the Red-winged pratincole *Glareola pratincola*.

studied, but pratincoles use striking wing displays during courtship.

Nest sites of all glareolids are in the open. Most pratincoles and a few coursers form definite nest scrapes in which to lay their eggs. The Australian pratincole and most coursers, however, merely clear a site of debris and lay their eggs on the flat ground. Nest sites are usually ringed with small objects thrown there by the birds. The Three-banded courser *Rhinoptilus cinctus* of Africa is unique in making a deep scrape filled with sand in which the clutch of two eggs is two-thirds buried during incubation. The Egyptian plover, which nests on sandbanks of large tropical African rivers, also buries its eggs, but only when it is disturbed from the nest; it may even bury its young and may regurgitate water over the spot to cool them.

Most coursers lay two eggs per clutch, but the Double-banded courser *R. africanus* lays only one, and the Bronzewing courser *R. chalcopterus* (also African) lays three. Pratincoles lay clutches of two eggs.

Glareolid eggs are pale off-white to yellowish in ground colour, marked with fine lines or blotches of black, brown and grey. Eggs of arid-zone species resemble the stones among which they are laid. The Double-banded Courser usually lays its egg among antelope droppings, where it is harder to see. The Red-winged pratincole lays dark coloured eggs: it prefers to nest on recently burnt areas or on newly ploughed dark earth. Some pratincoles nest on rocky islets in the middle of large rivers.

Incubation is by both sexes in all glareolids. Parents relieve each other on the eggs about every two hours. The off-duty parent spends much of its time near the nest, either in the shade of a shrub or on a slight eminence like a stone where the air temperature is a few degrees lower than at ground level. In warm weather coursers may merely shade their eggs (pratincoles apparently never do this), but in very hot weather they incubate their eggs in the usual way to keep them cool. The sitting bird lowers its own body temperature by panting, and therefore withdraws heat from the eggs. Some pratincoles wet their eggs in hot weather with water carried in their belly feathers.

Incubation periods of glareolids are usually just over 20 days. The young hatch with their eyes open and a covering of down on the body, but they are not as precocial as other wader chicks. They spend up to 24 hours in the nest and are then led by the parents to the nearest shelter, such as a shrub, grass tuft or even a burrow. The chicks remain in these 'refuges' and are fed by the parents until they can fly; chicks may be moved from one refuge to another during their dependent period, especially after disturbances.

Pratincole parents perform injury-feigning distraction displays to lure intruders from nests or young, but coursers never do so. Both groups have startle displays, flashing spread wings and boldly patterned tails when defending eggs against non-predatory animals.

Chick plumage patterns and colours vary more among glareolids than among any other group of waders. Chicks of the Red-winged pratincole are dark to tone in with burnt ground. Chicks of the Australian pratincole, however, are pale buff with a few dark markings and blend perfectly with the pale soil between the stones of the gibber plains on which the species usually nests. Courser chicks may be predominantly brown or grey with simple or complex patterns, presumably adapted to specific habitats.

Behaviour. Pratincoles are always highly gregarious. They nest in loose colonies. Non-breeding flocks may number hundreds of birds. Coursers of the genus *Cursorius* are also gregarious, although not as markedly so as pratincoles, occurring in flocks of up to about 30 birds. Even when breeding they tolerate small groups of their own species near the nest, but they do not nest in colonies. Coursers of the genus *Rhinoptilus* are never gregarious. Like most colonial birds, pratincoles are very vocal. They have pleasant piping calls. Coursers are far less vocal and their calls are somewhat sharper in quality.

Composition. The Glareolidae are divisible into two subfamilies, the Glareolinae or pratincoles, and the Cursoriinae or coursers. The Glareolinae number seven species in the genus *Glareola* and two monotypic genera, *Stiltia* and *Pluvianus*. The Cursoriinae are ground birds of plover-like size and appearance in two genera. The four plain brown-backed species of *Cursorius* are a closely related natural group. The strongly patterned dorsal plumage and/or banded chests of the four species of *Rhinoptilus* may indicate a natural grouping, but their chicks are all very different in pattern. These differences may be no more than a reflection of habitat differences. The Bronzewing courser is exceptional in this genus in that its back is unpatterned; it is also the most nocturnal of the coursers and may constitute a separate genus.

SEED SNIPE

The four species of seed snipe in the Thinocoridae are ground-living birds ranging in size from that of a large pigeon to that of a quail. They are well camouflaged by cryptically patterned dorsal plumage, in shades of brown, black and buff. They resemble sandgrouse or doves in their stocky bodies, small heads and short legs. The hind toe is well developed, but raised above the level of the three rather long front toes. The bill is shaped like that of a pheasant, and is characterized by shield-like coverings over the nostrils which open by a long slit on each side. In flight seed snipe look very like sandpipers or sandgrouse, with their long pointed wings.

Distribution. The seed snipe are confined to South America from the Andes of Ecuador in the north, to the southernmost islands of the Cape Horn region in the south. Three of the four species are largely montane; the fourth and smallest species, the Least seed snipe *Thinocorus rumicivorus*, occurs on low arid to semi-arid plains, even down to sea-level in the Atacama Desert of Chile and in Argentine Patagonia. All are birds of bleak open country where vegetation is sparse. The southernmost populations migrate north in winter and south in summer. The montane species, at all latitudes, have altitudinal migrations, moving to lower elevations in winter.

Feeding. Seed snipe are entirely vegetarian, eating mostly seeds and leaves. They appear to obtain all their water from succulent or subsucculent leaves, whether they live in the Andes where water is freely available, or in the deserts of Chile and Peru. Like most seed-eating birds, seed snipe have a well developed crop.

Nesting and the Young. Courtship in the seed snipe has not been documented. The nest is a well formed scrape in the ground, either in the open or against a shrub or grass tuft. The scrape is filled with bits of dry vegetation, soil and small stones before egg-laying. As each egg is laid, it is buried in the loose material. Only the female incubates from the completion of the invariable clutch of four eggs; whenever she leaves the nest, either when disturbed or to feed, she covers the eggs with nest material. While the female is on the nest, the male stands guard nearby on a stone or other vantage point.

The eggs have a pale creamy-pink or greenish ground, speckled or blotched with black, brown and grey. They have the typical peg-top shape of wader eggs, and usually lie with the pointed ends inward and downward in the nest material. After an incubation period of just over three weeks, the precocial chicks are led away from the nest as soon as they are dry. The downy plumage is brown, with black flecks and two whitish stripes on the back and off-white below.

Territorial Behaviour. Seed snipe are monogamous during the summer breeding season. Each male defends a small territory by characteristic flight displays accompanied by monotonously

The Least (or Patagonian) seed snipe *Thinocorus rumicivorus*, the smallest of the seed snipes and a resident of low, dry plains.

repeated *puku-puku* calls; this territorial song may also be uttered from a perch on a stone, fence post or bush. Adjacent territorial males fight frequently at their common boundaries, and chasing between rival males may continue uninterruptedly for hours. Outside of the breeding season seed snipe are gregarious and occur in flocks of over a hundred.

Composition. The Thinocoridae are a well defined family of uncertain relationships. They are undoubtedly charadriiform, however, as shown by numerous anatomical, serological, biological and plumage features. The four species fall naturally into two genera. *Thinocorus* contains the Least seed snipe and the Grey-breasted seed snipe *T. orbignyianus*, both having grey breasts and black chest bands in the males, as well as marked sexual dimorphism and relatively small size. *Attagis* contains the Rufous-bellied seed snipe *A. gayi* and the White-bellied seed snipe *A. malouinus*, both larger in size, sexually monochromatic, and without breast bands in the males. The Grey-breasted and Rufous-bellied seed snipe are mainly Andean in distribution. The White-bellied seed snipe is a bird of low mountaintops and bleak islands at the extreme southern tip of South America. Thus the smallest species live in warmer areas and the larger in colder parts, a common occurrence among animals.

A male Grey-breasted seed snipe *Thinocorus orbignyianus* stands guard while the female incubates.

SHEATHBILLS

The sheathbills are remarkable dumpy white birds about 18in (46cm) long with stout blunt bills surrounded by a horny sheath. They combine the appearance and habits of gulls and shorebirds, to which they are related, and which they tend to replace around part of the borders of the Antarctic, where they are the only native birds without webbed feet. In their general habits, pottering around colonies of other birds and human encampments, they somewhat resemble pigeons and also crows.

Distribution. Sheathbills breed on Kerguelen, Heard, the Crozet, Marion and Prince Edward islands south of the Indian Ocean, where they are sedentary, and on South Georgia, the islands of the Scotia Arc, and the Antarctic peninsula. In the winter, those members of the latter populations which are unable to find food disperse north to the coast of South America and to the Falkland Islands though they do not breed in these areas. Migrant sheathbills occasionally visit ships at sea.

Behaviour. Sheathbills are largely terrestrial, walking about seabird colonies, whaling bases and expedition camps and along the shore like so many chickens, though when necessary they can fly well, with quick beats of their short wings. They are territorial when breeding, nesting in scattered pairs, but sociable, albeit in a noisy, quarrelsome way at other times. When not persecuted they become very tame and inquisitive, and spend much time standing about or walking around human intruders, though in the past they were persecuted around such places as the whaling camps at South Georgia where consequently they became scarce and shy. The largest numbers occur in the summer around penguin and shag colonies, where they steal eggs and young birds and feed on carrion. In the winter they also frequent seal colonies and feed on afterbirth. Where other foods are lacking they forage along the shore for invertebrates and algae.

Sheathbills make a variety of hoarse calls and mutterings. They bow to each other in courtship, and when quarrelling together fight with their sharp carpal spurs. They are shy when breeding, and the nests, which are an untidy mass of litter hidden among boulders or in holes, are not easily found. Two or three off-white eggs with grey and brown markings are laid in about December and hatch approximately a month later. They are laid some days apart, while incubation starts immediately, which means that often only the first chick survives. The newly-hatched chicks are clad patchily in brownish down. They soon run about freely, though feeding takes place at the nest. Fledging occurs at between 1–2 months, by which

The two species of sheathbill, the only members of a gull-like family. (1) Snowy sheathbill *Chionis alba* and (2) the Black-faced sheathbill *C. minor*.

time the young have a white plumage and resemble the adults, though the bill is smaller and they retain traces of down at first, and the adults themselves then start to moult.

The Chionididae's population dynamics are of interest because, before the arrival of man and introduced mammals, it appears that adult sheathbills had few natural predators, though skuas and gulls would probably always have taken some eggs and chicks. In summer the food-supply is generally good around bird colonies and whaling-stations. The sheathbill population in such places soon increases and, if they are not persecuted, the birds become very tame. On the other hand, along the shores and on the inland meadows of the Indian Ocean islands sheathbills are scarce and widely-scattered. The extent to which they remain for the winter at the southern colonies in the west Antarctic is also determined by the food-supply. It would seem that the sheathbills maintain a large non-breeding population, presumably mainly composed of young birds, while those that do breed hide their nests more carefully than other Antarctic species, and tend to lay many eggs but succeed in rearing few young, as for example, do birds of prey in areas where the food supply is uncertain. Birds with this type of life-cycle may be rather vulnerable to new pressures resulting from human settlement, though the issue appears to have received little attention.

Composition. There are only two species of sheathbill, one with two races. *Chionis minor* of the Indian Ocean has a black bill, the race occurring on Heard and Kerguelen Islands having a more prominent sheath and paler pink legs than that occurring on the Crozets, Marion and Prince Edward islands, while *Chionis alba* in the American Antarctic has yellow, pink and red markings on the bill and blue-grey legs and feet.

SKUAS AND JAEGERS

The skuas and jaegers are a small but prominent group of aerial seabirds, looking rather like dark-plumaged gulls but distinguished by their elongated central tail feathers. They are renowned for their habit of harrying other birds on the wing and forcing them to disgorge their food, which they then catch in mid-air, though they also feed in other ways as well. The Stercorariidae falls naturally

Snowy sheathbills *Chionis alba* feed on the carcass of a Sea elephant.

into two groups. The great skuas or bonxies are large, stout dark-brown birds about 2ft (61cm) long from the bill to the slightly elongated central tail feathers; the small skuas or jaegers are of slighter build but have longer tails, so that both are the same in length. They are normally dark above though many populations are polymorphic and may be either dark or light below (the Antarctic great skuas show the same variation to a smaller extent). The bill is short and stout. The legs too are short, and the feet are webbed. The long and slender wings, usually held somewhat angled at the joints during flight, show a pale 'flash' formed by white shafts to the primary feathers in the middle of the terminal segment. The pale morphs normally have a dark cap, a pale chin, and a variably darker zone across the breast with a pale belly. They grade through scarce intermediate individuals to uniformly dark birds. The latter are commonest in the low-latitude breeding populations of the Arctic skua or Parasitic jaeger *Stercorarius parasiticus*, where they may form a majority, but are scarcer in the Arctic breeding populations of both this species and the Pomarine skua *S. pomarinus* and are very rare in those of the Long-tailed skua *S. longicaudus*. The young birds of all species are more or less barred with brown.

(1) The Great skua *Stercorarius skua* in dark phase and (2) the Pomarine skua (or jaeger) *S. pomarinus* in light phase.

Many skuas have light and dark phases of plumage colouration. (1) The Arctic skua (or Parasitic jaeger) *Stercorarius parasiticus* in light phase and (2) the Long-tailed skua (or jaeger) *S. longicaudus* also in light phase.

Distribution. Skuas breed along the coast and on bare ground inland in high latitudes in both hemispheres, and migrate into lower latitudes of the same or the opposite hemisphere at other times, where they remain while young. Member of the Stercorariidae perform some of the longest and most complex migrations found in birds. These movements are still incompletely understood. Some pass high over the land-masses, only coming down when they meet the sea (including such places as the Caspian Sea), while others pass down the centres of the oceans to winter in remote, little-explored regions where they are moreover hard to tell apart because they go through the moult there and for a time lose their distinctive central tail feathers.

The Northern great skuas *Stercorarius skua* breed on the Scottish islands, Faroes, Iceland and recently Bear Island and disperse throughout the temperate and subtropical North Atlantic and Mediterranean, while a few appear to reach the South Atlantic. The similar Brown skuas *S. antarcticus* breed around southern

South America and on the subantarctic islands and disperse north, apparently seldom crossing the equator. Another closely related form, MacCormick's Skua *S. maccormicki*, which breeds around the Antarctic continent, is known to migrate north across the equator into the Arabian Sea, to Japan and California, though it has not yet been detected in the North Atlantic, though it may have been overlooked there among local birds. The small skuas are stronger migrants, dispersing throughout the oceans and tending to 'leapfrog' over each other. The largest, the Pomarine skua, appears to stay largely in the tropics, where it concentrates in the biologically rich upwelling areas off west and southwest Africa, around the Indian Ocean and East Indies, and off the west coasts of the Americas. The Arctic skua goes further south to the southern cool temperate coasts, and the Long-tailed skua may go even further south off South America, though so far little is known about its winter quarters.

Feeding. The skuas have a fast, mobile, swooping flight whether foraging for themselves or pursuing other birds to make them disgorge their food. In the breeding area they also take young birds of other species. The Pomarine and Long-tailed skuas, which breed inland on the arctic tundra, catch many small mammals and will gather to breed where there are lemming plagues. In the autumn they will also take berries. The Arctic skua feed along the coast and out to sea, often parasitizing terns throughout the year, while some great skuas feed around seabird colonies in both hemispheres, though many feed at sea, where they may catch fish, eat goose-barnacles attached to driftwood, or sometimes fish-offal or garbage left by ships.

Nesting and the Young. The Stercorariidae breed in scattered pairs or loose colonies on open areas along the coast or inland. Thousands of pairs of great skuas have sometimes occurred together in the North Atlantic in recent years. The birds carry out spectacular aerial displays accompanied by staccato calls when they arrive on the breeding grounds, and the members of a pair then select regular look-out posts on a mound or rock somewhere near the nest site. One to three olive eggs with brown spots are incubated for 3–4 weeks in a scrape with a minimum of lining. The incubating bird leaves the nest ahead of an intruder, and mobs him or tries to decoy him away with tumbling distraction-displays, so that the nest may be hard to find. The chicks are covered with mottled grey-brown down and soon leave the nest to crouch nearby; they fledge in 6–8 weeks, and soon set out on their first migration. In the winter quarters the birds appear to spend all their time at sea and much of it on the wing, though they will settle on the water, on drifting objects, or the shore at times, and in the southern hemisphere the great skuas perch on ships.

Composition. The classification of the great skuas varies. They are sometimes treated as a distinct genus, *Catharacta*, perhaps with inadequate justification. The Brown skua of the southern cool temperate zone is sometimes also treated as a race of the Northern great skua, and sometimes as a separate species, and MacCormick's skua of the Antarctic is more often treated as a distinct species, although all three are plainly closely related. The three small skuas of the genus *Stercorarius* are clearly much more distinct.

GULLS AND TERNS

The gulls and terns are a very familiar group of largely aerial birds feeding mainly along the water's edge in temperate regions, though some occur far inland, others far out to sea, some in warmer regions, others in colder ones, and many move between different habitats at different seasons. Gulls tend to be grey above and white below when adult, with a streaked, cryptic brown immature plumage, but may be whiter in cold climates and browner in warm ones. Their long wings are adapted for easy, graceful flight and for soaring in updraughts. They have moderately long legs with webbed feet and can swim easily on the surface of the water. They will plunge for food but do not dive deeply. Gulls are usually diurnal though some may feed at night, especially out at sea. They have shrill voices with a fairly complex vocabulary though hardly a melodious song, and also indulge in complex visual displays. The sexes are similar except that males are usually slightly larger with heavier heads. They range in length from 10in to 30in (25–75cm). Terns tend to be smaller than gulls and have more slender bodies. The tail is often forked.

Three species of gull. (1) The Pacific gull *Larus pacificus*, (2) Herring gull *L. argentatus*, (3) Black-headed gull *L. ridibundus* in summer plumage and (4) in winter plumage.

Distribution. Gulls appear to have originally haunted the water's edge, but they have spread very widely, especially since they have taken to following man. Complex communities of half a dozen or more gull species which vary in size, feed in different ways, and migrate in different directions are now often found together. In general the large species tend to breed along shorelines, either by inland waters or along the sea coast, while the smaller ones often breed in marshes and swamps as well. Those which breed far inland often tend to go to the coast in the winter, though they are opportunists and also hang around man-made food sources, such as rubbish tips. These movements may vary greatly in length and regularity, from a dispersal of a few miles between different habitats, to sustained migrations crossing half a continent. Some species move east or west, and many into lower latitudes in the winter, though only two species carry out major transequatorial migrations. Franklin's gull *Larus pipixcan* breeds around inland lakes in North America and migrates to winter along the west coast of South America, while Sabine's gull *Larus sabini* breeds on the Arctic tundra and migrates down the eastern coasts of the Atlantic and Pacific Oceans to winter at sea off South Africa and Peru. Several other species such as the Mediterranean and Little gulls *Larus melanocephalus* and *L. minutus* also move out to sea to a lesser extent in the winter, though they never become as highly pelagic as the kittiwakes and Swallow-tailed gull *Creagrus furcatus*.

Terns have a similar distribution to gulls, occurring in coastal regions and sometimes in inland situations where there are marshes and rivers. The largest number of species is found in the region of the Pacific Ocean.

Feeding. Most gulls are prepared to accept a very varied diet, especially when it is provided by man. The larger species probably fed originally on fish and shellfish along the shore, small mammals inland, other birds and their eggs and young, and carrion. They have now become great scavengers as well, both on dumps inland and around fishing boats at sea, with consequently a vast expansion in range and increase in numbers. Originally the smaller gulls probably fed to a considerable extent on invertebrates, including insects when inland in summer, and plankton when out at sea in the winter, but now they also scavenge on waste tips and exploit agricultural ploughed land. They will take insects, including locusts in some areas, while on the wing; worms that have been brought to the surface of the ground by rain; young fish forced up in shoals by marine predators; and, of course, crusts and other tit-bits thrown to them by benevolent humanity. They sometimes bring an extraordinary array of food remains and inedible objects back to their nests. In some species at least, the young birds tend to adopt the simpler types of foraging along the shore and on rubbish dumps, while the old experienced birds use more difficult methods of hunting from the air both inland and out at sea. The characteristic method of feeding by terns is by plunge-diving, but they will also take insects when inland.

Nesting and the Young. There is great similarity in the nest and eggs throughout the family, but a wide variety of nest sites may be used even in the same species. In general the nest consists of a scrape lined with withered vegetation, which in marshy areas may be built up into a considerable pile, with a cup on top. Gulls lay 1–3 large eggs with heavy brown and grey markings on a buff, green, blue, or white ground. Incubation lasts from 3 to 4 weeks. The attractive chicks are covered with thick mottled down. They remain near the nest at first but when about half grown, they start to hide in surrounding cover, wherever this is available, until they fledge at 5–8 weeks. The parents usually feed them, by regurgitation, for a variable period after fledging. If nests, eggs, or small young are lost a new start is made, though gulls are otherwise normally single brooded, except in the case of the Australian Silver gull *Larus novaehollandiae* which may

have two breeding-seasons in the year. Some tropical species may also complete a full breeding and moulting cycle in a period of less than 12 months.

Gulls may nest alone, though most species are, to a variable extent, social in the breeding season. Terns, on the other hand, often breed in large colonies, especially when site conditions are favourable. The degree to which gulls nest together usually depends on the local food supply. Where it is good and there are secure sites available, colonies may become very large, running into thousands and tens of thousands of pairs. Some species are particularly faithful to their nest sites, returning to the same cliff-ledge year by year. The most usual sites include coastal sand-bars and shingle-ridges, salt-marshes, cliffs, offshore islands, lagoons or bogs behind the coast, the shores and islands of inland lakes, and inland marshes. Bonaparte's gull *Larus philadelphia* nests in trees, usually conifers, in North America, and other species may do so occasionally, while in many parts of the world, the larger species are turning more and more to nest on urban rooftops. Such species as the pelagic kittiwakes and the Swallow-tailed gull, with their short legs, specialized displays, and comparatively quiescent young, are particularly adapted for nesting on cliffs, though even kittiwakes will nest on the beach if nothing else is available.

Behaviour. Because they are large, numerous and relatively tame, and have conspicuous visual and vocal displays, gulls have been major subjects for the study of bird behaviour, and that of all species has been worked out and compared in considerable detail. In general, once they leave the nest the young birds tend to form loose flocks and remain sociable throughout their lives, except when defending the immediate vicinity of the nest-site. When searching for food they fly around the countryside in loose groups, gathering to soar where there are updraughts along hill-crests or on the windward side of a ship, and following promising sources of food such as a tractor pulling a plough or a trawler hauling its nets. When they have fed they spend much of the day standing, sitting or swimming about in idle groups in open spaces where they have a

(Black-legged) Kittiwakes *Rissa tridactyla* at a nest colony built on narrow cliff ledges. When conditions are favourable, such colonies may extend to tens of thousands of nesting pairs.

clear view of approaching predators. They usually feed by day, but will gather to feed over lighted fishing-boats or where the tide ebbs to expose mudflats at night, and the pelagic species may feed mainly at night on plankton which comes to the sea surface then. Otherwise the birds from a large area may gather at favourite roosts at night, on inland waters, coastal inlets or sand-bars, cliffs, islands, rooftops, or offshore. In areas where there is a large gull population very prominent movements may occur along regular routes between the roosting and feeding areas in the morning and evening.

Calls and plumage and other markings are used in display and for other communication between individuals. A particularly good example of the latter is provided by the red spot near the bill-tip of many of the large species: small chicks may be seen to peck at this spot, an action which stimulates the parent bird to regurgitate food. In the larger species various combinations of bill, eye-ring, and back and wing-tip colouration serve as recognition marks between members of the same species, and it has been found that by using paint to alter the markings it is possible to get different species to hybridize with each other. The dark head assumed in the breeding season by some of the smaller gulls provides an indication that the bird is in breeding condition, and is exhibited by one bird to another in threat displays but concealed by turning the head away as a mark of submission by birds with peaceful intentions.

Most terns breeding in northern areas migrate southwards during winter. The Arctic tern *Sterna paradisaea* migrates distances of 22,000mi (36,000km) each year.

Economic Importance. In parts of the world, gulls' eggs are regarded as a delicacy and the birds themselves are also eaten in some places. The smaller species are usually considered to be beneficial to agriculture as it is thought that they eat many potentially harmful invetebrates, though this view is debatable. The larger species are more often considered injurious because they attack other birds or take their eggs and young, and because they steal agricultural produce and take food from domestic animals such as pigs. They can create a major nuisance in towns, especially where they nest on buildings. Flocks of gulls frequenting airports present a major hazard to aircraft, and have been responsible for a great deal of expensive damage to jet engines. Gulls are probably one of the most important avian vectors of disease, including fowl pest, ornithosis, intestinal parasites, and food-poisoning. This is potentially serious where they commute regularly between sewage farms, rubbish dumps, reservoirs, and the roofs of factories and markets dealing with food. A certain way to reduce their numbers would be by the introduction of more efficient waste disposal. Yet gulls have seldom been proved to have caused infections in humans. They may even be said to perform a useful role in clearing up garbage.

Composition. The Laridae falls into two groups, the subfamily Larinae or gulls, and the Sterninae or terns. The gulls include some 45 species, nearly all placed in one genus *Larus*, though half a dozen or so specialized genera with one or two species are recognized by some authors. The large species allied to the Herring gull *Larus argentatus* in which the yellow bill is marked with a red spot, present a notorious taxonomic problem since a number of forms whose distribution overlaps all behave like distinct species in some places but hybridize freely in others. This is particularly common where species extending their range meet others for the first time, as happened when Herring gulls colonized Iceland and promptly started to interbreed with the Glaucous gulls *Larus hyperboreus*. Similar problems occur with the even more numerous small hooded gulls represented by the Black-headed gull *Larus ridibundus* in Britain and the Laughing gull *Larus atricilla*, among others, in North America. Some of these are undertaking even bolder enterprises, as for example in the case of the Old World Little gull *Larus minutus* which has recently colonized Canada. Most of the specialized genera have been mentioned already, but the small, graceful pink and white Ross's gull *Rhodostethia rosea* which apparently breeds in Siberia and winters in darkness in the centre of the Arctic Ocean also deserves notice.

The terns include only three genera: *Sterna*, the black-capped terns (30 species); *Anous*, the noddies (5); and *Larosterna*, the Inca tern *L. inca*.

SKIMMERS

Skimmers are elegant tern-like birds of sea shores, lakes and rivers mainly in the tropics. The family, Rynchopidae, contains three species; one in America, one in Africa and one in India and southeast Asia. They are similarly black above and white below, with long vermilion-and-black or -yellow beak, and short scarlet legs and toes with shallow webs. The tail is short and forked, and the wings very long with a spread two-and-a-half times the length of the bird. Only trivial characters of beak colour and head pattern separate the species. They live gregariously, nesting on the glaring white beaches and sand-bars of tropical rivers, feeding sociably over the water mainly at night, and resting by day in compact flocks on sand-bars or open grassland. To withstand the glare, skimmers have a vertical slit pupil, like a cat's. But an even more remarkable feature is the form of the bill; the lower mandible is up to 1in (25mm) longer than the upper, and is extremely thin and flexible. In flight the beak is held at a downward angle and skimmers feed with the beak wide open and the lower mandible knifing the water.

Distribution. The American Black skimmer *Rynchops nigra* is as much a bird of the coasts as of interior rivers, and breeds on the

Atlantic coast north to Massachusetts (42° N) and south to Buenos Aires and casually even to Santa Cruz (50° S), and on the Pacific coast from the Gulf of California south to the Gulf of Guayaquil in Ecuador. It does not breed in the West Indies, but is found locally on larger South American rivers. The Indian skimmer *R. albicollis* prefers lakes and rivers with extensive sand banks rather than coasts and is found in India, Burma and Indo-China; while the African skimmer *R. flavirostris* shuns the coast completely and has a wide distribution on rivers and lakes throughout the whole of sub-Saharan Africa south to the Orange River. It formerly occurred also on the lower Nile. In North America the Black skimmer is exclusively coastal and is migratory, wintering from North Carolina southward, and elsewhere this species and the other two are vagrant rather than migrant, wandering hundreds of miles along rivers according to the dictates of water levels.

The smallest and largest terns compared. (1) Little (or Least) tern *Sterna albifrons* and (2) the Caspian tern *S. caspia*. In the African skimmer *Rynchops flavirostris* (3) the lower mandible is longer than the upper mandible (4) and is used to skim food from the surface of shallow water (5).

Feeding. In common with gulls and terns, the downy chick is fed by its parents but from two weeks of age it also feeds upon such flies, beetles and sandhoppers as it can catch for itself on the sand banks and strands of its home. Chicks close to fledging still use the beak as forceps, standing at the edge of the water and making stabs at crustacea and small fish. Then the lower mandible begins to elongate and soon after fledging the bird can make its first attempt at skimming. Adults also feed to an extent by pecking at crustaceans while standing in shallow water, but skimming is far more important for them – a highly specialized method of feeding without parallel among birds. The bird makes air speed by banking across the breeze and with a few strong wing beats descends to the water surface and glides on slightly raised wings until momentum is lost, with the beak opened wide and the mandible slicing the water. They prefer calm water and are unable to skim if the surface is choppy. Over the very calm waters of broad tropical rivers, skimmers are generally obliged to use powered flight while skimming and do not just glide. The flight posture is extraordinary, the body being tilted down towards the beak and the long wings beating in an upheld, dihedral, position – yet the whole effect is of effortless and supremely graceful mastery of technique.

Small fish, crustaceans and other planters constitute the diet of skimmers. When the blade-thin mandible strikes one, the beak snaps shut as the head is moved down and back, then with barely perceptible pause skimming continues. Skimming is mostly at dawn and dusk and during the night, for during the day the plankton moves deep and is less readily available.

Behaviour. Little is known of courtship in skimmers because the sexes are indistinguishable by plumage in the field and much of the territorial ritual is at night. Before nesting skimmers become active and noisy, especially by night. After aerial chasing the pair land and the male, making a soft shrill cooing note, opening and closing the bill and jerking the head from side to side, has been seen to approach and mate with the squatting female.

Nesting and the Young. Skimmers nest in loose colonies from a score up to 4,000 pairs in size. A bird hollows out a shallow depression in the sand by turning on its breast, and a set of two or three tern-like eggs is laid. At higher latitudes the clutch is four, occasionally five. Both sexes incubate, and at equatorial locations where the mid-day sand temperature may exceed 140°F (60°C) they show increasing restlessness towards noon, and nest relief may occur every minute. The relieved bird flies over the water and dips its feet several times into the surface. It returns immediately to the nest with wet feet and splashed breast feathers, and the eggs are evidently wetted and cooled. The newly hatched chick is assiduously cared for, shaded and fed, and as the sun gets hot it is led to the edge of the water, where it lies in cooling moist sand. In spite of this care, the mortality of eggs and young is great, with high tides and storms washing eggs off low sand-bars and with nestlings; despite often taking cover in grass, falling ready prey to snakes, lizards and herons.

Composition. The three skimmers are very closely related, practically a single superspecies. While undoubtedly a tropical derivative of the shore terns, the Rynchopidae fully deserves familial status on account of the birds' unique mode of feeding and the correlated structural adaptations of the beak, head and neck.

AUKS

The auks are a highly successful group of short-winged marine diving birds forming the family Alcidae. There are 22 species, if we include the Garefowl, or Great auk *Alca impennis*, the large flightless species which became extinct in the 1840s. Two other

Three species of auklet to show head decoration. (1) The Crested auklet *Aethia cristatella*, (2) Rhinoceros auklet *Cerorhinca monocerata* and (3) the Whiskered auklet *Aethia pygmaea*.

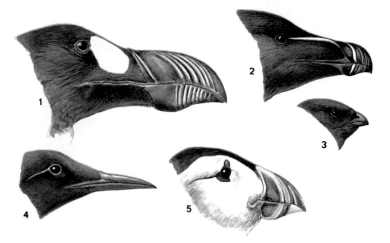

Five species of auk to show variation of bill shape. (1) The Great auk *Alca impennis* (now extinct), (2) Razorbill *A. torda*, (3) Little auk (or Dovekie) *Plautus alle*, (4) Guillemot (or Common murre) *Uria aalge* and (5) the Common puffin *Fratercula arctica*.

species are commonly known as 'auks': the Razorbilled auk or Razorbill *Alca torda* and the Little auk or Dovekie *Plautus alle*. Other species are known as guillemots or murres, murrelets, auklets, tystie and puffins.

Auks vary in length from $6\frac{1}{2}$–30in (16–76cm). The plumage is largely black above and white beneath, though two of the Pacific species have a cryptically coloured breeding dress. The tail, legs and neck are short, which, with the short wings, stocky body and large head, gives the bird its chunky appearance. There is a considerable variation in the bill characters of the group. In the guillemots it is long and pointed; in the Great auks, razorbills and particularly in the puffins, it is deep and laterally compressed. As with other birds which spend much of their time in the water, the principal distinguishing features are on the head. In the puffins and some of the auklets the bill plates are shed after the breeding season and replaced annually. Some species have ornamental plumes on the head and the lining of the mouth is generally brightly coloured. Some species also have brightly coloured feet.

Although rather feeble in flight, and taking wing with difficulty, auks are expert divers and underwater swimmers, using the wings in a half-open position to provide propulsion. The legs are placed well back on the body, for more efficient steering and the standing posture of auks is therefore rather upright. The Great auk in fact was very similar in appearance to a medium-sized penguin. The feet are seldom used for forward movement underwater, but function as steering vanes beneath the surface, and also in the air. They are of course webbed, although the hind toe – the first – is rudimentary or missing. The remaining three toes bear strong claws.

The Tufted puffin *Lunda cirrhata* has the usual striking puffin bill plates, but it also has pendant tufts of feathers falling down behind on each side of the head. The Rhinoceros auklet *Cerorhinca monocerata* has a peculiar short horn projecting upwards from the base of the upper mandible and a pair of white plumes running back on each side of the head, one from above the eye and the other from the corner of the mouth. Despite its name, it is in reality a type of puffin.

Distribution. Just as the penguins, which resemble the auks in many ways, belong to the southern seas so the auks, conversely, belong to the north. Their origin seems to have been in the area of the Bering Sea and their present distribution is in the North Pacific, North Atlantic and Arctic Oceans. The Bering Sea origin of the auks is suggested partly by the distribution of auks today. Some of them are circumpolar, but 16 species occur in the North Pacific, 12 of them nowhere else. The Pacific auks include the five auklets of the genera

A Razorbill *Alca torda* swims under the water's surface to catch fish prey. It propels itself with the wings and steers with the feet.

Ptychoramphus and *Aethia*, which are the ecological equivalent of the Little auk in the North Atlantic and the Tufted and Horned puffins.

The extinct flightless Great auk *Alca impennis*, the largest of the Alcidae, was found in subarctic and temperate waters – not in the far north as has often been stated – from north Britain and the Faeroes in the east, through Iceland and Greenland to Newfoundland in the west. In winter it moved farther south.

Feeding. Auks eat many kinds of marine organisms, including worms, shellfishes (both mollusc and crustacean) and even algae, but the principal item in the diet of most species is fish. The prey is usually captured in deep water as, outside the breeding season, auks live out at sea. A certain amount of bottom-feeding also takes place, but this is more frequent when the adults are feeding chicks. The feeding specializations are illustrated by the different kinds of prey given to the young of Little auks, razorbills, guillemots and puffins. Up to three of these species may be fishing in the same waters at the same time, but excessive competition is avoided by preferences for different types of prey. The Little auk feeds its young on plankton and crustaceans, carried in cheek pouches; puffins concentrate on small fish fry and Sand eels; razorbills takes fishes a little larger; and guillemots take the largest fishes of all.

Four species of auk to show size variation. (1) The extinct Great auk *Alca impennis*, (2) Little auk (or Dovekie) *Plautus alle*, (3) Ancient murrelet *Synthliboramphus antiquum* and (4) the Tufted puffin *Lunda cirrhata*.

Nesting and the Young. Auks are gregarious and usually breed in colonies. Some of these colonies are enormous and may consists of millions of birds. The sexes are externally very similar and both male and female share in the incubation of the egg or eggs and the feeding of the young. The nests, on rocky coasts or off-shore islands, are on ledges, fully exposed but usually inaccessible to climbers, or partially hidden in crevices or under boulders, or fully concealed in burrows. These burrows may be dug by the auks themselves or taken over from other animals, such as shearwaters or rabbits. A puffin has been seen to fly into a burrow which originally belonged to a rabbit and, after a short but sharp altercation, eject a shearwater.

The avoidance of direct competition between auks living in the same area is also shown in their choice of nest sites often on the same cliff. The Common guillemot, or Murre *Uria aalge*, and Brünnich's guillemot *U. lomvia*, lay their eggs on exposed ledges. The Razorbill tends to lay in more sheltered positions on the ledges, sometimes quite out of sight; the Black guillemot, and the Little auk lay under

Guillemots (or Common murres) *Uria aalge* circle each other in courtship.

cover of rocks; and the puffin nests in a burrow. The Black guillemot lays two eggs while all other auks lay only one.

The time of the departure of auk fledglings from the nest varies considerably with the species. The young of Common and Brünnich's guillemots, for example, spend from 18–25 days on the bare cliff ledges before they go to sea. For the first few days after hatching the chick is rather helpless and in great danger of falling off its ledge and from exposure to the elements. From about the sixth day chicks venture more frequently from beneath the parent, and soon begin to solicit food from any adult. The fledglings leave the nest and flutter down to sea before their primary wing feathers are fully developed and sea-going is therefore full of risks. Frequently the breeding ledges are hundreds of feet above the sea and the young birds may have to fly $\frac{1}{4}$mi (0·34km) or more in order to clear the rocks beneath. On this first flight they are usually accompanied by one or more adults. Sometimes the young try to take to the water before they are fully ready and in these circumstances they usually die of exposure or drown. The parents seem to actively try to prevent a premature departure by standing between the chicks and their destination.

Puffin chicks are reared in the security of the nest burrow and can thus afford to take their time, developing fully before going to sea, which may take as long as 50 days. The Pacific murrelets of the genera *Endomychura* and *Synthliboramphus*, however, are hatched in a highly advanced state and follow the adults to the water before they are two days old.

The nesting habits of the Marbled murrelet *Brachyramphus marmoratus*, the breeding range of which seems to be the coastal coniferous belt of the North Pacific region, are as yet unknown. Kittlitz' murrelet *B. brevirostris* is highly unusual among auks in being a solitary nester, laying on bare ground amongst patches of snow above the tree-line in the mountains of Alaska, or on islands off the coast. Both species have cryptic breeding plumage, from which we may deduce that the Marbled murrelet is also a ground nester.

Voice. Vocalizations outside the breeding season are infrequent, but on or near the nesting sites they are quite varied, from the sibilant whistle of the Black guillemot to the harsh grunts, growls and moans of the Razorbill and puffin. The calls mostly form part of the breeding displays, but aggressive notes are also used. The breeding displays also involve 'water dances' in a number of species, in which several birds swim around in lines and figures, or a pair of birds may perform mutual displays, with simple posturings and vocalizations and display of the coloured mouth lining. A considerable amount of billing also takes place, both on the water and at the breeding site.

Composition. The Alcidae is an ancient family divided into 13 genera. One member of the genus *Alca*, the Great auk *Alca impennis*, a flightless species also known as the Garefowl has been extinct for more than 100 years.

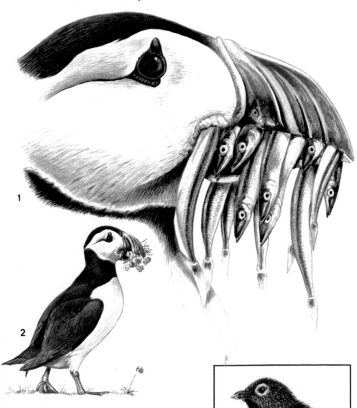

The Common puffin *Fratercula arctica* is able to hold large numbers of Sand eels in its large bill (1). A solitary puffin carries flowers in its bill; this may be interpreted as displacement activity reflecting the normal carrying of food (2). Puffin chicks develop inside burrows (3).

COLUMBIFORMES

The 255 species of pigeons include pink ones, blue ones and even some with spectacular crowns

SANDGROUSE — *Pteroclididae*
DODOS — *Raphidae*
PIGEONS — *Columbidae*

SANDGROUSE

The sandgrouse constitute a well defined family of pigeon-sized birds in the family Pteroclididae. Strictly ground-dwellers, sandgrouse are patterned cryptically in shades of brown, yellow, olive, grey and white, variously marked with black. The males are always more brightly coloured than the females and often have breast bands. The plumage is dense with a thick undercoat of down. The body is chunky with small head, short bill and short legs characteristically feathered down to, and sometimes including, the toes. The hind toe is rudimentary or absent. The nostrils are covered with feathers. Long and pointed wings betoken the excellent powers of flight which enable the sandgrouse to make daily visits to distant waterholes, where they may gather in hundreds or thousands to drink.

Distribution. Sandgrouse are mostly confined to arid or semi-arid zones of Africa and Eurasia. The greatest numbers of species are found in Baluchistan and the Thar Desert of India. Other centres of distribution are the southern Arabian peninsula, the Sahara, and the Kalahari Desert of southern Africa. A few species inhabit relatively dry woodland savannas, but most are birds of open country. Like many seed eating desert birds, sandgrouse are nomadic. Some appear to be migratory, but their movements are poorly understood.

Feeding. Sandgrouse feed almost exclusively on small hard seeds, hence their need to drink every day. The large crop in which seeds are softened before digestion is also used as a water store. Adults drink either during the morning or evening depending on the species and may make a round trip of up to 100mi (160km), between feeding ground and watering place.

Nesting and the Young. Courtship has not been well studied in the sandgrouse. The nest is a shallow scrape excavated by the female using her feet as she pivots on her breast. The scrape is usually lined or ringed with small stones and bits of dry vegetation tossed toward it with a sideways flick of the head. Nests are made among stones and shrubs, seldom under cover of a plant. The normal clutch in all species is three eggs, rather elongated in shape and equally rounded at both ends. The eggs are dull cream, pink or green, marked with spots and blotches of grey and darker tones of brown, red and olive. Sandgrouse eggs have a glossy finish which may serve to reflect heat if the parents are away from the nest, but they are nonetheless well camouflaged by their colouration. Normally the eggs are never left unattended. The female incubates by day from about two hours after sunrise to about two hours before sunset; the male incubates the rest of the time. The dense underdown must insulate sandgrouse against cold at night and heat by day, especially against the effects of direct sunlight. Incubating females may need to drink twice a day in hot weather.

Incubation lasts 21 to 31 days, according to the species.

The distribution of sandgrouse coincides with the arid or semi-arid regions of Africa and Eurasia.

Chicks of Pallas' sandgrouse *Syrrhaptes paradoxus* drink water carried in the male parent's belly feathers (1). Both the chicks (2) and eggs (3) of sandgrouse are almost invisible in their natural surroundings.

Sandgrouse chicks are highly precocial, leaving the nest as soon as their downy plumage is dry. They are among the most characteristically and attractively marked of all chicks, with a dorsal figure-of-eight pattern in white on a dark background of mixed brown, yellow and black. The belly down is pale coloured and unmarked. As soon as they have left the nest accompanied by both parents, sandgrouse chicks feed by themselves on tiny seeds. The female may peck at food to show the chicks what to eat, but neither parent ever actually feeds them. Because of the low water content of their diet, the chicks must have water to drink. They cannot fly, however, until five or six

The male (1) and female (2) Namaqua sandgrouse *Pterocles namaqua*, (3) the Pin-tailed sandgrouse *P. alchata* and (4) Lichtenstein's sandgrouse *P. lichtensteinii*. Males are more brightly coloured than females.

weeks old, and they cannot normally be brought to water because the distances involved are too great. The male parent therefore transports water to the young in his belly feathers which are structurally adapted for holding water in a fine bed of hairs that stand erect when the feathers are wetted. The water is held on the inside surface of each feather and, since the feathers overlap each other, evaporation is kept to a minimum.

It has been estimated that an adult male Namaqua sandgrouse *Pterocles namaqua* can deliver water to young up to a maximum of 20mi (32km) from waterholes. This means that breeding sandgrouse are restricted to the vicinity of watering places. Females may also occasionally transport water. Sandgrouse have probably evolved this curious method of water transport so that the adults' own water resources are not depleted by watering chicks from the crop.

The Tibetan sandgrouse *Syrrhaptes tibetanus* is apparently exceptional in not transporting water in its belly feathers because it lives in cold mountainous regions of Central Asia where water from snowmelt is always available close by. The chicks drink with the adults.

Territorial and Colonial Behaviour. Sandgrouse are highly gregarious at the waterholes. Non-breeding birds are gregarious at all times. Breeding sandgrouse are, however, monogamous and solitary nesters, although nests may be fairly closely grouped at times in favourable areas, for instance where localized rains produce isolated patches of food plants. Sandgrouse are never colonial nesters in the strict sense. Each species has a characteristic call to maintain contact with the flock, especially in flight. Flocks may consist of more than one species where the distributions and drinking times of two or more species overlap. Sandgrouse are usually rather silent when on the ground away from watering places.

Economic Importance. Sandgrouse have long been regarded as good sporting birds. The flesh is tasty but tough. Shooting sandgrouse at waterholes has happily been largely discontinued; even though their numbers were never seriously depleted by this unsporting practice, it is doubtful if sandgrouse could successfully be exploited by man as an important source of protein because the birds' reproductive turnover is rather low. Few species rear more than one brood a season. Seldom do more than one or two chicks of a brood of three survive. The success of sandgrouse may therefore be ascribed to good adult survival due to abundant food, and the ability to escape natural predators.

Research on sandgrouse may most profitably be done on feather structure, heat tolerance and kidney function. Sandgrouse can drink quite saline water without ill effect; since they have no functional salt glands to process extra salt (as have many seabirds and shorebirds), their kidneys must perform this function.

Composition. There are 16 species of sandgrouse in two genera – *Syrrhaptes* (two species) with no hind toe, and front toes feathered, and *Pterocles* (14 species) with a rudimentary hind toe and front toes naked. Alternatively, one subgroup (including *Syrrhaptes* and four *Pterocles* species) have two elongated central tail feathers, like the Namaqua sandgrouse, and another subgroup within the genus *Pterocles*, sometimes given the generic name of *Nyctiperdix*, and consisting of four savanna-dwelling species, has a black-and-white forehead pattern, heavily barred plumage and the habit of drinking at dusk or at night, like the Double-banded sandgrouse *Pterocles bicinctus*. The remaining sandgrouse are mostly desert-dwellers, morning drinkers, have simple tail feathers, and all but one species lack the black-and-white pattern on the head.

Sandgrouse cannot be confused with any other birds; they are remarkably uniform in body size and general habits. Despite their superficial resemblance to pigeons, they are almost certainly more closely related to the Charadrii or waders, as shown by similarities in feather structure, egg pigmentation, nest type, wing structure, egg white protein patterns and other features. They differ markedly from the doves in everything but skeletal morphology.

DODOS

This family, the Rhaphidae, is related to pigeons and was peculiar to the Mascarene Islands of the Indian Ocean and became extinct

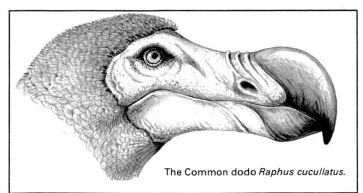

The Common dodo *Raphus cucullatus*.

during the 17th and 18th centuries. Three species, the Common dodo *Raphus cucullatus*, the Rodriguez solitaire *Pezophaps solitaria* and the Réunion solitaire *Raphus solitarius*, are well authenticated, but a fourth, the White dodo *Victoriornis imperialis*, was founded almost exclusively on 17th century water colour paintings, and is therefore not generally accepted as a valid species.

Much of the knowledge concerning the outward appearance of the three recognized species is based on contemporary descriptions and drawings of varying degrees of reliability. This evidence is supported by almost complete skeletons of the Common dodo and the Rodriguez solitaire.

Although the Common dodo was somewhat larger than the solitaires, both genera must have been about the size of the Turkey

Meleagris gallopavo. Both forms were massively built with short, strong legs and feet, and heavy bills which had the external nostrils situated towards the tip of the upper mandible. They had rudimentary wings, and an almost unkeeled sternum which rendered them flightless.

The Common dodo was a slow, clumsy bird with a large head, hooked bill and a tail which consisted of only a few curly feathers. The plumage was blue-grey, darker on the upperparts, but lighter on the throat, chest and under surface of the abdomen. Some of the variations found in drawings may be due to artistic licence, but others can only be explained as results of differences in age, moult or sexual dimorphism. Further, it is known that the bird had a fat and thin stage which is thought to have had seasonal significance. Variation of bill shape also occurred, probably as a result of moulting of the bill sheath after breeding; a feature seen also in some auks.

The Réunion solitaire *Raphus solitarius*. This and the Common dodo are two of the three valid species of dodo that lived on the Mascarene Islands until their defencelessness made them extinct.

The solitaires were less heavily built than the Common dodo, but had longer necks and legs. Their plumage was predominantly brown, although the female Réunion solitaire is thought to have been white with a yellow bill and legs. The Rodriguez solitaire is the best known of this group and had a relatively small head, a slender bill and almost no tail. The male in particular developed a round, bony outgrowth towards the end of each rudimentary wing the size of a table-tennis ball. From March to September the males became fat and often weighed as much as 45lb (20kg).

Distribution. The Raphidae were birds of high forests once found on the Mascarene Islands. Fossil remains of this family have only been found on the Mascarene Islands of Mauritius, Rodriguez and Réunion which are situated 600mi (966km) east of Madagascar in the Indian Ocean. The dates for the extinction of the three accepted species are: the Common dodo shortly before 1693; the Rodriguez solitaire sometime between 1761 and 1791, and the Réunion solitaire about 1746. The White dodo of Réunion is said to have died out between 1735 and 1746.

Behaviour. As these birds were completely flightless they must have been ground-feeders. There are but few direct references to their diet, but what there is states that they fed on fallen fruits and leaves. In addition, it is possible that they may have taken some animals such as crabs.

Only the nests of the Common dodo and the Rodriguez solitaire have been described. Both built nests on the ground in wooded areas. They were made up of mounds of vegetable matter on which one white, goose-sized egg was laid. The incubation period of the Rodriguez solitaire is stated to have been seven weeks with each parent taking turns on the nest. Pairings appear to have been for life.

Being flightless, dodos were easy to catch and, as their flesh was relatively palatable, they became an obvious source of protein for visiting explorers and passing sailors. However, although man obviously played an important part in their extermination, the main reason for the extinction of dodos was probably the introduction of domesticated pigs, which are notorious for destroying the nests and young of living birds.

Composition. It has been suggested that dodos may be related to the rails, but now it is generally accepted that they are members of the order Columbiformes (pigeons).

The Snow pigeon *Columba leuconota* from the Himalayan region.

Rock dove *Columba livia* (1) is the ancestor of all domestic pigeons. Other species: (2) the Orange dove *Ptilinopus victor*, (3) Masked dove *Oena capensis*, (4) the Magnificent fruit dove *Megaloprepia magnifica*.

PIGEONS

The Columbidae comprises some 255 species of pigeons found in most parts of the world except for polar and subpolar regions and some oceanic islands. The term 'pigeon' is sometimes used to denote the larger species, in contrast to the smaller species which are known as 'doves,' but the terms are not consistently used and are not based on any real biological distinction.

Pigeons have undergone a considerable degree of adaptive radiation and now vary in size from that of a lark to that of a hen turkey, from 6–33in (15–84cm) in length. They also vary considerably in plumage, some of them being among the most brightly coloured of birds, others rather drab. The most typical plumage is some pastel shade of grey, brown or pink, with contrasting patches of brighter colours. The feathers are soft and often loosely inserted in the skin, but are nevertheless strong and dense. Wings and tail show much variation in size and shape, but the legs are usually short, being rather long only in some of the terrestrial species. The body is compact, the neck rather short and the head small. The bill is usually small, soft at the base but hard at the tip, and at the base of the upper mandible is a fleshy 'cere,' a

naked area of skin which in some species is much swollen. This swelling is much more common in domesticated varieties. Some species have a noticeable crest. In most species the male is rather brighter than the female, but in a few species the sexes are similar and in others they are very different. Pigeons perch readily and regularly in trees, but some are terrestrial, others cliff-dwelling and some have taken to nesting on buildings in towns and cities. The feral pigeons which are so common in towns are all 'escapes,' or descendants of such, from stocks of domestic pigeons. All domestic pigeons are derived from the Rock dove *Columba livia* of Europe, which in the wild form nests on rock ledges, so that feral pigeons take naturally to breeding on buildings. Most species are gregarious, at least outside the breeding season, and some of them may be seen in large flocks. In the Passenger pigeon *Ectopistes migratorius*, now extinct, flocks of literally countless millions were common at all times of the year. Most pigeons are very strong on the wing.

Distribution. The generalized type of pigeon, which spends at least some of its time in trees and shrubs but obtains a proportion of its food on the ground, is found in all geographical regions inhabited by pigeons. Many species of great diversity of form are involved, but the long-legged and short-winged rather terrestrial species are not found in the northern regions where considerable powers of flight are needed to avoid severe winters and other periods of food shortage. Treeless areas have become colonized by species adapted to nesting in caves, cliffs and rock cavities. These are ground feeders. Other ground-feeding forms are found in areas such as the Americas, Australasia and some Pacific islands, where there are plenty of trees, and these nest above ground level. Some are quite bulky and highly terrestrial and live in regions (for example in New Guinea) where there is little competition from game birds. Australasia also has a number of species that normally nest on the ground, and this, like other aspects of Australasian zoology, is probably connected with the scarcity of carnivorous mammals in the region.

Pigeon species that are predominantly arboreal occur widely in tropical regions, but principally in Australasia and Indonesia. These include the fruit pigeons. Their abundance in such regions is probably correlated with the absence of monkeys which would be serious predators of eggs and young.

There are four subfamilies. The subfamily Columbinae includes the typical pigeons and doves, and also the small South American doves as well as the Pheasant pigeon *Otidiphaps nobilis*, a highly terrestrial species of New Guinea; the quail doves *Geotrygon* of South and Central America; and the Australian bronze-wing pigeons of a number of genera which in themselves show a high degree of adaptive radiation. Members of this last group are largely ground-feeders, some of them being quite partridge-like.

The subfamily Treroninae contains the arboreal fruit pigeons, in most of which the gut is specialized for digesting large fruits swallowed whole. The green pigeons of the genus *Treron*, however, have a well-developed gizzard for crushing the seeds of the wild figs on which they feed. The fruit doves of the genus *Ptilinopus* are brilliantly coloured species of the Indo-Malayan and Pacific regions, where the larger imperial pigeons of the genus *Ducula* are also found. The blue fruit pigeons of the genus *Alectroenas* are found on islands in the Indian Ocean. Other genera are found in Australia, New Zealand and the Philippines.

The other subfamilies are much smaller. The Gourinae contains only the three species of crowned pigeons of the genus *Goura* found in New Guinea. These are rather terrestrial, forest-dwelling species, with an outstanding fan-shaped laterally-compressed crest on the top of the head. The subfamily Didunculinae contains but the one species of Tooth-billed pigeon *Didunculus strigirostris* which is found in Samoa.

Feeding. A variety of food is taken, including berries, nuts, acorns, apples, seeds of many kinds and also buds and leaves. Many species also take animal food such as snails, worms and caterpillars. Food is stored temporarily in a crop which may be capacious. The distended crop of a Wood pigeon *Columba palumbus*, for example, after a successful day's feeding may be seen clearly as the bird flies home to roost. Most pigeons have a large, muscular gizzard which, with the enclosed grit deliberately swallowed, grinds up even the most intractable food. In some of the fruit pigeons, however, the gizzard does not have a crushing function and the rest of the gut is wider than in other species.

Pigeons drink in a manner unusual among birds. They immerse the bill and then, instead of lifting the head and tipping the water down the throat, they suck. This habit is said to be shared with the sandgrouse (Pterocliidae) and buttonquail (Turnicidae) and for this and other reasons the pigeons and sandgrouse have been said to be closely related. This, however, has been disputed, as sandgrouse seem to drink in a manner rather intermediate between pigeons and other birds. Nevertheless, the pigeons, sandgrouse and the dodo and solitaires are united in the order Columbiformes.

Nesting and the Young. Pigeons build a simple, rather insubstantial and usually platform-like nest of twigs, stems or roots, in a tree or brush, on a cliff or building ledge, or sometimes on or in the ground, or in a tree cavity. Two pale unmarked eggs form the usual clutch, and both sexes incubate. The young are helpless when first hatched and sparsely covered with a filamentous down. They are fed by both parents for the first few days on 'pigeons milk,' a curd-like material secreted by special cells lining the crop. This is scooped up by the broad, soft bill of the young inserted deeply into the parent's mouth to obtain the regurgitated material. Gradually it is supplemented with food partially digested by the parents.

Pigeon nestlings grow rapidly and in some of the smaller species the young can fly at two weeks of age. If eggs or young are lost through predation or other causes the female will usually lay again. In a successful season two or three broods may be produced. Such breeding habits must have contributed significantly to the success of pigeons as a group. The Collared dove *Streptopelia decaocto* which has spread northwestwards across Europe from Asia Minor during the 20th century is a many-brooded species which has put the less fecund Turtle dove *Streptopelia turtur* at a disadvantage.

Behaviour. The typical vocalization of pigeons is a cooing sound, usually produced while inflating the neck. Some species also produce harsher, sometimes whistling calls, without neck inflation. Cooing calls may be generally divided into two basic types: the advertising *coo* and the display *coo*. The display *coo* is usually given while the bird is performing its bowing display, which male pigeons direct towards females. In the bowing display the bird lowers its

Behaviour in pigeons. (1) A Wood pigeon *Columba palumbus* feeding its chick 'pigeons milk,' (2) a male Rock dove *C. livia* and (3) a Victoria crowned pigeon *Goura victoria* perform bowing displays during courtship.

head and leans forward, thus exhibiting its display plumage to best advantage. A considerable amount of variation in the bowing display may be seen in the family as a whole, and some species do not bow while uttering the display *coo*. In the Luzon bleeding heart dove *Gallicolumba luzonica*, which has a striking blood-red streak on the breast, the displaying bird throws its chest out and up to display the red patch, cooing as it returns to its normal posture.

The advertising *coo* is equivalent to the song of songbirds, usually being given by territory-owning males. It may, however, be uttered from the nest as well as from a perch well away from the nest. Males in breeding condition also perform display flights. Typically, these consist of a conspicuous flight with the wings beaten more slowly but over a wider arc, interspersed with glides, and the wings being clapped together from time to time.

Composition. The Columbidae is divided into 43 genera comprising some 255 species. There are four subfamilies: the Columbinae; the Treroninae; the Gourinae; and the Didunculinae.

PSITTACIFORMES

Specialized birds with short, hooked bills. Only one is native to North America

PARROTS — *Psittacidae*

PARROTS

The parrots are contained in the Psittacidae, a family of rather uniform structure placed in its own order, the Psittaciformes. Affinities with other birds are not known for certain, although parrots seem closer to the pigeons than to other groups. They vary from 3–40in (8–102cm) in length, and show wide variation in colouration, but all have more or less stout, hooked bills with an enlarged fleshy covering of the upper mandible – the cere. The upper mandible is attached to the skull by a flexible joint that allows it to move up and down freely. The neck is invariably short, and the body rather plump, with more or less rounded wings. The legs are short and covered with small granular scales and the feet are zygodactyl (two toes pointing forwards, two back).

Plumage is typically rather sparse and usually hard and glossy. Many species are very brightly coloured, but the two sexes are similar in appearance in the majority of species. The voice of most parrots is both loud and harsh, consisting of screeching and grating notes which are usually lower-pitched in large species than in small ones. A few species have musical whistled calls, and small lorikeets, hanging parrots and pygmy parrots give high-pitched squeaks. Many species whose normal voices are harsh and rasping can be trained to imitate the human voice with surprising fidelity.

Distribution. Parrots are mainly restricted to the tropics, but extend into high latitudes in the southern hemisphere. The extinct Carolina parakeet *Conuropsis carolinensis* formerly inhabited North America north to the Great Lakes, but no native parrot now occurs in North America north of Mexico. In Central and South America and the West Indies there are numerous genera and species, a few occurring as far south as Tierra del Fuego.

Africa has comparatively few parrots (four genera, 15 species), and a few others inhabit the islands of the Indian Ocean. Southern Asia has several genera, including most species of the large genus *Psittacula*, but the family reaches its greatest diversity in the

Australasian region, where all eight subfamilies are found. Species of the genus *Cyanoramphus* occur on sub-Antarctic islands south of New Zealand, and these and small lorikeets extend eastwards across the Pacific Ocean to eastern Polynesia.

Feeding. Vegetable foods make up the diet of most of the parrots. Many are frugivorous, others eat seeds, buds and other vegetable matter in addition to fruit, some such as the Budgerigar *Melopsittacus undulatus* eat mainly seeds, and the lories, lorikeets and hanging parrots of the genus *Loriculus* subsist mainly on nectar and pollen from flowers. Insects are probably taken in small quantities by many species, but they form an appreciable part of the diet of some small lories, such as the Marquesan lorikeet *Vini ultramarina*, and of some cockatoos, such as the Long-billed corella *Cacatua tenuirostris*. The Kea *Nestor notabilis* of New Zealand is unusual in taking a varied diet that includes fruit, seeds, buds, leaves, nectar, insects and animal carrion. It has been wrongly charged with killing sheep for food, though Keas will readily eat fat and meat from dying animals. The pygmy parrots of the genus *Micropsitta* are unique among birds in eating slime-like fungi and algae, as well as more the normal fare of insects and seeds.

Most parrots use the feet to hold their food; typically, a perching bird holds its food up with one foot. This habit is lacking in the flower feeding lories and hanging parrots. The Kakapo *Stringops habroptilus* eats a wide range of vegetable foods, including the leaves and buds of low-growing plants. These are extensively chewed before being swallowed, unusual behaviour for which the very strong bill of this species is specially modified. The larger bills of many parrots enable them to crack strong nuts to obtain the kernels. Captive Hyacinthine macaws *Anodorhynchus hyacinthinus* and Palm cockatoos *Probosciger aterrimus* are even able to cope with brazil nuts. Many of the smaller seed eating parrots use the bill to husk and crack seeds before they are swallowed.

The bill structure and tongue vary in different groups of parrots to suit their feeding habits. Those species that feed on fruit and seeds have very stout, strong bills and short, flat, muscular tongues which aid the manipulation of food. In contrast the lories and lorikeets have longer, more slender bills and longer tongues tipped with a brush of hair-like papillae. These adaptations facilitate probing into the corollas of flowers to extract nectar and pollen. The tongues of parrots have more taste buds than those of most other birds, but the reasons for this are not known.

Nesting and the Young. The vast majority of parrot species nest in holes in trees. Many will enlarge a hole that is not quite big enough, but the majority do little else before laying on wood fragments in the

A Blue-crowned hanging parakeet *Loriculus galgulus* roosting while suspended upside-down. The tail is used as a prop in this position.

Six parrot species. (1) The Kea *Nestor notabilis* feeding on sheep's wool, a habit not certainly known to occur; (2) Hawk-headed parrot *Deroptyus accipitrinus*; (3) Pesquet's parrot *Psittrichas fulgidus*; (4) Kea *Nestor notabilis*; (5) Kaka *Nestor meridionalis*; (6) Kakapo *Strigops habroptilus*.

bottom of the hole. Hanging parrots and lovebirds of the genus *Agapornis* build a nest, sometimes complete with dome, inside the hole. It consists mainly of strips bitten from leaves. The only parrot to build a nest in the open is the South American Quaker parakeet *Myiopsitta monachus*, in which a number of pairs cooperate to build a large, rounded communal nest of sticks in a tree, in which each pair has its own nest chamber. Some of the small lorikeets and the pygmy parrots excavate their own nest holes in the ball-like arboreal nests of forest termites or ants, and a number of other species will use holes in crags, or even in buildings. The Burrowing parrot *Cyanoliseus patagonus* nests in large colonies in burrows dug into earthy cliffs, and the Night parrot *Pezoporus occidentalis* and Ground parrot *P. wallicus* of Australia both nest in hollows in tussocks of grass.

All parrots lay glossless white eggs without markings. They are rather small for the size of the birds, and rounded or oval in shape. Lories, lorikeets and some of the large macaws and cockatoos lay only two eggs in a clutch. Many parrots lay three to five eggs, some of the small seed eating parrots commonly laying as many as eight. Incubation lasts from three to four weeks and is performed by both sexes in the majority of species, but by the female alone in some. The newly-hatched young are naked except for a variable amount of greyish or brownish down. They are fed by both parents on food regurgitated from the crop, and fledge after about four weeks in the nest in small species and eight weeks in the largest macaws. The young are fed by the parents for some time after fledging.

Behaviour. Many parrots inhabiting forest or woodland habitats occur in small groups or pairs and nest solitarily or in small colonies, but some species of arid regions occur in large flocks and nest in large colonies. Colonies of Budgerigars numbering over a million birds have been reported, and colonies of other species commonly include several hundred pairs. No parrot is known to defend an exclusive territory after the manner of many song-birds, although many will defend the immediate vicinity of the nest.

Economic Importance. For the most part, parrots are only of special interest to man as desirable cage and aviary birds. The Budgerigar is now one of the most widely kept of all cage birds, and many colour varieties have been bred from the original green-backed birds imported from Australia. The Cockatiel *Nymphicus hollandicus*, and the African Grey parrot *Psittacus erithacus* are also favourite cage birds.

A few tropical species are agricultural pests, notably some cockatoos and rosellas which damage grain crops and eat fruit in orchards in Australia, and some parakeets which consume large amounts of grain in southern Asia.

Composition. The family Psittacidae contains about 330 species classified into approximately 60 genera and six to eight subfamilies, which some zoologists consider should be regarded as separate families.

The Owl parrot or Kakapo is usually afforded a subfamily of its own, the Strigopinae, partly on the basis of anatomical peculiarities, and partly because of uncertainty about its relationships to other parrots. It is a large, heavily built parrot about 28in (72cm) long, with small wings and a reduced keel on the sternum. Its flying ability is limited to gliding downwards, so that it lives mainly on the ground.

The Kaka *Nestor meridionalis* and Kea are also placed in a separate subfamily, the Nestorinae. They are both confined to New

The five parrot species shown below are (1) Scarlet macaw *Ara macao*, (2) Red-capped pigmy parrot *Micropsitta bruijnii*, (3) Masked lovebird *Agapornis personata*, (4) Rainbow lorikeet *Trichoglossus haematopus* and (5) the Crimson rosella *Platycercus elegans*.

The Hyacinthine macaw *Anodorhynchus hyacinthinus* (1) and a close up of its beak (2) with which it is able to crack hard nuts. The lower jaw is adjusted to exert the maximum possible pressure. (3) Adult and (4) young Carolina parakeets *Conuropsis carolinensis*, a species that is now extinct and (5) the Sulphur-crested cockatoo *Cacatua galerita*.

Zealand, although there was formerly a distinct subspecies of the Kaka on Lord Howe Island. Both species have rather long, narrow bills and dull brownish plumage. Their closest affinities may be with the Loriinae, which has about 60 species found from Indonesia and the Philippines to Tasmania and eastern Polynesia. They are nearly all flower-feeders, and all have long tongues tipped with a brush of papillae and various other distinctive anatomical features. The smallest species, Wilhelmina's lorikeet is less than 4in (9cm) long, but the larger species of the genus *Domicella* reach 13in (33cm). Many lories and lorikeets have long, graduated tails, but in some they are short and nearly square, and in the Fairy lorikeet *Charmosyna papou* and related species of the New Guinea region the central feathers have long ribbon-like tips.

The Cyclopsittacinae with five species in the single genus *Psittaculirostris* is more closely related to the Loriinae than to other subfamilies, but differs in having the tongue deeply grooved with no papillae at its tip, and in various other anatomical features. All five species inhabit rain forests in New Guinea and adjacent islands and, in one species, Queensland. They are 4–7in (10–18cm) long, and have short wide bills used for eating fruit and seeds.

The subfamily Platycercinae has about 29 species classified into 8–10 genera. Most of the species are found only in Australia, but a few are confined to New Zealand and nearby islands, New Caledonia, and formerly the Society Islands. The familiar Budgerigar is the smallest species, and typical of the subfamily in having a short stout bill and long, wedge-shaped tail. The rosellas of the genus *Platycercus* are among the largest species, reaching a length of 16in (40cm). Two species, the Australian Ground parrot and Night parrot are terrestrial birds living concealed among ground vegetation. Both can only fly weakly, and both have concealing colouration marked by green upperparts with dark streaking and barring.

The bulk of the parrots is at present placed in the rather heterogeneous subfamily Psittacinae. These vary from tiny hanging parrots only 3½in (8–9cm) long to the largest macaws, and are found in the Americas, Africa, southern Asia, Indonesia, Australasia and islands of the Pacific and Indian Oceans. The subfamily is marked by possession of an unspecialized tongue and various other structural features, but it seems likely that it consists of a number of rather distantly related groups of parrots which show strong convergent similarities due to similarities in their ecology. All of the parrots of South and Central America are classified here, and they may all be more closely related to each other than to any of the Old World parrots, although there are striking superficial differences between such extremes as the small parrotlets of the genus *Forpus*, only 4½in (11–12cm) long, the large macaws, and the large amazon parrots which reach 16in (40cm) long and have broad, square tails.

The cockatoo subfamily, Cacatuinae, has 16 species placed in five or six genera. They are characterized by broad wings, broad, square tails and various anatomical peculiarities. A number of species have prominent crests, and the colouration is usually predominantly white, grey or black. One species, the Cockatiel, is considerably smaller than other cockatoos and differs in having a long, graduated tail. Most of the species are found in Australia, with other restricted to Indonesia, the Philippines, New Guinea and the Solomon Islands.

Six species of tiny pygmy parrots of the genus *Micropsitta* are placed in a subfamily Micropsittinae because their relationships are obscure, and because of a number of peculiarities. They range from 3–4in (8–10cm) in length and have stiff shafts to the tail feathers which they use to support the body as they walk up vertical tree trunks and branches, like tiny woodpeckers. Several species are found in New Guinea, the others in the Admiralty Islands, Bismarck Archipelago and Solomon Islands.

CUCULIFORMES

Many cuckoos are nest parasites and lay their eggs in nests made by other birds

TURACOS — *Musophagidae*
CUCKOOS — *Cuculidae*
HOATZIN — *Opisthocomidae*

TURACOS

Members of the Musophagidae are known by several common names. All are restricted to Africa. The brightly coloured species of the evergreen forest are known as turacos, as louries in South Africa, and as plantain-eaters in West Africa although there is no evidence that they feed on plantains or bananas. The grey-blue, grey or brown species frequenting woodland, acacia country, savanna and semi-arid thornbush are known as go-away birds.

Turacos are relatively large birds, 14¾–18½in (37·5–47cm) long,

Four species of turaco. (1) The Giant blue plantain-eater *Corythaeola cristata*, (2) Ross's turaco *Musophaga rossae*, (3) White-bellied go-away bird *Corythaixoides leucogaster*, (4) Livingstone's turaco *Tauraco livingstonii*.

with the exception of the Giant blue plantain-eater *Corythaeola cristata* which is 30in (76cm) long. All have exaggeratedly long, broad tails, graduated outwards, which may be expanded in flight (*Corythaeola*) and also help balance when running squirrel-like amongst forest branches or when perching.

The plumage is soft, thick and in some species inclined to be hairlike. All, with one exception, the Violet plantain-eater *Musophaga violacea*, have conspicuous crests, often tipped with white or red. The stout, strongly decurved bill, varies from red to yellow, yellow tipped red, greenish, bluish or black; the nostrils vary in shape from round to slit-shaped. The sturdy, black, rather long legs enable the forest species to move athletically among the tree-tops. The relatively short, rounded wings, make the undulating flight somewhat slow, and laboured. All are sociable and noisy.

The primary and secondary feathers of the wings in *Tauraco* and *Musophaga* are coloured with a unique red pigment containing copper, called turacin, which is erroneously thought to be soluble in rain. An equally unique green pigment called turacoverdin is found in the forest species.

Distribution. Turacos are widespread in Africa south of the Sahara, at altitudes from sea level to 11,000ft (3,350m). Only one genus – *Corythaeola* occurs deep within the tropical rain forest, though two others – *Tauraco* and *Musophaga*, frequent evergreen forest and, to a lesser extent, vegetation growing along river banks. Sedentary and often local, turacos are non-migratory, though *Corythaeola* moves considerable distances each day from its communal, nocturnal roost to feeding grounds.

Feeding. Turacos are reputed to feed exclusively on berries and wild and cultivated fruits such as guavas and ripe mangoes, as well as on other soft vegetable matter, but they will also consume various insects and caterpillars.

In southern Africa *Corythaixoides* feeds greedily on seeds of introduced Persian lilac, and in west and central Africa species of

Tauraco relish the fruit of the Umbrella tree, *Musanga smithi*. Most curious is the inclusion in its diet – without harm – of the highly poisonous berries of the *Acokonthera* tree.

Nesting and the Young. The nests of turacos are frail forms of twigs in low trees or lofty shrubs. Though inconspicuous, they are often revealed by the brooding bird's long tail. Two to three eggs are laid. Those of the forest species are rather rounded, smooth, white or creamy-white, except those of *Corythaeola* which are handsome greenish. Those of *Corythaixoides* and *Crinifer* are pale bluish, grey-blue or light greyish. The female usually incubates the eggs for a period of about 16–18 days. The nidicolous young, which remain helpless in the nest for some time after hatching, are at first thickly covered with greyish or brown down. They are fed a diet of regurgitated fruit pulp, and are able to fly at about six weeks.

Behaviour. The forest species tend to be local, but others accustomed to more open conditions range over larger areas. All are, to a greater or lesser extent, gregarious, the flocks being exceptionally noisy. Those of the savanna indulge in noisy spectacular aerobatics and will greet the hunter's intrusion with such cacophony as to put on the alert every wild creature within miles. A small party of *Crinifer zonurus* often indulges in a sort of 'follow-my-leader' game, towering above a tree-top suddenly to dive downwards to perch clumsily with tail ridiculously cocked forward.

The general pattern of courtship behaviour includes fluttering half-open wings (*Tauraco* and *Musophaga*) to display the bright red colouration, conspicuous crest raising, tail flipping and strident calling. The male follows the female and offers her food. Some extraordinary, commonly seen displays are not necessarily associated with courtship, and include hovering, diving, chasing and tail flirting.

Composition. The Musophagidae was at one time separated into nine genera, but only five are now recognized – *Corythaeola*, *Corythaixoides* and *Crinifer*, all lacking turacin, and *Tauraco* and *Musophaga*. The Bare-faced go-away bird *Gymnoschizorhis personata* is now included in the genus *Corythaixoides* and the gaudy *Proturacus*, *Gallirex* and *Ruwenzorornis* are all now included in *Tauraco*. The family has long been included in the order Cuculiformes, an arrangement confirmed by studies of their egg white proteins.

Seven species of cuckoo. (1) The Oriental cuckoo *Cuculus saturatus*, (2) Pied coucal *Centropus ateralbus*, (3) Lesser roadrunner *Geococcyx velox*, (4) Golden-bronze cuckoo *Chrysococcyx lucidus*, (5) Crested coua *Coua cristata*, (6) Long-tailed cuckoo *Eudynamis taitensis* and (7) the Smooth-billed ani *Crotophaga ani*.

CUCKOOS

Though exhibiting great superficial diversity, members of the family Cuculidae are all closely related, ranging in size from 6¼in–27½in (16–70cm) but sharing numerous similarities in the anatomy of the head, body, legs and feet. Many species of cuckoo, though not all, are parasitic in their breeding habits. Another characteristic is the usually loud and unmusical voice. The family includes species adapted for a cursorial life on the ground as well as entirely arboreal species.

Some members of the family are known as anis, couas, coucals, malkohas and roadrunners. There are six subfamilies. In general the body tends to be elongated, with a moderately long neck, and the tail varies from medium length to very long and graduated. The wings vary from moderately long and rounded to long and hawk-like. The legs are short in the majority of arboreal species, but long in those that live on the ground. In both arboreal and terrestrial species the feet are zygodactyl, having two toes pointing forwards and two pointing back, although the outer hind toe is reversible. The bill is moderately long, slightly decurved, and usually rather stout. In the anis of the genus *Crotophaga* the bill is extremely deep and laterally compressed.

Plumage is generally rather loose-webbed, although it is stiff and wiry in some species. Many have patches of bare, coloured skin around the eye, and prominent eyelashes. Colouration varies widely, although greys and browns are common, often with heavy streaking or barring on the underparts. Some species are predominantly black or have varied brighter colours. The sexes are usually similar in colouration, but juveniles often differ markedly from adults.

In some host-parasitic species of the subfamily Cuculinae remarkable mimesis occurs. In some species these mimetic plumages resemble those of potential hosts; in others they resemble the plumages of hawks or crows, giving the cuckoo an appearance alarming to a host bird.

Distribution. Of the six subfamilies, three are confined to the Old World (one to Madagascar); one is only found in the New World and another mainly so, and the sixth is widespread in both hemispheres. The typical subfamily Cuculinae ranges from Europe, Africa and Asia to Australia and the islands of the tropical south Pacific Ocean. The European cuckoo *Cuculus canorus* is the best known species, but the Greater spotted cuckoo *Clamator glandarius* also occurs in southern Europe. The African genera *Chrysococcyx* and *Cercococcyx* are noted for their very glossy plumage. The genera *Chalcites* and *Cacomantis* include a number of small species in the Oriental and Australasian zoogeographical regions. Several species of Cuculinae inhabiting high latitudes are long distance migrants. For example, the European cuckoo winters in Africa and various species of northern Asia winter south of the Himalayas. In the Southern Hemisphere, two New Zealand species have remarkable migrations: the Shining cuckoo *Chalcites lucidus* passes the southern winter north to the Solomon Islands and Bismarck Archipelago, and the Long-tailed cuckoo *Eudynamis taitensis* winters on the archipelagos of the tropical Pacific east to the Society and Tuamotu Islands.

The subfamily Phaenicophaeinae has three genera in the New World, among them *Coccyzus* which includes the Black-billed cuckoo *C. erythrophthalmus* and Yellow-billed cuckoo *C. americanus*, and the large Lizard cuckoos of the genus *Saurothera*. In Africa there is only the one species, the Yellowbill *Ceuthmochares aereus*, but tropical Asia has eight genera, most of them known by the name 'malkoha.' The Small green-billed malkoha *Rhopodytes viridirostris* and the Sirkeer *Taccocua leschenaultii* occur in India. The subfamily Crotophaginae is confined to warm and tropical

regions of the Americas. There are two genera, the monotypic *Guira*, and *Crotophaga* which contains the three species of ani. The latter, noted for their gregarious habits, are large all-black birds with very deep bills.

The subfamily Neomorphinae is unusual in having five genera in the Americas and one (*Carpococcyx*) in southeast Asia. The best known member of the subfamily is the Greater roadrunner *Geococcyx californianus*, a predominantly terrestrial bird inhabiting dry regions from the southern USA southwards into Central America. The 10 species of the subfamily Couinae, all of which are placed in the genus *Coua* and known as 'couas,' are confined to Madagascar and neighbouring islands. The coucals of the subfamily Centropodinae – about 27 species – range from Africa and Madagascar through tropical Asia to Australasia. Most species are large skulking terrestrial birds that fly only weakly. The Indian Crow-pheasant *Centropus sinensis* is a well-known Asian species.

The family as a whole occupies a great range of habitats, including most kinds of forest, woodland and scrub. Few species occur in open country, although the roadrunners will inhabit desert regions where there is only scanty ground vegetation.

Feeding. All species of the family for which information on the diet is available eat insects, often almost to the exclusion of other foods in the smaller arboreal species. Many of the small species regularly eat the more hairy caterpillars, which are generally rejected by most insectivorous Passerines. The larger cuckoos, particularly terrestrial species living in warm countries, commonly eat mainly lizards and small snakes. The Greater roadrunner will even kill and eat rattlesnakes, and the Lizard cuckoos of the West Indies specialize in capturing large lizards. These and other species also take occasional

A young European cuckoo *Cuculus canorus* being fed by its foster parent, a diminutive Reed warbler.

The European cuckoo *Cuculus canorus* is often found to have its stomach lined with caterpillar hairs. This insect is not immune from attack by cuckoos as it is from many other birds.

mice, small birds and other vertebrates. A few cuckoo species also eat snails, spiders and fruit in small quantities. Feeding behaviour varies. The large terrestrial cuckoos sprint after active running prey or dig among vegetation; arboreal species glean food from twigs and leaves, sometimes hanging upside-down to reach distant prey.

Nesting and the Young. The Cuculidae probably shows greater diversity in its breeding biology than any other family of birds. The most striking adaptation of many cuckoos, which is paralleled by honeyguides (Indicatoridae), cowbirds (Icteridae) and some weavers (Ploceidae), is the habit of nest parasitism, in which the eggs are laid in the nests of birds of other species, which alone care for and feed the growing nestlings.

Nest parasitism is restricted to the subfamily Cuculinae, all members of which are thought to be parasitic, and to three species of the Neomorphinae, the Striped cuckoo *Tapera naevia*, the Pheasant cuckoo *Dromococcyx phasianellus* and the Pavonine cuckoo *D. pavoninus*, all three of which are confined to the American tropics. All members of the subfamilies Phaenicophaeinae, Crotophaginae, Couinae and Centropodinae are non-parasitic, as are the genera *Morococcyx*, *Neomorphus*, *Carpococcyx* and *Geococcyx* of the subfamily Neomorphinae.

Considerable diversity is shown in the breeding of the non-parasitic cuckoos. The genera *Coccyzus*, *Piaya* and *Saurothera* of the Phaenicophaeinae build loosely constructed nests of twigs in trees and bushes, usually at no great height. Clutches are of two to six or seven pale blue eggs. Both parents take part in the incubation. As for all other cuckoos, the young are more or less naked when hatched, then attain a spiky or bristly appearance as the growing feathers appear enclosed in their sheaths. The Asian species of Phaenicophaeinae have generally similar breeding habits.

The anis (Crotophaginae) build communal nests in trees. Each of the several pairs involved has its own nest chamber within the large globular nest of sticks, and each female lays only in its own nest chamber. Clutches are small, consisting of pale blue eggs that have a chalky surface deposit. Incubation and feeding of the young is carried out by both parents, and other birds of the group often assist.

The Couas (Couinae) nest in trees and bushes and lay small clutches of pale-coloured eggs. Their breeding biology is not known in detail. Coucals (Centropodinae) build large globular nests of

grass, leaves, stems and other plant materials, usually near or touching the ground in dense vegetation. Some species build a short funnel-shaped nest entrance lined with leaves. Clutches are of 3–5 rounded white or very pale eggs. The parents share incubation, which in at least some species starts with the laying of the first egg, so that hatching is spread over several days and the members of the resulting brood vary markedly in size.

Most parasitic cuckoos that are larger than their hosts lay only a single egg in the host nest, but when cuckoo and host are of similar size, two, three or four eggs are often laid. As incubation is carried out by the host alone, the female cuckoo must first find a host nest that has either just received eggs or is about to do so. This is an easy matter for such species as the Koel *Eudynamis scolopaceus* which parasitize crows. Their nests are conspicuous and so a carefully-timed approach is all that is involved. Cuckoos such as the European cuckoo, on the other hand, tend to parasitize birds, like the Meadow pipit, whose nests are difficult to locate which makes their task that much more difficult. The female cuckoo must then lay her egg in the host nest and leave without causing too much disturbance. The superficially hawk-like appearance and behaviour of many cuckoos may facilitate this. Species that lay several eggs in a host nest must return daily to add their own egg.

The eggs of parasitic cuckoos show numerous adaptations to nest parasitism. If the cuckoo is larger than the host, then its egg is relatively small. The eggs are thicker-shelled than those of most birds, and at least in the European cuckoo, the embryo is partly developed when the egg is laid. Perhaps most striking, however, is the resemblance in colouration and markings between the cuckoo eggs and those of the host. It is now well established that individual female cuckoos lay only one type of egg, normally in the nest of only a single host species, the eggs of which it matches more or less well. Thus there are 'gentes' of female European cuckoos specializing in Dunnocks, Robins, Reed warblers, Meadow pipits, Tree pipits, Redstarts, Pied wagtails and less often other hosts.

There are occasional exceptions to the rule of close resemblance of cuckoo and host eggs, one of the most obvious being the poor resemblance of the dark eggs laid by European cuckoos in Dunnocks' nests to the immaculate blue of Dunnock eggs. However, a tendency towards poorer host resemblance in European cuckoo eggs collected this century, compared with earlier records, has been ascribed to the increased breaking up of habitats, so that an individual female cuckoo may find it harder to obtain a territory providing sufficient host nests of the correct species. As the European cuckoo may lay its single egg in each of 20 or more nests in one season this explanation seems plausible.

In cuckoos which are of roughly similar size to their hosts the young cuckoos are usually reared alongside the host nestlings. However, in species where the cuckoo is considerably larger than its hosts the newly-hatched cuckoo, while still appearing helpless, evicts the hosts' nestlings and any remaining eggs from the nest, in order to insure its own food supply. In the species where cuckoo and host nestlings are in the nest together the cuckoo nestlings often bear a close mimetic resemblance to those of the hosts, in voice as well as colouration. Young cuckoos continue to receive food from their hosts for some time after fledging.

Behaviour. The majority of cuckoos defend exclusive territories by means of loud calls or songs. In the European cuckoo each male defends a large territory by means of the familiar 'cuckoo' call, and females defend separate territories from other females within the male's territory. This kind of arrangement is probably common among the parasitic members of the Cuculinae, most of which have loud and distinctive calls.

Non-parasitic cuckoos of the Phaenicophaeine, Neomorphinae and Centropodinae apparently defend territories as a pair and nest

The Greater roadrunner *Geococcyx californianus* feeds on lizards and even rattlesnakes. In spite of its habits, it is related to the cuckoos.

within the territory. The coucals give loud series of hissing, bubbling or screeching noises from cover, sometimes as duets with one bird of a pair singing notes rhythmically alternating with the notes of its mate. The anis differ strikingly from other cuckoos in being gregarious throughout the year and in nesting communally. The nest is built by members of several pairs, each of which has a separate nest chamber within it. Groups of anis that nest together have definite home ranges, but it is not known to what extent these are defended from other groups.

Composition. The family Cuculidae has around 127 species that are classified into six subfamilies. Some subfamilies were regarded as distinct families by the early ornithologists, but closer study has emphasized their similarities.

HOATZIN

The Hoatzin *Opisthocomus hoazin* – sole member of the family Opisthocomidae – is a large untidy-looking bird, about 25in (64cm) long, with bottle-green upper plumage and white shaft-streaks and white edges to some of its feathers. The primary quills are chestnut with dark tips. The lower back is blackish, and the tail similar in colouring with a broad buff tip while the underparts are buff

The Hoatzin *Opisthocomus hoazin* feeding on marsh plants. Some authorities maintain it has a restricted diet, others that it is an omnivore.

shading to chestnut on the abdomen and sides. On the chest there are long ferruginous plumes, tipped with black. The eyes are bright red and the facial skin is electric blue. Hoatzin chicks have wing claws which are now regarded as a secondary adaptation and not, as was formerly believed, a primitive characteristic linking the bird with fossils such as Archaeopteryx. The heavily-muscled crop occupies most of the anterior third of the body. Considering the bird's size, the breastbone is extremely small. The bare callous of skin on the breast helps support the bird's weight when it perches on a branch, its crop heavily laden, after feeding. The wing feathers are only loosely attached and this, together with the small keel, gives the bird weak powers of flight, about 20–30yd (18–27m) being the normal flight range.

Distribution. Hoatzins are sedentary birds living in permanently flooded forests along the banks of some of the large rivers in the northeast of South America, occurring chiefly around the Amazon but being generally present in the area between Guiana and Brazil, and Colombia and Bolivia.

Feeding. The Hoatzin feeds largely on the leaves, flowers and fruits of marsh plants including *Montrichardia* (Araceae) and *Avicennia* (the arboreal white mangrove), with, according to some authorities, fish and crabs forming part of the diet. Others maintain that Hoatzins eat only leaves, buds and pulpy seeds. Early morning and late afternoon are the most active feeding times.

Nesting and the Young. Breeding coincides with the onset of the rainy season. So marked is this that in years of a double rainy season, the bird produces two broods and in dry years it does not breed. The nest is a crude construction of twigs and sticks, much like a heron's nest. Indeed it is so loosely made that the eggs can be seen from below. Clutches of 2–3 occasionally up to 5 buff eggs, dappled with brown or bluish spots are laid. Incubation, carried out by both parents, lasts 28 days beginning with the first egg and the young hatch in regular succession. According to some reports, mating among the groups of up to six individuals which the birds tend to form during the breeding season, can be indiscriminate with all members of the group participating in incubation and care of the young.

The young are naked when hatched but soon develop reddish down. They have a well-developed claw on the elongated thumb and on the point of the wing which, when only a few hours old, they use to help them scramble through the branches. When alarmed at the nest a young Hoatzin will dive into the water, submerge, and swim downstream to a safe distance before emerging. Once the danger has passed it will return through the undergrowth to the nest. The young begin to feed themselves at 10–14 days old. The nests are most usually situated over water, with a protective canopy above and an escape chute immediately below. Downstream from the nest there is often a convenient tangle of vegetation which helps the chick to climb out. Nests have, however, been found in conspicuous positions, fully exposed to direct sunshine.

Behaviour. When not breeding the Hoatzin forms flocks of up to 40, though gatherings of 'several hundreds' are on record. These flocks, as previously noticed, break up into groups of 2–6 in the breeding season. The bird has a variety of calls, among them: a clucking courtship call; a mewing feeding call; a wheezing alarm note and a sharp screech, which has been compared to the call of a guinea fowl.

Economic Importance. While the Hoatzin itself is not eaten, it has an unpleasant smell which has earned it the name 'stinking hannah.' Hoatzin eggs are popular, however, with the people of northeast South America.

Composition. The Opisthocomidae contains a single species, the Hoatzin *Opisthocomus hoazin*. Its systematic position has long been in doubt. For many years the Hoatzin was placed with the Galliformes, to which it bears a fairly strong external resemblance. Some authorities have demonstrated that the Hoatzin is more closely related to the cuckoos Cuculiformes. It seems advisable, however, to retain the bird's familial status until more is known about it.

The Hoatzin *Opisthocomus hoazin* with its young which display the wing claws that were once thought to indicate relationship with *Archaeopteryx*.

STRIGIFORMES

Usually creatures of the night, these birds of prey have a nearly soundless flight

BARN OWLS — *Tytonidae*
TYPICAL OWLS — *Strigidae*

BARN OWLS

Though closely related to the typical owls (Strigidae), barn owls and their relatives the grass owls and bay owls (Tytonidae) differ slightly in skeletal structure, and have a characteristic facial disc of pale, stiff feathers, centred about the eyes. The bill and claws are strongly curved, as in all other owls; the eyes, usually black, are forward looking and proportionately smaller than among the Strigidae; the plumage is barred or spotted, often in rich tones of golden or chocolate brown. The head, large and round, has no ear tufts; the neck is short, and the moveable edges of the face mask hide large ear openings. The long and slender legs are feathered on barn and bay owls, bare in grass owls; the wings are long and broad, with rounded tips and soft feathers which make little noise in flight.

All members of the family are nocturnal hunters, emerging in the half light of evening and quartering their feeding grounds silently in search of prey. Barn owls, best known of the group, range from 11–21in (28–53cm) in length, with wing span up to 36in (90cm). Grass owls lie centrally within this range; bay owls are smaller, seldom exceeding 14in (35cm) in length.

Distribution. The common Barn owl *Tyto alba* is perhaps the world's most widely distributed species, ranging through North, Central and South America, Britain and western Europe to the Black Sea, North, central and southern Africa, Madagascar, India, Burma, many islands of the East Indies, Australia and Tasmania. Over 30 geographical races have been described, some widespread, many restricted to individual islands, island groups or small forested localities. The remaining five species of barn owl occur in the Australasian region: they include the grey Sooty and Masked owls, *Tyto tenebricosa* and *T. novaehollandiae*, of eastern Australia and New Guinea, the Celebes and Minahassa; barn owls, *T. rosenbergii* and *T. inexpectata*, of Celebes; and the New Britain barn owl *T. aurantia*. The three species of grass owls, of Africa, Australasia, India, and Madagascar, form a closely-related trio, and the Eastern and Western bay owls, *Phodilus badius* and *P. prigoginei*, differ from each other only slightly in colour and length of bill and feet, and are found in India, Sri Lanka and southeast Asia, with one specimen recorded in the Congo. Barn owls seem equally at home in open forest, parkland and savanna, desert and moorland, and have adapted well to roosting and nesting in buildings. Grass owls are chiefly birds of the open grass-covered plain, and bay owls are inhabitants of wet tropical forest. Geographic variation occurs in all of the widely distributed species, suggesting that there is little movement between local populations.

Behaviour. Barn owls and their kin catch small mammals – voles, mice, rats, shrews, young rabbits, and even bats – and also take birds, lizards, frogs, insects and fish. Mostly they hunt by flying low along hedges, through woodland and over fields, occasionally perching on a post or low branch. Locating their prey by sound or sight, they hover and swoop, striking at the last moment with claws extended and taking off immediately with the food firmly held in the bill. Large animals they tear with bill and feet, smaller ones they swallow whole; indigestible bones, claws, feathers and fur are thrown up later, often accumulating in heaps under an owl's habitual roost.

They breed in spring, sometimes producing second broods later in the year if food is plentiful. The nesting site may be a deep crevice or cavity or a hollow tree, a sheltered cavern on a cliff face, or the corner of a loft or belfry; no nest is built, but the eggs, round and white, are laid on dirt, feathers or old castings, which help to keep them in place. Most barn owls normally lay 3–6 eggs, with larger clutches when food is plentiful. Only the females incubate, being fed daily by their partners for $4\frac{1}{2}$–5 weeks. The first eggs hatch several days before the last, so the first chicks have a permanent advantage over later ones: if food becomes scarce during the period of growth, the later chicks die first, giving the early ones an increased chance of survival. The young chicks have a covering of dense woolly down; they remain in the nest for 10–12 weeks where they are fed on mice and other prey which the parents bring home and dismember for them. On fledging, the young closely resemble their parents. Barn owls space themselves widely; their long screeches and chuckling

(1) A Barn owl *Tyto alba* with regurgitated pellets composed of indigestible remains of small prey, (2) Celebes barn owl *T. rosenbergii* and (3) a Barn owl with its field mouse prey.

trills, given in flight or from song posts, are probably territorial calls. Little is known of their social organization or courtship.

Composition. The Tytonidae includes nine species of barn owls and grass owls (genus *Tyto*, subfamily Tytoninae) and two species of bay owls (genus *Phodilus*, subfamily Phodilinae). Some authorities exclude the genus *Phodilus* from this family.

TYPICAL OWLS

The Strigidae is the larger of the two living families of owls. It includes about 120 species, all closely related to each other and only slightly removed from the Tytonidae (barn, bay and grass owls). Like all other owls, strigids have soft, dense plumage which makes them virtually soundless in flight. The feathers are cryptically coloured, usually brown, cream or buff with prominent speckles or bars. Many species are patterned to match the lichen-covered trunks and branches of their home forests, and are very difficult to see when roosting during the day or flying in the half-light of late evening. Females tend to be larger than males, though plumage patterns of the two sexes are similar. Colouring, the shape of the head (especially of the ear tufts) and distinctive calls help owls to identify their own species. Other birds seem to have no difficulty in identifying owls in the open, and many species mob them whenever they appear during daylight. Bill and claws are strong and curved; owls often strike at their prey with talons extended, crushing small

Four species of owl to show size variation. (1) The Eagle owl *bubo bubo*, (2) Oriental bay owl *Phodilus badius* (a barn owl), (3) Elf owl *Micrathene whitneyi* and (4) the Snowy owl *Nyctea scandiaca*.

mountains or grassland and one species – the great Snowy owl *Nyctea scandiaca* of the Arctic – lives on open tundra in the far north. Woodland species live mainly among mature trees, roosting quietly among them in daytime and hunting from their branches at night. A roosting site can often be identified by droppings and castings on the ground beneath though the occupant is usually too well camouflaged to be readily visible from the ground. Most owls are strongly territorial and require both roosts and nesting sites within their feeding territories. Several species inhabit cities, favouring parks and suburban gardens where birds and small rodents are plentiful. Farmland also is attractive to owls, with its combination of open cultivated land, hedgerows, mature trees and rambling buildings.

Territories are usually large, and breeding pairs of most species tend to be widely spaced. Short-eared owls *Asio flammeus* in Scandinavian marshland and tawny owls in British woodland require about 35–50 acres (0·14–0·2sq km) per pair; Snowy owls may require up to 4sq mi (10sq km). Malaysian fish owls space themselves about half a mile (0·8km) apart along the rivers which provide their food. Northern populations of Great grey owl *Strix nebulosa*, the Hawk owl *Surnia ulula*, the Snowy owl and the Long-eared owl *Asio otus* retain their territories throughout the summer breeding but move southward in winter, when the voles and other rodents which form their prey disappear under the snow.

Feeding. Owls are occasionally seen hunting in daylight, but most information about their prey comes from examination of their castings – pellets of indigestible material including fur, teeth, bones, insect casings and vegetable fibres which they disgorge between feeds. From this evidence, most owls feed mainly on birds, small rodents and insects, which they catch almost entirely between dusk and dawn. Many also take frogs, snakes, lizards and other small ground-living prey within the same size range, switching readily

The Hawk owl *Surnia ulula* has a hawk-like silhouette. Unlike most species, it often hunts by day, as does the Snowy owl *Nyctea scandiaca*.

prey with their bill or tearing flesh with bill and claws combined. The large, forward-looking eyes have overlapping fields of vision and, unlike those of tytonics, often have a brilliant yellow or golden iris. The eyes are tubular and move only slightly in their sockets, but owls rotate and bob their head to allow all-round vision and accurate judgement of distance. The retina is extended, with a high concentration of sensitive cells; owls have remarkable visual acuity and night vision, far exceeding those of most other birds and of man.

Most strigid owls have excellent hearing. The ear apertures, concealed by the edges of the face mask, sometimes occupy the whole side of the skull, and are often markedly asymmetrical. The ear tufts have no known connection with hearing, but the face mask and flaps of skin in front of the ears are believed to deflect sound into the apertures and help owls to locate their prey very precisely. Tawny owls *Strix aluco* and other strigids hear tiny sounds well below the threshold of human hearing. They are especially sensitive to high frequency sounds, of the kind made by small mammals on the woodland floor, and can strike with remarkable accuracy at a source of sound in complete darkness. Their normal methods of hunting are to fly slowly and silently a few feet above the ground, watching and listening for prey as they travel, or to perch on a low post or branch and rotate the head to locate sounds and movement about them. Nearly all the strigids are nocturnal predators, hunting small vertebrates and insects. A few species are diurnal, and some have adopted special methods of hunting, for example catching fish on the surface of lakes and rivers.

The earliest known fossil owl remains date from the late Cretaceous period, the earliest strigid remains from the upper Eocene or lower Oligocene. There is little or nothing in the fossil record to indicate affinities between owls and other families of birds, and their origins and kinships remain uncertain. Recent studies of egg white proteins have suggested that owls may be related fairly closely to nightjars, oilbirds and their kin (order Caprimulgiformes) and perhaps more distantly to falcons and other raptors.

Distribution. Strigid owls are found all over the world from the Arctic to cool temperate regions of the southern hemisphere. They live in a wide range of habitats. Most are birds of woodland, parkland or forest edge, but some inhabit hot deserts, bare

Black-and-white owl *Ciccaba nigrolineata* showing the way in which an owl can turn its head through an almost complete circle.

from one kind of food to another at different times of the year. Birds, bats, flying and ground-living insects and earthworms may alternate seasonally with rodents, or be hunted intensively at times when rodents are scarce.

The largest owls tend to take the largest prey; the Eagle owl *Bubo bubo* of Scandinavia, weighing up to 9lb (4kg), takes mice, voles, rats, lemmings, hedgehogs, squirrels, hares, ducks, birds of prey (including goshawks and buzzards) and hooded crows. It may also tackle deer and porcupines considerably heavier than itself, and foxes, weasels and other fierce predators. Small owls take smaller prey; the Elf owl *Micrathene whitneyi* of Arizona feed mainly on insects, centipedes and arachnids, including desert scorpions and spiders. Great grey owls, though large, feed mainly on voles, mice and shrews, migrating in winter when these preferred species are difficult to catch. Tawny owls of woodland feed mostly on mice and other small mammals, but those of urban areas take a much higher proportion of small birds. Fish owls of Africa and Asia, for example the Brown fish owl *Ketupa zeylonensis*, feed mainly on fish, which they strike with their talons at the surface of the water. They also hunt crabs and crayfish in the shallows, and may take small mammals and insects as well. Like other owls they hunt mostly at night, though they seem to rely more on sight than on sound for catching their main prey.

Owls often hunt the same ground as hawks and other raptorial birds and take a similar range of prey species, though their nocturnal hunting avoids direct competition. Peregrine falcons and other day-time predators often fall prey to owls, but probably only during the late evening when failing light favours the nocturnal hunter.

Nesting and the Young. Very few species of owls have been studied in detail at the nest. Generally they nest in natural holes or cavities, often adopting a site abandoned by woodpeckers, jackdaws or other species. They may also nest on open grassland or in the branches of trees, on cliffs or in buildings, usually taking over an old stick nest of

another species and adding a few feathers, twigs or moss fragments of their own. Desert species, for example the burrowing owls of North and South America, nest in the abandoned burrows of prairie dogs and other rodents, or among the rocks of dry scree slopes. Elf owls of the southern USA nest in woodpecker holes in tall cactus, or in the shade of shrubs or small forest trees – anywhere which gives them protection from extremes of cold and heat in their dry subtropical environment. Tundra and moorland species nest on open ground, usually among rocks or in low vegetation which shelters them from wind and the cold sting of drifting snow. Tawny owls and some other species take readily to nesting in boxes, especially in new or managed woodlands where there is a shortage of natural nesting sites.

Paired birds communicate with a repertoire of antiphonal calls and quieter conversational chatter. Courtship includes display flights, posturing and bobbing and wing-clapping, with males often bringing food to their mates at the nest site. Most owls lay white eggs, unmarked and often sub-spherical; tropical species lay one to three, those of higher latitudes four to six, with burrowing and ground-nesting species tending to produce the largest clutches. Exceptionally, seven to nine eggs or more may be laid when food is particularly plentiful. Females take almost exclusive responsibility for incubation, and are fed by the males.

In most species incubation starts when the first egg appears, and successive eggs follow at intervals of one to two days. The chicks hatch successively at similar intervals. By the time the last egg has hatched, the first chicks are several days old and already down-covered and well in advance of the youngest. When food is plentiful all the chicks of the brood may survive; in times of scarcity the nestlings compete for the food which the parents bring to them, older chicks surviving at the expense of younger. This ensures that one or two strong chicks, rather than four or five starvelings, leave the nest with reasonable chance of survival. Young owls fly with their parents for several weeks before dispersing from the home territory to fend for themselves.

Economic Importance. Owls are in general too sparsely distributed to affect man economically. Those which inhabit farmland and live in farm buildings may take significant numbers of small rodents from local populations, though on a broad scale their effects are likely to be slight. Those of moorland and spinney may take a small toll of gamebirds among their prey, and in consequence suffer harassment by gamekeepers; again, their effects are unlikely to be significant, and gamekeepers who expend time and shot on owls are probably wasting both.

Composition. The species of strigid owls fall into some two dozen closely-linked genera, which are currently divided into two subfamilies, mainly on the complexity of their earflaps. The Buboninae include the Screech owl *Otus asio*, the Scops owl *O. scops*, the Pygmy owl *Glaucidium passerinum*, the Eagle owl, the Hawk owl and the fishing and burrowing owls. The Striginae, with more complex flaps and (possibly) better hearing, include the Tawny, Short-eared, Long-eared and Snowy owls. This division, retained for want of a better one, emphasizes the basic similarities between owls of the family Strigidae.

Strigid owls differ from tytonid owls in having an unforked, rounded tail, a round head, often with distinctive 'ear tufts,' and a face mask of stiff feathers which, though usually marked, is seldom so complete as the heart-shaped mask of the Barn owl *Tyto alba*. In strigids the second toe is notably shorter than the third and none of the claws is serrated; the breastbone and furcula (wishbone) remain separate throughout life. In tytonids the toes are equal in length, one claw has a comb-like edge, and the breastbone and furcula are fused for additional strength. The eyes of strigid owls tend to be larger, and the bill relatively shorter, than in tytonids. These differences are trivial compared with the many common features which unite the two families in the order Strigiformes; owls of either family could hardly be mistaken for any other kind of bird.

Eagle owl *Bubo bubo*, largest of the owls. The ear-tufts are only feathers which help in camouflage concealment.

CAPRIMULGIFORMES
Mainly nocturnal birds, with long, pointed wings and gaping mouths for catching insects

OILBIRD — *Steatornithidae*
FROGMOUTHS — *Podargidae*
POTOOS — *Nyctibiidae*
OWLET-FROGMOUTHS — *Aegothelidae*
NIGHTJARS — *Caprimulgidae*

OILBIRD

The family Steatornithidae contains a single species, the Oilbird *Steatornis caripensis* of South America. The family is usually placed by itself as a suborder of the Caprimulgiformes, the order that comprises the nightjars and related birds. The Oilbird is about 18in (46cm) long, with a wing span of about 3ft (90cm). The beak is powerful and hooked, with long vibrissae (whisker-like feathers) at either side; the wings are long and wide, the tail long and ample. Oilbirds have extremely short legs and relatively weak feet. The plumage is rich brown, with blackish bars on wings and tail and there is a scattering of white spots which are especially large and conspicuous on the head and wing coverts and at the edges of the flight and tail feathers. The Oilbird's most outstanding characteristics are, however, ecological and behavioural. It is a nocturnal bird, living in colonies in caves, where it also nests, and leaving the caves at night to feed on the fruits of forest trees. Within the caves, which may be pitch dark even by day, the birds orientate themselves by echolocation, as bats do, but the sounds they emit are easily audible, not supersonic as in bats.

Distribution. Oilbirds are found in a limited area of tropical South America. They occur very locally in western Guyana, and from there westwards through Venezuela (including the island of Trinidad close to the Venezuelan coast) to Colombia, and south through the Andean foothills to northern Bolivia. Within this general area they are found in forested country wherever there are suitable caves. They fly long distances while foraging, but once a bird is an established member of a colony it almost certainly remains permanently based on its home cave. Stragglers, probably young birds, have however been recorded in Panama and other places well away from any known colonies.

Feeding. Oilbirds feed on the wing, plucking fruits from forest trees. With their powerful beaks and wide gapes they can wrench off and swallow relatively large fruits. The majority of fruits taken are from a few plant families, the most important being the palms, laurels and members of the incense family. Nearly all contain a single rather large seed surrounded by a layer of firm, rather dry pericarp (the outer flesh). Only the pericarp is digested, the seed being regurgitated intact. It is characteristic of the fruits eaten by Oilbirds that the flesh is highly nutritious, containing much more protein and fat than that of succulent fruits. Such fruits can thus provide a complete diet in themselves, though large quantities must be eaten. Great mounds of decaying seeds accumulate on the floors of caves colonized by Oilbirds. Some of these germinate, producing small forests of etiolated seedlings which, however, soon die through lack of light.

Although they use echolocation inside their caves, Oilbirds evidently have very acute night vision and can make use of what little light there is to locate food trees and pluck the fruit. In addition they have an unusually well developed olfactory organ, and almost certainly they make use of their sense of smell as a supplementary method of locating food. Many of their food trees are highly aromatic, and it is interesting that those that are not tend to go unexploited. The palms are not aromatic, but they have such a distinctive silhouette that Oilbirds probably have no difficulty in locating them by vision alone.

Oilbirds are known to fly up to 30mi (50km) in search of food, but usually they appear to forage within about 10mi (16km) of their caves. These distances are based on records of the food taken at colonies in Trinidad and on the known distribution of some of the trees used by birds from different colonies.

Nesting and the Young. Adult Oilbirds live permanently in pairs and roost at their nests throughout the year, whether breeding or not. The nest is a low roughly cylindrical mound, with a shallow central

In the permanent dark of the caves which it inhabits, the Oilbird *Steatornis caripensis* orientates itself by means of echolocation. This picture shows the difference in the frequencies of sound located by the human ear, by the Oilbird, and by Bechstein's bat. The upper limit of human hearing is around 20 kilohertz (20,000 cycles per second); frequencies above this are not perceived as sound.

depression; it appears to be made of mud, but in fact consists of semi-digested fruit pulp which the bird regurgitates. In addition, nests incorporate much fruit debris. This increases from year to year until eventually the nests fall away, to be repaired and built up again as the breeding season approaches.

The nesting cycle is extraordinarily long. The eggs, which are white but soon become stained brown from the decaying matter in the nest, are laid at intervals of several days. The laying of a complete clutch (up to 4 eggs) may thus take two weeks or more. Incubation begins with the first egg and lasts about 34 days; the young hatch at approximately the intervals at which the eggs were laid. At first they are covered with sparse grey down; later they grow a second, much thicker coat of down. They develop very slowly, being fed only on fruits, and become extremely fat. When about 70 days old they may weigh half as much again as the adult. They then lose weight, and at the same time their adult plumage grows (there is no juvenile plumage), until they are eventually ready to leave the nest at three or four months. The total period, from the laying of the first egg to the fledging of the last young, may take nearly six months.

Economic Importance. Young Oilbirds have traditionally been exploited for their oil, hence their name. The young from the Caripe cave in Venezuela, where Humboldt first discovered the Oilbird in 1799, were collected in huge numbers and boiled down, to provide oil for lamps and for cooking. The species is now protected by law in most of the places where it breeds; the cave at Caripe is a national monument. Now the threat to the birds' survival comes from the destruction of forest land rather than more direct human interference.

Composition. The Steatornithidae, containing a single species, the Oilbird *Steatornis caripensis*, is usually treated as a distinct suborder of the Caprimulgiformes.

FROGMOUTHS

Frogmouths are nocturnal birds that closely resemble the nightjars. There are 12 species generally assigned to two genera, endemic to southeast Asia, as far west as Sri Lanka, and to Indonesia and Australia. Like the nightjars they have a soft, cryptic plumage with a 'dead-wood' pattern; the feet and legs are weak, and the beak, although more massive than in the nightjars, has a very wide gape. While the frogmouths are undoubtedly closely allied to the much larger nightjar family, they differ from them in diet and feeding behaviour. They hunt in a manner reminiscent of that of some of the owls, and also of pounce-feeding birds like broadbills or rollers. Frogmouths eat a wide variety of invertebrates occasionally taking small vertebrates, and obtain the bulk of their diet on the ground. They are more arboreal than nightjars, roosting in trees by day, hunting from them at night, and nesting in them. These differences, in morphology and behaviour, are quite sufficient in degree to warrant the family rank accorded to the frogmouths. Other distinguishing features are the tuft of coarse, bristle-like feathers at the base of the beak and about the nostrils. These are directed towards concealing the external openings of the nostrils and, in part, the beak itself. The wings are rounded, owl-like rather than nightjar-like, and the flight is direct but neither powerful nor particularly agile; the tail is rather long and graduated. Irises are brown, red or yellow. In some ways frogmouths are strongly convergent with owls: the head is very large, some species have ear tufts, and the plumage – grey, brown or rufous with mottling, streaks, bars and vermiculations – has grey and 'red' phases in many species.

Distribution. The Tawny frogmouth *Podargus strigoides* is found in woodland throughout Australia and Tasmania. Two others occur in Australia, in rainforest and dense woods in the Cape York peninsula, both also inhabiting New Guinea and many adjacent islands. They are the Papuan frogmouth *P. papuensis* and the Marbled frogmouth *P. ocellatus*, the latter occurring also in northeast New South Wales and the Solomon Islands.

Thailand (with five species) and Borneo (with six) are the centres of distribution of the remaining frogmouths, all of which are in the genus *Batrachostomus*, which ranges from south and northeast India and Sri Lanka through the rainforest of Burma to the Philippines and Papuan region.

Behaviour. Frogmouths are retiring birds. When roosting during the day, they adopt a stiff, upright posture with the beak and forehead bristles pointing obliquely up. They flatten themselves against a branch or leaning trunk, often on a broken-off stump, with the tail pressed against the limb, and can be extremely difficult to see. Little is known about the family's feeding habits. Evidently they perch in trees at night and when an animal is spotted descend with fast flight and a direct glide, striking their prey with the beak and simultaneously landing on the ground. Studies of stomach contents show that a wide variety of arthropods are eaten – beetles, grasshoppers, bugs, spiders, centipedes, scorpions, land crustaceans and, rarely, molluscs. These are probably crushed by the huge beak on impact, but larger arthropods and certainly the odd small rodent are beaten before being swallowed whole. Some of the Oriental species also eat fruit.

The nest is an open cup built in a tree fork or on a horizontal branch. In some species it is a loosely built platform of thin twigs, like that of a pigeon, and in others it is a highly cryptic flattened cup or pad composed of the bird's own down with bits of bark, lichen and moss. Tropical species lay a single white egg, Australian species, clutches of 2 (usually) to 4.

Composition. The Podargidae is divided into two genera: *Podargus* has no oil gland and builds a felt nest; *Batrachostomus* makes a twig platform nest and has an oil gland; otherwise the two are very similar.

POTOOS

Potoos, the Nyctibiidae, are popular relatives of the nightjars or goatsuckers (Caprimulgidae), found only in the American tropics. The Victorian naturalists called them 'tree-nighthawks', but the Creole name 'potoo,' originally used for only one of the five species, is now used for all of them.

Potoos vary from 16–19½in (41–50cm) in length and are rather stoutly built. The wings are long and fairly pointed, the tail moderately long and the legs very short. The toes are strong and flattened beneath. The exposed culmen of the bill is small and narrow with a downcurved tip, but the gape is very large, partly because the large lower mandible can be greatly deflexed when gaping, and partly because the upper mandible can be reflexed.

The plumage is soft and fluffy, with modified cheek feathers forming fans of bristles on either side of the gape. All five species have concealing colouration of grey, buff, blackish-brown and white forming elaborate barred and mottled patterns. The White-winged potoo *Nyctibius leucopterus* has conspicuous white wing patches, and the Rufous potoo *N. bracteatus* has white tips to the tail feathers. Adults of each sex are very similar in size and colouration, but unfledged immatures have a ghost-like whitish plumage with few dark markings.

The drab colouration with elaborate barring and mottling admirably camouflages potoos while they perch upright. Their choice of perches on sloping branches or broken-off stumps readily enables them to be passed by as pieces of dead or broken branch.

Distribution. The Nyctibiidae is confined to the Neotropical zoogeographical region. Only two of the five species have ranges extending beyond the South American continent. One of these, the Common potoo *Nyctibius griseus* is widespread in central America from southern Mexico southwards, and also inhabits Hispaniola, Jamaica and Trinidad. Various subspecies occur widely in South America, from the Guianas, Venezuela and Colombia, to eastern Ecuador, western Ecuador, eastern Peru, most of Brazil, and Argentina south to La Rioja and northern Santa Fe.

The Great potoo *N. grandis* occurs in Guatemala and Panama and has a wide range in South America, from the Guianas, Venezuela, Colombia and eastern Ecuador to eastern Peru and Brazil in Amazonia and from Bahía to São Paulo and Mato Grosso in eastern Brazil.

The Long-tailed potoo *N. aethereus* ranges from Guyana and southern Venezuela to western Colombia in Chocó and eastern Colombia in Vaupes, eastern Ecuador and eastern Peru, much of Brazil and Paraguay. The White-winged potoo *N. leucopterus* has a smaller range, from the Táchira district of Venezuela to eastern Colombia and eastern Ecuador, and the Bahía region of Brazil. The Rufous potoo *N. bracteatus* ranges from Guyana and eastern Colombia, south through eastern Ecuador to eastern Peru.

All Potoos inhabit forests, but the Common and Great potoos, and perhaps other species, prefer light forest and extend into plantations, savanna with trees and cerrado. All five species are thought to be sedentary.

Behaviour. Potoos are solitary, nocturnal birds that pass the day sitting on a tree branch or stump. Characteristically they perch upright so as to be passed over as a piece of dead branch, but they sometimes also lie along a horizontal or sloping branch. Day-time roosting sites of individual birds are often used for weeks or months on end.

They become active at night, especially when there is bright moonlight. The diet of plant bugs, moths, beetles, crickets, termites and other flying insects is obtained by flycatcher-like flights from exposed perches. When each insect is captured it is carried back to the original perch and consumed there.

Varied repetitive calls are given at night, including series of six to eight chanting whistles descending the scale, a barking *wow*, a rich *oorrr*, *oooorrooo*, quacking notes and a cat-like mewing.

No nest is built, the single egg being laid in a crevice in the bark of a tree or on a stump, sometimes near to the ground, but at least occasionally at a great height. The egg is oval, without much gloss, and white with small lilac and brown spots. The breeding season apparently varies greatly between different regions. Incubation is thought to be carried out by both sexes, but the incubation period, care of the nestlings and fledging period are not known. Incubating birds rely on their colouration to escape detection, so they may be closely approached or even handled before they react.

Composition. The closest relatives of the five species included in the Nyctibiidae are probably the nightjars (Caprimulgidae), although such geographically distant caprimulgiformes as the frogmouths (Podargidae) and owlet-frogmouths (Aegothelidae) may also be allied to them.

OWLET-FROGMOUTHS

Owlet-frogmouths, also known as owlet-nightjars, are intermediate in many respects between nightjars and frogmouths, and also have some convergent resemblance to owlets. The family consists of seven species found in New Guinea and Australia. All are nocturnal insectivores and catch their food both on the ground and by

Nocturnal insectivores. (1) The Tawny frogmouth *Podargus strigoides* uses its enormous beak like a missile head to strike its prey on landing. Even greater precision is needed to capture insects in midflight, as does the Common potoo *Nyctibius griseus*, seen here on its perch (2) and about to seize a moth (3). The Owlet-nightjar *Aegotheles cristatus* (4) feeds both in midair and on the ground.

hawking; they are less adept and agile in flight than nightjars (which feed entirely by hawking insects) and have a small, weak beak in contrast with the massive bill of the frogmouths (which feed by pouncing on large insects on the ground). But the owlet-frogmouths should not be thought of as intermediate in the systematic sense; although they seem to be rather more closely related to the nightjars than to the frogmouths, it is best to regard the three families as separate radiations from a distant common stock.

Owlet-frogmouths are similar in size to the nightjars, being 8–12in (20–30cm) long and weighing 1½–4oz (45–115gm). The sexes are alike or very nearly so, having plumage varying from ashy-grey to buff, brown or rufous, and variously mottled, vermiculated and spotted with cream, cinnamon or black. As with other nocturnal birds, some species have grey and 'red' phases of plumage. In general the species of owlet-frogmouths are plainer than other caprimulgiform birds. They are dumpy birds, with soft plumage, looking large-headed and long-tailed, and their stance is more upright than nightjars. When perching in trees they sit across branches, rather than perching longwise, and the upright, rather owl-like appearance is heightened by the fact that the tarsus is sufficiently long to be clearly visible – again in contrast with nightjars.

The beak is nightjar-like, with a wide gape. Long bristles with hairlike barbs arise in the lores and chin, pointing forwards and outwards and partly concealing the bill. The eyes are set more

forwards than in nightjars and it is likely that a great proportion of the field of vision is stereoscopic. Owlet-frogmouths further differ from nightjars in lacking a comb-like middle toe nail and in having rather more rounded wings.

Distribution. New Guinea is the centre of distribution, with five species. One of these, the Owlet-nightjar *Aegotheles cristata*, is also widely distributed in Australia and Tasmania, but is not found in the more arid areas nor in tropical Queensland. Other species are found in the Moluccas and New Caledonia.

Behaviour. The birds inhabit tropical rain forest and in Australia all manner of woodland and even arid shrub country in the interior. By day they roost in hollow trees and tree-holes and are difficult to disturb. At dusk they become active, leaving their roost to forage in forest or woodland. The flight is erratic and curiously butterfly-like, and hawking after insects has been described, although it appears that they feed mainly on the ground, since stomach-contents comprise non-flying arthropods like millipedes, spiders and ants as well as beetles and moths. Owlet-frogmouths spend much of the night standing on the ground, rising to make short erratic chases after passing insects. They are quite vocal both during the day and at night, with owl-like hissing, whistling and squeaking, and a churring recalling that of nightjars.

For most of the year owlet-frogmouths are solitary. Their courtship has not been described. Nesting takes place in a hollow in a tree, the clutch being laid on a rudely fashioned platform of dry leaves and bits of wood and vegetable matter or simply on a bare floor. The eggs are white; clutch size varies from 2–5. The Australian Owlet-nightjar lays two clutches in the southern spring, from September to December. Nestlings have a dense whitish down that is shed as the feathers grow beneath it.

Composition. Seven, or eight, species are recognized (the variation depending on the taxonomic treatment of some island forms) and they comprise a single natural genus *Aegotheles*. The species differ in size but are all very similar in plumage (nocturnal birds tend to vary specifically in vocal, behavioural and ecological characteristics rather than in visual ones). Owlet-frogmouths resemble frogmouths in some anatomical characteristics and nightjars in others.

NIGHTJARS

The Caprimulgidae has approximately 70 species and forms the principal family of the order Caprimulgiformes. The related families Nyctibiidae, Podargidae and Aegothelidae have fewer species that differ from most Caprimulgidae in catching prey in short flights from perches rather than in sustained flight.

Nightjars, or goatsuckers or nighthawks as they are called in America, are rather small to medium-sized birds, varying in length from $7\frac{1}{2}$–$11\frac{1}{2}$in (19–29cm), although a few species have very long tail feathers that may add as much as $8\frac{1}{2}$in (21·5cm) to the length. The head and eyes are proportionately large, the neck rather short and the legs very short, with feathered tarsi in some species. The bill is small and weak, but very wide so that the gape is large. This adaptation for catching flying insects is enhanced by long bristles, called rictal bristles, that tend to direct prey into the mouth, and by special adaptations of the jaw muscles which cause the mouth to snap closed like a mouse-trap when prey hits the top of the palate. Most species have rather long and more or less pointed wings, those of some American nighthawks being similar in shape to the wings of falcons. A few species have greatly elongated inner primary feathers that form streamers trailing from the middle part of the wing. Others have very long tail feathers that form similar streamers, although the tail is of medium-length and squared or forked in the

majority of species. The feet and toes are invariably small and slender, with three toes pointing forwards and one pointing back. The claw of the middle toe has comb-like ridges which probably assist in preening the head and neck feathers as the birds scratch their heads.

The plumage is soft and fluffy and mainly buff, brown, rufous, grey or blackish in colour. Many species have elaborate barred, streaked or vermiculated patterns that conceal them when they perch motionless. White patches on the wings or tail occur in many species and often serve to distinguish the sexes. For example, males of the European nightjar *Caprimulgus europaeus* have three white spots near each wing-tip and conspicuous white tips to the outer tail feathers, but these markings are absent in females.

Most nightjars are active at dawn and dusk or throughout the night. During the day they mostly lie in concealment on the ground or perching along the branch of a tree.

Distribution. The Caprimulgidae has virtually a world wide range, only being absent from the colder northern parts of North America and Asia, southern South America, New Zealand and most oceanic islands. As is to be expected of birds that feed on large flying insects, the greatest diversity of species occurs in tropical and sub-tropical regions.

The European nightjar *Caprimulgus europaeus* is the only species breeding in Britain and most of Europe. It breeds as far east as western Siberia and south to North Africa, and the entire population migrates in early autumn to spend the winter in tropical Africa, whence it returns in late spring. The only other species breeding in Europe is the Red-necked nightjar *C. ruficollis* which occurs in Spain, Portugal and North Africa; it winters mainly on the southern fringes of the Sahara.

Africa is rich in nightjar species, including numerous *Caprimulgus*, the Standard-winged nightjar *Macrodipteryx longipennis*, the Long-tailed nightjar *Scotornis climacurus* and the Pennant-winged nightjar *Semeiophorus vexillarius*. Several of the African nightjars are inter-tropical migrants, although the details of the movements of these elusive birds are not well known.

Southern Asia has fewer species than Africa and these are mostly of the genus *Caprimulgus*. Australasia has still fewer, of the genera *Caprimulgus* and *Eurostopodus*. The family is absent from most islands of the Pacific, although single species occur in the Palau Islands, Solomon Islands and on New Caledonia.

North America has six species, although only the Chuck-will's-widow *Caprimulgus carolinensis*, the Whip-poor-will *C. vociferus*

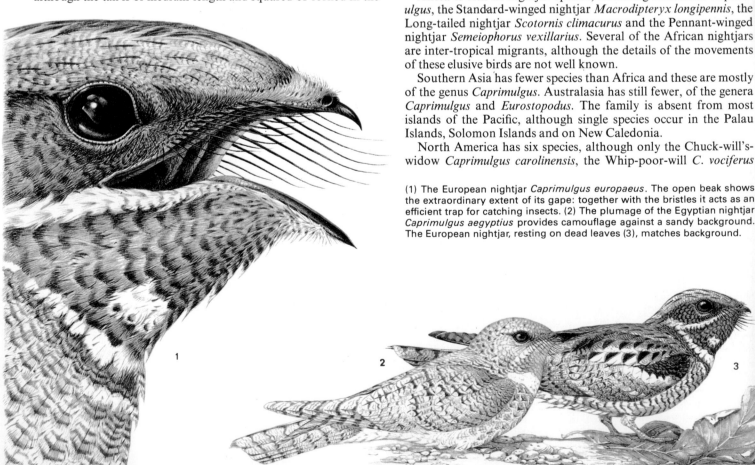

(1) The European nightjar *Caprimulgus europaeus*. The open beak shows the extraordinary extent of its gape: together with the bristles it acts as an efficient trap for catching insects. (2) The plumage of the Egyptian nightjar *Caprimulgus aegyptius* provides camouflage against a sandy background. The European nightjar, resting on dead leaves (3), matches background.

Males of the nightjar family during the breeding season. Magnificently long tail feathers are developed by the Long-tailed nightjar *Macropsalis creagra* (1), while the Standard-winged nightjar *Macrodipteryx longipennis* (2) and the Pennant-winged nightjar *Semeiophorus vexillarius* (3) exhibit streamers formed from elongated primary feathers. (4) The Common night-hawk *Chordeiles minor* repeatedly dives onto the female with whirring wings, skidding to a halt and flying up again. (5) The courtship flight of the Standard-winged nightjar. As he circles the female, the rapid beating of his wings creates an air-current which lifts the pennants.

and the Common nighthawk *Chordeiles minor* occur in the east. The Lesser nighthawk *Chordeiles acutipennis* is common in the southwestern USA, the Poorwill *Phalaenoptilus nuttallii* is wide-spread in the west, and the Pauraque *Nyctidromus albicollis* is a large subtropical species that ranges north to southern Texas. All of these species, except the Pauraque, migrate from northern regions to winter further south.

South America has no fewer than 27 nightjar species, including such spectacular birds as the Lyre-tailed nightjar *Uropsalis lyra*, and the Long-trained nightjar *Macropsalis creagra* as well as numerous rather drably-coloured species of *Caprimulgus*. Several species occur in Central America and the West Indies that are absent from both North America and South America, among them the peculiar little Eared poorwill *Otophanes mcleodii*, which has ear-like tufts of feathers on the sides of the head. The endemic Puerto Rican whip-poor-will *Caprimulgus noctitherus* was long feared extinct, but it was rediscovered in small numbers some years ago.

It has recently been discovered that the Poorwill is among the few birds that hibernate, others being certain hummingbirds, and a few swifts which may become temporarily torpid. Poorwills apparently hibernate in rock holes for months on end and they may return to the same hole in successive winters. The body temperature falls as low as 64–66° F (18–19° C) when they are torpid, compared with the normal 104–106° F (40–41° C).

Feeding. Nightjars feed on insects caught in flight, especially moths, beetles and crickets. The European nightjar is typical in that it feeds mostly by flying to and fro over and among vegetation, periodically hovering to pick insects from the foliage or less often from the ground. The American nighthawks are somewhat more aerial than this, commonly flying high above the ground like large nocturnal swifts. In contrast, some *Caprimulgus* such as the Fiery-necked nightjar *C. pectoralis* hunt by flying out in pursuit of prey from fixed perches, rather like nocturnal flycatchers.

Nesting and the Young. So far as is known, all nightjars are monogamous and nest solitarily. The nest is placed on the ground and consists of a hollow among dead leaves, fallen logs or ground vegetation. Some species tend to accumulate a few dead leaves, pieces of twig or small stones at the nest.

The clutch is of one or two (very rarely three) eggs that are oval in shape and of a white to pinkish-buff ground colour with elaborate blotched and marbled patterns of black, brown and violet. Both parents incubate. In the European nightjar the incubation period is about 18 days and the female alone incubates during the day, being relieved by the male in the evening and probably also at dawn.

The newly-hatched young are covered with fluffy down of a general buff, brown or grey colour that makes them inconspicuous against the nest background. Both parents feed them on insects carried to the nest in the bill.

Adults of several species perform elaborate distraction displays when they are disturbed at the nest. In the European nightjar these consist of aerial displays in which the bird flies about with very rapid wing-beats, holding the wings in a peculiar position and the tail spread, and of similar flapping displays performed on the ground.

Behaviour. Many nightjars are more easily detected by their nocturnal calls or songs than by sight. The name 'nightjar' is derived from the sustained nocturnal jarring or churring song of *Caprimulgus europaeus*. Various other species also have churring songs, but some give nasal whistles. Among those that whistle, the Whip-poor-will, Chuck-will's-widow, Pauraque and Poorwill have names that imitate their repetitive nocturnal songs. Besides the song, most if not all species also give calls or communicate by clapping their wings together.

The European nightjar and various American species are known to defend territories in which they nest and feed. As other species give similar songs and are similarly spaced-out when breeding it seems very likely that they are also territorial.

Composition. The Caprimulgidae has about 70 species that are generally grouped in around 18 genera. Two subfamilies are recognized on the basis of anatomical differences, the Caprimulginae for the majority of nightjars, and the Chordeilinae for the American nighthawks. Because of the difficulties of finding many nightjars it seems likely that a few species and subspecies still remain undiscovered in tropical regions.

APODIFORMES

Birds capable of fast and acrobatic flight on slender, pointed wings. Their feet are extremely small

TYPICAL SWIFTS — *Apodidae*
CRESTED SWIFTS — *Hemiprocnidae*
HUMMINGBIRDS — *Trochilidae*

TYPICAL SWIFTS

The Apodidae are the most aerial of birds, far surpassing any swallow or hawk in their ability to continue rapid flight for days on end. They commonly collect nest material and copulate in the air, drink and bathe while swooping low over water, and even pass the night on the wing.

Everything about the structure of swifts fits them for constant flight. Their wings are long and pointed with short secondary feathers but long and strong primaries, the body is compact, the neck short, and the tail varies from short and square to long and forked. The legs are extremely short, with small strong feet that have sharply pointed claws. Swifts do not normally land on the ground or

on vegetation, so that their short legs and strong feet with a reversible hind toe serve only to enable them to cling to steep rock, bark or masonry while at their nests or roosting.

The bill is very short and slightly downcurved, with a very wide gape to receive insect prey caught in flight. The plumage is strong and compact with feathered tarsi and sometimes even feathered toes. The colouration is predominantly black, blue-black or blackish-brown, although numerous species have white patches of variable extent, most often on the rump and underparts. The Chestnut-collared swift *Cypseloides brunneitorques* is alone in having extensive chestnut markings on the neck and underparts.

Species of the subfamily Chaeturinae have the strong shafts of their tail feathers projecting beyond the vanes as spine-like tips. These aid the birds in clinging to vertical surfaces. Species of the subfamily Apodinae lack these modified tail feathers and rely on the strength of their feet for clinging.

Distribution. The family Apodidae has virtually a world wide range, with representatives in every zoogeographical region. The scarcity of flying insects in the Arctic and in windier parts of the north temperate zone has prevented swifts from becoming established there, and the same factor probably accounts for their absence from New Zealand, the southernmost parts of South America and many small oceanic islands.

Europe has four breeding species, although only the Swift *Apus apus* is widespread. The entire population of *Apus apus* migrates in early autumn to winter quarters in southern Africa. In Europe the Pallid swift *A. pallidus* breeds only around the Mediterranean coasts; this species also migrates to winter in Africa. The large Alpine swift *A. melba* breeds from southernmost Europe north to Switzerland and winters in tropical Africa, although not as far south as *A. apus*. The small White-rumped swift *A. caffer* was first discovered breeding in southern Spain in 1966; this small colony remains the only one known in Europe.

The other swifts of the Palearctic region are the Needle-tailed swift *Hirundapus caudacutus* of Asia, which has straggled occasionally to Europe; the Himalayan swiftlet *Collocalia brevirostris* which breeds from the Himalayas to central China and the Indo-Chinese countries; the House swift *Apus affinis* which is widespread in Africa from Morocco southwards and in southern Asia; the Plain swift *A. unicolor* which breeds only in the Cape Verde, Madeiran and Canary Islands, and the large White-rumped swift *A. pacificus* which breeds in eastern Asia and winters from Malaysia to Australia.

All of the swifts which breed in temperate parts of Asia also breed in tropical Asia. In addition, tropical Asia has numerous species of the genus *Collocalia*, a few large swifts that are not found further north, and the Palm swift *Cypsiurus parvus*.

Tropical Africa is rich in swift species, including numerous typical swifts of the genus *Apus*, the small Palm swift, and several spine-tailed swifts of the subfamily Chaeturinae. Australasia has far fewer species. Excepting swiftlets, only the New Guinea spine-tailed swift *Chaetura novaeguineae* breeds there, although *Chaetura caudacuta* and *Apus pacificus* occur as winter visitors from Asia. New Guinea has four breeding species of *Collocalia* swiftlets, but Australia has only two. Other species of this genus range through the islands of the western Pacific to as far east as Tahiti (*C. leucophaea leucophaea*) and the remote Marquesas Islands (*C. leucophaea ocista*).

North America has only four breeding species: the Chimney swift *Chaetura pelagica* which is widespread east of the Missouri and Mississippi Rivers, the very similar Vaux's swift *C. vauxi* which replaces it west of the Rockies, and two other western species, the Black swift *Cypseloides niger* and White-throated swift *Aeronautes saxatilis*.

Central and South America are as rich in swifts as the tropics of the Old World. There are numerous spine-tailed swifts of the genera *Chaetura* and *Cypseloides*, two species of swallow-tailed swifts *Panyptila* which have very deeply forked tails, various large swifts of the genera *Steptoprocne* and *Aerornis*, and the White-throated swift of North America.

Feeding. All swifts feed entirely on small animals caught in the air. Tiny insects naturally make up the bulk of this 'aerial plankton' which they eat, although tiny spiders are also drifted aloft at times. Such insects as two-winged flies, small beetles, flying ants, plant bugs and aphids figure prominently in the diets of those species that have been studied in detail, although tiny moths, lacewings and other insects may be taken in small quantities.

Although swifts evidently see and pursue individual insects at times, their normal mode of feeding is probably to locate concentrations of flying insects, then to fly back and forth among them with the large mouth held wide agape. Some species commonly feed at great heights above the ground where insects are drifted up in thermals, but at other times they may skim only inches above the ground or water.

Nesting and the Young. Different genera of swifts use a remarkable diversity of nest sites. The species of *Chaetura* under natural conditions nest mostly in hollow trees, but some have adopted the habit of using chimneys, fixing their nests to the vertical interior walls. Swiftlets of the genus *Collocalia* mostly nest in caves. Some species nest in total darkness, where they find their way to fly by means of echolocating clicks, much as bats do, or aeroplanes using radar. *Cypseloides* and related genera of American swifts mostly nest in shallow caves or rock cracks near water, sometimes under waterfalls.

The Old World genus *Apus* mostly nest in holes in cliffs or buildings, although a few species burrow into sand banks and one appropriates the disused nests of swallows. The Palm swift builds a tiny cup-shaped nest in the open and stuck to the inner side of a palm leaf. The egg is glued to the nest with saliva and incubation is carried out with the bird in a vertically upright position. *Aeronautes* nests in holes in cliffs and *Tachornis* places a bag-shaped nest in palm foliage. The swallow-tailed swifts build hanging sleeve-shaped structures of plant materials which are suspended from branches or rock. The nest-entrance is at the bottom of the sleeve, the nest-chamber at the top.

Many different kinds of nest sites are found among swifts. (1) The Alpine swift *Apus melba* often takes advantage of holes in cliffs (2), while the African palm swift *Cypsiurus parvus* (3) commonly glues its nest to the under side of a palm leaf (4) using saliva. The eggs in turn may need gluing to the nest — a problem which the Fork-tailed palm swift *Tachornis squamata* (5) avoids by building a bag-shaped nest (6) to hold the eggs securely. *Collocalia* species usually nest in caves, like those of the Andaman Islands (7). The cross-section (8) shows how they site their nests high up to escape the dangers of stormy weather (9). (10) The Edible-nest swiftlet *Collocalia fuciphaga* builds nests largely or even entirely of dried and hardened saliva; from these comes the oriental delicacy bird's-nest soup.

Most swifts build their nests of plant materials held together by sticky saliva, but some *Collocalia* build nests of saliva alone – the 'edible-nest swiftlets.'

Clutches vary from one to six eggs in different species, some habitually laying only a single egg, but others normally laying four to six. The eggs are nearly oval and unmarked white with slight gloss. Both sexes incubate, for incubation periods that are rather long for the size of the bird. The European swift, for example, incubates for 19–20 days, whereas the heavier (unrelated) Blackbird *Turdus merula* takes only about 14 days.

The young are blind and helpless when hatched and lack natal down. Both parents feed them on sticky boluses of insects regurgitated from their throats. The nestling periods are long and unusually variable, that of the European swift taking from five to eight weeks depending on the weather.

Behaviour. Most swifts nest in colonies, which may be of just a few nests in a cave, tree-hole or crack in a mountain crag, or as many as hundreds together. Some *Collocalia* nest in vast colonies, with hundreds of thousands of nests concentrated on the roofs and walls of a large cave system. Colonial nesting in swifts may partly be a consequence of restrictions on the availability of the specially sheltered nesting places that most species prefer, although it may also benefit the birds in other ways, such as by providing easy interchange of information about the location of good feeding places.

Most swifts feed in loosely associated flocks or groups. Most likely they tend to congregate where food is abundant and concentrated, but to scatter when it is scarcer or more scattered.

The calls of most swifts are short rasping or twittering notes; a few give more musical twitters or shrill screaming or squealing calls.

Economic Importance. Most swifts are of little direct economic interest, but being almost exclusively insectivorous they no doubt consume quantities of harmful insects. Swift nests in buildings may occasionally constitute a fire hazard, but House sparrows and Starlings are very much worse offenders in this respect.

Some *Collocalia* swiftlets are of considerable economic importance to a few scattered villages in southern Asia. These swiftlets provide the 'edible' birds' nests used in oriental soup. The accumulated droppings on the floors of these caves where swiftlets nest in large numbers are rich sources of organic fertilizer, although of limited extent.

Composition. The Apodidae contains 75–80 species that are usually classified into two subfamilies, the typical swifts in the Apodinae and the spine-tailed swifts in the Chaeturinae. Different taxonomists have recognized very different numbers of swift genera, mainly because of the considerable structural similarities of most swifts coupled with the diversity of their breeding habits. A fairly conservative modern classification would use about five genera for the Apodinae and four or more for the Chaeturinae.

Taxonomists have also found it difficult to decide how many species to recognize in some swift genera. This is because of the tiny differences separating some forms that are known to be distinct species because they breed close together, such as certain *Collocalia*.

CRESTED SWIFTS

The Hemiprocnidae is a small family containing four species of swifts that are most closely related to the true swifts of the Apodidae. They differ from the latter in hawking insects from high perches after the manner of shrikes (Laniidae) or Wood swallows (Artamidae), in having a crest on the forehead, and in various small anatomical peculiarities. They are also more brightly coloured than most true swifts.

Like most swifts, the crested swifts or treeswifts are rather small, ranging from 6½–13in (16·5–33cm) in length, with a small narrow body and short neck. The wings are extremely long and pointed, and the legs are very short, with four small weak toes. The hind toe points forwards with the other three and is not reversible. The bill is small, flat, and broadly triangular, with a broad gape facilitating the capture of flying insects, as do the very large eyes. The tail is long and deeply forked, with considerable emargination of the outermost pair of feathers. All four species have a short crest on the forehead and a patch of long silky feathers on the flanks.

The body plumage is generally rather soft, with a fluffy or silky texture. Different species have the upperparts brown or soft grey, often with a green or blue gloss. The underparts are brown or grey, often with blue gloss on the breast, with a white chin and in some forms a white lower belly and under tail coverts. Two species have conspicuous white stripes extending from the base of the bill, above the eye as superciliary stripes, and beneath the eye; these end as tufts on the nape and shoulder. Males of all species have chestnut cheeks. In the Crested treeswift *Hemiprocne coronata* these chestnut patches extend across beneath the chin.

Unlike the true swifts, all species of crested swift show sexual dimorphism and some age differences in plumage colouration. Females and immature birds are generally duller than adult males.

Distribution. The family ranges from India through southeast Asia to the islands of the southwest Pacific. The Moustached swift or Greater treeswift *Hemiprocne mystacea* occurs in both the Oriental and Australasian zoogeographical regions, with a range extending from the Moluccas to New Guinea, the Bismarck Archipelago and the Solomon Islands. It has three or four distinct subspecies, and reaches 4,000ft (1,200m) elevation in New Guinea.

The other three species are restricted to the Oriental zoogeographical region. The Grey-rumped treeswift *H. longipennis* has several subspecies and ranges from the Tenasserim district of Burma southwards through Malaya and the small islands of Malaysia to Java and Celebes. The Crested treeswift has often been regarded as a subspecies of *H. longipennis* but is probably distinct from it, although there is room for some doubt. It ranges from Ceylon and India, except the dry parts of northwest India, to eastern Assam and southwards through Burma to Laos and Cambodia. The Lesser treeswift *H. comata* has five subspecies found from the southern Tenasserim district of Burma southwards through the Malay Peninsula, Sumatra and Borneo to all of the Philippine Islands. Its range overlaps parts of the ranges of *H. coronata* and *H. longipennis*.

None of the species is a migrant. All four are found in a variety of habitats that offer exposed perches high on tree limbs and open spaces over which the birds can watch for flying insects. Open woodland on hillsides and the trees about clearings in forests are favoured habitats, but Crested swifts can also be found in and around garden trees, and trees bordering fields and roadsides. The Greater treeswift sometimes inhabits tall forest where there is a closed canopy overhead. Here it perches on high branches projecting from the canopy and is difficult to detect from beneath, except by its screaming calls.

Feeding. Unlike the true swifts of the family Apodidae, crested swifts habitually perch in trees. Typically they feed by watching from perches high in forest trees, from which they make fast dashing flights with quick turns and short glides to catch insects. The insect

prey taken includes flies, small beetles, plant bugs and ants – venomous bees and wasps are apparently avoided. Insects are swallowed as they are caught, and several are often caught on a single circuitous hunting flight. As with many of the true swifts, the call is a loud screeching or screaming note, and it is given both from perches and in flight. There is no elaborate song. Long flights made between hunting perches are fast and wheeling, and often noisy when a small group of crested swifts are associating. Although crested swifts are somewhat gregarious, they usually hunt singly and nests are generally widely spaced.

Nesting and the Young. The nest is an extremely small and shallow cup-shaped structure that is attached to the side of a tree branch, often where a small lateral twig makes a narrow fork. It is constructed of fragments of tree bark and feathers bound together with the birds' glutinous saliva and is surprisingly strong for all that it is paper-like in texture. However, the nest supports mostly just the weight of the single, large, pale blue-grey egg, the incubating bird resting its own weight mainly on the branches supporting the nest. Both parents incubate the egg for an unknown period. The newly-hatched nestling is almost helpless and clothed only in fluffy greyish natal down. It is fed by both parents on insect food that is regurgitated into the gape of the waiting nestling in the form of round boluses of compacted, and partly digested, insect matter.

Composition. The four species of Hemiprocnidae are all closely related and placed in the genus *Hemiprocne*. Formerly, two other genera were used for two of the species, and the family was variously called the Macropterygidae or Dendrochelidonidae.

HUMMINGBIRDS

The hummingbirds are tiny, nectar drinking birds of the New World which take their name from the noise made by their rapid wing-beats. There are 319 species contained in the family Trochilidae.

In rapid movements such as this squabble between two male Rubythroats *Archilochus colubris*, a hummingbird may be momentarily upside-down.

Hummingbirds are mainly aerial and are related to the swifts. Like the swifts they have very small legs and feet and the bony structure of the wings is also very much reduced. The hummingbirds move solely by flying, the short legs and little feet being used merely for perching. They feed on the wing and even bathe while airborne – in fine spray or rain, or by brushing against wet foliage. Hummingbirds do not tuck the bill into the feathers of the back when sleeping, but squat on a twig with body feathers fluffed; the head tilted back a little and the bill pointing up at an angle. The head is large in relation to the rest of the body but this is not obvious in most species because of the relatively large size of the wings and tail.

Crested swifts. (1) Crested treeswift *Hemiprocne coronata*, (2) Lesser treeswift *H. comata*, seen also catching an insect in midflight (3). (4) Moustached swift (or Greater) treeswift *H. mystacea* incubating an egg. Not only the parent but also the newly-hatched chick (5) must rest its weight on the branch, since the nest itself (6) is small and relatively delicate.

Nine species of hummingbird to show variety of bill shape. (1) The Giant hummingbird *Patagona gigas*, (2) the Sword-billed hummingbird *Ensifera ensifera*, (3) the White-tipped sicklebill *Eutoxeres aquila*, (4) the Spatuletail *Loddigesia mirabilis*, (5) the Bearded helmetcrest *Oxypogon guerinii*, (6) the Ruby-topaz hummingbird *Chrysolampis mosquitus*, (7) the Frilled co-quette *Lophornis magnifica*, (8) the Amethyst woodstar *Calliphlox ame-thystina* and (9) the Bee hummingbird *Mellisuga helenae*.

Hummingbirds are, in general, small, fast and extremely active. The largest species, the Giant hummingbird *Patagona gigas* of the Andes, is a little over 8in (20cm) in length, of which half is tail. The smallest, the Bee hummingbird *Mellisuga helenae* of Cuba, is virtually the size of an insect. The body is about 1in (2·5cm) long, the bill and tail adding another inch to this. In the majority of species the body size is about 2in (5cm) or less.

It is generally the case that the smaller a bird is the faster it needs to move its wings to keep airborne. In this connection the hummingbird has an additional problem associated with its mode of feeding. When taking nectar from blossoms hummingbirds must, in the absence of a convenient perch nearby, hover while feeding then move backwards to withdraw the bill from the flower. As a result the flight is specialized. The wingbeat is highly efficient and, proportionally, the hummingbird uses fewer beats than other birds. Some of the larger hummingbirds have a rate of 20–25 beats per second, which is comparable with that of the considerably larger and slower tits. In small hummingbirds the rate rises to 70–80 beats per second but in the Giant hummingbirds it is surprisingly slow, 8–10 beats per second. The wings are kept more rigidly extended throughout the beat than those of other birds and they rotate through a narrow ellipse during each beat.

In normal forward flight the body is horizontal and the wing-beat almost vertical, but in hovering the body is more vertical and the wingbeat horizontal, the wing-tip moving through a figure-of-eight. To reverse, the wings are raised and rotated and the hummingbird may momentarily fly on its back before rolling over. The speed of direct flight is from 30–40mph (50–65kph).

The bill is long and fine, an exceptionally short one being only about half as long again as the head, while the longest, that of the Swordbilled hummingbird *Ensifera ensifera* is straight and as long as head, body and tail combined. Such a bill is designed for probing long tubular flowers. A number of species have the bill slightly decurved, while in the Sicklebill *Eutoxeres aquila* the bill is long and strongly arched downwards, and a few hummingbirds have a slight upward curve to the bill. The tongue is slender and elongated. It can be extended well beyond the tip of the bill and the edges are rolled in to form a double tube up which the nectar is sucked.

The displays of the hummingbirds are relatively unspectacular in terms of movement, usually being very rapid swoops terminating in a hover in front of the female, but the brilliance of the display lies in the vivid iridescent colours of the male's plumage and the often elaborate plumage decorations such as crests, ruffs, beards and tail-streamers. Most of the more vividly iridescent plumage is on the throat and crown – brilliant shapes of red, yellow, pink, purple, blue or green. In many cases this is only really conspicuous from one angle, usually from the front, so that it shows to best advantage when the male hovers before the female. The head colour may be enhanced by decoration such as the long tapering green or violet crests of the plovercrests *Stephanoxis*, the green and red paired horns of *Heliactin cornuta* or the black and white paired crests and pointed beard of *Oxypogon guerinii*. In addition to a bright crest, the coquettes *Lophornis* have erectile fan-shaped ruffs on the sides of the

neck, boldly coloured and with contrasting bars or spots at the feather-tips. When the male hovers before the female the other visible parts of the plumage are the undersides of wings and tail. The body plumage of most hummingbirds is glossy green or blue and the underwings may have a contrasting chestnut-red tint. The tails of some show an overall bronze or purple iridescence on the undersides of tail feathers, visible in display but not obvious from above.

In addition the tails may have a variety of shapes. Broad fans are frequent, and forked tails vary from blunt forks to the long scissor-shapes of the trainbearers *Lesbia* and the slender tail streamers of the Streamer-tail *Trochilus polytmus*. Others show different degrees of tapering and elongation of the central tail feathers, as in the hermits *Phaethornis*. The racket-tails *Ocreatus* have the two outer feathers elongated to long wires terminating in large rounded vanes and show the additional decoration of white down patches like powder puffs around the legs, which are also found in some other species.

Distribution. Hummingbirds are restricted to the New World where they are found from Tierra del Fuego in the south to Alaska in the northwest and Labrador in the northeast. Many are forest-dwellers, but they may also occur in a wide range of habitats, extending into open country where flowering plants are present and also to high altitudes in mountain regions. In some areas they are nomadic or subject to seasonal movements in order to take advantage of the flowering seasons of different plants. Several species are migratory and three move into North America to nest in the southern parts of Canada or Alaska. Other species, and particularly those of tropical or subtropical mountain regions, may be very localized in distribution at all times.

Feeding. The variety of bills in the hummingbirds indicates their adaptation to different types of flowers as sources of food. In taking

Aspects of behaviour in hummingbirds. (1) The nest attached to a drooping leaf is occupied by the Long-tailed hermit *Phaethornis superciliosus*. More common is the simple cup-shaped nest (2) built here by the Black-chinned hummingbird *Archilochus alexandri*. (3) The Rufous hummingbird *Selasphorus rufus* hovers almost motionless over a flower while extracting nectar with its tongue – actions which are paralleled by the Hummingbird hawkmoth. (4) The Broad-billed hummingbird *Cynanthus latirostris* hovers in midair by moving the tip of its wings in a figure of eight. The hummingbird family is highly aggressive. Typically, the Rufous-throated sapphire *Hylocharis sapphirina* drives away a hawk many times its own size (5).

nectar from the flowers the birds may also transfer pollen from one flower to another and be important agents of fertilization. It would seem that some plants have adapted to attract hummingbirds and so aid cross-fertilization for, in areas where hummingbirds are migrants, the flowers needing such pollination tend to have a similar red colour so they can be quickly recognized by a bird new to the area. Where hummingbirds are resident the flowers are more variable and there may be a more direct relationship between one type of flower and a particular hummingbird species. Although nectar forms the staple part of the diet, a large number of tiny insects are also taken, usually by being snatched in mid-air.

With their small size and fierce activity the hummingbirds quickly burn up their reserves of energy. During active periods they appear to feed about once in every 10–15 minutes. Like swifts, hummingbirds are at a disadvantage in prolonged periods of rain and low temperatures, but may compensate for this by their ability to become torpid, appearing lifeless and saving energy until the weather improves. Migrating hummingbirds overcome the need for frequent feeding by laying down sufficient fat reserves to enable them to undertake a long journey.

Nesting and the Young. The nests of hummingbirds are built of fibres, plant down and similar fine material and moss and lichen, bound together with spiders' webs. Some nests are smooth neat cups on twigs, others are domed, and some are pendent, or built onto hanging plants. They are often decorated externally with lichens. The female builds the nest, incubates and cares for the young. She lays two white eggs, which are very large in proportion to her body size and very bluntly elliptical. Incubation takes about a fortnight and the young are born naked. The female feeds them by inserting her bill well into the chicks' gullets and regurgitating food. The young take three to four weeks to fledge, the period varying apparently in response to the food supply available.

Behaviour. Although hummingbirds may occur in numbers where food is plentiful they are aggressive and quarrelsome among themselves. They are territorial when nesting, and outside the breeding season may defend small feeding territories. Not only do they attack and chase each other but they will also boldly attack much larger birds, which their speed and agility enable them to dominate.

Composition. In spite of the fact that the Trochilidae contains over 300 species, the family is remarkably homogeneous. All its members share the specialized anatomical features that make rapid wingbeats and hovering flight possible and it is extremely likely that they are the result of a relatively recent radiation.

COLIIFORMES

Small birds with long tails composed of ten feathers of varying length. Their name comes from their creeping habits

MOUSEBIRDS — *Coliidae*

MOUSEBIRDS

The Coliidae is a small family of six species called mousebirds or colies. They are exclusively African and easily recognized by their extremely long, stiff, sharply graduated, attenuate tails which are composed of 10 feathers and are at least twice as long as the small body. A most unusual anatomical characteristic of the family is the ability of its members to direct all four toes forwards.

All six species of mousebirds are similar in shape and generally drab in appearance, being brown or greyish. Their plumage is thick, soft and hair-like, and both sexes have conspicuous crests. Aptly called mousebirds from specific creeping habits, these birds occur in small flocks of half to two dozen. Mousebirds have long, sharp claws and fairly powerful, sharply decurved, short bills, well suited to tearing open tough-skinned fruit, but suggesting that animal food is also occasionally taken

Distribution. Mousebirds occur throughout Africa south of the Sahara, from sea level to over 8,000ft (2,438m) in bush, savanna, woodland and acacia country. They are sedentary and do not migrate. The White-headed mousebird *Colius leucocephalus* and the Chestnut-backed mousebird *C. castanotus* are restricted respectively to a limited area of eastern Kenya, and from Congo (Zaire) north to part of Angola. The White-backed mousebird *C. colius* is found in the Cape region and South Africa, while the Blue-naped mousebird *C. macrourus* is widespread in eastern Africa and to Senegal north of the equatorial rain forest. The Bar-breasted or

Mousebirds hang from twigs and clamber about in a rather unbirdlike fashion. Shown here is the Blue-naped mousebird *Colius macrourus*.

Speckled mousebird *C. striatus* is found in west, east and southeast Africa, and the Red-faced mousebird *C. indicus* in southeast Africa from Tanzania to Cape and in southwest Africa to the mouth of the Congo.

Behaviour. Mousebirds feed greedily and destructively on all manner of vegetable matter – fruit, flowers, buds and leaves; in a short time a few will strip a sprouting hedge of every leaf, as well as ravaging orchards, returning daily to complete the process.

Nests vary from shallow, softly lined, twig cups which are sometimes decorated with flower heads, to the loosely constructed, often bulky, untidy structures built by the Bar-breasted mousebird, a casual breeder which is likely to desert should it be disturbed at laying time or during early incubation. The nests are usually well concealed on leafy branches or thick bush, sometimes not far above the ground. Often, eggs seem to be laid at irregular intervals. The general breeding pattern is rather curious; both sexes incubate, and those not on the nest join up into feeding flocks, composed of either male or female birds. More than one male may help to look after the same nest and young. Two to seven eggs are laid, but if more than five are present, these may be the result of two females laying in the same nest. Indeed, two females have been observed incubating side-by-side on the same nest. The eggs are dull surfaced, almost rough, relatively thick shelled, immaculate whitish or creamy in the Bar-breasted mousebird or white sparingly spotted with dull red, sepia or brown.

Mousebirds are sociable and gregarious. Their flight is direct and swift – the result of a sharp flap and glide on stiffened wings. They leave cover explosively with whirring wings, in quick succession, soon joining up into close flock, a party of Blue-naped mousebirds in speedy transit suggesting a flight of arrows. When landing they crash headlong into cover. Some climb to the tops of bushes or small trees prior to take-off, another curious characteristic.

All utter a clicking *tsik tsik* which according to intensity, may be an alarm cry or a recognition call enabling members of a flock to keep in touch with one another. Before take-off the flock indulges in considerable twittering which is continued in flight, and the Blue-naped mousebird similarly has an unmistakable, attractive 'peeping' call. When courting, the male Bar-breasted mousebird twitters to the female, while Red-faced mousebird females will call to males.

Economic Importance. Mousebirds are most destructive, causing severe, persistent damage to fruit crops, as well as to leaf buds; locally a pest.

Composition. The genus *Colius* comprises six species, four showing subspecific variation—*C. striatus* at least 14; *C. macrourus* 4; *C. indicus* 3; and *C. leucocephalus* 2. All six species resemble one another closely, and the validity of the genus is unquestionable.

TROGONIFORMES

Brightly plumaged tropical birds with delicate skins.
They are only remotely related to other bird families

TROGONS — *Trogonidae*

TROGONS

The Trogonidae is the only family of the order Trogoniformes, a group of highly colourful birds that have numerous anatomical pecularities and show only distant relationship to any other bird family. All trogons are short-necked arboreal birds, varying in length from 9–13¼in (23–34cm). They have rather short, broad bills that, in some species, have serrated edges to the mandibles. The legs and feet are very small and weak, with the tarsi feathered and the toes arranged in a unique way: the first and second being turned backwards and the third and fourth forwards. The eyes are relatively large and surrounded by a bare ring of brightly coloured orbital skin. The wings are short and rounded, with 10 primaries; the tail is long, composed of 12 rather broad feathers that are of graduated length in most species and have modified tips in a few.

The skin is unusually delicate and easily torn, so that the feathers are readily lost. Adult males of all the American and African species have the breast and belly brightly coloured, either red, pink, orange or yellow, usually in strong contrast to the glossy green, greyish or brownish colour of the rest of the plumage. In the Asian species the males lack metallic gloss, but often have red or pink on the head, breast, rump or tail. Females of the Asian species are mainly duller than the males, but those of the African and American species are usually much like the male. The colouration of newly-fledged juveniles mostly resembles that of the adult female, but bright abdominal colour is lacking and there are usually some pale spots on the wings. In the quetzals of the genus *Pharomachrus* the upper tail coverts are greatly elongated and hang over the tail, hence their old vernacular name of 'trainbearer.'

Distribution. The family Trogonidae occurs in the Neotropical, Ethiopian and Oriental zoogeographical regions, but the discovery in southern France of fossil bones thought to be those of a trogon suggests that the family's range was more extensive when the climates of the northern hemisphere were warmer, during the Eocene and Oligocene eras.

The largest number of trogon species is found in the Americas, where it seems probable that individuals are also commonest. The monotypic genus *Euptilotis* is restricted to Mexico, but the genera *Pharomachrus* and *Trogon* are widely distributed throughout Central and South America. The Elegant trogon *Trogon elegans* of Central America has a range extending northwards into the USA in southern Arizona, and other species of this genus reach sub-temperate latitudes in South America. Two monotypic genera are both restricted to islands in the West Indies, the Cuban trogon *Priotelus temnurus* to Cuba, and the Hispaniolan trogon *Temnotrogon roseigaster* to Hispaniola. Although the American trogons are mainly restricted to tropical latitudes, some species occur at high elevations in mountain forests, exceeding 12,000ft (around 4,000m) in some places.

Only three species occur in Africa, the Bar-tailed trogon *Heterotrogon vittatus*, and the two species of the genus *Apaloderma*, the Narina trogon *A. narina* and the Bare-cheeked trogon *A. aequatoriale*. The Narina trogon has a wide range extending from Liberia east to Eritrea and south to Cape Province.

The only Asian trogons are the eleven or so species of the genus *Harpactes*, which range from western India and Ceylon eastwards to southeastern China and south through much of Indonesia and the Philippines. The Red-headed trogon *H. erythrocephalus*, with many subspecies, ranges from central Fukien to Nepal, Malaya and Sumatra.

All trogons are arboreal and most species are confined to forests or woodlands, although some occur in small groves of trees or tall brush. In tropical America it is common for several species occurring in the lowland forests to be replaced by fewer montane species at higher elevations. All members of the family are believed to be sedentary.

Mousebirds feed voraciously on plant matter. (1) The Red-faced mousebird *C. indicus* and (2) the White-headed mousebird *C. leucocephalus*.

Typical postures of trogons. (1) The Quetzal *Pharomachrus mocinno*, (2) the Red-headed trogon *Harpactes erythrocephalus*, (3) the White-tailed trogon *Trogon viridis* and (4), catching an insect in midflight, the Scarlet-rumped trogon *Harpactes duvauceli*.

Feeding. Insects and spiders form the bulk of the diet, although a number of American species also eat substantial quantities of berries and other small fruit. The Quetzal *Pharomachrus mocinno*, for example, is especially fond of small fruits of a tree related to the avocado, and these are swallowed whole. Lizards, snails and small tree frogs are also sometimes eaten, by a variety of species.

Nesting and the Young. Nests are flimsy structures placed either in cavities or in holes excavated in the arboreal nests of wasps or termites. The clutch is of 2–4 white or pale-coloured, unspotted eggs. Incubation is by both parents, for periods of around 17–19 days. Newly hatched nestlings are helpless and have no down. They are fed by both parents on food (mainly insects) regurgitated from the throat.

Behaviour. Most trogons are usually seen sitting motionless on a branch or vine beneath the tree canopy, or in quick undulating flights through the trees. The normal posture of a perching trogon is erect, with the tail hanging down almost vertically and sometimes with the neck hunched. Most species normally occur singly or in pairs. Their calls are simple, usually consisting of hollow whistles, squeaks, hoots, caws or cooing noises, varying between species in their number, rhythm and pitch. In some species a number of males may gather together and 'sing' within a short distance of each other. They infrequently hop or walk along branches, and most of their food is caught in the air, either while fluttering or hovering in front of foliage or while flying from one perch to another after the manner of a flycatcher.

Composition. The family Trogonidae contains between 34 and 40 species, the exact number depending on taxonomists' judgements of species-limits in little-known American and Asian forms. Nine genera are usually recognized: *Apaloderma* with two species, *Euptilotis* with one species, *Harpactes* about 11 species, *Heterotrogon* one species, *Pharomachrus* with 3–5 species, *Priotelus*, *Temnurus* and *Temnotrogon* with one species each, and *Trogon* with around 15 species.

CORACIIFORMES

The Kookaburra and its relatives tend to be noisy and social. All nest in tree holes or other cavities

KINGFISHERS — *Alcedinidae*
TODIES — *Todidae*
MOTMOTS — *Momotidae*
BEE-EATERS — *Meropidae*
CUCKOO-ROLLER — *Leptosomatidae*
TYPICAL ROLLERS — *Coraciidae*
HOOPOE — *Upupidae*
WOOD-HOOPOES — *Phoeniculidae*
HORNBILLS — *Bucerotidae*

KINGFISHERS

The Alcedinidae comprises 87 species of kingfisher in two subfamilies: the Alcedininae and the Daceloninae, the former being the familiar fishing kingfishers with long narrow sharp-pointed bills, and the latter the forest kingfishers which often live far from water and whose bills are broader, flatter and sometimes hooked at the tip.

Kingfishers vary in length from about $4\frac{1}{2}$in (11·4cm) in the Malachite crested kingfisher *Corythornis cristatus* to 18in (45·7cm) in the Giant African kingfisher *Megaceryle maxima*. The Common kingfisher *Alcedo atthis* is a dumpy bird only $6\frac{1}{2}$in (16·5cm) long. The azure feathers of its back can also look emerald green depending upon the angle of the light. The tail feathers are a darker cobalt, as are those of the head and wings where the striae glow with rows of azure speckles. In contrast the underparts are a warm chestnut orange. It has a white throat or bib, white neck patches and orange cheek patches behind the eye. The 1½in (3·8cm) dagger shaped bill is the only external indication of the sex. In an adult male it is wholly black, but the female usually has a partially or completely rose-coloured lower mandible. The small feet and legs are sealing wax red.

Distribution. Europe has only one species, the Common kingfisher which is also found in Africa and the Far East, eastward to the Solomon Islands. The fishing kingfishers live mainly on unpolluted rivers, lakes and streams, canals and fen drains. They also inhabit tidal estuaries, salt marshes, gutters and rocky sea shores, especially in the winter when driven to the coast because inland fresh water has frozen over.

The North American Belted kingfisher *Megaceryle alcyon*, 13in (33cm) has habits similar to those of the Common kingfisher. This blue-grey bird has a belt across its white chest and has a slight crest. It is commonly seen perched high upon telegraph posts and wires along the roadside ditches. The Texas kingfisher *Chloroceryle americana* ranges southwards from Mexico and is very similar to the crested Amazon kingfisher *C. amazona*, 11in (28cm) whose brilliant green upperparts contrast with its white underparts. The male is distinguished by his chestnut breast. These birds live along the tropical jungle streams.

The largest kingfisher is the Giant African kingfisher. It is grey speckled, with a chestnut breast. The Pied kingfisher *C. rudis* is common south of the Sahara. Its plumage is black and white. Among the forest kingfishers are the inland kingfishers of the genus *Halcyon*. The Grey hooded kingfisher *H. leucocephala*, 7in (18cm), with a striking red beak, has a brilliant cobalt and turquoise back and chestnut underparts, and lives on beetles, grasshoppers and small reptiles. Another inland kingfisher is the Striped kingfisher *H. chelicuti* which nests in ready-made holes and will often evict swallows from their nests under the eaves.

New Zealand has only one kingfisher, the yellow Sacred kingfisher *H. sancta*, which also occurs in Australia. Also in Australia, the Forest kingfisher *H. macleayii*, an insect eater, nests in termite nests on the sides of eucalyptus trees. Best known in Australia is the Kookaburra *Dacelo gigas*, 17in (43cm), whose diet of snakes and lizards makes it popular among the bushmen, though it loses its good name by raiding farmyards for chicks and ducklings. Widely distributed with about 50 known local races is one of the noisiest species, the White collared kingfisher *H. chloris*, 8in (20cm). It has brilliant turquoise upperparts and white underparts. It ranges from the Red Sea to Samoa, where it frequents the mangrove swamps and coastlines. The greatest numbers of kingfishers are to be found in Southeast Asia, the most elegant being the Raquet-tailed kingfisher *Tanysiptera galatea* found from the Moluccas to northeast Australia. Living on the dry uplands of India is the White-throated kingfisher *H. smyrnensis*, 11in (28cm), which has a scarlet bill, as has the Stork-billed kingfisher *Pelargopsis capensis*, 14in (35·5cm).

Feeding. The chief prey of the Common kingfisher is fish, which it secures underwater by grasping the fish between its mandibles, not by stabbing as is the popular misconception. The bird will watch from a perch, usually overhanging the water, until it sights its prey, and then, having aimed, it tenses and dives headlong into the water straight as an arrow, beak open and the opaque nictitating membrane, or third eyelid, closed. On grasping the fish it pivots and, using the buoyancy of its body, flaps its way back to the surface, propelling itself out of the water on the downstroke of the wings. The whole action takes about a third of a second. Once back on the perch the kingfisher prepares to kill the fish, which is banged vigorously and repeatedly against the perch until it stops wriggling. A kingfisher may also hover prior to diving and it has been known to

The Common kingfisher *Alcedo atthis* beats its prey against a branch to stun it.

catch dragonflies and spiders in this manner. The diet also includes tadpoles, small molluscs and crustacea.

Some of the forest kingfishers never go near the water but feed in the forests and on the savannahs catching insects, small mammals, amphibians, and reptiles. The Malachite crested kingfisher, a very common African species, lives on flies, water invertebrates and small fish. The Shoe-billed kingfisher *Clytoceyx rex* of the New Guinea forests differs from all the others, having a flattened bill with which it digs for earthworms. The Kookaburra *Dacelo gigas* of Australia feeds mainly on snakes and lizards.

Nesting and the Young. Early in the year the Common kingfishers fly high in a courtship flight, after which they look for a suitable place

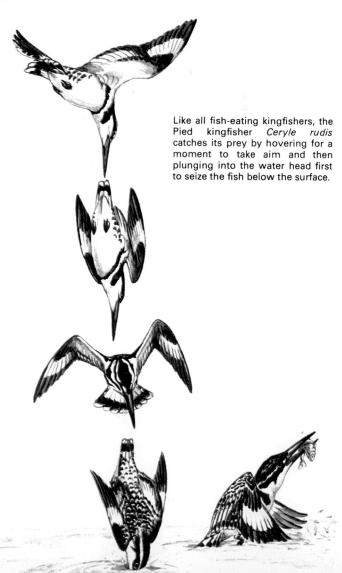

Like all fish-eating kingfishers, the Pied kingfisher *Ceryle rudis* catches its prey by hovering for a moment to take aim and then plunging into the water head first to seize the fish below the surface.

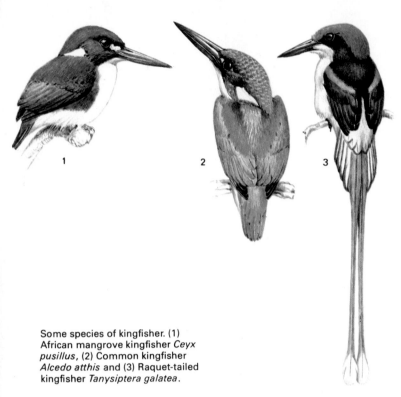

Some species of kingfisher. (1) African mangrove kingfisher *Ceyx pusillus*, (2) Common kingfisher *Alcedo atthis* and (3) Raquet-tailed kingfisher *Tanysiptera galatea*.

TODIES

The Todidae is a West Indian family of five species of closely related birds all between $4\frac{1}{4}$–$4\frac{1}{2}$in (10–11cm), in length, with short squared tails, rounded wings, short slender legs and a rather long, laterally expanded bill. All are bright green above with a crimson throat patch in adults that is preceded by dull grey in juveniles. The underparts vary from pale yellowish or greenish to white, with pink flanks in all but the Puerto Rican tody *T. mexicanus*. The under tail coverts are bright yellow in all species, the bill dark with an extensive orange patch on the lower mandible, the iris pale grey and the legs black. When perching todies usually hold the bill pointing upwards at an angle of 45° above the horizontal.

Distribution. The Todidae is restricted solely to the West Indies, where it is found on the larger islands of the Greater Antilles. Four of the species appear to be closely related and replace each other on different islands, forming a 'superspecies.' These are the Puerto Rican tody (on Puerto Rico), the Broad-billed tody *T. subulatus* (Hispaniola and Gonâve), the Cuban tody *T. multicolor* (Cuba and the Isle of Pines) and Jamaican tody *T. todus* (Jamaica). The fifth species, the Narrow-billed tody *T. angustirostris*, also occurs on Hispaniola. It inhabits mainly humid mountain forests, although it sometimes occurs at lower elevations in forests inhabited by the Broad-billed tody. The difference in bill-shape between these two species is probably related to differences in diet that allow them to coexist where their ranges overlap.

Two species of tody. (1) Narrow-billed tody *Todus angustirostris* and (2) Jamaican tody *T. todus*.

to nest, in a chamber at the end of a tunnel in a bank of the stream. Sometimes they return to the nest of the previous year. If the banks of the streams are not high enough they may choose the earthy roots of an up-rooted tree, a hole in a wall or bridge, or they may travel overland to a sand, gravel or chalk pit. The tunnel may measure up to 3ft (0·9m) long and slope slightly upwards. At the end a spherical chamber is formed where the eggs are laid in a depression on the bare soil. Once the nest is complete the ritual of courtship feeding takes place. The female sits bolt upright, beak in the air, wings drooped and juddering, and utters a pleading, bleating call. The male bird catches a fish and returns with it presented head first. The female takes it and eats it, coition usually following.

The eggs are a delicate translucent pink about $\frac{3}{4}$in (1·9cm) long, and are laid upon the bare soil; there are normally seven in a clutch. Incubation, which is shared, starts once the clutch is complete.

After 19–21 days the eggs hatch and at three weeks old the young are fully feathered and spend much of their time preening and stretching their wings. They are duller than their parents with shorter black bills and black feet. Between 24 and 26 days they leave the nest of their own accord scattering up and down the streams and sometimes joining up in twos and threes. They will attempt to fish for themselves on the day they leave the nest though their parents will continue to feed them until they are good at fishing. There is, however, a high mortality rate through drowning. A second brood is laid if the first has failed, and sometimes there is a third brood.

Behaviour. Kingfishers pair for life and share a common territory throughout the year, defending it by chasing off aggressors. An encounter starts with a series of aggressive stances, on opposite perches, and when one kingfisher judges he has caught the other off guard he dashes towards his opponent in an attempt to knock him off his perch and duck him in the water.

Composition. There are 87 members of the Alcedinidae, currently divided into two subfamilies: the Alcedininae, which includes the Common kingfisher *Alcedo atthis*, and the Daceloninae, including the forest kingfishers and the Kookaburra *Dacelo gigas* of Australia. Some authorities recognize an additional subfamily, the Cerylinae, comprised solely of certain fish-eating species.

All five species inhabit woodland and forest, but details of their habitat preferences differ. The Puerto Rican tody occurs in open woodland and groves of trees in dry coastal regions as well as in more characteristic, wetter forests. The Cuban tody inhabits most woodland and forest, including small groves of trees near rivers and streams, and the Jamaican tody has equally varied preferences, but is most common on wooded hills and mountain slopes.

Behaviour. Todies characteristically perch quietly on thin twigs amid the leaves of shady trees and bushes, usually at no great height. From such half-concealed perches they make short flights to catch their insect food with audible bill snaps. Prey is caught both in the air and on leaves and twigs, and sometimes includes tiny lizards.

Although their colouration, habits and small size make todies inconspicuous, they are not shy of human observers and can often be approached to within a few yards. They are most readily detected by their characteristic calls, a chattering in the Cuban tody, a harsh *cherek* note that is probably similar in the Puerto Rican and Jamaican todies, a rather plaintive, repeated *terp-terp-terp* in the Broad-billed tody and a very different harsh *tick-cherek* or chattering in the Narrow-billed tody.

Todies occur singly and in pairs and are apparently sedentary within the territories they defend. The flight is weak and usually of short duration. Sometimes it is accompanied by a whirring, rattling sound, apparently made by the short outermost primary. This noise is made by both sexes and appears to be under the birds' control; it is heard most often in the mating season.

The nest is a tunnel varying from a few inches to two feet long, excavated by both male and female in the face of an earthy bank. Because of their small size they are able to use quite small vertical elevations for nest sites, including even deep ruts made by the wheels of vehicles. Nest holes are only about 1¼in (3cm) in diameter, although a chamber 3–5in (7–12cm) long and about 3in (7cm) high is excavated inside. Clutches are of two or three, sometimes four, unmarked white eggs. They are laid on the bare earth of the nest floor and often become soiled, particularly when the soil is the common red clay of the tropics. Both parents incubate the eggs in turn, for an unknown incubation period. The young are helpless when hatched and are fed by both parents.

Composition. The five species in the family Todidae are placed in a single genus, *Todus*. Their closest allies are the motmots Momotidae of tropical America, although they are also closely related to the kingfishers Alcedinidae. Various anatomical peculiarities suggest they are best placed in a distinct family.

MOTMOTS

The Momotidae form a small, brightly coloured, neotropical family. The group as a whole must be one of the most attractive of all bird families, and although regarded as being stupid because of their habit of sitting motionless for long periods and allowing close approach, they rightly deserve the commonly used West Indian name of 'King of the Woods'. For all their bright colouring they are not easy to see in their natural forest environment as the colours blend remarkably well into the background, and for this reason are said to be rare or very local.

They vary in length from 6–20in (15·2–50cm), have short rounded wings, a large tail (except *Hylomanes*) and a fairly long bill which is somewhat decurved with well marked serrations in the horn along its edges. In all but *Hylomanes*, *Aspatha* and two subspecies of *Baryphthengus*, the tail is long, graduated and racket-tipped. The development of the rackets is unusual in that the two elongated, central tail feathers grow quite normally, but in the sub-

terminal parts the barbs are loosely attached and fall off during normal preening. The result is that part of the vane becomes naked, while at the end of the vane the barbs remain intact leaving the characteristic racquets. The long-tailed motmots often sit on a perch swinging their tails from side to side rather like a pendulum which has lost much of its momentum.

The majority of motmots are greenish, olive or rufous brown with brighter colouring about the head, and a dark spot on the breast. The legs are very short, with the two outer toes joined for a good part of their length, and only a single toe diverted backwards.

Distribution. Members of the family are only found in neotropical parts of the New World, and are restricted to well forested areas from Mexico to Paraguay and northeastern Argentina. The Blue-crowned Motmot, which has the widest range, also inhabits the islands of Trinidad, Tobago and Cozumel.

Behaviour. The diet of motmots is mainly made up of insects of

The tail of the Rufous motmot *Baryphthengus ruficapillus* is often swung like a pendulum (right). The Blue-crowned motmot *Momotus momota* (below) produces the spatulate tail by removing some of the barbs.

many kinds, including beetles, caterpillars and butterflies, but spiders, lizards, worms and fruit are also taken. They catch their prey by making a quick sally from a perch usually plucking their victims from the foliage, and returning immediately to the perch, against which they beat their prey with great ferocity before swallowing it. The noise made by the heavy bill against the perch during this process often indicates a motmot's presence even though it may be out of sight. Motmots are also known to catch insects on the wing, in a way similar to that employed by flycatchers, and will at times forage for caterpillars on the ground. In some inhabited areas, which have good cover nearby, they will come to bird tables where they become remarkably tame, and will even take food from the hand.

The call of the motmot is not very inspiring and consists of rhythmical, low-pitched, hooting or cooing notes uttered singly or in series from a low perch. Two birds often sing together, one calls and the other replies almost immediately.

Motmots nest in a small rounded cavity at the end of a long burrow which they usually excavate themselves in a bank or in the ground.

It is a paradox that these beautiful birds are hatched and reared in an insanitary hole, which may be a crevice in rocks or in a chamber at the end of a long burrow in a bank or in the ground. The burrows are excavated by the birds with the aid of their powerful bills, and may be 5–15ft (1·6–5m) in length. The 3–4 white, roundish eggs are laid in the chamber which has no lining, and take about three weeks to hatch. The young are born naked and do not leave the nest for at least another four weeks. Both parents share in all the nesting duties. Motmots are usually found alone or in pairs. They roost in burrows with their young during the breeding season.

Composition. The Momotidae contains six genera; *Aspatha*, *Baryphthengus*, *Electron*, *Eumomota*, *Hylomanes* and *Momotus*, containing in all eight species, some with numerous subspecies. They appear to be closely related to the kingfishers the Alcedinidae.

BEE-EATERS

Bee-eaters (family Meropidae) are bright-plumaged insect-eating birds of the Old World. They closely resemble the jacamars Galbulidae, insectivorous birds of tropical America, though the two are not related. Bee-eaters live on flying insects, caught in graceful pursuit flights, and have pointed, rather long decurved beaks, pointed wings and very short legs. The sexes are similar. The best known species is the 11in (28cm) long European bee-eater *Merops apiaster*. Its cinnamon crown and shoulders, gold scapulars, blue-green wings, green tail, black eye-stripe, yellow throat and apple-green underparts command attention as much as its confiding gregariousness and liquid trilling *pruik* call-note. Like other bee-eater species, it prefers open countryside and the vicinity of water, and breeds in colonies of a few to a hundred or more pairs, in holes excavated in sandcliffs or flat ground.

All other members of the genus *Merops* have equally bright plumage, chiefly of greens, blues and yellows, hence the common name Rainbow-bird for the Australian *M. ornatus*. All possess a black mask across the eyes, sometimes accentuated by a narrow pale blue or yellow line above and below it, and the chin and throat of most species are bright yellow or scarlet, contrasting with the surrounding plumage and delineated by a narrow black breast band. The West African Rosy bee-eater *M. malimbicus* is slaty black with a white moustache and pink underparts and Carmine bee-eaters *M. nubicus* of Africa are entirely carmine except for their blue heads.

The two species in the genus *Nyctyornis*, found from southwest India to Indo-China and Borneo, are large, forest dwelling birds with rather stout beaks and a principally green plumage; the throat and breast feathers are elongated and pendent, blue in the Indian *N. athertoni* and scarlet in the Malayan *N. amicta*.

Distribution. The European bee-eater is a summer visitor to the Mediterranean countries, and western Asia, being found north of the Pyrenees, the Camargue, the Alps and Carpathians, 500mi (800km) north of the Black and Caspian seas and east to Kashmir.

It spends the winter in Africa south of the Sahara. Populations also winter in southwest Arabia and in northwest India. For many years now, small isolated colonies are known to have nested in a few localities in the Union of South Africa during the southern summer. This population is surely derived originally from migrant European bee-eaters, but it is not known whether, after nesting in South Africa, the same birds accompany other wintering bee-eaters back to Europe and Asia to nest there again, six months later. Occasionally European bee-eaters nest north of their usual range, in Germany and Denmark.

The genus of forest dwelling bee-eaters *Nyctyornis* is found from southwest India to Indo-China and Borneo. Another forest bee-eater, *Meropogon forsteni*, the affinities of which, within the family, are not understood, lives in Celebes and somewhat resembles three dark plumaged forest species of western and central Africa.

Several species are trans-continental migrants. Large green bee-eaters from India, *Merops philippinus*, winter in the East Indies, and those from West Pakistan and trans-Caucasia, *M. superciliosus*, migrate to Africa as do the European bee-eaters. Rainbow-birds *M. ornatus* fly to New Guinea after breeding in Australia and most of the African species migrate regularly within that continent.

Feeding. Bee-eaters are well named, for practically all the species which have been investigated in detail feed exclusively on airborne insects, with bees and their allies (Hymenoptera) comprising 80% or more of their diet. There are two principal ways of feeding: the smaller species keep watch for passing insects from a vantage-point like a bush, fence-post or telephone wire, while the larger species hunt on the wing. In either case an insect is pursued with a fast and dextrous flight and snapped up in the bill. Generally the bird returns to its perch, where it beats the prey against the perch until it is inactive. Over much of the family's range, the various bee-eaters subsist largely on honeybees. The venomous workers of honeybees and other stinging Hymenoptera have their stings removed. The insect is held in the beak near the tip of its abdomen, which is rubbed against the perch so that the venom is discharged. Apart from bees, most other suitably-sized flying insects are also preyed upon: demoiselle-flies, termites, butterflies, bugs, beetles, and, particularly by the Carmine bee-eater of Africa, grasshoppers. After a rainstorm in Africa, flying ants and termites emerge in great profusion and are hunted by many kinds of birds; an excited flock of wheeling bee-eaters is often in attendance. Members of the genus *Nyctyornis* take a generalized diet of insects, spiders and woodlice, but will catch some insects in flight, including bees.

Nesting and the Young. The breeding biology of all bee-eaters seems to be very similar. Migrants start to excavate their nesting holes in

The Cuckoo-roller (or Courol) *Leptosomus discolor*. (1) The male, seen also in flight and (2) the female.

Four species of bee-eater showing the long, decurved beaks. (1) European bee-eater *Merops apiaster*, (2) Red-throated bee-eater *M. bulocki*, (3) Red-bearded bee-eater *Nyctyornis amicta* and (4) Celebes bearded bee-eater *Meropogon forsteni*.

sand banks or earth cliffs as soon as they arrive at their summer quarters, but sedentary species like the Red-throated bee-eater *Merops bulocki* of Africa, which breed at the end of the dry season when the ground is rock-hard, dig their nest holes in softer earth at the end of the previous rainy season, months in advance. In some species the tunnels are up to 8ft (2·4m) long, being straight or just a little angled, and end in an oval chamber 6–10in (15–25cm) long. Here 2–6 spherical white eggs are laid, without benefit of nesting material other than a thick carpet of the indigestible hard parts of insects, regurgitated in the chamber by adult birds.

The young hatch naked and blind, but long before their eyes open at 10 days they have learned to shuffle quickly forward on their swollen horny 'heel' pads when they hear a parent alight at the tunnel entrance with a meal. Fledging occurs after four weeks in the nest and for several more weeks the young birds are tended and fed, not only by their parents, but by other non-breeding adults as well. Juvenile plumage is identical with that of the adults.

Composition. The Meropidae is divided into three genera containing 24 species in all. *Merops* contains 21 species; *Nyctyornis*, 2 species; and *Meropogon*, a single species *M. forsteni*.

CUCKOO-ROLLER

The Cuckoo-roller or Courol *Leptosomus discolor* is the only species of the family Leptosomatidae. Cuckoo-rollers are 16–18in (41–46cm) long, with a rather slender body. The head is large and rounded, the neck rather short and the bill stout and slightly downcurved with a small hook at the tip of the upper mandible. The wings are long and pointed, the tail long with a squared tip and the legs extremely short. The feet are unusual in having two long toes that always point forwards, a short hind toe that always points backwards and a mobile third toe which can point either forwards or back. The female is substantially larger than the male.

The plumage is rather loose and scanty, with long thin throat feathers and a short crest in both sexes. The adult male is mainly glossy dark grey on the upperparts which have strong green and coppery iridescence, but dull grey on the underparts and hind neck. Females and immature males differ from adult males in having the hind neck barred with rufous and black and the underparts pale rufous with bold black spots.

Cuckoo-rollers were described as 'lazy and stupid' by 19th-century ornithologists, but in fact they are active, noisy birds. They are tame towards man, so were probably described as stupid because of the ease with which they could be shot. They spend a good deal of time hopping about in the treetops or flying above them with slow flapping wing-beats that result in a rapid and graceful straight or bounding flight.

Distribution. Confined to Madagascar and the Comoro Islands. The Leptosomatidae is one of a few bird families forming a distinctive Malagasy subregion avifauna. The subspecies *L. d. discolor* is widespread in Madagascar and also inhabits the Comoro Islands of Moheli and Mayotte. Grand Comoro has a small subspecies *L. d. gracilis* which differs in having the breast and belly paler coloured in male birds and the tail and upperparts red-brown in females. The birds of Anjouan resemble *L. d. discolor* in colour, but are smaller in size so that they are separated as *L. d. intermedius*.

Feeding. The diet consists mainly of large insects and lizards captured in the foliage and branches of trees. After lizards and other large prey are captured they are held in the bill and beaten against a branch before being swallowed. Studies in Madagascar have suggested that the species prefers hairy caterpillars to other prey, often taking so many that the stomach becomes lined with their hair. However, hairy caterpillars were not found in stomachs of birds collected in the Comoro Islands, where chameleons, grasshoppers, caterpillars, mantids, phasmids and cockroaches were the main foods.

Nesting and the Young. Very little is known of the breeding biology of the Cuckoo-roller. Display flights occur mainly in the wet season and it is thought that breeding occurs then. In these flights, a bird flies rapidly upwards with swift wing-beats followed by a rapid swoop downwards with the wings held still.

The nest is placed in a hole in a tree trunk, and according to local people also in holes in banks. A clutch of unmarked white eggs has been reported, possibly three in number. The young and the breeding behaviour have not been described.

Behaviour. The Cuckoo-roller is a noisy bird that is often heard calling as it flies over the treetops at times when it might otherwise pass unnoticed. The usual call is a rich, loud, whistled *kwiii-yu, kwi-yu, kwi-yu, kwi*, the first note being loudest. This call is probably only made by the male, and the birds will often approach closely if it is imitated. Other calls include a loud, whistled *wheee* note repeated at intervals. Calling birds puff out the throat in time with each call, presenting a very distinctive appearance as the long throat feathers project.

Cuckoo-rollers are often seen in small groups that fly together above the forest treetops. It has been claimed that the species is likely to be polyandrous because males were thought to greatly outnumber females. However, recent studies suggest that males only appear to outnumber females because they are more conspicuous, not more numerous.

Composition. The closest relatives of the Cuckoo-roller are the typical rollers (Coraciidae). However, it differs from the typical rollers in a number of anatomical features that suggest it has been pursuing a separate evolutionary course for a long time.

TYPICAL ROLLERS

Rollers are stoutly-built perching and terrestrial birds related to the Cuckoo-roller (Leptosomatidae) and also to the superficially dissimilar Hoopoe (Upupidae) and wood-hoopoes (Phoeniculidae).

Coraciidae vary from $9\frac{1}{2}$–13in (24–33cm) in length, although some species have a few elongated tail feathers that may add as much as 6in (15cm) to this. The bill is moderately long, downcurved, stout and broad, and has a slight hook at the tip. The typical rollers of the subfamily Coraciinae have long rounded wings and rather long tails with a square or forked tip, a few species having the outer tail feathers elongated with tips that are either pointed or spatulate. This subfamily have rather short necks and very short legs with strong feet in which the second and third toes are united at the base. The Madagascar ground-rollers (Brachypteraciinae) have shorter rounded wings, longer legs and more pointed tails that are very long in some species.

Most species of the Coraciinae are brightly coloured, with patches of blue, blue-green, green, violet and brown. They are mostly unmarked, although a few species have streaks on the underparts. The ground-rollers are duller with more buff, brown or black in the plumage, which is usually barred or mottled. The sexes are similar or identical in colouration in all species of the family.

Rollers are named from their habit of rolling or somersaulting in display flights. All of the Coraciinae are strong-flying birds and most of them are known to have display flights. However, the Brachypteraciinae are terrestrial and differ from the Coraciinae in running rather than hopping when on the ground.

Distribution. The Coraciidae is confined to the Old World and has more species in the tropics and subtropics than in temperate regions. Europe has only the European roller *Coracias garrulus* which is widespread in southern and eastern Europe, but only a vagrant in the British Isles. European rollers migrate to winter in tropical Africa.

Africa, with 11–12 species, is richer in rollers than any other continent. Nine species of *Coracias* make up the bulk of this number, the others being broad-billed rollers of the genus *Eurystomus*. Among the *Coracias*, the Raquet-tailed roller *C. spatulata* is of special interest because of its long outer tail feathers with spatulate tips.

Asia has only a few rollers, among them the Indian roller or Blue jay *Coracias benghalensis* which ranges from eastern Arabia to Indo-China and Temminck's roller *C. temminckii* which is restricted to Celebes and nearby islands. The Broad-billed roller or Dollar-bird *Eurystomus orientalis* ranges from northern India and China

Seven species of rollers. (1) Blue-headed ground-roller *Atelornis pittoides*, (2) Crossley's ground-roller *A. crossleyi* and (3) Long-tailed ground-roller *Uratelornis chimaera*. (4) European roller *Coracias garrulus*, (5) Raquet-tailed roller *C. spatulata*, (6) Broad-billed roller (or Dollar-bird) *Eurystomus orientalis*, seen also in the rolling display flight which gives the group its name and (7) Scaled ground-roller *Brachypteracias squamigera*.

south through Indonesia to Australia and the Solomon Islands. The numerous subspecies of *E. orientalis* are the only rollers in the Australasian zoogeographical region. The Australian subspecies *E. o. pacificus* migrates northwards in the southern autumn to winter in New Guinea and nearby islands.

The ground-rollers of the subfamily Brachypteraciinae are confined to Madagascar. The Short-legged ground-roller *Brachypteracias leptosomus*, Scaled ground-roller *B. squamigera*, Blue-headed ground-roller *Atelornis pittoides* and Crossley's ground-roller *A. crossleyi* inhabit rain forest and the Long-tailed ground-roller *Uratelornis chimaera* is a desert bird.

Feeding. Rollers of the subfamily Coraciinae characteristically perch on posts, bushes, wires or other open sites from which they swoop to catch prey on the ground. Some species also pursue flying insects. The diet consists mainly of large insects, spiders, lizards and small mammals, but small birds are also taken at times. The ground-rollers have a similar diet, but chase after prey on the ground.

Nesting and the Young. The Coraciinae nest in holes in trees, banks or rocky crags. No lining is added to the hole, although old nests of other species may sometimes be present and this may give the misleading impression that a nest has been built. Clutches are of 3–6 unmarked white eggs that are incubated by both parents. In the European roller the incubation period is 18–19 days. The young are helpless and lack down when hatched. Both parents feed them, and continue to do so for some time after fledging. The fledging period is about four weeks in the European roller and probably similar in the other species.

No ornithologist has seen a nest of any of the five species of Brachypteraciinae. Natives report that the nests are in holes in trees or holes dug in the ground or a bank and that the eggs are white or spotted, although the latter seems unlikely.

Behaviour. The typical rollers are normally encountered evenly spaced on conspicuous perches. Their bright wing patches and bold behaviour apparently suffice for territory defence and make up for the absence of any well-developed song. The European roller is known to defend exclusive territories both on its breeding grounds and in the African winter quarters, and some of the sedentary species probably also defend territories throughout the year. However, some species are known to migrate in small flocks or to flock when feeding at swarms of locusts or temporary concentrations of insects disturbed by brush fires. The calls of Coraciinae consist of loud harsh notes, those of some species being frequently uttered.

The Brachypteraciinae call infrequently, giving low soft notes or chuckling calls. It is unknown whether or not they defend territories. The Long-tailed ground-roller is unusual in being a terrestrial bird of sandy sub-desert country. When alarmed it runs and bounds into scrub where it usually stands quietly with the head and tail raised.

Composition. The Coraciidae includes about 16 species that are generally classified into two subfamilies. The typical subfamily Coraciinae has two genera, *Coracias* with about eight species and *Eurystomus* for which three to five species are recognized by different authorities. The Madagascar ground-rollers of the subfamily Brachypteraciinae are placed in three genera, *Atelornis* with two species, *Brachypteracias* with two, and *Uratelornis* with one. Some authors have regarded the Brachypteraciinae as a separate family, but the modern tendency is to treat it as a subfamily of the Coraciidae.

HOOPOE

The Hoopoe *Upupa epops*, sole member of the Upupidae, is a very distinctive species, noted for its striking appearance – the plumage is cinnamon-pink, the wings boldly patterned with black and white bars – and as a bird of myth and folklore, being used as a hieroglyph in ancient Egypt and featuring in the Greek classical literature. Hoopoes differ from their closest relatives the wood-hoopoes Phoeniculidae in having open, rounded nostrils, the tail shorter than the wing and in lacking a metallic gloss to the plumage. They vary in length from between $10\frac{1}{2}$–12in (26–30cm) and are further characterized by their slender curved bills and the erectile head-crest of black-tipped, pink feathers.

The Hoopoe *Upupa epops* in defensive attitude with wings and tail spread as a hawk passes.

Distribution. Hoopoes are widely distributed in the Old World, breeding in the central and southern portions of the Palaearctic, northwest Africa and throughout the Middle East to India, Ceylon and Mongolia, extending in winter on migration to tropical Africa. They have also been recorded as far north as Spitzbergen. During the breeding season Hoopoes frequent wood borders, parks and orchards; and are often seen in cultivated areas round villages, particularly in Asia. During the winter months they tend to inhabit open bush and low scrub. One of the earliest migrants to return in southern Europe, they arrive from Africa between March and mid-May, with a peak in April. The return migration begins in August, lasting through September and October.

Feeding. The food consists chiefly of insects, particularly larvae, and other small invertebrates such as spiders, earthworms, woodlice and centipedes. These are mainly taken on the ground. In areas around human settlement hoopoes are often seen probing lawns, paths or manure heaps.

Nesting and the Young. Hoopoes mate on the ground, and there is no nuptial display. The nest is usually a hole in a tree or wall, but many other holes are utilized. In treeless areas crevices in rocks are often used. No nest is constructed but the hole is usually filled up with a heap of rags, straws and other rubbish on which the eggs are laid, and only a very narrow entrance is left. Clutches of 5–8, occasionally up to 12, are laid. The eggs vary in colour, being usually white or bluish-white, but sometimes yellowish, pale olive-green, grey or olive-brown, and generally unmarked. They are oval, porous and unglossed and rapidly become nest-stained. Incubation, carried out solely by the female, lasts 16–19 days, the hen bird being fed on the nest by her mate. The young hatch at intervals and are at first brooded by the female and fed by the male. Later both sexes take part in feeding. Fledging takes 20–27 days.

Behaviour. Hoopoes usually occur singly or in pairs, but often come together in small flocks when on migration. They will perch in trees, on buildings and on walls and have occasionally been recorded climbing up the trunks rather in the manner of the woodpeckers. The flight is curiously desultory and butterfly-like, but is in fact much stronger than it appears for the birds can easily evade falcons. They are fond of taking dust and sand baths. The normal call, a soft low *hoop-hoop-hoop* from which the name derives, carries a great distance and is generally heard in the breeding season. There is also a harsh chattering warning call, and a catlike mew.

Hoopoes have a remarkable defensive attitude, which they strike chiefly when threatened by birds of prey. They sit on the ground with wings and tail spread, the wings so extended that their tips almost touch, while the head is thrown back and the bill pointed into the air.

Composition. The Hoopoe *Upupa epops* is the only member of the Upupidae. There are about 6 or 7 subspecies, formerly considered species, but now combined as geographical races. These differ only in minor details of plumage.

WOOD-HOOPOES

Wood-hoopoes, sometimes called tree-hoopoes, are members of an exclusively African family, the Phoeniculidae. Prominent characters include a slender body and a long, wedge-shaped tail composed of 10 feathers; a rounded wing; and a conspicuous, long, decurved bill which is much exaggerated and sickle-shaped in the scimitar-bills, members of the genus *Rhinopomastus*. The plumage is iridescent with metallic blue, green, violet or purple. The juveniles are more blackish. The sexes are alike, but the males have longer bills.

All wood-hoopoes have an offensive body smell that emanates from a rump preen gland, as well as filthy nesting habits.

Distribution. Wood-hoopoes are restricted to Africa south of the Sahara in woodland, bush savanna, acacia and thorn bush country and to certain extent in riverine forest. The Buff-headed wood-hoopoe *Phoeniculus bollei* is a montane forest species living at heights of up to 8,500ft (2,578m). One species, *Rhinopomastus cyanomelas*, is specially dependent on the ant-gall acacia, *Acacia drepanolobium*.

Mostly strictly arboreal, wood-hoopoes are non-migratory residents, though it has been suggested that some may indulge in coastal movement in West Africa.

Feeding. Wood-hoopoes feed mainly on insects and their larvae, primarily beetles, grasshoppers, ants and termites – some species explore flowers and leaf-buds for insects – also berries and small wild fruits. Their short, stout, abruptly curved, acutely tipped claws, assist them in creeping like tree-creepers in any position along tree trunks and branches to probe crevices methodically and meticulously with their long, thin bills. They have the curious habit of dropping vertically down tree-trunks and expertly clinging on again.

Nesting and the Young. Description of courtship behaviour is lacking, but bowing between members of flocks of the Green wood-hoopoe *Phoeniculus purpureus* has been observed. Nests are not constructed, and abandoned nest-holes of woodpeckers and barbets, and natural tree-hollows are utilized. Eggs may be laid on accumulated dead leaves or wood chips. The filth and stench of a nest with its rotting food remains and its droppings, is incredible.

The Hoopoe *Upupa epops* (1) is a ground-feeding bird which uses its bill to root around for insects. Its erratic flight has been likened to the flight of butterflies. (2) Green wood-hoopoe *Phoeniculus purpureus*, (3) Buff-headed wood-hoopoe *P. bollei*, (4) Scimitar-bill *Rhinopomastus cyanomelas*, (5) Forest wood-hoopoe *Scoptelus castaneiceps* and (6) Abyssinian scimitar-bill *Rhinopomastus minor* feeding its young.

Only the female incubates, but is fed by the male. During incubation the long tail becomes considerably frayed.

Egg colouration varies, but consists mostly of shades of blue, olive or grey, sometimes mottled with brown. They soon become nest-stained and dirty. Three to five eggs are laid. Both sexes feed the nestlings, and family feeding of the incubating female and young is common. There is a tendency to community breeding in the Green wood-hoopoe in which several nests are built close together. The incubation period lasts about 18 days, and fledging 3–4 weeks.

Behaviour. Wood-hoopoes are sociable and gregarious, forming noisy flocks consisting of family parties, especially in the Green wood-hoopoe. Members of the genera *Rhinopomastus* and *Scoptelus* are less gregarious and more often occur in pairs or singly.

Wood-hoopoes are noisy while flying, but the voice varies. The Afrikaans word 'kakelaar' (chatterer), describes the exceptionally noisy Green wood-hoopoe, but can be applied to all species which, besides having a raucous cackling call, may also have pleasanter whistling cries. In South Africa, native names liken their weird noisy cries to the piercing shrieks of hysterical women.

Composition. Wood-hoopoes *Phoeniculidae* are most closely related to the Hoopoe (Upupidae), and more distantly to kingfishers, bee-eaters, rollers and hornbills. Phoeniculidae contains three genera – *Phoeniculus*, *Scoptelus* and *Rhinopomastus*.

HORNBILLS

The hornbills form the Old World family, the Bucerotidae, a group of medium-sized to large birds with large, brightly-coloured and often elaborately structured bills. There are two subfamilies: the Bucoracinae which comprises the two mainly terrestrial African ground hornbills *Bucorvus* and the Bucerotinae, which contains rather more than 40 mainly arboreal species.

Hornbills are characterized by a relatively large bill which is usually surmounted by a large decorative casque from which their name is derived. Both bill and casque are often brightly coloured while the bill itself may be ridged and grooved. The casque is sometimes enormous and reaches its extreme development in males of the Black-casqued hornbill *Ceratogymna atrata* of West Africa, the Great hornbill *Buceros bicornis* of India and much of southeast Asia and the Rhinoceros hornbill *B. rhinoceros* of Malaya, Sumatra, Java and Borneo. The casque is very light, being composed of a thin outer covering of horn which is filled with a sponge-like cellular tissue, except in the Helmeted hornbill *Rhinoplax vigil* of Malaya, Sumatra and Borneo which has a solid casque, with the consistency of ivory, red on the outside but golden inside. After being specially processed this is known as hornbill ivory, or *ho-ting* to the Chinese who, in ancient times, valued it more than jade or ivory.

Many hornbills have brightly coloured patches of bare skin on the throat and around the eyes. The most common colours are blue, red and yellow and the colours may differ between the sexes. In addition, the Black-casqued hornbill and the Yellow-casqued hornbill *Ceratogymna elata*, both of West Africa, have bright, cobalt blue neck wattles. Another rather bizarre peculiarity of hornbills is their eyelashes which are long, thick, black and curly. Most species also have a distinct and rather hairy crest. The plumage of hornbills tends to be boldly patterned in black or brown and white. The sexes are usually similar in general appearance, although the casque is often bigger and more brightly coloured in the male.

Hornbills vary greatly in size ranging from the 15in (38cm) long Red-billed dwarf hornbill *Tockus camurus* of West African forests to the turkey-sized ground hornbills of African savannahs and the 4ft (1·2m) Great hornbill of Asian forests. Most species have rather thick tarsi while the toes are broad-soled, the three that point forwards being partially united to form a pad. The two ground hornbills have much longer and thicker tarsi, clearly an adaptation to their terrestrial habits. The flight of the larger species is rather slow and laboured, consisting of a series of wing beats followed by a glide. In the smaller species flight is light and swooping, the tail appearing disproportionately long and cumbersome.

Noisy and conspicuous birds, hornbills produce a great variety of whistling, cackling, grunting and roaring noises. They frequently form flocks and a number of species are known to form communal roosts of up to 100 or more individuals during the non-breeding season. In tropical forests the habit of forming communal roosts seems to be confined to fruit-eating species.

Distribution. Hornbills are distributed almost throughout the Old World tropics: 25 species occur in Africa, although there is none in Madagascar, while the remaining 20 species occur across southern Asia from India through Burma, Thailand, Indo-China, Malaya, the Greater and Lesser Sunda Islands and Celebes to the Philippines and New Guinea, but not Australia. They occupy a variety of habitats ranging from rain-forest to grassland with scattered trees. The presence of at least some trees is essential as hornbills are dependent upon hollow trees for nest sites, although the ground hornbills occasionally make use of holes in cliffs.

Feeding. Hornbills are catholic in their feeding habits. Most species consume fruit when it is available but otherwise eat almost any animal which they can overpower. Even small birds and bats are readily taken, while poisonous animals make up a high proportion of the animal diet of at least a number of the Asian species. A number of hornbills, such as the White-crested hornbill *Tropicranus albocristatus* which lives below the continuous canopy of rain-forest where fruit is scarce, eat little else but insects.

Hornbills are exceedingly dextrous in the way they manipulate objects with the bill. Combined with the length of the bill this is of great importance in dealing with small poisonous animals. Snakes, centipedes and scorpions are caught and held in the very tip of the bill, and repeatedly squeezed along their whole length as they are manipulated backwards and forwards. Free-flying tame Rhinoceros hornbills, Wreathed hornbills *Aceros undulatus* and Black hornbills *Anthracoceros malayanus* will treat any long flexible object, such as a piece of rope, in precisely the same way and also spend much time playing with twigs and leaves, tossing them up in the air, catching them and passing them backwards and forwards in their bills. Such 'play' has also been observed in the wild in several

Four species of hornbill. (1) Rhinoceros hornbill *Buceros rhinoceros*, (2) Giant hornbill *B. bicornis*, (3) Helmeted hornbill *Rhinoplax vigil* and (4) Von der Decken's hornbill *Tockus deckeni*.

species and can probably be regarded as practice for a feeding pattern that demands skill and precision. This ability to manipulate delicately is also related to their fruit-eating behaviour and hornbills are quite capable of peeling the unpalatable outer skin from a fruit using no more than their bills.

Nesting and the Young. The breeding behaviour of hornbills is even more remarkable than their appearance because the females of all species except the ground hornbills are walled into the nest chamber during incubation, presumably as a defence against predators, and are fed by the males. The wall, which blocks the entrance to the nest hole, is built by the female with her own droppings which are viscid at first but harden on exposure to air. In some species the male assists by bringing pellets of clay mixed with saliva. When the wall is completed there remains only a narrow slit just large enough to allow the male to feed the female. The female of Von der Decken's hornbill *Tockus deckeni*, and presumably the females of other *Tockus* species, breaks out of the nest hole when the young are 2–3 weeks old and about half-grown, and thereafter helps the male to feed them. It is particularly remarkable that the young replaster the hole after the female has departed. The young, usually 2–4, are fed on insects which are brought one or two at a time. The females of some species, for example the Silvery-cheeked hornbill *Bycanistes brevis*, remain in the nest until the young fledge.

The female hornbills' long sojourn in the nest raises problems of nest sanitation. This has been solved by her defaecating at high velocity through the narrow entrance slit. It is not clear at what age the young become capable of this performance. Fruit stones are cast out of the nest hole and scavenging insects take care of any remaining refuse. While in the nest the female usually, though not invariably, undergoes a complete moult and may indeed become temporarily flightless although this is no disadvantage in her prison. Only the Ground hornbills, which do not wall up the nest cavity, follow the more normal procedure of moulting after breeding.

Composition. The Bucerotidae is divided into two subfamilies. The Bucoracinae contains the genus *Bucorvus* while the Bucerotinae contains all other genera of the family.

PICIFORMES

Birds in which the feet usually have two toes pointing forwards and two backwards. All have specialized bills and feeding habits

JACAMARS — *Galbulidae*
PUFFBIRDS — *Bucconidae*
BARBETS — *Capitonidae*
HONEY-GUIDES — *Indicatoridae*
TOUCANS — *Ramphastidae*
WOODPECKERS — *Picidae*

JACAMARS

The jacamars are a small, but extremely interesting family (Galbulidae) of birds from the New World tropics. They are related to the puffbirds (Bucconidae), also found in South and Central America. Both families are currently classified in the order Piciformes, along with barbets, toucans, woodpeckers and honey-guides, although they also show many features linking them with

the Coraciiformes. They are beautiful birds, several with brightly iridescent upperparts, long pointed bills, and long tails. Their general shape and appearance are reminiscent of hummingbirds, although they are much larger – from 7–11in (18–28cm) long. The resemblance is heightened by their excitable behaviour. They have short legs and rather weak feet, with two toes directed forwards, and two back; one species, the Three-toed jacamar *Jacamaralcyon tridactyla*, has lost one of the hind toes.

Distribution. The principal region occupied by the family is northern South America. The most widely distributed species is the Rufous-tailed jacamar *Galbula ruficauda*, which extends as far south as northeastern Argentina. In the north, its range includes eastern Panama, and two other species, including the Great jacamar *Jacamerops aurea* – also extend into this area.

Feeding. Jacamars typically feed entirely on flying insects, for which they wait perching until one comes near, when it is deftly seized, sometimes after a swift and agile chase. Their prey includes a large proportion of bees, ants or wasps. Unlike the Old World bee-eaters, which their habits in many ways closely resemble, they seem to have no special procedure for making such prey release their venom before they are eaten; probably they possess some immunity to the effects of the venom. Other frequent prey include large grasshoppers and katydids, dragonflies and butterflies – sometimes the huge blue Morphos butterflies which are such a spectacular feature of South American forests. Another difference from the bee-eaters is that none of the jacamars feed in continuous flight although their aerial sallies are frequent – about one every two or three minutes for much of the day. The most atypical species with regard to feeding habits is the Great jacamar, which frequently takes insects from foliage, and in some respects seems more like a puffbird in habits. It is a bird of forest clearings, as are the small jacamars of the genus *Brachygalba*. Most others feed in more open scrub or forest edges. The Paradise jacamar *Galbula dea* in particular is typical of forest edges, and its feeding perches are often very high in contrast to most other jacamars, which make their sallies from quite low positions.

Nesting and the Young. Jacamars are hole-nesters, choosing for preference a sandy bank in which to excavate a tunnel 1ft–1ft 6in (30–45cm) long. Sometimes cavities in termite nests are used. The species whose nesting habits have been most thoroughly studied is the Rufous-tailed jacamar. It lays from 2–4 white glossy eggs in a widened chamber at the end of the burrow. This is lined by a deposit of insect remains which are regurgitated by the birds and which gradually accumulate. Incubation lasts 20 to 23 days, and is performed by both sexes. The young which hatch are clothed in long white down, and are equipped with heel pads like the young of many other hole-nesting birds. They remain in the nest for 21 to 26 days, and are fed by both parents.

Jacamars are not colonial nesters as are bee-eaters, but in suitable areas nests may be 100yd (91m) or less apart. When not nesting, they may sometimes be seen in small groups, though more usually in pairs. They are excitable birds, and social interactions are usually accompanied by much calling – often a high pitched and far carrying trill.

Composition. Fifteen species of jacamars are currently recognized, though some authorities recognize more. Eight of these are contained within the genus *Galbula*, most members of which resemble the Rufous-tailed jacamar in general appearance, with iridescent green upperparts and more or less rufous on the underparts. An exception is the Paradise jacamar, which has almost

---

Typical of hornbills are the long eyelashes and brilliantly coloured wattles of the African ground hornbill *Bucorvus cafer*. Above, feeding in open savannah, the omnivorous *B. cafer* takes a puff adder.

black upperparts – though with brilliant bronze iridescence – and dull black underparts with a white throat. It is further distinguished by its greatly elongated central tail feathers. *Brachygalba* is a genus of four species, all of them small and rather dull in colouration. The remaining three species are each assigned to a different genus. The Chestnut jacamar *Galbalcyrhynchus leucotis* is a distinctive species from western South America; besides its mainly rufous colouration it is characterized by an exceptionally heavy kingfisher-like bill. The Three-toed jacamar *Jacamaralcyon tridactyla* in addition to having three toes has a dark, dull colouration with a distinctive streaked crown. The Great jacamar *Jacamerops aurea* resembles species of *Galbula* in colouration, but is much larger, with a relatively shorter, more robust bill.

Some aspects of the Rufous-tailed jacamar *Galbula ruficauda* showing (1) the long, slender bill for seizing insects; (2) the small foot, with two toes pointing forwards and two backwards, which facilitates balance and grip when perching; (3) a male offering an insect to a female in courtship and (4) a female emerging from the nest burrow in a bank.

Four species of jacamar. (1) Great jacamar *Jacamerops aurea*, (2) Paradise jacamar *Galbula dea*, (3) Rufous-tailed jacamar *G. ruficauda* and (4) White-throated jacamar *Brachygalba albogularis*. The Rufous-tailed jacamar is also seen waiting for its prey (5). When a flying insect appears, the bird darts out to seize it (6), returning to the perch to enjoy its meal.

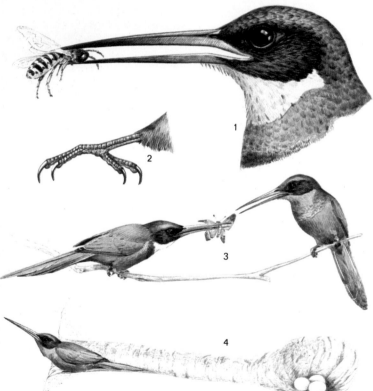

life. They spend much of their time sitting quietly on some vantage point – not, as a rule, very high up – and from this they make short flights at infrequent intervals to seize food. This may be a large insect, or occasionally perhaps a small frog or lizard, captured from neighbouring foliage or from the ground. Aerial captures are also made, especially in species of the genus *Monasa*, the nunbirds. One puffbird, the Swallow-wing *Chelidoptera tenebrosa*, has become entirely dependent on aerial prey. It perches on exposed branches in fairly open country, and from these makes regular aerial sorties to capture small insects, of which ants form a large part. Some extended flights last up to a minute. Species of the genus *Nonnula*, the nunlets, are small puffbirds which seem to be more active than most of the family, moving about through foliage in somewhat warbler-like fashion.

Nesting and the Young. Like jacamars, puffbirds are hole-nesters, either excavating in the ground, or making cavities in termite nests. Ground nests, in the few species which have been studied, generally slope downwards from an entrance sited in level or slightly shelving ground. The White-whiskered softwing *Malacoptila panamensis*

Four species of puffbird. (1) White-eared puffbird *Nystalus chacuru*, (2) Pied puffbird *Notharchus tectus*, (3) White-fronted nunbird *Monasa morphoeus* and (4) Swallow-wing *Chelidoptera tenebrosa*.

PUFFBIRDS

The Puffbirds are a tropical New World family (Bucconidae), related to the jacamars. This relationship is clearly shown by their many common anatomical features, yet in external appearance they are very different. Most puffbirds are solid-looking, chunky birds with shorter bills and tails than jacamars. They lack iridescent plumage, and are clad either in browns and buffs, or in pied plumage. They are more sluggish in their habits, and most of them are much less given to vocalization. The Bucconidae is a larger family than the Galbulidae (the jacamars), and contains 32 species which show more variety of form and habit.

Distribution. Puffbirds are found in the lowlands of South America, from southern Mexico in the north, to Paraguay in the south. They are most common in the Amazon basin.

Feeding. Typical puffbirds resemble some of the forest-dwelling Old World kingfishers of the genus *Halcyon* in their shape and way of

and White-fronted nunbird *Monasa morphoeus* surround the entrance of the burrow with sticks, reducing its conspicuousness. There is no trace of freshly dug earth to give away the location of the nest. In the Black-fronted nunbird *Monasa atra* nests are built with a complete tunnel of sticks running along the surface of the ground to the entrance of the burrow. The Swallow-wing, on the other hand, places no camouflage around the mouth of the burrow.

The parents share the duties of excavation, incubation and feeding the young. Two or three white eggs are laid, and the young, when hatched, soon learn to make their way up to near the tunnel entrance. This may be a considerable distance – 20in (50cm) in the White-whiskered softwing, about 40in (100cm) in the nunbirds and up to 80in (200cm) in the Swallow-wing. The young retire to the chamber at night, and in at least one species, screen themselves off with dead leaves taken from the nest lining.

Behaviour. Puffbirds are not colonial, but at least one species exhibits a quite distinct form of social behaviour in its breeding biology. This is the White-fronted nunbird, a bird which is in any case commonly seen in parties of up to six. It appears that the young are commonly fed by other individuals in addition to their true

(1) Swallow-wing *Chelidoptera tenebrosa* with a nest in a vertical burrow. As soon as they are able, the chicks will climb up to the top to take food from the parent. (2) Collared puffbird *Bucco capensis* hunting an insect.

parents – a form of behaviour seen in, for example, some New World jays. Nunbirds are also among the most vociferous of puffbirds – generally a quiet group. They have a wide vocabulary of cackling calls, some of which are uttered in a coordinated chorus by the members of a party.

Composition. The family is divided into 10 genera, which fall roughly into four groups. The largest of these, consisting of the genera *Notharcus*, *Bucco*, *Nystalus*, *Hypnelus* and *Malacoptila*, includes 20 species of medium or medium to large birds, with heavy bills and short tails. The monklets and nunlets, *Micromonacha* and *Nonnula*, consist of six small species with more slender bills, and in the case of the nunlets, tails of normal length. The nunbirds *Hapaloptila* and *Monasa* consist of five species of medium size with long tails and bright red or yellow bills. Finally, the distinctive Swallow-wing *Chelidoptera* stands apart, both because of its appearance and habits. It is a small species with short bill and tail, and relatively long and broad wings.

BARBETS

Barbets (the Capitonidae) are generally strongly-built, thick-set birds with rather large heads and stout sharply-tipped bills and may perhaps be considered as intermediate between woodpeckers and

rollers. The name barbet comes from the distinctive 'beard' of feathers and bristles around the base of the bill. The legs are comparatively short, and the feet are zydactylic – having two toes pointing forward and two back – and so are well adapted for clinging to trees; when doing this barbets often use their tails as supports, although the feathers are not stiffened for the purpose. Although the Asiatic barbets are heavy, clumsy birds, some of the smaller species are very agile: for example the Red-headed barbet *Eubucco bourcieri* of South America may frequently be seen probing and boring into rotten wood while hanging head downwards. The wings are rather short and rounded and flight, although rapid, is not usually sustained for long distances and appears to be somewhat weak. On the ground the birds progress by means of rather clumsy hops.

Most of the barbets are brightly coloured, some of the Asiatic and South American species being among the most beautifully plumaged of all birds. In these green predominates, with red, blue and yellow markings around the head. In African barbets black, yellow and red predominate, with a greater tendency towards spotting and barring than is found in species from Asia and South America. Although some South American species are sexually dimorphic, the sexes of those from Africa and Asia are not easily identifiable by plumage. There are, however, curious exceptions to this: for example, the Asian genus *Megalaima*, in which the sexes are generally alike, has one species, the Gaudy barbet *Megalaima mystacophanes*, in which male and female are very dissimilar, while the African genus *Trachyphonus* has also just one easily-sexable species, the Red-and-yellow barbet *Trachyphonus erythrocephalus*.

Distribution. Barbets are mainly birds of tropical forests and are

Five species of barbet. (1) Double-toothed barbet *Lybius bidentatus*, (2) Red-and-yellow barbet *Trachyphonus erythrocephalus*, (3) Red-fronted tinkerbird *Pogoniulus pusillus*, (4) Many-coloured barbet *Megalaima rafflesi*, (5) female Red-headed barbet *Eubucco bourcieri* and (6) the male.

Barbets have strong bills for tearing fruit and crushing hard berries. (1) Toucan barbet *Semnornis ramphastinus*, (2) Fire-tufted barbet *Psilopogon pyrolophus* and (3) Naked-faced barbet *Gymnobucco calvus* with zydactilic foot – two toes pointing backwards and two forwards, giving the bird an unusually firm grip.

found in Central and South America, Africa and in most of Asia as far east as the Philippines and Indonesia. Some of the African species have adapted themselves to live in drier savannah country and are thus more likely to be seen on or near the ground than the typical forest barbets, which rarely descend from their tree-top habitat. As a family they are non-migratory, usually moving only in search of food, tending especially to follow the seasonal fruiting of wild figs.

Feeding. Barbets feed chiefly on fruits, berries and buds, although most species include a certain amount of live food – principally insects – in their diet and many rear their young mainly on insects; the larger species occasionally take young birds, mice and lizards. The African ground barbets are, with the possible exception of one of the South American species, the most insectivorous of all and are reputed to eat large numbers of termites. Some species work over the bark of trees like woodpeckers and bore into rotten wood in search of insects. Although most indigestible matter such as insect wings and legs and vertebrate remains are regurgitated as pellets, the skins and seeds of grapes, berries and other fruit are passed in the faeces.

Fruit eating barbets are very wasteful feeders, plucking and rejecting many of the berries and small fruits which they attack, while they so persistently shake their heads and wipe their bills to rid themselves of pieces of fruit which adhere to them that more seems to be cast away than is swallowed.

Nesting and the Young. Barbets usually excavate their own nest holes in rotten trees, termites' mounds, sand or earth banks, or euphorbia stems. D'Arnaud's barbet *Trachyphonus darnaudii* bores a tunnel almost vertically downwards into level ground, swinging horizontally at the bottom to form a nest-chamber. The Pied barbet *Lybius leucomelas* appears to be the only species which, in the absence of suitable trees, frequently takes over the deserted nests of other birds, such as swallows and martins.

In most cases there is little formal courtship apart from the chasing of the female by the male, although in the ground barbets the male struts and postures around the female with his erectile crown feathers raised.

No nest material is used, the 2–5 white eggs resting on the bottom of the nest-hole. Incubation and rearing is by both parents, food being carried to the young in the bill except in the case of a few of the smaller species, such as the Red-fronted barbet *Tricholaecua diadematum*, which regurgitate semi-digested food deep into the throats of the nestlings.

The young remain in the nest for an unusually long time and emerge well-developed and, in most cases, able to fly well, although they continue to demand food from their parents long after they appear well able to fend for themselves. Red-and-yellow barbets not only tend to remain in family parties but have been recorded as raising a family by communal effort. More than two adult birds have been seen to carry food into a nest-hole and ringing has shown that the young of a first brood will assist in rearing a second, and even that a precocious young male will attempt to mate with his mother prior to the laying of the second clutch of eggs.

Behaviour. Except as mentioned above, most barbets live singly or in pairs, although some of the smaller species may, out of the breeding season, be seen hunting in the tree tops in parties, sometimes in the company of other birds. Little seems to be known about their territorial requirements, although it is noteworthy that in captivity some barbets are extremely pugnacious towards other members of either sex of their own species except when nesting.

Most barbets can hardly be described as possessing a song in the usual sense of the word, uttering instead oft-repeated single or a short series of very monotonous notes, in many cases quite unmusical and resembling honks, chirps or the tapping of a hammer on a hollow object. In some species the males make a very rapid version of the *poo-poo-poo* of the Hoopoe *Upupa epops*. An especially interesting exception is the East African Red-and-yellow barbet, which is one of the best-known avian duettists. A pair of birds, usually sitting close together, will simultaneously burst into loud (though not altogether unmusical) songs, composed of different notes and not necessarily in the same tempi but which rhythmically synchronise so well that it is difficult to tell which bird is producing which notes. Although usually described as a duet, it is sometimes a chorus of the combined efforts of a family party.

Composition. Barbets are usually divided into 13 genera and 76 species, although it has been suggested that some – such as the Pied barbet and the Red-fronted barbet from Africa – are con-specific and some authorities claim only 72 species. There is a wide range in size – from about $3\frac{1}{2}$in (8·9cm) in the tiny African 'tinker barbets' of the genus *Pogoniulus* to 13in (33cm) or more in the larger members of the Asiatic genus *Megalaima*. Despite the fact that the former are agile, energetic little birds with superficially slight resemblance in habit or external form to the heavy, sluggish and rather clumsy members of the latter, the grouping of the various genera into one family is more than a matter of convenience. Even the East African ground barbets of the genus *Trachyphonus*, which are slim, rather long-tailed and long-legged birds with many passerine characteristics, are clearly correctly classified as barbets.

HONEY-GUIDES

The Indicatoridae is a distinctive family of small birds found in the Old World tropics. They appear to be most closely related to the toucans, but have quite distinctive characteristics of their own. For one thing, they are brood parasites which are as much adapted to that end as are cuckoos. Indeed, of the six bird families that contain brood parasites, the Indicatoridae is the only one that is, so far as it is known, wholly parasitic. Another characteristic is that honey-guides eat wax, a habit unique among birds, and assuming that they can assimilate it, they must also have unique digestive enzymes. The family names, both common and scientific, derive from the extraordinary habit of two species of guiding mammals to bees' nests which, when broken open, provide honey on which the birds feed.

Honey-guides of the principal genus *Indicator* are robust birds weighing 1–2oz (28–56gm) with thick skins that may provide protection against bee stings. They have drab brown or olive-green and whitish plumage, a strongly graduated tail with more or less white in the outer feathers; and a short, blunt conical beak. Like woodpeckers, honey-guides' legs are short and strong and the feet are zygodactylous (with toes pointing forwards and backwards) with strongly curved claws. The two species of *Prodotiscus* are warbler-like, and while being parasitic and wax-eating, are set apart from the other honey-guides by their small size and thin beaks.

Distribution. The Orange-rumped and Malaysian honey-guides *Indicator xanthonotus* and *I. archipelagicus* inhabit southern Asia; the other species are all African, mostly inhabiting lowland rain forest. The Dwarf honey-guide *I. pumilio* is a highland forest bird, and a few species are found in the wooded savannas of Africa. None is known to migrate.

Feeding. The honey-guides of the genus *Indicator* feed on a variety of insects and have a predilection for bees, while the species of *Prodotiscus* eat mainly smaller, soft-bodied arthropods. But each also eats wax, the former as a constituent of bees' honeycombs and the latter as scale insects (bugs of the family Coccidae), which secrete a thick white waxy substance over their bodies). Black-throated and Lessers honey-guides, *Indicator indicator* and *I. minor*, are so fond of wax that they have been said to enter churches to peck the candles; and certainly a piece of honeycomb lodged in a tree will quickly attract both species. Both these birds, and probably most members of the genus *Indicator*, feed avidly upon honey bees *Apis mellifera* and their products: larvae, pupae and wax comb. But only Black-throated honey-guides and another woodland species, the scarce Scaly-throated honey-guide *I. variegatus*, have the guiding

habit. If a bird finds a bees' nest and then comes across a person or a Honey-badger *Mellivora capensis*, it begins a loud attention-demanding chattering, accompanied by short restless flights from bough to bough. Gradually the mammal will be led to the bees' nest, which may be as much as ½mi (0·8km) away. By the nest the bird abruptly ceases chattering, and sits quietly while the nest is broken apart (the Honey-badger is a major predator of bees' nests). Afterwards the honey-guide forages the remains.

Nesting and the Young. All honey-guide species whose eggs have been discovered are brood parasites. Black-throated honey-guides lay their egg (or eggs – the clutch size is not known; but never more than one egg is found in a host's clutch) in the clutches of hole-nesting birds. Woodpeckers, barbets, hoopoes and bee-eaters are important hosts; they all lay white subspherical eggs, from which the honey-guide's egg is exceedingly difficult to distinguish. There is evidence that the female honey-guide pips some eggs in the host's clutch, preventing their development. The newly hatched honey-guide chick is naked, pink and blind and closely resembles the host's chicks, save that the honey-guide's beak has strongly angled and needle-sharp tips which cross each other. This organ is put to use when the young honey-guide repeatedly bites any of the host's chicks that hatch. The victims quickly die of multiple lacerations, leaving the honey-guide to grow rapidly in the absence of competition for food. Red-throated bee-eaters *Merops bulocki* are a common host, and the insistent food-soliciting call of a young

Young of the Lesser honey-guide *Indicator minor* being fed by a Red-throated bee-eater *Merops bulocki*. Honey-guides parasitize hole-nesting birds and in the first few weeks of life have sharp, hooked bill-tips for killing the young of the host.

honey-guide sounds like the begging call of not one, but two bee-eater chicks: a powerful stimulus for the fosterers. The incubation period is the same as that of the bee-eaters (21 days, assuming that incubation does not begin in the oviduct before the egg is laid, as is the case in some cuckoos); but the nestling period is longer, 38–40 days, during which time the honey-guide grows to a fledging weight of 1·6–1·8oz (47–53gm), which is twice its host's adult weight. By three weeks of age the beak needles become blunted.

Behaviour. Most honey-guides are quiet and inconspicuous, but the commonest African species, the Black-throated honey-guide, has a loud, far-carrying song, the repeated disyllable *whit-gurr* that is heard throughout the year. It is essentially a courtship call, and is usually given from a special singing site that is used year after year, apparently by a succession of males. On attracting a female, the male's courtship includes a wide ranging flight with short dives that produce a bleating noise in the fanned tail feathers. The comparable courtship of the Lyre-tailed honey-guide *Melichneutes robustus* consists of aerial display with steep dives above the forest canopy, when an extraordinary loud booming rattle is produced by the curiously curved and graduated tail feathers.

(1) Black-throated honey-guide *Indicator indicator*, (2) Cassin's honey-guide *Prodotiscus insignis*, (3) Orange-rumped honey-guide *Indicator xanthonotus* and (4) Lyre-tailed honey-guide *Melichneutes robustus*.

Composition. Four genera are usually recognized. *Indicator* has nine species in Africa and two more in Asia. The Lyre-tailed honey-guide *Melichneutes robustus* has a similar plumage and form and (so far as known) habits; generic separation is warranted only by the tail shape. Cassin's and Wahlberg's honey-guides *Prodotiscus insignis* and *P. regulus* are small, olive green birds resembling warblers in their delicate build and their thin, insectivorous beaks. Structural characters show the rare Zenker's honey-guide *Melignomon zenkeri* to be closer to *Prodotiscus* than to *Indicator*; like them, it has a thin beak and feeds on scale insects rather than bees. The family is a single natural assemblage, as shown by the common possession of brood parasitism, wax eating, and – uniquely among flying birds – only nine primary feathers in the wing.

TOUCANS

Toucans (family Ramphastidae) are among the few tropical birds that are widely known to non-ornithologists, but surprisingly little is known of many aspects of their biology. They vary from about 12–24in (30·5–61cm) in length and are distinguished by their very large, laterally compressed bills. The bill is relatively larger in the larger species and often brightly coloured. The wings are short and rounded, the tail rather long and varying from rounded to graduated at the tip, and the legs are short and strong with the toes arranged in the zygodactyl pattern (two toes forward, two back).

The plumage is soft and lax, most species having a patch of bare skin around the eye and lores (the region between the eyes and the bill). The plumage is brightly coloured in most species, being black above with combinations of white, orange, red or yellow on the underparts in the genus *Ramphastos*, and predominantly green or greenish with bright markings of yellow, blue, orange or red in most species of the other genera.

The sexes are alike in colouration and size in most species, although the females are duller than males in a few of the small araçaris, species of the genus *Pteroglossus*. Immatures resemble the adults in colouration, or are slightly duller.

The large bill, which is commonly brightly coloured with contrasting shades of green, yellow, red or blue, apparently serves various functions. Its length enables distant fruit to be plucked with ease and its colouring serves to intimidate potential predators and to intimidate small birds while their nests are being robbed.

Distribution. The Ramphastidae is confined to the Neotropical zoogeographical region. The overall range extends from Vera Cruz in Mexico, southwards through Central America to almost all of South America south to southern Brazil, Paraguay and northern Argentina.

Most Toucans are forest birds, although a few also inhabit scrub and patches of trees in savanna regions. Several species are confined to forests at high elevations, up to around 9,000ft (3,000m) in places, or to humid tropical forests of the lowlands. Most of the lowland species are sedentary except for local roaming in search of food. Some of the toucanets living in mountain forests are thought to make altitudinal movements at certain seasons.

Behaviour. Most Toucans are gregarious, occurring in small flocks that roam together through the treetops in search of the varied diet of fruit, insects, bird's eggs and many other foods. The flight of the smaller species is swift and direct, but larger forms alternate bursts of flapping with glides, producing an undulating flight path.

Toucans lack elaborate songs and usually only give rather harsh calls. These include monotonous croaking and yelping notes, gull-like mewing sounds, sharp rattling bursts and high, sharp notes. Some larger toucans of the genus *Ramphastos* give more musical series of calls at dusk which may function as songs.

Toucans are neo-tropical fruit-eating birds with heavy bills.(1) Toco toucan *Ramphastos toco*, Spot-billed toucanet *Selenidera maculirostris* and (3) Green aracari *Pteroglossus viridis*.

Araçaris and probably other toucans roost throughout the year in holes in trees, often old woodpecker holes. Each flock has a number of such dormitories, into which several adults crowd with their tails folded over their backs to save space.

Toucans nest in holes in trees, using natural holes or woodpecker holes, and often enlarging the cavity by removing soft, rotten wood. The holes chosen are commonly very high above the ground, although low holes may be used for lack of alternatives. The nest cavity is unlined, except for regurgitated seeds which soon accumulate and an occasional green leaf carried in as if for decoration.

Clutches are of 2–4 white eggs which are incubated by both parents. The incubation period has been recorded as 16 days in a small toucanet, but is probably longer in the large toucans. The young are naked when hatched and have thickened heel pads. They are fed by both parents and fledge after around 40–50 days in the nest.

Composition. The Ramphastidae includes about 42 species which are usually classified in five or six genera. The genus *Andigena* has four species which inhabit montane forests and are known as mountain toucans; *Aulacorhynchus* has seven species known as toucanets; *Baillonius* a single species of uncertain affinities; *Pteroglossus* 14 species known as araçaris; *Ramphastos* about 11 large species of toucan, and *Selenidera* five small species of toucanet.

WOODPECKERS

Woodpeckers are birds specialized for digging prey out of wood or from in or under the bark of trees. They vary in size from 6–22in (15–56cm) and exhibit considerable variation in plumage. Some species are soberly coloured in greens, browns and greys, sometimes patterned with spots or bars, a few showing extensive yellow or red colouring, and a large number are boldly patterned in black and white, the last being barred, spotted or with large contrasting areas of black or white. Many species have signal patches of red or yellow on the head, rump or upper tail coverts; and a number possess a short crest. Woodpeckers are highly adapted to their tree-climbing and wood-boring life style. They cling to trees by means of strong claws, with second and third toes directed forward, the fourth out to the side and the first, or smallest toe, below. The first toe is lacking in the Three-toed woodpecker *Picoides tridactylus* and in some other species of the genera *Picoides*, *Dinopium* and *Sasia*. Stiff tail feathers or rectrices also support them against vertical surfaces. Woodpeckers have straight, powerful bills that grow continuously against their being worn down.

But perhaps the most remarkable feature of these birds is the long protrusible tongue. This is supported by hyoid bones so long that they extend around the back of the skull, then over to the base of the bill. Further extensions, depending on species, may circle the right orbit or go to the end of the hollow inside the upper mandible. The hyoids are attached to muscles that enable woodpeckers to dart their tongues in and out with great rapidity. Species that feed on ants, such as the Green woodpecker *Picus viridis* and the Common flicker *Colaptes auratus* can extend their tongues for 2in (5cm) beyond the bill. The tongues of these two have small barbs at the tip and are coated with a sticky saliva. Tongues of other species have sharp, horny tips for spearing wood-boring larvae and those of the sapsuckers have brush-like tips for taking sap.

Distribution. Woodpeckers are found in the wooded areas of all continents and large islands with the exception of Australia, and of Greenland, Madagascar, New Guinea and New Zealand. Some, such as the Common flicker of North America and the Green woodpecker of Europe, although nesting in trees, spend much of their time on the ground. This latter habit is developed most extensively in the Ground woodpecker *Geocolaptes olivaceous* of

South Africa, the Andean flicker *Colaptes rupicola* and the Campos flicker *C. campestris* of the South American pampas. All of these species live in treeless areas and both nest and feed on (or in) the ground.

Most woodpeckers live in the same areas the year around, with only three species undertaking annual migrations. These are the Wryneck *Jynx torquilla* of Eurasia that migrates to tropical India and Africa; the Common flicker to the southern portions of its breeding range and the Yellow-bellied sapsucker *Sphyrapicus varius* from breeding grounds in Canada and the northern USA, to the south as far as the West Indies and Panama. For some reason female sapsuckers go farther south in winter than the males. Red-headed woodpeckers *Melanerpes erythrocephalus* and Lewis woodpeckers *Asyndesmus lewis* are opportunists, migrating irregularly to areas where mast is abundant in the fall.

Feeding. Woodpeckers show considerable diversity in feeding. The pied woodpeckers of Europe and the Hairy woodpecker *Dendro-*

The long tongue of the Green woodpecker *Picus viridis* has an adhesive tip and is used for extracting ants and their larvae from deep inside ants' nests.

copos villosus of North America are adept at extracting wood-boring larvae. In contrast, the Black woodpecker *Dryocopus martius* lives mainly on wood-tunnelling ants. Wrynecks with bills too weak for digging into wood, use their tongues to glean prey from trees and other surfaces. Some woodpeckers that breed in open country are expert flycatchers, for example, the American Lewis woodpecker with its specially rounded wings, can fly after many successive insects before returning to its perch. Some species also feed on sap. Although this habit is best developed in the true sapsuckers it is also developed in the American Acorn woodpecker *Melanerpes formicivorus* and the European Great spotted woodpeckers *Dendrocopos major*.

Nesting and the Young. The courtship of woodpeckers varies among species. Head-swinging; slow, exaggerated flights; abortive copulations, and exchanges of low notes can all be involved, with many of these activities centring on a prospective nest site. Males and females of many species register attachment to these sites by a slow, rhythmic form of drumming or tapping. Members of pairs of Red-bellied woodpeckers *Centurus carolinus* perform this drumming together. These and the related Red-headed woodpeckers engage in reverse mounting in which the female mounts the male before he mounts her. Bill-touching is a form of courtship seen among Crimson-crested woodpeckers *Campephilus melanoleucos*. Both sexes of woodpeckers excavate the nest cavity with males doing the larger share of the work. While some species use dead,

When the Great spotted woodpecker *Dendrocopos major* feeds on seeds of pine cones, it first makes a hole and wedges the cone into it. It is then able to keep the cone steady and extract the seeds.

decaying stubs others, such as the Hairy woodpeckers and the Red-cockaded woodpeckers *Dendrocopos borealis* prefer to excavate in living trees whose centres have decayed. The latter dig their holes in pines, circling the trunk above and below the nest with gashes that promote a heavy flow of sticky pine gum. This sheet of pitch, extending from 3ft (1m) above and below the hole prevents attacks by tree-climbing snakes. Among other unusual nests are those of the Indian Rufous woodpecker *Micropterus brachyurus* that carves its nest in the papier-maché-like nests of arboreal ants *Crematogaster*. Although they bite quite viciously, these ants do not, remarkably, disturb the incubating bird or the nestling.

Clutches vary from 3–5 entirely white eggs. Incubation is extremely short, taking from 12–17 days. Both parents take turns in incubating as well as in feeding the young. Feeding methods vary between species. Great spotted woodpeckers carry food in their bills, flying to the nest many times in an hour. The Black woodpecker and the flickers, and other long-tongued ant-eating species feed by regurgitation, coming to the nest only at relatively long intervals of 40 minutes to 2 hours. Nestling woodpeckers excrete faeces in tough membranous sacs which facilitate their removal by the parent birds. This means that woodpecker nests are generally kept clean, at least until within a few days of fledging. Adult wrynecks are unusual among woodpeckers in making a snake-like distraction display in defence of their young.

As the nestlings grow they climb the walls of the nest cavity. Fighting may then take place as the one occupying the hole, and hence being the first to be fed, strikes down at the others. The young leave the nest within 3½–4 weeks. In all species of woodpeckers, it is the male that spends the night on the nest. Juvenile woodpeckers follow their parents for from 2 weeks to 2 months and longer.

Behaviour. Woodpeckers exhibit territorial behaviour by fighting with rivals along common borders early in the breeding season. By the time of nesting, defence becomes limited to the vicinity of the nest hole. Woodpeckers that store food in the fall defend the areas where their stores are kept against intruders, which mostly belong to other species. This behaviour is seen in Red-headed, Acorn and Great spotted woodpeckers. Acorn woodpeckers are highly social, living in groups of 4–8 or more individuals throughout the year. All of the members defend the territory, harvest acorns and care for the young. Although differing in ecology, Red-cockaded woodpeckers also live in groups based on nest and roost trees that are used year after year. Golden-naped woodpeckers *Tripsurus chrysauchen* lead their young, after fledging, back to the nest hole which the entire family then uses as a communal roost. Drumming in woodpeckers takes, to some extent, the place of song in other birds. It is used, among other things, in the defence and advertisement of territory. Woodpeckers also utter loud, harsh notes that carry for considerable distances and are sometimes rapidly repeated to produce 'laughing' calls.

Composition. The Picidae is divided into three subfamilies. Of these the Picinae or true woodpeckers consist of 33 genera with 179 species. The Junginae or wrynecks have soft plumage, which is grey, brown and black in colour. There is one genus with two species, one in Eurasia and one in Africa. They lack the stiff tail feathers which aid climbing in true woodpeckers, but have the same type of undulating flight as do the piculets Picuminiae. These are tiny birds, some under 3in (8cm) and the largest 5in (13cm) long. They are olive, green, or brown in colour, with lighter underparts. Piculets are divided into four genera, having 25 species in the American tropics, 3 in Southeast Asia, and one in Africa.

Six species of woodpecker. (1) Ivory-billed woodpecker *Campephilus principalis*, (2) Wryneck *Jynx torquilla*, (3) Arrowhead piculet *Picumnus minutissimus*, (4) Red-headed woodpecker *Melanerpes erythrocephalus*, (5) White woodpecker *Leuconerpes candidus* and (6) Great spotted woodpecker *Dendrocopos major*.

PASSERIFORMES

An order containing more than a third of all living families and over half the living bird species. The passerines are the so-called perching birds and have feet adapted to cling to branches, reeds or even man-made objects such as telephone wires, in such a way that the grip automatically tightens when the bird falls backwards. Passerines include all those birds noted for their ability to sing, and are sometimes called the 'song birds' as a result.

BROADBILLS – *Eurylaimidae*
WOODCREEPERS – *Dendrocolaptidae*
OVENBIRDS – *Furnariidae*
ANTBIRDS – *Formicariidae*
ANTPIPITS – *Conopophagidae*
TAPACULOS – *Rhinocryptidae*
COTINGAS – *Cotingidae*
MANAKINS – *Pipridae*
TYRANT FLYCATCHERS – *Tyrannidae*
SHARPBILLS – *Oxyruncidae*
PLANTCUTTERS – *Phytotomidae*
PITTAS – *Pittidae*
NEW ZEALAND WRENS – *Acanthisittidae*
ASITYS – *Philepittidae*
LYREBIRDS – *Menuridae*
SCRUB-BIRDS – *Atrichornithidae*
LARKS – *Alaudidae*
SWALLOWS – *Hirundinidae*
WAGTAILS AND PIPITS – *Motacillidae*
CATERPILLAR BIRDS -- *Campephagidae*
BULBULS – *Pycnonotidae*
FAIRY BLUEBIRDS AND LEAFBIRDS – *Irenidae*
SHRIKES – *Laniidae*
VANGAS – *Vangidae*
WAXWINGS – *Bombycillidae*

PALMCHAT – *Dulidae*
DIPPERS – *Cinclidae*
WRENS – *Troglodytidae*
MOCKINGBIRDS AND THRASHERS – *Mimidae*
HEDGE SPARROWS – *Prunellidae*
THRUSHES – *Turdidae*
BABBLERS – *Timaliidae*
OLD WORLD WARBLERS – *Sylviidae*
AUSTRALIAN WREN WARBLERS – *Maluridae*
OLD WORLD FLYCATCHERS – *Muscicapidae*
PENDULINE TITS – *Remizidae*
LONG-TAILED TITS – *Aegithalidae*
TITMICE – *Paridae*
NUTHATCHES – *Sittidae*
AUSTRALIAN TREECREEPERS – *Climacteridae*
TYPICAL CREEPERS – *Certhiidae*
FLOWER PECKERS – *Dicaeidae*
SUNBIRDS – *Nectariniidae*
WHITE-EYES – *Zosteropidae*
AUSTRALIAN CHATS – *Epthianuridae*
AUSTRALIAN HONEYEATERS – *Meliphagidae*
BUNTINGS AND AMERICAN SPARROWS – *Emberizidae*
AMERICAN WOOD WARBLERS – *Parulidae*
HAWAIIAN HONEYCREEPERS – *Drepaniidae*
VIREOS – *Vireonidae*
AMERICAN BLACKBIRDS AND ORIOLES – *Icteridae*
CHAFFINCHES AND LINNETS – *Fringillidae*
WAXBILLS – *Estrildidae*
TYPICAL WEAVERS – *Ploceidae*
STARLINGS – *Sturnidae*
OLD WORLD ORIOLES – *Oriolidae*
DRONGOS – *Dicruridae*
WATTLEBIRDS – *Callaeidae*
MUDNEST-BUILDERS – *Grallinidae*
WOOD-SWALLOWS – *Artamidae*
BELL-MAGPIES – *Cracticidae*
BOWERBIRDS – *Ptilonorhynchidae*
BIRDS OF PARADISE – *Paradisaeidae*
CROWS, JAYS AND MAGPIES – *Corvidae*

BROADBILLS

The broadbills form a small but extremely attractive group, the Eurylaimidae, of Old World suboscine passerines. As their name suggests, the bill in most species is broad and heavy. Early classifiers usually placed these birds with the Old World flycatchers Muscicapidae; indeed, it was not until well into the present century that the African species were recognized as broadbills. With the discovery that they had a primitive syrinx and a primitive condition of the tendons of the feet, broadbills were placed with the families of suboscines rather than with the more specialized oscine songbirds. They are now generally considered to be the most primitive living group of passerines and are most probably relics of an ancient larger and more widespread assemblage. Although the family appears to be a natural one, the genera are rather diverse and not particularly closely related. Once accorded their own suborder, members of the Eurylaimidae have been shown in fact to differ little from other primitive suboscines such as the cotingas Cotingidae of the New World, to which they may be distantly related.

In size, the broadbills range from small to medium-large (5–11in (12·7–30cm)). Bill width is usually great, although in the green broadbills *Calyptomena*, the bill is not of such abnormal proportions. In contrast, that of the Dusky broadbill *Corydon sumatranus* is the widest and most grotesque of any of the Passeriformes, having almost the appearance of the bill of a frogmouth Podargidae. The legs are short, the feet normally developed, with the third and fourth toes fused for over half their length. The tail varies from quite short, as in Grauer's broadbill *Pseudocalyptomena graueri*, to long and graduated in the Long-tailed broadbill *Psarisomus dalhousiae*, with the remaining forms falling somewhere in between. Colouration is variable. The Dusky broadbill is predominantly dull black; the species of *Smithornis* are brownish and streaked; and the remaining species exhibit a beautiful array of colours including deep maroon, yellow, blue and dazzling green. The sexes are alike in the four genera containing the Dusky, Long-tailed, Grauer's, and the Black-and-red broadbill *Cymbirhynchus macrorhynchus*. In the females of the green broadbills the feathers are duller both in colour and gloss. In the Wattled broadbill *Eurylaimus steerei* the male is purplish below, where the female is white. In the Banded broadbill *E. javanicus* and the Black-and-yellow broadbill *E. ochromalus*, the males have a complete breast band, lacking in the females, whereas in the Collared broadbill *Serilophus lunatus* the reverse is true, the females of most races possessing a silvery crescent on the breast which is absent in the males. In two of the species of *Smithornis* the crown of the males is black and in the females it is grey or brown. In *Smithornis* and the Dusky broadbill there are patches of white or orange display feathers concealed in the back.

Broadbills are usually described as lethargic, tame, almost stupid birds, often not even responding to the sound of a gun shot. Some are solitary and sit still for long periods; others, like the Long-tailed broadbill, move about actively in small flocks, sometimes climbing parrotlike up small vines.

Distribution. The Eurylaimidae are confined to forests of the Old World tropics. They are most numerous in southeast Asia, from Indochina and Malaya south to Borneo and Java, with one species in the Philippines and two ranging into India and Nepal. The three

The hanging nest with the side entrance is typical of broadbills. Shown here are the male (1) and female (2) of the Green broadbill *Calyptomena viridis* and (3) the same species displaying the large gape which gives broadbills their common name.

Five species of broadbill. (1) Dusky broadbill *Corydon sumatranus,* (2) Long-tailed broadbill *Psarisomus dalhousiae,* (3) Green broadbill *Calyptomena viridis,* (4) female Collared broadbill *Serilophus lunatus,* (5) and (6) female and male Black-and-yellow broadbills *Eurylaimus ochromalus.*

species of *Smithornis* and Grauer's broadbill are found in Africa south of the Sahara.

Several species have very restricted ranges. Whitehead's broadbill *Calyptomena whiteheadi* and Hose's broadbill *C. hosei* are found only on a few mountains in Borneo. Grauer's broadbill, which was not discovered until 1908 and for a long time was known from a single specimen only, is confined to a narrow belt of montane forest about 150mi (240km) long, in central Africa. None of the broadbills is migratory, but some undergo seasonal local movements. They are forest birds, being found in dense undergrowth as well as in treetops, and seem to prefer the proximity of water.

Feeding. The diet consists mainly of insects gleaned from leaves and branches. Some species catch insects in flight. Beetles, cicadas, caterpillars, grasshoppers, mantises, ants, spiders, snails and even tree frogs have been recorded in their diet. Seeds, fruits, and buds are also taken.

Nesting and the Young. Displays and courtship behaviour are poorly known. The males of the Red-sided broadbill *Smithornis rufolateralis* perform a short circular flight, covering about a foot from their perch. During this flight a toadlike croaking is made with the primaries. The function of this display is not known. Both sexes of the African broadbill *S. capensis* are said to perform similar displays. Nests are built low down, usually over a stream. These are attached to a single pendent vine and are large, bulky, pear-shaped structures of leaves, roots, stems, and grass, often decorated with spider webs. The nests have been described as looking like a mass of debris left after a flood. The entrance is on the side, usually with an overhanging porch. The clutch size is 2–3 in most species, 4–8 in the Long-tailed and Collared broadbills. The eggs are immaculate creamy white in *Smithornis* and *Calyptomena* and speckled, sometimes intensely, with chestnut, brown, or purple in the other genera. Both sexes partake in nest building and incubation. In the Dusky broadbills several individuals may share in building the nest.

Vocalizations vary considerably within the family. The Long-tailed broadbill gives a shrill whistling call and goes about in noisy flocks. Other broadbills are commonly silent but a variety of coos, jay-like notes, hoarse grumbles, grinding noises, wheezes, cicada-like churring, liquid bubbling and ringing sounds, or repeated unmelodic notes have been attributed to the various species.

Composition. There are 14 species of broadbills, divided into 8 genera, 5 of which contain one species only. The genus *Calyptomena* has at times been placed in its own subfamily, but seems no more distinctive than some of the other genera. Several internal features suggest that *Smithornis* is the most advanced genus of the family. The Wattled broadbill *Eurylaimus steerei* is restricted to the Philippines and is unique in possessing a ring of fleshy wattles about the eyes, for which it was once separated in its own genus *Sarcophanops*. The species of the two African genera *Smithornis* and *Pseudocalyptomena* are the smallest in size but do not appear to be closely related. The three species of *Calyptomena* are distinct in having peculiar tufts of feathers enveloping the bill, somewhat in the manner of a cock-of-the-rock *Rupicola* (Cotingidae).

Black-and-red broadbill *Cymbirhynchus macrorhynchus*, shown here feeding on caterpillars.

WOODCREEPERS

Woodcreepers or woodhewers are climbing relatives of the ovenbird family (Furnariidae), and so closely related to them that some ornithologists regard them both as members of a single family. Long outer toes and thickened tail-feather shafts, climbing adaptations of woodcreepers, differentiate them from ovenbirds.

Woodcreepers vary in length from 5·5–14in (14–36cm), and look like enlarged versions of the Brown creeper *Certhia familiaris* of northern latitudes. They are brown with russet overtones, especially on the wings and tail; many are streaked with buff or white or

Six species of woodcreeper showing bills adapted in various ways for capturing insects in trees. (1) Red-billed scythebill *Campylorhamphus trochilirostris*, (2) Strong-billed woodcreeper *Xiphocolaptes promeropirhynchus*, (3) Straight-billed woodcreeper *Xiphorhynchus picus*, (4) Olivaceous woodcreeper *Sittasomus griseicapillus*. Below are (5) Barred woodcreeper *Dendrocolaptes certhia* and (6) Wedge-billed woodcreeper *Glyphorhynchus spirurus*.

barred with black; one species is almost white underneath. Males are coloured like females, but at times are slightly larger or longer-winged. Unlike clambering ovenbirds, which normally keep their tails slightly off the trunks, woodcreepers usually perch vertically with the spines at the tips of their tails resting on the trunks.

Woodcreepers display striking variation of bill shape, from short and wedge-tipped in the Wedge-billed woodcreeper *Glyphorynchus spirurus* to a long sword in the Long-billed woodcreeper *Nasica longirostris* and thin scimitars up to 3in (8cm) long in the Scythebill *Campylorhamphus falcularius*. Bills are usually dark, but those of some are red, while those of Long-billed woodcreepers and a few others are yellowish. Their feet are generally dark, short but strong with long and strong toes and claws. The eyes are usually medium-sized and reddish-brown, and the wings moderately long and pointed. The flight is fast and direct or downward, sometimes with brief periods of gliding or hurtling.

Distribution. Woodcreepers live in the shade or edges of tropical forests and woodlands from northern Mexico to central Argentina on the mainland of South America, and on the islands of Trinidad and Tobago. None reach Chile or the Antilles. They are most numerous in moderately wet forests of lowland regions where up to 15 species occur together in some areas; fewer species occur in montane habitats, wet or dry forests, and toward the edges of the geographic range. Narrow-billed woodcreepers *Lepidocolaptes angustirostris* are said to migrate to the Buenos Aires region during summer.

Scythebill *Campylorhamphus falcularius* extracting a larva from a dead trunk (1), flying off with the larva (2) and depositing it in its own nest (3).

Feeding. Many woodcreepers climb up trees in mixed-species forest flocks and peck insects off trunks and limbs, especially under and near lianes, epiphytes, or crevices. Some woodcreepers, such as the Plain-brown woodcreeper *Dendrocincla fuliginosa*, sally out like flycatchers to distant leaves or trunks. Scythebills probe deep in crevices. Red-billed woodcreepers *Hylexetastes perrotii* dig in debris or wasp nests, and several other large-billed species dig in logs or other material on or near the ground. Foods range from arthropods to frogs and even small snakes. Most woodcreepers follow swarms of army ants at times, and a few species regularly feed on these insects.

Nesting and the Young. Some woodcreepers, such as the Plain-brown woodcreeper, pair only for copulation, and chasing is the main courtship activity. Others, such as the Barred woodcreeper *Dendrocolaptes certhia*, form long-lasting pair bonds in which the male becomes ruff-headed and flees as if terrified when his mate comes near. Females of the first group care for eggs and young alone, while pairs do so in the second group. The breeding seasons are short and one brood per year is the rule. Nests are in natural cavities of tree trunks, woodpecker holes, hollow fence posts and the like and are barely lined with a few bits of leaves or strands. One to three white eggs are laid. Incubation lasted 15 days in one record of a Streak-headed woodcreeper *Lepidocolaptes souleyetii*, and the nestling period for it and a few other species is 19–24 days. The young emerge short-tailed but well feathered, and are soon indistinguishable from their parents except in having blacker bills and in making begging squeaks. Young are fed occasionally for up to 5 months, but remain with adults until the next breeding season only in a few species, such as the large and dominant Red-billed woodcreeper.

Behaviour. In many species pairs or family groups hold territories and eject trespassers. In Plain-brown woodcreepers, mature females

hold separate areas while adult males separately maintain their own overlapping mosaic; there are many wandering birds that do not maintain a territory. Pair-forming woodcreepers sing loudly, producing sounds from weird whistles to rather rough descending or ascending trills, as if announcing territories; they often sing at dawn or dusk. In many species, singing seems to function as a means of communication to mates or young. Woodcreepers have loud alarm calls but utter few other notes; when in danger they more commonly duck behind tree trunks or flee.

Composition. There are some 47 species in at most 13 genera. The family is closely related to the ovenbirds, the Furnariidae, with which it shares anatomical features such as partially joined front toes.

OVENBIRDS

The ovenbirds (Furnariidae) are one of the largest and most important families of passerine birds of the New World. Their common name refers to the fact that members of this family build well constructed domed nests of clay or reinforced mud, shaped outwardly like an old-fashioned baker's oven. By definition, all members of this family breed in a closed nest or within a cavity, although this behaviour has become modified in one species. The North American *Seiurus aurocapillus* is also called 'ovenbird' in English because it builds a dome-shaped nest of plant material on the ground, shaped somewhat like an oven, but this bird is a wood warbler of the family Parulidae which is quite unrelated to the Furnariidae.

Ovenbirds are usually small and unpretentious in appearance and their wing length, which is a good index of general size, normally varies between about $2\frac{2}{5}$–$3\frac{1}{2}$in (6–9cm). They are occasionally

(1) Rufous ovenbird *Furnarius rufus*, (2) White-cheeked spinetail *Schoeniophylax phryganophila*, (3) Des Murs's spinetail *Sylviorthorhynchus desmursii*, (4) Firewood-gatherer *Anumbius annumbi*, (5) Striated earthcreeper *Upucerthia serrana* and (6) Plain xenops *Xenops minutus*.

characterized, and dismissed, as merely a large assemblage of 'small brown birds' but, in fact, they probably constitute the most diverse of all bird families. Despite their undeniable interest, no comprehensive account of the family has been published to date. They are difficult to study, mainly because they consist of a large number of species. Moreover, the family continues to be enlarged at a good rate; new species became known only in 1969 and 1971 and, since then, distinct new forms have been discovered which may or may not represent separate species.

Distribution. The Furnariidae is found throughout South America. Members have spread to Coiba Island off Panama, Trinidad and Tobago, and to the small islands of the Cape Horn Archipelago at

(1) Plain xenops *Xenops minutus* digging a nest hole in a bank. (2) Rufous-fronted thornbird *Phacellodomus rufifrons* constructing a large communal nest of thorny twigs in which each pair has a separate nest cavity.

the extreme tip of the continent, but not far from the continent with the exception of the Falkland (or Malvinas) Islands, and Masafuera Island in the Juan Fernandez Archipelago, respectively about 250 and 466mi (400 and 750km) off the mainland. Ovenbirds occupy all the niches that South America can provide for a land bird, from the absolute desert on the coast of Peru and Chile, to swamps, streams, grasslands, wooded steppe, gallery or any sort of forest, to the high puna and paramos of the Andes, or from sea level to a height of well over 16,400ft (5,000m).

The ovenbirds have invaded every possible habitat and adapted themselves to each so successfully that many have become very similar in appearance to, and behave in the same way as, unrelated groups which normally fill the habitat concerned in other parts of the world. There are ovenbird 'equivalents' of chats, wheatears, and other thrushes, pipits, dippers, crested larks, wagtails, long-tailed tits, some true tits, North American marsh wrens and thrashers, some Old World warblers, treecreepers and nuthatches. In all cases the family or group mentioned is not represented at all in South America, or only very marginally so, and their niche is filled by the ovenbirds, often to an astonishingly perfect degree of convergence.

Feeding. Almost all ovenbirds are insectivorous, but the types of insects taken are extremely varied as is indicated by the variety of habitats colonized. Some species of *Cinclodes* are unique amongst passerines in that they obtain their food from a marine habitat.

Nesting and the Young. The ovenbirds breed in a closed nest which can be located at the end of underground burrows, in a cavity, or built of clay or of sticks, twigs, or plant material above the ground.

The nests of a large number of species are still unknown but, with a single exception, all the species for which it is known adhere to the closed pattern. The burrow or cavity is sometimes dug by the ovenbird itself, or is adapted from, for instance, a hole excavated by a woodpecker, a burrow dug by a small rodent or another bird, or caused by decay of a branch or root. The 'typical' ovenbirds (*Furnarius*) build 'ovens' of clay or reinforced mud above the ground, but in the other birds which build above ground, the nest is constructed of sticks, twigs, or other plant material such as moss and lichens and is usually very well constructed, often very elaborate and bulky. So much variation exists that it is not possible to do justice to this subject in an article of this length, but one must stress that the ovenbirds are the most inveterate nest builders of all birds and among the most skillful. Most species have very long breeding periods which may last as much as nine months or more, during which they keep working on the nest, remodelling, adding or subtracting, no doubt 'improving' it until it becomes a real

Rufous ovenbird *Furnarius rufus* transporting lumps of mud with which to construct its nest (1) and duetting perched on the completed nest (2). Inset is a horizontal cross-section of the nest showing the entrance tunnel and the nesting cavity. The nest's resemblance to a primitive native oven gives the group its name of ovenbird.

monument out of all proportion to the generally modest size of the architect. In the case of the cachalotes, members of the genus *Pseudoseisura* of Argentine, a nest is built which is roughly spherical, and which may attain a diameter of 5ft (1·5m) and is constructed of stout sticks with an elaborate entrance gallery. As much as 70lb (32kg) of sticks and twigs have been recovered from such nests which are so strongly made that W. H. Hudson reported standing and stamping on the top of the nest 'without injuring it in the least'.

The nests of the cachalotes and of other genera of ovenbirds are a conspicuous feature of the more open regions of South America. They usually survive the winter intact and are often adapted for nesting by other birds, or as a source of construction material for other ovenbirds which also construct large nests of sticks and twigs. Two general rules concerning the nest of the Furnariidae can be made. One, with no proved exception, is that the nest is not used again by the same pair for two consecutive breeding cycles, no matter how elaborate, perfectly preserved, or conveniently situated it may be. The other rule, to which important exceptions exist, is that all the species of the same genus build the same type of nest in the same location.

The only species in which the normal habit of breeding in a burrow, cavity, or closed nest has been modified is *Spartonoica maluroides* which inhabits beds of reeds and rushes in southeastern Brazil, Uruguay, and Argentina. The author of this article has pursued its study and all the nests known so far vary in structure, from more or less open platforms, sometimes with one side built up and raised above the eggs, to spherical nests that are nearly closed, but with an opening at the top abnormally wide for a so-called closed nest.

Composition. The ovenbirds are conveniently divided into three subfamilies: Furnariinae, Synallaxinae, and Philydorinae. The Furnariinae include the true ovenbirds of the genus *Furnarius* and four other genera of dull and rather coarse birds that are all terrestrial, and in which the nest is normally situated underground, at the end of a burrow or in another suitable location, such as a crevice among rocks. The Synallaxinae form the largest group with 17 genera. They vary a great deal but are all arboreal and nest above the ground in a nest which is usually elaborate, and often bulky, and normally constructed of twigs and other material. The largest genus is *Synallaxis* with 37 species, inappropriately called 'spinetails' for, in spite of their name, their tails are not spiny. The Philydorinae include 12 genera; they are nearly all forest birds which search the foliage for food, or hunt through the litter on the floor of the forest; the majority nest in holes in trees or underground.

ANTBIRDS

The Formicariidae is the eleventh largest family of birds in the world, and includes a wide variety of birds, from warblerlike 'antwrens' or larger 'antshrikes' which live in the tree canopy and other foliage, to walking 'antthrushes' and hopping bob-tailed 'antpittas' which live on the ground in tropical forests and scrublands of the New World. Antbirds vary in size from 3–14in (8–36cm). Their bills are moderately thick and long, hooked at the tips, with notches on their edges that help hold and cut prey. Only two species of 'bushbirds' have flattened bills, one for slitting stems of bananalike plants. Their eyes are usually reddish, becoming bright red in 'fire-eyes' and some others, and are surrounded by bare skin which is bright blue, green, or red in a few species such as 'bare-eyes', and which forms an eyespot design that may be useful in scaring competitors or predators. Colour patterns are often striking and usually composed of brown, black, white, or shades of

The distinctive silky white feathers of the crest and beard of the White-fronted antbird *Pithys albifrons* stand out a little from the head when the bird is in repose (1), but stream back when in flight (2). Antbirds are so called because they often rely on army ants to do their hunting for them, preying on the small creatures which flee in panic from the ants' path (3).

yellowish to greenish brown. Males and females generally differ in plumage, except in antthrushes and antpittas. The body plumage is usually loose, becoming plushlike and dense only on the foreheads of fire-eyes. Many species have buff or white patches on the centre of the back which are exposed mainly during disputes. The oddest plumage is that of White-fronted antbird *Pithys albifrons* which, because of their white crests and beards, appear like small arrows in flight. The wings are moderately long but very rounded, an adaptation for life amongst vegetation, and the feet are long, especially in ground-foraging species, with strong to moderately strong claws and toes. The tails are rounded, rarely pointed, and are seldom longer than the wings.

Distribution. Antbirds are preeminently birds of lowland tropical forests of Central and South America, and 30 to 40 species live together in many places in the Amazon valley. Numbers of species decrease rapidly as one moves into swamps, up mountains into cooler zones, or out into open and dry zones. None reach beyond the Andes into Chile, beyond La Plata in Argentina, or beyond northeastern Mexico. Only two species are restricted to Central America; others that occur there occur also in South America. None have reached Caribbean or Pacific islands unless those islands were connected to the mainland at one time; and there are often different species on opposite banks of a large river in Amazonia.

Feeding. Antbirds rarely eat ants, and only one in eight species (27 species in 12 genera) actively follows ants. However, many, if not all, species casually follow army ants. Both active and casual followers capture insects, frogs, lizards, and other small animals flushed by these ants, which are mainly two carnivorous species (*Eciton burchelli* and *Labidus praedator*) that hunt in wide swarms on the forest floor or in grass or other shade. Antbirds pay little attention to other ants, even to species of army ants that do not flush prey.

Where several species of antbirds occur together, there is always a peck order in which larger species dominate small ones. The largest species occupies the centre of the swarm, the next occupies the zone around it, and the next smallest occupies the far margins or wanders above. Large birds enforce this arrangement, and do so because more insects are flushed the closer one approaches the swarm centre.

The many antbirds that rarely follow ants capture arthropods and small vertebrates from the forest canopy to the forest floor. Commonly in Amazonia one finds one or two species of antwren in the canopy, another in the midlevels, yet another somewhat above head height, and a final species or two near the ground.

Antbirds often join other insectivorous species in the famous mixed-species flocks of the tropics, where up to 50 species move about together. Usually the birds forage very diversely, and only a few alert species gain when other species flush flying prey. The main reason for assemblage seems to be that birds are safer from hawk or snake attack when together – the alert species give the alarm for species that forage intently. Members of mixed-species flocks generally differ from members of ant-following flocks.

Nesting and the Young. Antbirds pair for life, and remain together until the death of one mate; divorces are rare. Courtship feeding, a juicy insect taken to the female by the male, commonly takes place. Nests are composed of leaves or strands, and occur as cups in forks of twigs or in small crotches, and occasionally in tree cavities or on the ground; some ground nests are oven-shaped. Both the male and female birds build the nest.

Three species of antbirds. (1) Great antshrike *Taraba major*. The plumage of the male, seen here on the left, is characteristically darker than that of the female. The ornamental white feathers on the head of the White-fronted antbird *Pithys albifrons* (2) are unusual for this family, unlike the inconspicuous markings of the Ocellated antbird *Phaenostictus mcleannani* (3).

The strikingly-marked male Barred antshrike *Thamnophilus doliatus* perches right up against the nest while the female feeds their young. This task, like nest-building and incubation, is shared equally by both of them.

Unusually stocky antbirds are the Chestnut-crowned antpitta *Grallaria ruficapilla* (1) and the Wing-banded antbird *Myrmornis torquata* (2).

Two, or sometimes three eggs, are laid two days apart, and incubation is by male and female and lasts for about 14 days. They are usually white, heavily to sparsely marked with purple or other dark spots; antthrush eggs are white. The young stay in the nests for 9–15 days, and fly poorly when they leave. Both the male and female brood and feed their young but, as in incubation, only the female stays on the nest at night. As in all forest birds, there is a high mortality of nests due to predators – reaching 90 or 95% loss in Panama, where up to 10 or 13 nestings may be attempted by a single pair in one year and only one or two succeed. Loss rates are lower in the Amazon, where nesting rates are lower and breeding more sporadic.

In some antbirds a few young stay with their parents for several months; and Ocellated antbirds *Phaenostictus mcleannani* form clans, in which young males bring back mates and associate loosely with their parents for several years.

Behaviour. Commonly antbirds are territorial and live as separate pairs. They sing back and forth across their boundaries or in disputes – series of deep whistles are the rule – and display back patches, spread tails or wings or bodies, and chase trespassers. In several ant-following species the local territorial pair allows other pairs to stay, but dominates them. Disputes are accompanied by harsh sounds and end in songs.

Alarmed antbirds flick their tails upward or pound them downwards, according to the species. Arboreal species commonly flick the wings. Harsh *chirr* notes or rattles are used in mobbing a human or other mammal, and sharp chipping notes are produced

Black-spotted bare-eye *Phlegopsis nigromaculata* feeding off an insect flushed by a column of army ants (1), in flight (2) and poised with open beak to seize another meal (3).

when fleeing a hawk.

Composition. Some 237 species are recognized and 53 genera, when one includes antthrushes (9 species, 2 genera), gnateaters (8 species, one genus) and antpittas (38 species, 5 genera).

ANTPIPITS

Little is known about the Conopophagidae, a South American family of 10 or 11 small, sombre plumaged, sedentary species commonly known as antpipits. There are two genera, *Conopophaga* and *Corythopis*. The antpipits in the genus *Conopophaga*, sometimes known as 'gnateaters', are rather rounded, long-legged birds with short necks, tails and wings. They are not unlike small pittas (Pittidae) in general shape, and it is interesting to find a parallel similarity in habits, for the antpipits also spend most of their time on the ground, particularly where there is leaf litter, scratching with their large feet in search of food. They range in

Two species of the retiring and rarely-observed antpipit family. (1) Black-cheeked antpipit *Conopophaga melanops* and (2) Silvery-tufted antpipit *Conopophaga lineata*.

length from about 4–5½in (10–14cm) but as with the pittas, length is a somewhat deceptive indication of size because their tails, though it may not be apparent at first sight, are extremely short. The plumage, generally loose-textured and soft, is quite long and dense on the lower back. Males of most species sport a short tuft of white feathers which form a streak running back from the eye. There is usually quite marked sexual dimorphism. The Black-bellied antpipit *Conopophaga melanogaster*, is one of the more striking species, the male having a black head and underparts, chestnut back, wings and tail and a white stripe behind the eye; the female being mainly grey and brown though the back and wings resemble those of the male.

The two species in the genus *Corythopis* are more like pipits of the genus *Anthus* in the family Motacillidae in general shape, having longer tails than *Conopophaga*. The Ringed antpipit *Corythopis torquata* is dark reddish brown above and white below with a broad belt of black streaks on the breast which merge at the front to form a continuous band. The Southern antpipit *C. delalandi* is very similar but its upperparts are somewhat lighter in colour and tinged with olive.

Distribution. The antpipits are strictly Neotropical. Members of the genus *Conopophaga* are mainly of tropical and subtropical distribution and in only three or four species do ranges overlap. The Chestnut crowned antpipit *C. castaneiceps* is confined to the dense rain forests on the Andean slopes of Colombia, eastern Ecuador and northeast Peru while the Slaty antpipit *C. ardesiaca* occurs in similar terrain further south in Bolivia and southeastern Peru. The Ashy-throated antpipit *C. peruviana* occurs to the east of the Andes at low altitudes in eastern Ecuador and Peru and extreme western Brazil. The Chestnut belted antpipit *C. aurita* also occurs here and in Bolivia but its range extends northeastwards to the Atlantic coast of the Guianas. The remaining species are chiefly or entirely of Brazilian occurrence.

Both species of *Corythopis* also have distinct ranges, the Ringed antpipit being found throughout most of tropical South America, except the northwest, whereas the Southern antpipit ranges from eastern Bolivia, Paraguay and northeast Argentina eastwards to the coast.

The male, upright, and incubating female of the Black-bellied antpipit *Conopophaga melanogaster*. The nest is in a hollow on the ground.

Behaviour. Though occupying different habitats, all species frequent low level vegetation and spend much time on the ground. Insects and other small invertebrates are believed to be the staple diet. Knowledge of breeding biology seems to be restricted mainly to nest structure and eggs. The bowl-shaped nest is usually placed near the ground and the normal clutch consists of two creamy eggs, speckled or streaked with pink or brown.

A number of species have harsh hissing calls but simple whistles are also recorded.

When excited, tapaculos move their tails into an upright position. (1) Ocellated tapaculo *Acropternis orthonyx*, (2) Grey gallito *Rhinocrypta lanceolata*, (3) Black-throated huet-huet *Pteroptochos tarnii* and (4) Silvery-fronted tapaculo *Scytalopus argentifrons*.

Composition. The Conopophagidae, currently divided into two genera, *Conopophaga* and *Corythopis*, clearly requires further study. The eight or nine *Conopophaga* species appear to be fairly uniform but their relationship within the suborder Tyranni is tentative. Taxonomists may consider certain structural characters sufficiently important to warrant separate family rank. Recent work suggests that the two *Corythopis* species may belong in the family Tyrannidae.

TAPACULOS

The Rhinocryptidae is a small Central and South American family including a variety of drably-coloured birds, bearing a superficial resemblance to wrens, but being most closely related to the ovenbirds Furnariidae and antbirds Formicariidae. They differ from these in having a large movable flap over the nostrils, whence the scientific name of the family is derived. Another anatomical peculiarity is the presence of four notches on the back edge of the sternum (metasternum).

Tapaculos vary in length from $4\frac{1}{2}$–10in (11–25cm). All species have plump, compact bodies, relatively small rounded wings and large and strong legs and feet associated with terrestrial habits. The tail varies from short (as in the genus *Scytalopus*) to strikingly long (in the genera *Merulaxis* and *Psilorhamphus*), but is always soft, so that it is not very helpful for steering in flight. The bill is sharply pointed and varies from small and slender in small species to rather stout and heavy. In the Ocellated tapaculo *Acropternis orthonyx* the culmen or dorsal ridge of the upper mandible is flat.

Distribution. A few species are found in Central America in Costa Rica and Panama, but the family reaches its greatest diversity in South America, where several species coexist at numerous localities. Most tapaculos are forest and woodland birds, occurring from humid lowland forests to scrub high on mountains. A few live in scrub and brush in more open country or even tall grassland or among reeds. No member of the family is known to be a migrant, but many species are little known so that local movements may have passed unnoticed. Chile is particularly rich in tapaculos, with eight species.

Feeding. Tapaculos are all skulking birds and inhabit areas of thick vegetation. They live mainly on the ground and walk rather than hop. Some species have been described as 'creeping about like mice' on the ground, and most can run at great speed, when the long-tailed species usually hold the tail erect. Insects, including larvae, form the bulk of the diet, but seeds and spiders have also been found in the stomachs of collected specimens.

Three species of tapaculo. (1) Chucao tapaculo *Scelorchilus rubecula* entering its ground-nest. (2) Grey gallito *Rhinocrypta lanceolata*, running. Tapaculos are weak fliers, and usually run rather than fly from danger. (3) Black-throated huet-huet *Pteroptochos tarnii* nesting in a tree-trunk.

Nesting and the Young. Nest sites of tapaculos vary from genus to genus, although the nests of many species have not yet been discovered. The Black-throated huet-huet *Pteroptochos tarnii* and other species nest in hollow tree trunks up to several feet above the ground or in holes in the ground. The White-throated tapaculo *Scelorchilus albicollis* and Chucao tapaculo *S. rubecula* both excavate their own nest holes in the ground. These hole-nesting species build a cup-shaped or domed nest of varied plant materials such as moss and dry grass.

The Ochre-flanked tapaculo *Eugralla paradoxa* builds a ball-shaped nest of grass, moss and twigs in a thicket about three feet above the ground. The adult birds enter and leave through a small hole in the side of the nest. The White-breasted babbler or White-breasted tapaculo *Scytalopus indigoticus* builds a similar ball-shaped nest on the ground amid dense vegetation.

All tapaculos whose nests are known lay clutches of 2–4 relatively large eggs. They are uniformly white, but often become stained in the nest so as to appear blotched or spotted. Both parents share in incubation, but the incubation period is not known. The young are helpless when hatched and covered with scanty down. They are fed by both parents on food carried to the nest in the bill.

Behaviour. Most if not all tapaculos are as easily heard as they are difficult to see. In most species the song consists of repeated, monotonous calls. These are rather harsh in tapaculos of the genus *Scytalopus*, but distinctly musical in *Pteroptochos* and a few other genera. Both sexes sing in at least a few species, and the singing bird is often difficult to locate because of its 'ventriloquistic' voice. The Slaty bristlefront *Merulaxis ater* sings a strikingly musical ascending or descending scale, and the White-throated tapaculo gives a loud, whistled *tee-kettle-ettle-ettle-ettle* song. The alarm calls of tapaculos are short and monosyllabic.

Composition. The Rhinocryptidae contains 26–27 species that are currently placed in 12 genera, six of which have only a single species. *Scytalopus* with 12 species is much the largest genus. The genus *Psilorhamphus*, with a single species, the so-called Spotted bamboowren *P. guttatus*, was formerly placed in the Muscicapidae.

COTINGAS

The cotingas are arboreal perching birds of the New World, so heterogeneous, in size, general appearance and structural characters that there is no general agreement as to the proper limits of the family. As usually defined, they include the larger frugivorous members of the Tyranni, as well as a variety of smaller species, some of which should perhaps be transferred to the manakins or tyrant-flycatchers. The largest cotinga, the Umbrella-bird *Cephalopterus ornatus*, is the size of a crow, about 19in (48cm) long; the smallest, the Kinglet calyptura *Calyptura cristata*, is only about 3in (7·6cm) long. Most species are 6–10in (15–25cm) long. Body proportions and beak shape vary greatly within the family, but the wings are generally of moderate length, the tail is not usually long, the beak is hooked at the tip (but otherwise very variable in shape), and the legs are generally rather short. In the males of several genera some of the outer flight-feathers are curiously modified. The outstanding character of the family, however, is the development of brilliant plumage and bizarre ornamentation in the males of many species. Deep reds and purples are characteristic colours.

Distribution. The cotingas are essentially tropical in distribution. One species, the Rose-throated becard *Pachyramphus aglaiae*, just crosses the Mexican border into the extreme south of the USA, and a few extend south of the tropics in southern Brazil, Uruguay and Paraguay. Several species occur at subtropical altitudes in the

Bellbirds are highly distinctive in appearance. (1) Bearded bellbird *Procnias averano*, (2) Three-wattled bellbird *Procnias tricarunculata* and (3) Bare-throated bellbird *Procnias nudicollis*.

Andes, one being common in the páramo (temperate moorland) zone at altitudes of over 10,000ft (3,000m). Only one species, the Jamaican becard *Pachyramphus niger*, is found in the Antilles. Most cotingas, as far as is known, are sedentary.

Feeding. Some cotingas eat only fruit, some are entirely insectivorous, and others have a mixed diet of fruit and insects. The specialized frugivores typically pluck fruits in flight and swallow them whole. The most specialized species have short beaks and very wide gapes, which enable them to swallow relatively large fruits. These species depend primarily on the fruits of forest trees belonging to a few families, whose fruits are especially nutritious (most importantly, the Lauraceae, Burseraceae and Araliaceae). Only the pericarp (the outer flesh) of the fruit is digested, the seeds being regurgitated intact.

The larger insectivorous species typically search for their prey by perching motionlessly, scanning the surrounding vegetation, and making an occasional sally to snatch an insect from branch or foliage. The small insectivorous becards, however, forage with active, restless movements more in the manner of warblers, and often accompany the mixed feeding parties of insectivorous birds which move through the forest tree tops. The purple-tufts *Iodopleura* are exceptional in hawking for flying insects from the tree tops.

Courtship. The elaborate and spectacular courtship behaviour of some of the cotingas has attracted a good deal of attention. The Guianan Cock-of-the-rock *Rupicola rupicola* is the most famous.

Four species of cotingas. (1) Capuchinbird (or Calfbird) *Perissocephalus tricolor*, (2) Masked tityra *Tityra semifasciata*, (3) Pompadour cotinga *Xipholena punicea* and (4) Swallow-tailed cotinga *Philabura flavirostris*.

The adult males are almost entirely brilliant golden orange, with a semicircular casque-like crest and long filamentous fringes to the modified secondary flight-feathers. The female is dull earth-brown. The males gather at traditional dancing grounds, where each bird clears a small area, or 'court', on the forest floor. The distance between neighbouring courts may vary from a few feet to 10–15yd (9–14m). For much of the time the males perch in the trees above their courts, but on the arrival of a female they fly down, each to his own court, to crouch on the bare earth with plumage spread and head tilted sideways to display the flattened crest, and there they remain motionless, like brilliant orange flowers, gazing up at the female with the single exposed eye. The females are attracted to the

The Umbrella-bird *Cephalopterus ornatus* showing its umbrella-like crest and its large scarlet air sac. It produces a low-pitched bellowing sound, which has been compared to the bellowing of a bull.

displaying males and visit them on their courts, where mating probably takes place. The final stages of the courtship have, however, not been recorded.

In the bellbirds *Procnias* the males attract females by uttering extraordinarily loud, bell-like or hammer-like calls from tree perches, where the females visit them. In the Bearded bellbird *P. averano*, the species that has been most thoroughly studied, the male uses high calling perches for his general advertising, and in the second phase of courtship attracts the female down to a special 'mating perch' on a small under-storey tree well below the forest canopy. Mating takes place after a ritualized ceremony involving calls and special display movements.

Male Capuchinbirds (or Calfbirds) *Perissocephalus tricolor* gather at traditional display grounds, each bird occupying a length of some more or less horizontal branch near the top of a second-storey tree below the forest canopy. Here they advertise themselves by uttering cow-like lowing calls, accompanied by grotesque posturings. As in all such leks, the males are attracted together but at the same time are intensely aggressive to one another. Overt aggression is largely suppressed as long as each bird keeps to its recognized perch.

Nesting and the Young. The nests of cotingas are very diverse. The tityras *Tityra* nest in holes in trees; the becards *Pachyramphus* build bulky, globular, covered nests, suspending them from

terminal twigs or placing them in high tree forks. The Cock-of-the-rock attaches a bracket-like nest of mud to a vertical cliff-face or cave wall. Other species build open nests in trees. Some of these nests are extremely small for the size of the bird, so that the incubating female appears to be crouching on a perch rather than sitting on a nest. Very small nests of this sort have been recorded in the bellbirds, the pihas *Lipaugus*, and the Pompadour cotinga *Xipholena punicea*. Becards may lay up to four eggs in their covered nests and tityras 2–3 eggs in their tree holes. The Cock-of-the-rock lays a clutch of two. In all species known to build extremely small open nests the clutch consists of a single egg. The eggs as a rule are blotched with dark brown on a whitish or olive-coloured ground. Little is known about the length of the incubation period.

The young, in the few species for which there is information, are more or less thickly covered with down. In the open-nesting species the down probably has a cryptic function as well as protecting the nestling against heat loss. Thus the young Swallow-tailed cotinga *Philabura flavirostris* is covered with down resembling lichen, and the young of the Shrike-like cotinga *Laniisoma elegans* are thickly covered with down resembling a fruiting moss.

Composition. The family Cotingidae contains some 27 genera and 79 species. A high proportion of the genera contain a single species or a small group of closely related species that replace one another geographically. *Pachyramphus*, with 15 species, is the only large genus. No satisfactory subdivisions have beeen proposed for the family. The following are some interesting genera: *Lipaugus*, the pihas, dull-plumaged birds whose extremely loud piercing calls are among the most characteristic sounds of the South American

Three male Guianan cocks-of-the-rock *Rupicola rupicola* on display ground. When a female appears (top left), the males fly down from the trees and display themselves, sometimes tilting their heads so that the crest can be seen sideways.

Cotingas range in size from 3in (7.6cm) to 18in (46cm), while their plumage ranges from inconspicuous browns to a dazzling array of red, purple, orange and white. (1) Kinglet calyptura *Calyptura cristata*, (2) Umbrella-bird *Cephalopterus ornatus*, (3) Peruvian cock-of-the-rock *Rupicola peruviana* and (4) the brilliantly-coloured male and more dowdy female of the Guianan cock-of-the-rock *Rupicola rupicola*.

forests; *Cotinga*, the blue cotingas, specialized frugivores of lowland forest, in which the males are brilliant blue with purple throats; *Xipholena*, the Pompadour cotinga and its allies, in which the males have deep purple or purple-black body plumage with modified laminated feathers, and white wings; *Procnias*, the bellbirds, in which the males are wholly or partly white, with wattles or bare skin on the throat and round the base of the beak; *Cephalopterus*, the umbrella-birds, in which the males have an umbrella-like crest and a large pendent wattle on the breast; and *Rupicola*, the cocks-of-the-rock, in which the males are brilliant golden orange (Guianan species) or intense orange or red (Andean species).

MANAKINS

The manakins are small forest-living birds of the family Pipridae found in the New World tropics. The limits of the family are hard to define, because of the existence of a number of species which link the manakins to the cotingas (Cotingidae) or to the tyrant flycatchers (Tyrannidae). Typical manakins, however, are small, active birds in which the males are brightly coloured with brilliant areas of red, orange, yellow, blue or white, usually on a black background, and the females are more or less uniformly olive-green. They are compact in shape, with short beaks slightly hooked at the tip, and short tails. Manakins fly rapidly, with great manoeuvrability, but on a perch their movements are confined to small quick side-steps or rapid about-turns; they do not hop along a perch or from perch to perch like most small perching birds. In several species some of the flight feathers are modified, with thickened shafts and curiously distorted vanes.

Distribution. Manakins are confined almost entirely to the American tropics. At the northern limit two species reach southern Mexico; at the southern limit a small number of species extend a few degrees south of the equator in southern Brazil, Argentina and Paraguay. One species occurs on islands off the coasts of Panama and Venezuela, two in Trinidad, and one in Tobago. As far as is known, all manakins are sedentary.

Feeding. Manakins feed partly on fruit and partly on insects. Fruits are plucked in flight by rapid sallies from a perch; insects are seized from the vegetation in much the same way. Many of the fruits are taken from shrubs and small trees growing in the lower strata of the forest or along forest edges.

Courtship. The manakins' courtship behaviour is among the most elaborate of any family of birds. Some species display in close groups (leks); in others the males display singly, at a little distance from one another.

The three best known types of courtship display are those shown by the genera *Manacus* (White-bearded manakin and allies), *Pipra* (Golden-headed manakin and allies) and *Chiroxiphia* (blue-backed manakins). In the genus *Manacus* the males display at traditional leks, which may persist in the same place for years. Each male clears for itself a small 'court' on the forest floor, a yard or so across, from which it removes all dead leaves and twigs. To be suitable for display, a court must have two or more small saplings growing round its edge. Neighbouring courts may almost touch one another or may be a few yards apart, and a large lek may contain anything up to 70 courts spread over an area of more than 30yd (say 30m) across.

Manakins of the genus *Pipra* display on high perches up in the trees. Several species have been studied and the details of the performance vary; but all use horizontal perches on which they execute striking movements, such as rapid 'slides' from side to side, lightning about-turns, and very rapid wing movements producing snapping sounds. The most spectacular element in the display is an

The White-bearded manakin *Manacus manacus*.

by the surrounding vegetation. In the Blue-backed manakin *C. pareola* the main advertising displays are always performed jointly by two males. First they utter a series of loud synchronized calls in the trees above the display perch; then they descend to the perch and perform a joint dance.

Two other species, the Long-tailed manakin *C. linearis* and the Lance-tailed manakin *C. lanceolata*, have displays that are very similar to that of the Blue-backed, but in the rather different Blue manakin *C. caudata* it is usual for three males, or sometimes even more, to take part in a 'catherine wheel' dance in front of the female.

The displays of some other species, which have been seen only rarely and not studied in detail, are probably as elaborate as those described above. Species which are very closely related, and in which the females may be almost identical, may show striking differences in the plumage and associated display of the males.

Nesting and the Young. The typical manakins build shallow cup-shaped nests, bound by cobweb and vegetable fibres in a horizontal fork between two lateral twigs or frondlets of a small tree or fern. The cup of the nest is thinly woven of vegetable fibres, rootlets and the like, and there may be a lining of finer materials. The eggs, normally only two, are thickly spotted or blotched with brown on a

extremely rapid flight to the perch with a curved trajectory from a distance of 20 or 30yd (say 18–28m), in the course of which the bird utters a series of loud calls and may make a tearing noise, apparently with the wings, at the lowest point of the trajectory. As the bird alights it may make another loud call accompanied by conspicuous fanning of the wings. As in *Manacus*, all the displays may be carried out in the absence of any female, but they are intensified when a female comes near. The rapid flight to the perch may culminate in the male landing on top of the female, but mating may also follow other display sequences.

The blue-backed manakins of the genus *Chiroxiphia* have a system of courtship which appears to be unique. In this genus the males have a red cap; in three of the species the rest of the head and body is black, with a sky-blue patch on the back, while in the fourth the whole of the body is blue. All four species have a basically similar display. Groups of males display on traditional perches close to the ground. A typical display perch consists of a slightly sloping or arched branch or series of branches usually somewhat concealed

Manakins are noted for their conspicuous colouring and highly developed displays. Opposite are (1) Long-tailed manakin *Chiroxiphia linearis*, (2) Cirrhate manakin *Teleonema filicauda*, (3) Lance-tailed manakin *Chiroxiphia lanceolata*, (4) Golden-headed manakin *Pipra erythrocephala* and (5) Gould's manakin *Manacus vitellinus*. Below, the Yellow-thighed manakin *Pipra mentalis* showing two of the display movements which birds of this genus perform on tree-top perches.

Long-tailed manakin *Chiroxiphia linearis*. The plumage of the male, seen here in flight (1) and in close-up (2), differs markedly from that of the female (3). (4) Typical of the manakin family, the toes of the foot are partially fused.

pale ground colour. Only the female attends the nest; incubation lasts 18 or 19 days, and the fledging period about 14 days. The young are fed on small insects, with an increasing admixture of fruits as they grow bigger.

The Thrush-like manakin *Schiffornis turdinus* builds a very different nest, bulky and deep and made of different materials. For this and other reasons it is likely that it is not closely related to the typical manakins. The nests of other untypical manakins have not been recorded.

327

Composition. The family Pipridae, as currently recognized, consists of 18 genera and 52 species. As mentioned above, it is rather heterogeneous, consisting of several genera of typical manakins, sexually highly dimorphic and with elaborate courtship displays, and a few more or less aberrant genera which perhaps should be excluded from the family. The typical manakins, in addition to those mentioned above, include the genera *Ilicura*, *Antilophia*, *Masius* and *Allocotopterus*. The aberrant genera include *Piprites*, *Chloropipo*, *Xenopipo*, *Schiffornis* and *Sapayoa*. Except for *Piprites*, they agree with the typical manakins in foot structure (the toes are partly united), but little is known of their behaviour and further research may show that some of them should be placed among the tyrant flycatchers Tyrannidae, while *Schiffornis* may need to be transferred to the cotingas Cotingidae.

TYRANT FLYCATCHERS

The large and diverse family Tyrannidae forms one of the largest groups of primitive perching birds classified in the suborder Tyranni of the Passeriformes. Tyrant flycatchers vary from tiny tit-like or warbler-like birds only 3in (8cm) long to large flycatchers 9in (23cm) long, the elongated tail feathers adding several inches to this length in a few species. The wings vary from long and pointed in forms that pursue flying insects to short and rounded in those that glean prey from foliage. The tail is typically of medium length with a square or shallowly forked tip, although it is short in some groups, rather long

Five species of tyrant flycatcher to show the family's diversity. (1) Fork-tailed flycatcher *Muscivora tyrannus*, (2) Great crested flycatcher *Myiarchus crinitus*, (3) Black phoebe *Sayornis nigricans*, (4) Vermilion flycatcher *Pyrocephalus rubinus* and (5) Buff-breasted flycatcher *Empidonax fulvifrons*.

The male Royal flycatcher *Orychorhynchus coronatus* has a brilliantly coloured crest which, when erect, spreads out across its forehead like a fan (1), but which the rest of the time is almost invisible (2).

in others, and very long and deeply forked in a few. The legs and feet are small and weak in the majority of genera, but stronger in a few that live mainly on the ground. The form of the bill is remarkably varied. Species that pursue insects in flight mostly have straight, rather broad bills, often with a slightly hooked tip. A few of these genera have the bill greatly expanded at the sides, paralleling the Old World flycatchers of such genera as *Machaerirhynchus* and *Myiagra*. The small forms that pick insects from foliage tend to have rather slender bills that are upcurved or downcurved in a few species. The groups that catch flying insects, and to a lesser extent others, usually have prominent rictal bristles about the base of the bill.

Some genera are notorious among ornithologists because of the great difficulties in identifying their very similar species. The tropical crested flycatchers of the genus *Myiarchus* and kingbirds of the genus *Tyrannus* include groups of species that are almost identical in size, proportions and colouration, although the voice differs. The identification problems are worst of all with the small flycatchers of the genus *Empidonax*, which has several widespread North American species that are very difficult to distinguish except by their calls. As they call frequently on their breeding grounds the observer should then have few problems in identifying them, but the problems of identifying some individuals on migration seem almost insurmountable.

Distribution. The normal ranges of all Tyrannidae are confined to the New World, although several species have been recorded as storm-blown vagrants to Europe.

A total of 31 species breeds in the United States, some of them ranging north into Canada. Nearly all of them migrate to pass the winter in Central America or the West Indies. In the eastern United States familiar and widespread species include the Eastern kingbird *Tyrannus tyrannus*, Great crested flycatcher *Myiarchus crinitus*, Eastern phoebe *Sayornis phoebe* and Eastern wood pewee *Contopus virens*. The Olive-sided flycatcher *Nuttallornis borealis* and Yellow-bellied flycatcher *Empidonax flaviventris* breed in northern coniferous forests and pass through the southern states on migration, and the similar Acadian flycatcher *Empidonax virescens*, Traill's flycatcher *E. traillii* and Least flycatcher *E. minimus* are all widespread, although only the Acadian flycatcher breeds in the southeastern states. The Grey kingbird *Tyrannus dominicensis* breeds in Florida, although it is more widespread further south.

The western United States has more tyrant flycatchers than the east, familiar species including the Western kingbird *Tyrannus verticalis*, Ash-throated flycatcher *Myiarchus cinerascens*, Black phoebe *Sayornis nigricans*, Say's phoebe *Sayornis saya*, various *Empidonax* and the Western wood pewee *Contopus sordidulus*.

Central America has at least 106 species of Tyrannidae, many of them common and widespread, but others are confined to a few remote highland regions. Whereas most of the North American tyrant flycatchers feed by catching insects in flight, many of the species in Central and South America glean food from twigs and leaves after the manner of a warbler. The West Indies have numerous local representatives of the genera that occur in North America, and many of the northern species occur there as migrants.

The family reaches its greatest numbers and diversity in South America, where there are more than 200 species. Most of the South American species are forest birds living in the tropical and subtropical regions, but others are confined to open country. The temperate regions of the southern part of the continent have about 30 species, including ten of the genus *Muscisaxicola*. Many of these southern species migrate north to avoid the worst part of the southern winter.

Two species of tyrant flycatcher with broad, slightly curved bills adapted to catching insects on the wing. (1) Golden-crowned spadebill *Platyrinchus coronatus* and (2) Boat-billed flycatcher *Megarhynchus pitangua*.

A male Royal flycatcher *Onychorhynchus coronatus* about to seize a dragonfly in midflight.

The range of habitats occupied by the Tyrannidae as a whole is vast. All kinds of forest from northern coniferous scrub through the broadleaved temperate woodlands to tropical rain forest have their characteristic species. Others inhabit open country with bushes, scrubby deserts, or even mountain slopes that are almost devoid of vegetation in the case of some species of *Muscisaxicola*. A few species are associated with waterside habitats, such as the brightly coloured Many-coloured rush-tyrant *Tachuris rubrigastra* which inhabits reed beds from Brazil south to Chile, and the Pied water-tyrant *Fluvicola pica* which occurs near rivers and streams from eastern Panama into tropical South America.

Many of the forms inhabiting southernmost South America are ecologically similar to the wheatears and other chats (Turdidae) of the Old World. For example, the White-fronted ground-tyrant *Muscisaxicola albifrons* breeds in the puna zone of the Andes of Chile and Peru, between 13,000–17,000ft (4,300–5,600m) elevation. It nests in holes under rocks or in cracks in banks and feeds either by hopping about on the ground or by flying down to pounce on insect prey from a prominent perch. Like many wheatears (*Cenanthe*) this species and some other *Muscisaxicola* sing on aerial song flights over their territories.

Feeding. Tyrant flycatchers are predominantly insectivorous birds, although some species also take vertebrate prey and fruit. The kingbirds, phoebes, pewees and others feed mainly by pursuing flying insects spotted from prominent perches, although the larger species often also fly to the ground to catch lizards, frogs or mice, and they sometimes even pursue small birds. A variety of small species feeds by making short flights to pick insect prey from twigs and leaves and others glean prey from the foliage while they hop about actively like warblers. Only a few feed mainly on the ground.

Many species of Tyrannidae are regular participants in the mixed feeding flocks of insectivorous birds that are a conspicuous feature of South American forests.

Nesting and the Young. It is no surprise in view of the great ecological diversity of the Tyrannidae to find that there is great diversity in their nesting habits. The commonest type of nest is an open cup-shaped structure placed in the forking branches of a bush or tree or on a flat branch. Kingbirds build bulky and untidy cup-shaped nests of plant materials, but nests of species of elaenias *Elaenia* are beautifully rounded and recall nests of large hummingbirds. In the genus *Euscarthmus* the nest is an extremely flimsy cup-like structure built of thin stalks. The nests of some phoebes are lined with mud, but most species use hair, feathers or fine plant fibres.

The crested flycatchers *Myiarchus* and Baird's flycatcher *Myiodynastes bairdii* build untidy cup-shaped nests in holes in trees, and species of the genus *Muscisaxicola* build similar nests in old rodent holes or hollows beneath rocks. Ball-shaped structures with an entrance hole at the side are built by members of a number of genera, including *Tolmomyias*, *Pitangus* and *Camptostoma*, and the tiny tody-tyrants *Tachuris* build long hanging masses of plant materials with a concealed nest chamber inside.

Some species of the genera *Tolmomyias* and *Comptostoma* usually nest in bushes or trees where colonial wasps or ants are nesting, presumably because of the protection from predators afforded by the bites or stings of these neighbours.

Most tropical tyrant flycatchers lay clutches of two or three eggs, although some lay four and a few only lay one. As with most perching birds, the clutch-size is larger in species of temperate regions, clutches of 3–5 eggs being normal for most of the North American species and some in southern South America. The majority of the species that have been studied lay one egg daily until the clutch is complete, although species of *Comptostoma* apparently

Flycatchers are highly aggressive towards intruders. Here an Eastern kingbird *Tyrannus tyrannus* (1) drives away the much larger Red-shouldered hawk *Buteo lineatus* (2).

lay at intervals of two days. The eggs are white, cream, buff or pale olive, many species having spots, blotches or irregular patches of brown, black and other dark colours.

Only the female incubates in the majority of species, although the male has been found to help in such duties in a few that have been studied intensively. The incubation period varies from around 14–18 days in most kingbirds, elaenias, pewees and others to as long as 19–23 days in some tropical genera. The reasons for this wide range are unknown. The newly-hatched young are nidicolous and have scanty down on their upperparts. Both parents feed them on food carried to the nest in the bill. The young fledge after periods of 14–24 days in the nest, the nestling period tending to be longer in hole-nesters and large species and shorter in small species that build open nests. The young receive food from their parents for at least a short time after fledging in most if not all genera.

Behaviour. All of the more familiar North American tyrant

Fork-tailed flycatcher *Muscivora tyrannus* taking advantage of the large number of insects driven up by a fire. The long tail streamers give it increased manoeuvrability in flight.

flycatchers defend exclusive territories by repeating simple songs and by chasing away intruders. For example, the Eastern wood pewee gives a plaintive whistled *pee-oo-wee, pee-oo* phrase with monotonous regularity and the Olive-sided flycatcher repeats a phrase sounding like *whip-three-beers*. The song apparently also serves in species recognition in at least some genera where the species are very similar in colouration. This has been studied experimentally in *Empidonax*, where it was found that the Acadian flycatcher (song *peet-suh!*), Traill's flycatcher (song *fee-bee-o*) and Least flycatcher (song *che-bek*) would respond only to tape recordings of the songs of their own species.

The social organization of most of the tropical species is unknown, although some have been found to defend exclusive territories and it seems likely that the majority do so. Simple grating, rasping, hissing or whistling calls are characteristic of the family, but a few species give more tuneful whistled notes. Notably, the Black-crowned pepoaza *Xolmis coronata* of Argentina is said to give doleful whistles with such a markedly human character that they regularly deceive dogs.

Composition. The family Tyrannidae has long been in need of a thorough systematic revision, but the totals of around 360 recognized species in about 115 genera have daunted most ornithologists. When studies being carried out at present are completed it seems likely that fewer genera will be recognized as some currently in use are defined on trivial characters.

The Sharpbill *Oxyruncus cristatus* has often been placed in a subfamily Oxyruncinae of the Tyrannidae, the remainder of the family being treated as the subfamily Tyranninae. However, some authorities prefer to afford the Sharpbill a family of its own (the Oxyruncidae), a convention that is adopted in this volume.

SHARPBILL

The Sharpbill or Crested sharpbill *Oxyruncus cristatus* is the only species in the family Oxyruncidae.

It is a stoutly-built perching bird $6\frac{1}{2}$–7in (16·5–17·5cm) long, with a moderately long, squared tail, rather long rounded wings and short legs with short strong toes. The bill, from which the English name is derived, is rather long and straight, tapering gradually from the base to a sharply pointed tip. Males have the outermost primary feather peculiarly serrated on its outer fringe, an adaptation lacking in females, but of unknown function. Both sexes have a short, bushy crest on the forehead and crown, but it is often held lowered so as to be inconspicuous to the field observer.

Plumage is predominantly dull olive-green above, with blackish-brown wing and tail feathers that are narrowly fringed with dull olive. The crest is scarlet or orange-red, tending to be paler in females, and bordered with blackish-brown streaks in both sexes. The forehead, sides of head and throat are white with narrow blackish bars and the underparts are nearly white with conspicuous thrush-like black spots. The black bill has a lighter brown cutting edge and lower mandible, the iris is brown, and the legs and feet are black.

Distribution. The range of the species is curiously discontinuous, as with many other birds of the humid forests of South and Central America. One population inhabits humid mountain forests in Costa Rica and adjacent parts of western Panama, another the Darien region of eastern Panama, a third ranges from Guyana to southern Venezuela on the tropical and subtropical zones of the lower mountain slopes, a fourth is restricted to the Chanchamayo Valley in eastern Peru, at around 4,000ft (1,300m) elevation on forested mountainsides, and the fifth population has an extensive range in central and southern Brazil, extending to parts of Paraguay. Despite the wide and fragmented range of the species subspecific variation is slight and confined to small differences in size and colouration.

Behaviour. The species usually occurs singly or in pairs in the leafy canopy of tall forest trees, often where they are covered with epiphytic vines and ferns. The birds fly strongly from tree to tree and perch among the higher branches. The stomach contents of small numbers of specimens collected for scientific study were long ago reported as fruit pulp and seeds extracted from fleshy fruit, so it has often been assumed that Sharpbills eat mainly or entirely fruit. However, the structure of the bird's bill might suggest that insects are also eaten, and that seeds taken from fruit may be a more important part of the diet than the fruit pulp.

The rarely-observed Sharpbill *Oxyruncus cristatus*. Although most aspects of its habits are a mystery, its diet is known to include fruit.

As only single birds and pairs have been reported by field observers it can probably be assumed that the species is normally solitary. However, it is not known whether territories are defended, whether or not individuals roam widely, or what the call is. It is perhaps surprising that no calls or song have been reported for such a widely distributed bird and one which is often common where it does occur. This may suggest that it is a relatively quiet species, or at least that it lacks loud or distinctive vocalizations. The nest and eggs are also unknown, although a number of observers have searched for them in the hope of shedding some light on the systematic relationships of the bird.

Composition. The Sharpbill is the only member of the Oxyruncidae and is sometimes considered to be a member of the Tyrannidae, the tyrant flycatchers, with which it shares a few small anatomical similarities.

PLANTCUTTERS

The three species of plantcutter, all of which are placed in the genus *Phytotoma*, are stocky birds with finch-like bills. The early naturalists regarded them as finches, but anatomical studies quickly revealed that their resemblance to finches was purely superficial and that their true allies are the tyrant flycatchers (Tyrannidae) and other groups of primitive perching birds known collectively as the suboscines. All three species are $6\frac{1}{2}$–7in (16·5–17·5cm) long, with rather long tails, broadly rounded wings, short strong legs and short conical bills with a curved, bulging upper mandible and saw-like cutting edges on both mandibles.

Adult males all have grey upperparts with blackish streaks, black tails tipped with white and blackish wings with two broad white bars formed by white tips to the covert feathers. The male of the Peruvian plantcutter *Phytotoma raimondii* has a greyish head, light grey breast with rufous in the middle and rufous under tail coverts. In contrast, males of the White-tipped plantcutter *P. rutila* and the Rufous-tailed plantcutter *P. rara* have the forehead, crown and underparts mainly orange; the Rufous-tailed plantcutter has yellow streaks on the nape and mantle and rufous in the tail feathers, features lacking in the White-tipped plantcutter. The females and juveniles of all three species have grey-brown upperparts with dark streaks and light grey breasts streaked with brown; their tail patterns resemble those of the males, but are duller.

Distribution. Plantcutters are confined to South America. The Peruvian plantcutter inhabits coastal regions of northwestern Peru, the White-tipped plantcutter inhabits the highlands of Bolivia and Paraguay south to Argentina, and the Rufous-tailed plantcutter inhabits northern Chile and northern Argentina west of the range of the White-tipped. The southern populations of the White-tipped plantcutter migrate to spend the southern winter as far north as northeastern Argentina and eastern Uruguay. The Rufous-tailed plantcutter has straggled out to the Falkland Islands, although it is not thought to be a regular migrant.

Behaviour. The name plantcutter is derived from the way in which these heavy-billed birds bite into buds, soft stems and other plant foods. The bill has serrated cutting edges to the upper mandible and a serrated ridge of horny material on the lower mandible, enabling the birds to bite through quite tough stems. Other foods include a variety of fruit and seeds. The Rufous-tailed plantcutter eats considerable quantities of seeds, which may form the bulk of its diet during part of the non-breeding season.

Male White-tipped plantcutters sing from high up in trees and bushes on their breeding territories, giving a discordant song of a few notes that have been likened to the bleating of sheep; they also produce a series of loud squeaks ending in a frog-like croak. The song of the Rufous-tailed plantcutter consists of a series of rasping metallic notes. The alarm calls of these two species are of the same tone as their songs, but short and abrupt. The only display which has been recorded is a distinctive slow flight from tree to tree by breeding male White-throated plantcutters. They then fly with very rapid wing-beats, quite different from their normal weakly bounding flight.

Plantcutter nests consist of a platform of twigs with a cup-shaped lining of plant fibres. Those of the Rufous-tailed plantcutter are usually placed high up in the fork of a tree, often in an orchard, but the White-tipped plantcutter usually nests in the interior of a thorny bush, sometimes even in cacti. All three species lay clutches of 2–4

Two Rufous-tailed plantcutters *Phytotoma rara* to show the difference in plumage between the female (1) and the male (2). (3) Another member of the Phytotomidae, the Peruvian plantcutter *Phytotoma raimondii*.

oval eggs of blue-green ground colour with dark brown spots and blotches. The incubation and fledging periods have not been recorded, although incubation is known to be mainly or entirely by the female in the case of the White-tipped plantcutter.

Composition. The three species included in the Phytotomidae are members of a single genus, *Phytotoma*, and are closely related to the tyrant flycatchers (Tyrannidae).

PITTAS

The Pittidae is a small distinct family of 23 species of plump, short-necked birds, noted for their brilliant plumage. Commonly known as pittas, they are all rather similar in general structure and behaviour, ranging in length from 6–11in (15–28cm). The bill is typically stout, the legs are long and powerful and the wings short and rounded. The proportions of their legs reflect their mainly terrestrial habits, the majority of species spending most of the time on the ground, scratching and picking for food among leaf litter, but they do perch in vegetation, occasionally quite high up, to roost or sing.

Pittas are among the most colourful of birds, with various shades of bright and often glistening blues, greens, reds, chestnuts and yellows contrasting with black and white markings, often on the head and wings.

With such plumage, the alternative vernacular name of 'jewel thrushes' is not surprising, and in fact most English names refer to some aspect of colouration, for example, the Blue-winged pitta *Pitta brachyura* and the Red-breasted pitta *P. erythrogaster*. A few species have more general, descriptive names such as the Rainbow pitta *P. iris* or the Garnet pitta *P. granatina*. Phayre's pitta *P. phayrei*, a species from southeast Burma and Siam, is unusual in having long, pointed plumes on each side of the nape.

Distribution. The pittas are exclusively Old World birds; two species are confined to Africa while the rest are of southeast Asian, Papuan and Australasian distribution. The African pitta *P. angolensis* occurs throughout much of tropical Africa and southwards in the eastern half of the continent almost as far as the Cape. Its near relative, the Green-breasted pitta *P. reichenowi* has a more restricted occurrence in west equatorial Africa from Cameroon to the eastern Congo. The Blue-winged pitta is widespread, ranging from India eastwards to China, Korea and Japan and south into Australia. The more widespread species occur as numerous distinct subspecies, sometimes treated as separate species. The majority of pittas are rather locally distributed and some of these are understandably little known. The Blue-headed and Blue-banded pittas *P. arcuata*, for example, are confined to Borneo.

The family is typically found in dense, moist, evergreen or deciduous forests, but they also frequent mangroves, scrublands and wooded ravines in otherwise quite open country. Some species are sedentary but most are migratory to a considerable extent, though their migration patterns are little understood. During migration, they often appear in rather 'unlikely' places like villages and seem particularly prone to collide with lighted buildings at night. The flight is quite strong and direct but seldom sustained except during migration.

Feeding. The diet consists of small terrestrial animals such as spiders, beetles, ants, termites and snails though some species will consume larger prey such as small lizards or crabs. The Noisy pitta *P. versicolor* uses stones as anvils on which to break open snails in the manner of the Song-thrush *Turdus philomelos*, while a Blue-winged pitta collected by an ornithologist was reported to have eaten a large number of small shrimps.

(1) The Garnet pitta *Pitta granatina*, alert to the faintest signals of danger. (2) The Noisy pitta *Pitta versicolor* feeds off snails, first smashing the shells against a stone.

Nesting and the Young. Little is known about the breeding biology of the pittas. However, it is known that the nest and eggs are remarkably similar throughout the family. The nest is a large globular or oval, untidy structure of twigs and rootlets, lined with finer materials, with an entrance at the side or at one end. It is sometimes built on the ground or against a bank or fallen tree but quite often the preferred site is low down in a tangled clump of vegetation or a thorny bush. The 2–7 eggs are rounded, glossy and white or buffish with fine greyish or lavender specklings and bolder blotching of reddish or purplish brown. As far as is known, both sexes share in nest building and incubation.

Pittas are noted for the beauty of their colouring. (1) Blue-winged pitta *Pitta brachyura*, shown also in flight. (2) Phayre's pitta *Pitta phayrei* with its rich chestnut colours and distinctive pointed plumes.

Behaviour. Pittas are usually seen singly or in pairs, except during migration when larger groups may occur. The song is characteristically a shrill, high-pitched whistle usually of two or sometimes three notes, most often heard at dawn and dusk, before rainstorms and on moonlit nights, when a number of neighbouring birds can often be heard singing against each other in chorus. The aggressive display of the African pitta involves crouching with fluffed out feathers and bill held high.

Composition. The Pittidae are placed in the mainly New World suborder Tyranni. The family is so uniform that all species are generally placed in the same genus, *Pitta*. Among their more interesting anatomical features are the muscles of the syrinx and the 10 full-length primary feathers in each wing; in many other passerine families, the outermost primary is much reduced and sometimes virtually absent.

NEW ZEALAND WRENS

The New Zealand wrens are an ancient, endemic family of obscure relationships (the Acanthisittidae or Xenicidae) with a long history of geological isolation during which three groups each with its own ecological preferences have evolved. They include the diminutive Rifleman *Acanthisitta chloris* living in the indigenous *Nothofagus* beech forests, not always readily seen but clearly heard by its characteristically high-pitched call.

Members of the genus *Xenicus* include the Bushwren *X. longipes* of the North and South Islands, which is seldom seen and may be extinct, and the Rock wren *X. gilviventris* which is one of a number of alpine adaptations of bush-inhabiting species, and lives in the mountains of the South Island. Although elusive, often skulking

under rocky debris, members of the latter group are not uncommonly seen by patient ornithologists and may yet be studied fully. The Stephen Island wren *Traversia lyalli* has a spectacular history of simultaneous discovery and extinction.

Distribution. The New Zealand wrens occur within large areas of forest of both islands, the mountains above, and on one group of off-shore islets. Although Bush wrens are now greatly reduced in numbers and distribution, the Rifleman is, perhaps, New Zealand's commonest bird in beech forests. The Rock wren occurs throughout the length of the South Island mountains ranging from 3,000–8,000ft (900–2,500m).

Feeding. Riflemen feed in a characteristic manner, searching incessantly, with strong wing-flicking, along the trunks and branches of trees for insects and spiders. They work their way up the trunk spiral fashion to perhaps 20 or 30ft (6–9m), dropping down to the base and beginning up another tree. Ground feeding is less common. Bush wrens feed on insects and other arthropods but fly from tree to tree rather than working upwards. Ground feeding is frequent and accompanied by continual bobbing movements. The Rock wren searches for insects (especially beetles and grasshoppers) and spiders amongst rocky debris, both above, below, and in the tussock grass and plants of mountain slopes with a 'restless zig-zag hopping' contrasting with the more sedate Bush wren with which it shares the characteristic bobbing.

Nesting and the Young. Riflemen breed from August to January, and more than one brood may be reared. Nests, of roots, leaves, moss or ferns and lined with feathers, are well hidden in holes in tree trunks, sometimes in banks or walls, fence posts or under eaves of

Three species of New Zealand wren. (1) Rifleman *Acanthisitta chloris*, (2) Rock wren *Xenicus gilviventris* and (3) Bush wren *Xenicus longpipes*.

buildings. Eggs are white and average $\frac{3}{5} \times \frac{1}{2}$in (16 × 12mm). The clutch size ranges from two to four or five. The interval between laying is about 48 hours, and incubation lasts 20–21 days. The young fledge in about 24 days. Both parents share nest building, incubation and feeding of the young.

Stead's bush wren *Xenicus longipes variabilis*, found on small southern islets off Stewart Island, is largely terrestrial, nesting in holes in the ground or in logs. Nests are often in musty or wet conditions and the feathers lining them are replaced frequently. Little is known of their breeding biology, but eggs have been found in November and December and measured $\frac{4}{5} \times \frac{3}{5}$in (21 × 15mm). Chicks have been seen at the end of November. Both parents incubate, and the young appear to be fed on moths and flies. Few nests of the South Island bush wren *Xenicus longipes longipes* have been found.

The extinct Stephen Island wren *Traversia lyalli* on coastal rocks. In 1894, a lighthouse keeper's cat on this New Zealand island brought in 15 specimens. No others have ever been found since that time.

The Rock wren's nest, set amongst loose rocks or in roots of alpine scrub and tussock, is made of grass, leaves, twigs or roots, lined with a variety of feathers. Laying occurs between September and November and the clutch may be two to five eggs. Chicks have been seen in late November, but nothing is known of incubation or fledging periods. Both parents incubate and feed the young. Intervals between feeding are much longer than for the Rifleman, being half to hourly visits.

Voice. The high-pitched, rapidly repeated needle-sharp *zsit-zsit* of the Rifleman is a clear indication of the presence of this tiny bird although well hidden by its cryptic colouring. The Bush wren's call is a rapid succession of merging cheeps or a subdued trill. Stead's bush wren makes a 'faint rasping sound, the noise of a small wristwatch in process of winding'. An alarm note is a loud cheep. The Rock wren has a whirring call of three notes and a thin piping.

Composition. The family Acanthisittidae (or Xenicidae as it is officially called by New Zealand ornithologists) contains three genera, *Acanthisitta*, *Xenicus* and *Traversia*, in the first two of which

South Island riflemen *Acanthisitta chloris* foraging on a trunk. They work their way up the tree in a spiral and when they have reached the top, fly down to the foot of a neighbouring tree to begin the process again.

some geographic and ecological speciation is evident. *Xenicus* is clearly allied to *Acanthisitta* but the Stephen Island wren, *Traversia lyalli*, seems to represent a very distinct genus. New Zealand ornithologists, however, generally lump all the wrens in the genus *Xenicus*.

Superficially, the New Zealand wrens differ only in plumage characters, and a number of subspecies are recognized. The Rifleman occurs as the South Island rifleman *Acanthisitta chloris chloris* and the North Island rifleman *A. c. granti*. A larger form has been described as an 'Alpine rifleman' *A. c. citrina* but is now held to be invalid. The Bush wren has three subspecies: the North Island form *Xenicus longipes stokesi*, the South Island form *X. l. variabilis*, and the Rock wren which has been described as the 'Fiordland' form *Xenicus longipes rinegi*.

ASITYS

The four species of the Philepittidae are all confined to Madagascar. Two species are placed in each of two genera, the asitys in *Philepitta* and the false sunbirds in *Neodrepanis*.

Both *Philepitta* species are about 6in (15cm) long and have a plump body, short neck, broad-based bill shorter than the head, moderately long rounded wings and a short tail. Their tarsi are stout and the feet rather large and strong with pointed claws. Females and immature males of the Velvet asity *P. castanea* are olive-green above and pale green scaled with white on the underparts. Adult males in fresh plumage are black with narrow yellow fringes to most feathers. The yellow fringes rapidly abrade away to leave an all-black bird. As the plumage becomes all-black a large fleshy wattle of greenish colour develops over the eye, running from the sides of the hind-crown to the forehead, where it rises in a short point on either side.

Schlegel's asity *P. schlegeli* is generally similar to *P. castanea*, differing in having the green colouration more suffused with yellowish, in having the black of the adult male confined to the top of the head, and in having the wattle of the adult male entirely surrounding the eye.

The false sunbirds of the genus *Neodrepanis* are about 4in (10cm) in length. They are of generally similar build to the larger *Philepitta* species, but have much longer bills which are more slender and curve downwards to a sharp point. Females of the False sunbird *N. coruscans* are dark green above and yellowish below. Adult males are iridescent blue on the upperparts and dull yellow on the underparts, and have a large wattle around the eye. *N. hypoxantha* is closely similar to *N. coruscans*, differing mainly in having brighter colouration and a more slender bill.

Distribution. The family Philepittidae is restricted to Madagascar. It is thus one of a few groups of birds characteristic of the Malagasy zoogeographical subregion.

The Velvet asity inhabits the humid forests of eastern Madagascar, Schlegel's asity the forests of western Madagascar. The False sunbird is also a bird of humid forests, but *N. hypoxantha* is known only from a few specimens collected in eastern Madagascar. Whether this species overlaps the range of the False sunbird or replaces it locally is still uncertain.

Feeding. The asitys of the genus *Philepitta* are solitary birds of the undergrowth and saplings in humid forests. Their behaviour is rather sluggish and their diet appears to consist mostly of the small fruit of forest shrubs, although they are little known and might also take insects.

The False sunbird is also a quiet, sluggish bird of the forest undergrowth. Its diet is thought to consist mainly of insects picked from twigs and branches with the long bill, but it has also been seen feeding at flowers by poking the long bill into the corolla tubes like a sunbird (Nectariniidae). The food taken from flowers probably includes both nectar and pollen. *N. hypoxantha* has a similarly shaped bill to that of the False sunbird, although more slender, so it probably feeds in similar ways to that species.

Nesting and the Young. The nests of the false sunbirds *Neodrepanis* are unfortunately unknown, but one nest of the Velvet asity has been described. It was a hanging pear-shaped structure built of moss and palm fibres placed high in a tall bush. The top of the nest was woven around the branches from which it was suspended, and the entrance was at the side near the top and covered by a sheltering roof of nest material. This nest contained three unmarked white eggs of an elongated oval shape. Details of the incubation and nestling periods, shares of the sexes and the nestling are all completely unknown.

The only known type of nest built by the Velvet asity *philepitta castanea* (1) is a suspended pear-shape. The female is shown with her head emerging from the nest's entrance. Another member of the Philepittidae is the Wattled false sunbird *Neodrepanis coruscans* (2). False sunbirds are notable for their long, tapering curved bills.

Behaviour. The Velvet asity has usually been described as a sluggish, solitary and quiet bird that allows close approach and does not fly far when disturbed. Some observers have reported that it occasionally gives a whistled thrush-like song, and this might function in territory defence. The only call reported for the False sunbird is a soft hissing note. This species is also solitary, and might well defend territories. The voice and social organization of Schlegel's asity and *N. hypoxantha* are completely unknown.

Composition. The two genera *Philepitta* and *Neodrepanis* are not very closely related, although there is ample evidence that they should be regarded as members of a single family.

LYREBIRDS

The lyrebirds of Australia, together with the scrub-birds, form the suborder Menurae and are of especial interest because of the spectacular nature of their song and display and their remarkable use of mimicry. Their ability to learn and reproduce a wide variety of complex sounds is all the more remarkable because of the simple structure of their syrinx or voice-producing organ. There are two species in the family Menuridae.

Normally shy and difficult to observe, the larger of the two species, the Superb lyrebird *Menura novaehollandiae* was commonly known to the early settlers as a pheasant and many were shot for their beautiful tail feathers. The general colour above is brown, the underparts being a lighter brown. The throat and tail covers are rufous. Adult males can be distinguished from females and young males by the tail, which grows up to 30in (76cm) in length and consists of two large outer feathers which have brown crescent-shaped markings on the upper side, two black wire-like feathers and 12 filamentary feathers which are dark on top and silver underneath, as are the outer tail feathers. This combination of feathers can be erected to give the shape of a lyre, the musical instrument after which the bird was named, though it is seldom carried in this position.

The Albert lyrebird *Menura alberti* is smaller in size and darker in colour than the Superb lyrebird and is less well known than its sole close relative.

Distribution. The lyrebirds are restricted to eastern Australia. The Superb lyrebird is plentiful in an area between the Great Dividing Range and the sea from southern Queensland through to the Dandenong Ranges in southern Victoria. Although it is now strictly protected, numbers are decreasing as further areas of forestland are cleared. The Albert lyrebird is now limited to a relatively small area of rain-forest close to the borders of New South Wales and Queensland between the Great Dividing Range and the coast.

Feeding. Food is gathered from the forest litter and extensive scratching of litter and top soil is carried out as the birds look for the litter fauna.

Nesting and the Young. Breeding takes place from May to October, but principally in the winter months of June and July when the single egg is laid. Where the lyrebird breeds at high altitudes the large domed nest is often covered with snow. The female builds the nest, incubates the egg and feeds the young unaided. The egg is remarkably resistant to cold and in the early stages of incubation can be left for 24 hours or more without damage. Although the nest is large and may measure up to 24in (61cm) in width, nesting females can be distinguished by their bent tail feathers, which are curled round the body when in the nest. Incubation takes about six weeks and the chick spends a further six weeks in the nest which may be on the ground, in a tree stump, on a cliff ledge, or even in a tall tree.

Behaviour. Territorial behaviour is highly complex among the lyrebirds. Superb lyrebird males occupy territories of 2–10ac (0·8–4ha). They make small clearings from which all vegetation is removed and scratch earth up into the form of a low mound some 6in (15cm) high and 36in (91cm) in diameter on which they sing and display. Usually from 4–6 such mounds, at various vantage points in the territory, are in use at any one time but several more may be built and discarded during the breeding season. These mounds are kept well tended and before a male commences to sing he carefully scratches the surface of the mound until any accumulated litter has been removed. Scratched earth is attractive to the females who will visit mounds and scratch around even when the male is not present.

The territorial song with its accompanying stream of mimicry and the very loud *pilik pilik* calls which accompany full display are largely directed to rival males.

Of the two species of lyrebird, the male Superb lyrebird *Menura novaehol-landiae* (1) has an even more extravagantly decorative tail than the male Albert lyrebird *Menura alberti* (2). The female Superb lyrebird takes any faeces and leaves them somewhere well away from the nest so as to lessen the chances of detection by predators (3); the nest and its single occupant (4) are her sole responsibility. (5) For a brief moment when the male Superb lyrebird is in full display, the tail may be laid back in the shape of a lyre.

Lyrebirds are said to mimic many sounds such as the noise of axe blows, cross-cut saws, barking dogs and a variety of other bushland noises. But generally, mimicry is restricted mainly to the calls of other bird species and the rustling of feathers in flight. Nevertheless the performance is often extraordinary, for example when the bird mimics a chorus of several Kookaburras or a flock of parrots passing overhead – calls, wingbeats and all. In dense vegetation, in which visibility is reduced to a few feet, the constant output of mimicry forms an effective directional beacon which gives a clear indication of the male's location and of the extent of his territory as he moves from one song point to another. As the female approaches and the song is directed to the now visible mate, different mimicked sounds are used. These do not have such strong directional characteristics, simply serving to retain the attention of the female for a short period until the song merges into a continuous clicking noise of low intensity which may continue for several minutes. This sound is the prelude to copulation which generally takes place near the display mound.

Females will sometimes sing and mimic for short periods. Such occurrences are often the result of a bird being disturbed by the presence of humans.

In the case of the Albert lyrebird male territories can be much larger, up to 30ac (12ha) and the males do not make display mounds. They do, however, have preferred song points and sometimes scratch the ground while displaying. The Albert lyrebird is also an accomplished mimic but its song differs in form from that of the Superb lyrebird, the territorial song being much louder and the mimicry generally much more subdued.

Composition. The Menuridae contains two species in a single genus *Menura*, the Superb lyrebird *M. novaehollandiae* and the Albert lyrebird *M. alberti*. Together with the scrub-birds (Atrichornithidae) they form an interesting link between the primitive songbirds (Tyranni and Eurylaimi) and the more advanced songbirds (Oscines).

SCRUB-BIRDS

Scrub-birds are rare Australian birds, more often heard than seen owing to their loud voice, shyness and general buff-brown appearance, which blends perfectly with the environment. The family Atrichornithidae contains two species. The Noisy scrub-bird *Atrichornis clamosus* measures 8¾in (22cm) in length. The upperparts are brown flecked with darker brown on the back and tail. Throat and breast are dull white and the male is distinguished from the female by black markings on the chest. The tail is long and the strong legs are greenish-white. The Rufous scrub-bird

Atrichornis rufescens is similar to the Noisy scrub-bird but is smaller, measuring 6½in (16·5cm) in length.

Distribution. One of the world's rarest birds, the Noisy scrub-bird is known only in one small area near the town of Albany in the southwest of the state of Western Australia. Formerly it was more widely distributed but numbers decreased rapidly following European settlement.

The Rufous scrub-bird is confined to the wetter parts of a few areas of rain-forest on the eastern slopes of the Great Dividing Range from southern Queensland to the middle of New South Wales. Though more numerous than its relative, its numbers are nevertheless low and have decreased as a result of forest clearance.

Behaviour. Noisy scrub-birds breed in very thick scrub in the wetter hollows and steep gullies in the eucalypt forest. Owing to the dense nature of the vegetation and the scrub-bird's cryptic habits, nests are very difficult to find. The nest is domed and lined with a hard dry substance rather like cardboard. It is usually situated near the ground and a narrow sloping platform projecting from the entrance provides access for the female. She alone builds the nest, incubates the egg and feeds the young. The single egg is creamy white speckled with reddish-brown. Breeding generally takes place in mid-winter (June) but can also occur as late as September.

Although it is mainly a ground-living bird, running rapidly through the eucalypt litter from which it gathers much of its insect food, it is not flightless and may often be seen making short flights from branch to branch up to 6ft (1·8m) from the ground. Display,

Four species of larks. (1) Crested lark *Galerida cristata*, (2) Black lark *Melanocorypha yeltoniensis*, (3) Desert lark *Ammomanes deserti* and (4) Shore (or Horned) lark *Eremophila alpestris*.

The elusive and now sparsely-populated scrub-birds were once widely distributed across Australia. (1) A male Rufous scrub-bird *Atrichornis rufescens* compared with (2) a male Noisy scrub-bird *Atrichornis clamosus*. (3) In display Noisy scrub-birds lower their wings and tilt their tails upwards and forwards. (4) The female Rufous scrub bird may take a month to complete her nest, having to allow time for the woodpulp lining to dry out.

which can take place either on the ground or on a low branch, is quite spectacular and resembles that of the lyrebirds. The long tail assumes a wide fan-shape and is drawn up and over the back, the short stubby wings are drooped and the whole body and tail quivers rapidly, to the accompaniment of the bird's song. The loud voice, for which the bird is named, is by no means harsh. The varied song is generally melodious and has been compared with that of the Nightingale. Though the male is a competent mimic and will sing duets with other species, this rarely occurs during the breeding season.

The Rufous scrub-bird breeds in the spring, from September to November, and it is the only member of the suborder Menurae (the scrub-birds and the lyrebirds) which lays two eggs and is not a winter breeder. The nest and eggs are similar to that of the Noisy scrub-bird, though smaller. It is primarily a ground feeder and runs rapidly over the ground in search of the litter fauna on which it feeds, its appearance and gait being rather mouse-like.

Display is similar to that of the Noisy scrub-bird but the song, though very loud, is much simpler and more stereotyped, being a series of short notes of rapidly descending frequency. It is also an excellent mimic and will reproduce many of the songs and calls of other species, especially when disturbed.

Composition. The Atrichornithidae contains two species in a single genus *Atrichornis*, the Noisy scrub-bird *A. clamosus*, and the Rufous scrub-bird *A. rufescens*.

LARKS

Larks are small terrestrial song birds which are usually streaked

underparts and usually chestnut above, whereas the females are a sombre brown. They are cheerful little birds of sandy or bare stony ground, often occurring in large flocks outside the breeding season. Among the most desert-loving of all larks are the desert larks *Ammomanes* occurring extensively in the deserts of Africa and southwest Asia. They are almost uniformly brown, the intensity of the colour being closely related to the colour of the soil on which they live. One of the largest of the larks, the Bifasciated or Hoopoe lark *Alaemon alaudipes* is also a bird of absolute desert, being found right across the great north African and south Asian desert belt from Morocco to the Punjab. The long, decurved bill, long legs and striking black and white wing markings make the bird unmistakable.

The mainly Asiatic genus *Melanocorypha* contains six species of large, heavy-billed larks including the Calandra lark *M. calandra* of southern Europe and southwest Asia. The Thick-billed lark

In its brilliant songflight, the Skylark *Alauda arvensis* spirals high into the air and then drops back to earth, emitting its exquisite song all the while.

(1) Bifasciated (or Hoopoe) lark *Alaemon alaudipes* in flight. (2) The Thick-billed lark *Rhamphocorys clot-bey*.

brown above and more or less streaked below. The hind claw is often much elongated, an adaptation to a terrestrial way of life. The lark family differs from all other perching birds in that the back of the tarsus is rounded and covered in scales, instead of being sharp and unsegmented. Together with certain primitive features of the syrinx, this has led to larks being generally regarded as the most primitive of true songbirds.

The colouration of larks is highly cryptic. Desert-loving species are generally uniform brown, whereas larks of grassland are more or less heavily streaked. Behavioural traits, such as crouching in vegetation, or standing motionless in the presence of danger, assist in this camouflage. The similarity between the colour of the upperparts and the colour of the ground on which the birds live has developed to a remarkable degree in the Desert lark *Ammomanes deserti*. As the soil colour changes, so does the mantle colour of the lark, and it is possible in some areas to find pale sandy forms on sand desert and blackish forms on black lava within the space of a few miles.

Distribution. Larks are almost entirely Old World in distribution, and are particularly well represented in Africa, all genera and no less than 80% of the species occurring there. Larks live in a great variety of open habitats, from cultivated meadows and steppe country, wasteland and semi-arid sparsely vegetated areas, to sandy and rocky wastes, arctic tundra and absolute desert. The Alaudidae contains both purely sedentary species and true migrants. In addition, many desert species, although showing no regular migration, are wanderers, moving about in search of fresh feeding grounds especially after sand or dust storms.

Twenty-three species are included in the mainly African genus *Mirafra*, the bush larks, one of which, the Singing bush lark *M. javanica*, occurs from East Africa across southern Asia to New Guinea and Australia. Bush larks prefer more heavily vegetated areas than do other larks, inhabiting semi-arid grassland with scattered bushes, and occasionally even open woodland. The Karoo and Long-billed larks *Certhilauda* are restricted to Africa, and are characterized by their long bills and upright stance. The finchlarks *Eremopterix* of Africa and southern Asia have very stout finch-like bills, and are unusual in that they show marked sexual dimorphism, the males being strikingly coloured, black and white on the

Rhamphocorys clot-bey is clearly closely related to the above genus, but has become adapted to desert conditions and has an unstreaked desert-coloured plumage. The genus *Calandrella* contains 12 species of small, short-tailed larks inhabiting sandy patches in poor cultivated areas, semi-arid plains and, more rarely, in absolute desert in Africa, southern Europe and southern Asia. The genus *Galerida* contains six species with prominent crests. They are partial to poor agricultural land and waste ground with scattered bushes. The Crested lark *G. cristata* has extended its range in Europe along with the cultivation of steppe areas, especially along roadsides and railway lines, and is often found in village streets and suburbs. The Woodlark *Lullula arborea* of Europe and southwest Asia is particularly fond of sparsely wooded sandy areas, and is one of the few larks which regularly perches in trees. The familiar Skylark *Alauda arvensis* of Europe and northern Asia east to Japan is a bird of damper ground than most larks, favouring cultivated and natural meadows, open heaths and moors.

The Horned or Shore lark *Eremophila alpestris* is one of the most attractive of the larks, with pinkish-brown upperparts, a contrasting facial pattern of black and yellow and small black tufts or 'horns' above and behind the eye. In Europe and Asia, the Horned lark is restricted to high mountains, stony plateaux and arctic tundra. However, in North America, the absence of other larks has enabled it to colonize a wide variety of habitats from the arctic tundra of the north through the plains and cultivated meadows of the central states, to rocky and sandy deserts in the south. This species is also the only lark to have reached South America, a very isolated population inhabiting the high plateau of Colombia. A closely related species, Temminck's horned lark *E. bilopha*, occurs in the stony and sandy deserts of north Africa and the Middle East.
Feeding. The diet of larks is varied, the wide variety of bill shapes being adapted to a wide range of foods. The large-billed species, such as the finchlarks, the Calandra lark, and bush larks, are chiefly seed-eaters; species with intermediate-sized bills, such as the Crested lark and the Skylark, have a mixed diet of small seeds and insects; and the fine-billed species, such as the Woodlark and the Horned lark, are mainly insect eaters, although both take some seeds in winter. The Horned lark, where it occurs on the coast in winter, is particularly fond of small molluscs and crustaceans, which it obtains by searching through dead seaweed on the tide line. The long-billed larks of the genera *Alaemon* and *Certhilauda* feed largely on insect pupae, for which they dig as deep as 2in (5cm). Within the single genus *Calandrella* there is a complete range of bills, from blunt and almost conical to fine and pointed, and the diets of the species range from almost entirely seeds to mainly insects.
Nesting. Larks are invariably ground nesters. The nest is a loose cup of dead grass and occasionally hair or wool, placed in a depression in the ground, usually in the shelter of a tuft of grass or a rock. In some species of Bush larks and Long-billed larks, the nest is a more complex structure, partially domed, and very well hidden. In several desert species, particularly of the genera *Ammomanes* and *Alaemon*, a small wall of pebbles, up to $\frac{3}{4}$in (18mm) high, is erected on the exposed side of the nest, presumably to afford some protection from the wind. The usual clutch is 3–5 eggs which are generally white or whitish, or very pale blue, heavily streaked or speckled with grey or brown.
Song. The song of many larks, particularly of the genera *Alauda*, *Lullula*, *Melanocorypha* and *Alaemon*, is remarkable for its melodious quality, and the vehemence with which it is delivered, often from a prolonged song flight. The Skylark delivers a loud and clear warbling, which may be sustained for as long as five minutes, while hovering in the air above its territory, sometimes at a great height. Bush larks tend to have shorter songs associated with more aerial acrobatics.

Composition. The Alaudidae comprises 75 species of larks in 15 genera. They constitute one of the most clearly defined song bird families.

SWALLOWS

The swallows are a distinctive and successful cosmopolitan group. Many are more commonly known as martins though there is no significant difference between 'swallows' and 'martins'. All have long wings and agile flight and feed almost entirely on insects they catch in the air. One species, *Riparia riparia*, is known as the Sand martin in Britain and the Bank swallow in America. They are all rather small birds, varying from $3\frac{3}{4}$–9in (9·5–22·9cm) in length, and in a number of species much of this is taken up by the long, forked tail. The plumage is generally dark; black, brown, green, or blue, often with a metallic sheen. Several species show white in the spread tail, and many species are paler on the underside of the body. The neck and legs are short, and the feet small and weak. Swallows perch readily on wires, branches and other vegetation, but due to their leg

Five species of swallows. (1) Common (or Barn) swallow *Hirundo rustica*, (2) Red-rumped swallow *Hirundo daurica*, (3) Cliff swallow *Petrochelidon pyrrhonota*, (4) Tree swallow *Iridoprocne bicolor* and (5) Sand martin (or Bank swallow) *Riparia riparia*.

and foot structure they are clumsy on the ground. In several species the whole of the legs, sometimes even the toes, are feathered.

One of the swallow's most outstanding features is the short, broad, and flattened bill which can be opened to a very wide gape forming a highly efficient insect trap. It also acts as a trowel for scooping up mud for nest-building.
Distribution. Swallows have a world-wide distribution, some individual species being found in both Old and New Worlds. Only the extreme latitudes and some oceanic islands are without one or more species of swallow. Most species are gregarious and all are migratory. In temperate climates especially, birds which depend on the aerial plankton are forced to migrate for that part of the year when the insects on which they feed are not flying. Some of these migrations are of very great length. The European swallow *Hirundo*

rustica, for example, may fly 7,000mi (11,000km) between northern Europe and South Africa.

Three genera of swallows are cosmopolitan in distribution: *Hirundo*, containing 13 species, *Petrochelidon* with 10, and *Riparia* with four. The swallow, itself, is found through most of the Palearctic and Nearctic regions, its original habitat apparently having been steppe country with large grazing animals which would disturb insects on which it could feed. Ten species of *Hirundo* are restricted to Africa. Two of these, the Red-chested swallow *H. lucida* from tropical West Africa, and the Angola swallow *H. angolensis* from Central and East Africa, have been said to be conspecific with *H. rustica*. Another similar species is the Coast swallow *H. tahitica*, which is widely distributed in Southeast Asia and Polynesia. In parts of China and Formosa it is found breeding alongside *H. rustica*. The Welcome swallow of Australia and Tasmania is sometimes regarded as a race of the Coast swallow and sometimes given specific rank as *H. neoxena*.

The genus *Petrochelidon* contains three species in America, four in Africa, one in Asia and two in Australia. In America the Cliff swallow *P. pyrrhonota* is a well-known bird, breeding from Canada and Alaska, in the north, to Mexico, in the south. It winters in South America. The Sand martin or Bank swallow is another successful holarctic species, being equally well known on both sides of the Atlantic. Two other species of the genus *Riparia* are purely African while another is found in both Africa and Asia.

Seven genera of swallows are found only in the Old World. There are three species of *Delichon*, two of them Asiatic, and the House martin *D. urbica* which is found throughout the Palearctic as far north as the 50°F (10°C) July isotherm. There are a few unusual instances of this species breeding in southern Africa. The genus

Ptyonoprogne contains three species in Africa and Asia controversially distinct from the Crag martin *P. rupestris*, which breeds across the Palearctic. Birds of this group tend to be sedentary rather than migratory. Of the genus *Cecrophis*, four species are African, one Asian and the other, the Red-rumped swallow *C. daurica*, has a discontinuous distribution across parts of southern Europe, southern Asia, and central Africa.

The remaining Old World genera are *Phedina* with two species in Africa and Madagascar, and *Cheramoeca* with the one species of Black-and-white swallow, *C. leucosternum*, in Australia.

In the New World there are nine genera of swallows not found elsewhere. The Tree swallow *Iridoprocne bicolor* is a well-known species of the north temperate region breeding from Alaska southwards. It is clear white beneath and a green- or blue-black above. There are five other species in the genus, three of them restricted to South America. The Rough-winged swallow *Stelgidopteryx ruficollis*, not closely related to the African rough-winged swallows of the genus *Psalidoprocne*, is so-called by reason of the serrations on the web of the outer primary wing feathers. It breeds in a variety of subspecific forms from southern Canada southwards to the Gulf of Mexico.

A particularly well-known American species is the Purple martin *Progne subis*. This is a rather large species in which the male is uniformly blue-black above and below, while the female is light-bellied.

The Golden swallow *Kalochelidon euchrysea* with green upperparts glossed with blue or bronze, is restricted to Hispaniola and Jamaica where it is largely found in the higher regions in the mountains.

Feeding. Swallows feed on aerial plankton, the insects and other invertebrates which are carried by, or fly weakly in, the air currents. Occasionally some species, for example the Tree swallow *Iridoprocne bicolor*, will feed on berries.

Nesting and the Young. Most species breed more or less colonially. The nest may be made in a hole in a tree or rock face, or even a building; or a tunnel may be excavated in the ground – usually in a bank – with the actual nest perhaps several feet underground; or a mud structure may be built – either cup-shaped or enclosed, with an opening in the side – and placed on a branch, beam, rock surface or fixed to a rock face. Buildings make good substitute cliffs and some species, such as the House martin *Delichon urbica* have taken to applying their mud nests to the walls under the eaves of buildings. Where nests are made of mud it is common for the female to do the building while the male carries the material. The female also seems to play the major role in incubation. The clutch contains 3–7 white, sometimes speckled eggs, according to species. The newly-hatched young are helpless and almost naked, and the developmental period is an extended one as the young must be able to fly well on leaving the nest. The fledgling period may thus be longer than three weeks.

Composition. The Hirundinidae comprises some 78 species in 19 genera. Three genera *Hirundo*, *Petrochelidon* and *Riparia* are cosmopolitan. Some authorities do not recognize the genus *Cecrophis* and place its six species in the genus *Hirundo*.

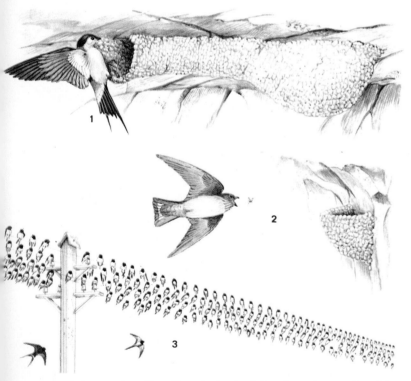

(1) Red-rumped swallow *Hirundo daurica* hangs from the outside of the long, tubular structure which opens out into a bulbous-shaped nest at the end. Also made of a clayey mud which will adhere to rock is the bowl-shaped nest of the Crag martin *Hirundo rupestris* (2), seen here with beak gaping to seize an insect in midflight. (3) The Common (or Barn) swallow *Hirundo rustica* assembles for the marathon journey to South Africa as soon as the insect population drops too far to provide an adequate diet.

WAGTAILS AND PIPITS

The family Motacillidae can be conveniently divided into two main groups, the wagtails and pipits. All are medium to small birds varying in size from 5–8¾in (12·7–22·2cm) in length. All have thin slender bills, long legs, upon which they run and walk rather than hop, relatively long toes and long tails. In some species the hind claw is elongated and spur-like, reaching 2in (5cm) in length in the Yellow-throated long-claw *Macronyx croceus*, which is a bird about

Wagtails are extremely varied, different forms occuring in small geographical regions. A good example of such variation is shown by members of the wagtail genus *Motacilla*. (1) Grey wagtail *Motacilla cinerea*, (2) Yellow-headed wagtail *M. citreola*, (3) Moroccan white wagtail *M. alba subpersonata*, (4) Egyptian white wagtail *M. alba vidua*, (5) Blue-headed wagtail *M. flava flava*, and (6) Iberian blue-headed wagtail *M. flava iberiae*.

Male (in the air) and female White wagtails *Motacilla alba alba*.

the size of a Skylark *Alauda arvensis*. The tail is more developed in the wagtails than in the pipits and is constantly wagged up and down, except in the Forest wagtail *Dendronanthus indicus* where it is moved from side to side while the bird is at rest. All have a strong undulating flight which is more accentuated in the wagtails.

The most intriguing feature of the genus *Motacilla* is the perplexing geographical variation some species exhibit. This reaches such a complex situation in one species, *M. flava*, that taxonomists differ widely in the number of species they recognize. Some treat each form as a geographical race or subspecies, while others give them species rank. They are mainly separated by the colour of the male's head in breeding plumage which may be yellow, blue, grey, black and even white. The main reason for treating such morphologically distinct population as races, rather than distinct species, is the frequency of interbreeding where races come into contact with one another.

The pipits are placed within three genera *Anthus*, *Macronyx* and *Tmetothylacus*. The 34 species placed in *Anthus* are generally small, somberly coloured birds which are brown above, buffish-white below and more or less heavily streaked, with prominent white outer-tail feathers. The sexes are similar. The genus *Macronyx* contains eight species of aberrant pipits known as long-claws. The group is confined to Africa, and its members are larger and stouter than the *Anthus* pipits, with bright yellow or pink underparts and a more or less well defined black pectoral band. The Golden pipit *Tmetothylacus tenellus* is the only representative of its genus. The male is almost entirely yellow, except for dark streaking on the back, and a black pectoral band, whereas the female is dusky brown.

Distribution. The Motacillidae has a world-wide distribution occurring in both the Old and New Worlds. In the north they occur as far as Iceland and Greenland and the coasts of the Arctic Ocean;

Pied wagtail *Motacilla alba yarrellii* (1) in symbiotic relationship with a fallow-deer: the deer is relieved of the flies clustering round its eyes while the bird gains food for its young, which may be sitting on the deer's back as they wait to be fed. Wagtails can be distinguished from similar birds by their characteristic tail movements. Here a Forktail thrush *Enicurus immaculatus* (2) is contrasted with a Pied wagtail (3).

in the south they extend to Tierra del Fuego in southern South America, South Georgia and New Zealand and other adjacent islands. The wagtails, however, are almost entirely restricted to the Old World with only one race of the Yellow wagtail *M. flava tschutschensis* finding its way into Alaska.

The group as a whole are all strong fliers, and the birds breeding in the extreme southern and northern limits of their range are strongly migratory, covering great distances and often wintering far into the tropics. Birds living at high altitudes usually move down into the valleys in winter.

Feeding. The food of wagtails is mainly made up of small insects and includes flies, mosquitoes, beetles, and grasshoppers which are actively hunted on the ground. They catch their prey either by picking it off the ground or by making short rapid runs to capture flying insects that they have flushed. Flocks of Yellow wagtails are often found in association with herds of large grazing mammals that disturb large quantities of insects as they walk, thus providing an easy supply of food; they may be cows in a European meadow or 'big-game' in the winter quarters. Insects also make up the bulk of the food of pipits, although some seeds and other vegetable matter may be taken in winter months, and certain African species are particularly fond of termites. The Rock pipit *Anthus spinoletta* has a more varied diet than most other species found in the family, and is known to take small worms, sandhoppers and periwinkles, in addition to insects.

A subspecies of wagtail found in the Balkans and Black Sea area, the Black-headed wagtail *Motacilla flava feldegg*.

Nesting and the Young. Wagtails and pipits are almost invariably ground-nesters, but holes in banks of streams and crevices in rocks or buildings may be used. The nest is a well-made cup of dried grasses, lined with finer materials and is usually well concealed in a depression in the ground in low vegetation. There is a tendency for the clutch size to vary with latitude; species living in equatorial regions lay as few as 2–3 eggs, while those inhabiting the higher latitudes may have a clutch size of 7.

The eggs are typically whitish or dirty pink, heavily streaked or spotted, and take about 15 days to hatch. On hatching the young have a thick coating of down on the upperparts and do not leave the nest for 15 days, after which they are fed for a few more days by the parents. The nesting duties are sometimes shared by both sexes but in some instances all the work is undertaken by the female.

Behaviour. Courtship behaviour in wagtails and pipits is comprised of short song-flights which commonly take the form of a rapid ascent to some height and then a slow fluttering descent to earth or perch. In the Pied wagtail *Motacilla alba* the display tends to be more elaborate than in most small passerines. It begins with the female being chased in erratic flight by two or more males, which endeavour to display to her by crouching with heads thrown up to show the black gorgets. After pairing, the male approaches on a zigzag course with the head depressed or with a bowing action which is accompanied by various wing movements. Before coition the male has been seen to run round the female in ever decreasing circles, at the same time bowing and stretching the head. Throughout the male's courtship the female remains relatively passive.

As a rule the call notes of their song varies little, being composed of series of repeated phrases. The name pipit is derived from the call which can be a series of tinkling, rather thin feeble notes which may end in a trill. The song is usually delivered from a short song-flight, which is less extensive and varied than that found in the larks.

Different from European wagtails, the Forest wagtail *Dendronanthus indicus* of Manchuria moves the tail laterally, not up and down.

Composition. The Motacillidae is made up of 48 species which are placed in five genera: *Motacilla*, *Dendronanthus*, *Anthus*, *Macronyx* and *Tmetothylacus*. Apart from the single species of Forest wagtail *Dendronanthus indicus* the wagtails can be regarded as representatives of only one genus, *Motacilla*, although some authors have placed the yellow wagtails in a separate genus 'Budytes'. *Motacilla* contains only seven species, but these show a considerable amount of geographical variation.

Five species of caterpillar birds. (1) Ground cuckoo-shrike *Pteropodocys maxima*, (2) Large cuckoo-shrike *Coracina novaehollandiae*, (3) Pigmy triller (or Pied shrike) *Hemipus picatus*, (4) White-browed triller *Lalage leucomela* and (5) Scarlet minivet *Pericrocotus flammeus*.

CATERPILLAR BIRDS

Many species in this unusual family, the Campephagidae, are found only on remote oceanic islands and in tropical forests and as yet the group as a whole has been relatively little studied, which accounts in part for the proliferation of vernacular names such as caterpillar birds and minivets, and the whole range of local compound names using the word 'shrike' – cuckoo-shrike, caterpillar-shrike, flycatcher-shrike, wood-shrike, pied-shrike. The family can be conveniently divided into two groups: the cuckoo-shrikes proper and the minivets.

The different species vary considerably in size, ranging from 5–12in (13–31cm). The cuckoo-shrikes are generally rather drab birds of varying shades of blue or brownish grey, or black, and white with varying degrees of barring. Sexual dimorphism is only slight, the females tending to be but duller versions of the males. Cuckoo-shrikes have long, pointed wings and longish rounded tails, rather small legs and weak feet. They are also characterized by having stiff, modified hairlike feathers known as rictal bristles on each side of the bill which in some species are sufficiently well developed to partly conceal the nostrils. The Wattled cuckoo-shrike *Campephaga lobata* is unusual in having yellow wattles of skin near the gape, providing a striking contrast with its red eyes.

By comparison, the minivets in the genus *Pericrocotus* are brightly coloured and form a more distinct group. They have something of a wagtail-like shape and show marked sexual dimorphism, the males having red and black plumage and the females a combination of yellow or orange and black or grey.

A peculiar feature of most species in the family are the stiff and erectile feathers of the lower back. These are loosely attached and their shafts, being formed into a spike-like point, may serve some

defensive purpose. The Whitewinged triller *Lalage sueurii* of the Australasian region, is apparently unique in the family, though not among birds generally, in having two complete moults a year instead of one.

Throughout the family, flight is buoyant and often powerful but seldom sustained for any great distance.

Distribution. The Campephagidae is found only in the eastern hemisphere, the majority of species occurring in the southeast Asian, Papuan and Australasian regions, with the remainder in Africa. Some species are of wide distribution, such as the Large cuckoo-shrike *Coracina novae-hollandiae* of which there are about 19 races throughout much of southeast Asia, from India, Nepal and China southwards – including many isolated islands – to New Guinea, Australia and Tasmania. In contrast, many species are restricted to small oceanic islands or groups of islands. For example, *Coracina typica* and *C. newtoni* are found only on Mauritius and Réunion respectively and *C. caerulescens* on Luzón and Cebú in the Philippines.

Most members of the family are sedentary or nomadic, undergoing only seasonal wanderings.

Feeding. The food consists entirely of invertebrates such as spiders, beetles, flies and grubs, or fruit of various sizes, collected from foliage or occasionally from the ground. Caterpillars are a favourite food of some species, hence the name Campephagidae – 'caterpillar-eaters.'

Nesting and the Young. The nest is typically a rather shallow, but neat and sometimes beautiful, saucer-shaped cup or platform constructed of small twigs, rootlets and dried grass, often bound together with spider-webs and well camouflaged with bark fragments and lichens to merge into the horizontal branch on which it is usually placed, so that it is frequently invisible from below. The Ground cuckoo-shrike occasionally uses the old nests of other species.

The clutch size varies from one, in the Varied triller *Lalage leucomela*, to as many as five in some species, though two or three is the more usual number. The eggs may be white, various shades of green, or blue and are frequently speckled or blotched with a contrasting colour such as reddish-brown or purplish-grey, and are incubated by both sexes, or in some cases by the female alone. The

Unlike most birds of its genus, the Flame-coloured minivet *Pericrocotus ethologus* is both colourful and vocal. Here a male (1) and female (2) attend to a nest of young.

343

nestlings sometimes have a white plumage which is subsequently replaced with one resembling that of the female and this is retained until maturity. Sometimes nests are built in close proximity and the Ground cuckoo-shrike takes the community spirit to the stage where neighbouring pairs may indiscriminately feed chicks in several closely placed nests. The breeding biology of a number of species is little known or completely undescribed.

Behaviour. Most members of the family are frequently seen in pairs, family parties or larger flocks, but this behaviour reaches the extreme in some of the minivets which gather in family parties of as many as 150 birds. Some species are rather quiet with soft, wheezy voices, while others are often very noisy especially when in flocks, uttering a variety of shrill whistles and sometimes harsh calls.

Composition. The family consists of 69 species grouped in nine genera, three of which contain only one species. The largest genus is *Coracina* with around 40 species, which have in some cases diverged, through isolation on remote islands, to an extent warranting their separation into races or subspecies; *Coracina tenuirostris*, for example, may be divided into 33 subspecies, and 10 other species contain between 10 and 20 races. The next largest genera are *Lalage* and *Pericrocotus* with 9 and 10 species respectively.

(1) Red-whiskered bulbul *Pycnonotus jocosus*, (2) Red-vented bulbul *Pycnonotus cafer* and (3) Black bulbul *Hypsipetes madagascariensis*.

In courtship display the male Black cuckoo-shrike *Campephaga phoenicea* (1) may open its mouth wide revealing a contrast in colour between its gape and its plumage. Both male and female (2) lift the feathers on their backs.

long or oval more or less operculate nostrils and well developed rictal bristles. The legs and toes are rather weak, usually short and often very short, the wings rather short and rounded, and the tail comparatively long with a rounded, squared or graduated tip.

The plumage is rather long and soft, with long, fluffy feathers on the lower back. Adults of both sexes invariably resemble each other in plumage. Immature birds are unspotted and resemble adults, although they are commonly more dully coloured.

Distribution. The Pycnonotidae is widely distributed throughout Africa, where it is absent only from desert regions. Bulbuls also occur in Madagascar and the Mascarene islands, and in southern Asia from Syria, Afghanistan and central China southwards through the Malay Archipelago to the Philippines and Moluccas. The large genus *Pycnonotus* has numerous species in both Africa and Asia, as does the genus *Criniger*. The Black bulbul *Hypsipetes madagascariensis* ranges from Madagascar to eastern Asia, and many species have restricted ranges in both Africa and Asia. The Red-vented bulbul *Pycnonotus cafer* has been introduced in Fiji and on other tropical island groups.

Behaviour. Many bulbuls are shy birds that remain hidden in dense forest vegetation, but some of the species living in open country are tame birds of tropical gardens that will feed readily on household scraps. Outside the breeding season many species are gregarious, roaming about in noisy bands and often roosting communally, although when breeding the pairs defend exclusive territories around the nest. Fruit, including berries, is the main food of most species, but others glean insects from foliage after the manner of

A group of Red-whiskered bulbuls *Pycnonotus jocosus* reacting to a snake with an aggressive display.

BULBULS

The Pycnonotidae is a fairly large family of tropical perching birds varying in length from $5\frac{1}{2}$–$11\frac{1}{4}$in (14–29cm). Bulbuls have rather small, notched bills, that are slender in all genera but *Spizixos*, with

warblers, and some species eat both insects and fruit. Species of the genus *Hypsipetes*, and probably others, also feed on the nectar and pollen of flowering trees and bushes, and sometimes eat the buds of woody plants.

Many forest bulbuls are exclusively arboreal, whereas open country forms are usually partly or mainly terrestrial. Non-breeding flocks commonly include several species, and often associate with groups of starlings and babblers. The voices of most species are loud and varied, typically consisting of short loud notes and whistles, some of which are musical, but most harsh. Numerous species have varied whistled songs that, in some, include mimicry of the songs of other birds.

The nests are cup-shaped and usually rather bulky, although some genera build semipensile cups that are more flimsy and supported only at the rim. They are built of twigs, stems, dry grass and other plant materials with a lining of fine roots and grasses. Most species nest in bushes or low trees 3–10ft (1–3m) above the ground, although the forest-living species of *Hypsipetes* normally nest 25–50ft (8–17m) up in a forest tree.

The clutch is typically of 2–3, less often 4–5 eggs, varying from white to pink with heavy markings of dark brown, black or grey. Both parents incubate the eggs in turn for periods of about 12–15 days. The young are fed by both parents on insect food that is carried to the nest in the bill. The nestlings are helpless when hatched and have little or no natal down. When small they are brooded by the parents, but later both parents devote their efforts to finding food. The young fledge after 14–18 days in the nest and continue to be fed by the parents for at least a few days afterwards.

Composition. The Pycnonotidae is a natural group of about 120 species usually classified into 15 genera. Ten of the genera are confined to Africa or Madagascar, or both; two are confined to southern Asia, and three genera occur in both Asia and Africa. One of these three, the typical genus *Pycnonotus*, contains nearly 50 species and is much the largest genus of the family. Differences between species in the African and Madagascar genus *Phyllastrephus* are often very slight, as revealed by the recent discovery of two hitherto unknown species *P. apperti* in eastern Madagascar and *P. hallae* in Zaire.

FAIRY BLUEBIRDS AND LEAFBIRDS

The Fairy bluebirds and leafbirds of the family Irenidae are a small group of Asian passerines that are probably closely related to the bulbuls (Pycnonotidae), although some of their characters also suggest affinity with the drongos (Dicruridae) and caterpillar birds (Campephagidae). They vary in length from $4\frac{3}{4}$–$9\frac{1}{2}$in (12–24cm) and are characterized by a fairly long, more or less slender bill with the upper mandible slightly hooked or at least decurved. The legs and toes are short, but not weakly built. The wings are of short to medium length and rounded.

The plumage of members of the Irenidae is long, dense and fluffy, as in many bulbuls. In the ioras of the genus *Aegithina* the colouration is predominantly yellow-green or olive-green, with black on the head, wings and tail and some white markings. The true leafbirds of the genus *Chloropsis* are mainly bright leaf-green, often with bright markings of blue, yellow, orange or black on the throats of adult males. In the third genus, *Irena*, the larger fairy bluebirds are boldly marked with blue or light blue and black. The sexes are mainly dissimilar in colouration in all three genera, the females generally being duller than the males.

Distribution. The Irenidae is confined to the Oriental zoogeographic region, where different species occur from western India to southern China and southwards through Malaysia and the Philippines. The

greatest diversity of species occurs in Malaysia. Although some species make local movements, no member of the family is a long-distance migrant.

Feeding. Leafbirds are all purely arboreal. The bulk of their food is composed of the pulp of large fruit such as guavas and the seeds and pulp taken from berries, figs and similar fruit. The ioras probably eat a higher proportion of insects than of fruit, and members of the other genera also eat insects at times. Insects are either gleaned from foliage or pecked from flowers or fruit. Buds and the dry seeds of herbaceous plants have also been recorded in the diet of fairy bluebirds. The true leafbirds of the genus *Chloropsis* commonly poke into the corollas of tubular flowers to obtain nectar and pollen.

Nesting and the Young. Members of all three genera build neat, cup-shaped nests placed high in the concealing foliage of tall trees or tall bushes, where they are commonly slung between two twigs. Clutches are of 2–4, usually 3–4 eggs. The eggs have a grey, cream or pinkish ground colour and are speckled or lined with brown or red-

Fairy bluebirds and leafbirds of the family Irenidae. (1) Blue-black fairy bluebird *Irena puella*, (2) Common iora *Aegithina tiphia*, (3) male Lesser green leafbird *Chloropsis cyanopogon* and (4) female of the same species.

brown. The sharing of incubation between the sexes appears to have been recorded only for the Common iora, in which each parent takes roughly an equal share.

Behaviour. Leafbirds have cheerful whistling or chattering calls and whistled songs. The fairy bluebirds usually sing regular whistled

The courtship of the Common iora *Aegithina tiphia* includes an acrobatic songflight in which the bird makes a steep ascent into the air and then descends in a slow spiral, singing all the while and fluffing out its feathers to give it a curiously ball-like appearance.

sequences from exposed perches, but the true leafbirds sing short whistled phrases from the concealment of the leafy forest canopy. Details of the territorial behaviour and social organization are unknown, but it seems probable that most if not all species occur in defended territories in which they nest. Several species regularly occur with roaming mixed-species flocks of insectivorous birds.

Composition. The 15 species of the Irenidae are classified in three apparently closely related genera: *Aegithina*, 4 or 5 species; *Chloropsis*, 8 species; *Irena*, 2 species.

SHRIKES

Shrikes are medium-sized to rather large perching birds, ranging from $6\frac{1}{4}$–$14\frac{1}{2}$in (16–37cm) in length, with strong hooked bills reminiscent of those of the smaller falcons, while the bold predatory habits of some species emphasise this superficial resemblance. The strong or moderately strong bill with a hooked upper mandible is a characteristic of the family, and some species also have a distinct tooth in the upper mandible with a corresponding notch in the lower. The legs and feet are strong, with sharp claws that are used for grasping prey. The tarsi are always scutellated (having rather large overlapping scales) in front, but vary from lamellated (finely scaled) to scutellated behind. The tail varies from rather short in the genus *Nilaus* to very long in the genus *Urolestes*, but it is moderately long in the majority of species. The colour and texture of the plumage varies widely.

Distribution. The Laniidae are primarily an Old World family, with two species in North America that doubtless represent a fairly recent colonization. One of the American species, the Northern or Great grey shrike *Lanius excubitor*, ranges from Mexico to Canada in the New World and is also widespread in Europe, Asia and North

Africa. The second American species, the Loggerhead shrike *Lanius ludovicianus*, is confined to North America.

Europe has five species, all of the genus *Lanius*. The Great grey shrike has a fairly extensive European range, as do the Red-backed shrike *L. collurio*, Woodchat shrike *L. senator* and Lesser grey shrike *L. minor*, but the Masked shrike *L. nubicus* is restricted to a small part of southeastern Europe. The last four of these migrate to winter quarters in Africa, European Great grey shrikes travelling only from northern to southern Europe or remaining near their breeding grounds throughout the year.

Africa is much richer in Laniidae than any other continent, having numerous representatives of the subfamily Laniinae as well as all of the species of bush-shrikes (Malaconotinae) and helmet-shrikes (Prionopinae). Laniiae are widespread on the African continent, but do not extend to Madagascar. Among familiar African species of this subfamily are the Grey-backed fiscal shrike *Lanius excubitorius*, Magpie shrike *Urolestes melanoleucus* and the Long-tailed shrike *Corvinella corvina*. The 39 species of Malaconotinae, classified into 7–9 genera, range from Morocco south to the Cape of Good Hope. The puffbacks of the genus *Dryoscopus* and the brightly coloured species of the genus *Chlorophoneus* are included in this subfamily, as are the distinctive tchagras of the genus *Tchagra*. The Prionopinae are also confined to continental Africa, from the southern fringes of the Sahara to Cape Province. The Plumed helmet-shrike *Prionops plumata* occurs in most parts of

Three species of shrikes. (1) Woodchat shrike *Lanius senator*, (2) Plumed helmet-shrike *Prionops plumata* and (3) Grey-headed bush-shrike *Malaconotus blanchoti* with prey.

Male Red-backed shrike *Lanius collurio* displaying to the female.

Here, in a scene witnessed by the artist, a Lesser grey shrike *Lanius minor* (1) unsuccessfully attempts to chase from its territory a Spotted flycatcher *Muscicapa striata* (2) and a Black-eared wheatear *Oenanthe hispanica* (3).

tropical Africa and is the most widespread species of the subfamily. Various African shrikes make seasonal movements, but none of them are long-distance migrants.

Shrikes of the genus *Lanius* (Laniinae) are widespread in Asia, from the temperate north to the tropics of Malaya and Indonesia. The Rufous-backed shrike *L. schach* has a vast range extending from continental Asia to New Guinea, being the only shrike to occur in the Australasian zoogeographical region. The only member of the subfamily Pityriasinae, the Bornean bristlehead *Pityriasis gymnocephala*, is restricted to Borneo. However, its allocation to the Laniidae is provisional and perhaps incorrect. It is about 10in (25cm) long, and has a mainly drab plumage relieved by scarlet on the throat and head. Parts of the head are bare of feathers and have wart-like protuberances and stiff bristle-like feathers.

Feeding. All shrikes are carnivorous and most are bold and aggressive predators of insects, small reptiles, small mammals and small or nestling birds. Many species (including most of the genus *Lanius*) usually hunt from exposed perches, swooping to catch prey in flight or on the ground nearby. The feet as well as the bill are used to manipulate prey, and some species habitually impale dead prey on thorns, stalks or the metal barbs on fences of barbed wire. Other species will hang prey from the forks of twigs and stems. These unusual feeding techniques may have derived from methods of killing live prey, but they also seem to serve as a means of storing food. The maintenance of a so-called 'larder' by the Red-backed shrike led to its alternative English name of 'Butcher bird.'

Many species of the subfamily Malaconotinae hunt among the branches and foliage of trees, gleaning insects and pursuing prey. In contrast the tchagras and some others run beneath bushes and ground vegetation in pursuit of small animals, and a few large species of the genus *Lanius* commonly hover rather in the manner of small falcons.

Nesting and the Young. Most shrikes nest in trees, bushes or hedgerows, building cup-shaped nests of dry leaves, thin twigs, stems and other plant materials with a lining of fine plant fibres or hair. Some species build very compact nests, but in the Black-crowned tchagra *Tchagra senegala* and other species it is rather flimsy. The Little blackcap tchagra *T. minuta* often ornaments the rim of its nest with pieces of snake skin.

Clutches are of 2–8 eggs that are spotted or blotched and vary widely in colouring, with white, pink, pale blue, pale green or buff ground colour and brown, grey, black or violet markings. In most species incubation is performed mainly or entirely by the female. The newly-hatched young have a covering of down. Both parents feed them on food carried to the nest in the bill, and they are brooded when small.

Behaviour. Social organization varies widely in the Laniidae, although paired birds of most species defend discrete territories within which they nest, as in the Red-backed shrike and Great grey shrike. In contrast the Long-tailed shrike is notably gregarious and some of the Malaconotinae are usually seen in small parties.

The helmet-shrikes are the most gregarious members of the family, occurring in parties of 5–20 birds at all seasons and often nesting in small colonies.

The calls of many shrikes are harsh, their name itself being possibly derived from the Middle English word for 'shriek.' However, the songs of many shrikes are rich and musical and often incorporate phrases mimicked from the songs of other species. Some members of the genus *Laniarius* have particularly rich whistling songs, and have been known as 'bell-shrikes.' Many Malaconotinae habitually sing antiphonal duets, with each bird of a

(1) Laden down with the weight of its prey, a Great grey (or Northern) shrike *Lanius excubitor* shifts the mouse from its beak to its claws. (2) South African gonolek *Laniarus atrococcineus* feeding its young, a duty which is performed by both parents. The nest is built of bark and cobwebs.

pair singing alternate notes and producing one half of the distinctive song.

Composition. The Laniidae has about 72 species that are normally classified into four subfamilies: the true shrikes in the subfamily Laniinae with about 25 species; the bush-shrikes in the Malaconotinae with about 39 species; the helmet-shrikes or wood-shrikes, 9 species in the Prionopinae; and the single species of Bornean bristlehead in the Pityriasinae. The similarities between the Malaconotinae and the Laniinae may be due to convergence rather than affinity, so that some ornithologists recognize a family Malaconotidae. The Prionopinae or Prionopidae have similarly uncertain affinities, although various characteristics suggest they are related to the Malaconotinae. Although the Bornean bristlehead's bill is distinctly shrike-like it has other features suggesting that its true affinities may lie in another family group and so it is only tentatively placed in the Laniidae.

VANGAS

The vangas or vanga-shrikes of the family Vangidae are perching birds of rather variable appearance. Some resemble shrikes (Laniidae), others recall wood swallows (Artamidae) or Australian honeyeaters (Meliphagidae), and the Helmetbird *Aerocharis prevostii* looks at first sight like a barbet (Capitonidae) or a small toucan (Ramphastidae).

Vangas vary from 5–12in (13–31cm) in length and show a remarkable range of structural variation. The wings vary from short

The markedly curved bills of vangas probably represent an adaptation to different kinds of prey. (1) Helmetbird *Aerocharis* (= *Euryceros*) *prevostii* with a tree frog. (2) Hook-billed vanga *Vanga curvirostris* with a chameleon.

Sicklebill *Falculea palliata* with a locust. The bird is also shown in flight.

to rather long and are rounded, the tail is moderately long with either a square or rounded tip, and the legs and feet are moderately strong. The bill is moderately long and stout with a hooked tip in the genera *Vanga* and *Leptoptera* among others, but it is short in *Calicalicus*, long, slender and sickle-shaped in *Falculea* and large and very heavy with a prominent swelling on top of the upper mandible in *Aerocharis*.

The Coral-billed nuthatch or Madagascar nuthatch *Hypositta corallirostris* shows numerous differences from the other vangids, so that its affinities to this family have only recently been recognized and are still not accepted by all ornithologists. Its general shape recalls that of a true nuthatch (Sittidae), although the bill is short and fine with a slightly hooked tip, the tail is longer and the hind toe is remarkably long.

The colouration of Vangas is as variable as their structure.

Distribution. The family Vangidae is found only in Madagascar. Unlike many groups of birds of the Malagasy subregion, none of the Vangidae occurs in the Comoro Islands. All of the species are sedentary birds of either wet or dry forests, although a few prefer dry bushy areas in the southwest part of Madagascar.

Several species are fairly common, but the Sicklebill, Van Dam's vanga *Xenopirostris damii*, Pollen's vanga *X. polleni* and Lafresnaye's vanga *X. xenopirostris* are among the rarest and least-known Madagascar birds. The Coral-billed nuthatch is confined to humid forests in eastern Madagascar.

Feeding. So far as is known, all vangas are active arboreal birds that feed mostly on insects and other small animals which are captured among the twigs and branches. The great variation in bill shape in the family suggests that different species are specialized to catch very different prey. The Helmetbird is known to readily take lizards and tree frogs and it seems likely that some other species also do so. The Coral-billed nuthatch behaves like a treecreeper (Certhiidae) as it feeds by climbing up one tree trunk before flying down to climb up another. Unlike the true nuthatches it has not been seen climbing head-first down tree trunks.

The Sicklebill presumably uses its long downcurved bill for poking or probing for food, either in flowers or in the crevices of tree bark. However, the information available on the feeding techniques used by vangas is so scanty that we can only speculate on the functions of their varied bills.

Nesting and the Young. Very little is known of the breeding biology of vangas. *Falculea palliata* is known to build a shallow cup-shaped nest of sticks lined with grass that is placed high in a tree, usually in a fork. The eggs of only a few species have been described and they are white or greenish with brown spots. Nothing is known of incubation, the duties of each sex or of the development of the nestlings.

It is noteworthy that the eggs and nest of *Falculea* appear to be similar to those of many shrikes (Laniidae), supporting the anatomical evidence for the affinity of this family to the Vangidae. However, information on the breeding of the more unusual genera such as *Hypositta* will be of much greater interest for the light it may shed on their relations to other birds.

Behaviour. The few ornithologists who have seen living vangas have mostly described them as strong-flying, active, gregarious birds that live in groups of from three or four to several dozen individuals. The Coral-billed nuthatch apparently does not associate with others of its species in the same way as do most vangas, although it is said to accompany mixed feeding flocks of other insectivorous forest birds.

The voice of the Coral-billed nuthatch has not been described, although several observers have commented that it is usually silent. Other vangas have been reported to give harsh repetitive calls, shrill whistles and chattering notes, both from perches and while flying. Whether or not any vanga has an elaborate song, details of the social organization, and the territorial behaviour (if any) are all unknown.

Composition. The affinities of the Vangidae are not clear. They are conventionally listed near the Laniidae or the Artamidae, but future studies may show this to be misleading. The Vangidae has usually been regarded as including 12–14 species in eight or nine genera. Recent work suggests that the Coral-billed nuthatch is a vangid rather than a member of the Sittidae, although it is perhaps best placed in a separate subfamily Hyposittinae apart from the other vangas. It has also been suggested that an oriole genus *Tylas* should be classified with the vangas.

Blue vanga *Leptopterus madagascarinus* (1) and Pollen's vanga *Xenopirostris polleni*, (2) watching for insects.

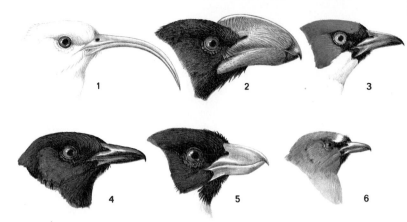

The shape of the bill varies widely among different species of vangas. (1) Sicklebill *Falculea palliata*, (2) Helmetbird *Aerocharis* (= *Euryceros*) *prevostii*, (3) Blue vanga *Leptopterus madagascarinus*, (4) Bernier's vanga *Oriolia bernieri*, (5) Lafresnaye's vanga *Xenopirostris xenopirostris* and (6) Coral-billed (or Madagascar) nuthatch *Hypositta corallirostris*. (7) Lafresnaye's vanga as it incubates its eggs.

The striking bill shape of *Aerocharis* (= *Euryceros*) *prevostii* led the 19th-century ornithologists to place it in a monotypic family Eurycerotidae, and they placed *Falculea* either in a monotypic family Falculidae or with the starlings in the Sturnidae. However, anatomical studies have shown that both of these genera are closely related to vangas of more typical appearance.

For a family of passerine birds with only 12–14 species the Vangidae shows remarkable diversity in structure, particularly in the size and shape of the bill. An obvious question with regard to their evolutionary history is whether they are the remnants of some formerly widespread group of shrike-like birds, or whether they have evolved into a wide range of ecological types from only one or a few ancestral types that colonized Madagascar.

The apparent absence of close relatives of the vangas away from Madagascar makes it seem more likely that they evolved there, and if this is so, it is evident that a great deal of evolutionary change has occurred.

WAXWINGS

The family Bombycillidae consists of only eight species grouped in three subfamilies, the waxwings, silky flycatchers and the single species *Hypocolius ampelinus*. They are similar in general behaviour, feeding habits and nest structure but above all in physical characteristics, such as the structure of the palate. All species have soft, sombre plumage, a prominent crest, a short, broad-based, slightly downcurved and sometimes notched bill, and short, stout legs and toes with long claws.

Five species of waxwings. (1) Bohemian waxwing *Bombycilla garrulus*, (2) Japanese waxwing *Bombycilla japonica*, (3) Long-tailed silky flycatcher *Ptilogonys caudatus*, (4) Hypocolius *Hypocolius ampelinus* and (5) Phainopepla *Phainopepla nitens*.

Waxwings, some $6\frac{1}{2}$–$7\frac{1}{2}$in (16·5–19cm) long, with rich fawn, grey and chestnut plumage, have a black throat and eyebrow streak, dark grey, pointed wings and a short tail. The generally sombre colours contrast strongly with white or white-and-yellow in the wings, and the red, waxy tips to the innerwing (secondary) flight feathers; hence the vernacular name. The grey tail darkens to black near the bright yellow tip; in the Japanese waxwing *Bombycilla japonica* the extreme tip is, in addition, bright red. The undertail plumage is red, chestnut or white, depending on species, sex and age.

Silky flycatchers, so called because of their soft, shiny plumage, are slighter than waxwings with relatively longer wings and tail giving an overall length up to 9in (23cm). Being little known, they, like *Hypocolius ampelinus* often lack a vernacular name. One which does not, the Grey silky flycatcher *Ptilogonys cinereus*, is pale grey, greyish-brown and bluish-grey with black wings. There is a bright yellow patch under the black tail which has a white transverse bar on its underside. The larger, Long-tailed silky flycatcher *P. caudatus* is similar, with a greenish-yellow head and longer, graduated tail. The Phainopepla *Phainopepla nitens* is completely glossy-black except for a large white patch in each wing. The females are mainly greyish-brown without wing patches. Salvin's phainoptila *Phainoptila melanoxantha* is also glossy-black but with bright yellow flanks.

Hypocolius ampelinus is pale or bluish-grey above and pale pinkish-brown below with a buff forehead and a prominent black band encircling the head. The long tail is black-tipped and the wings have white tips and a black leading edge.

Distribution. The ranges of the three subfamilies are quite different. The Cedar waxwing *Bombycilla cedrorum* breeds from southeast Alaska across subarctic Canada and the northern United States to Newfoundland, while the Waxwing *B. garrulus*, known as the Bohemian waxwing in America to distinguish it from the Cedar waxwing, occurs throughout much of the subarctic region, ranging from southern Alaska and northwestern parts of the United States across Canada to Hudson Bay, and from northern Scandinavia across northern Russia and Siberia as far as the Kamchatka Peninsula and the Sea of Okhotsk. The breeding range of the Japanese waxwing is centred on eastern Siberia. The Cedar waxwing occupies a variety of open deciduous and coniferous wooded habitats including orchards and also, where trees are available, bogs and lakesides. The other two species are more typically coniferous forest birds, though mixed or deciduous woodland is also frequented.

Waxwings are noted for the irregularity both of their breeding distribution and periodic eruptive, mainly southerly, winter dispersals, believed to occur when low fruit yield coincides with high bird numbers. It is then that they are seen as far south as Algeria and Iran, and in China, Japan and southwestern United States, particularly in areas with small berry- and fruit-bearing trees, often near human settlements.

The habitat of the silky flycatchers is different and varies both within and between species and from region to region. The two species of the genus *Ptilogonys* inhabit pine and oak woodland, often at high altitudes, and also open, thinly timbered areas, while

The wings of the Cedar waxwing *Bombycilla cedrorum* (1) and the Phainopepla *Phainopepla nitens* (2) display a marked difference in shape, the former being sharp and pointed while the latter are well-rounded. In maturity the Cedar waxwing normally feeds on both fruit and insects, but chicks are fed almost entirely on insects (3). The secondary feathers of waxwings commonly terminate in a red-shaped tip (4), the waxy appearance of which gives the group its common English name.

The highly co-operative and gregarious Palmchat *Dulus dominicus*. The nests are built close together to form one great mass, each nest with a separate entrance and cavity, and usually situated in the crown of a palm.

Phainopepla prefers arid scrubland within reach of watercourses and species of *Phainoptila* are more typical of woodland edges and undergrowth. The subfamily is confined within the region from the southern United States southwards throughout much of Central America. *Phainopepla* ranges the most widely, extending as far north as central California, while the rest breed in various parts of Mexico, Costa Rica, Guatemala and Panama.

Feeding. The food consists of small fruits and berries, and insects, often caught in flight, with the emphasis on berries in the waxwings and *Hypocolius ampelinus* and on insects in the other species.

Nesting and the Young. Knowledge of the breeding biology is sparse for some species. All construct rather loose, bulky nests of interlocked, not woven, twigs, lined with rootlets, grass, pine needles or hair and sometimes a few feathers, and placed often quite high in a bush or tree. The 3–6 eggs are pale bluish-grey or greenish-blue with variable amounts of black or blackish-brown speckles which in *Hypocolius ampelinus* and *Phainoptila* may merge round the broader end of the egg to form a distinct ring. Nest building, incubation and chick feeding duties vary with species; for example, the female Waxwing performs most of the 10–15 days' incubation but the job is shared in *Phainopepla*.

Behaviour. During the breeding season, waxwings are not territorial but merely defend the immediate vicinity of the nest. This behaviour is associated with the lack of a well-developed song, although the calls are sometimes quite striking and musical.

Composition. The inclusion of the three subfamilies within the family Bombycillidae is somewhat tentative for, although taxonomists generally agree upon their close relationship, some prefer to divide them up in various ways, for example as three separate families while recently, others have also included the family Dulidae. More universal agreement may result from further studies of the lesser-known species.

PALMCHAT

The Palmchat *Dulus dominicus* is the only species of the Dulidae. It is about 7in (18cm) in length, with rather rounded wings of medium length, a moderately long tail with a slightly forked tip and rather stout legs and feet having fairly long toes and claws. The bill is rather long, stout and laterally compressed.

The plumage is strong and somewhat coarse in texture. Adults of both sexes have similar colouration, with grey-olive upperparts, tail and wings, and white to cream underparts with bold longitudinal stripes of dark brown. The feathers of the head have dark shafts so that the head appears darker than the back, and the rump feathers are tinged with green. The bill is yellowish, the iris red-brown, and the feet and legs are blackish-grey. Juveniles differ from adults in having the throat and neck mainly dark brown, with faint pale streaks formed by narrow whitish edges to the feathers, and in having the rump buffy rather than dark olive-green.

Distribution. The Palmchat is confined to the island of Hispaniola in the West Indies, where it occurs both in Haiti and the Dominican Republic, and on the offshore islands of Gonave and Saona. It is sedentary except for local feeding movements. The preferred habitat of the Palmchat is open country or scrub with groves of tall trees. It particularly favours groves of Royal palms *Roystonea*, although these are absent from some localities where the species breeds.

Feeding. The Palmchat's diet consists mainly of small fruit, the berry-like fruit of certain palms being particularly favoured. Flower buds and open flowers of such trees as *Cordia* are also eaten, and probably also nectar and pollen from flowers. When feeding in a fruiting bush or tree, flocks of Palmchats move agilely through the branches and individuals commonly hang half-inverted to reach distant fruit.

Nesting and the Young. Palmchats build large communal nests of sticks, twigs and vine stems in trees. Favoured sites are in tall Royal palms, where the nest is woven about the top of the smooth trunk and the bases of the fronds. When the palm dies and the fronds fall the nest falls to the ground. In mountain regions where palms are scarce the nest is usually only a small structure occupied by one or two pairs, but dozens may use the same nest in the lowlands. In less favourable habitats the nest may be placed in a variety of trees.

New nests are built and old ones are repaired for reuse during the months from March to June. Each pair of birds using a communal nest adds sticks to the main structure, although each builds its own nest chamber with a private entrance to the outside. The nest may thus be visualized as a block of flats, rather than as a truly communal structure. The nest chambers are lined rather roughly with fine grass or other plant stems, dead leaves or shredded bark. Clutches are of 2–4 white eggs that are heavily spotted and blotched with dark purple-grey, or sometimes with a rough band of spots of this colour around the large end. Incubation is probably carried out by both sexes. The young are probably naked of down when hatched. They receive food from both parents, which carry it to the nest in their throats then regurgitate it into the gapes of the nestlings. Fledged young are fed for at least a short time after they leave the nest.

Behaviour. The Palmchat is gregarious throughout the year. Outside the breeding season it feeds in groups and roosts communally with individual birds huddled together in a row along a branch. It is noisy at all seasons, although perhaps especially so when nesting. There is no true song. The calls consist of whistling, scraping, twittering and warbling notes, some of them harsh and others more melodious.

Composition. The Palmchat has peculiarities which suggest it is not very closely related to any of the major passerine groups. Its closest relatives appear to be the waxwings (Bombycillidae).

DIPPERS

Dippers are rather wren-like song birds of the family Cinclidae, and suborder Oscines. There are four species contained in a single genus *Cinclus*. The dippers resemble wrens in their short wings and tail, copious plumage and type of nest, but are specialized for feeding in or under running water, with the tarsus long and sturdy and with stout claws for gripping the river bed. The different species vary in size from between that of a sparrow to that of a Song thrush. They have thin bills and are predominantly grey or brown.

Distribution. Dippers are confined to hilly and mountainous regions. Several races of the White-capped dipper *Cinclus leucocephalus* inhabit the Andes. The range of the American dipper *C. mexicanus* extends from western Panama to Alaska and the Aleutians. The European Dipper *C. cinclus* ranges from Britain eastwards to northwest Africa and central Asia, reaching 16,000ft (4,920m) in the Himalayas and nearly 17,000ft (5,230m) in Tibet. In Turkestan, the Himalayas and western China, its range overlaps with that of the Brown dipper *C. pallasii* which prefers lower, wider rivers and inhabits northern Asia eastwards to Japan.

Feeding. The dipper's feeding habits have always aroused interest representing as they do a special form of adaptation to an unusual mode of life. Dippers have been filmed swimming under water, propelled by their wings and not their legs. They are also quite commonly seen walking upstream in shallow water searching for prey on the river bed, or swimming in slightly deeper water – not usually more than 18in (45cm) deep – and diving from the surface. They will readily plunge directly into the water from a river bank, a boulder or the margin of ice.

Their food consists mainly of the larvae of aquatic insects, and small aquatic molluscs and crustaceans. Small fishes are also taken but they are not very expertly dealt with and form, together with worms and tadpoles, only a small proportion of the dipper's known prey.

Nesting and the Young. The breeding of the dipper has been studied in North America, Czechoslovakia and Britain. Nests are usually built on rock faces (including waterfalls), on man-made structures, for example on sluices, mills, culverts and bridges, and under overhanging banks and against tree trunks. The entrance is normally over water.

The large nest is like that of a wren and usually fits into a roofed cavity which determines its dimensions. In Britain the nest's outer shell is made of mosses. These are mostly gathered along the river bank although some aquatic mosses may be used. The material, collected by both cock and hen, is dipped into the river before use, presumably to make it easier to work with. When the outer shell is completed, a lining of dried grasses and finally an inner cup of leaves are added.

Nest-building begins as early as February and proceeds slowly. Eggs may be laid in mid-March but more usually in April. Later nests may be built in as little as nine days. Four or five thin-shelled white eggs are usually laid, sometimes only three, rarely as many as seven. They hatch in about 16 days and the young are fed by both parents. There are sometimes two broods.

Young dippers remain in the nest for about three weeks, and reach a weight of 2oz (50–60gm). Their first plumage, which they begin to moult at nine weeks, is more mottled than that of the parent birds, and the white feathers at chin, throat and upper breast are tipped with dark brown, giving a rather thrush-like appearance. The young are fed by their parents until about five weeks old and then disperse. They can be distinguished from adults by the white tips of the greater wing coverts which persist until the following April.

Behaviour. The territorial habits of the dipper are striking. Both sexes take up territories in winter, as well as in spring and summer. It is possible to pursue a dipper along the bank of a stream or river

Four species of dippers. (1) American dipper *Cinclus mexicanus*, (2) Brown dipper *C. pallasii*, (3) European dipper *C. cinclus* with prey, (4) White-capped dipper *C. leucocephalus* and (5) European dipper with nest of young on a river bank.

The European dipper *Cinclus cinclus* hunting for small fish and insects.

until it suddenly doubles back, thus revealing the limit of its territory. Winter territories have been found to be as little as 1,050–1,200ft (320–365m) long in North America where dippers are forced downstream by ice, but a distribution of one dipper to 2,100–3,300ft (650–1,015m) is more usual in Czechoslovakia and Scotland.

Summer territories also vary markedly in size, from about 1,200ft (365m) in Britain, and 1,650–1,950ft (505–600m) in Germany to nests $1\frac{1}{4}$–2mi (2–3km) apart in the USSR. Territory size may be determined by the availability of nest sites.

Territories are defended by song, often delivered from favoured boulders near the margin of the territory and by ritualized forms of display. Dippers sing loudly so as to be heard above the rush of water and throughout the whole year except July and August. Both sexes sing. Display consists largely of bobbing up and down with wing-flicking, dropping into the water and swimming ashore during pursuit flight, and a form of upright posturing to display the breast colouring. There is also a display flight, rarely seen, in which two dippers fly much higher than usual, at 50–100ft (15–30m), with loud and continuous song. Normal flight is directly along the water-course at about 1–6ft.

Winter occupation of a territory may be by either sex or by both birds of a pair which remain to nest in the same place the following spring. Some dippers stay for two or three years in the one territory, changing mates during that time.

Composition. The Cinclidae comprises four species in a single genus *Cinclus*, the Dipper *C. cinclus*, the American dipper *C. mexicanus*, the White-capped dipper *C. leucocephalus*, and the Brown dipper *C. pallasii*.

WRENS

Wrens are small or, exceptionally, middle-sized passerines, ranging in size from $3\frac{3}{4}$ to $8\frac{3}{4}$in (9·5–22·2cm). Their plumage comes in shades of brown, rufous, greyish to blackish, often with dull white or chestnut areas and sometimes streaked, banded or spotted with buff, brown or black, especially on the wings and tail. Male and female are alike. The bill is slender and somewhat curved, adapted for probing into crevices. The legs are strong, with long claws. Most species are plump, apart from the largish and relatively conspicuous cactus wrens, and many have short tails which can be cocked. All species are active, bustling birds but unobtrusive apart from their songs. Species have become adapted to many different kinds of habitat, varying from rain forest to moorland, marsh and semi-desert, island cliffs and mountain highlands. In general they feed fairly close to the ground and thread their way readily through undergrowth. The Wren *Troglodytes troglodytes* (or Winter wren as it is called in America) is particularly adaptable and can make itself at home in forests, off-shore islands or suburban gardens where it is welcomed because of its cheerful song, diminutive size, intriguing ways and interesting domed nest. Wrens move their wings rapidly in flight and mostly avoid coming out into the open.

Distribution. Apart from the Winter wren the Troglodytidae is confined to the New World. Species are most numerous in or near the Tropics where apparently the family originated. About 8–9,000 years ago when temperatures rose and the polar ice receded, the Winter wren crossed to Asia in the region of the Bering Strait and gradually extended its range through much of the continent, apart from areas too hot, cold or arid. It then colonized Europe and reached North Africa, where there are two subspecies. Few species are migratory but the House wren goes south from the United States and there are wren passage movements along the east coast of Britain and the Channel Islands.

Feeding. All wrens are insectivorous although some species eat a small amount of vegetable matter. Spiders are quite commonly taken and, exceptionally, wrens have been observed catching tadpoles and small fish.

Nesting and the Young. The Winter wren and House wren build nests, or their foundations, as a preliminary to securing a mate. Some species make a number of nests – the Winter wren occasionally as many as 10. Such multiple nesting is related to the pair bond and roosting behaviour. It may have evolved in the tropics. The cock wren prefers moist material and is stimulated to build by a downpour after a dry spell. His mate lines the nest with feathers and a little moss. In many tropical species the sexes work together but the contribution of male and female may vary. A female Carolina wren *Thryothorus ludovicianus* sometimes completes a nest begun by the male. In the Winter wren, courtship display is related to the nest. The male attracts a roving female with his song and, when she approaches, he sings in a subdued way, fluttering his wings, and thus displaying leads her to the nest. He induces her to enter by going inside, emerging and singing again. The courtship of the Long-billed marsh wren *Telmatodytes palustris* is somewhat similar. In some species the nature of the habitat and the abundance or otherwise of food has a bearing on whether the pair bond is monogamous or polygamous. Male Winter wrens holding favourable territories are most prone to form a multiple pair bond. In more austere habitats, as on some of the island groups north of mainland Britain where distinct subspecies occur, polygamy has not been noted. The form of polygamy is usually bigamy; a contemporaneous pair bond with three mates is rare. Some 6% of House wrens are bigamous and between a quarter and a third of Prairie marsh wrens *Telmatodytes palustris dissaeptus* but, as with the Winter wren, the nature of the habitat may be significant. In a favourable area polygamy in the Winter wren may approach 50%. So far as is known, most tropical wrens are monogamous.

The eggs of most species are white, speckled to greater or lesser extent with brown, and the clutch may number from 2–8 – the smaller clutches being typical of some tropical species and the larger of the Winter wren in the most northerly continental parts of its range. The incubation rhythm may be complete the day after the last egg is laid or not until the fifth day after – hence discrepancies between records of the incubation period varying from 12 to 16 or more days. In all species only the female incubates.

Occasionally the female wren is responsible for all, or nearly all, the feeding but the male commonly helps after the first week and may take entire charge of the nestlings for the last week or more if misadventure befalls his mate. The average nestling period is 16–17 days. In most tropical species both parents feed the nestlings, but young of an earlier brood of Neotropical house wrens sometimes help to feed the chicks of a later brood and auxiliaries may help at the nests of Banded wrens *Thryothorus pleurostictus*.

Behaviour. Wrens of all species are territorial and defend their holding vocally but occasionally a Winter or House wren may have

The Winter wren *Troglodytes troglodytes*, like most species of wren, constructs covered nests, often in a recess or cavity.

beak and claw encounters with another male. A Winter wren may defend the same territory for five years but, casualties being heavy, this is unusual. Tropical species appear to retain the same territory and mate from one year to the next. The family includes notable songsters, such as the Organ bird or Quadrille wren *Leucolepis arada* of South America and the Song wren *L. phaeocephalus* of Central America. Some tropical species sing antiphonally or 'duet.'

All species roost in a sheltered nook which may be one of their own nests. Some species sleep in nests which are similar to the breeding nest in construction and location but others make dormitory nests which are different, being less substantial. The Chinchirigüi wren *Thryothorus modestus* builds a sleeping nest of different design from the breeding nest. The dormitory nests of the Lowland wood wren *Henicorhina leucosticta* have flimsy sides and are situated some feet up in the undergrowth but the breeding nest is built lower, has much thicker walls and is better concealed. In some species the dormitory nests have such shallow cups that eggs would roll out. Sub-adult Northern cactus wrens build incomplete dormitory nests. Carolina wrens have been found sleeping in the pocket of an old coat. They sometimes roost in pairs.

When young Winter wrens fledge they are led at dusk or earlier by the male or female to a roosting-place which may be one of the cock's unused nests or the disused nest of some other species. Fledged Winter wrens may return for a night or two to their nest. Sometimes the female may spend the night with them. So far as is known it is usual for the fledged young of most temperate and tropical wrens to be guided to the nest by means of a procedure rather similar to that used by the Winter wren in enticing a female to his nest. When auxiliaries help Banded-backed wrens *Campylorhynchus zonatus* with tending the chicks all may sleep together.

The social roosting of Winter wrens in winter is a family pre-adaptation which has been important in enabling this small bird, normally non-social, to extend its range so widely. When cold weather sets in a male calls or sings at dusk and attracts others. At first he may try to repel more than one or two from entering the nest or other roosting niche which he is occupying but, eventually, defence is abandoned and if severe weather continues large numbers may crowd into a nest or nesting box.

Most wrens have a retiring disposition and avoid coming out into the open. (1) Winter wren *Troglodytes troglodytes*, (2) Long-billed marsh wren *Cistothorus palustris*, (3) Lowland wood wren *Henicorhina leucosticta*, (4) Northern cactus wren *Campylorhynchus bruneicapillus*, (5) Canyon wren *Salpinctes mexicanus*, (6) Rock wren *S. obsoletus* and (7) White-headed wren *Campylorhynchus albobrunneus*.

Composition. The family consists of 63 species divided into 12–14 genera according to different authorities.

MOCKINGBIRDS AND THRASHERS

The family Mimidae is often referred to as the mockingbird family but the actual mockingbirds constitute only about half the total species, most of the remainder being known collectively as thrashers and a few others as catbirds. In all there are over 30 species. Medium-sized birds of some 8–12in (20–30cm) in length, they have long tails and rather short, rounded wings. Many species have strong, fairly long bills, which are downcurved, in some species to a marked extent; a few have straighter medium-length bills. The family is not remarkable for bright plumage, most species being various shades of grey, reddish to greyish brown or almost white, generally darker above than below and often with faintly or distinctly spotted or streaked underparts. A number of species have patches or bars of white in the wings and tail; these are particularly noticeable in flight. Several species have dark eye patches, and in some, the bright yellow iris gives the eyes a rather staring appearance. A general feature of the family is the lack of any marked sexual or seasonal plumage differences.

Distribution. Mockingbirds occur in the temperate, subtropical and tropical regions of the American continent and its neighbouring islands, from southern Canada, through central America and the West Indies south to southern Argentina and Chile. The species vary considerably in the extent of their range; for example one species, the Galápagos mockingbird *Nesomimus trifasciatus*, is confined to the Galápagos Islands whereas the Common catbird

occurs from southern Canada south to the Gulf States and winters as far south as Panama, and the Northern mockingbird *Mimus polyglottos* ranges through much of central, eastern and southern United States and southwards to Mexico and various islands in the Gulf.

The family is best represented in Central America where about half the species are endemic and a number of other more widely distributed species also occur. The tropical populations tend to be sedentary while those from higher latitudes are often markedly migratory, moving to warmer regions for the winter. Not surprisingly habitats vary considerably from deserts to swampy woodlands, plantations, gardens and forest edges, but the greatest number are found in arid areas of dense bushes and small trees or cacti.

Feeding. The range of diet throughout the family is not large, most species feeding on fruits and seeds or various invertebrates such as

Some variations in plumage among mockingbirds. (1) Galápagos mockingbird *Nesominus trifasciatus*, (2) Northern mockingbird *Mimus polyglottos*, (3) Common (or Gray) catbird *Dumetella carolinensis*, (4) Black catbird *Melanoptila glabrirostris*, (5) Blue mockingbird *Melanotis caerulescens* and (6) Blue-and-white mockingbird *M. hypoleucus*.

Brown thrasher *Toxostoma rufum* in full flight with a larva in its beak.

insects, spiders, centipedes and worms. Differences exist chiefly in the types of food taken and these are related to a diversity of structural adaptations in the skeleton, musculature, legs and bills, of the different species. The bills of the 10 species of thrashers of the genus *Toxostoma*, varying considerably in length and curvature as they do, illustrate the principle best. The longest, most decurved bills in the genus are found in the California thrasher *T. redivivum*, the Le Conte thrasher *T. lecontei* and the Crissal thrasher *T. dorsale*, which are adapted for digging and probing in search of prey in soft soil and leaf litter. Their terrestrial habits have led to decreased development of the wings and wing musculatures and a corresponding improvement in running ability.

Nesting and the Young. The nests are generally rather bulky, open, cup-shaped structures of twigs lined with rootlets, hair or grass. They are built, often by both sexes, low down in a bush or even on the ground and frequently last for several seasons, although they are normally used only once. The two to six eggs (the larger clutches are characteristic of higher latitudes and the smaller ones of tropical regions) vary in colour from species to species but are often speckled with brown. The ground colour may be various shades of pale buff, blue or green or, as in the Bahama mockingbird *Mimus gundlachii*, creamy or pinkish white. In the majority of species, incubation is performed by the female alone, but in others, such as some of the thrashers, the duties are shared. After about a fortnight's incubation, the helpless, sparsely down-covered nestlings are hatched and tended by both parents for a further 13–19 days, after which the fledglings gradually become independent. The California thrasher is unusual in being able to nest during the autumn as well as the normal spring breeding period.

Behaviour. The mockingbirds never gather in flocks and are generally solitary and highly territorial, defensive behaviour being often conspicuous and not always confined to the breeding season. Territorial aggression in some species may take the form of physical attacks on such invaders as dogs, cats and even humans. However, at other times, they can be extremely tame. The intensity of defensive behaviour is often reflected in the degree to which the song is developed, some species being renowned for their vigorous, musical voices. The song does not adhere to a fixed pattern,

although phrases are repeated, sometimes successively. It contrasts strongly with the alarm notes which are extremely harsh and unmusical. The name 'mockingbird' is associated with the ability to imitate the songs of other species, though this is sometimes exaggerated as many of the vocal similarities are believed by scientists to be coincidental; true mimicry probably constitutes only about 10% of the repertoire of the better mimics such as the Northern mockingbird.

Singing is not solely by the male nor is it always confined to the breeding season or to daylight hours, although nocturnal singing usually occurs only during the breeding period. Mostly, the song is uttered from a conspicuous perch, but members of the genus *Mimus* and the Sage thrasher *Oreoscoptes montanus*, sing during a short aerial display flight over the nesting grounds.

The Brown trembler *Cinclocerthia ruficauda* and the White-breasted trembler *Ramphocinclus brachyurus* are worthy of special mention because of their unique and peculiar habit of trembling the wings and body vigorously, the significance of which is not understood. Attractive birds, unfortunately restricted to a few islands in the West Indies and nowhere common, they are also noted for their remarkable tameness and inquisitiveness.

Composition. The *Mimidae* are divided into 13 genera, the largest of which are *Mimus* with 9 species and *Toxostoma* with 10. *Melanotis* contains two species, sometimes regarded as races of the same species. Ten of the genera contain only one species, and these tend to be restricted to remote islands such as the Galápagos Islands and Socorro, and St Lucia, Martinique, St Vincent and other West Indian islands, where they have evolved in isolation from the mainland species. The Galápagos species is particularly interesting in that different islands in the archipelago now support different subspecies or races. The family appears to have considerable affinities both with the thrushes *Turdidae* and the larger wrens *Troglodytidae*.

HEDGE SPARROWS

The accentors, represented in Europe by the familiar Hedge sparrow or Dunnock *Prunella modularis* and Alpine accentor *P. collaris* are small, rather sombre-plumaged birds from 5–7in (12·5–17·5cm) long, forming a distinct group of 12 species. They range in colour from dark brown or grey to buff, chestnut or russet, being generally though not always darker above than below. Most

All members of the Prunellidae are shy, skulking or inconspicuous, spending most of the time in cover. (1) Siberian accentor *Prunella montanella* and (2) Radde's accentor *P. ocularis*.

species are streaked, especially on the upper parts, and the chin and breast are often spotted or of a contrasting colour to the rest of the plumage. The dark-brown or blackish bill is rather slender, though wide at the base, and finely pointed. The wings of some species are rather short and rounded but others, usually of the more migratory species, are rather longer and more pointed, while the tail is of medium length in all species. The legs and feet are strongly constructed, indicative of the accentors' habit of feeding largely on the ground where they move by hopping or running. Some species also perch in trees or bushes, particularly to sing. The flight is usually low, infrequently sustained but quite strong and undulating, with rapid wing-beats. The plumage of the sexes is identical though the male may be somewhat brighter. The juveniles are usually mottled on the upperparts and often distinctly spotted on the breast.

Distribution. The accentors are chiefly confined to the temperate latitudes of the Palearctic Region in North Africa, Europe and Asia, though the Dunnock has been introduced elsewhere as in New Zealand and South Africa. The family is typically associated with high mountainous regions and frequently occurs above the tree line. Species of these areas migrate to lower altitudes in winter while

The Dunnock *Prunella modularis* has a wide range of habitats, but hedge sparrows typically like open country with sparse, shrubby vegetation. (1) Alpine accentor *Prunella collaris*, (2) Dunnock and (3) Maroon-backed accentor *P. immaculata*.

those of more northerly populations migrate southwards, either completely or partially. The Dunnock is chiefly sedentary in Britain but mainly migratory on the European continent. The Himalayan accentor *P. himalayana* breeds between about 12,000 and 17,000ft (3,600–5,100m), while the Nepal race of the Alpine accentor *P. c. nipalensis* has been recorded at 21,000ft (6,300m) although it is only known to breed up to about 18,000ft (5,400m). The Alpine accentor has the widest range, though because of its specialized habitat it is a markedly discontinuous one. It occurs in the high mountains of southern and eastern Europe, northwest Africa, the Caucasus, Iran, the Himalayas, Central Asia and southern Siberia, eastwards to China and Japan.

By comparison, the Dunnock is much more abundant over a more compact, almost entirely European range. There are two main

populations, one extending from Ireland eastwards to the Urals, but absent from the extreme south and north and from southern European Russia, and the other found only in the Crimea and Caucasus and from Turkey eastwards to the southern Caspian region.

The Japanese accentor *P. rubida*, restricted to Japan and neighbouring islands, closely resembles the Dunnock in many respects and the two species are probably eastern and western relics of a single species once occurring right across the Asian continent. The breeding distributions of five species, the Himalayan accentor, the Brown accentor *P. fulvescens*, the Robin accentor *P. rubeculoides*, the Maroon-backed accentor *P. immaculata* and Rufous-breasted accentor *P. strophiata*, are centred at high altitudes on the Himalayan and associated mountain ranges, while the Siberian species, *P. montanella*, is apparently confined to northern and central Siberia, migrating to southeast Asia in winter. The Black-throated accentor *P. atrogularis* is chiefly Himalayan but with an isolated population in the northern Urals. Two other species occur entirely outside the Himalayas; Kozlov's accentor *P. kozlowi* is found only in Mongolia and Radde's accentor *P. ocularis* is restricted to two distinct populations, one in the Yemen and the other in the mountains of northeast Turkey, Armenia and northern Iran.

Feeding. Details of food of most species are sparse or lacking but the Dunnock and Alpine accentor are probably representative, taking mainly small seeds and fruits, particularly in winter, or small invertebrates such as flies, caterpillars, beetles, spiders and worms, especially in summer.

Nesting and the Young. In spring, the male's repeated, brief, rather thin, trilling warble from a prominent bush or rock signals the start of breeding. Courtship and displays are not elaborate and this, coupled with the often remote breeding areas, has led to a paucity of recorded observations. However, the Dunnock, which has been best studied, takes part in communal displays when two or more birds hop around in vegetation or on the ground, repeatedly flicking up one or both wings, while uttering short staccato calls. Another

A pair of Dunnocks *Prunella modularis* (1) with a nest of eggs. The female is shown in flight. (2) Black-throated accentor *P. atrogularis* at take-off.

peculiar aspect of Dunnock behaviour is 'cloaca pecking,' where the female crouches on the ground, fluffs out her feathers, and progressively raises the tail to expose the distended cloaca (reproductive opening) which is repeatedly pecked by the male. This generally leads to copulation, achieved as the male very briefly mounts the female. The female alone usually builds the nest, either virtually on the ground or up to several feet above it, generally well concealed by dense vegetation or a rock, tussock or crevice depending on species and habitat. The eggs, usually 4–5 but occasionally 3–6, are bluish or greenish-blue and incubated by the hen or, in some species, both sexes for 11–15 days. The young are hatched naked and helpless and fed in the nest by both sexes for about a fortnight and subsequently until well able to fly.

Composition. Most authors regard the accentors as a distinct family group but their relationship to other families is the subject of considerable debate, the wagtails, warblers and thrushes all having been involved at some time. All species are generally placed in one genus *Prunella*, reflecting the view that the family is homogeneous.

THRUSHES

The thrushes, chats, robins and solitaires of the family Turdidae form a large and distinctive group in the vast assemblage that includes the Old World warblers and flycatchers, and perhaps the babblers (Timaliidae). Members of the Turdidae vary in length from $4\frac{1}{2}$–13in (11–33cm), most species being of medium size. The wings vary from short and rounded to longer and pointed and the

Five members of the thrush family, to show variation in plumage. (1) Wheatear *Oenanthe oenanthe*, (2) Nightingale *Luscinia megarhynchos*, (3) Stonechat *Saxicola torquata*, (4) Black redstart *Phoenicurus ochruros* and (5) Eastern bluebird *Sialia sialis*.

The thrush family probably originated in the Old World, but has been established in the Americas for a very long time. (1) (European) Blackbird *Turdus merula*, (2) Rock thrush *Monticola saxatilis*, (3) Townsend's solitaire *Myadestes townsendi* and (4) Wood thrush *Hylocichla mustelina*.

tail varies from short to rather long. A few species have the tail tip forked, but it is square or rounded in most. The legs and feet are typically of moderate length and rather stout, but some genera have shorter tarsi. The bill is more or less slender in all species, and generally has at least a few rictal bristles at its base.

Plumage is glossy in a few species but rather soft in the majority. Colouration is varied, with brown, grey, olive, black or blue usually predominating, often with orange or red markings. Green and yellow occur only in a few species. The sexes are similar in many species, but very different in colouration in others. Juvenile plumages are usually spotted or have scaly markings, especially on the underparts.

Distribution. The Turdidae as a whole has a vast range, including all continents except the Antarctic and most major islands except for New Zealand, where, however, the Song thrush *Turdus philomelos* and Blackbird *T. merula* have been introduced.

Characteristic European species include the Blackbird, Song thrush, Mistle thrush *Turdus viscivorus*, Redwing *T. iliacus* and Fieldfare *T. pilaris*, the last two breeding north into the Arctic. The chat-like group is represented by the familiar European robin *Erithacus rubecula*, and the Nightingale *Luscinia megarhynchos*, Redstart *Phoenicurus phoenicurus*, Black redstart *P. ochruros*, Wheatear *Oenanthe oenanthe* and Stonechat *Saxicola torquata*. Various other chats occur in southern Europe, including several other species of wheatear.

Tropical Asia has additional representatives of all of these groups, including a considerable diversity of small chats of *Erithacus*, *Luscinia* and related genera. The primitive shortwings of the genus *Brachypteryx* are found only in India and southeast Asia, as are the peculiar forktails of the genus *Enicurus*. The Australasian zoogeographical region has few thrushes, other than numerous forms of the Island thrush *Turdus poliocephalus* and a few related species, ground-thrushes of the genus *Zoothera*, two species of the genus *Saxicola* and the scrub-robins of the genus *Drymodes*. The Island thrush is the only species inhabiting Polynesia, where its varied subspecies are found as far east as Samoa. Africa is rich in chat-like thrushes, but has fewer representatives of the true thrushes of such genera as *Turdus* and *Zoothera*. Chats of the genera *Cossypha*, *Alethe*, *Cercomela* and *Erythropygia* are particularly abundant and represented by numerous species.

North America has many thrushes, among the most familiar being the American robin *Turdus migratorius* and a variety of small species of the genera *Hylocichla* and *Catharus*. The bluebirds in the genus *Sialia* are widespread and colourful, but the solitaires of the genus *Myadestes* are inconspicuous forest birds. Most of these range south to central America and the West Indies, at least as migrant visitors. The American tropics have a considerable number of peculiar species of *Turdus*, as well as a few solitaires and small thrushes. The Hawaiian Islands are inhabited by the two small species of the genus *Phaeornis*, which are thought to have been derived from migrant solitaires, and Tristan da Cunha has the endemic genus *Nesocichla*.

Many thrushes inhabiting temperate regions are long distance migrants and others make more local movements. Examples of long distance migrants are the Whinchat *Saxicola rubetra* and Nightingale, both of which breed in Europe and winter in tropical Africa. Local migrants include some such as the Fieldfare which may move from Finland to Italy or Britain, and others where the more northern and eastern populations make long movements, but their more southern and western counterparts are sedentary, as in the European robin.

Most Turdidae are terrestrial or partly terrestrial, but some are

Four species of thrush shown in flight. (1) (European) Blackbird *Turdus merula*, (2) Song thrush *T. philomelos*, (3) Rock thrush *Monticola saxatilis* and (4) the White's thrush *Zoothera dauma*, seen also (5) from below.

(European) Blackbird *Turdus merula* (1) and Song thrush *T. philomelos* (2) alighting on their nests. (3) A (European) Blackbird defeats a Song thrush in a tug-of-war for a worm. This bird's disability in having only one leg is compensated for by its typical aggressiveness.

predominantly arboreal. The range of habitats occupied by the family as a whole is vast, from rich tropical rain forests to the bare desert habitats of the Desert wheatear *Oenanthe deserti*. Other species of chat prefer open grasslands or scrub, and some of the true thrushes breed in arctic tundra. Various members of the family have become familiar town and garden birds, notably the European robin, Blackbird and Song thrush and the American robin.

Feeding. Thrushes as a whole take varied diets, including a variety of small animals and of vegetable materials. The animal foods include many kinds of insects, spiders, molluscs, earthworms, small crustaceans, and occasionally such tiny vertebrates as baby snakes, lizards and fish. Vegetable foods include quantities of berries and other fruit, and to a lesser extent seeds, buds and stems. Those species living near human habitations often adapt to a diet including quantities of bread and other scraps.

A variety of hunting techniques is used. Such species as the American robin and Song thrush will glean insects from the foliage or limbs of trees or hop about on grassland ready to pounce on any exposed insect or hidden earthworm they encounter. In contrast, wheatears and other chats often wait on low perches for insects to appear, then catch them on quick, shrike-like flights.

Nesting and the Young. Virtually all Turdidae build open cup-shaped nests, although domed nests have been reported for a few species whose position in the family is questionable. The nest materials are typically stems and leaves of plants, including thin woody twigs in the larger species. The lining is often of finer stems and leaves and may include moss, lichens and occasionally feathers. The Song thrush builds a hard nest-lining of dried mud, cattle dung or wood pulp, and the Blackbird's nest has a similar solid lining but covered with fine plant stems and fibres.

Nest sites vary widely, from enclosed holes in the ground or among rocks, as in the wheatears, to open sites among vegetation. The Redstart nests in tree holes, holes in stumps or in holes in the ground, whereas the Black redstart prefers less enclosed cavities in rocks or buildings. Both Stonechats and Whinchats *Saxicola rubetra* choose concealed sites in thick ground vegetation, often in dense clumps of grass, gorse or heather. Most of the typical thrushes and many chats nest in bushes, trees or hedges, at heights varying from near ground level to high in trees. Some of these species will nest on buildings where sites in trees are scarce, or occasionally on the ground where bushes are almost or completely absent.

Many species raise several broods each season, as many as five having been recorded for a pair of Blackbirds, although three or four are more usual. Other species are double or single brooded. In the multi-brooded species the same nest may be used for all of the later broods or a new nest may be built for each.

Clutches contain 1–7 eggs, 3–6 being the range for most species. The eggs vary from unmarked white to pale green, blue, buff or reddish with heavy spots and blotches. The egg colour of particular species is closely related to the kind of nest site chosen. Thus the Redstart which nests in holes lays immaculate light blue eggs, the Stonechat nesting in concealment on the ground lays blue eggs with fine reddish spots, and the Mistle thrush nesting in the open branches of a bush or tree lays eggs with bold spots of red-brown and grey. The relationship of the egg colour to the nest site apparently reflects adaptations to the conflicting requirements for camouflage from predators in open sites and for the eggs to be visible to the parents in dark places.

Both nest building and incubation are performed by the female alone in at least the large majority of species. Incubation periods vary from 12–15 days, tending to be long in the larger species and in those small species that nest in holes.

The newly-hatched young have fluffy dark-coloured down on the head and back. The eyes open within a few days, and feathers begin to grow within a week. Fledging periods vary from around 12–15 days, tending to be long in the hole-nesting species and short in those which nest in concealed sites on the ground. The young are fed by both parents on food carried to the nest in the bill or in both bill and throat. Feeding rates are often as high as one feed every three or four minutes, but sometimes as low as every 10 to 15 minutes.

After fledging the young continue to receive food from their parents for a few days, begging with fluttering wings and high-pitched calls. Soon after they have begun to obtain their own food, they disperse from the vicinity of the parent's nest or territory.

Behaviour. The vast majority of Turdidae defend exclusive territories by aggressive posturing, fighting and song. The Fieldfare is among the few which do not defend exclusive territories, this species nesting in loose colonies. Many species flock outside the breeding season, but others become solitary or remain in pairs.

The songs of thrushes are usually rich and musical, species such as the Nightingale, Song thrush, Blackbird, European robin and others being considered among the best singers of all birds. However, such rich and varied whistled songs contrast with the rattling or scratchy notes of many chats. The alarm calls of most species generally consist of a harsh rattling or chattering.

Composition. The Turdidae includes about 300–310 species that are classified in around 35 genera, the exact number of genera being very much a matter of convenience and thus subject to differing opinions. The Wren-thrush *Zeledonia coronata* has often been placed in a distinct family, because of its syndactyl feet (in which two toes are joined for part of their length) and other peculiarities.

Some authorities have classed the Turdidae as a subfamily, Turdinae, within a family Muscicapidae, that includes Old World warblers, flycatchers and babblers.

BABBLERS

The babblers are a large, diverse group of ten-primaried Old World passerines: the Timaliidae. Though often placed near or within the thrush-warbler-flycatcher assemblage (the muscicapids), they have many distinctive behavioural characteristics which set them apart, the similarities with the muscicapids and a number of other passerine families seeming to be largely due to convergent evolution. The Timaliidae appears to be an ancient family which has undergone a remarkable radiation, centred on Southern Asia (with its many, more or less isolated mountain chains), which has produced a variety of forms superficially like other groups – as the names tit-babbler, wren-babbler, shrike-babbler, thrush-babbler, jay-thrush and the like indicate.

Typical babblers range in size from the small wren-like and tit-like species, through others about as big as a European robin *Erithacus rubecula* or a Song thrush *Turdus philomelos*, to those like the larger laughing-thrushes of the genus *Garrulax* which are the size of a Chough *Pyrrhocorax pyrrhocorax*. They have soft, loose, fluffy plumage; strong stout feet and legs (the latter often quite long in ground-living species); and short or fairly short wings. The often notched bill varies greatly in form, while the tail of 12 feathers may be long (and often graduated) to very short. Unlike any muscicapid and most other passerines, many babblers scratch their heads 'directly', bringing the foot straight up; also, again unlike true muscicapids, they use the foot to grip food, rather like a tit or crow. Babblers bathe by hopping in and out of the water repeatedly, not by standing in it throughout in the manner of most other passerines,

Five species of babblers. (1) White-crested laughing-thrush *Garrulax leucolophus*, (2) Red-billed leiothrix *Leiothrix lutea*, (3) Red-winged shrike-babbler *Pteruthius flaviscapis*, (4) Slender-billed scimitar-babbler *Xiphirhynchus superciliaris* and (5) Nullarbor quail-thrush *Cinclosoma alisteri*.

Grey-crowned scimitar-babbler *Pomatostomus temporalis* (1) building a co-operative nest. Typically a group of birds combine to attend the nest of just one pair. (2) Pair of Reedlings or Bearded tits *Panurus biarmicus*, the female with prey, attending a nest. The male is also shown in flight.

including the muscicapids. Unlike the latter, they are 'contact' birds, having no inhibitions in 'clumping' up closely with their mates or flock companions, and frequently allopreening – mates, for instance, each preening the other's head-parts and inviting such preening in return.

Most species have cryptic plumage to a greater or lesser extent, often with disruptive bars, streaks or spots, and sometimes with pale (often white) underparts to provide countershading. Among the more terrestrial babblers, brown, red, chestnut, buff, grey and black predominate; the more arboreal species, however, tend to be olive, yellow and green. Within this general scheme there is a wide range of other markings, mainly on the head, throat, breast, wings and tail. Some species also have well-developed crests. Among the plainest timaliids are the jungle-babblers and their allies, most of the wren-babblers, and the members of the genera *Turdoides* and *Babax*; among the brightest, some of the laughing-thrushes, the two leiothrixes, and the Fire-tailed myzornis *Myzornis pyrrhoura*. In most genera, the sexes look alike; only in some song-babblers (for example, the genus *Leiothrix*) are they dissimilar with the male the brighter.

The true babblers can be divided into four tribes: the Pallorneini; the Pomatorhinini; the Timaliini; and, comprising more than half the family, the Turdoidini (the song-babblers).

Distribution. The true babblers are a wholly Old World group centred firmly in the Oriental Region from the Indian subcontinent (including Ceylon), Burma, Indochina, Malaysia and southern China, with an outlier the White-eyed Warbler-babbler *Hapalopteron familiare* on the Bonin Islands. Just one genus (*Pomatostomus*) extends to New Guinea and Australia, but a number of other genera occur in Ethiopian Africa – *Lioptilus*, *Ptyrticus* and *Phyllanthus* entirely, *Trichastoma*, *Turdoides* and *Alcippe* partly – while the four jerys *Neomixis* are confined to Madagascar. The only timaliids found in or near the Palearctic Region (in North Africa, the Sahara, Arabia and the Near East) belong to the genus *Turdoides*; these include the Arabian babbler *T. squamiceps*, and the Fulvous babbler *T. fulva* which extends as far west as the southern Maghreb. The *Turdoides* babblers are mostly birds of drier areas, inhabiting almost any kind of thick scrub, but the other timaliids are predominantly forest birds, living in a wide variety of deciduous and evergreen, often dense and wet woodland, both montane and lowland. Within these habitats, they are weak fliers and largely sedentary.

Feeding. Though some species (for example, many tit-babblers and some tree-babblers) are arboreal or at least live mainly above ground in grass and bushes, many timaliids feed terrestrially and among the undergrowth where even the larger forms weave their way through dense vegetation with remarkable, almost rodent-like agility. On the ground, they forage by probing, digging and flicking things over with the bill; the gait, especially of the larger species such as laughing-thrushes, tends to be strong and springy, and short, jerky flights are often made between the floor and an elevated perch. Some species are omnivorous, taking a wide variety of insects and other invertebrates, fruit and seeds, and have relatively simple bills. Others are much more specialized as is shown by the striking number of bill-types. Thus, for example, we find timaliid 'wrens', 'tits', and 'shrikes', some of the latter (the smaller *Pteruthius*) in fact being more like New World vireos (Vireonidae). Most wren-babblers resemble wrens in the genus *Troglodytes* (Troglodytidae) but the Long-billed wren-babbler *Rimator malacoptilus* is more like one of the cactus-wrens in the genus *Campylorhynchus*. The Wedge-billed wren-babbler *Sphenocichla humei* has a pointed, conical bill like some of the caciques of the genus *Cacicus* (Icteridae) and may similarly use it to prise things open. The typical scimitar-babblers of

Bare-headed rockfowl *Picathartes gymnocephalus* (1), Grey-necked rockfowl *P. oreas* (2). Young of latter in mud nest on the wall of cave.

the genus *Pomatorhinus* resemble, with their decurved bills, New World thrashers of the genus *Toxostoma* (Mimidae); this bill-type reaches its extreme in the closely related genus *Xiphirhynchus* which is more like one of the Neotropical woodhewers *Campylorhampus* (Furnariidae). Mention must also be made of the Fire-tailed myzornis which, with its decurved bill and modified tongue, is a specialized nectar feeder, as are the arboreal sibias. Some of the laughing-thrushes, with their stout, jay-like bills, have proved to be specialized acorn-eaters and hoarders. Ants figure prominently in the diet of some timaliids, such as the Ferruginous jungle-babbler *Trichastoma bicolor*, but many species have another and more peculiar relationship with certain types of ants, applying them to the wing-feathers – such 'anting' apparently being part of the elaborate feathercare system.

Almost without exception, the babblers are highly sociable, keeping in small flocks while foraging for food and at most other times, more or less throughout the year. These bands are often a typical component of the mixed-species feeding parties so characteristic of tropical forests. Though some species are relatively silent and secretive, many others keep in contact with their mates and flock companions by frequent, often noisy calling, especially when alarmed (hence the name 'babbler'). The laughing-thrushes often have particularly loud, harsh chattering or screaming voices.

Nesting and the Young. Relatively little is known about the breeding habits of many of the babblers. Most members of the tribes Pellorneini, Pomatorhinini and Timaliini build domed, often rough, ball-shaped nests of moss, dead leaves and the like, access being through a side-hole; many species place such nests near or on the ground but some are quite high up in trees. Most of the song-babblers, however, make open, cuplike nests in trees, bushes and creepers. All babbler nests are usually well concealed and widely dispersed so as to reduce the risk of predation; this does not, however, prevent their being favourite hosts for parasitic cuckoos (Cuculidae) in many areas.

Babbler eggs vary much in colour and size but, in most cases, the shell has a fine, compact texture, often producing a smooth, satiny surface with a variable amount of gloss. The following examples give some idea of the range of egg-types, and an indication of clutch-size. The 2–4 broad, oval eggs of the jungle-babblers in the genus *Pellorneum* are heavily marked with reddish brown with underlying spots of light grey on a greenish or yellowish white background. The 2–5 (often 3–4) pure white eggs of the scimitar-babblers *Pomatorhinus* are elongated oval in shape. Those of the tree-babblers (3–4) are also white, or faintly marked red or brown. Among the song-babblers, the oval eggs of the laughing-thrushes *Garrulax* (2–5 most often three) are blue and often very glossy, unmarked or with a few brownish markings; those of the *Turdoides* babblers (2–5 usually 3–4), are a pure, highly glossy blue and of broad oval shape. The eggs of other song-babblers, however, tend to be heavily and richly marked. Those of the Red-billed leiothrix *Leiothrix lutea* (usually three), for example, are spotted, blotched, and speckled red-brown and varying shades of purple, with subsidiary streaks and smudges of pale lilac, all on a white, pale green or greenish blue ground; as in many babblers, the markings tend to gather towards the broader end of the egg where they often form a ring.

Behaviour. The local bands of at least two *Turdoides* babblers maintain group territories throughout the year, defending them against other bands of the same species. Such a system is probably widespread among timaliids, with the members of the band breeding within the group territory – either co-operatively or as dispersed pairs. The extent to which individuals, especially males, and solitary pairs are independently territorial (either within a group territory or quite separately) seems, however, uncertain.

The males of a number of species, especially among the song-

Four species of parrotbill babblers. (1) Rufous-headed parrotbill *Paradoxornis guttaticollis*, (2) Reedbed parrotbill *P. heudei*, (3) Short-tailed parrotbill *P. davidianus* and (4) Ashy-eared parrotbill *P. nipalensis*.

babblers, do have loud, far-carrying (and sometimes beautiful) songs. Notable songsters include the Red-billed leiothrix and the Melodious laughing-thrush *Garrulax canorus*, both favourite cage-birds. The utterance of such species has all the characteristics of territorial advertising song. In the case of some laughing-thrushes, however, the males include imitations in their songs, thus identifying themselves individually, and their females respond with simpler calls; such behaviour generally appears to be important in maintaining bonds between mates and members of the same band, and there are indications that reciprocal calling or singing, whereby two birds duet by uttering the same or different vocalizations, simultaneously or antiphonally, may be found widely in the family. Antiphonal calling, for instance, has been described in two widely spaced genera, *Pomatorhinus* and *Garrulax*.

Composition. In all, there are about 230 species of typical babblers. Of the 41 genera, 15 are monotypic and most of the rest consist of nine or fewer species. Only five genera are large: *Trichastoma* and *Alcippe* (17 species each), *Stachyris* and *Turdoides* (both 24), and *Garrulax* (47).

The Timaliidae is usually considered to be polyphyletic, that is, having more than one origin: although taxonomic revisions have removed some of the more obviously disparate elements, others still remain in current classifications. However, the 'core' of true babblers seems to be a really natural group, as shown, for example, by a study of their egg white proteins.

OLD WORLD WARBLERS

The Sylviidae is one of the biggest passerine families, and includes about 325 species in 60 genera. All have 10 primary feathers contrasting with the nine found in the American wood warblers (Parulidae). Old World warblers are generally small insectivorous birds, from 4–8in (10–20cm) long, with pointed bills. Many groups are drably coloured and contain species which resemble each other closely. Unlike some of their closest relatives, the Thrushes (Turdidae) and Old World flycatchers (Muscicapidae) the juvenile plumage is unspotted and generally similar to that of the adults. Many species, particularly some from Europe, have very pleasing and melodic warbling songs – from which their family name is derived.

Distribution. Almost half the Old World warblers breed in Africa and many others winter there. Otherwise the majority are found in Europe, Asia and Australia – the Fernbird *Bowdleria punctata* is the only representative in New Zealand. Two species of the genus *Regulus*, there known as kinglets, and one of *Phylloscopus* breed in North America but, apart from these and 12 species of gnatcatchers, Old World warblers are not found on the American continent. Although some genera contain only resident species many, particularly from higher latitudes, contain species that migrate long distances. For example, the high arctic breeding Arctic warbler *Phylloscopus borealis*, whether breeding in northern Scandinavia or Alaska, winters in southeast Asia (mostly Indonesia) and all Willow warblers *P. trochilus* whether from western Ireland or eastern Siberia, winter in Africa. Within Europe, most populations choose to circumnavigate the Mediterranean to allow for an easier crossing of the Sahara. Sometimes all individuals of a species take the same route – for example, all Lesser whitethroats *Sylvia curruca* move southeast in the autumn – but with other species there is a definite 'migratory divide' in central Europe with western populations going southwest and eastern ones southeast in the autumn. The classic examples of species which display a migratory divide are the Blackcap *Sylvia atricapilla* and the Garden warbler *S. borin*. In some genera, closely related species migrate in different directions – for instance Melodious warblers *Hippolais polyglotta* all move southwest and Icterine warblers *H. icterina* southeast.

Feeding. All Old World warblers are basically insectivorous although some vegetable material has been found in the diet of most studied in detail. A few species will form into loose flocks and feed together but most usually they are either solitary or family party feeders. Food items are picked individually from the vegetation or, less often, from the ground. Some species take food items whilst in flight either by hovering in front of vegetation as in some species of *Regulus*, or by catching flying prey – the gnatcatchers of North America, for example, do this regularly. Although many species live

Eight species of Old World warblers. (1) Fernbird *Bowdleria punctata*, (2) Arctic warbler *Phylloscopus borealis*, (3) Willow warbler *P. trochilus*, (4) Blackcap *Sylvia atricapilla*, (5) Whitethroat *S. communis*, (6) Common fan-tailed warbler *Cisticola juncidis*, (7) Great reed warbler *Acrocephalus arundinaceus* and (8) Graceful prinia *Prinia gracilis*.

in habitats rich in weeds, grasses and reeds, very few take seeds – the grassbirds *Megalurus* of southeast Asia and Australia are, however, one of the exceptions.

Several species eat fruit before migrating to put on fat to use as fuel – the Whitethroat *Sylvia communis* particularly takes blackberries. During winter, Blackcaps in the Mediterranean area often eat figs and their vernacular name in several countries is 'figeater'.

Nesting and the Young. With so many species it is rather difficult to generalize about the breeding behaviour of Old World warblers. Most species form territories with single pairs breeding within each. A few, for instance the Reed warbler *Acrocephalus scirpaceus* and possibly some related species, seem to form multiple territories with males within the colony co-operating in singing to attract females to their restricted breeding area, however, even within the colony, individual nesting territories are still defended. Many species build very elaborate nests normally using fine grasses and hairs but also, in the case of the gnatcatchers, some species of *Hippolais* and several of *Cisticola*, spiders webs and, particularly with the kinglets and Leaf warblers, mosses are used. The structure of the nest varies to suit the habitat. For instance, species breeding in grasslands or reed-beds usually suspend their nests from stems and the structures may be open, cup-shaped, domed or flask-shaped. The tailorbirds *Orthotomus* and two species of *Cisticola* (*C. cantans* and *C. erythrops*) actually sew the edges of large leaves together to form envelopes for their nests. Other species generally build simple nests in thick scrubby bushes or other concealing vegetation. Several groups, including the leaf warblers, build domed nests generally at ground level and often within dense vegetation. The kinglets and gnatcatchers build domed and open nests respectively in trees, sometimes at heights of over 65ft (20m).

Clutches vary from 2–3, for some of the more tropical species, to 4–7 in species of temperate and colder areas, with the record clutches of 10 or 11 being laid by kinglets. Whilst a few species lay boldly marked and brightly coloured eggs the typical warbler's egg has a pale background, often white or pink, with some brown or grey markings. Many species are parasitized by the local species of cuckoo and the European cuckoo *Cuculus canorus* can mimic very closely the eggs of some. Most species hatch between 12 and 14 days after incubation. Both sexes help feed the nestlings which stay in the nest for a further two weeks or so. A number of species are habitually double-brooded, and in some others the adults undergo a rapid, complete moult immediately after nesting; thus the period during which the young are dependant on their parents is often very short.

Voice. Song plays an important part in the breeding cycle both in defending territory and in males advertising to females. Ornithologists can often identify almost identical species because they have very different songs. In Britain, for instance, the three breeding species of *Phylloscopus* are very much alike but their songs are completely different. A number of the reed and grassland breeding species have long, repetitive songs which are sometimes confused with insect sounds. One species, the Marsh warbler *Acrocephalus palustris*, is a renowned mimic and individuals have been recorded with a repertoire including the songs or calls of more than 20 other species. To the human ear the song of the Blackcap is particularly fine and many rate it above that of the Nightingale *Luscinia megarhynchos*.

Economic Importance. Bearing in mind their small size, it is astonishing that members of the Sylviidae should feature as human food, but migrants are still caught in some Mediterranean countries for consumption. Cyprus is a particularly bad example and, since

Species of Old World warblers to show differences in facial colouring. (1) Firecrest *Regulus ignicapillus*, (2) Formosan goldcrest *R. goodfellowi*.

there are far flung expatriate Cypriot communities in many countries, there is an international trade in 'pickled birds' taken on migration with lime-sticks – these are even imported into Britain and can be bought in London.

Composition. The Sylviidae contains 60 genera of which more than half have only one or two species; only examples from a few can be mentioned. Typical genera include a variety of small, long-tailed, scrub-dwelling birds whose distribution is centred on the Mediterranean – although one, the Dartford warbler *Sylvia undata*, spreads as far north as Britain. The Great reed warbler *Acrocephalus arundinaceus* is one of the largest members of the family and can be found in reed-beds in Europe, Asia and Australia. The wren warblers *Prinia* of Africa and Asia include some drably coloured relatives of the more brightly coloured African genus *Apalis*. This genus includes some scrubland birds reminiscent of the tits coloured with yellows, greys and black. They, in turn, are related to the tailorbirds, whose astonishing nest-building abilities give them their name, and the African woodland warblers including *Seicercus*. This genus includes some species that are astonishingly similar to the *Phylloscopus* warblers of the Palearctic. The kinglets include Europe's smallest birds the Goldcrest *Regulus regulus* and Firecrest *R. ignicapillus* and their North American counterparts. These species have bright crown feathers, which can be raised as crests, and are particularly adapted to feeding in conifers and, during

Nests of Old World warblers. (1) Long-tailed tailorbird *Orthotomus sutorius* with a nest made between two leaves pulled together with plant down. (2) Blue-grey gnatcatcher *Polioptila caerulea* with a nest of moss, lichen and cobweb. (3) Goldcrest *Regulus regulus* with a nest of moss.

the winter, they are the most northerly representatives of the family. Finally, the North American gnatcatchers are rather different from most members of the Sylviidae and have sometimes been considered as a separate subfamily. They are small grey warblers with long tails.

AUSTRALIAN WREN-WARBLERS

The Maluridae were for many years regarded as an Australasian offshoot from the Old World warbler family, the Sylviidae, but are now regarded as a rather disjointed assemblage of wren and warbler-like birds which have evolved in that region. Nothing is yet known, from the fossil record, of their ancestors and their relationships are very imperfectly understood.

Most Australian wren-warblers that have been studied build enclosed, often domed nests concealed low in vegetation. (1) Male Black-backed blue wren *Malurus melanotus* with nest. (2) A Pilot-bird *Pycnoptilus floccosus* follows a Superb lyrebird *Menura novaehollandiae* in order to pick up any titbits left over from the lyrebird's scratching of the ground.

Four species of Australian wren-warblers. (1) Superb blue-wren *Malurus cyaneus*, (2) Mallee emu-wren *Stipiturus mallee*, (3) Blue-and-white wren *Malurus leucopterus* and (4) Brown thornbill *Acanthiza pusilla*.

Australian wren-warblers are small birds, often with (sometimes exceptionally long) cocked tails, measuring from 4–8in (10–20cm) overall. Most species spend their time foraging within, or on the edge of, whatever cover of vegetation is locally available. Some groups are drably and cryptically coloured showing little sign of sexual dimorphism but in others males are brightly coloured.
Distribution. The Maluridae is confined to Australia, New Zealand and New Guinea and the adjacent islands. Some species, even amongst those breeding on the mainland of Australia, have very restricted ranges. Many of those with more extensive ranges show wide variation in both colour and size between different populations. Some are partial migrants, probably influenced by the climatic vagaries of the country.
Behaviour. Most species feed almost exclusively on invertebrates, but a few have been recorded eating vegetable material – usually grass seeds. Species in areas where the weather has set annual patterns tend to have set annual breeding cycles but others, which are dependant on the unpredictable rainfall of the interior of Australia, may only breed after the rains have come. The breeding behaviour of only a few species has been studied in detail. The fairy

wrens *Malurus* breed as social groups with several adults at a single nest. In this genus the dominant males have very distinctive and splendid, brightly coloured breeding plumages which they may retain for many months. Other males within the breeding group usually retain a drab non-breeding plumage but, if anything happens to the dominant male, one of these drab birds will very quickly moult into the bright breeding plumage and take top position in the group. Group breeding in these species, as with many others, is thought to have evolved to ensure successful breeding at every opportunity that is offered by a very variable and often adverse climate. However this sort of group breeding behaviour is not the rule amongst most of the 24 other genera. Most other species hold territories and form pairs in the conventional way. Many have attractive songs that are sometimes very loud and penetrating.
Composition. The Maluridae is divided into 25 genera, of which 6, *Malurus* (the fairy wrens), *Todopsis*, *Chenorhamphus*, *Clytomyias*, *Stipiturus* and *Lamprolia*, are divided from the rest because they have characteristic feather tracts and special behavioural traits.

OLD WORLD FLYCATCHERS

Flycatchers are insectivorous song birds of the wooded regions of the world. More than 600 species are called 'flycatcher' in English but they belong to two very distinct and quite unrelated groups, one in the Americas, the tyrant flycatchers (Tyrannidae), and the other in the Old World, the Old World flycatchers or, simply, flycatchers (Muscicapidae).

Flycatchers typically feed by catching flies or other flying insects on the wing. This is normally accomplished from the top of some favoured and exposed perch, or look-out, from which the bird repeatedly launches itself on short forays. They are small, or fairly small birds averaging 5–5½in (12·5–14cm) in length, with strong, flattened bills which are broad at the base and well supplied with conspicuous bristles at the gape. Their legs are short.

The flycatchers are a rather heterogeneous assemblage and have been divided into three groups which are usually accorded the rank of subfamily. These are: the fantails, Rhipidurinae; monarchs or paradise flycatchers, Monarchinae; and the 'typical' flycatchers, Muscicapinae.
Distribution. Flycatchers are found throughout the Old World, and are most abundant in Africa and India, southeast Asia and Australasia. The fantails are almost entirely restricted to the Oriental and Australian regions; the monarchs are best represented in Africa and the Oriental region but some species such as

365

Some striking flycatcher species. (1) Black paradise flycatcher *Terpsiphone atrocaudata*, (2) Paradise flycatcher *T. paradisi* (red phase), (3) male and (4) female Pied flycatcher *Ficedula hypoleuca*, (5) Blue-and-white flycatcher *Cyanoptila cyanomelana*, (6) Scarlet robin *Petroica multicolor* and (7) Wattleeye *Platysteira cyanea*.

Terpsiphone atrocaudata and *T. paradisi* occur in colder Japan, Manchuria and Turkestan. Finally, the 'typical' flycatchers are widely distributed in all regions of the Old World from Europe and Siberia to South Africa, Madagascar, Indo-Malaya and Australia.

Feeding. Flycatchers display a great diversity of feeding methods within limits defined by their basic insect eating habit. Whereas some species such as the Pied flycatcher *Ficedula hypoleuca* is something of a 'machine for catching flies', repeatedly returning to its perch after having caught its prey in mid air, others such as the Spotted flycatcher *Muscicapa striata* seldom, if ever, return to the same perch after catching an insect, and will also glean insects from foliage or the surface of the ground.

Nesting and the Young. A typical member of the family is the Pied flycatcher. It breeds in holes in trees or the walls of buildings, and the securing of a desirable hole and its defence against rivals take up much of the bird's energy during the breeding season; it is believed that at this time the conspicuous white spot on its forehead is used for territorial display, and warns would-be competitors that the hole has been preempted. The female arrives in the breeding area after the male, and the latter tries to lure the female to an inspection of the nesting cavity through song and parade, during which the white areas of the plumage are displayed to their utmost, including the white borders of the tail that are flashed on and off by spreading and closing the tail. If the cavity is accepted, most of the nesting material is contributed by the female.

The courtship and breeding behaviour of other flycatchers, for example the Spotted flycatcher, is simpler. It consists chiefly of mutual nuptial flights and chases during which the male lifts its wings over its back and vibrates them; he also offers food to the female.

Composition. The three subfamilies of the Muscicapidae are the fantails Rhipidurinae, monarchs or paradise flycatchers Monarchinae, and typical flycatchers Muscicapinae. The fantails are characterized, as their common name indicates, by having a long tail shaped like a fan which they constantly unfold and close. Another peculiarity consists in the number of bristles at the gape which are twice as numerous as in other flycatchers. The monarchs or paradise flycatchers are difficult to characterize as they are the most heterogeneous group of all. Most of their numerous species are colourful birds with black, white, red, blue, or yellow areas in their plumage, some of which are glossy, and with or without crests, plumes, or vivid eye-wattles, and can be small or large. Some taxonomists believe these birds do not constitute a natural assemblage and one can readily grant that – at least in general appearance – the short stubby *Batis* with their bold pied colouration and the puffy plumage of their back, or the equally small *Platysteira* and *Diaphorophyia* with their vivid eye-wattles are, indeed, strikingly different from the extremely elegant and regal, well-named paradise flycatchers of the genus *Terpsiphone*.

The 'typical' flycatchers of the Old World are included in the subfamily Muscicapinae which contains about 113 species. The subfamily is not very sharply defined but 12 genera have been recognized in a recent revision of the group.

The African paradise flycatcher *Terpsiphone viridis* builds a typical bowl-shaped nest of plant filaments, pieces of leaves and spiders' webs.

PENDULINE TITS

The penduline tits (the Remizidae) are active and acrobatic passerines, generally found in small parties or family groups. Most species have small bodies, short wings and long tails and are birds of open scrubland. In general their bills are more finely pointed than those of the true tits or titmice Paridae, and three of the four genera build very elaborate and characteristic nests.

Distribution. The Eurasian species, the Penduline tit *Remiz pendulinus* is extremely variable, and has a rather discontinuous distribution, almost from the Atlantic to the Pacific. Many areas

Flycatcher species. (1) Spotted flycatcher *Muscicapa striata* nesting in a hole in the wall and hunting a dragonfly. (2) Male Paradise flycatcher *Terpsiphone paradisi* (white phase) hunting a wasp. A typical nest is also shown. (3) Pied fantail *Rhipidura rufifrons* at a nest with two young.

within its range lack suitable breeding habitats and this has gradually led to isolation of populations each being characterized by quite marked variation. The species is beginning to establish itself in western Europe, breeding pairs being recorded in Denmark and Holland. The African genus *Anthoscopus* contains six species of kapok tit which inhabit varied types of open woodland and scrub that occur from the southern edge of the Sahara to Cape Province. They are, of course, absent from the dense equatorial forests but do occur in some of the very arid thornscrub areas of the major deserts. Both these Old World groups are gregarious, with parties of 10, 15 or 20 busily feeding through trees, bushes or even reed-beds, a common sight. Apart from the Verdin *Auriparus flaviceps*, the only other species in the family is the insectivorous Fire-capped tit *Cephalopyrus flammiceps* found only in the Himalayan area. It is tiny, and an altitudinal migrant breeding as high as 11,000ft (say 3,000m) but wintering lower down, in small flocks.

Feeding. Penduline tits do not normally associate with other species. They are mainly insectivorous but do take some seeds. Although they are not strongly migratory, nomadic feeding parties are sometimes seen some distance from breeding centres. The Verdin is the North American representative of the family. Very similar in shape to the European Penduline tit, Verdins occur in the dry scrublands of the southwest USA and north Mexico. They are not so gregarious as the Eurasian and African groups although they are seldom seen singly. Verdins also feed on insects and, sometimes, berries. Often found many miles from water, their food probably supplies their needs for fluid even under the very hot, dry conditions of the desert areas they inhabit throughout the year.

Nesting and the Young. The Remizidae generally builds elaborate and distinctive nests. The one exception is the Fire-capped tit whose nest is always placed in a hole in a tree-trunk or branch at heights from 6–40ft (2–12m). The nest is lined with grass, rootlets and feathers and a clutch of 3–5 blue-green eggs is laid. Sitting birds hiss at intruders as do the typical tits Paridae – indeed, there seems every

reason for shifting this monotypic genus to that family. The remaining Old-World species have a highly involved social life and breeding pairs are quite often assisted by 'nest-helpers'. It is thought that these may be birds raised by the 'senior pair' at previous nesting attempts.

Building is generally started by the male. He weaves a hoop of grasses and roots about the tip of a thin branch, several feet – in at least one case as high as 60ft (18m) – above ground level. This is then used as the basis for building upwards, from the inside, a felted structure made from the hairy seed heads of willows, poplars or reeds (in areas where these are not available grass is used).

Penduline tits make flask-shaped nests with a slight tunnel at the entrance, in the upper part of the nest. Six to eight white eggs are laid and incubated for a fortnight by the female and fledging occurs after a further 16–18 days. The kapok tits *Anthoscopus* build very similar nests but often use animal fur if vegetable fluff is not available. An added refinement is that the entrance, at the very top of the nest, closes or can be closed so that a much more obvious 'dummy' entrance below the real entrance will attract any inquisitive predator. The tiny white eggs are usually laid in rather smaller clutches (seldom more than five) than in the Eurasian species but many cases of two, or more, hens laying in the same nest have been recorded. Nests are also used outside the breeding season for roosting purposes and up to 18 of these tiny birds have been recorded roosting in a single nest.

The Verdin's nest is normally built from very thorny twigs intricately woven together to form a conspicuous but tough and well-nigh impregnable ball about 8in (20cm) in diameter. These nests are also used for roosting but by single birds and are so sturdy they can last for several years. The inside is lined with grass and feathers and a clutch of 3–6 blue-green eggs with reddish speckles is laid. This nest structure is really very different from that of the Old World members of the family but one race of Verdin (the nominate form from Lower California) builds a different type of nest, one only rarely armoured with thorns. This race starts to build in the same way as the Penduline tits, with a hoop of grasses or rootlets. It then builds up a vegetable down nest, again like the Penduline tits, but with the entrance at the bottom.

Behaviour. All species are very active when feeding and both

367

penduline and kapok tits are extraordinarily acrobatic. They are gregarious and have a variety of thin, whistling contact calls which are uttered incessantly in order to keep the flock together. It may be that flocking enables them to make the most of food supplies, to keep a good look out for predators and, since they roost close together (with some species in specially constructed nests) to conserve heat overnight. The songs are simple and tit-like. Nest-helpers have been recorded in the Old World genera except for *Cephalopyrus*, but not in the case of the Verdin.

Composition. The single species of *Remiz* shows great variation across the two continents that it inhabits. Basically a pale buff, chestnut and black species, the European (and adjacent races) has a black eye-patch. This is much suppressed in the Manchurian race and extended round the back of the head in some central Asian races. There are two races from east of the Caspian in which the head is black. The kapok tits *Anthoscopus* are mostly brown and yellow birds showing considerable geographical and specific variation. These two genera are definitely very closely related. The Verdin *Auriparus* is basically grey with yellow on the head and a rusty patch on the carpal joint. Young birds lack these distinctive field marks and they are also sometimes difficult to identify even in adult birds. Although one race makes a very similar nest to the previous two genera, recent comparative work suggests that *Auriparus* might be more closely related to the honeyguides Coere-bidae, although there can, as yet, be no certainty about this. The genus *Cephalopyrus* contains a single species *C. flammiceps* in which the male has a very bright plumage: scarlet head, orange chin and throat, yellow cheeks and underparts and also yellow on the rump and back. The female is much duller. Since their nesting habits differ so considerably from those of the other Remizidae it seems likely that this genus will eventually be placed in the Paridae.

(1) Penduline tit *Remiz pendulinus*. (2) Cape penduline tit *Anthoscopus minutus,* its nest with a false entrance also seen in cross-section showing the real entrance first closed and then open. (3) Verdin *Auriparus flaviceps*.

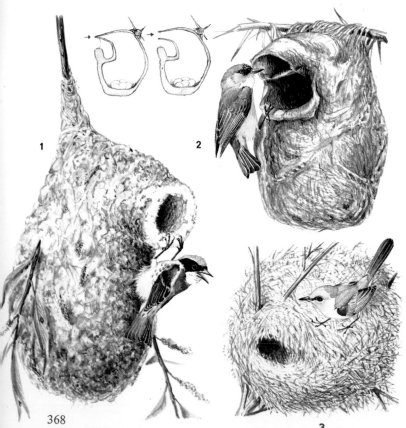

LONG-TAILED TITS

The long-tailed tit family Aegithalidae contains eight species of tiny tree- and bush-living birds with obvious affinities to the tits (Paridae) and penduline tits (Remizidae). They build elaborate, enclosed nests and several of the species whose breeding has been studied have 'nest helpers'. They are generally gregarious although, unlike the Paridae, the flocks they form are usually only with their own species.

In most species of long-tailed tit more than half the overall length of 4–6in (10–15cm) is taken up by the tail. Healthy individuals weigh as little as a $\frac{1}{5}$oz (5·6gm). They are very active creatures constantly moving through woodland, scrub or hedgerows looking for food and keeping in contact with high and, considering their diminutive proportions, surprisingly penetrating calls.

Some long-tailed tits. (1) Long-tailed tit *Aegithalos caudatus* southern type and (2) northern and eastern type. (3) Red-headed tit *A. concinnus*. (4) Common bushtit *Psaltriparus minimus*.

Distribution. The most widespread and best known species is the Long-tailed tit *Aegithalos caudatus* which can be found over most of Europe and through Asia to Japan and Kamchatka. The other species in this genus are all centred around the Himalayas and spread into China. Most are basically black and white with graduated tails – the outer feathers being progressively shorter than the central ones – having some pink, chestnut or red in their plumage. The Red-headed tit *A. concinnus* is a particularly attractive bird. The head, flanks and breast-band are chestnut, the chin is black, surrounded by white, and there is a distinctive black eye-stripe. The only other Old World genus is monotypic, consisting of the Javan pygmy tit *Psaltria exilis*, found only in central and western Java. This species is basically pale grey with off-white underparts. In the New World the family is represented by the two bushtits of the genus *Psaltriparus* which range along the western part of the United States from California southwards through Mexico to Guatemala. The Common bushtit *P. minimus* is the northern species and the Black-eared bushtit *P. melanotis* takes over in Mexico. Both *Psaltriparus* and *Aegithalos* species show a great deal of variation – over 20 races of the Long-tailed tit were recognized in a recent revision, and some feel that the two species of *Psaltriparus* should be amalgamated as one species, *P. minimus*.

Feeding. Constant call notes announce the presence of a feeding party usually long before the birds themselves are seen as they go searching through areas of vegetation for the small invertebrates which make up the major part of their diet. The Aegithalidae are extremely agile and with their short stubby bills are able to search out the minutest prey items. During the breeding season larger prey,

3

such as caterpillars are readily seized upon. Unlike most species living in temperate areas, apart from colonial nesters, foraging parties of several adults can often be seen together during the breeding season.

Nesting and the Young. In those species most studied, it seems that nests are often attended by more than two birds. In the case of the Long-tailed tit often four adults and, on at least one occasion, as many as six have been recorded at a single nest. In all species the nest itself is an amazingly large, intricate and beautiful structure. It is made from mosses, lichens and cobwebs and is basically a bag hung from a branch with an entrance, towards the top of the bag, leading to a nesting chamber in the bottom.

In general the genus *Aegithalos* build nests similar in shape to an egg, hanging from the branch by its pointed end and being up to 7in (18cm) long. Astonishing numbers of feathers, mostly from species other than the tits, are used in the lining – 2,379 have been counted from a single nest. The clutch size ranges from 3–12, more if two females are laying in the same nest. The European Long-tailed tit lays the largest clutches since the species is very vulnerable to cold weather during the winter. The Javan pygmy tit builds a similar nest and also uses other birds' feathers in the lining. Some of these feathers may be almost as big as the pygmy tit itself. Bushtits sometimes make much longer nests – 7in (18cm) would be short and 12in (30cm) is not rare while a nest 21in (49cm) long has been recorded. Such elaborate nests take a long time to build and pairs have been known to work on a nest for as long as seven weeks, though generally the process is far less protracted. Long-tailed tits may take as little as 10 days from starting a nest to laying the first egg but usually construction takes about three weeks. The Javan

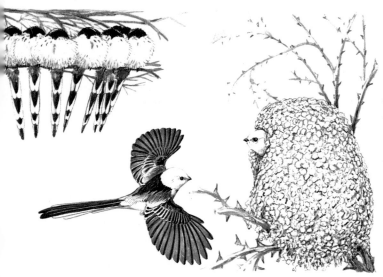

Pair of Long-tailed tits *Aegithalos caudatus,* the female in the nest. At night groups of these birds sleep pressed together to stay warm.

pygmy tit has two breeding periods each year – March to May and August to November – but the others only breed during the summer. Repeat clutches are common in European Long-tailed tits as the first nests, built before deciduous trees are in leaf, are frequently raided by predators. Bushtits often have second, and sometimes third, clutches in the same nest. The young of all species remain with their parents after they have fledged – they may even help feed later broods – and will roost in tightly packed groups to conserve heat.

Composition. From their structure and behaviour the long-tailed tits

of the genus *Aegithalos* and the bushtits *Psaltriparus* are obviously very closely related with such features as graduated tail-feathers, nest-construction, social behaviour and voice in common. However the plumage differences between the two genera, and the marked similarity of plumage within the genus *Aegithalos* warrant the generic distinction. The single *Psaltria* species, found only in Java, resembles the bushtits more closely than it does the long-tailed tits.

TITMICE

The Paridae is a family of some 46 species of typical tits, titmice or chickadees, all active, highly acrobatic and gregarious wood or scrubland birds, ranging in length from about $4\frac{1}{2}$–8in (11–20cm),

Two species of titmice. (1) Blue tit *Parus caeruleus* and (2) Boreal chickadee *P. hudsonicus*.

weighing from $\frac{1}{3}$–1oz (9–30gm), and characterized by their relatively short bills and strong feet which are specially suited to their mainly arboreal way of life. Titmice are predominantly insectivorous but depend quite considerably on a seed diet through the winter months. Most lay fairly large clutches and all those studied nest in holes or crevices, normally in trees. A high proportion are obviously very closely related and all but two are placed in a single genus *Parus*.

Distribution. Tits can be found all over the wooded parts of Europe, Asia, Africa, India and North America as well as some of the western islands of the Pacific. Although they are normally thought of as being relatively sedentary, large-scale long distance movements take place irregularly in many species, while regular migrations are seen in some temperate species. Movements involving millions of Blue tit *Parus caeruleus*, Great tit *P. major* and Coal tit *P. ater* have been recorded in Europe when populations are high. In North America invasions of Boreal chickadees *P. hudsonicus* occur during some winters. Many species have adapted to man-made situations and they are among the best-known visitors at bird tables.

Feeding. During the breeding season titmice are completely insectivorous and most species in temperate areas are dependent on caterpillar crops when rearing their young. Many species will feed on seeds, particularly from trees, during the autumn and winter – beech mast, for example, is a great favourite. At feeding stations

Roving parties of hungry titmice have been known to attack putty in window-frames. (1) Sultan tit *Melanochlora sultanea*, (2) Great tit *Parus major*, (3) Blue tit *P. caeruleus*, (4) Azure tit *P. cyanus*, (5) Willow tit *P. montanus*, (6) Crested tit *P. cristatus* and (7) Tufted titmouse *P. bicolor*.

almost all food is taken and most species will investigate the possibilities of anything that looks remotely edible. The male helps feed the female at the start of the breeding season.

Nesting and the Young. The gregarious feeding practised during the autumn and winter often carries through to the early part of the breeding season and birds defending territories will also join feeding flocks. Most species have penetrating, whistling, rhythmic calls and songs and will defend their nesting territories from both males and females of neighbouring pairs. The male usually chooses the nesting hole – sometimes an old woodpecker hole – though a few species will excavate all or part of the nest themselves, as does, for example, the Willow tit *P. montanus*. Holes in the ground are occasionally taken by most species (particularly the Coal tit) but generally nest sites are from 6–20ft (2–6m) from the ground. Titmice readily accept nest-boxes. Sometimes moss and grasses are used to line the nest cavity to which are added hair, fur and feather to form the actual nest cup. This is normally placed as far from the entrance hole as possible. The clutch is generally from 6–10 eggs although clutches of as many as 15 are not at all unusual in some species. The eggs of most species have a pale background speckled with reddish-brown flecks and spots.

Hatching occurs after about 12 days incubation, mainly by the female who is still fed, on the nest, by the male. The fledging period is generally long – up to 21 days – and the parents provide vast quantities of food to produce a nestful of fledglings which often exceeds their combined weight by eight or nine times. Immediately on fledging the nest is vacated only to be used for roosting by the female. The family party will then meet and join up with other families of its own and other species.

Behaviour. In the winter, roving flocks will cover ill-defined feeding territories and if the season has been poor, the seed crops having failed, the flocks remain active right throughout the daylight hours searching, in crevices in the bark and branches of trees for insects, their eggs and pupae. They will also attack buds, which contain food items such as weevils and bugs. Some species habitually feed off parasitized fir cones, apparently detecting the grub's presence by the

hollow sound the cone makes when tapped. Feeding flocks use a generalized soft, high-pitched whistle to keep in touch, although the characteristic calls of each species can be heard at most times of the year as well. Winter feeding flocks of over 100 individuals of five or more species are quite common in temperate Europe and Asia.

In America, the Boreal chickadee and its Old World counterpart the Siberian tit *P. cinctus* survive winter temperatures as low as −50°F (−45°C) and other species can cope well with cold weather conditions provided that glazed ice does not cover the crevices in tree-bark where they find most of their food.

Composition. The Paridae contains three genera, the main genus *Parus* containing about 44 species. Some, like the Great tit, range very widely and have many races. There are 30 races of Great tit, and 19 races of Coal tit. The two other genera are both monotypic and from Asia. The Sultan tit *Melanochlora sultanea* is the largest of the family. The other species, the Yellow-browed tit *Sylviparus modestus* is less well-known. A small bird, it resembles the leaf-warblers of the genus *Phylloscopus* in colouring and comes from their strong-hold in the Himalayas. But its voice is tit-like and its nest, which was found for the first time in 1973, is in a hole in a tree. The Yellow-browed tit's place in the Paridae is thus vindicated. It may well be the most primitive member of the family now surviving.

NUTHATCHES

The family Sittidae consists of rather small, mainly arboreal birds known commonly as nuthatches. They are plump and short-tailed, with robust bills (though elongated, even curved, in a few cases),

Blue tits *Parus caeruleus* have large broods which may fill the nest cavity with the more hungry birds rising to the top. A Blue tit is also shown carrying the faecal sac away from the nest.

short legs, long toes and strong claws adapted for climbing. Most species are characterized by a great agility in climbing on tree-trunks, moving upwards, sidewards or downwards; the creepers (Certhiidae) are able to ascend in this manner but not descend. Adaptations to the feet permit this extraordinary agility in the nuthatches which can even walk upside-down under overhanging branches, like flies on a ceiling. Unlike the creepers and woodpeckers, whose specially stiffened tails act as supports, nuthatches do not use their tails, which are short and soft, while climbing. Some atypical Old World species, the so-called rock nuthatches *Sitta neumayer* and *S. tephronota*, live among cliffs and gorges, and show similar agility when clambering along rock faces; and this also applies to the peculiar Wallcreeper *Tichodroma muraria* of central Eurasia.

In plumage, the typical nuthatches are variations on a theme of blue-grey upperparts and black eye-stripes; characteristics of species are variations of head patterns in black, white, and blue-grey, and in the colour of the underparts, which vary from white through buff to rufous, coloured on the whole undersurface in some, or a limited area (such as a breast-band) in others. The Wallcreeper, on the other hand, has no close relatives, and is readily distinguished by its decurved bill and distinctive wing pattern of black and red with white spots on the primaries. The sittellas of Australia are currently regarded as conspecific, though there are some striking plumage differences between populations, mainly in head patterns of black and white, grey, or wholly white, while they all have white rumps and conspicuous flashes of white or rufous in the otherwise dark wings.

Distribution. The nuthatch family – there are 25 species distributed between 4 genera – is represented in the New and Old Worlds, but not in South America or Africa; the so-called Coral-billed nuthatch

Hypositta corallirostris of Madagascar is now believed to belong to the Vangidae. Four species are native to North America, and there are three species of Sittella in Australia and New Guinea. The remaining 18 occur in Eurasia, and the largest number in any one region is 13 – in the mountainous region of central Asia; 12 of these are *Sitta* species, which, however, are ecologically isolated from one another. Some live in tropical and subtropical lowland forest (with further selection between dry or moist, deciduous or evergreen trees), others in temperate forest (divided between coniferous, broad-leaved or mixed woodland, and with altitudinal separations), in alpine-zone forest, or on rocky hill-slopes. *Sitta whiteheadi*, which occurs only in pine forest on the Mediterranean island of Corsica, is probably the most localized of all European breeding birds, though it is not believed to be endangered.

Feeding. The typical nuthatches have earned their vernacular name from their fondness for eating nuts and other tree seeds in autumn. West European Nuthatches chiefly take hazel-nuts, but acorns,

Some nest types among the Sittidae. (1) (European) Nuthatch *Sitta europaea*. Mud has been used to reduce the size of the nest's entrance. (2) Western rock nuthatch *S. neumayer* with nest built of mud and attached to the rock face. (3) Wallcreeper *Tichodroma muraria* nesting in a rock cavity.

Six species of nuthatches. (1) (European) Nuthatch *Sitta europaea*, (2) Western rock nuthatch *S. neumayer*, (3) Coral-billed nuthatch *Hypositta corallirostris*, (4) Velvet-fronted nuthatch *Sitta frontalis*, (5) Corsican nuthatch *S. whiteheadi* and (6) Red-breasted nuthatch *S. canadensis*.

beechmast, and seeds of various conifers have also been recorded. Nuts with thick shells will be broken open by wedging them in tree bark or some other crevice, and then hammering them open with the beak. For this reason, nuthatch species adapted to deciduous woodlands tend to have stouter beaks than do those that haunt conifers. At other seasons, the nuthatches are mainly insectivorous, as are the Wallcreeper and the sittellas at all times. Diptera, lepidoptera, coleoptera and hymenoptera species are eaten, along with eggs and grubs, found by searching as the birds climb over tree branches or rock faces. The Sittidae is one of the few bird families whose species are known to use tools (at least occasionally) to obtain food; both the Australian Orange-winged sittella *Neositta chrysoptera* and the Brown-headed nuthatch *S. pusilla* of North America have been seen using small twigs to draw grubs out of concealment.

Nesting and the Young. All members of the Sittidae are solitary breeders, each pair having its own defended territory. Courtship displays between male and female vary between species, but always involve drawing attention to brightly-coloured parts of the plumage. Thus the male Nuthatch ruffles his flank feathers to exhibit the chestnut colouration, and spreads his tail to show off its white spots; while the male Wallcreeper flutters and climbs around the female with half-spread wings to reveal the striking red, black and white wing pattern. The arboreal nuthatches adopt, or excavate in some American situations, a suitable hole in a tree branch to nest in, though artificial nest-boxes will be used on occasion. Old World species plaster mud around the entrance hole to make it smaller, presumably to discourage intruders; however, American species do not do this, though the Red-breasted nuthatch will smear pitch around the hole entrance – possibly a relic of the plastering habit. On the debris at the bottom of the hole a clutch of 6–10 will be laid (only 3–5 by the cliff-nesting Wallcreeper). The eggs are white, spotted or freckled with reddish-brown. They are incubated for 14–15 days, by the female alone; but the male assists in feeding the young for their 23–25 days in the nest. The sittellas differ markedly from the above in their breeding biology, for they are not cavity-nesters. Instead, a cup-shaped nest is built of plant fibres and cobwebs, camouflaged externally with flakes of bark, and sited in a forked branch up to 60ft (say 18m) above ground; the eggs, normally three, are whitish with olive and grey markings.

Four distinct forms of the sittella. (1) Male and (2) female Striated sittella *Neositta striata*, (3) White-headed sittella *N. leucocephala*, (4) female and (5) male Black-capped sittella *N. pileata*. The nest of the Orange-winged sittella *N. chrysoptera* (6) is covered with pieces of bark for camouflage.

Behaviour. The true nuthatches are not notably gregarious, though sometimes in autumn and winter one or two may associate with a foraging flock of tits and kinglets; such behaviour is possibly more usual in North America than it is in Europe where some defend a territory all through the year. Once family parties have broken up in autumn, it is unusual to see more than two nuthatches together, although small flocks of the Red-breasted nuthatch are not unknown. The Wallcreeper remains a solitary bird. In contrast, the sittellas always form small flocks outside the breeding season, and move about restlessly from tree to tree, constantly uttering a high-pitched twitter. Nuthatch songs are mainly repetitions of a single note, almost a trill in some species, or a loud, piping *twee-twee-twee* by the European bird which also proclaims its presence by a loud, metallic *chwit* call-note.

Composition. As at present constituted, the family comprises three subfamilies: Sittinae for the 21 species of true nuthatch, the monotypic Tichodromadinae for the Wallcreeper, and Daphoeno-sittinae for the three sittellas of Australasia. This classification may not be a natural one. There has long been a dispute as to whether *Tichodroma* should be allied to the creepers (Certhiidae) or the nuthatches; while the sittellas have characteristics (especially in breeding habits and social behaviour) which set them apart from both.

AUSTRALIAN TREECREEPERS

The Australian treecreepers, the Climacteridae, consist of six species that are similar in size and proportions. They are small, being 5–6¾in (12·5–17cm) long, robust birds with fine, slightly downcurved bills and relatively long wings and short tails. The feet are strong and the claws well-developed, especially the hindclaw. Rictal bristles are absent. The upper surface varies from sooty brown to greyish; the undersurface is usually streaked. There is a light chestnut wing-bar, revealed conspicuously in flight, and a dark subterminal bar on all tail feathers except the middle pair (this is obliterated in two black-tailed forms). In four of the species there is a well-defined eyebrow. Sexual dimorphism of plumage occurs in all six species.

These treecreepers are usually seen hopping up the sides of tree trunks and larger branches, probing for insects in the bark with the bill. The feet are not particularly adapted for climbing, nor is the tail used as a brace as in some other tree-creeping species such as woodpeckers and creepers, which suggests that the habit has evolved comparatively recently in this group. Three of the species also spend a good deal of time on the ground, and all six may occasionally perch on twigs in the manner of other perching birds. The flight is direct, often swooping, usually from the upper branches of one tree to the lower bole of the next.

Distribution. The Climacteridae is restricted to Australia (excluding Tasmania) and New Guinea. All six species occur in Australia, between them covering most of the continent; the White-throated treecreeper *Climacteris leucophaea* also occurs in New Guinea. The habitats of the different species range from the mulga scrub and desert oak parklands of the semi-arid regions to montane rain forest. The species are apparently sedentary, and often locally common; in some areas of northern Australia, for instance, the Black-tailed tree-creeper *C. melanura* is one of the most frequently seen birds.

Feeding. The food of Australian treecreepers consists of insects and other small arthropods, obtained mainly from fissures in the trunks of standing or fallen trees, and sometimes from fenceposts. Three species, the Brown, Rufous and Black-tailed treecreepers, *C. picumnus*, *C. rufa* and *C. melanura*, also feed directly on the ground, where they hop about turning over leaves and other litter.

contains only the White-throated treecreeper. In the second group the eggs are pale pinkish and heavily-marked, and the females differ from the males in having the centre of the throat or upper breast streaked or spotted with orange- or maroon-brown, this area in the male being streaked or spotted with blackish, or plain. The affinities of the family have long been a matter of debate. Its members have been included with the typical creepers (Certhiidae), but another opinion suggests that they are related more closely to the Australian honeyeaters (Meliphagidae).

TYPICAL CREEPERS

The treecreeper family Certhiidae contains eight very similar species distinguished by their feeding behaviour – that of literally creeping on the trunks and branches of trees seeking food in the cracks in the bark. All the species are quite small, up to 6in (15cm) long, with brown and white spotted and barred plumage, long strongly decurved bills and long claws adapted for climbing on trees. One of the three genera concerned, *Certhia*, shares with the woodpeckers the strong stiff tail feathers which lend it support in climbing. The central feathers are the most important and they are moulted after the rest of the tail has been renewed, so that the tail can still serve as a support while the most important feathers are themselves renewed. The other two genera, *Rhabdornis* and *Salpornis*, lack this adaptation and have probably had different ancestors from those of the *Certhia*.

At all times of the year the treecreeper is dependent on trees for

Six species of Australian treecreepers. (1) Red-browed treecreeper *Climacteris erythrops*, (2) Brown treecreeper *C. picumnus*, (3) White-browed treecreeper *C. affinis*, (4) Rufous treecreeper *C. rufa*, (5) Black-tailed treecreeper *C. melanura* and (6) male White-throated treecreeper *C. leucophaea*, shown passing food to the female.

Some typical creepers. (1) Short-toed treecreepers *Certhia brachydactyla*, the female in a nest behind detached bark. (2) Treecreeper (or Brown creeper) *C. familiaris*, (3) Spotted treecreeper *Salpornis spilonotus* with prey. (4) Stripe-headed treecreeper *Rhabdornis mystacalis* and (5) Plain-headed treecreeper *R. inornatus*.

Nesting and the Young. The breeding biology of the Climacteridae is poorly-known. The indications are that both sexes take part in building the nest, incubating, and feeding the young. The nest is generally placed in a hole in a trunk, spout or stump, sometimes a fencepost, or in a sheltered crevice in a tree or building. Nests have been found from near ground-level to a height of 90ft (27m). The nest is usually a pad of grass and bark, lined with vegetable down, feathers or fur (possum fur and rabbit fur is frequently used). Often the cavity below the nest is filled by the birds with grass and kangaroo, horse or cow dung.

The eggs are of two distinct types. Those of the White-throated treecreeper are ivory white with a few scattered spots of dark brown and lavender grey; disregarding size, these are remarkably similar to the eggs of the White-eared honeyeater *Meliphaga leucotis* and the Lesser lewin honeyeater *M. notata*. The eggs of the remaining five species are quite different, having a pale pinkish ground densely blotched and spotted with purplish-brown and lavender grey, sometimes similar to the eggs of the Long-billed honeyeater *Melilestes megarhynchus* and the Little friarbird *Philemon citreogularis*. The clutch size is usually 3–4.

In the breeding season the birds are found in pairs; at other times they may occur in small parties. The calls are usually rapid series of short, high-pitched whistles.

Composition. The six species are contained in a single genus, *Climacteris*. On the basis of their mode of sexual dimorphism and egg-colouration they may be divided into two groups. In the first the eggs are whitish and lightly-marked, and the female differs from the male in having an orange spot beneath each cheek; this group

both food and shelter. Other rough surfaces with cracks and fissures are sometimes searched but typically a feeding treecreeper works its way spirally up the trunk of a tree, incessantly searching for food, before dropping down to within a few feet of the ground to start the process again on another tree. In the autumn and winter they will join up with nomadic parties of tits (Paridae) and other woodland species but will always retain their mode of feeding – up the trunks and main branches of the trees.

Distribution. The *Certhia* species are widely distributed through Europe and Asia, particularly round the Himalayas, with a single species in North Africa. The Treecreeper *C. familiaris* is distributed through Eurasia from Japan to Ireland and, as the Brown creeper, from Newfoundland to California in North America. The Spotted creeper *Salpornis spilonotus* is found in open bush areas in Africa south of the Sahara and in India. The genus *Rhabdornis* only occurs in the Philippines.

Feeding. The treecreeper's long curved bill is specially adapted for feeding on insects, their eggs and larvae, and other invertebrates to be found in cracks, crevices and holes. In times of plenty, such as during the breeding season when caterpillars are generally abundant, larger food items found crawling on the bark are easily and frequently taken. However, the full significance and advantage of the long, curved bill is easily seen during the winter. Any area of woodland with mature trees contains a vast surface of vertical bark. Many invertebrates winter in cracks and crevices in this bark and though safe from the small, stubby bills of the tits, can readily be found and taken by tree-creepers (they can also be excavated by nuthatches and woodpeckers).

The Spotted creeper's feeding habits closely resemble those of the true treecreepers. It has been recorded searching trees downwards, head first, like a nuthatch and, of course, the species lacks the very useful support of stiff tail feathers. The Stripe-headed and Plain-headed creepers, *Rhabdornis mystacalis* and *R. inornatus*, normally feed in the usual creeper fashion but are often seen in open situations feeding at flowers, possibly taking nectar. They have the brush-tipped tongue normally associated with flower feeding. The other tree creepers have pointed tongues for probing in cracks.

Nesting and the Young. All the treecreepers are basically hole nesters apart from the Spotted creeper. This species makes a cupped nest high up in a tree and lays a clutch of 2–3 pale blue eggs with black, brown and lavender markings. For *Certhia* species clutches of 5–6 are normal and the male, which is slightly larger than but similar to the female, may assist with incubation. The young fledge about a month after the clutch has been completed and some pairs may have a second brood. The eggs are very similar to those of the tits, having a pale ground colour sprinkled with reddish spots. Family parties often keep together for at least the first part of the autumn.

Behaviour. All species have rather weak songs and thin, sibilant contact calls which are used continually between the birds of a foraging group during the autumn or winter or between the male and female after the pairs have formed and taken up territory in the spring. *Certhia* species are generally inconspicuous but there are a surprising number of records of really violent conflicts between two nesting pairs. The courting flight and song seem to occur only during a very short period in the early spring.

Composition. The five *Certhia* species are very similar indeed. The two widely distributed species, the Treecreeper and the Short-toed treecreeper, are hard to distinguish in the field or even in the hand except by really experienced ornithologists. In the Himalayas three extra species can be distinguished from the Treecreeper. The Himalayan treecreeper *C. himalayana* has barred tail-feathers: the Brown-throated treecreeper *C. discolor* has a brown throat and underparts: and Stoliczka's treecreeper *C. nipalensis* has a rufous belly and undertail coverts.

FLOWER PECKERS

The Dicaeidae is a family of small and often brightly coloured birds that feed on nectar and berries. The true flower peckers are members of the genera *Dicaeum* and *Prionochilus*; they have tongues adapted for nectar eating, the muscular stomach or ventriculus reduced to a blind sac, and build hanging, purse-like nests. The so-called berry peckers and pardalotes or diamond birds do not all share these features and, although classified in the Dicaeidae, they may in fact be unrelated.

Distribution. The species of *Dicaeum* occur in wooded habitats from

Male Short-toed treecreeper *Certhia brachydactyla,* shown scanning the sky in flight and alighting on the vertical surface of a tree-trunk within which the female is nesting.

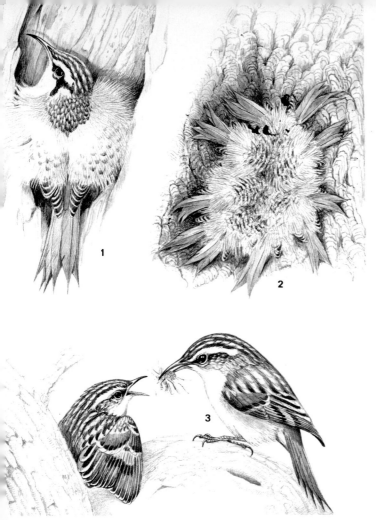

Treecreepers tend to use regular sleeping-places such as this cavity which Short-toed treecreepers *Certhia brachydactyla* have hollowed out in the soft bark of a tree (1). In exceptionally cold weather a number of birds may roost together (2). (3) A young bird being fed.

India and southern China through Malaysia, Indonesia and the Philippines to Australia, Irian and the Solomon Islands. They are frequently associated with mistletoes. Regular migrations are unknown, though in the Mistletoe bird, *D. hirundinaceum*, nomadism occurs. *Prionochilus* occurs on the Malay Peninsula, Sumatra, Java, Borneo and the Philippines, mainly in primary and secondary forest. The species are thought to be sedentary, and may be locally common. *Melanocharis* and *Rhamphocharis* are confined to Irian, New Guinea, where they dwell mainly in the understorey of montane forest. The Tit berry pecker *Oreocharis arfaki* is restricted to the mountains of Irian, where it occurs mainly in the lower levels of the forest in loose flocks of 15–20 birds, often assembling to feed with other species at fruiting trees. The Crested berry pecker *Paramythia montium* is also restricted to Irian, where it is abundant in the moss-forests between 6,800 and 13,000ft (2,073–3,962m). In the non-breeding season this species usually travels in loose bands of 3 to 12 birds, though a flock of over 75 birds has been recorded.

The pardalotes inhabit Australia where the species between them cover the greater part of the region. They are mainly foliage gleaners, and prefer large leafy trees. Some species are migratory; the Yellow-tipped pardalote *Pardalotus striatus*, for instance, breeds in Tasmania and winters in Queensland.

Feeding. Numerous species of *Dicaeum* have been noted as feeding extensively on the nectar and fruits of mistletoes; the nectar and the juicy pulp surrounding the mistletoe seed are a rich source of easily-digested glucose. *Dicaeum* species also eat other fruits, and small invertebrates such as spiders, aphids and leaf-hoppers. Whereas the fruits and seeds pass rapidly straight through the digestive system, the spiders and other small animals are diverted into the protein-

digesting ventriculus and their chitinous remains finally ejected through the mouth as pellets.

The berry peckers are so-called because they feed mainly on berries and fruit, though some *Melanocharis* species eat insects too. The pardalotes feed mainly on small arthropods gleaned from the foliage of large trees.

Species of *Dicaeum* are the chief pollinators and seed-dispersers of many Indo-Australian mistletoes. The tongue of *Dicaeum*, like that of *Prionochilus*, is adapted for nectar feeding.

Nesting and the Young. In *Dicaeum* and *Prionochilus* the nest is a bag with a side entrance (often hooded) near the top, suspended from a leafy twig. It is a well felted construction of moss, plant down and spiders' silk, decorated outside with spiders' cocoons, seeds and the excrement of various insects. The eggs, usually two, are pure white in most species, but spotted or speckled in a few. In *Dicaeum* at least, the female alone builds the nest and incubates the eggs.

Of the berry peckers, the nesting of *Rhamphocharis* and *Oreocharis* has not been described. In *Melanocharis* the nest is a smooth, deep, felted cup of plant down and fibres, coated externally with spiders' silk and decorated with flakes of lichen, the whole attached to a slender branch or fork. The eggs, apparently two, are white or pinkish white, blotched and spotted with browns and greys, the blotching denser near the large end. The Crested berry pecker

(1) Male and (2) female Mistletoe bird *Dicaeum hirundinaceum*, (3) Spotted diamondbird *Pardalotus punctatus*, (4) Tit berry pecker *Oreocharis arfaki*, (5) male and (6) female Orange-bellied flower pecker *D. trigonostigma*, (7) male and (8) female Scarlet-backed flower pecker *D. cruentatum*, and (9) Crested berry pecker *Paramythia montium*.

Paramythia montium builds a deep, loose, untidy cup 3–7ft (0·9–2·1m) up in a shrubby tree, composed of stems, rootlets and lichens with a thick pad of golden chaff from the bases of treefern leaves in the bottom. The single egg is white with spots of dark browns and greys making a wreath about the large end and sparingly scattered over the rest of the shell. The female alone incubates, and both sexes feed the young.

In the pardalotes the nest is cup-shaped or domed, of grasses, bark strips and feathers, usually in a hole in a tree or at the end of a tunnel excavated by the parent birds in a bank. The Red-tipped pardalote *P. substriatus* and the Yellow-tipped *P. striatus* have been reported as occasionally using old nests of the Fairy martin *Petrochelidon ariel.* The eggs, usually four, are pure white. Both sexes excavate, build nests, incubate and feed the young.

Composition. The latest revision of the flower peckers recognizes six species of *Prionochilus* and 36 of *Dicaeum* (including the extinct *D. quadricolor* of Cebu in the Philippines). These are small, stump tailed, short billed birds about 3½in (8·9cm) long. In some species the sexes are similar and plain; in others the male is very brightly coloured. In *Prionochilus* the outermost primary is well-developed, in *Dicaeum* (except *D. melanoxanthum*) vestigial. The five known species of *Melanocharis*, 4½–6in (11·4–15·2cm) long, are black or olive above and grey or olive-grey below, often with a conspicuous tuft on either side of the breast, and with longer tails than the flower peckers. The Spotted berry pecker *Rhamphocharis crassirostris* is similar to *Melanocharis* but has a longer bill, and the female is strikingly spotted. *Oreocharis arfaki*, 5in (12·7cm), with its yellow, green and black plumage, is similar in appearance to some species of titmice, *Parus*. The exquisite *Paramythia montium*, 8–8½in (20·3–21·6cm), is mainly green above and blue below.

The pardalotes (five or eight species, depending on how one treats the *Pardalotus striatus* complex) are small – 4in (10·1cm), short tailed, short billed birds. All species but one are brightly coloured, with patches of yellow, red and black, the last often strikingly spotted or streaked with white.

Some flower pecker species nesting. (1) Male Scarlet-backed flower pecker *Dicaeum cruentatum* in flight and landing at the pendent nest. (2) Mistletoe bird *D. hirundinaceum* bringing mistletoe berries to the young. (3) Spotted diamondbird *Pardalotus punctatus* bringing insects to the young in a domed nest of grasses at the end of a tunnel excavated in a bank.

SUNBIRDS

For over one hundred years the name sunbird has been applied to the Nectariniidae, a family of brightly plumaged birds, widely spread over the warm parts of the Old World. Ranging in size from 3½–8½in (8·9–21·6cm), with metallic iridescence in the plumage, they invite comparison with the hummingbirds (Trochilidae) of the New World. The two families are in no way related. The sunbirds show their closest affinity to the Australian honeyeaters (Meliphagidae) and the flower peckers (Dicaeidae).

The following characteristics separate sunbirds from their two nearest relatives: strong sexual dimorphism, with bright metallic colouration in the males, dull colouration in the females; and an eclipse or non-breeding plumage in the males of some species. The nostrils are oval and covered. The bill, whether long or short, slender or decurved, has fine serrations near the tip – an adaptation for holding large flying insects taken as food. The tongue is tubular in all sunbirds for two-thirds of its length, with the tip split into a fork for extracting nectar from blossoms of flowering plants. Ten primary wing feathers may be counted in each rounded wing. The legs are strong and protected with scales. The toes are short, with sharp claws. Tails may be long, square, or graduated with much variation among the species.

Distribution. Sunbirds are widely distributed in the warmer parts of the Old World in forests, scrubland and mangroves. The largest concentration occurs in tropical Africa, where more than one half of the known species live. Numerous representatives occur in India,

Ceylon, Burma, Malaya, the East Indies and Australia. Palestine has its own sunbird which is related to the African forms. Arabia claims four species and one of the Indian species is found in Baluchistan.

Feeding. Sunbirds feed on insects and upon nectar, extracting the nectar both on the wing and from a perch. The fleshy pulp of fruits and berries are also eaten. Some sunbirds may be seen hovering with rapid wing beats over spider webs or searching leaves for insects. Large blossoms and those with long tubular corollas are pierced at the base with the long pointed bills to obtain food.

Nesting and the Young. Courtship is unknown in many species of sunbirds. Subtle relationships develop between male and female, involving emotional swaying, bobbing, pivoting, upside-down swooping and swinging, wing-dropping and fluttering. All of this takes place with the sexes perched side by side and it is accompanied by soft sub-songs. These events are far too seldom seen and recorded. Vent-pecking is characteristic of the breeding season,

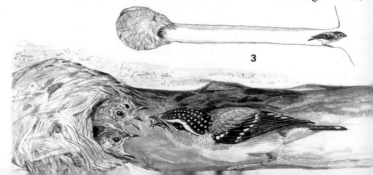

especially during the nest-building period, and even more so just prior to egg laying. Presumably this habit must provide a precopulatory stimulus.

The typical sunbird nest is a long, hanging, purse-shaped pouch constructed of matted fibres and grasses, woven together with spider webs. The nest is usually hung from a branch fairly near the ground, seldom more than 12ft (3·7m) above it. A few species make neat, compact nests, but most nests are ragged. The bottoms of most nests are extended with loose trails of fibres with a leaf or two wedged in to give the appearance of a bit of accumulated rubbish. The female alone builds the nest, but when she has completed the framework and moved inside to line the nest, the male brings materials for her. Plant down, hair or feathers are used for the lining. Upon completion, the nest is closed from the top to prevent water

Sunbirds inhabit all types of country. In Africa brilliant species live in the open, duller ones in forest. (1) Female and (2) male Yellow-backed sunbird *Aethopyga siparaja,* (3) Regal sunbird *Nectarinia regia,* (4) Shelley's sunbird *Aethopyga shelleyi,* (5) female and (6) male Ruby-cheeked sunbird *Anthreptes singalensis,* (7) Long-billed spider hunter *Arachnothera robusta* and (8) Yellow-eared spider hunter *A. chrysogenys.*

Four sunbird species showing differences in the bill and the shape of the tail. (1) Emerald sunbird *Nectarinia famosa,* (2) Golden-winged sunbird *N. reichenowi,* (3) Black sunbird *N. amethystina* and (4) pair of Yellow-bellied sunbirds *N. jugularis,* female with prey. Female also in nest.

from running into it. A porch-like projection is made above a side entrance and the male uses this porch when feeding the female in the nest. The entrance hole usually faces the centre of the tree.

The normal clutch of eggs is two, although sometimes three are found in a nest. The eggs are white or bluish-white in colour with brown or grey spots and streaks. The females incubate the eggs from 14 to 17 days before the chicks appear as nestlings. The eyes of the chicks are closed when hatched, but are fully opened on the seventh or eighth day. The bill is straight in the chicks at the time of hatching. In the species with curved bills, the curve begins to take shape at 9–10 days of age as the bill lengthens.

The body is covered with soft grey down at hatching to protect the delicate skin. When 11 or 12 days old, true feathers appear as small pin-feathers in feather tracts on the body, head, tail and wings. The chicks are fed by the female alone for the first few days after hatching. Males will bring in small insects to the brooding female, she will accept the food and then feed the chicks within the nest. As the chicks grow larger and require additional food, the female then permits the male to assist in feeding the young. A fledging period of 15 to 17 days has been recorded before the nestlings leave the nest. Once out of the nest, chicks are attended by both parents who feed them and teach them to fly, perch and seek security from their natural enemies.

Behaviour. Though sunbirds often gather together to feed when some favoured tree or patch of flowers comes into bloom, they do not show colonial behaviour. Some are pugnacious and defend feeding stations as well as nesting territories against unwelcome visitors. Many species take up fixed song-posts and use them not only for courtship singing but as lookout stations from which to intercept intruders into their territories.

The constant search for flowering shrubs and trees causes the sunbirds, especially the long-billed ones, to move about locally in search of food and with no definite migration route. Some species moving from one area to another cover 70–75mi (130–139km) a day.

The voice is usually poorly developed and their thin metallic calls do not carry far. In a few, the voices are sharper or husky with metallic undertones. Some males in courtship offer a subdued series of sibilant twittering warbles, rapid and excitable, in a medium-pitched key. Only the Black sunbird *Nectarinia amethystina* is outstanding in song.

Composition. Sunbirds are a relatively uniform group. In the family Nectariniidae 8 genera and 105 species are recognized by most systematists. This family may be divided into three groups which differ from one another in the length and shape of the bill: the size,

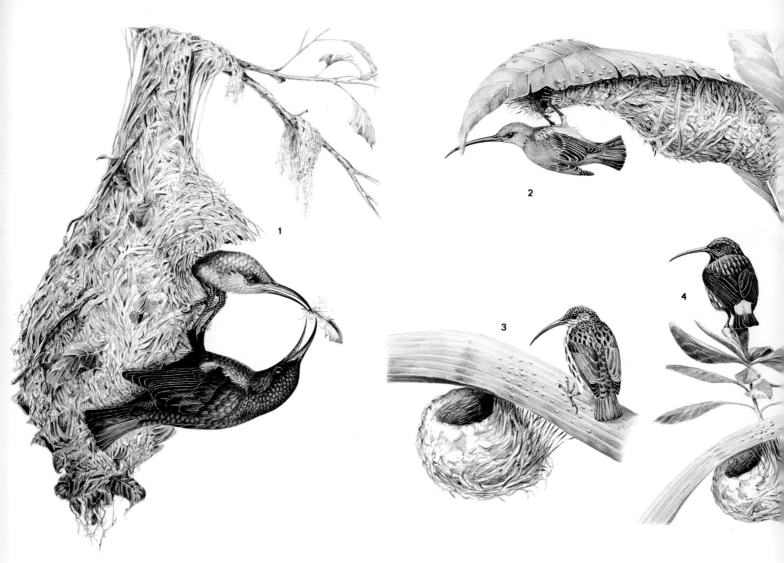

Purple sunbirds *Nectarinia asiatica* (1) build nests of plant fibres and dead leaves which may assist in camouflage; here the female is holding a feather to be used in the lining. Spider hunters fix their nests to the underside of a broad leaf; their sharp-pointed bills force the ends of plant fibres or cob-webs through the leaf from below and the cut surfaces close together gripping the material. (2) Long-billed spider hunter *Arachnothera robusta* at a nest with a long entrance tube, (3) Streaked spider hunter *A. magna* and (4) Whitehead's spider hunter *A. juliae.*

and shape of the tail; and in the number of lobes in the tongue.

The largest group, *Nectarinia*, includes 74 species of several subgenera; *N. cyanomitra*, the Olive sunbird of Rhodesia; *N. chalcomitra*, the Black sunbird in the Cape Province; *N. leptocoma*, Van Hasselt's sunbird in the Philippines; and *N. nectarinia*, the Golden-winged sunbird in eastern Africa.

The second group, *Anthreptes*, with 16 species, is distinguished from *Nectarinia* by having shorter, less curved bills, a smaller size and metallic plumage in both sexes in several species. This group contains the Violet-back and Blue-throated sunbirds, *Anthreptes longuemarei* and *A. reichenowi*, of South Africa.

The third group, *Aethopyga*, contains 14 species and differs from all other sunbirds in the structure of the tongue, which terminates in three lobes instead of two. In the Malay Peninsula, over 25 species of sunbirds have been recorded. The Yellow-backed sunbird *Aethopyga siparaja* on the islands of Cebu and Negros in the Philippines is a member of this group. The largest species of sunbird is the Great sunbird *A. thomensis*, which is $8\frac{1}{2}$in (21·6cm) long,

which is restricted to the Island of Sao Tome in the Ethiopian region. The family is represented in Australia by 13 species of which the Yellow-bellied sunbird, *Nectarinia jugularis*, is one of the best known.

WHITE-EYES

The Zosteropidae is an homogeneous family of Old World passerines commonly known as white-eyes. They are all small or very small birds, $3-5\frac{1}{2}$in (7–14cm) long, with slightly decurved, pointed bills that are short in most species, wings with only nine primary feathers, and usually a brush-tipped tongue. All but a few aberrant species have a distinctive ring of white feathers around the eye from which the family takes its name. In a typical species of the genus *Zosterops* the upperparts are dull green and the underparts yellow or greyish, with no prominent pattern. Many island forms have lost the yellow lipochrome pigment, so that they are coloured in various shades of brown and grey. The sexes are similar in plumage in every species of the family. The small species of the genus *Zosterops* have short slender legs and a rather short tail, but some of the larger species of other genera, being partly terrestrial, have longer and stronger legs. They also have relatively longer tails.

Distribution. The white-eyes are found throughout Africa south of the Sahara, on many islands off the coast of Africa and in the Indian

the bill and tail tips of an incubating bird can be seen from the side. Clutches of 1–3 white or pale blue eggs, are incubated by both parents for $10\frac{1}{2}$–13 days. At hatching the young are helpless and naked except for thin patches of down. They are fed on insects by both parents for a period of $9\frac{1}{2}$–12 days after which the parents continue to feed their fledged brood for at least a few days.

Behaviour. Those typical species of the genus *Zosterops* that have been investigated all live in groups of 5–20 birds that roam about together, feeding as they go. The movements of these groups are not extensive, although they sometimes overlap the ranges of other groups. As they move about the birds keep in touch with soft, plaintive calls which are short and high-pitched.

Composition. The Zosteropidae has about 85 species, of which about 62 are in the central genus, *Zosterops*. The remaining species are placed in a number of small genera whose affinities to each other and to *Zosterops* are unclear. *Speirops* has three species, larger than any *Zosterops*, which lack yellow colouration: they are found on the three islands in the Gulf of Guinea and on Cameroon Mountain. *Woodfordia* has two large brown species, with long bills and no eye-ring, found on Rennell and Santa Cruz Islands: *Rukia* has four large species found in the Palau and Caroline Islands: *Tephrozosterops* and *Madanga* have one species each in the mountains of Ceram and Buru in the Moluccas: *Lophozosterops* has six species in Indonesia and the Philippines, and *Heleia* has two species and *Oculocincta* and *Chlorocharis* one each in the same region. The single species of the Philippine genus *Hypocryptadius* is tentatively placed in the Zosteropidae, but its affinities are at present uncertain.

Five species of white-eyes. (1) Chestnut-flanked white-eye *Zosterops erythropleura*, (2) Grey-breasted white-eye *Z. lateralis*, (3) Olive black-eye *Chlorocharis emiliae*, (4) Cinnamon white-eye *Hypocryptadius cinnamomeus* and (5) Oriental white-eye *Zosterops palpebrosa* brooding on the thin nest which is suspended between forked twigs.

Two male Pygmy sunbirds *Anthreptes platurus* in flight (1), showing the long tail feathers which aid rapid changes in direction. (2) Orange-tufted sunbird *Nectarinia osea* and (3) Splendid sunbird *N. coccinigastra* extracting the nectar which is an important part of its diet. (4) Pair of Van Hesselt's sunbirds *N. sperata*, the female occupying the pendent nest.

Ocean, throughout southern Asia, and south through Indonesia and the Philippines to the whole Australasian region. Many species have colonized islands of the southwest Pacific, from New Zealand and the Solomon Islands eastwards to Samoa and north to the Caroline Islands.

White-eyes of different species inhabit most wooded or forest habitats from coastal mangroves to high mountain scrub. In continental regions they do not usually occur inside dense rain forest, but some island species inhabit the thickest of tall forests.

Feeding. Most white-eyes have a varied diet of insects, fruit, nectar and pollen. Characteristically they roam about in small groups feeding as they go, often in association with flocks of other insectivorous birds. When feeding on fruit, they pierce the skin of the ripe fruit with the bill and use the brush-tipped tongue to extract juice and pulp. Some of the larger island species live mainly near the ground in thick undergrowth of forests, and these are probably largely insectivorous.

Nesting and the Young. In all known cases, the nests are cup-shaped structures of plant fibres, plant down and cobwebs hung in a fork of a bush or tree. The cup of the nest is usually very deep, so that only

AUSTRALIAN CHATS

The Australian chats (Epthianuridae) are small short-tailed terrestrial or semiterrestrial birds, 4–5in (10–12·5cm) long, at least three of which have brush-tipped tongues. Excepting one species, the males are more brightly coloured than the females, at least in the breeding season. The nest is cup-shaped and placed on or near the ground. The eggs are whitish and spotted, and similar to those of some honeyeaters.

Distribution. The five species of Australian chat are confined to Australia, including Tasmania. The Crimson chat *Epthianura tricolor* and the Orange chat *E. aurifrons* range through the greater part of the semi-arid interior of the continent, frequenting flat open shrubland such as saltbush and samphire plains, and shrubby sandplains and gibbers. Both species are highly nomadic, often

The colourful Australian chats are largely terrestrial. (1) Female, (2) male Crimson chat *Epthianura tricolor* and (3) Gibber chat *Ashbyia lovensis*.

moving into an area after it has received rain. In dry years the Crimson chat especially may irrupt into the wetter coastal districts. In the interior the White-fronted chat *E. albifrons* inhabits similar country, but in coastal districts usually frequents saltflats, moist grassland, cultivated regions and the fringes of swamps, and may sometimes be resident in such areas.

The distribution and ecology of the Yellow chat *E. crocea* are very much under review at present. Until recently, this species was known only from a few scattered coastal and subcoastal swamps in northern and northeastern Australia, and was thought to be sedentary. In 1972 it was discovered in good numbers in reedy artesian swamps on the gibber plains of southwestern Queensland. It now seems possible that its centre of distribution is the Lake Eyre Basin, and that the peripheral records may represent transient or established vagrants.

The Gibber chat *Ashbyia lovensis* is an inhabitant of the open grassy plains and gibbers of the Lake Eyre Basin. It is mainly sedentary, though some local movement does occur.

Behaviour. Australian chats are basically insectivorous, and feed mainly on the ground. In the Crimson, Orange and Yellow chats at least, the tongue has a brush-tip; this is presumably an adaptation to nectar feeding, for the Crimson chat has been observed inserting its bill into nectar-containing flowers.

Pair of White-fronted chats *Epthianura albifrons* showing the similarity of their colour pattern to that of the wagtails. The female is seen with prey.

In the Crimson chat at least, both sexes build the nest, incubate, and feed the young. In all species the nest is cup-shaped, of stalks, grasses and rootlets, often lined with finer rootlets, hair and plant down. The Gibber chat places its nest in a depression in the ground; in the other species the nest is built close to the ground in a bush or tussock. The eggs, normally three, are, with their white or creamy ground colour and sparse markings of purplish black, brownish black, reddish brown and orange brown, strikingly similar to those of some honeyeaters. All species may give an injury-feigning display to draw an intruder away from the nest.

Australian chats are gregarious in the non-breeding season, and may also nest in loose communities. In the Crimson chat, each nest in a community is the centre of a territory that is strongly defended by both sexes; in one community these territories were estimated to be about ½ac (0·2ha). After breeding, the family parties congregate on common ground.

Composition. The 5 species are placed in two genera, *Epthianura* (4) and *Ashbyia* (1). In the Crimson chat the male has a scarlet crown and underparts, white throat and brown mask. Males of the Orange and the Yellow chat are mainly yellow on the head and underparts, the former having the face and throat black and the latter a black breast-band. The male White-fronted chat has the white head and upper breast completely encircled by a broad black band. In the foregoing species the females, and sometimes the non-breeding males, are duller and less boldly marked. In the Gibber chat the sexes are similar, yellow beneath and light brown above.

The taxonomic position of the family as a whole is not clear, but recent studies of egg white proteins suggest that it is close to the Australian honeyeaters (Meliphagidae), an hypothesis supported by their tongue shape and egg colouration.

The Yellow chat *Epthianura crocea*, another of these Australian species, showing the cup-shaped nest in which the female is brooding.

AUSTRALIAN HONEYEATERS

Honeyeaters are small to medium-sized song birds that, as the family name Meliphagidae pointedly implies, feed at least partly on nectar. For this, they have a deeply-channelled, prolonged and protrusible tongue that is characteristically fringed at the tip and conducts food to a modified alimentary tract that allows easy passage of nectar from oesophagus to intestine while retaining solid matter in the stomach for digestion.

From time to time it has been suggested that honeyeaters are polyphyletic and comprise unrelated songbirds linked by a single, convergently adaptive character, the brush-tipped tongue; and it has become apparent that some genera such as the African sugar-birds *Promerops* have been misplaced in the family. Apart from structure and function of tongue however, honeyeaters have a number of other characteristics that unify them, and they may in fact represent a monophyletic group. In appearance, they are generalized songbirds with 10 primary flight feathers in the wing and prevailingly soft, sombre plumage. Contrasting colour patterns on the sides of the head, effected either by patches of bright, frequently yellow and/or black plumage, bare skin and wattles, and varicoloured eyes, are common features.

Also characteristic are the slender, downcurved bills of varying length that, notwithstanding frequent microscopic toothing, are better fitted for probing than gripping. Slit-like semi-operculate nostrils and the almost total reduction of rictal bristles about the bill are also apparently adapted to the mode of feeding. Honeyeaters have unelaborate, often metallic harsh calls and songs, ascending display flights, suspended cup-shaped nests, similarly-coloured eggs, and the prevailingly secondary role of the male in nest building.

Distribution. Although a number of species range through the islands of the southwestern Pacific as far as Hawaii and through Timor and the Moluccas to the eastern Lesser Sundas, honeyeaters are centred in Australia and New Guinea. They comprise the largest single bird group in these avifaunally rich continental islands and dominate the inland bird faunas there.

Though essentially arboreal, some species descend occasionally to the ground to feed. Unlike other Australo-Papuan song bird families with their geographically or ecologically restricted distributions, honeyeaters are ubiquitous: in Australia they are found from coastal mangroves, rain forests and heaths through the eucalypt woodlands to the sandhill vegetation of inland deserts; and in New Guinea they are partitioned throughout all forested altitudes up to alpine shrubbery at heights of 13,125ft (4,000m) in primary and secondary vegetation and all strata within the forest.

In keeping with their ecological versatility, honeyeaters may be sedentary, migratory or nomadic.

Feeding. More has been said than is known about the feeding habits and methods of honeyeaters, and their role in pollination and the evolution of ornithophilous flowers. Nevertheless it does appear that those central genera, typified by *Meliphaga* itself, and most of the larger honeyeaters, for example, the New Guinean and Australian wattlebirds *Anthochaera*, *Melidectes* and friar-birds *Philemon*, with moderately long bills and brush-tipped tongue of basic structure, are generalized nectar suckers, insect gleaners and fruit eaters that exploit whatever food is conveniently offering.

Nervously active, noisy and pugnacious when feeding, honey-eaters often congregate in loose single- or multi-species feeding flocks, particularly in flowering food trees. Threat postures and submissive gestures are feeble, most controversies being accompanied by real fighting as the larger species displace by rank the smaller in their feeding; several species possess fighting songs.

Nesting and the Young. Females alone normally construct the nest and incubate, and males assist only in the raising of young. Nests are usually flimsy and cup-shaped, constructed roughly of vegetable fibre, lined with similar but finer materials, and slung from the branchlets and leaves of small shrubs at levels from close to the ground to the tops of forest trees. Hanging domed nests are made only by the two species of the Austro-Papuan genus *Ramsayornis* and possibly by the New Guinean Pigmy honeyeater *Oedistoma pygmaeum*.

Eggs are usually white to salmon pink and spotted and blotched with shades of red-brown and sepia prevailingly towards the larger end. Some species, for example, the Australian Singing honeyeater *Meliphaga virescens*, have plain eggs; others, such as the Pied, Banded and Spiny-cheeked honeyeaters, *Certhionyx variegatus*, *Myzomela pectoralis* and *Acanthagenys rufogularis*, of inland and northern Australia, have buff-brown, blackish marked eggs that belie their relations with myzomeline honeyeaters and Australian wattle-

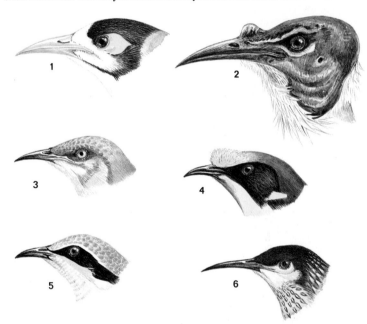

Bill and head ornamentation among honeyeaters. (1) Noisy miner *Manorina melanocephala*, (2) Noisy friarbird *Philemon corniculatus*, (3) Lewin's honeyeater *Meliphaga lewinii*, (4) Helmeted honeyeater *M. cassidix*, (5) Mangrove honeyeater *M. fasciogularis*, (6) Macleay's honeyeater *M. macleayana*, (7) Scarlet honeyeater *Myzomela sanguinolenta*, (8) Black-chinned honeyeater *Melithreptus gularis* and (9) Cockerell's honeyeater *Lichmera cockerelli*.

birds respectively. Size of clutch varies predictably from one or two in most tropical and rain forest inhabiting species to two to four in most temperate and open forest- to arid scrub-inhabiting species. The period of incubation ranges from 13 to 16 days and the nidicolous young grow extraordinarily rapidly to fledge about 10 to 16 days after hatching.

Behaviour. Most honeyeater species appear to hold territory only when breeding. Notable exceptions are the miners *Manorina* and Blue-faced honeyeater that form sedentary colonies with complex social organization throughout Australian eucalypt woodlands. During nesting, moreover, various members of these colonies assist parents in the feeding of young. Little is known of the permanence of pair bonding or the rituals of courtship. Honeyeaters in general have characteristic territory-advertizing flights accompanied by strongly metallic or repetitively whistled songs. The parabolic flights made from perches by species of the Australian genus *Lichenostomus* typify the pattern. Interesting variants are exhibited by the Australian Tawny-crowned *Gliciphila melanops* and Pied honeyeaters with their respective spiralling and vertical dives, and in the miners which describe slow circling flights with head raised at an awkward angle. Both sexes sing, and synchronized duet- and group-singing is highly developed in some species such as the friar-birds.

Composition. The Meliphagidae contains some 170 species, of which Australia shares about 70, New Guinea about 62, Timor, the Moluccas and Lesser Sundas about 22, the Melanesian and Micronesian archipelagos and islands about 31, New Zealand 3, Hawaii 5, and the Bonin Islands 1.

They can be grouped into two or three subfamilies, depending on whether the Australian chats are included in the family. The typical honeyeaters, which probably include all genera except three and the majority of species, occur throughout the range of the family. Among them are the large Australo-Papuan friar-birds with their noisy, clanking calls and partly or completely bald heads. Related to them are the Australian miners which have differing piped calls to warn of the approach and departure of predators and crane inquisitively with cross-eyed aspect. Colonies of one of these, the Bell miner *Manorina melanophrys*, call incessantly throughout the day, each bird repeating at intervals an echoing, sucked-in *tink*. At the other extreme in size is the Pigmy honeyeater, the smallest bird in New Guinea and less than $2\frac{1}{3}$in (6cm) long. Of others, the Australian spinebills often hover hummingbird-like to take nectar from flowers; the spotted-eyed honeyeaters *Lichmera*, with their musical, reed warbler-like calls, disperse easily and have colonized islands, particularly to the northwest of Australia as far as Bali; the energetic New Zealand Tui *Prosthemadera novaeseelandiae* re-

Honeyeaters have produced very varied forms. (1) The extinct 0-o *Moho nobilis* from Hawaii, (2) Leatherhead *Philemon novaeguineae* from New Guinea, (3) Cape sugarbird *Promerops cafer*, (4) Tui *Prosthemadera novaeseelandiae* from New Zealand and (5) Blue-faced honeyeater *Entomyzon cyanotis* from Australia.

Pygmy honeyeater *Oedistoma pygmaeum* (1), Cardinal honeyeater *Myzomela cardinalis* (2), Yellow-winged honeyeater *Phylidonyris novaehollandiae* (3) and Cape sugarbird *Promerops cafer* (4) showing the long-tailed male in flight and the female nesting in a protea.

sembles a starling in its metallic green-black plumage and possesses rich and resonant calls; and the similar, endangered Hawaiian O'os *Moho* search noisily for insects along the branches of trees with much movement of their long, trailing tails.

The second group, the myzomeline honeyeaters, comprises about 25 species in the single genus *Myzomela*. Small in size and distinguished by their structure of tongue and varying amounts of metallic red in their plumage, they are as facile tramps as the spotted-eyed honeyeaters and have spread widely through the Melanesian archipelagos.

The third group contains the Australian chats. These are thought by some ornithologists to be valid members of the Meliphagidae, but by others to represent a separate though closely related family. In this volume it is described separately.

Traditionally, honeyeaters have been thought of as close relatives of the sunbirds (Nectariniidae) and flower peckers (Dicaeidae). New Guinean long-bills *Toxorhamphus* appear to confirm this view in that they display features intermediate between the sunbirds and flower peckers and the honeyeaters.

BUNTINGS AND AMERICAN SPARROWS

The Emberizidae, a large family with 554 species in 133 genera, can be divided into three main groups: the buntings and American sparrows, the cardinal-grosbeaks, and the tanagers. In a family of this size there is, as might be expected, a good deal of variation in habitat preference, food, behaviour and plumage patterns. The buntings and American sparrows are generally of sober appearance, patterned in black, white and browns, having the fairly stout bills associated with seed eating; the majority are sexually dimorphic. In spite of their lack of bright colouring, some are of quite striking appearance: examples are the handsome male Lapland bunting *Calcarius lapponicus*, which has its black face and throat marked off from the black crown and chestnut nape by a V-shaped white band; and the male Snow bunting *Plectrophenax nivalis*, which in summer is pure white, apart from black on the back and in the wings and tail – an eye-catching contrast. The cardinal-grosbeak group also have the stout 'seed eater' bill; they, however, are more brightly coloured. For instance, the male Blue grosbeak *Guiraca caerulea* has uniformly dark blue body plumage (with blackish tail and wings, the latter with buff bars); the male Painted bunting *Passerina ciris*, which is not a true bunting at all, is a gaudy bird, having red underparts, purple head and green back; and the male Cardinal *Pyrrhuloxia cardinalis*, one of the few crested emberizids, is red all over except for a black facial mask. Among the tanagers, which have more slender bills due to different feeding habits, plumage colouration is even more striking, its brilliance surpassing even that of the humming-birds. The Paradise tanager *Tangara chilensis* is one of the gaudiest, with black upperparts, crimson rump, purple throat, and brilliant blue underparts; while even unicoloured species, such as the Blue-grey tanager *Thraupis episcopus*, are notable for their brightness of hue.

Distribution. The family belongs predominantly to the New World. The cardinal-grosbeaks and tanagers are found only in the Americas, where the buntings and allies are also best represented. There are, however, 40 species of bunting in the Old World, 37 of them in the genus *Emberiza*; these are mainly found in cool-temperate regions, and are more strongly represented in Asia than in Europe or Africa, indicating that *Emberiza* evolved in Asia, perhaps following a spread across the Bering Straits by an ancestral stock. The only bunting breeding in tropical Asia is the Crested bunting *Melophus lathami* of India and Indo-China; however, the African tropics possess seven native *Emberiza* species, plus the House bunting *E. striolata* which is shared by the Palearctic and

Brightly coloured birds in the bunting family. (1) Cardinal *Pyrrhuloxia cardinalis*, (2) Lapland bunting (or longspur) *Calcarius lapponicus*, (3) Paradise tanager *Tangara chilensis* and (4) Crested bunting *Melophus lathami*.

Buntings occupy a very wide variety of habitats. (1) Painted bunting *Passerina ciris*, (2) Blue grosbeak *Guiraca caerulea*, (3) Yellow-hammer *Emberiza citrinella*, (4) Little bunting *E. pusilla* and (5) pair of Swallow tanagers *Tersina viridis*, the more dull-coloured female emerging from the nest-hole and showing the broad gape of the bill.

Ethiopian regions. The two other Old World breeding species are the Lapland and Snow buntings, both Arctic birds of circumpolar distribution, which therefore breed in North America also.

The American sparrows show much diversity in the north temperate region, but are nevertheless well represented in the Neotropics also, while *Zonotrichia* and *Melanodera* have representatives as far south as Tierra del Fuego and the Falkland Islands. The rarest, and now endangered, species is the Zapata sparrow *Torreornis inexpectata*, found only in two small areas in Cuba; some rare forms in maritime North America, the Cape sable sparrow, Dusky seaside sparrow and Ipswich sparrow, are now regarded as races of widespread continental species. The cardinal-grosbeaks and tanagers show greatest speciation in the New World tropics, but a number of species penetrate into the cooler regions, south and north: the Rose-breasted grosbeak *Pheucticus ludovicianus* and Western tanager *Piranga ludoviciana* breed as far north as the Great Slave Lake in Canada.

Overall the tendency is for the many tropical species to be more or less resident, but with the degree of seasonal movement increasing with latitude so that subarctic and arctic breeding populations are truly migratory.

Feeding. The stout bills possessed by typical members of this family denote their mainly granivorous diets, and many species have a bony hump in the roof of the mouth against which seeds can be

Snow buntings *Plectrophenax nivalis* in winter plumage: immature female (1) and adult female (2), and immature male (3) and adult male (4). In summer plumage is McKay's bunting *P. hyperboreus* (5). Adult snow buntings are shown in summer plumage resting (6 and 7).

crushed; berries are also consumed freely in autumn. Because of its wetland habitat, the Reed bunting *E. schoeniclus* feeds mainly on the seeds of marsh plants and grasses, whereas the Yellow-hammer *E. citrinella*, inhabiting drier (usually cultivated) ground, takes mainly grain and weed seeds. In North America, the White-crowned sparrow *Zonotrichia leucophrys* feeds mainly on seeds in winter, and (when available) fleshy fruits such as mulberry and crowberry; on their return to northern breeding grounds in the spring they eat the green capsules of the hairy-cap moss *Polytrichum*, which become available as soon as tne snows melt and before many insects emerge. Insects form an important minority part of the diets of buntings and American sparrows, and nestlings are fed almost exclusively on insectivorous matter. Adult buntings in both America and Europe feed predominantly on vegetable matter.

Tanagers are mainly insectivorous and frugivorous, and their beaks are more slender than those of the buntings and sparrows; typically, they are birds of forest edge and forest canopy.

Nesting and the Young. In *Emberiza* a characteristic form of sexual behaviour occurs in the period after pairing and before the hen reaches breeding condition; this involves sexual chasing, a headlong twisting pursuit of the female by the male, commonly ending in a mêlée as the birds tumble from branch to branch or to the ground.

Individual territories are established and defended. Songflights are more pronounced in some species than others; the male Snow bunting, for example, rises 20–30ft (6–9m) into the air, with expanded wings and tail, and peculiar fluttering wing beats, descending with the wings held at 45°.

Nest sites vary according to habitat; thus *Emberiza* species generally select a low site in a hedge or bush, while the American sparrows may use similar sites or simply nest on the ground. Lapland buntings nest in a ground depression or in the hollow of a hummock on the tundra, while Snow and Rock buntings build among loose rocks or in screes. Nests are compact cups of whatever material is available – dry grasses, reed stems, dead weeds, small twigs, mosses, lichens, with a lining of finer grasses, wool, hair or feathers. Three to five eggs constitute the normal clutch, but Arctic nesters may lay six or even (rarely) seven eggs; colouration is variable, but the general pattern is for a pale ground colour, spotted, blotched or scrolled with black or shades of brown. These are incubated for 12–13 days, generally by the hen, though males assist in some species. The Corn bunting *Emberiza calandra* is polygamous, and males having up to seven hens have been recorded; this is one of the few species where the male does not usually assist in feeding the young, which in most emberizids remain in the nest for two weeks or a little less. Two or even three broods may be reared in a season, though in the arctic the short summer leaves insufficient time for more than one.

In keeping with the general rule that birds nesting in the tropics lay smaller clutches than those in temperate or cool regions,

Neotropical tanagers generally lay two eggs; but there are exceptions in the cases of the general *Chlorophonia* and *Euphonia*, which lay 4–5. The migratory tanagers *Piranga* of North America lay 3–5 eggs. According to species, the open, cup-shaped tanager nests may be built in tree tops or low bushes or even in a tree hole or other cranny; *Chlorophonia* and *Euphonia* again differ, for they build dome-shaped nests with a side entrance. Only hen tanagers incubate, though both parents tend the young. Most are double-brooded.

Behaviour. Though strictly territorial while breeding, the emberizids are mostly gregarious at other seasons, feeding and roosting in flocks that may be large in migratory species. Roosting may be on or close to the ground, or well above it in trees, bushes, or haystacks. Some species, notably European ones, may associate with other buntings, sparrows or finches in feeding and roosting. Flocks, including those of non-migratory species, will wander considerable distances to feed, for example, on stubble fields.

Inevitably, in such a large family as this, there are exceptions. The saltators of South America (part of the cardinal-grosbeak assemblage) remain paired throughout the year; and this seems to apply to a number of the tanagers, in which males may at any time offer food to their mates as pair bonding maintenance behaviour, and with increasing frequency as the breeding season approaches.

The emberizids as a family are not notable as songsters; this is particularly true of the tanagers, which for the most part have poorly developed songs, or even no true song at all. However, the migratory North American species and the ant-tanagers *Habia* have quite pleasant songs, while the aberrant Thrush tanager is decidedly musical. Among the American sparrows, one must single out the Song sparrow *Melospiza melodia*, with its sweet, musical song, which is variable to an unusual degree from one male to another; this song may be delivered all through the year, except when the bird is moulting.

Economic Importance. It is inevitable that a large family of seed eaters should contain a couple of species which have offended local agricultural interests; but very few emberizids occur in such concentrations as to constitute major problems. This is the case, however, with Yellow-breasted buntings that winter in large flocks in the rice fields of southeast Asia; they are netted extensively and used for food, and in Thailand this practice reaches massive proportions with over 2 million birds taken annually. The Black-faced bunting *Emberiza spodocephala* is likewise trapped extensively for food in Taiwan; while the rice farmers of the Burmese Shan States regard the Chestnut bunting *E. rutila* as a major pest in its winter quarters there.

Composition. The taxonomy of the Old and New World seed eaters has been a controversial issue; and some quite recent publications have lumped the buntings and their allies with the cardueline finches and Galapagos finches in an enlarged family Fringillidae, while at the same time keeping the tanagers apart in a family of their own. The arrangement used in this article is believed to reflect most recent thoughts, based on reports of distinctive morphological characters (especially those concerning palate and gut structure) between the buntings and tanagers on the one hand, and the true finches on the other.

The 554 species now placed in Emberizidae fall naturally into three groups. The buntings and American sparrows (subfamily Emberizinae) consist of 278 species in 65 genera, found mainly in the Americas though two genera (containing 38 species) are restricted to the Old World; there are also three species endemic to isolated Gough Island and Tristan da Cunha in the South Atlantic: *Rowettia* and *Nesospiza*, whose closest affinities seem to be with *Melanodera* of South America. The cardinal-grosbeaks Cardinalinae consist of 37 species in nine genera; and the tanagers Thraupinae 239 species in 59 genera (including the aberrant, monotypic *Catamblyrhynchus* and *Tersina*, which until recently were placed in subfamilies of their own). The 239 tanagers further include *Hemispingus parodii* of Peru, a species new to science when it was first described in 1974.

AMERICAN WOOD WARBLERS

Warblers are small nine-primaried song birds with slender bills. Many species are brightly coloured, and although yellow predominates, there may be areas of orange, red, blue or chestnut as well as duller markings. Members of the tropical genus *Ergaticus* are almost completely red. In tropical species the sexes usually have a similar appearance. Females and immatures of North American species are often dull coloured and the males of some brightly coloured species moult into a drabber plumage for the winter months. Thus, identification of migrants in the autumn poses a real challenge to bird watchers as so many look alike. Warblers are small, most having a length of only 5in (12.5cm), but the Yellow-breasted chat *Icteria virens* is about 7in (17.5cm). Warblers flit about actively in search of food and seem always to be on the move.

Distribution. Warblers are widely distributed in the western hemisphere, inhabiting North, Central and South America and the West Indies. The various species make up a large proportion of breeding bird populations in some areas. For example, in the coniferous forests and associated habitats in the northern United States and Canada, 10 or more species may live within hearing distance of each other. The North American species are largely migratory, some such as the Blackpoll warbler *Dendroica striata* travelling thousands of miles to a winter home in northern South America from its breeding grounds in northern North America.

Many species have broad geographic ranges and occur in a variety of habitats, but some are more restricted. For example, Yellow warblers *Dendroica petechia*, Yellowthroats *Geothlypis trichas* and Yellow-breasted chats breed from Canada to Mexico

Honeycreepers are small and brightly coloured, like the Old World sunbirds. (1) Pair of Red-legged honeycreepers *Cyanerpes cyaneus*, the male shown also in flight, (2) Green honeycreeper *Chlorophanes spiza* and (3) Purple honeycreeper *Cyanerpes caeruleus* puncturing the base of a petal in order to reach the nectar.

Four species of American wood warblers. (1) Yellow-breasted chat *Icteria virens*, (2) Prothonotary warbler *Protonotaria citrea*, (3) Kirtland's warbler *Dendroica kirtlandii* and (4) Red-faced warbler *Cardellina rubrifrons*.

and from the Atlantic to the Pacific. Another wide-ranging species, the Orange-crowned warbler *Vermivora celata*, breeds in shrubby areas, both deciduous and coniferous forest, and from dry hillsides to damp willow thickets. On the other hand, the newly discovered Elfin Woods warbler *Dendroica angelae* occupies only about 1,125 ac (450ha) of a particular forest type in Puerto Rico.

Feeding. Warblers are largely insectivorous and obtain their food in a variety of ways. A close relationship often exists between structure, particularly of the bill, and manner of feeding. In the spring Blue-winged warblers *Vermivora pinus* and other members of this genus probe in buds and flowers seeking insects, and their bills are especially slender and sharply pointed. On the other hand, the American redstart *Setophaga ruticilla* has a flattened bill and prominent rictal bristles, which are characteristics of feeders on aerial insects, and this species obtains much of its food by making short flying sallies in the manner of a flycatcher. Most species glean insects from foliage. However, the Black-and-white warbler *Mniotilta varia* forages on tree trunks and branches. Some species, such as the Ovenbird *Seiurus aurocapillus*, forage on the ground.

Nesting and the Young. The nest may be placed in various locations. Most species construct their nests in trees or shrubs, but some nest on the ground or even in crevices in banks or rock ledges. The Prothonotary warbler *Protonotaria citrea* nests in cavities in trees. The nests of most species are simple cup-shaped structures, but the Ovenbird and some tropical warblers build domed nests with side openings. Females usually do all the nest building.

The eggs are generally creamy with blotches and speckles of brown, although a few species lay white eggs. The usual clutch size for North American species is four, although tropical warblers typically have smaller clutches. The Bay-breasted warbler seems to adjust its clutch size according to food supply. In years of spruce budworm outbreaks they have clutches averaging six eggs, in other years typically five. The Brown-headed cowbird *Molothrus ater* often lays its eggs in warbler nests, and cowbird parasitism may be an important problem for Kirtland's warbler, which has such a small breeding population. Incubation is conducted by the female, and it usually lasts for about 12 days. When the young hatch they are fed by both parents and remain in the nest for 8–12 days. They

may still be dependent on their parents for a few weeks longer.

Behaviour. Very little is known of the breeding behaviour of tropical warblers, but some North American species have been well studied. Males, on return from migration in the spring defend a territory against intruding males of the same species. Territorial boundaries are delineated by song and visual displays. When male American redstarts confront a neighbour near the mutual boundary, they perform a complicated series of displays. Each male takes his turn in a stylized circling pattern in which he first approaches to within a few feet and then circles away from his opponent. The circling evidently serves to reinforce the position of the boundary.

Territory size is variable, ranging from about 0·3 to 8 ac (8 to 20ha). One of the factors affecting territory size in Ovenbirds is food availability. Ovenbirds feed on small invertebrates in leaf litter of the forest floor, and their territories are larger when invertebrates are sparsely distributed.

The quality of song is quite variable in wood warblers. Some species have simple insect-like trills and buzzes, while others have more complex melodious songs.

Most North American species form monogamous pair bonds

Pair of Northern parulas *Parula americana* (1) at their nest made of Spanish moss built into a hanging tuft of the same material. (2) Pair of Prothonotary warblers *Protonotaria citrea* at their nest built in a hollow stump.

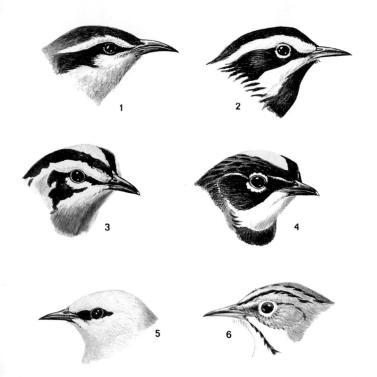

When in breeding plumage the American wood warblers show a notable variety of colour and pattern on the head. (1) Bananaquit *Coereba flaveola*, (2) Black-and-white warbler *Mniotilta varia*, (3) Blackburnian warbler *Dendroica fusca*, (4) Yellow-rumped warbler *D. coronata*, (5) Blue-winged warbler *Vermivora pinus* and (6) Ovenbird *Seiurus aurocapillus*.

Distribution. Of the 22 full species of drepanids, eight are already extinct and eight others are currently considered to be in danger of extinction. The six remaining species have at least one valid race each in danger of extinction. The genus *Psittirostra* has one species, *P. cantans* that is restricted to the Leeward Islands, Nihoa and Laysan. Formerly, Laysan Island was also inhabited by a distinct race of Apapane, *Himatione sanguinea freethi*. All other species of Hawaiian honeycreepers are confined to the six main islands: Kauai, Oahu, Molokai, Lanai, Maui and Hawaii.

When the first comprehensive field studies of the drepanids was carried out, at the turn of the century, some species of honeycreepers were observed in the lowlands, but today very few honeycreepers are found below 3,000ft (914m) on any of the main islands in the chain. Most of the drepanids inhabit high elevation tropical rain forests where an annual rainfall of more than 100in (254cm) is common. The only area in which all the endemic birds still occur is the Alakai Swamp region on Kauai where over 600in (1,524cm) of rain have been recorded in a single year, on Mt. Waialeale 5,000ft (1,524m). The rain forest on the northeast slope of Maui's Haleakala Crater – elevations of 5,300ft (1,615m) and 6,800ft (2,073m) – is also good honeycreeper habitat.

American redstart *Setophaga ruticilla*.
This strikingly patterned species builds a cup-shaped nest set in a fork of a branch.

that last for a single breeding season; tropical species may have more enduring pair bonds.

No species are known to be colonial during the breeding season, although the Yellow-rumped warbler lives in flocks during the non-breeding season. Many migratory species feed in mixed species flocks in the tropics during the winter, associating with other warbler species, tanagers and honeycreepers.

Composition. About 113 species in 26 genera are currently recognized as belonging to the Parulidae, although the precise number varies according to the opinions of different taxonomists. The wood warblers appear to be closely related to some other groups of nine-primaried song birds, particularly to the emberizine finches (buntings) and perhaps to the tanagers as well.

HAWAIIAN HONEYCREEPERS

The Hawaiian honeycreepers constitute a family of small birds endemic to the Hawaiian Islands. The largest living species, the Kauai akialoa *Hemignathus procerus*, is only 7¾in (19·6cm) in total length; the Anianiau *Loxops parva*, one of the smallest, is 4¼in (10·8cm) long. The extreme diversity of structure within the family (especially in bill shape) illustrates allopatric speciation and adaptive radiation from an assumed single ancestral species, far better than does any other bird family in the world. The akialoas *Hemignathus procerus* and *H. obscurus* have strongly decurved bills over 2in (5cm) in length, or nearly one-third the total length of the bird. The Akiapolaau *Hemignathus wilsoni* has a strongly decurved upper mandible and a lower mandible that is short, straight, and only about half the length of the upper mandible.

Although the study of adaptive radiation within the Drepaniidae has received considerable attention it is unfortunate that so little is known about the ecology, behaviour, and breeding biology of this unique family. The nests, eggs, and newly hatched young were never described for any of the recently extinct species (approximately 40% of the family).

A second habitat type which supports a large population of honeycreepers is the dry forests located on the south and southwestern slopes of Mauna Kea (on the island of Hawaii) at elevations between 6,000–9,300ft (1,829–2,835m).

Feeding. The variation of bill types between different members of this family reflects the variety of foods eaten – insects, seeds, flower buds and petals, and nectar. The Akiapolaau retracts its longer decurved upper mandible and pounds the lower mandible into dead trees in search of insects and their larvae. This species appears to fill the woodpecker niche in Hawaii. The Iiwi has a strongly decurved bill that fits as easily into native lobeliad flowers as hand into glove.

It has been suggested that this relationship expresses coevolution. The Palila has a finch-like bill which it uses to bite through and extract the tough seeds of the Mamane tree.

Nesting and the Young. Detailed investigations on the breeding biology of the Hawaiian honeycreepers are few. However, four species living on Kauai (Apapane, Iiwi, Anianiau, and the Kauai race of Amakihi *L. virens stejnegeri*) have been studied in detail Intraspecific groups of Amakihi, Anianiau, Apapane, and Iiwi, common during the nonbreeding season, break up with the onset of the breeding season, at which time the birds travel in pairs.

Courtship display is species-specific for Amakihi and Anianiau, and probably for Apapane and Iiwi. Sexual chasing, singing, aggression towards other males of the same species, and courtship feeding are characteristics shared by the four species.

The nests of the Amakihi, Anianiau, Apapane, and Iiwi are similar in construction. The body of the nest and the nest cup are compact and the latter is well lined. Both the male and the female share in building the nest, an operation taking from 4–8 days, but the female assumes the more active role. The eggs of all four species have a whitish background with irregular shaped markings varying in colour from tan to reddish-brown to dark chocolate. Three eggs generally constitute a clutch for Amakihi, Anianiau, and Apapane and two for Iiwi.

Both the Apapane and Iiwi begin laying in late February, with the Apapane still laying in early June and the Iiwi ceasing to lay by mid April. The Amakihi and Anianiau begin egg laying in early March

Some Hawaiian honeycreepers. (1) Mamo *Drepanis pacifica*, (2) Crested honeycreeper *Palmeria dolei*, (3) Grosbeak finch *Psittirostra kona* and (4) Iiwi *Vestiaria coccinea*.

Specialized methods of feeding among the Drepaniidae. (1) Akiapolaau *Hemignathus wilsoni* scraping away the bark of a tree with its lower beak in order to loosen larvae which are then removed with its upper beak. (2) Kauai akialoa *H. procerus* picking insects or larvae out of cracks and holes with its long curved beak.

and both species lay complete sets in April, May and June. All four species begin incubation with the laying of the last egg and only the female incubates. The incubation period of the Amakihi, Anianiau and Iiwi is 14 days and that of the Apapane 13 days. In all four species both adults feed the nestlings but the female makes more frequent trips to the nest with food.

Composition. The Drepaniidae can be divided into two subfamilies, Psittirostrinae and Drepanidinae. The Psittirostrinae have plumage that is dense and fluffy, without lanceolate or stiffened feathers. The primaries are not truncate or angular at the tips and therefore the birds produce no whirring sound in flight. The females and young are usually dull coloured, with much olive-green or grey-green in the plumage. The males are usually yellow, orange, or red, but sometimes dull like females.

The subfamily Drepanidinae has plumage that is not as soft and fluffy as in the Psittirostrinae. Lanceolate and stiffened feathers may be present, especially on the head. A whirring sound in flight (especially in the Apapane and Iiwi) is produced by primaries obliquely truncated at the tips. The young are dull coloured, grey or spotted with black, and go through several intermediate stages before attaining full adult plumage. The adults are brightly coloured (except the Black mamo *Drepanis funerea*) with black, yellow, and red plumage. The sexes are alike.

It seems advisable as the family exhibits great morphological diversity to define genera more broadly than in conservative families. Nine genera with 22 full species are recognized.

The origin of the Drepaniidae remains an unsolved question. One theory links the drepanids with American neotropical honeycreepers, largely on the basis of the number of functional primary flight feathers (nine). The second theory envisions derivation from the cardueline finches of Eurasia (claiming that the founder population had finch-like bills). With what little we know about the behaviour, breeding biology and anatomy of the drepanids no certain answer can be given.

VIREOS

Vireos are small to medium-sized perching birds varying from 4–7in (10–18cm) in length. They have rather short, but strong legs, tails of medium length, a short neck, and wings varying from short and rounded to rather long and pointed. In the typical vireos of the subfamily Vireoninae the bill is of medium length with a slightly hooked tip and the front three toes are joined at their bases. In the shrike-vireos (Vireolaniinae) the bill is stouter with a hooked tip, and in the pepper-shrikes (Cyclarhinae) the bill is heavy and laterally compressed with a large hook at the tip.

The Vireoninae are all plainly marked birds with olive, greenish, yellowish or greyish upperparts and white, buff, yellow or light grey underparts. Some species have prominent light wing bars, light eye rings, or light superciliary stripes and a few have moustachial streaks, but the plumage otherwise lacks any barred, spotted or streaked pattern, even in juveniles. Some species have prominent white or red irises, but they are brown or blackish in the majority.

The shrike-vireos have brighter colouration, with green or olive-green upperparts, a bright blue or grey crown-patch, and often bands of yellow, white, black or grey on the sides of the head. The underparts are greenish-yellow or white, with a chestnut breast-band and flank patches in one species. The pepper-shrikes have olive-green upperparts, the crown being brown or grey in some forms, a broad chestnut supercilliary stripe, grey cheeks, and underparts varying from bright greenish-yellow to pale buff.

Distribution. The Vireonidae is confined to the New World. There are more species in North and Central America and the West Indies than in South America, so it has been suggested that the Vireonidae is one of a few bird families to have originated in warmer parts of North America. The Red-eyed vireo *Vireo olivaceus* has occasionally occurred in Europe as a storm-blown vagrant.

Familiar species in eastern North America are the Solitary vireo *V. solitarius*, White-eyed vireo *V. griseus*, Red-eyed vireo and Warbling vireo *V. gilvus*. The Philadelphia vireo *V. philadelphicus* is widespread in the east, but uncommon and difficult to identify, and the distinctive Yellow-throated vireo *V. flavifrons* is also uncommon. The only other eastern species, the Black-whiskered vireo *V. altiloquus*, occurs in the United States only in southern Florida, although it is more widespread in the West Indies.

Western North America is richer in vireos than the east, with

seven or eight species, of which the most widespread are the Solitary vireo, Grey vireo *V. vicinior*, Bell's vireo *V. bellii*, Hutton's vireo *V. huttoni* and Warbling vireo.

Most of the species breeding in North America migrate to winter in Mexico and Central America. Northern populations of Red-eyed vireos are unusual in travelling as far as the upper parts of Amazonia and neighbouring regions of South America, where they mingle with sedentary local forms during the winter. In contrast, most Central American vireos are more or less sedentary, although

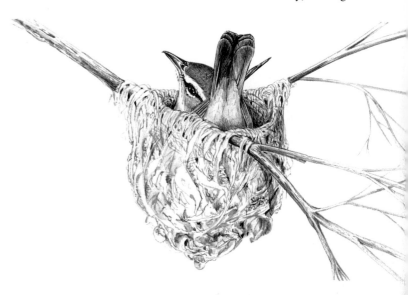

Red-eyed vireo *Vireo olivaceus* in the typical bag-like nest slung between the forks of twigs.

the local populations of the Red-eyed vireo migrate to winter in South America like their northern counterparts.

Feeding. All of the typical vireos whose feeding habits have been described eat mainly insects that are gleaned from the foliage of bushes or trees. Some species of this subfamily also eat fruit at times. The shrike-vireos eat mainly fruit, although they perhaps also take insects, and the pepper-shrikes regularly eat both insects and fruit.

Nesting and the Young. Typical vireos and pepper-shrikes build cup-shaped nests of plant fibres and stems in horizontal forks of trees or bushes. Typically, only the rim of the nest is attached to the supports so that the cup is semi-pendent. Nests of shrike-vireos have not been discovered.

Typical vireos lay clutches of from 2–5 white eggs with very small spots of brown or blackish that are often concentrated around the large end. Incubation in this subfamily is carried out by both sexes, or by the female alone. The young have no down, or just a little on the upperparts and are fed by both parents on food carried to the nest in the bill.

Pepper-shrikes lay two or three pale pink eggs that are blotched and spotted with brown. Both sexes probably incubate, but this observation needs confirmation. The young are naked of down when hatched and they receive food from both parents.

Behaviour. Typical vireos from North America all defend breeding territories with loud songs and aggressive behaviour. Some species give elaborate whistling and warbling song-phrases recalling the songs of such birds as the American robin *Turdus migratorius*, but others have simple songs, such as the monotonously repeated two-note phrase of Hutton's vireo. The call notes of *Vireo* species are typically short and harsh with a scolding tone.

The shrike-vireos repeat simple phrases of sweet whistled notes

Six species of vireos. (1) Solitary vireo *Vireo solitarius*, (2) White-eyed vireo *V. griseus*, (3) Tawny-crowned greenlet *Hylophilus ochraceiceps*, (4) Chestnut-sided shrike-vireo *Vireolanius melitophrys*, (5) Green shrike-vireo *V. pulchellus* and (6) Rufous-browed pepper-shrike *Cyclarhis gujanensis*.

and give rattling and screeching calls. The pepper-shrikes give loud, sweet, warbling songs at frequent intervals and harsh, scolding call notes. It is not known whether species of these two subfamilies defend territories, although this seems the most likely function of their loud songs.

Many of the greenlets of the genus *Hylophilus* and typical vireos of tropical regions are regular members of the mixed feeding flocks of insectivorous birds that roam through the forests. Some of the species involved are known to defend territories, so it seems likely that mainly non-breeding birds join the flocks, or that breeding birds only do so when flocks travel through their territories. Feeding in flocks may be advantageous to these insectivorous forest birds if the combined activity of many birds tends to flush concealed insects that might remain hidden from a single feeding bird.

Composition. The Vireonidae has about 44 species that fall into three natural groups, each of which was formerly treated as a family although they are now regarded as subfamilies. The largest group, the Vireoninae, has about 39 species of which 13 are placed in the genus *Hylophilus* and given the vernacular name 'greenlet'. The remaining 26 species are placed in the typical genus *Vireo* and called 'vireos'.

The three species of shrike-vireo are placed in a subfamily Vireolaniinae and classified into either the single genus *Vireolanius*, or into *Vireolanius* and *Smaragdolanius*. The third subfamily, the Cyclarhinae, contains only the two species of pepper-shrike of the genus *Cyclarhis*.

Although there can be little doubt that the Vireonidae is a natural group of advanced passerine birds, there is little evidence of their relationships to other groups. The bill-shape, anatomy and general appearance have led some ornithologists to suggest they are closely related to shrikes (Laniidae), but the smaller, warbler-like species have led others to suggest affinities with the Parulidae.

AMERICAN BLACKBIRDS AND ORIOLES

The Icteridae is a diverse family of perching birds notable for its remarkable adaptive radiation. It includes the cowbirds, oropendolas, caciques, grackles, American blackbirds, American orioles, meadowlarks and the Bobolink *Dolichonyx oryzivorus*. Though ranging from 6–21in (20–53cm) in length, icterids can typically be considered as medium-sized birds. All members of the family have nine functional flight feathers per wing and an identical arrangement of scales on the legs. Being strong, direct fliers, their pointed wings are long or of moderate length, while the tails, which vary in length and form, are usually rounded. Legs and feet are stout and relatively long in the terrestrial forms. Probably the most characteristic feature of the family is the unnotched, sharply pointed, conical bill. Due to the exploitation of various dissimilar feeding areas, bill proportions vary, but the bill is never much longer than the head.

Most icterids, especially the northern migratory species, show marked sexual dimorphism, both in colour and size. Male and female Great-tailed grackles *Quiscalus mexicanus*, in particular, differ to such an extent that a novice may easily regard them as representing two different species. Plumage brilliance tends to be a male characteristic, the females having a more sombre garb. Although black is the predominant family colour, the basic pattern is frequently relieved by shades of brown, green, orange, red, white and yellow. Streaked plumage is rare and mostly limited to females. As for size differences, most males are conspicuously larger than their respective females.

Distribution. Although best represented in the New World tropics, icterids range over all the western hemisphere, including the

Some American blackbirds and orioles. (1) Male and (2) female Boat-tailed grackle *Quiscalus major*, (3) Bobolink *Dolichonyx oryzivorus*, (4) Red-winged blackbird *Agelaius phoeniceus*, (5) Military (or Red-breasted) blackbird *Leistes militaris* and (6) Rusty blackbird *Euphagus carolinus*.

Falkland Islands where the Military or Red-breasted blackbird *Leistes militaris* occurs. The Red-winged blackbird *Agelaius phoeniceus*, which nests from Alaska to Central America, is the most widespread member of the family, while the Rusty blackbird *Euphagus carolinus* can be considered the most northerly representative as it breeds within the Arctic Circle.

Most icterids inhabiting the temperate regions, whether of the north or the south, are migratory. But most notable of them all is the Bobolink which flies some 5,000mi (8,000km) from its summer territory in the northern USA or southern Canada to winter as far south as the Argentine. Even though the tropical species are not migratory, seasonal movements do occur locally.

Being such a diverse and highly adaptable group, icterids are found throughout the New World in virtually all habitats suitable for land birds. The greatest variety of species is supported in the humid tropical jungles, but almost every type of temperate forest and even the coniferous forests of the higher latitudes, are commonly associated with several forms. Other areas frequently inhabited by these birds include fresh- and salt-water marshes, open grasslands and prairies.

Feeding. Food preferences of the Icteridae are remarkably varied. Grackles, for instance, can truly be considered omnivorous. They will eat almost anything ranging from small vertebrates, insects and meat to plants, bread and acorns. Specialized jaw muscles and a cutting ridge in the roof of the mouth which works like a can opener, aid in the shelling of the latter. Orioles and oropendolas, in contrast, are essentially fruit eaters and also sip large quantities of nectar. Generally speaking, all members of the family eat insects, especially during the breeding season, and most feed on seeds and grains.

Nesting and the Young. Few avian families exceed the remarkable diversity and complexity of icterid nesting structures. Master architects are the caciques and oropendolas which weave pensile grassy sleeves measuring 3–6ft (approximately 1–2m) in length. Groups of up to 100 tightly packed nests, gently swaying like stockings on a washing-line, are sometimes built in the outer reaches of the forest canopy where they present a most impressive sight. Most orioles construct finely knit purse-like pouches – before the advent of the automobile these were often largely composed of horsehair – which they make fast to the forked branches of broad-leaved trees. In contrast, the Bobolink and the meadowlarks fashion relatively simple but well concealed nests on the ground by digging a hollow or merely remodelling a hoofprint or other depression. Various fine materials form the bedding which is often further camouflaged by a dome-shaped roof of interlaced growing grass stems. Other ground feeding species nest in a wide variety of places, but usually build bulky or compact, open-cupped nests lined with fine plant material and mudlike substances. Among grackles, the composition of the nests depends to a considerable extent on the availability of nesting material in the vicinity, a fact clearly demonstrated near human habitations, in contrast to those in rural areas, where pieces of cloth, paper, plastic, string, yarn, and other man-made articles are commonly incorporated. In the majority of cases, nest construction is performed entirely by females.

Like the well-known cuckoos, honeyguides and a few weaver-finches of the Old World, almost all cowbirds refrain from preparing nests of their own. Instead, they habitually drop their eggs into the nests of other birds. Such brood parasitism frequently involves birds of the same or of smaller size, and may either be random or restricted to members of a single species. The highly successful Brown-headed cowbird *Molothrus ater*, for instance, parasitizes more than 200 other species, while the Screaming cowbird *M. rufoaxillaris* only victimizes the non-parasitic Bay-winged cowbird *M. badius* which itself appropriates other birds' nests.

Pronounced latitudinal variation in clutch size is apparent among icterids, two being the normal set in the tropics as against 3–8 eggs in the temperate zones. The eggs are mostly white, bluish or greenish, and marked with black, brown, purple or reddish blotches, dots and irregular scrawls. Incubation, carried out by the female alone, ranges from 11–14 days. Although the males of some species may

The tree-nesting orioles vary from the large grotesque Wagler's oropendola *Zarhynchus wagleri* (1) to the small slender Northern oriole *Icterus galbula* (2), shown with its deep pendent nest.

A colony of Montezuma's oropendola *Gymnostinops montezuma* showing their peculiar elongated bag-like nests which are entered at the top.

assist, feeding of the young is usually the exclusive responsibility of the female. Nesting periods are highly variable, the minimum and maximum values being represented respectively by young Brown-headed cowbirds which rapidly fledge in nine or ten days and the larger oropendolas which need as many as 37 days.

Behaviour. While some species are solitary in habits, most icterids are conspicuously gregarious, wintering in flocks and roosting communally in enormous numbers. In the breeding season, the birds typically nest in colonies where no permanent bonds are formed, individual males mating successively with several females.

Most icterids possess large repertoires of calls, whistles and harsh, rapping notes. Orioles, however, produce clear, liquid melodies which make them outstanding songsters. In general, full song consists of a number of different phrases and tend to be accompanied by conspicuous display postures. Although males often fly with heavy resonant wing beats, flight songs are heard only

Oriole displays. The Eastern meadowlark *Sturnella magna* (1) shows the conspicuous markings of its breast to the female, while the uniformly-coloured Giant cowbird *Scaphidura oryzivora* (2) pulls in its head and fluffs out a ruff of neck feathers.

when the Bobolink and a few other species are engaged in display.

Composition. With close to 100 species, this New World assemblage of song birds can be compared with the most complex of all bird families. Allied to the tanagers (Thraupidae) and Cardinal finches (Fringillidae), it forms an extremely heterogeneous group. The many familiar common names testify to their remarkable diversity. However, none of these distinctive groups is truly representative of the entire family. Confusion also exists with the unrelated Old World Blackbirds (Turdidae), larks (Motacillidae) and orioles (Oriolidae) which they only superficially resemble. For these reasons, the term icterid is nowadays in widespread use to unequivocally depict the family.

CHAFFINCHES AND LINNETS

The Fringillidae is a family of small songbirds, with stout conical bills, strong skulls, large jaw muscles, and powerful gizzards; all adaptations for dealing with hard seeds. They are distinguished from the various other seed eating birds by certain details of skull structure, the presence of 9 (instead of 10) large primary feathers in each wing, 12 large tail feathers, and the fact that the hen is responsible for building the cup-shaped nest and for incubating the eggs. Some of these features are shared with other groups, and it is the combination of characters that distinguishes the Fringillidae. The family contains a variety of species, ranging between 0·3–3·5oz (8·5–100gm) in weight, some of them highly coloured and, within the limits imposed by a seed diet, showing great variation in the shape of their beaks, according to the types of seeds they eat. They are usually seen in flocks.

The family is split into two subfamilies. The Fringillinae contains only three species, the Chaffinch *Fringilla coelebs* and Brambling *F. montifringilla* of Eurasia, and the Blue chaffinch *F. teydea* of the Canary Islands. The Carduelinae contains around 122 species, of which 16 are found in Europe and 14 in North America. The main distinction between these subfamilies is seen in the food of the young, and in their nesting habits.

Distribution. The family is widely distributed and is represented naturally in North and South America, Eurasia and Africa (except Madagascar), and by introductions in Australasia. They occupy a range of habitats from closed forest, through scrubland and savannah, to open tundra, steppe and desert, though no one species is so widespread. In some regions, certain species have successfully colonized man-modified environments, and breed commonly in town parks and gardens, and in farmland. They are thus some of the most familiar birds in western Europe and in eastern and northern America. Populations of arctic and temperate regions tend to be migratory, and others resident.

Feeding. The beak of all finches is modified internally for holding and shelling seeds. Each seed is wedged in a special groove at the side of the palate and crushed by raising the lower jaw onto it. The husk is then peeled off with the aid of the tongue, thus releasing the kernel, which is swallowed. In cardueline finches the bill is also used for extracting seeds from the seed-heads of plants. Species differ in the size of seeds they prefer, and in the types of seed-head they can best exploit, and these differences are related to differences in the size and shape of their bills, and in the way the bill is used. Hawfinches *Coccothraustes coccothraustes* have big powerful bills

Some boldly coloured finches. (1) American goldfinch *Carduelis tristis*, (2) Serin (or Canary) *Serinus canarius* and (3) Chaffinch *Fringilla coelebs*.

for crushing large hard tree-fruits; goldfinches and siskins have long tweezer-like bills for probing into thistles and other seed-heads; Bullfinches *Pyrrhula pyrrhula* and Pine grosbeaks *Pinicola enucleator* have rounded bills adapted for bud eating; while crossbills have crossed mandibles which help them extract seeds from hard closed cones. Moreover, the three species of crossbills in Europe have different sized bills and feed primarily from different cones: the slender-billed Two-barred crossbill *Loxia leucoptera* eats

Some species of finches showing variety of bill shape. (1) Hawfinch *Coccothraustes coccothraustes* seen also flying, (2) Parrot crossbill *Loxia pytopsittacus* and (3) Redpoll *Carduelis flammea*.

seeds are most available: in larch forests this is mainly in late summer or early autumn, in spruce forests in autumn to winter, and in pine forests in spring. If spruce and pine are available in the same area, breeding can occur continuously for 10 months.

In all Fringillidae, courtship involves song and special displays and posturing, but most cardueline finches also have elaborate song flights over the nesting area. The female is responsible for building the nest, incubating and brooding the young, and during this period is fed on the nest by the male. When the young are feathered and can keep warm, both parents collect food. All species build open, cup-shaped nests, mostly in trees or shrubs, and lay 3–6 eggs, which in most species are whitish with brown spots. Incubation takes up to two weeks, and the young then stay in the nest for another two weeks or so (longer in crossbills). Predation on eggs and young is heavy, but in most areas, more than one brood is raised in a season. The young are born naked, but can fly within a few days after leaving the nest.

The fringilline finches defend large territories while breeding, and pairs spread themselves fairly evenly through the habitat. The food is obtained from the territory itself, and the young are fed at frequent intervals. The carduelines nest solitarily or in loose colonies, within which each pair defends only a small area around its nest; they forage away from the colonies in flocks, wherever food happens to be abundant at the time.

After breeding, adult finches undergo a complete moult, and at

European goldfinches *Carduelis carduelis* feed mainly on weed seeds. The group shown here are on one of their favourite foods, the thistle. The young bird (top right) has not yet acquired the bright markings on its head.

mainly the small soft cones of larch, the medium-billed Common crossbill *L. curvirostra* mainly the medium cones of spruce, and the large heavy-billed Parrot crossbill *L. pytopsittacus* mainly large, hard cones of pine. The various species also differ in the proportion of food they obtain directly from vegetation, as opposed to the ground, and in the extent to which they use their feet in feeding, both being connected with differences in body weight and leg length.

While the main food of all finches is seeds, the Fringillinae feed their young entirely on insects (especially caterpillars), while the Carduelinae feed their young either on a mixture of seeds and insects or on seeds alone. The raising of young entirely on a seed diet has been recorded in crossbills, siskins, redpolls and Linnets *Carduelis cannabina*, but is comparatively rare among birds. Also, while the Fringillinae carry insects to their young one or a few at a time in the bill, the Carduelinae carry large quantities of seeds in their throats and regurgitate them to their young.

Nesting and the Young. Like other birds, finches breed when their food is most plentiful, but this occurs at a different time in different species, according to what they eat. The Chaffinch, which needs caterpillars, has a short breeding season in late spring; while the cardueline finches which need seeds, have long and varied seasons, in which individual pairs often raise more than one brood. Thus the Greenfinch *C. chloris*, Linnet and Bullfinch, which in Britain eat a variety of seeds, breed for almost the whole growing season, continually changing their diet as different plants come into seed. The European Goldfinch *Carduelis carduelis*, which likes the seeds of thistles and related plants, breeds later in summer, while the American goldfinch *C. tristos* which depends even more on thistles, breeds later still. The crossbills nest in any month, whenever conifer the same season the juveniles have a partial moult, replacing only the soft body feathers and retaining the large flight and tail feathers for another year.

Economic Importance. Because of their song, bright colours, engaging habits and simple seed diet, finches have for centuries been kept in cages as pets. Some species breed readily in captivity, and from the wild Serin *Serinus canarius* of the Canary Islands all the various strains of domestic Canary were derived. Certain finches are also important as pests, especially the Bullfinch which eats buds of fruit trees, sometimes devastating orchards and causing a major problem to the industry.

Composition. The word 'finch' has at one time or another been applied to at least nine other groups of seed eating birds, beside the Fringillinae and Carduelinae, all of which have the same specializations for dealing with hard seeds. Yet these various groups differ so much in the other details of their anatomy and behaviour, that they are without doubt derived from several ancestral stocks. They provide an example of convergent evolution – of unrelated animals growing to look like one another because they have the same way of life. The two subfamilies which at present comprise the Fringillidae differ markedly in food of young, breeding dispersion and other behaviour and there seems little sense in linking them together in the same family. The whole seed eating complex is in need of review, taking full account of behaviour as well as morphology and anatomy.

The estrildine waxbills vary in colour. (1) The domesticated piebald form of the Striated finch *Lonchura striata*, (2) the Zebra finch *Taeniopygia guttata*, (3) the Blue-faced parrot finch *Erythrura trichroa*, (4) the Violet-eared waxbill *Uraeginthus granatinus* and (5) the Waxbill *Estrilda astrild*.

WAXBILLS

Waxbills are grain eating song birds. Their plumage is often coloured and attractively patterned. The two main characteristics that distinguish the waxbill family Estrildidae from other granivorous song birds, for example the finches, buntings and

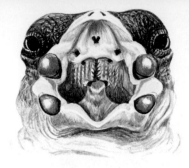

Nestling of the Blue-faced parrot finch *Erythrura trichroa* showing the light-reflecting papillae on the gape of the bill.

weaverbirds, are certain behaviour patterns and the structure of the digestive tract. Today it is assumed that the waxbills are derived directly from insectivorous song birds.

A typical feature of the waxbills is the highly differentiated palate marking of the nestlings. Many species show conspicuous points on the palate, the tongue and the bill, and in several species these points are fused to form a horseshoe-like pattern. In addition, the gouldian finches and parrot finches have light-reflecting papillae. The properties of these papillae enable the young nestling to be seen in the dark of the nest.

Distribution. Waxbills occur in the tropics of the Old World. It is probable that they initially inhabited Africa, from which their distribution has extended to the east.

Most waxbills inhabit the steppe and dry open forests. In Africa and the South Pacific Islands, several forest forms of waxbill have developed. The seed-crackers *Pirenestes* that possess very thick bills, and the blue-bills *Spermophaga* are found only in the lowlands of the Congo. In the bamboo-jungle of Borneo and the Philippines, the Green-tailed parrot finch *Erythrura hyperythra* lives at an altitude of up to 8,667ft (2,600m); the Blue-faced parrot finch *Erythrura trichroa* is found in the secondary forests of New Guinea at an altitude of 13,300ft (4,000m). A few species have extended into semi-desert areas: the Cut-throat *Amadina fasciata* in South Africa and the Zebra finch *Taeniopygia guttata* in Australia.

Feeding. The staple diet of waxbills of the savanna and the steppe is composed of grass seeds, but during the breeding season they also eat termites. However, in contrast to the feeding habits of birds living in such dry zones, those waxbills that inhabit forest areas generally have a much broader spectrum diet and eat seeds both of grasses and dicotyledons. The Antpecker *Parmoptila woodhousei*, a species that inhabits the forests of Central Africa, represents a peculiarity among waxbills in that it only eats ants and has insectivorous characteristics. Some species of parrot finches of the South Pacific Islands are also specialized in that in addition to seeds of mono- and dicotyledons they eat fresh fruit and wild fig seeds.

Nesting and the Young. The courtship behaviour of waxbills has been thoroughly investigated and can be considered as one of the best studied behaviour patterns among birds. In most species, the following ritualized movements can be observed during nest building: the male picks up a feather or a grass shoot in its bill and hops around his partner singing and, at the same time, moving the nesting material up and down in front of her face. In some genera, for example *Lonchura*, this ritual is performed without a feather or grass shoot. In addition to this basic movement, some species introduce a ritualized begging movement of nestlings into the display. Copulation may occur after this ceremony; alternatively, copulation takes place in the nest.

A display behaviour completely different from this basic pattern has been found in some species of parrot finches (for example in the Blue-faced parrot finch *Erythrura trichroa*): in this species, after the male has performed some elements of the display, the female flies away uttering loud calls. The male, also singing, follows and, after a short flight which is clearly different in character from normal flight, the female lands on a branch and starts to warble. As soon as the male arrives, the female again flies away. In most instances, this ritualized ceremony termed 'pursuit flight' stops abruptly and does not lead to copulation. However, shortly before the eggs are laid, the 'pursuit flights' become longer and more excited. After one of these long flights the female remains sitting on the branch, waits for the male and copulation takes place. In waxbills, the position of the female during copulation is very different from the corresponding position in other song birds so far investigated. The female crouches in front of the courting male with a very rapidly vibrating tail.

All the investigated waxbills are monogamous and in many species the pair bonds continue during sexual quiescence. In the Purple grenadier *Uraeginthus ianthinogaster* and the Violet-eared waxbill *U. granatinus* pair bonds are developed at the age of seven weeks, long before sexual maturity is reached.

Most waxbills breed during, or shortly after, the rainy season. Their nests are always covered and are built in a spherical form with a diameter of 4–8in (10–20cm). Grass is the main nesting material, and many species line the grass on the inside with feathers. Both partners share the work of nest building; the male is responsible for collecting nesting material, and the female incorporates newly brought grass and feathers into the nest. In addition to breeding nests, many species build roosting nests in which 20 or more individuals may sleep together at one time.

The clutches of waxbills consist of 4–6 white eggs. The male and female take turns sitting on the eggs, and change over at regular intervals of about $1\frac{1}{2}$ hours.

The eggs hatch after 12–16 days. In most species the begging position of the nestlings is very different from that of other song birds: the head turns round through 90–160°, the bill opens and the head gyrates.

Waxbills feed their young in a similar way to the finches, pigeons

The elaborate tail plumes of male parasitic whydahs are used in advertisement flights. (1) Paradise whydah *Steganura paradisaea* with the duller female, (2) Fischer's whydah *Vidua fischeri,* (3) Queen whydah *V. regia,* (4) Paradise whydah in flight, (5) Sakabula *Euplectes progne* and (6) Pin-tailed whydah *Vidua macroura.*

and parrots, that is, by using their crops. However, a striking difference between the finches and waxbills is that the latter can regurgitate the whole content of the crop in a single attempt, whereas the finches take several attempts. This technique of regurgitation makes the waxbills unique among all song birds.

The parent birds look after the nestlings for many weeks after the young have left the nest. When they are fully independent, the young birds organize themselves into groups. Pair bonds are developed within these groups before the start of the initial breeding season.

Many species of waxbills become mature by the age of 6–8 months. In the Zebra finch it has been observed that the males become mature extremely early, at the age of 10 weeks. However, this peculiarity is considered to be an ecological adaption to the conditions of the climate in central Australia, where rainfall is scarce and irregular. Sufficient seeds to feed the young can only be found during or shortly after the rainy season, and consequently the early maturity attained by this species is advantageous since two cycles of breeding can rapidly occur within the span of one wet season.

In general, the waxbill species that inhabit forest areas defend specific territories, not only during the breeding season, but throughout the whole year. In contrast, species that inhabit dry areas are very gregarious and live in groups both in and out of the breeding season.

Composition. Thirty-five waxbill genera with approximately 125 species have been described. Some species have been discovered as recently as the present century. Classification of waxbills is complicated by parallel evolution and convergence between members of different genera.

TYPICAL WEAVERS

The Ploceidae is a rather large assemblage of small to medium-sized seed eating passerines, varying from $4\frac{1}{2}$–20in (11–50cm) in length. Most species are rather stoutly built, with a short, strong bill that varies considerably in depth, although the culmen (the dorsal ridge of the upper mandible) is usually arched. The legs and feet vary from rather slender to moderately heavy, with the usual passerine arrangement of toes. The wings are more or less rounded and have 10 primaries, the outermost of which is considerably reduced in size, but which remains in the primitive position beneath the ninth primary. The tail varies from rather short to very long and is composed of 12 rectrices, the outermost of which are usually shorter than the innermost. In the larger species the tail tends to be very long. Other family characteristics are that the nest is always domed or covered in some way, that the nestlings lack patterns of spots inside their bills (which also distinguishes them from the estrildine finches, Estrildidae), and that the voice consists of unmusical clicking, chirping, buzzing or chattering songs and calls.

Most true weavers of the subfamily Ploceinae have bright red, orange, yellow and black patterned adult male plumages with duller, mainly brown females and immature males that are often streaked. Some species are all-black. The sparrows and related genera of the subfamily Passerinae mainly lack bright colours and are marked with varied shades of brown, buff or grey, often with markings of black or white. Some rock-sparrows of the genus *Petronia* are marked with bright yellow. Most Passerinae show some sexual dimorphism in colouration, the females being duller.

Distribution. The natural distribution of the Ploceidae is confined to the Old World, and includes much of the Palearctic, Oriental, Ethiopian and Malagasy zoogeographical regions. Africa is much richer in species and genera than any of the other regions.

Six species of weavers. (1) House sparrow *Passer domesticus*, (2) (European) Tree sparrow *P. montanus*, (3) Snow finch *Montifringilla nivalis*, (4) White-headed buffalo-weaver *Dinemellia dinemelli*, (5) Madagascar fody *Foudia madagascariensis* and (6) Cuckoo-weaver *Anomalospiza imberbis*, which lays its eggs in warbler nests.

The two species of the subfamily Bubalornithinae, known as buffalo-weavers for no very obvious reason, both inhabit the drier parts of Africa. They are the Black buffalo-weaver *Bubalornis albirostris* and White-headed buffalo-weaver *Dinemellia dinemelli*.

The Passerinae as a whole is widespread in the Palearctic, Oriental and Ethiopian regions. The snow finches of the genus *Montifringilla* are all mountain birds, six species being confined to Asia, and one, the Snow finch *M. nivalis*, occurring also in Europe. The five species of rock-sparrow of the genus *Petronia* all occur in Africa; one, the Rock sparrow *P. petronia*, extends to Europe and three occur also in southwest Asia. The typical sparrow genus *Passer* includes about 15 species. Of these, the Tree sparrow *P. montanus* is widely distributed in Europe and Asia and has been introduced in the United States, Australia and parts of Indonesia, and the House sparrow *P. domesticus* has a similar wide range, inhabiting also parts of North Africa. It has been very widely introduced in the Americas, Australasia and elsewhere, and may now be the most widely distributed of all land bird species. The Spanish sparrow *P. hispaniolensis* occurs in Spain, Portugal, North Africa and Asia east to India; five species of *Passer* are found only in Africa, three only in the Far East, and two have very limited ranges in western Asia.

Sparrow-weavers of the genus *Plocepasser* (four species), *Histurgops* (one species), *Pseudonigrita* (two species) and *Philetairus*

(one species) all inhabit dry parts of Africa and have mainly rather limited ranges, although the Black-billed sparrow-weaver *Plocepasser mahali* ranges from Ethiopia to northern Cape Province.

All the true weavers of the Ploceinae are confined to Africa south of the Sahara, excepting a few on islands of the Indian Ocean and islands along the African coasts, and five species ranging from India to Malaysia. The genus *Foudia*, species of which are known as fodies, occurs only on the Mascarene Islands, Madagascar and the Seychelles; some of its species are now rare. There are around 57 species in the genus *Ploceus*, 52 African and five in southern Asia. The commonest of the Asian species is the Baya weaver *P. philippinus*, which ranges from Pakistan and Ceylon to Sumatra, but is absent from the Philippines. One species, the São Thomé grosbeak *Neospiza concolor*, is known only from two specimens collected on São Thomé in the 1880s. It may now be extinct.

Various species of the Passerinae make wandering local movements, sometimes covering hundreds of miles, but they are not regular long-distance migrants.

The Ploceidae as a whole occupies a vast range of habitats from desert fringes to agricultural land, high mountain slopes and tropical rain forest. The African Ploceinae includes species characteristic of dry and wet forests, brush, marshes and grassland habitats, and the Palearctic Passerinae range from montane to desert environments. The House sparrow, and Asian populations of Tree sparrows, depend largely on man for their food.

Feeding. Most Ploceidae eat mainly the seeds of grasses and other herbaceous plants, supplementing their diets with insects in variable quantities, often feeding small young entirely on insects, and taking small quantities of buds, other plant materials and such oddments as small snails. The size range of seeds making up the bulk of a species' diet is related to the size of its bill; massive-billed species such as the Black swamp weaver *Amblyospiza albifrons* crack large seeds and nuts, whereas rather slender-billed forms such as some species of *Ploceus* take small seeds and a large proportion of insects. Town-dwelling populations of House sparrows and Tree sparrows take almost any potentially edible kind of waste that becomes available. These and many other species are equally at home feeding on the ground or in the vegetation of bushes and trees. Others feed mainly on the ground, and various weavers in the genus *Ploceus* are

Grenadier weavers *Euplectes orix* showing the male with his plumage puffed out in display and the female in the typical domed nest slung between growing stalks.

Two types of nests found among typical weavers. (1) Village weavers *Ploceus cucullatus* may suspend a number of nests from twigs in a single tree. (2) The Sociable weavers *Philetairus socius* build their nests side by side to form a huge structure like a haystack, often in a solitary small tree. The entrances to the individual nests are all on the underside of the mass, as shown in the inset, in a section of the communal nest viewed from below.

exclusively arboreal, particularly forest species that include a high proportion of insects in their diet.

Nesting and the Young. A general feature of the Ploceidae is that the nest is variously domed or otherwise covered, but details of its structure vary considerably. Species of the genera *Passer*, *Petronia* and *Montifringilla* usually nest in holes or cavities, building an untidy domed nest of leaves and stems with a lining of hair, feathers or plant fibres. In very small holes nests may be reduced to a mere pad-like lining. Both species of buffalo-weavers build untidy domed nests of thorny twigs in the branches of trees. Typical weavers of the genus *Ploceus* build suspended pouch-, pocket- or sleeve-like nests elaborately woven from vegetable fibres and hung from the branches of trees or bushes. Details of nest structure in this genus vary considerably from one group of species to another and have provided information on the relationships of the species. Their nests commonly have special structures protecting the entrance tunnel, and they are often placed close to the habitations of wasps or large birds or near human dwellings, probably to gain extra protection.

Bishops of the genus *Euplectes*, fodies and a few other genera have ball-shaped nests, in long grass in the case of the bishops, and in trees in fodies. The Grey-headed social weaver *Pseudonigrita arnaudi* and Black-headed social weaver *P. nigrita* both build stout, prickly nests from strong grass stems. These nests commonly have two entrances and are placed in the protection of thorny trees.

The Cuckoo-weaver *Anomalospiza imberbis* is unique among the Ploceidae in being a brood-parasite, placing its eggs in nests of Grass warblers of the genera *Cisticola* and *Prinia*. Details of its biology are unfortunately unknown.

Clutches of Ploceidae range from one or two to as many as seven or eight eggs, 3–6 being most common in species of temperate regions, 2–4 in the tropical species. The eggs vary enormously in colour, markings and variability within the family. Those of buffalo-weavers are white or nearly white with heavy speckles and streaks, although one subspecies of the Black buffalo-weaver has unmarked pale blue eggs. Most species of the genus *Ploceus* have extremely variable eggs, probably because their colonial nesting and protective nest structures reduce selection for egg colour. Eggs of the Black-headed weaver *P. melanocephalus* for example vary from white to pink, brown, green or blue, with or without purplish or brown spots of variable extent. Cavity-nesting Passerinae also often have rather variably coloured eggs, those of the House sparrow varying from white to pale green or blue with variable spots or blotches of grey, brown or black. In contrast the eggs of bishops and whydahs of the genus *Euplectes* are much less variable.

Incubation is carried out by the female alone in some species and by both parents in others; it typically lasts for a period of 12–15 days. The newly-hatched young are helpless and have either a thin covering of down or are entirely downless. In the majority of species both parents feed the young on food carried to the nest in the throat, or in both throat and bill. Most species continue to feed the young for some days after they fledge, which is usually 10–15 days after hatching. Fledged young typically beg for food with high-pitched calls and shivering movements of the slightly opened wings.

Behaviour. The wide range of types of social behaviour in the Ploceidae has provoked a great deal of investigation. The majority of species are more or less gregarious, although some such as the monogamous snow-finches defend exclusive territories during the breeding season and only flock at other times. House and Tree sparrows, among others, will often nest solitarily or in small groups, but will also nest in large colonies when suitable nest cavities are concentrated together. These and many other species normally flock all year round and often occupy large communal roosts.

Most species in the genus *Ploceus* nest in large and dense colonies and flock throughout the year, their sociality as in other gregarious birds being thought to facilitate finding a scattered food supply and to reduce predation.

Bishops and whydahs are polygamous, males of most species defending exclusive territories in grassland areas within which several females build nests and rear the young.

Most Ploceidae have elaborate displays, involving special postures, calls, and often display of brilliant plumage colours. The displays of bishops and whydahs are among the most spectacular, with fluffed rump feathers, sizzling calls, and in some species aerial display flights. No member of the family has notably musical calls; the Passerinae either lack elaborate songs, or have simple songs, and their calls consist of chirping, clicking and cheeping notes. Many Ploceinae have rapid clicking, rattling, buzzing or whirring songs which vary from loud to very faint and high-pitched.

Economic Importance. Being gregarious seed eating birds, it is not surprising that various species in the Ploceidae have become pests of cereal crops and gardens. The House sparrow often ravages crops of wheat, oats, barley and other cereals over large areas in Europe and Asia, and the same occurs where populations have been introduced in the Americas and New Zealand.

Composition. The family Ploceidae is here considered to include about 130 species in 18 genera. Three subfamilies are recognized in the treatment adopted here: the Bubalornithinae for the monotypic genera *Bubalornis* and *Dinemellia*: the Passerinae for the 37 species comprising the genera *Histurgops, Montifringilla, Passer, Petronia, Philetairus, Plocepasser, Pseudonigrita* and *Sporopipes*; and the Ploceinae for the remaining 91 species in the genera *Amblyospiza, Anomalospiza, Euplectes, Foudia, Malimbus, Neospiza, Ploceus* and *Quelea*.

The whydahs or cambassous of the genus *Vidua* are here regarded as forming a subfamily of the Estrildidae, although they have often been placed in the Ploceidae or as a distinct family, Viduidae. The whydahs appear, in various respects, to be intermediate between the Ploceidae and Estrildidae, but the modern tendency is to consider them as estrildid, although doubt remains.

The Passerinae has often been divided into additional subfamilies, such as the Plocepasserinae and Sporopipinae. Recent biochemical studies of egg white proteins suggest that the typical sparrows of the genus *Passer* are not closely related to the Weavers of the Ploceinae, and should probably be placed in a separate family. Thus, wholesale revision of this group of genera may be needed when better information is available, and such genera as *Montifringilla, Petronia, Sporopipes* and *Plocepasser* may then be placed very differently from their position in any of the existing provisional classifications.

STARLINGS

The Sturnidae is a large family of robust perching birds varying from 7–17in (18–43cm) in length. Anatomical features suggest their closest allies are such large passerines as the drongos Dicruridae, Old World orioles Oriolidae and even the crows Corvidae, but the nest structure of a few species and some structural characters also suggest relationship to the typical weavers Ploceidae.

Most starlings are of stocky build with strong legs and bill, moderately long, rounded or somewhat pointed wings and squared tails. The bill is short and stout in the two oxpeckers in the genus *Buphagus*, but is characteristically rather long, and often somewhat downcurved. Many species are black or predominantly black in colour, often with considerable iridescence. A few species such as the Superb glossy starling *Spreo superbus*, which is mainly glossy blue and green with an orange belly, are particularly attractive, but many bear a strong general similarity to the familiar Common starling *Sturnus vulgaris*. Some species have coloured wattles, lappets or short bristly feathers on the head, giving them an ugly, vulturine appearance. The attractive Crested starling *Basilornis*

Jackson's weaver *Ploceus jacksoni* (1) tears thin fibrous strips from palm leaves to construct a tough, resilient nest. Some weavers build long entrance tubes on the rounded, pendent nests. Two are shown here, the Baya weaver *P. philippinus* (2) and Cassin's weaver *Malimbus cassini* (3).

In addition to the Starling *Sturnus vulgaris* (1), the starling family includes the brightly coloured Superb glossy starling *Spreo superbus* (2), the steppe-dwelling Rose-coloured starling *Sturnus roseus* (3), the Hill mynah *Gracula religiosa* (4) well known for its mimicry, the Red-billed oxpecker *Buphagus erythrorhynchus* (5) and the very rare Rothschild's mynah *Leucopsar rothschildi* (6).

galeatus is unusual in having a large erect crest of lacy feathers extending the full length of the head.

Distribution. The natural distribution of the family is restricted to the Old World, where it occurs in Europe, Africa, Asia, Indonesia and Australasia, reaching the Cook Islands in eastern Polynesia. The Common starling has been introduced in many parts of the world, and is now a familiar bird in North America.

Europe has only three species, the Common starling, Spotless starling *Sturnus unicolor* of southern Europe, and the Rose-coloured starling or Rosy pastor *Sturnus roseus* which is a wanderer from the Near East. Africa has numerous starlings, including all representatives of the genera *Lamprotornis* and *Spreo*, and the peculiar Wattled starling *Creatophora cinerea*. The two species of oxpecker are also confined to Africa.

Two species that inhabited small islands near Magagascar became extinct a century or more ago; their place has now been taken by mynahs of the Asian genus *Acridotheres* which man has introduced to the area. Southern Asia and Indonesia are rich in starlings, including the mynahs of the genera *Gracula* and *Acridotheres*, various arboreal species of *Aplonis* and numerous typical starlings of the genus *Sturnus*. The attractive Rothschild's mynah *Leucopsar rothschildi* is confined to Bali, near Java, and is now apparently rare owing to the destruction of its forest habitat. Another peculiar species, the Celebes starling *Scissirostrum dubium*, which has a large, strong bill, is confined to Celebes, and various other species of the genera *Basilornis* and *Aplonis* have restricted ranges in Indonesia.

The New Guinea region is inhabited by the Papuan mynah *Mino dumontii* and various species of the genera *Aplonis*, one of which is the only starling native in Australia. The widespread genus *Aplonis* also ranges from Micronesia and Melanesia to the Cook Islands in Polynesia. Species of this genus have become extinct in the Society Islands (*A. mavornata*) and on Kusaie of the Caroline Islands (Kusaie Mountain starling *A. corvina*).

Indian mynahs *Acridotheres tristis* have been widely introduced on islands in the Pacific, Indian and Atlantic Oceans, and are now established on such widely separated islands as St. Helena, Mauritius, Fiji, Tahiti, Hawaii and the Marquesas Islands.

Some northern starlings are migratory, notably the northern populations of the Common starling, which winter south of their breeding grounds in Europe and Asia. Other species such as the Rose-coloured starling and Wattled starling make irregular movements following locust swarms and other food sources. Most tropical starlings are, however, sedentary.

The family includes birds of a wide range of habitats, although inhabitants of forests and agricultural land predominate. The Common starling occurs in the centres of the largest cities, many of which are favoured as roosting sites, and some of the Asian mynahs are familiar city birds. Rose-coloured starlings and some African species inhabit arid open country, and the oxpeckers are restricted to the vicinity of large game animals and livestock.

Feeding. The starlings as a whole include omnivorous species, specialized fruit and insect eaters and many species which take a somewhat restricted variety of foods. The Common starling and various of the Asian mynahs are as omnivorous as any birds, eating insects, fruit, offal, domestic scraps and a very wide range of other foods, many of which are obtained near houses or on refuse tips. These and other starlings which commonly eat insects often use the 'zirkeln' method of probing for food in grassland and other substrates: pushing the closed bill in, then opening it while peering to find any prey exposed by the action. The omnivorous species also resemble the fruit eaters in commonly holding food down with one foot while pecking at it.

In contrast, many forest starlings eat mainly fruit obtained from trees and bushes, supplementing this diet with insects. The Rose-coloured and Wattled starlings habitually follow flocks of locusts and eat mainly insects.

The two African species of oxpeckers or tick-birds are unique among birds in habitually associating with herds of large mammals in order to feed on parasites obtained from their hides.

Nesting and the Young. Most members of the Sturnidae nest in holes in trees, although some have secondarily adapted to using holes in and around buildings, nest boxes, and holes in rocks. A few such as the Bank mynah *Acridotheres ginginianus* excavate holes in earthy banks, and the Celebes starling uses its strong bill to excavate holes in trees while supporting itself woodpecker-like with its tail. The hole-nesting species normally build an untidy nest of dry plant materials and rubbish, the size of which depends very much on the size of the cavity available.

Some species build untidy globular nests with a side entrance and a lined chamber within. The Indian mynah is unusual in sometimes nesting in a hole and sometimes building an untidy nest outside. The Long-tailed starling *Aplonis metallica* of New Guinea is unique among the Sturnidae in building a suspended, pouch-like nest of dry plant materials hanging from a tree branch like the nests of some weavers Ploceidae and oropendolas Icteridae.

Clutches are of 2–9, usually 3–4 eggs, which are pale blue, pale green or white in most species, those of oxpeckers having brown spots. Incubation is by the female alone in most species and lasts from 14–16 days in the few species for which it has been recorded. Newly hatched nestlings are blind and helpless with a variable covering of grey or brownish down. They are fed by both parents on food carried to the nest in the bill or crop, or both, and fledge after 15–25 days in the nest. Juveniles are fed for at least a short time after fledging. In species with metallic plumage, the juveniles are usually dull and glossless, but those of most species moult into adult plumage within a few months of fledging. Several species raise two or three broods of young each breeding season.

Behaviour. Most starlings are gregarious both during the breeding season and at other times, but the habit of hole nesting prevents many species from nesting in large colonies. Common starlings and Indian mynahs will nest at high density in groves of old trees or on suitably decayed buildings where there are plenty of cavities. In these and other loosely colonial nesters only the vicinity of the nest hole is defended as a territory. The Long-tailed starling suffers no such restrictions in the availability of nest sites, building its hanging nests in large colonies in tall trees. Some arboreal species of the genus *Aplonis*, such as the Rarotonga starling *A. cinerascens*, probably nest solitarily or in very small groups as they are usually seen singly or in pairs. Many starlings are extremely gregarious outside the breeding season; for example, both Common starlings and Indian mynahs congregate in communal roosts which may include millions of birds.

None of the Sturnidae has a really pleasing song, although many species give a variety of musical whistles. Some, including the Common starling and several species of mynah, freely imitate other birds and environmental noises and as a result have a very varied vocabulary, much of which consists of harsh and discordant notes. Several species of mynah will learn to imitate the human voice, often with as much ability as the most 'articulate' parrots.

Economic Importance. A number of species are of economic importance. The Common starling and various African and Asian species are agricultural pests, eating fruit and seeds from growing crops and in orchards. The Indian mynah is a particularly troublesome nuisance in tropical orchards where it pecks pieces from bananas, paw-paws, pineapples, guavas and other fruit, damaging far more than it actually eats. This species was misguidedly introduced on to many Pacific islands in the hope that it would control insect pests in orchards, but it now causes more damage than the insects ever did.

The Common starling was originally introduced into many parts of the world for sentimental reasons, but it has often become a serious agricultural pest and has caused considerable damage to native birds by usurping their nest-holes. In the United States bluebirds in the genus *Sialia* have suffered particularly badly from its competition. Large urban roosts of Common starlings on buildings in European and American cities have also become a nuisance. The vast quantities of droppings they leave are both a health hazard and, because of their uric acid content which corrodes the stonework, a threat to the buildings themselves. Various methods of removing the birds, including the broadcasting of Starling distress calls, the use of falcons, shooting, poisoning and

This Yellow-billed oxpecker *Buphagus africanus* has a highly specialized manner of feeding, removing insects from the skin of large grazing animals.

illumination of the buildings have all been tried with limited success. Now a jelly painted on the roosting ledges is being used in some areas and this appears to be quite successful in deterring the birds from perching.

Composition. The Sturnidae includes about 110 species classified into 25 genera. The two species of oxpeckers are usually placed in a subfamily Buphaginae apart from the other starlings, although they were formerly afforded a separate family because of their peculiar habits.

OLD WORLD ORIOLES

The Oriolidae is a small family of mainly arboreal Passeriformes, containing about 28 species. They are medium-sized birds generally characterized by a predominantly yellow plumage. They have short tarsi and decurved red, blue or black bills. Their nostrils are concealed by short fine bristles. The sexes usually have different plumages and the young often have striped underparts.

Distribution. The family is mainly a tropical one but has representatives in Eurasia as well as Africa, East Indies, Philippines and Australia. A few species, notably those not confined to tropical evergreen forest, show migratory tendencies to various degrees, the most developed being those of the Golden oriole *Oriolus oriolus* which breeds in Europe and western Asia and winters south of the Sahara.

Orioles show most evidence of speciation in the eastern part of their range, particularly where there are many islands. A few forms have lost the characteristic brilliant yellow plumage. For example *Oriolus crassirostris* of São Tomé in the Gulf of Guinea is a much duller species with very short and rounded wings. In the Moluccas, *Oriolus bouroensis* is considered to be an example of a Batesian mimic. This is a form of mimicry where a weak species may derive some protection by resembling a pugnacious one. In this case these Indonesian orioles have evolved to become dull brownish birds resembling the friar birds of the genus *Philemon*. In Australia the Yellow figbird *Sphecotheres vieilloti* of the Northern Territory and northeast Queensland frequently form a nesting relationship with the Drongo *Chibea bracteata* or the Helmeted friar bird *Philemon yorki*. Both are pugnacious species and will drive away marauders of all kinds, thus giving the Yellow figbird a good deal of fortuitous protection. The Golden oriole has no need of this protection as when it is breeding it is a fervent defender of its territory attacking birds as large as crows – even the Kestrel *Falco tinnunculus* does not escape its attention.

Feeding. The orioles are mainly insectivorous and consume a wide variety of invertebrates which inhabit the tree canopy, such as beetles, cicadas, caterpillars and flies. They appear to be particularly

The conspicuously coloured irises of these starlings become suddenly more obvious when they are excited, because the pupils contract. (1) Purple glossy starling *Lamprotornis purpureus* and (2) Black-breasted glossy starling *L. corruscus*.

fond of caterpillars. Hairy caterpillars are beaten against branches to remove most of the hairs, before being swallowed. Late in the summer when berries and fruit ripen, orioles augment their diet and show a preference for cherries, mulberries, currants, figs and loquats. The Golden oriole is not always popular in the Mediterranean region because of its appetite for figs as it passes through on its autumn migration.

Nesting and the Young. Most of the orioles make rather attractive, closely woven cup-shaped nests of grass and strips of bark decorated with moss and lichens. The nest which is very tough and will withstand quite severe storms, is usually slung like a hammock from a forked branch. If a convenient fork is not available, the female, who usually does the nest building, will form one by weaving several adjacent branches together. The male tends to confine his activities to collecting building material. The figbirds of Australia and New Guinea differ from other orioles by building very flimsy shallow saucer-shaped nests composed mainly of twigs. They are so loosely constructed that the eggs can be seen through the bottom of the nest.

Very little is known about some of the orioles: in fact the nests and eggs of several species have still to be described. The best documented species are the Golden oriole and the Indian Black-headed *Oriolus xanthornis*. In the case of the Golden oriole the clutch can vary from 3–5 eggs though normally four eggs are laid. The eggs are generally very handsome with a white or pinkish ground, strongly marked with black or brown speckles which increase in size and density towards the blunt end of the egg. The eggs of the figbirds have a greenish background. The incubation is mainly by the female but the male occasionally takes her place. In the few tropical species studied the male plays an even smaller part in the breeding cycle and confines his activities to feeding the female on the nest.

Incubation lasts between 13–15 days for the species so far studied and the young which are born blind and have their bodies covered with long yellowish down remain in the nest another two weeks before they fledge. They are fed with insects and larvae together with the occasional berry. Usually there is only one clutch per year. If eggs and nest are destroyed at the beginning of the incubation the birds will try again. The nesting season is usually confined to between May and early July. This contrasts with the Indian Black-headed oriole whose nesting season can, in Ceylon, last from May to October, two or even more broods being quite common. Australian orioles *O. flavocinctus* and *O. sagittatus* as well as the figbirds have breeding seasons from September to January, leaving plenty of time

Male orioles are boldly coloured, though inconspicuous when resting in foliage. (1) In flight and perching beside the duller female, the Golden oriole *Oriolus oriolus*, (2) Black-naped oriole *O. chinensis*, in flight, (3) Yellow figbird *Sphecotheres flaviventris* and (4) Maroon oriole *Oriolus traillii*.

for more than one brood. The young of the Golden oriole tend to keep together in families which break up in August just prior to migration.

Behaviour. In the spring the males appear on the breeding grounds up to 10 days earlier than the females but pair off as soon as the latter arrive. The courtship is quite spectacular with the male chasing the female in and out of the tree canopy. They are so close in the chase that the male's bill almost touches the female's tail and yet he is able to conform to all her sudden movements. This behaviour is apparently triggered off by the female dashing at the male.

Orioles are well-known for their melodious song. The true song does not carry far but call notes and alarm cries can be heard from a considerable distance.

Composition. The word oriole is an English derivation from the Latin *aureolus* which means yellow or golden, though of the 28 species some are not predominantly this colour. A Malaysian species, *Oriolus cruentus*, is mainly black with crimson patches; *O hosii* of Borneo is completely black except for chestnut undertail coverts. The four species of figbirds are distinguished from the other orioles mainly by the bare skin (reddish in the male) around the eye and by the very short bill. The little known *Tylas* of the Madagascan jungles is sometimes included in the Oriolidae. Systematicists place the Oriolidae between the drongos (Dicruridae) and the crows (Corvidae). They do not, however, have any striking characteristics and tend to be rather a homogeneous group. Old World orioles are not related to the American orioles which belong to the family Icteridae.

The nest of the Golden oriole *Oriolus oriolus* is made of long fibrous material and slung between twigs. Here the male is seen incubating.

DRONGOS

Drongos are a family of elegant insect eating song birds (Dicruridae) that are similar to, though not related to, the tyrant flycatchers (Tyrannidae). They are birds of medium size which vary in length from about 7–15in (about 18–38cm), not counting the elongated tips of the outer tail feathers of some species which may add another 15in (38cm) or more. In the species with the greatly elongated tail feathers, the shaft is completely bare of barbs in the adult, and is wire-like, except at its tip which is feathered, forming a paddle- or racquet-shaped tip. The shape of the tip of the tail also varies a great deal in other species, from truncate to very deeply

Drongos have evolved long elaborate tail feathers and sometimes filament-like crests. (1) Lesser racket-tailed drongo *Dicrurus remifer*, (2) Ashy drongo *D. leucophaeus*, (3) King-crow *D. macrocercus*, (4) Spangled drongo *D. hottentottus* and (5) Greater racket-tailed drongo *D. paradiseus*.

forked, or with the tips of the outer feathers tightly curled, but, typically, the tail is long and deeply forked with the tips of the outer feathers curving outward, but not curled. The wings are long, pointed, and handsomely tapered in all species and the combination of these beautifully designed wings with the long and deeply bifurcated tail enables the drongo to manoeuvre with great buoyancy. The Ashy drongo of India *Dicrurus leucophaeus* is noted for being 'a magnificent flier, turning and twisting with extreme speed and skill', according to one of the most competent of the bird observers of India. Crests and hackles also add to the appearance and interest of the drongos. The hackles are glossy and the crests, when present, vary a great deal from species to species and from one population to another of the same species. The crest may consist of only a rather short tuft of erect feathers on the forehead, little plumes curling over the crown, or broad well-webbed feathers which curl gracefully over the back of the head and over the nape; or the feather may be partly or completely denuded of barbs and extend posteriorly like a thick hair for about 5in (13cm) or a little more.

Distribution. The Dicruridae are divided into two genera, one of them with only one species, the Papuan mountain drongo *Chaetorhynchus papuensis*, which inhabits the mountains of New Guinea. The other 19 species are contained in the genus *Dicrurus*. Three species are African, but the Comoro Archipelago, Madagascar, and the Aldabras Islands, not far from Madagascar and the Comoros, boast the best representation anywhere with four species. Madagascar shares a handsome species, *D. forficatus*, with Anjouan Island in the Comoros, and Grand Comoro Island, Mayotte Island, and the tiny Aldabras each have their own interesting species. The other 12 species inhabit southern Asia and the Indo-Australian region but three of them have penetrated far beyond the tropics, west to Iran and north to beyond the Amur River in Siberia.

Feeding. The drongos are usually solitary, perching on some vantage point from which they can fly out or swoop to catch their prey in flycatcher or roller fashion. They feed mainly on insects, although on some occasions they may take some nectar.

Behaviour. The life history and habits of most species are unknown and none have been studied thoroughly, not even that of the King-crow *Dicrurus macrocercus*, which is certainly one of the most abundant and familiar birds of India, as well as one of the most conspicuous. The King-crow holds forth noisily from telephone or telegraph wires and owes its picturesque name to the fact that it is fearless and so intolerant of crows, or other large, dangerous birds,

that it drives them away. However, the King-crow is not a mere bully as it does not molest small birds, or larger birds such as doves that are harmless. It is also well known that many species of birds build their nests in the same tree where a drongo has built its own, presumably to 'take advantage of the protection' of the drongo. Other interesting aspects of behaviour that have been reported are that drongos are normally the leaders in the mixed bands of insectivorous birds that roam the forest hunting for food; that they associate with cattle and man; and that some individuals are superb mimics, especially the Greater racket-tailed drongo *D. paradiseus* which is celebrated for this ability. But courtship has not been studied, and the role played by the sexes in other activities, such as nest building and incubation is not known, although it is believed both sexes share these activities. The nest, when known, appears to be frail but is said to be unusually strong, and consists of a rather shallow, semi-pendent cup constructed of small flexible twigs, roots, or shreds of plants, well bound by cobwebs, within the fork of a slender branch at the outer edge of the crown of a tree, usually at a good elevation above the ground.

Composition. The family Dicruridae is composed of two genera one of which, *Chaetorhynchus*, contains a single species; the other, *Dicrurus*, contains 19 species. The Spangled drongo *D. hottentottus* is one of the most variable of all birds, with well over 30 subspecies.

WATTLEBIRDS

The two living members of this small but interesting endemic New Zealand family Callaeidae are distinguished by the fleshy wattles growing at the gape of the bill. These wattles are brilliantly coloured in orange or red in all except the North Island subspecies of the Kokako *Callaeas cinerea*, in which they are blue. Although the common name of the Kokako is Wattled crow, the family Callaeidae is probably not closely related to the corvids of the northern hemisphere, and it is far from certain what their closest relatives may be.

In the extinct Huias *Heteralocha acutirostris* (1), the male's bill was short and stout and the female's long and slender. This was probably not to enable them to help each other but to ensure that they did not compete too closely for food. (2) Kokako *Callaeas cinerea* and (3) Saddleback *Philesturnus carunculatus*.

Wattlebirds are medium sized passerines ranging from 9–13in (23–34cm) in length. The plumage is mostly blue-grey and black, relieved in the Saddleback *Philesturnus carunculatus* by a broad splash of bright chestnut across the back and both sets of wing coverts.

An unusually large number of New Zealand birds have either become flightless or else have very limited powers of flight. The wattlebirds are good examples of this tendency, the three genera being characterized, in varying degrees, by their feeble flight. The weakest flier is the Saddleback. Its short, rounded wings are notably small for its body size and can support level flight for only a few yards. Indeed, this species represents the closest surviving approach to a flightless passerine.

Distribution. Until about the end of the last century wattlebirds were widely distributed throughout New Zealand, although the Huia *Heteralocha acutirostris* was not abundant. By the early years of this century, however, numbers of all species suddenly dropped to very low levels – the Huia to virtual extinction, the Saddleback to small populations on islands in the extreme north and south with small pockets of survivors in Southland forests, and the Kokako to scattered groups in remote forested areas. The reasons for this sudden decline are not clear but certainly their feeble flight and ground feeding behaviour made the wattlebirds particularly vulnerable to introduced predators such as stoats, feral cats and rats. The Huia was literally hunted into extinction by both Maoris and Europeans. Their large black tail feathers, handsomely barred with white across the tips, were worn in the hair by tribal chiefs as a mark of their high status. Unfortunately, the same fashion spread to the European community after a visiting dignitary wore a Huia feather in his hatband.

Extra pressure on the Huias came from collectors who wanted specimens with which to show the extraordinary differences of size and shape between the beaks of the male and female. The male's beak was robust, of moderate length and slightly downcurved, whereas the female's was very long, thin and strongly curved. So great were the differences that it was difficult to believe that the two sexes could belong to the one species. The few feeding observations made suggest that the pair may have had a cooperative foraging regime – the male breaking open the dead wood and rotting logs on the forest floor with his powerful beak while the female secured grubs from narrow crevices not accessible to the male. No other species showing such an extreme difference betwen the sexes in bill size and shape has ever been discovered, and thus it is a matter of great regret that this unique feeding adaptation is no longer available for live study.

Feeding. The wattlebirds live in dense evergreen rain forests that formerly clothed most of New Zealand. These vary from luxuriant sub-tropical forests in the north to the beech forests in the south, where species of the southern hemisphere evergreen *Nothofagus* cover extensive areas. The two surviving wattlebird species have very different diets and feeding habits. The Saddleback is mainly insectivorous, constantly searching dead wood, bark crevices and clumps of epiphytes for insects. The closed beak, which is notably strong and pointed, is thrust firmly into dead wood or into the pith cavity at the end of a broken dead branch or under a flake of bark, and then the jaws are forcibly opened to split open the wood. The power with which the beak can be opened is quite remarkable and is made possible by special adaptations of the muscles and bones of the head.

Behaviour. Wattlebirds form very firm pair bonds. For example, Saddleback pairs stay together for life and do not separate even in the winter. Indeed, the two birds of a pair keep in constant touch by sight and sound from dawn to dark, parting company only at dusk when they go to sleep in separate roost holes. They build simple loose nests of grass and plant fibres in hollow trees and usually lay two eggs. Each pair occupies a large territory which is defended throughout the year but the exact boundaries are hard to distinguish owing to the denseness of the habitat. Territory is proclaimed by a variety of very loud chattering songs. Postural displays and fighting are seldom seen, perhaps because in leafy evergreen vegetation vocal threats carry a message much further than visual ones can, and defending such a large perimeter by fighting would need a great deal of time and energy. The Kokako builds a bulky nest high in the forest canopy. This species has an extraordinary song consisting of a series of steady-toned harmonious organ-like or bell-like notes interspersed with shorter harsh sounds. The longer notes characteristically commence softly and swell to great volume.

Detailed study of individually marked Saddlebacks has revealed that male birds in given areas counter-sing against each other using extremely similar song versions. However the songs used are so strikingly different from those of neighbouring areas that each area can be said to have its own dialect. Where the song areas meet the boundary residents regularly sing both dialects. Young males reared in one dialect area do not take their father's song with them if they happen to settle to breed in another dialect area but rather learn the song types of the new area.

Composition. The family Callaeidae contains three genera two of which, the Saddleback and Kokakos, each have a North Island and a South Island subspecies, while the extinct Huia is not so subdivided. The distinction between the Saddleback subspecies is unique in the bird world in that it is made on the grounds that the South Island form, *P. carunculatus carunculatus*, passes through an all-brown juvenile plumage phase lasting about a year whereas the North Island birds, *P. c. rufusater*, assume the adult black and chestnut 'saddled' plumage from the nest.

MUDNEST-BUILDERS

There are only four species in the family Grallinidae and these are grouped together largely because they all build mudnests, hence the common family name. Little is known about the New Guinea Torrent-lark *Grallina bruijni* but the other three species all build very similar bowl-shaped mud nests, usually upon horizontal branches, a process which requires a rather specialized building

Apostlebirds *Struthidea cinera* (1) live and nest in groups, while pairs of Magpie-larks *Grallina cyanoleuca* (2) defend a territory against others.

technique. Apart from this similarity they are not a very convincing family unit and for the purposes of this book are best considered as two subfamilies, the Grallininae and the Corcoracinae.

The Grallininae. This subfamily consists of two species, the familiar Magpie-lark *Grallina cyanoleuca*, and the Torrent-lark. Both these species are pied, black and white and in both, the sexes are clearly marked by different patterns, while the young birds have a compromise plumage. The feathering is shiny and neat, compared to that of the Corcoracinae which have a matt, fluffy, finish.

Both the Magpie-lark and the Torrent-lark feed mainly on the ground, but both are very capable, if not fast, fliers. The Magpie-lark is found throughout Australia and reaches parts of southern New Guinea, thriving wherever there is water, open spaces and a scattering of trees. Nearly every stock dam therefore has its resident pair of Magpie-larks, with windmills or telephone poles sometimes fulfilling the need for a nest tree. Breeding is generally in the spring and the offspring tend to be shed into large juvenile nomadic flocks in the autumn, while the parents remain resident on their territories.

Little is known about the Torrent-lark except that it is rarely, if ever, encountered away from the fast-flowing streams that drain the mountainous interior of New Guinea. It forages along the water's edge and is particularly at home on mid-stream boulders. It is extremely agile in this habitat and appears to occupy the niche filled by forktails in southeast Asia and the dipper in the northern temperate regions.

Both species in the Grallininae are mainly insect eaters although crustaceans, snails and other water life are probably snapped up as encountered, as the birds forage over the ground and particularly at the water's edge.

As with so many birds that pair permanently and maintain resident territories there is no elaborate or spectacular courtship display. An essential part of the territory is a suitable nest tree though as already mentioned substitutes are accepted. Nest building generally starts in August and takes several days because each layer needs to dry and set, before the next is added. Three to five white eggs with purplish-brown spots and blotches are laid and incubated by both parents for 17–18 days. Both parents feed the nestlings for about three weeks and the young tend to stay with their parents, gradually being less dependent, until they are three months old. At this stage the juveniles leave the parental territory and join large nomadic flocks, generally near water.

A Magpie-lark territory is generally about 20ac (8ha) in size and both sexes take part in defending the area. Like several other bird species, they indulge in 'antiphonal' singing in which one pair member starts a song that is continued by the mate and then by the initiator again – so that each member sings alternately. Each pair has a 'signature tune' that is different from that of its neighbours and which helps to keep the pair together and show that that territory is occupied.

Pair of White-winged choughs *Corcorax melanorhamphos*. The female, in the nest, is eyeing her prey.

Magpie-larks are known to feed on freshwater snails which act as an intermediate host to the liver fluke. They are, therefore, probably of economic importance to sheep and cattlemen.

The Corcoracinae. This subfamily contains two species, the White-winged chough *Corcorax melanorhamphus* and the Apostlebird *Struthidea cinerea*. Both these species have soft fluffy plumage and occur in large sociable groups throughout the year, in contrast to the pairs of the Grallininae.

Although both White-winged choughs and Apostlebirds are strictly-speaking omnivorous the former are chiefly insectivorous and the latter seed eating. The bills of these birds emphasize the different diets dealt with, for the White-winged chough has a long curved bill for raking and probing in the litter while the Apostlebird's bill is broad, strong and stubby like that of a finch. Both species are restricted to Australia where they are found throughout most of the eastern half of the country, being unknown in the west. They generally haunt the same area throughout the year, wandering through a home range of about 2sq mi (5–6sq km).

White-winged choughs eat a wide range of insects and other small animals, from frogs to ants. During the breeding season one of the main items brought to nestlings is scarab larvae dug from rotting timber lying on the ground; in the autumn and winter, seeds quite often form part of the diet. Apostlebirds eat mainly insects in spring and summer, turning to seeds for the rest of the year.

The members of a group stay together all the year round and the group generally grows larger each year as young birds are added to the family. It appears that when the male dies the group breaks up and the fragments may either serve as the basis of a new group or may recombine with other birds to achieve a satisfactory social unit. The nests of Apostlebirds are very hard to distinguish from those of the Magpie-lark; those of the White-winged chough are nearly twice as large, though they are constructed in a similar way. In both species the eggs are off-white in colour and are spotted and blotched with brown, grey and blackish markings. Clutches normally contain from 2–5 eggs but clutches of eight and more are not uncommon and are the result of two females laying in the same nest. It is very rare, however, for more than three nestlings to be raised despite all the helpers. The eggs are incubated for 19–20 days and the nestlings remain in the nest for 23–28 days, generally leaving the nest before they can fly properly.

The social groups formed by these birds are usually expanded families, constant throughout the year except for the annual increment as a result of successful breeding. Group members contribute to most aspects of the nesting cycle; they all help build the nest and all except first-year birds share in incubation. By the time the eggs hatch even the first-year birds have begun to catch on and they and the older members all help to feed the nestlings and to brood them. It is not uncommon to see a number of birds queuing up to present food to the nestlings. At times there is even competition over which of the attendants shall be the next to brood.

Composition. The family Grallinidae consists of two rather different subfamilies and is best regarded as a temporary solution to a complex problem. It is not clear where the Grallininae should be placed but there are strong arguments to support the view that the Corcoracinae have more in common with the babblers Timaliidae than with Grallininae.

WOOD-SWALLOWS

Wood-swallows are largely insectivorous birds, characteristically stout, varying in length from 5¼–8in (13–20cm), with short legs and long strong wings indicative of a mainly aerial life-style. The tail is short and the birds present a flight silhouette very similar to that of

Some species of wood-swallows. (1) White-breasted wood-swallow *Artamus leucorhynchus*, (2) Little wood-swallow *A. minor*, (3) Black-faced wood-swallow *A. cinereus*, (4) adult and (5) young Masked wood-swallow *A. personatus*, (6) Dusky wood-swallow *A. cyanopterus*, seen also nesting in a tree trunk, (7) male White-browed wood-swallow *A. superciliosus* and (8) the female, pursuing her prey in midflight.

Wood-swallow nests are generally very frail structures and are frequently placed in the tops of hollow stumps, behind shedding bark and even inside other birds' nests. However when nests are built in bushes their frailty is made obvious for one can generally see the eggs through the bottom of the nest. The outer bowl of fine twigs is lined with thin green plant stems. Not only is nest-building rapidly accomplished but the whole sequence from courtship to egg-laying may be extremely quick in response to rainfall in arid areas. Nests are known to have been completed within six days of rain falling (after a long drought) and eggs laid within 12 days.

Most wood-swallows lay 3-egg clutches and the eggs are white, with reddish spots generally more concentrated towards the blunter end. The young hatch with tufts of powder-down that are unusual among passerines and the purpose of which is unknown. As the nestlings feather up, the juvenile mottled plumage becomes evident and until the next moult young are easily distinguished from their parents. Both parents help build the nest and incubate and feed the young; sometimes a third and even a fourth individual may help to feed the nestlings. Young wood-swallows generally leave the nest before they can fly properly, for their tails develop slowly, but their sharp claws enable them to clamber to some convenient perch in the sun. The parents feed them for about a month and since they may become merged with the flock soon after fledging other birds may also help in the feeding. Most wood-swallows do not breed until they are more than two years old, but exceptions do occur, under the arid conditions of inland Australia, where breeding pairs in immature plumage have been recorded.

Behaviour. Wood-swallows are sociable birds and in between bouts of feeding, several individuals may be seen lining a branch, preening each other or just sitting side by side. This companionable life reaches a climax at night, for most species roost communally and huddle together in some sheltered spot, so closely that they resemble a swarm of bees. Clusters of more than 100 have been recorded, but 15–20 is a more representative figure. No one knows why these birds roost like this for they do it even when the nights are above 80°F (26·7°C) so that any need for warmth may be largely discounted. Nevertheless wood-swallows are decidedly sluggish early in the morning and may start to cluster in the middle of the day if the temperature falls suddenly, so that their temperature regulation may be different from that found in other birds.

When breeding, wood-swallows become a little less sociable. They will defend the immediate area of the nest from trespass by other wood-swallows, but most species tend to breed in 'neighbourhoods' – a term covering cases of territoriality where the distribution of territories is not random but where birds tend to cluster in particular localities.

Although wood-swallows have no true song they maintain an almost constant twittering contact call while hawking for insects. They are extremely aggressive towards other species, usually potential predators such as hawks and crows, and have a conspicuous call which they use whenever they encounter such birds.

Composition. The Artamidae has a single genus *Artamus*, consisting of at least nine species. These fall into three groups on the basis of colouration. First, the dusky birds that are mainly uniform grey or brown *A. cyanopterus*, *A. minor* and *A. cinereus*; secondly the piebald birds which are mainly black and white *A. leucorhynchus*, *A. maximus*, *A. monachus* and *A. insignis*; and thirdly the multicoloured species *A. superciliosus* and *A. personatus*.

BELL-MAGPIES

Bell-magpies, butcher-birds and currawongs are the common names of the three highly distinctive genera in the family

the Common starling *Sturnus vulgaris*. All members of the family have blue-grey bills tipped with black. The plumage is generally black, grey and white, though a chestnut-brown colour occurs in some cases.

Distribution. The Artamidae is for the most part an Australasian family and may be found in every part of that continent. Several species occur in the islands to the north of Australia while one is frequently encountered in India and southeast Asia. Woodswallows combine the characteristics of both the shrikes (Laniidae) and the swallows (Hirundinidae) but are not closely related to either. Although they spend much of their time trawling for insects high in the sky with their broad bills agape, they also spend a lot of time perched on conspicuous twigs and flying brief sorties as prey is espied.

Most species remain in the same area all the year round but at least three species (*Artamus personatus*, *A. superciliosus* and *A. leucorhynchus*) are nomadic over extensive tracts of country, exploiting both tropical and temperate environments as the season suits. Two species, the Masked wood-swallow *A. personatus* and the White-browed *A. superciliosus*, forage in mixed flocks and it is one of the unsolved puzzles pertaining to these birds that in the west of the continent such flocks are predominantly of the former species while in the eastern states the latter predominates.

Feeding. All wood-swallows are largely insectivorous but they possess brush-tongues so that they may occasionally utilize nectar and pollen as a food source rather as the honeyeaters do.

Nesting and the Young. Courtship in wood-swallows may involve one bird presenting the other with a morsel of food. Later, one or other of the pair will start to flutter its partly-opened wings and to rotate the spread tail; the other partner may respond and take up the performance so that the pair are busy displaying for more than a minute. Suddenly the male will fly the few feet to the female and, landing on her back, mate with her.

Members of the Cracticidae are often seen at bird tables where they tend to dominate other species. (1) Adult and (2) young Pied butcher-bird *Cracticus nigrogularis*, (3) Black butcher-bird *C. quoyi*, (4) Grey butcher-bird *C. torquatus*, (5) White-backed magpie *Gymnorhina hypoleuca* and (6) Pied currawong *Strepera graculina*.

Cracticidae. The family bears no relation to the corvids – crows, jays, magpies – despite the common name. Its members tend to be black, white and grey stockily built birds with strong dagger-like bills usually coloured blue-grey and tipped with black. All are fine songsters that enliven the Australian bush with their calls and carolling. Of the three genera, the butcher-birds *Cracticus* are the smallest, being little larger than a Blackbird *Turdus merula*; the magpies *Gymnorhina* are intermediate while the currawongs *Strepera* are the largest, being nearly 20in (50cm) in length.

Distribution. Butcher-birds and magpies are chiefly found in woodlands and savannahs while currawongs are more birds of the forests and scrublands. Taken together they may be said to occupy the niches filled by jays, crows and jackdaws in other continents, for the family Corvidae is poorly represented in Australia. One species of magpie and four species of butcher-bird occur in New Guinea. Magpies have been introduced to New Zealand, where the family is not endemic. Apart from these examples the Cracticidae is confined to Australia. Few parts of the country have less than three representatives of the family and these are frequently among the commonest local birds.

Both butcher-birds and magpies tend to be resident all the year round while the currawongs are much more mobile. Once breeding is completed large flocks wander through the forests and, quite commonly in winter, into the towns and cities.

Feeding. All the Australian magpies are largely insectivorous although when such food is scarce they may eat seeds and carrion. Butcher-birds generally take their prey after a swift flight from some convenient vantage point, in typical shrike manner; prey is taken both in the air and on the ground. In contrast the magpies usually forage as they walk over the ground, probing into soft areas of soil and turning over sticks, cow-pats and other likely hiding places for insects. Currawongs have the largest and strongest bills of the family and probably concentrate on larger prey.

Nesting and the Young. No particular courtship display has been observed in members of this family. Their nests are stick bowls placed well off the ground and lined with grass, bits of bark, wool, fine roots and branchlets. The female does the major share of nest-building and all the incubating. Once the young have hatched both parents and even some of the previous year's offspring help to feed the nestling butcher-birds but with magpies, despite the fact that they live in groups, it is mainly the female who feeds and tends the young. The eggs vary in ground colour from brown to blue-green and have dark brown spots and blotches. The young fledge in about four weeks and continue to be fed by other members of the group for the next two months.

Behaviour. The territorial behaviour of the Black-backed magpie *Gymnorhina tibicen* has been closely studied. Not only are these birds strictly territorial throughout the year, holding areas of 10–30ac (4–12ha), but they also tend to live in groups of two or three adults plus immatures. A group may contain, say, seven adults but never more than four individuals of either sex; groups of as many as 10 have been recorded, but these generally contain several immature birds. The whole group helps to defend the territory but beyond that offers surprisingly little help to the dominant female who does nearly all the work involved in nesting and rearing young. Where two females nest and lay eggs in the one group-territory it is unusual for both nests to be successful.

Suitable breeding territory is at a premium and its quality may vary considerably between groups. A stable group will invariably hold a territory containing good nesting trees, plenty of pasture and some water supply. Elsewhere, where the terrain is less hospitable, the birds congregate in large flocks, often containing several hundred individuals. Such flocks usually consist of immature birds that have left the group in which they were reared, adult birds not yet able to attain territorial status and others whose groups have disintegrated, as when a dominant male dies, leaving the remaining adults unable cohesively to defend their territory. New groups will form within the flock and try to force their way into the territorial mosaic early in the spring but they usually have to wait some months before a suitable vacancy occurs.

Not only do many magpies not belong to territorial groups but many established groups occupy sub-optimal habitats. Where this is so the birds may build nests, lay and hatch eggs but rarely rear the young successfully. From experimental work, where caged intruders were placed in otherwise excellent territories, it has been found that females can fail to breed when their territory is continually in dispute and where song battles and constant attacks directed at the intruder distract her from the job in hand, thus emphasizing the importance of a settled environment.

Most Australian magpies sing magnificently. The carolling of members of the genus *Gymnorhina* serves to advertise territory and so is heard at its best in early spring when boundaries are being adjusted and disputes are frequent. These birds also have a harsh aggressive note generally used in flying attack and a plaintive distress call when alarmed or when contact with the rest of the group has been lost. Young magpies have an unlovely and insistent, loud begging call which they use frequently during the months when they depend on others for food.

The butcher-birds perform magnificent flute-like duets which are among the most impressive bird songs. Owing to something of a ventriloquial talent it is often very hard to make out which member of a particular duo is actually singing. Currawongs cannot be said to sing but they have distinct, ringing, bell-like calls that carry well through their forest habitat and which presumably serve to keep pairs in contact and to show that a particular territory is occupied.

Economic Importance. Currawongs have been found to be of economic importance in the control of forest-defoliating phasmatids – large mobile leaf eating stick-insects which can cause serious losses in commercial plantations. The Pied currawong *Strepera graculina*, for example, will eat such large numbers of these insects that, in years when they are not abundant, entire populations have been eliminated in some areas.

Composition. The numbers of species and even of genera included in the Cracticidae has been much debated over the years. Recent opinion regards the three genera already mentioned – *Cracticus*, *Gymnorhina* and *Strepera* – as being valid. There are four species of butcher-bird in Australia, the Black-headed butcher-bird *Cracticus mentalis*, the Pied butcher-bird *C. nigrogularis*, the Black butcher-bird *C. quoyi*, and the Grey butcher-bird *C. torquatus*; a fifth species, the Black-headed butcher-bird *C. cassicus* is confined to New Guinea. Most authorities recognize two if not three species of magpie, but recent taxonomic opinion regards these as subspecies since there is a considerable zone of hybridization and the species are known to interbreed in the wild where they meet. *Gymnorhina dorsalis* and *G. hypoleuca* are therefore regarded as races of the Black-backed magpie *G. tibicen*. Although in the past many species of currawong have been named, present opinion reduces these to three species, the Pied currawong *Strepera graculina*, the Black currawong *S. fuliginosa* and the Grey currawong *S. versicolor*.

Although the Grey butcher-bird *Cracticus torquatus* is a predator, it cannot hold the prey with its feet and wedges it in a twig fork.

BOWERBIRDS

The bowerbirds are perching birds noted for their very elaborate sexual displays. In all there are 18 species in the family Ptilonorhynchidae, found in New Guinea and the surrounding islands, and in north and east Australia. Bowerbirds are closely related to the birds of paradise. They vary from 9–15in (23–38cm) in length and show a wide range of colours and patterns in their plumage. Bold patterns of green, orange, lavender, and yellow with grey or black are found in many species; some have a plain grey or brown plumage and a few are spotted. In the more brightly coloured species the male bird is much brighter than the female, but the sexes are alike in the dull-coloured forms. Some of the species have a crest of elongated feathers, the crest often being brilliantly coloured. In a few species it forms an elaborate ruff or a mane hanging over the upper back. The bill is slightly hooked at the tip in all of the bowerbirds, but in some it is slightly downcurved, in others straight, in some it is thin and weak, in others heavy. In a few species the upper mandible has some small tooth-like notches along its cutting edge.

Distribution. Bowerbirds are most numerous in New Guinea, where five of the eight genera are found. The other three genera only contain one species each and are confined to Australia.

The genus *Ailuroedus* has three dull-coloured species known as catbirds. One of these is confined to New Guinea, one is found in Australia and New Guinea and one is confined to Australia. They are bright green above and pale brown or pinkish-brown below, boldly patterned with black.

The Stagemaker or Tooth-billed bowerbird *Scenopoeetes dentirostris* is found only in Australia. It is an olive-brown bird, about 11in (28cm) long, with pale stripes on the underparts.

In another monotypic genus is Archbold's bowerbird *Archboldia papuensis* of the mountains of New Guinea. This is a rather large species that varies from 12–15in (30–38cm) long. The male is black or sooty grey with a crest of golden yellow feathers; the female is dull grey with pale brown markings on the wings.

The genus *Amblyornis* contains four species that are again confined to the mountains of New Guinea. They are 9–10in (23–25cm) long, rather short-billed, with red-brown plumage. The females lack crests, but the males of all but the Vogelkop gardener bowerbird *A. inornatus* have brightly coloured crests; red, orange or yellow according to the species.

The genus *Prionodura* has only one species, the Golden bowerbird *P. newtoniana*, which is found only in the mountain forests of northern Queensland, Australia. It is about 9in (23cm) long and rather short-billed. The male is bright olive-green with yellow underparts, head, neck and tail, while the female is dull yellow-green with grey underparts.

The three species of the genus *Sericulus* vary from 9–11in (23–28cm) long and are found in both Australia (one species) and New Guinea (two species). The males have large areas of orange, red or bright chrome yellow in their plumage, and an erectile cape of brightly coloured feathers; the females are brown or pale yellow above with grey or olive-brown underparts marked with a dark, scaly pattern.

The Satin bowerbird *Ptilonorhynchus violaceus* is the only member of its genus and is confined to eastern Australia. About 12in (30cm) in length, it is rather long-billed, the bill also being heavy and straight. The plumage is glossy black in the male and grey-green in the female.

The last genus, *Chlamydera*, has four species. Two of these are confined to Australia, one is found in New Guinea and in the Cape York area of Australia, and the other is restricted to New Guinea. In two species the sexes differ in plumage, the male being grey-brown or yellow-brown with a spotted or scaly pattern on the underparts and a glossy violet-pink crest on the back of the neck. The females are duller and only occasionally have a crest. In the other two species both the male and female are dull grey-brown or olive-brown with a salmon-pink wash on the body plumage.

Feeding. So far as is known, all of the bowerbirds live mainly on the fruits of trees and bushes, supplementing this diet with insects, larvae, spiders, and sometimes small snakes and lizards, tree frogs and seeds. It is this predominantly frugivorous diet that enables the males to have the time necessary for bower building, as tree fruits are abundant for most of the year. This abundance of food also enables them to nest polygamously, the female bird carrying out all of the nesting duties without encountering any difficulty in feeding herself and her offspring.

Nesting and the Young. Bowerbird nests vary from bulky cups in *Ailuroedus*, *Amblyornis* and *Chlamydera* that are built in bushes, to a bulky cup in a tree-hole in *Prionodura*, and a frail, shallow cup built in a bush in *Scenopoeetes*, *Sericulus* and *Ptilonorhynchus*. In *Prionodura*, as in many other hole-nesting birds, the eggs are pale in colour (cream) without markings. In *Ailuroedus* the eggs are a deep rich cream, but they are fairly well hidden from predators, being inside a deep nest-cup. In the other species the eggs are cream, white or light blue or grey, variously spotted, mottled and streaked with grey, lavender or brown to hide them from predators, as they rest in the open cup of the nest.

Except perhaps in the genus *Ailuroedus*, the female bird builds the nest alone, lays the clutch of 2–5 eggs, incubates them and then feeds the young until they fledge and for a week or two afterwards. Incubation periods of between 12–15 days have been recorded and approximate fledging periods of from 13–20 days, though some of these were probably inaccurately recorded.

Behaviour. The bowerbirds are so-called because of the complicated, and often highly decorated, structures that the males of some species use when they are displaying. These structures sometimes take the form of cleared areas containing a domed tunnel of sticks, decorated with brightly coloured stones, fresh flowers, spiders' webs and coloured insects' skeletons.

In the genus *Ailuroedus* no bower is built, though the males appear to defend a territory near the forest floor. In display the male rustles its wings, jumps spasmodically upwards on slender, leaning saplings, chases the female and gives a head-jerking display accompanied by a rasping call.

In the genus *Scenopoeetes* the male defends a perch from which it sings, above a cleared patch of ground among slender young trees. It decorates its private lawn with large leaves laid upside down and a few snail shells. In display the male flicks its wings open, bobs its head from side to side with its bill gaping, hops about erratically, fluffs its breast feathers and holds a leaf in the bill for long periods.

In the genus *Archboldia* the male has one, or sometimes more, perches on which it sits waiting for females to approach. The perches are usually about 10–20ft (3–6m) up on a tree branch above a cleared ground court which is decorated with pieces of vegetation, snail shells, pieces of insects and chips of tree resin. In display the male crawls about in front of the female for up to 20 minutes or more, pausing occasionally to make short hops towards or away from her. He faces the female for most of the time as she moves around the edges of the cleared area. Whilst doing this the male carries a small twig held crosswise in the bill.

The males of the genus *Amblyornis* defend perches that are often closer together than they are in the three preceding genera. The perch is usually from 15–30ft (4·5–9m) up in a tree near to a cleared ground court. The court surrounds a moss-covered stage which is built around a sapling ringed with sticks. In two of the three species the stage is roofed and ornamented with coloured fruits and berries, fungi and charcoal; in the other species the stage is not roofed and has few ornaments. In display the male has a strange song, ventriloquial and imitative of many sounds of the forest, and it also makes whistling, crackling and rattling noises.

In the genus *Prionodura* the males defend territories that are grouped together, each male's territory being a fairly large area surrounding the private court and bower. The male sits for most of the time on a stick or creeper above the bower structure. The bower itself is remarkable; it may be up to 7ft (2m) tall, surrounded by smaller towers and decorated with moss, berries and flowers. In display the male bird hovers around the bower, jerks its head from side to side, flutters the wings and carries sticks and flowers to the bower.

Little is known of the behaviour of the species of the genus *Sericulus*, but two of them are known to build a walled bower.

In the genus *Ptilonorhynchus* each adult male defends a separate court and bower inside a traditional courtship area. The bower consists of a solid mat of small sticks with a wall of sticks on each side. The whole structure is painted with a paint made of vegetable juices and is brilliantly decorated by the male with shells, flowers,

Bowerbirds build elaborate display grounds made of twigs and often decorated with a variety of small objects; the female visits the male at the bower and mating takes place there after the complex display. Shown here are four species of bowerbirds with their bowers numbered correspondingly. (1) Satin bowerbird *Ptilonorhynchus violaceus*, (2) Regent bowerbird *Sericulus chrysocephalus*, (3) Golden bowerbird *Prionodura newtoniana* and (4) MacGregor's bowerbird *Amblyornis macgregoriae*.

leaves and dead insects. In display the male spends most of its time at the bower, uttering scraping, grating, cackling, churring and squeaking notes. It dances about with its tail raised over its back, jumps right over the bower, points the bill to the ground and becomes so excited that its eyes bulge outwards.

In the four species of the genus *Chlamydera* the males have bowers in groups in the forests, but they are widely spaced within these groups. Each male defends a private bower consisting of a wide range of brightly coloured objects.

It seems that there is a fairly close relationship between the complexity of bowerbirds' plumage patterns and the complexity of the bower that is built. In the species that build no bowers, or only clear a ground court, the plumage is often coloured with red, orange, yellow, green or black in varying combinations of brilliance, but in the species that build the most elaborate and brilliantly decorated bowers the birds are disappointingly dull in colour, with the exception sometimes of the crest.

Composition. The Ptilonorhynchidae comprises 18 species in eight genera. Growing understanding of the similarities between the bowerbirds and the birds of paradise is leading some authorities to consider including the former in the Paradisaeidae.

BIRDS OF PARADISE

Birds of paradise are generally rather stout, heavy-billed, strong footed birds varying in size from that of the Starling *Sturnus vulgaris* to the typical crows *Corvus*; 8–18in (20–46cm). These measurements do not, however, include ornate flank and tail plumes. The Ribbon-tailed Astrapia *Astrapia mayeri* would measure 46in (117cm), including its 36in (93cm) tail.

The crow-like resemblance of the group has resulted in it being considered to have derived from an ancestral crow (Corvidae) stock although starlings (Sturnidae), honeyeaters (Meliphagidae) and other families have been considered.

Adult male birds of paradise of most species are remarkably colourful and ornate in plumage as an adaptation to a rare and peculiar promiscuous breeding system called polygyny which involves complex display sequences. Polygyny is found in only approximately 1% of all birds, involving 12 families and about 100 species. Intricate display feathering on the head of certain species has brought about marked modifications in skull shape. Attainment of adult male plumage takes five to six years in several species, as may prove the case in most, if not all, of the sexually dimorphic birds. The females are drab and cryptically coloured, being fairly uniform in appearance throughout the family. The degree of ornate plumage in males (and thus differences between the sexes) is correlated with the type of breeding behaviour; thus the less colourful species are sexually similar and practice normal avian reproductive behaviour (monogamy).

The promiscuous breeding of most members of the family has brought about drastic, and evolutionarily rapid, development of ornate plumages by sexual selection, the females selecting finer dressed and displaying males for mating. As a result, the family members are remarkably diverse in appearance but are genetically very close as indicated by the existence of 14 intergeneric and five intrageneric hybrids in the wild.

Distribution. Birds of paradise are confined to the Australasian region being predominately abundant on New Guinea where the family undoubtedly originated. Several species are confined to off-shore islands of New Guinea. Two species are peculiar to the Mollucan Archipelago and four occur in eastern and northeastern Australia, two of which are restricted to that continent.

Altitudinal distribution on mainland New Guinea is important as it maintains isolation of populations of separate species, as it does in many other New Guinea birds. For example the Blue bird of paradise *Paradisaea rudolphi* confined to the central mountains of eastern New Guinea at 4,500–6,300ft (1,372–1,920m) fringes on the range of Count Raggi's bird *P. raggiana*, which is found from sea level to 5,000ft (0–1,524m). Where these populations meet (probably as a result of recent vegetational changes) hybridization occurs.

All birds of paradise are sedentary forest birds.

Feeding. Fruits form the basic diet, whilst berries, seeds, insects, frogs and reptiles have been seen to be taken.

Nesting and the Young. Nest building and raising of the young is carried out exclusively by the female in all promiscuous genera. Of the remaining seven genera only a little is recorded of the habits of three. In Macgregor's bird *Macgregoria pulchra* the female builds

the nest and both parents feed the young. Both sexes of manucodes *Manucodia* brood and feed the young but what part males play in nest building and incubation is unknown. Both sexes of the Trumpet bird *Phonygammus keraudrenii* share nesting duties.

The majority of known nests are bulky basin-shaped structures of twigs placed on or in the forks of branches. One exception is the King bird *Cicinnurus regius* which nests in tree holes.

Only one or two eggs of pale ground colour, marked with irregular and longitudinal lines, are laid. Upon hatching young are either naked or downy, and blind (nidicolous).

Behaviour. Territorialism in birds of paradise has been given little attention and almost nothing is recorded. Communal displaying males are known to chase one another from favoured perches within the 'arena'. No doubt birds such as the six-wired species *Parotia*, which display on individual cleared areas within earshot of other males, defend their areas. Most species have very loud, clear, calls which carry considerable distances and probably function to advertise the presence of individuals and their territory to other males as well as to prospective mates. It is possible that nesting females of the promiscuous species maintain territory, but this is uninvestigated.

The courtship displays and postures of wild birds of paradise were first reported by Alfred Russel Wallace in 1857 and have attracted considerable attention ever since. The displays executed by males of the various genera and species are as diverse and splendid as the plumages developed for them.

The rifle birds *Ptiloris* display in groups high in the forest. They wear iridescent metallic-like feathers on the throat and breast which are displayed by raising the head and bill vertically and spreading the peculiarly rounded wings on either side of the throat.

Males of Wallace's standard wing *Semioptera wallacei*, a generally pale brown bird, display communally, erecting large iridescent green breast shields and waving two with 'flag plumes' from the bend of each wing. The sickle-bills and the King bird of paradise

Extreme variation in display plumage among birds of paradise. (1) Greater bird of paradise *Paradisaea apoda*, (2) Magnificent riflebird *Ptiloris magnificus* and (3) King of Saxony bird of paradise *Pteridophora alberti*.

Cicinnurus regius perform displays incorporating the erection of peculiar flank 'fans' of iridescent-tipped feathers from beneath each wing. The Superb bird *Lophorina superba* is velvety black and displays by raising an iridescent green breast shield. It lacks white 'flag plumes' as in Wallace's bird but wears a huge triangular 'cape' which is raised above and behind the head.

The six-wired birds are generally velvety black and 'dance' alone on cleared perches and soil by presenting iridescent areas of violet, blues and olives on the breast, shining patches of gold and silver on the head and six 'flag plumes' which are raised over the head, three originating behind each eye. In addition, elongate flank plumes are raised and spread to form a 'skirt' about the bird.

The little King of saxony bird *Pteridophora alberti* appears to do little more than raise two unique enamel-like 'flag plumes' of extreme length above the head, erect the back feathers, and bounce about on branches.

The Magnificent and Wilson's birds, *Diphyllodes magnificus* and *D. respublica*, have exceedingly intricate plumage and perform on vertical saplings in cleared areas of forest. Both utilize brightly coloured mouth-parts in display.

The male 'plumed' birds of paradise of the genus *Paradisaea* are adorned with elongate lace-like flank plumes. Groups of males gather at traditional tree-top 'arenas' and display by hopping about, often inverting themselves on a perch, and spreading the flank plumes over the back and head in a colourful cascade of feathering whilst quivering the wings. Two exceptions are the Blue bird and the Emperor of Germany bird *P. guilielmi* which perform rather static postures whilst hanging upside down.

Several species produce loud rustling noises with the wings in flight, the function and mechanics of which are little known.

Courtship of the species with mono-coloured males and normal breeding behaviour is believed to consist of simple flight chases and vocalizations, but little is known about these.

Economic Importance. Adult plumaged male bird of paradise skins are used by the natives of New Guinea as adornments and currency. These are hunted at the birds' traditional display grounds with bow and arrow, nooses, and more recently shot guns.

Between the years 1600 and 1914 vast numbers of male birds, mostly of the genus *Paradisaea*, were collected to satisfy a huge fashion market in Europe requiring plumes mostly as colourful hat accessories. Today all birds of paradise are protected from commercial trading, whilst they are still hunted by native peoples with traditional weapons.

Composition. The family Paradisaeidae contains 42 species divided into 20 genera. Great diversity within the group is reflected by the fact that 11 genera each contain only a single species.

Recent anatomical studies of skull characters indicate the presence of two natural groups within the family. The subfamily Cnemophilinae contains the genera *Loria*, *Loboparadisea*, *Cnemophilus* and *Macgregoria*; the subfamily Paradisaeinae contains the remaining genera. It is not known to which subfamily the genus *Macgregoria* should be allocated. The Cnemophilinae is considered the ancestral stock of the family and bridges the gap between birds of paradise and bowerbirds (Ptilonorhynchidae).

Another authoritative opinion, based predominately upon behavioural considerations, is that the birds of paradise and bowerbirds are so close that the latter should be placed with the birds of paradise in the Paradisaeidae. An interesting aspect of this arrangement is the theory that bowerbirds have 'descended' to the forest floor, to display, from tree-top displaying bird of paradise ancestors; having subsequently developed the habit of constructing bowers and losing their bright plumage as a result. Marked correlations between the degree of bower building and display plumage in the bowerbirds strongly support this theory.

CROWS, JAYS AND MAGPIES

The Corvidae includes a variety of robust perching birds which at first sight seem dissimilar to each other. However, such divergent types as choughs, nutcrackers, jays, magpies and ravens all share a number of structural characters pointing to their close relationship. The bill is more or less stout, fairly long, and often has a small hook at the tip; the nostrils are usually round, partly concealed and shielded by small bristly feathers, and the legs and feet are strong.

They vary in length from 7–30in (18–77cm) and include the largest passerine birds. The wings are strong and usually more or less rounded and the tail varies from short and squared to long and graduated or forked. A number of species have head crests.

Much of their behaviour suggests a highly developed mentality, and it has been suggested that the corvids are the most highly evolved of birds. This is supported by the behavioural adaptability of many species and by the performance of crows in laboratory tests of intelligence. Other characteristics of the family include the absence of any musical song, a tendency to be gregarious and aggressive and powerful flight.

The typical crows of the genus *Corvus* are mainly black or black and white in colour, often with a strong metallic gloss, although a few species have secondarily acquired a dull brownish colouration. The choughs in the genus *Pyrrhocorax* are also glossy black, although they have red legs and in the Chough *P. pyrrhocorax* a red bill, or a yellow bill as in the Alpine chough *P. graculus*. In contrast, the jays and magpies mainly have bright colouration, in which green and blue are prominent. The sexes are similar in plumage in nearly all Corvidae species. There is no seasonal change of plumage.

Distribution. The family is almost cosmopolitan, but absent from New Zealand and most other archipelagos of the Pacific Ocean. Europe has four species of typical crow: the Raven *Corvus corax*, the Carrion and Hooded crows *C. corone*, Rook *C. frugilegus* and Jackdaw *C. monedula*; both species of chough; the European jay *Garrulus glandarius*; the Magpie *Pica pica*; the Azure-winged magpie *Cyanopica cyanus*; the Nutcracker *Nucifraga caryocatactes*, and the Siberian jay *Perisoreus infaustus*.

Africa has several species in the genus *Corvus*: the peculiar Black magpie *Ptilostomus afer* and Stresemann's ground-crow *Zavattariornis stresemanni*, and an outlying population of choughs in Ethiopia, but lacks the numerous species of jay and magpie present in the tropics of Asia and America.

The small ground-jays in the genera *Podoces* and *Pseudopodoces* are restricted to desert and semi-desert areas of northern and central Asia, where magpies and choughs also occur. Tropical Asia has many species of jay and magpie, including the primitive Shrike-jay *Platylophus galericulatus* and White-winged magpie *Platysmurus leucopterus*. The Jungle crow *Corvus macrorhynchos* and House crow *C. splendens* are the common typical crows of the region.

The New Guinea region, Australia and the islands of the western Pacific Ocean have only typical crows of the genus *Corvus*. In Australia this genus appears to have undergone considerable recent evolution, resulting in a number of very similar species of black crow, all of which were formerly classified as *C. orru*.

North America is even richer in corvids than Europe, with the typical crows represented by the Raven; the Common crow *C. brachyrhynchos*; the Fish crow *C. ossifragus*, and the Northwestern crow *C. caurinus*, as well as several species confined to islands of the West Indies. Besides the Magpie, the Yellow-billed magpie *Pica nuttallii* occurs in California; the nutcrackers are represented by Clark's nutcracker *Nucifraga columbiana* and the Siberian jay by the Grey jay *Perisoreus canadensis*. Nearly 36 species of jay in eight genera are confined to North and tropical America. Of these, the Blue jay *Cyanocitta cristata*, Steller's jay *C. stelleri* and the Scrub (or

Variation of plumage in the crow family. (1) White-naped raven *Corvus albicollis*, (2) Jackdaw *C. monedula* seen also (2a) in flight, (3) Chough *Pyrrhocorax pyrrhocorax* seen also (3a) in flight, (4) Raven *C. corax* seen also (4a) in flight, (5) (Eurasian) Nutcracker *Nucifraga caryocatactes*, (6) (Black-billed) Magpie *Pica pica* seen also (6a) in flight, (7) Jay *Garrulus glandarius*, (8) Steller's jay *Cyanocitta stelleri*, (9) Green magpie *Cissa chinensis* and (10) Red-billed blue magpie *Urocissa erythrorhyncha*.

Florida) jay *Aphelocoma coerulescens* are familiar North American birds. Two monotypic genera found only in Central America deserve special comment; in the genus *Psilorhinus*, the Brown jay *P. morio* is characterized by its inflatable throat sac which enables it to produce loud snapping noises; while in the genus *Calocitta* the Magpie-jay *C. formosa* is distinguished by its very long tail.

The Hawaiian Islands have been colonized by the Hawaiian crow *Corvus tropicus*, which is now very rare.

Most corvids are sedentary, or make only local movements, but some northern species are long-distance migrants. Different species of the family occupy a wide range of habitats, from deserts in the genera *Podoces* and *Pseudopodoces* and in the Fan-tailed raven *Corvus rhipidurus*, to tropical jungle in many jays and magpies.

Feeding. Many of the typical crows are well-known as omnivorous scavengers which will at times eat almost anything they can swallow. Carrion crows, for example, have been recorded eating such diverse fare as insects, molluscs, seeds, fruit, nuts, animal carrion, mice, eggs, fish, domestic scraps, rubber, putty and plastic insulation material. However, most species have more restricted diets, and some such as choughs are primarily insectivorous while nutcrackers and jays often specialize, taking nuts or seeds from a few species of trees. The larger crows will kill small or sick animals for food, although carrion is more commonly eaten, and a few tropical crows, such as the Papuan crow *Corvus tristis* eat mainly the fleshy fruit of forest trees.

The apparent intelligence of crows is well reflected in the versatility of their feeding behaviour. Carrion crows and Rooks will fly in to the air with hard-shelled molluscs or walnuts and drop them onto hard surfaces, whereas gulls drop them indiscriminately. Several species habitually wash sticky food items, and the feet are used to hold and manipulate food while it is pecked.

Nesting and the Young. Some corvids are known to pair for life, and it seems likely that most if not all of them do. Courtship is marked by courtship feeding and allopreening, and by displays, but this behaviour is also used to maintain pair bonds.

The nest is typically a bulky structure of twigs with a lining of grass or hair. In a few species it has a dome of twigs. Nest sites are usually in trees or bushes. The Jackdaw usually nests in holes in rocks, trees or buildings; choughs use shallow holes, and ground jays use the deep burrows of small desert rodents.

Clutches are of 2–4 eggs in most tropical jays and some species in the genus *Corvus*, but up to nine in magpies and others. The eggs are buff, cream, green, pale blue or white, usually with spots and blotches of brown, black or grey. Incubation, carried out by the female bird alone, usually lasts 16–21 days.

The young are blind and helpless when hatched, with a scanty covering of down. Because incubation starts when the first egg is laid, the young hatch over a period of several days, so that they differ in size until late in the nestling period. When food is scarce the smaller young usually die because they are unable to compete for food with their larger siblings. Both sexes feed the young on food carried to the nest in the throat and crop. Fledging periods vary from about 20–45 days, being longer in the larger species, and the young are fed by their parents for at least a few weeks after fledging. No crow is known to rear more than one brood of young each year, and young birds of most species do not breed until they are two years old. In some American jays helpers at the nest additional to the parent birds have been recorded. These supernumerary adults may be young from earlier years.

Behaviour. Many corvids are highly gregarious, nesting in dense colonies, as is most notably the case with the Rook. Others, such as Jackdaws, nest in less dense colonies, and some such as the Magpie, Raven and jays nest solitarily and defend large territories. The colonial nesters normally flock throughout the year and occupy communal winter roosts, as do young birds of some of the solitary nesters. The voices of all crows are loud, and usually harsh, varying from the repeated cawing of Rooks to soft notes and screeching or chattering in Jays and Magpies. Some species have whispered 'sub-songs' composed of less harsh notes.

Economic Importance. Several of the typical crows and magpies are minor agricultural pests because they eat fruit and grain or interfere with new-born or sickly livestock. Only Rooks do great damage.

Composition. The Corvidae contains about 103 species classified in 26 genera. The family as a whole is a rather uniform group of forms which are closely related.

INDEX

Page numbers in **bold** type refer to illustrations.

Reader's Digest Fund for the Blind is publisher of the Large-Type Edition of *Reader's Digest*. For subscription information about this magazine, please contact Reader's Digest Fund for the Blind, Inc., Dept. 250, Pleasantville, N.Y. 10570.